ACCOUNTING STANDARDS

A comprehensive question book on
International Financial Reporting Standards

NINETEENTH EDITION

OPPERMANN
BOOYSEN
VAN DER MERWE

juta

Accounting Standards
A comprehensive question book on International Financial Reporting Standards

First published 1985
Sixteenth edition 2015
Seventeenth edition 2017
Eighteenth edition 2019
Nineteenth edition 2023

Juta & Company (Pty) Ltd
First Floor
Sunclare Building
21 Dreyer Street
Claremont
7708

PO Box 14373, Lansdowne 7779, Cape Town, South Africa

ISBN 978-1-48512-281-3

Production specialist: Samantha Simmons
Proofreader: Martin Rollo
Cover designer: Simplicitas Design
Typesetting: Wouter Reinders
Printed in South Africa by xxxxx

Contents

IN CHRONOLOGICAL ORDER

Contents

STANDARDS ARRANGED BY THEME

Note the following

1. The book includes a number of questions that are either excluded or at an awareness level in the SAICA syllabus, for institutions that cover these topics voluntarily or in accordance with syllabi of other professional bodies. The content page of each chapter indicates which questions are excluded or at an awareness level of the SAICA syllabus.
2. Tax rates and allowances are not necessarily those currently applicable but were chosen for convenience and for illustration of the accounting principles.
3. The main changes since the previous edition relate to updates for any changes in IFRS pronouncements since the previous edition was published.

Any suggestions or comments may be addressed to:

Nico van der Merwe
School of Accounting Sciences
North-West University
POTCHEFSTROOM 2520
Email: nico.vandermerwe@nwu.ac.za

About the Authors

S F BOOYSEN
DCom (Acc) (Pret), CA(SA)

R R DE VILLIERS
PhD (Accountancy), CA(SA), Associate Professor, NWU

G FORTUIN
MCom (Accounting Sciences), CA(SA), Lecturer, US

H S FOURIE
MCom (Accountancy), CA(SA), Senior Lecturer, NWU

N P FOURIE
BAcc (Hons) (UFS), CA(SA), Senior Lecturer, Milpark

K R HEATHCOTE
MCom (International Accounting) (UJ), CA(SA), Senior Lecturer, UJ

S LAMPRECHT
DAcc (UFS), ACMA (UK), CGMA, CA(SA), Associate Professor, US

Y MEYER
MCom (International Accounting) (UJ), CA(SA)

A MOSTERT
MCom (Accountancy) (NWU), CA(SA), Senior Lecturer, NWU

H R B OPPERMANN
BCom (Hons) (Acc) (Pret), CA(SA)

A SMIT
MCom (Acc) (UP), CA(SA), Associate Professor, Academic One

T TOMES
MCom (Accounting Sciences) (UP), CA(SA), Senior Lecturer, UP

N VAN DER MERWE
PhD (Accountancy), CA(SA), Professor, NWU

L VAN STADEN
MCom (Accountancy) (NWU), CA(SA), Senior Lecturer, NWU

HA VAN ZYL
MCom (Accounting) (UFS), CA(SA), Senior Lecturer, UFS

L VENTER
MCom (South African and International Taxation) (NWU), CA(SA),
Senior Lecturer, NWU

Preface

The publication is meant to introduce students to general accounting principles and the disclosure requirements of financial statements prepared in accordance with International Financial Reporting Standards (IFRS). Terminology and concepts implemented in the revised standards and interpretations issued by the IASB are applied.

The publication follows an approach whereby principles are illustrated by way of questions and solutions. Self-study is encouraged by the inclusion of questions for which the solutions are available to lecturers of prescribing institutions only. Questions become progressively more difficult, thereby gradually broadening the student's understanding of the principles involved.

We would like to extend a word of gratitude to the publishers for their willingness to participate in this contribution to the accounting field.

The authors
October 2022

Solutions to all questions are made available to lecturers who prescribe the book. Please refer to https://juta.co.za/pages/juta-passmasters for details.

Framework

Conceptual framework for financial reporting

❑ SUMMARY

Proposed approach to answering questions on the Conceptual Framework

❑ QUESTIONS AND SOLUTIONS

FRW.1	Objective of general purpose financial reporting
FRW.2	Qualitative characteristics
FRW.3	Event after reporting date
FRW.4	Objective of financial statements and the purpose of the Conceptual Framework
FRW.5	Application of the asset definition
FRW.6	Application of the asset definition
FRW.7	Application of the asset and expense definition

❑ QUESTIONS

FRW.8	Fundamental qualitative characteristics of financial statements
FRW.9	Application of the asset and expense definitions
FRW.10	Application of the asset definition
FRW.11	Application of the liability definition
FRW.12	Application of the asset definition and recognition criteria; selecting an appropriate measurement basis

PROPOSED APPROACH TO ANSWERING QUESTIONS ON THE CONCEPTUAL FRAMEWORK

The issue is normally to decide whether an item is:

- *An asset or expense – e.g. cost to plant a crop, development costs, etc.*
- *A liability or income – e.g. deposit received, etc.*

(Bear in mind that most, if not all, transactions will influence two elements in the financial statements due to the nature of the double entry system. We are not looking at the obvious leg but at the less obvious one, e.g. money borrowed to purchase goods will obviously be a liability, but will the goods purchased be an asset or an expense?).

Approach to solving this kind of problem:

1. *Classify the item according to the criteria in Chapter 4 of the Conceptual Framework – The Elements of Financial Statements (i.e. asset/liability/equity/income/expense). Pay special attention to the definitions in table 4.1. The recommended approach for proving an expense/income is to first apply the definition of an asset/liability to the item in question. Only if an item fails to meet the definition of an asset/liability, will the definition of an expense/income be applied and proved.*

2. *Take note of Chapter 5 of the Conceptual Framework – Recognition and Derecognition to determine whether the item should be recognised in the financial statements. Only items that meet the definition of an element will be recognised accordingly, e.g. if the definition of an asset is met it will be recognised as such in the statement of financial position and if the definition of an expense is met it will be recognised as such in the statement of profit or loss (Conceptual Framework 5.6).*

3. *Furthermore, an element is only recognised if recognition provides useful information to the users of financial statements, i.e. provides relevant information and a faithful representation (Conceptual Framework 5.7).*

4. *Take note of the important distinction between* ***recognition*** *(the process of capturing an element in the appropriate statement),* ***measurement*** *(the result of applying a measurement basis to an element) and* ***disclosure*** *(effective communication of information in financial statements about an element).*

❑ QUESTION FRW.1

What is the objective of general purpose financial reporting as defined by the Conceptual Framework?

❖ Suggested solution FRW.1

To provide financial information about the reporting entity that is useful to existing and potential investors, lenders, and other creditors in making decisions about providing resources to the entity.

❑ QUESTION FRW.2

Zet (Pty) Ltd has disclosed the model of motor cars driven by its directors in its financial statements over the past few years. Explain with reference to the qualitative characteristics of financial statements whether the information is useful.

❖ Suggested solution FRW.2

For information to be useful it must both be *relevant* and provide a *faithful representation* of what it purports to represent (fundamental qualitative characteristics of useful financial information). Comparability, verifiability, timeliness, and understandability enhance the usefulness of such information (enhancing qualitative characteristics).

Although the information about the model of motor cars driven by Zet (Pty) Ltd's directors may be **faithfully represented, comparable, verifiable, timely,** and **understandable**, it is **not relevant** because it will probably not influence the economic decisions of existing and potential investors, lenders and other creditors about providing resources to Zet (Pty) Ltd. Information is relevant if it has predictive value, confirmatory value or both. Disclosure of the model of motor cars driven by directors has no predictive value and it does not confirm any fact that is useful for decision-making.

To conclude, information in respect of the model of motor cars driven by Zet (Pty) Ltd's directors will not enhance the usefulness of financial statements or make a difference to the decisions of users.

❑ QUESTION FRW.3

A company's financial year ended on 30 September 20.8. On 15 October 20.8 it came to light that a debtor who owed R45 000 and had been experiencing financial difficulties for a number of months had been declared insolvent. The financial statements for the year ended 30 September 20.8 have not been prepared yet and the accountant does not want to account for the R45 000 as an allowance for credit losses at 30 September 20.8, although the amount is material. The auditors, however, insist that it should be done.

By only referring to the criteria of the Conceptual Framework, explain why one should agree with the auditors' requirement that the valuation adjustment and expense should be reflected in the financial statements.

❖ Suggested solution FRW.3

The debtor is measured at historical cost, updated over time to depict the effects of events that cause part of the historical cost of the debtor to be no longer recoverable (Conceptual Framework 6.7(b)). Confirmation of the situation (impairment) was obtained on 15 October 20.8. This confirmation improved the verifiability of this information. The amount is also material and recognition of the expense is therefore relevant for decision-making. Recognition of the expense will also be a faithful representation of the particular economic phenomenon (i.e. the weakening in credit quality of the debtor).

The carrying amount of the debtor should thus be updated on 30 September 20.8 to depict this subsequent change in measurement that was present (already existed) at the reporting date.

Explanatory note:

The question requires that reference should only be made to the criteria of the Conceptual Framework in agreeing with the auditors' requirement. It is therefore not necessary to take into account the requirements and principles of IFRS 9 *Financial Instruments*, IFRS 7 *Financial Instruments: Disclosures*, and IAS 10 *Events after the Reporting Period.*

❑ QUESTION FRW.4

'The Conceptual Framework is a coherent system of interrelated objectives and fundamentals that is expected to lead to consistent standards and that prescribes the nature, function, and limits of financial accounting and reporting. It is expected to serve the public interest by providing structure and direction to financial accounting and reporting to facilitate the provision of even-handed financial and related information that is useful in assisting capital and other markets to function efficiently in allocating scarce resources in the economy.'

(FASB – Statement of Financial Accounting Concepts No. 2.)

Required

With reference to the Conceptual Framework:

a. Discuss the objective of financial statements.
b. Briefly discuss the purpose of the Conceptual Framework.
c. Briefly state how the Conceptual Framework contributes to the mission of the IFRS Foundation.

❖ Suggested solution FRW.4

a. The objective of financial statements is to provide financial information about the reporting entity's assets, liabilities, equity, income and expenses that is useful to users of financial statements in assessing the prospects for future net cash inflows to the reporting entity and in assessing management's stewardship of the entity's economic resources (Conceptual Framework 1.2 and 3.2).
b. The purpose of the Conceptual Framework is to assist the IASB to develop IFRS Standards that are based on consistent concepts, assist preparers to develop consistent accounting policies when no Standard applies, or when a Standard allows an accounting policy choice and to assist parties to understand and interpret Standards (Conceptual Framework SP 1.1).
c. The mission of the IFRS Foundation is to develop Standards that bring transparency, accountability and efficiency to financial markets around the world (Conceptual Framework SP 1.5). The Conceptual Framework provides the *foundation* for such Standards that contribute to *transparency* by enhancing the international comparability and quality of financial information, enabling users of such information to make informed economic decisions. Standards based on the Conceptual Framework provide information to hold management *accountable*. The Conceptual Framework contributes to economic *efficiency* by helping investors to identify opportunities and risks across the world, thus improving capital allocation.

❑ QUESTION FRW.5

Puff-Puff Farming Entities are renowned for the high-quality tobacco they produce on their farms. During the year ended 30 June 20.5 they planted tobacco on all available land at a cost of R1,5 million. At the financial year end it appears from projections that they will reap a record harvest which will yield a return of about R5 million. (This was calculated by multiplying the expected crop size by the current price of tobacco.) A further four months will elapse after the year end before the tobacco is ready for sale.

The managing director (MD) and the financial director (FD) have a difference of opinion regarding the treatment of the planting costs of the tobacco. In the previous year the MD insisted that the planting costs of the crop be treated as an asset. After the financial statements had been issued, unexpected hail and rain resulted in the loss of a substantial part of the crop and they were unable to recover their costs.

The FD now insists that the planting costs should be treated as an expense in the 20.5 financial year. The MD does not support this approach as he argues that it will not be consistent with the previous year, and it will also result in two years' expenses being recognised in 20.5 with no income. He suggests that the planting costs should be treated as an asset once again. The crop is insured this year against rain and hail damage.

A well-known cigarette manufacturer, Lucky Pakkie Ltd, contracted with Puff-Puff Farming Entities to buy half of the current harvest for R2,5 million. The contract was finalised during June 20.5.

Required

Conceptually discuss the appropriate element that the planting costs should be classified as in the financial statements of Puff-Puff Farming Entities for the year ended 30 June 20.5, by referring only to the requirements of Chapter 4 of the Conceptual Framework.

❖ Suggested solution FRW.5

Definition of an asset

- A present economic resource controlled by the entity as a result of past events.

Definition of an economic resource

- A right that has the potential to produce economic benefits.

Applying it to the tobacco crop

- *Present right:* Puff-Puff Farming Entities already planted the tobacco which results in a present right to receive cash when it harvests the tobacco and sells it to Lucky Pakkie Ltd and in the market. Even if hail or crop disease result in the loss of a substantial part of the crop, Puff-Puff Farming Entities still has a right to receive cash from its insurance company.
- *Potential to produce economic benefits: For this potential to exist, it does not need to be certain that the right will produce economic benefits and it is only necessary that in at least one circumstance this right would produce for the entity economic benefits beyond those available to all other parties.* Puff-Puff Farming Entities expects to reap a record harvest which will yield a return of about R5 million. Furthermore, there is already a sales commitment for half of the crop for more than the total input cost. Even if natural causes like hail or

crop disease destroy the harvest or the market for tobacco crashes before the crop is sold, a successful claim from its insurance company will result in a cash receipt.

- *Controlled by the entity:* Puff-Puff Farming Entities has the present ability to direct the use of the crop and obtain the economic benefits that may flow from it, i.e. they control the crop. The crop is planted on the entity's land and is being developed and maintained by the entity.
- *The past event:* The planting of the crop and incurring the related costs.

Conclusion

In the absence of evidence to the contrary, it can be assumed that the crop will result in a potential return in excess of the input cost. The cost of planting the crop should therefore be treated as an asset in the 20.5 financial statements. This will be consistent with the previous year and result in comparability from year to year.

Explanatory note:

The question requires that the planting costs should be discussed by referring only to the criteria of the Conceptual Framework, therefore no mention was made of the requirements of IAS 41 *Agriculture* for recognising planting costs as an asset.

❑ QUESTION FRW.6

Woodpecker Ltd bought a farm in the Witels Mountain area that is suitable for growing pine trees. They paid R1 million for the farm and immediately started to develop the land. This involved making roads to the various planting areas, dividing the farm into sections, and creating fire- and windbreaks. Holes were also dug and young trees planted and fertilised. This was done at a cost of R100 000 per hectare.

After the trees had been planted they had to be watered and the weeds had to be controlled. The trees also had to be pruned to ensure that they grew straight and tall. This was an ongoing operation with costs being continually incurred.

After a period of about 10 years the trees should be ready for harvest and should yield a return in excess of 20% per annum on the costs incurred to establish them.

During the financial year ended 31 December 20.4, Woodpecker Ltd developed 10 hectares at a cost of R1 million and spent R300 000 on watering and maintaining the trees.

The accountant reflected the cost of R1,3 million as an expense in the statement of profit or loss and other comprehensive income. The financial director, however, feels that there are enough reasons to justify treating the R1,3 million as an asset in the statement of financial position as at 31 December 20.4.

Required

Conceptually discuss whether the cost of planting and maintaining the plantation is an asset or an expense, by referring only to the requirements of Chapter 4 of the Conceptual Framework.

❖ **Suggested solution FRW.6**

Definition of an asset

- A present economic resource controlled by the entity as a result of past events.

Definition of an economic resource

- A right that has the potential to produce economic benefits.

Applying it to the cost of modifying the software system

- *Present right:* Woodpecker Ltd already incurred the cost of planting and maintaining the plantation which results in a present right to receive cash when the trees are felled and the wood is sold.
- *Potential to produce economic benefits: For this potential to exist, it does not need to be certain that the right will produce economic benefits.* Even though the period prior to expectation of the benefits is quite long and there is some uncertainty involved (e.g. drought, fire, market after 10 years, etc.), this right has the potential to produce cash inflow in excess of 20% per annum on the costs incurred to establish the trees.
- *Controlled by the entity:* Woodpecker Ltd has the present ability to direct the use of the plantation and obtain the economic benefits that may flow from it, i.e. the plantation is under the control of the company. The plantation is on the company's land, and is being developed and maintained by the company. Woodpecker Ltd can also prevent other parties from directing the use of the plantation and from obtaining the cash when the trees are felled and the wood is sold.
- *The past event:* Incurring the cost and the development of the plantation.

Conclusion

Although a long time will pass before the trees produce any income, it is fair to assume that they have the potential of earning a return over and above the costs incurred. There are sufficient reasons for treating the costs incurred as an asset. At regular intervals the recoverable amount of the plantation should be determined and if the costs incurred are higher than the recoverable amount, the costs should be written down to the recoverable amount.

Explanatory note:

Since the definition of an asset was proved, it is not necessary to also disprove the definition of an expense. The question requires that the costs of development and maintenance should be classified by only referring to the criteria of the Conceptual Framework, therefore no mention was made of the requirements of IAS 41 *Agriculture* for the recognition of the costs of development and maintenance as an asset.

❑ QUESTION FRW.7

Zero Ltd incurred cash costs amounting to R15 million during its financial year ended 31 December 20.9. The costs relate to the modification of its existing software system to make it compatible with its new operating system. The expenditure incurred will only enable the software system to continue to perform as it did originally.

The financial director of Zero Ltd has, however, decided that in view of the amount involved, the amount should be capitalised as an asset at 31 December 20.9.

Required

Discuss, by referring only to the requirements of Chapter 4 of the Conceptual Framework, whether or not you agree with the financial director's decision. Assume that the amount is material.

❖ Suggested solution FRW.7

Definition of an asset

- A present economic resource controlled by the entity as a result of past events.

Definition of an economic resource

- A right that has the potential to produce economic benefits.

Applying it to the cost of modifying the software system

- *Present right:* Zero Ltd is the legal owner of the software system.
- *Potential to produce economic benefits: For this potential to exist, it does not need to be certain that the right will produce economic benefits.* The expenditure incurred will only enable the software system to continue to perform as it did originally and there is no potential to produce economic benefits which had not already existed before the modification.
- *Controlled by the entity:* Zero Ltd has the present ability to direct the use of the software within their business operations and obtain the economic benefits that may flow from it.
- *The past event:* Acquiring and updating the software.

Conclusion

The costs incurred to modify the existing software system to make it compatible with its new operating system fails the definition of an asset as it does not have the potential to produce economic benefits which had not already existed before the modification.

Definition and application of an expense

- *Decreases in assets, or increases in liabilities, that result in decreases in equity*: The cash payment of R15 million will result in a decrease of cash that will result in a decrease in equity;
- *other than those relating to distributions to holders of equity claims:* Not the case, because it is costs incurred to modify an existing software system; not distributions to shareholders.

Conclusion

The cost of the modification incurred is seen as a decrease in assets. Therefore, I disagree with the financial director's decision and the cost of R15 million must be recognised as an expense according to the requirements of the Conceptual Framework.

❑ QUESTION FRW.8

Mr De Jager, a director of Jagter Manufacturers Ltd, questions the recognition and disclosure of a lease entered into for machinery to the value of R3 million, which is used in the company's manufacturing process.

Mr De Jager is of the opinion that it is unnecessary to capitalise the machinery and the corresponding liability, and that too much information will be disclosed when doing so.

Required

Explain to Mr De Jager, by referring only to the fundamental qualitative characteristics of the Conceptual Framework, why the lease should be capitalised and disclosed as such. Assume that the amount is material.

❑ QUESTION FRW.9

Sepi Ltd has developed a unique soft drink. It is very healthy and yet tastes like the top-selling unhealthy brands. Unfortunately, the product does not sell very well. Sepi Ltd has identified the following reasons for this:

- The product is not being correctly marketed.
- The marketing problem is attributed to the fact that the product does not have a trademark.

Sepi Ltd therefore set about developing a trademark for this product. All indications are that it will be called Sepi Sola.

In developing the trademark, Sepi Ltd incurred the following expenses up to 30 June 20.5:

	Rand
Design of logo	900 000
Legal fees for registration	200 000
Advertising campaign to promote the trademark	600 000
Total	1 700 000

From budgets prepared and experience so far it seems that Sepi Ltd will enjoy benefits from the trademark for the next 10 years. Sepi Ltd is already experiencing an upswing in the demand for its product.

Required

Conceptually discuss how Sepi Ltd should record the costs incurred in developing the trademark in its financial statements for the year ended 30 June 20.5 by referring only to the requirements of Chapter 4 of the Conceptual Framework.

❑ QUESTION FRW.10

Renewal Ltd manufactures a special rejuvenating product with no side effects. It apparently induces a feeling of youth and vitality when it is used. This product is manufactured on a farm owned by the company situated in the Agter-Witsenberg valley. One of the main ingredients used in the product is the water from a mountain stream which flows through the farm. In terms of the water rights, Renewal Ltd may use the water but it must allow 50% to flow through to farms in the lower valley.

Renewal Ltd needs further financing but is unable to borrow any more money from the bank as its debt-to-equity ratio is too high (due to high outstanding loans and few assets). The managing director thought it was a pity that one of the company's most important resources, the mountain stream, was not reflected on the company's statement of financial position.

The financial director reacted to this by indicating that he is more than willing to place a value on this asset and include it in the statement of financial position. He suggests that they should assume that the mountain stream will be perennial and unpolluted for the next 10 years.

Renewal Ltd has annual sales of R15 million and, due to the low input cost (mainly mountain water), has a high gross profit percentage. As Renewal Ltd is operating in an environmentally sensitive area, management is concerned about achieving environmental excellence.

Required

Provide a well-reasoned argument as to whether or not the mountain stream may be recorded as an asset in the financial statements of Renewal Ltd. Include in your argument any reservations you might have in this regard. Use Chapter 4 of the Conceptual Framework as a basis for your discussion.

❑ QUESTION FRW.11

Xilo Ltd is dependent upon its software to process its purchase and sales transactions and has a year end of 31 January.

On 15 January 20.5, Xilo Ltd approached a computer consultant to establish whether or not its software was compliant with its own new open-source operating system. On 31 January 20.5, the consultant informed Xilo Ltd that the software was not compliant and that Xilo Ltd would need to spend about R3 million to make it so.

The financial director of Xilo Ltd has decided to recognise a liability for the amount of R3 million in its accounting records for the financial year ended 31 January 20.5. Xilo Ltd has not yet appointed a contractor to do the modifications.

Required

Discuss the financial director's decision to recognise a liability of R3 million in the financial statements of Xilo Ltd for the year ended 31 January 20.5. Assume that the amount is material. Justify your answer by referring only to the requirements of the Conceptual Framework.

❑ QUESTION FRW.12

Novecy Ltd acquired 100 Bitcoins on 1 December 20.8 that will be used exclusively to purchase manufacturing equipment at a future date. The reason for acquiring Bitcoins to fund these future purchases, is because cryptocurrency has reduced transaction costs, and the sophisticated security inherent to cryptocurrency appeals to the financial director of Novecy Ltd.

Even though the Bitcoin price has significantly decreased during the period November 20.7 to December 20.8, it seems as if the price has stabilised since. The financial director is an investment specialist and believes that the Bitcoin price will be driven up by market factors during 20.9.

Although it is not Novecy Ltd's intention to trade with their Bitcoins, they have established that there is a principal, active market for Bitcoins with freely available quoted prices. You may assume that selling the Bitcoins on the principal market represents the highest and best use for this cryptocurrency, and no inherent restrictions pertaining to the Bitcoins are applicable.

Required

a. Conceptually discuss the classification and recognition of the Bitcoins in the financial statements of Novecy Ltd for the financial year ended 31 December 20.8 by referring only to the requirements of the Conceptual Framework.
b. Recommend the appropriate measurement basis for the Bitcoins purchased in terms of the Conceptual Framework.

IAS 1

Presentation of financial statements

❑ SUMMARY

Illustrative example – statement of financial position
Illustrative example – statement of profit or loss and other comprehensive income (expenses by function)
– statement of profit or loss and other comprehensive income (expenses by nature)
Illustrative example – statement of changes in equity

❑ QUESTIONS AND SOLUTIONS

IAS 1.1	Objective of IAS 1: discussion
IAS 1.2	Components of a complete set of financial statements: discussion
IAS 1.3	Explanation of the term 'material': discussion
IAS 1.4	General features of financial statements: discussion
IAS 1.5	Information to be displayed in financial statements to ensure the information presented is understandable: discussion
IAS 1.6	Distinction between current and non-current assets and liabilities: discussion
IAS 1.7	Presentation and disclosure of a refinanced financial liability: discussion
IAS 1.8	Statement of profit or loss and other comprehensive income and separately disclosable items: presentation
IAS 1.9	Ordinary dividend per share: calculation and disclosure

❑ QUESTIONS

IAS 1.10	Accounting treatment of a refinanced financial liability in accordance with the requirements of IAS 1: discussion
IAS 1.11	Disclosure requirements of separately disclosable items: discussion
IAS 1.12	Statement of changes in equity: presentation
IAS 1.13	Ordinary and preference dividend per share: calculation and disclosure

Illustrative example

NKOSI LTD GROUP
STATEMENT OF FINANCIAL POSITION AS AT 31 DECEMBER 20.2

	20.2 Rand	20.1 Rand
ASSETS		
Non-current assets	x	x
Property, plant and equipment	x	x
Goodwill	x	x
Other intangible assets	x	x
Investment in associates	x	x
Investment in equity instruments	x	x
Current assets	x	x
Inventory	x	x
Trade receivables	x	x
Other current assets	x	x
Cash and cash equivalents	x	x
Total assets	x	x
EQUITY AND LIABILITIES		
Total equity	x	x
Equity attributable to owners of the parent	x	x
Share capital	x	x
Retained earnings	x	x
Other components of equity	x	x
Non-controlling interest	x	x
Total liabilities	x	x
Non-current liabilities	x	x
Long-term borrowings	x	x
Deferred tax	x	x
Long-term provisions	x	x
Current liabilities	x	x
Trade and other payables	x	x
Short term borrowings	x	x
Current portion of long-term borrowings	x	x
Current tax payable	x	x
Short-term provisions	x	x
Total equity and liabilities	x	x

NKOSI LTD GROUP
STATEMENT OF PROFIT OR LOSS AND OTHER COMPREHENSIVE INCOME FOR THE YEAR ENDED 31 DECEMBER 20.2
(Illustrating the classification of expenses by function)

	20.2 Rand	20.1 Rand
Revenue	x	x
Cost of sales	(x)	(x)
Gross profit	x	x
Other income	x	x
Distribution costs	(x)	(x)
Administrative expenses	(x)	(x)
Other expenses	(x)	(x)
Finance costs	(x)	(x)
Share of profit of associates	x	x
Profit before tax	x	x
Income tax expense	(x)	(x)
Profit for the year	x	x
Other comprehensive income		
Items that will not be reclassified to profit or loss	x	x
Property revaluation	x	x
Gain on property revaluation	x	x
Tax expense	(x)	(x)
Investments in equity instruments	x	x
Gains arising during the year	x	x
Tax expense	(x)	(x)
Share of other comprehensive income of associate	x	x
Items that may subsequently be reclassified to profit or loss	x	x
Cash flow hedges	x	x
Gains arising during the year	x	x
Tax expense	(x)	(x)
Exchange differences on translating foreign operations	x	x
Gains arising during the year	x	x
Reclassification adjustment for gains included in profit or loss	(x)	(x)
Tax expense	(x)	(x)
Share of other comprehensive income of associate	x	x
Total comprehensive income for the year	x	x
Profit attributable to:		
Owners of the parent	x	x
Non-controlling interest	x	x
	x	x
Total comprehensive income attributable to:		
Owners of the parent	x	x
Non-controlling interest	x	x
	x	x
Basic earnings per share	x	x
Diluted earnings per share	x	x

NKOSI LTD GROUP
STATEMENT OF PROFIT OR LOSS AND OTHER COMPREHENSIVE INCOME FOR THE YEAR ENDED 31 DECEMBER 20.2

(Illustrating the classification of expenses by nature)

	20.2 Rand	20.1 Rand
Revenue	x	x
Other income	x	x
Changes in inventories of finished goods and work in progress	(x)	(x)
Work performed by the entity and capitalised	x	x
Raw material and consumables used	(x)	(x)
Employee benefit expense	(x)	(x)
Depreciation and amortisation expense	(x)	(x)
Impairment of property, plant and equipment	(x)	(x)
Other expenses	(x)	(x)
Finance costs	(x)	(x)
Share of profit of associates	x	x
Profit before tax	x	x
Income tax expense	(x)	(x)
Profit for the year	x	x
Other comprehensive income		
Items that will not be reclassified to profit or loss	x	x
Property revaluation	x	x
Gain on property revaluation	x	x
Tax expense	(x)	(x)
Investments in equity instruments	x	x
Gains arising during the year	x	x
Tax expense	(x)	(x)
Share of other comprehensive income of associate	x	x
Items that may subsequently be reclassified to profit or loss	x	x
Cash flow hedges	x	x
Gains arising during the year	x	x
Tax expense	(x)	(x)
Exchange difference on translating foreign operations	x	x
Gains arising during the year	x	x
Reclassification adjustment for gains included in profit or loss	(x)	(x)
Tax expense	(x)	(x)
Share of other comprehensive income of associate	x	x
Total comprehensive income for the year	x	x
Profit attributable to:		
Owners of the parent	x	x
Non-controlling interest	x	x
	x	x

	20.2 Rand	20.1 Rand
Total comprehensive income attributable to:		
Owners of the parent	x	x
Non-controlling interest	x	x
	x	x
Basic earnings per share	x	x
Diluted earnings per share	x	x

NKOSI LTD GROUP
STATEMENT OF CHANGES IN EQUITY FOR THE YEAR ENDED 31 DECEMBER 20.2

	Share capital Rand	Revaluation surplus Rand	Translation reserve Rand	Retained earnings Rand	Total Rand	Non-controlling interest Rand	Total equity Rand
Balance at 1 January 20.1	x	x	(x)	x	x	x	x
Changes in accounting policy				(x)	(x)	(x)	(x)
Restated balance	x	x	(x)	x	x	x	x
Changes in equity for 20.1							
Total comprehensive income for the year		x	x	x	x	x	x
Profit or loss				x	x	x	x
Other comprehensive income		x	x		x	x	x
Dividends (Rx per share)				(x)	(x)	(x)	(x)
Issue of share capital	x				x		x
Transfer to retained earnings		(x)		x			
Balance at 31 December 20.1	x	x	(x)	x	x	x	x
Changes in equity for 20.2							
Total comprehensive income for the year		x	x	x	x	x	x
Profit or loss				x	x	x	x
Other comprehensive income		x	x		x	x	x
Dividends (Rx per share)				(x)	(x)	(x)	(x)
Issue of share capital	x				x		x
Balance at 31 December 20.2	x	x	(x)	x	x	x	x

❑ QUESTION IAS 1.1

Explain what the objectives of IAS 1 are and how this standard aims to achieve this.

❖ Suggested solution IAS 1.1

IAS 1 prescribes the basis for the presentation of general purpose financial statements to ensure that the entity's own financial statements will be comparable from year to year, and also with those of other entities.

To achieve this objective, IAS 1 sets out overall requirements for the presentation of financial statements, guidelines for the structure of financial statements and minimum content requirements.

❑ QUESTION IAS 1.2

General purpose financial statements should provide financial information to users in respect of financial position, performance and cash flows of an entity in order to facilitate decision-making.

According to IAS 1, what are the main components of a complete set of financial statements?

❖ Suggested solution IAS 1.2

A complete set of financial statements comprises:

- A statement of financial position.
- A statement of profit or loss and other comprehensive income.
- A statement of changes in equity.
- A statement of cash flows.
- Notes, comprising significant accounting policies and other explanatory information.
- Comparative information in respect of the preceding period.
- A statement of financial position as at the beginning of the preceding period when an entity applies an accounting policy retrospectively or makes a retrospective restatement of items in its financial statements, or when it reclassifies items in its financial statements that have a material effect on the information in the statement of financial position at the beginning of the preceding period.

❑ QUESTION IAS 1.3

The accounting standard IAS 1 requires each material class of similar items to be presented separately in the financial statements. Items of dissimilar nature or function should be presented separately unless they are immaterial. Explain what is meant by the term 'material'.

❖ Suggested solution IAS 1.3

IAS 1 states in its definitions (IAS 1.7) that information is material if omitting, misstating or obscuring it could reasonably be expected to influence decisions that the primary users of general purpose financial statements make on the basis of those financial statements, which provide financial information about a specific reporting entity.

Materiality depends on the nature or magnitude of information, or both. An entity assesses whether information, either individually or in combination with other information, is material in the context of its financial statements taken as a whole.

❑ QUESTION IAS 1.4

a. Explain, by referring to the requirements of IAS 1, what is meant by the following terms and what their implications for the preparation of financial statements are:

- Going concern basis
- Accrual basis

b. Briefly discuss whether 'offsetting' of the elements of financial statements is permitted by IAS 1.

❖ Suggested solution IAS 1.4

a. **Going concern basis:** This is the assumption that an entity will continue to operate into the foreseeable future (which covers a period of at least 12 months from the end of the reporting date). Management is required to assess the entity's ability to meet this criterion and unless management intends to liquidate the entity or to cease trading (or has no realistic alternative but to do so), the financial statements should be prepared on a going concern basis (IAS 1.25).

Accrual basis: Under the accrual basis of accounting, items are recognised as assets, liabilities, equity, income and expenses (the elements of financial statements) when they satisfy the definitions and recognition criteria for those elements in the *Conceptual Framework*. Accordingly, an entity should prepare its financial statements, other than cash flow information, under the accrual basis of accounting.

b. **Offsetting:** IAS 1 does not permit offsetting of the elements of financial statements unless it is permitted or required by an IFRS. Accordingly, an entity shall report separately both assets and liabilities, and income and expenses.

❑ QUESTION IAS 1.5

The accounting standard IAS 1 requires an entity to clearly identify each financial statement and the notes. List the additional information an entity is required to display prominently in its financial statements to ensure the information presented is understandable.

❖ Suggested solution IAS 1.5

The following information should be displayed prominently according to IAS 1.51:

- The name of the reporting entity or other means of identification, and any change in that information from the preceding reporting date;
- Whether the financial statements presented relate to an individual entity or a group of entities;
- The date of the end of the reporting period or the period covered by the set of financial statements or notes;
- The presentation currency; and
- The level of precision of the amounts presented in the financial statements (e.g. R'000).

❑ QUESTION IAS 1.6

A distinction is made in the accounting standard IAS 1 between current and non-current assets, and current and non-current liabilities. Explain the distinctions.

❖ Suggested solution IAS 1.6

According to IAS 1.66, a current asset is an asset that:

- is expected to be realised in, or is intended for sale or consumption in the entity's normal operating cycle;
- is held primarily for the purposes of being traded;
- is expected to be realised within 12 months after the reporting period; or
- is cash or a cash equivalent, unless it is restricted from being exchanged or used to settle a liability for at least 12 months after the reporting period.

According to IAS 1.69, a current liability is a liability that:

- is expected to be settled in the entity's normal operating cycle;
- is held primarily for the purpose of being traded;
- is due to be settled within 12 months after the reporting period; or
- the entity does not have an unconditional right to defer settlement of for at least 12 months after the reporting period.

All other assets and liabilities are to be classified as non-current assets or non-current liabilities.

❑ QUESTION IAS 1.7

Long-term financial liabilities (e.g. borrowings) would normally be classified as current liabilities if they are due for repayment within the next 12 months after the entity's reporting date.

However, an entity could enter into an agreement to refinance, or to reschedule payments, on a long-term basis, thereby changing the substance of the financial liability back to long term.

Briefly discuss the appropriate presentation and disclosure of a financial liability due for repayment within the next 12 months after the entity's reporting date, in its financial statements, if:

- the entity applied to reschedule the payments on a long-term basis before its reporting date; and
- the rescheduled payments were only approved by the issuer of the financial liability after the reporting date, but before the financial statements are authorised for issue.

❖ Suggested solution IAS 1.7

An entity presents its financial liabilities as current when they are due to be settled within 12 months after the reporting period, even if:

(a) the original term was for a period longer than 12 months, and
(b) an agreement to refinance, or to reschedule payments, on a long-term basis is completed after the reporting period and before the financial statements are authorised for issue.

Therefore, the financial liability shall be presented as a current liability at year end.

Events after the reporting period are those events, favourable and unfavourable, that occur between the end of the reporting period and the date when the financial statements are authorised for issue (refer IAS 10).

The rescheduled payments on a long-term basis were only approved after the reporting date, but before the financial statements were authorised for issue. This is indicative of conditions that arose after the reporting period, i.e. this represents a non-adjusting event after the reporting period.

Accordingly, the entity shall disclose the nature of the refinancing agreement and an estimate of its financial effect.

❑ QUESTION IAS 1.8

The following amounts were taken from the trial balance of Birdie Ltd for the year ended 31 December 20.5:

	Rand
Revenue	600 000
Cost of sales	200 000
Gain on disposal of vehicle	5 000
Gain on revaluation of owner-occupied land	8 000
Finance cost	20 000
Lease expenses – Offices (short-term leases)	20 000
Depreciation – Vehicles	25 000
Employee cost	50 000
Write-down of inventory to net realisable value	2 000
Administrative expenses	4 000
Current tax expense	81 000
Deferred tax income (P or L)	2 000
Deferred tax expense (OCI)	1 792

Additional information

1. Assume that all amounts are material for purposes of disclosure.
2. Birdie Ltd accounts for its owner-occupied land on the revaluation model of IAS 16.

Required

Prepare the statement of profit or loss and other comprehensive income and profit before tax note of Birdie Ltd from the available information for the year ended 31 December 20.5 in accordance with the requirements of International Financial Reporting Standards (IFRS). Birdie Ltd classifies its expenses by function and prepares its statement of profit or loss and other comprehensive income in one statement. Comparative amounts, accounting policy and tax notes are not required.

❖ **Suggested solution IAS 1.8**

BIRDIE LTD
STATEMENT OF PROFIT OR LOSS AND OTHER COMPREHENSIVE INCOME FOR THE YEAR ENDED 31 DECEMBER 20.5

	Note	Rand
Revenue		600 000
Cost of sales		(200 000)
Gross profit		400 000
Other income		5 000
	Note	**Rand**
Administrative expenses		(4 000)
Other expenses (1)		(97 000)
Finance cost		(20 000)
Profit before tax	2	284 000
Income tax expense (2)		(79 000)
Profit for the year		205 000
Other comprehensive income		
Items that will not be reclassified to profit or loss		6 208
Gain on property revaluation		8 000
Tax expense		(1 792)
Total comprehensive income for the year		211 208

(1) 20 000 + 25 000 + 50 000 + 2 000 = 97 000
(2) 81 000 – 2 000

BIRDIE LTD
NOTES FOR THE YEAR ENDED 31 DECEMBER 20.5

2. Profit before tax

Profit before tax is stated after taking the following into account:

	Rand
Expenses	
Lease payments on short-term lease contracts (1)	20 000
Depreciation (2)	25 000
Employee cost (2)	50 000
Write-down of inventory to net realisable value (3)	2 000

(1) Disclosure requirements of IFRS 16.53(c)
(2) IAS 1.104 disclosure requirement
(3) IAS 2.36(e) disclosure requirement

Items to be disclosed separately (4)	
Gain on disposal of vehicle	5 000

(4) Disclosure requirements of IAS 1.97 – material items

❑ QUESTION IAS 1.9

Ape Ltd was incorporated on 1 January 20.1. On this date, it issued 100 000 ordinary shares which remained unchanged for the years ended 31 December 20.1 and 20.2.

Ape Ltd had the following transactions, relating to dividends, for the year ended 31 December 20.1:

- Paid an interim ordinary dividend of R10 000 on 30 June 20.1.
- The directors proposed a final ordinary dividend of R20 000 on 31 December 20.1.

The dividends proposed by the directors on 31 December 20.1 were approved by the shareholders at the annual general meeting held on 31 March 20.2. These dividends were paid on 8 May 20.2.

Interim dividends of R15 000 were paid to the ordinary shareholders on 30 June 20.2.

On 31 December 20.2 the directors proposed a final ordinary dividend of R25 000.

Required

Calculate and disclose dividends paid and dividend per share for Ape Ltd for the year ended 31 December 20.2 in accordance with the requirements of International Financial Reporting Standards (IFRS).

❖ Suggested solution IAS 1.9

APE LTD
STATEMENT OF CHANGES IN EQUITY FOR THE YEAR ENDED 31 DECEMBER 20.2

	Retained earnings Rand
Balance 1 January 20.1	x
Changes in equity for 20.1	
Dividends paid – ordinary	(10 000)
Balance 31 December 20.1	x
Changes in equity for 20.2	
Dividends paid – ordinary (1)	(35 000)
Balance 31 December 20.2	x

	20.2 Rand	20.1 Rand
Dividend per ordinary share (2) (3)	0,35	0,10

APE LTD
NOTES FOR THE YEAR ENDED 31 DECEMBER 20.2

15. Dividends not recognised as a distribution to owners

A final ordinary dividend of R25 000 (R0,25 per share (4)) was proposed on 31 December 20.2.

(1) 20 000 + 15 000 = 35 000
(2) 10 000/100 000 = 0,10
(3) (20 000 + 15 000)/100 000 = 0,35
(4) 25 000/100 000 = 0,25

❑ QUESTION IAS 1.10

Ace Ltd has the following loan from a financial institution:

• Date incurred	1 January 20.1
• Interest rate	12% p.a.
• Instalments (payable monthly in arrears)	R19 750
• Period	4 years
• Outstanding amount	
– 1 January 20.1	R750 000
– 31 December 20.3	R222 292

Ace Ltd entered into a refinancing agreement with the financial institution on 10 January 20.4 in terms of which the outstanding amount may be repaid in two annual instalments of R127 800 each, i.e. Ace Ltd will only pay the final instalment on 31 December 20.5.

Ace Ltd has a 31 December year end. The financial statements for the year ended 31 December 20.3 were authorised for issue on 25 February 20.4.

Required

Explain how the above-mentioned matter should be accounted for in the financial statements of Ace Ltd for the year ended 31 December 20.3 in accordance with the requirements of IAS 1.

❑ QUESTION IAS 1.11

You are preparing the financial statements of Africa Media Ltd for the year ended 30 September 20.2. The company is a leading publisher of popular magazines and publications that deal with music and related entertainment. An analytical review of the general ledger accounts revealed the following:

1. Salary bonuses of R22 million, compared to an average of R5,8 million during the previous few years, have been paid to employees. The financial manager explained that a new incentive scheme was adopted in terms of which all employees share in the benefits of increased sales figures.

2. Amortisation of copyrights paid to publish articles from overseas magazines in a local publication – R2,5 million.

3. A loss of R1,8 million is attributable to the loss suffered after an uninsured property was destroyed by an earthquake.

4. During the current year the company was responsible for the formation of the Africa Media Foundation with its main purpose being to donate funds to welfare organisations. This foundation forms part of Africa Media Ltd's social investment programme. The company contributed R3 million to the fund.

Required

Briefly discuss the disclosure requirements (if any) of the above-mentioned matters in the notes to Africa Media Ltd's financial statements according to the requirements of IAS 1. Africa Media Ltd classifies its expenses by function in its statement of profit or loss and other comprehensive income.

❑ QUESTION IAS 1.12

Arium Ltd has the following balances at 30 June 20.5:

	Rand
Share capital	300 000
Revaluation surplus	185 600
Foreign currency translation reserve	335 000
Retained earnings	405 000

During the year ended 30 June 20.6, the following movements in the entity's equity occurred:

	Rand
Profit for the year	225 500
Dividends paid	75 000
Revaluation of land (surplus)	105 000
Deficit on currency translation, debited directly against foreign currency translation reserve	50 000
Shares issued (10 000 ordinary shares)	40 000

The opening retained earnings should be credited with an amount of R37 500 as a result of an accounting policy change during the year ended 30 June 20.6.

Required

a. Prepare the other comprehensive income section of Arium Ltd's statement of profit or loss and other comprehensive income for the year ended 30 June 20.6. Ignore taxation.
b. Prepare Arium Ltd's statement of changes in equity for the year ended 30 June 20.6. Ignore comparative amounts and taxation.

Your answer must comply with the requirements of International Financial Reporting Standards (IFRS).

❑ QUESTION IAS 1.13

Milo Ltd had 500 000 10% participating preference shares and 4 000 000 ordinary shares in issue throughout the two financial years ended on 30 June 20.7 and 30 June 20.8.

The 10% participating preference shares have an additional right to earn dividend income of one-tenth of the total dividend paid/proposed to the ordinary shareholders while Milo Ltd is a going concern or on liquidation of Milo Ltd.

On 30 June 20.7 an ordinary dividend of R0,50 per share was proposed by the directors. This dividend was approved by the shareholders at the annual general meeting held on 15 October 20.7.

During the financial year ended 30 June 20.8, an interim ordinary dividend and preference dividend was paid on 31 December 20.7. The directors proposed a final ordinary dividend on 30 June 20.8 of R1 million. Total dividends paid in cash during the year ended 30 June 20.8 amounted to R3 155 000.

Required

Calculate and disclose dividend per share of Milo Ltd for the year ended 30 June 20.8 in accordance with the requirements of IAS 1.

IAS 2

Inventories

❑ QUESTIONS AND SOLUTIONS

IAS 2.1	Measurement of inventories – cost of conversion: Calculations
IAS 2.2	Measurement of inventories – net realisable value: Calculations
IAS 2.3	Cost formulas: Calculations and presentation
IAS 2.4	Measurement of inventories – allocation of production overheads: Calculations
IAS 2.5	Presentation and disclosure of inventories in the financial statements
IAS 2.6	Use of different valuation methods for inventories: Discussion
IAS 2.7	Joint products and by-products: Calculations
IAS 2.8	Inventory valuation: Calculations and disclosure
IAS 2.9	Cash discount and settlement discount: Journal entries

❑ QUESTIONS

IAS 2.10	Net realisable value of finished goods and raw materials: Calculations
IAS 2.11	Inventory valuation and calculation of net realisable value of raw materials: Calculations
IAS 2.12	Inventory valuation and profit calculation: Calculations
IAS 2.13	Inventory valuation: Presentation, disclosure and discussion
IAS 2.14*	Allocation of production overheads: Presentation and disclosure
IAS 2.15*	Inventory valuation and net realisable value: Calculations, discussion, presentation and disclosure

* *These questions are not in the textbook, but are available in the electronic guide for lecturers containing the suggested solutions for questions without answers.*

❑ QUESTION IAS 2.1

Bata Ltd manufactures takkies (shoes). The normal production capacity of the plant is 500 000 pairs of takkies per annum. Due to an increase in local demand, abnormally high production volumes were reached during the financial year ended 31 December 20.2 with the manufacture of 550 000 pairs of takkies.

There were 20 000 pairs of takkies on hand at 1 January 20.2, and 540 000 pairs of takkies were sold during the year. No raw material inventory is maintained as purchases are matched to production demand.

The following information is available for the year ended 31 December 20.2:

	Rand
Opening inventory (pairs of takkies in rand value)	160 000
Raw material purchased	1 375 000
Auditors' remuneration	120 000
Directors' remuneration	125 000
Telephone cost	70 000
Advertising	220 000
Depreciation	
Plant	143 000
Equipment (20% factory; 80% administration)	42 000
Delivery vehicles	112 000
Furniture (20% factory; 80% administration)	31 000
Electricity and water – plant	50 000
Repairs and maintenance	
Plant (60% fixed)	150 000
Delivery vehicles	25 000
Cost of factory management	120 000
Consumable inventory used in production process	165 000
Wages	2 420 000
Salaries	300 000
Pension fund contributions	55 000
Medical aid fund contributions	35 000
Unemployment insurance fund (UIF) contributions	30 000

It is estimated that 60% of salaries and related contributions to pension fund, medical aid fund and UIF, are attributable to the management of the manufacturing activities. Wages represent direct labour costs incurred in the production of takkies.

There was no work in progress at the beginning or the end of the year.

The estimated net realisable value exceeds the cost of the unsold inventory.

Required

Calculate the value of the closing inventory of Bata Ltd as at 31 December 20.2 in compliance with the requirements of International Financial Reporting Standards (IFRS).

❖ **Suggested solution IAS 2.1**

Closing inventory	**Pairs of takkies**
Opening inventory	20 000
Manufactured	550 000
Sold	(540 000)
	30 000

Allocation of fixed production overheads	**Rand**
Total fixed production overheads	619 600
Depreciation – plant	143 000
Depreciation – equipment (1)	8 400
Depreciation – furniture (2)	6 200
Repairs and maintenance – plant (3)	90 000
Cost of factory management	120 000
Salaries (4)	180 000
Unemployment insurance contributions (5)	18 000
Pension fund contributions (6)	33 000
Medical aid fund contributions (7)	21 000

(1) 42 000 × 20% = 8 400
(2) 31 000 × 20% = 6 200
(3) 150 000 × 60% = 90 000
(4) 300 000 × 60% = 180 000
(5) 30 000 × 60% = 18 000
(6) 55 000 × 60% = 33 000
(7) 35 000 × 60% = 21 000

Allocation of variable production overheads	**Rand**
Total variable production overheads	275 000
Electricity and water	50 000
Repairs and maintenance – plant (1)	60 000
Consumable inventory used in production process	165 000

(1) 150 000 × 40% = 60 000

Unit cost of finished goods	**Rand**
Raw materials (1)	2,50
Labour cost (2)	4,40
Fixed production overheads (3)	1,13
Variable production overheads (4)	0,50
	8,53

(1) 1 375 000 / 550 000 = 2,50
(2) 2 420 000 / 550 000 = 4,40
(3) 619 600 / 550 000 = 1,13
(4) 275 000 / 550 000 = 0,50

According to IAS 2.13, in periods of abnormally high production, the amount of fixed production overheads allocated to each unit of production is reduced so that inventory is not measured above cost, therefore the allocation of fixed production overheads was based on actual production of 550 000 pairs of takkies and not on normal capacity of 500 000 pairs.

Inventory valuation	**Rand**
Closing inventory (1)	255 900

(1) 30 000 × 8,53 = 255 900

❑ QUESTION IAS 2.2

Rascall Ltd is a diversified entity whose reporting date is 31 December. The following information, relating to inventory, is available:

Telebunken radios

Units manufactured	10 000
Production cost per unit	R500
Selling price per unit	R600
Units on hand – 31 December 20.2	6 000
– 31 December 20.3	5 700

On 31 December 20.3 the Minister of Finance announced the scrapping of import duties on imported radios. According to the marketing director, this announcement will enable the company to import a similar product at R380 per unit which could be sold at an estimated selling price of R450 per unit.

Product 'Blush'

Rascall Ltd concluded a contract with Group Six Ltd to deliver 10 000 units of product Blush at a fixed price of R1 600 per unit. Delivery of the units took place evenly over the negotiated delivery period. Rascall Ltd manufactured 12 000 units. The production cost per unit of Blush is R1 000. The units produced in excess of the contract requirements (more than 10 000) are sold at R800 per unit.

On 31 December 20.3, inventory on hand of Blush was as follows:

	Units	**Selling price per unit Rand**
Units contracted for	6 800	1 600
Units not contracted for	1 400	800

Product 'Jax'

On 31 December 20.2, 2 000 units of Jax were on hand. The cost per unit of Jax is R3 000 and the selling price is R5 000. On 31 December 20.2 the marketing director informed the board of directors that a competitor would introduce a similar product to the market on 1 January 20.3 at a selling price of R2 000 per unit. The board decided to reduce the selling price of Jax to R2 000 per unit as from 1 January 20.3 to be able to compete in the marketplace.

On 31 December 20.3 the competitor was liquidated and Rascall Ltd increased the selling price of Jax to R5 000 per unit. On 31 December 20.3, 1 200 units of Jax were on hand.

Raw material 'Dol'

Raw material Dol is used in the production of Kosp. Dol was originally purchased at R120 per unit but purchases of raw material are now made from a new foreign supplier, which resulted in a reduction of the unit cost to R30. On 31 December 20.3, 20 000 units of Dol were on hand (purchased at a unit cost of R120). The cost of production of a unit Kosp is R1 000. The drop in cost price per unit of Dol (due to the new supplier) resulted in the selling price of Kosp being reduced to R940 per unit. Three units of Dol are used to produce one unit of Kosp.

Required

a. Calculate the value of inventory of Rascall Ltd at 31 December 20.3.
b. Calculate the amount written off or written back (in profit or loss) in relation to inventory during the year ended 31 December 20.3 in accordance with the requirements of International Financial Reporting Standards (IFRS).

❖ **Suggested solution IAS 2.2**

Rascall Ltd

a. Inventory valuation

	Rand
Telebunken radios (1)	2 565 000
Product Blush (2)	7 920 000
Product Jax (3)	3 600 000
Raw material Dol (4)	2 000 000
	16 085 000

(1) 450 × 5 700 = 2 565 000
(2) (6 800 × 1 000) + (1 400 × 800) = 7 920 000
(3) 1 200 × 3 000 = 3 600 000
(4) 20 000 × ([940 – {1 000 – (120 × 3)}] / 3) = 2 000 000

b. Amounts written off

	Rand
Telebunken radios (1)	285 000
Product Blush (2)	280 000
Raw material Dol (3)	400 000
	965 000

(1) 5 700 × (500 – 450) = 285 000
(2) 1 400 × (1 000 – 800) = 280 000
(3) 20 000 × (120 – 100) = 400 000; the write-off on raw material Dol is limited to the loss made on the finished product Kosp, since each finished product is manufactured using three units of raw material (see IAS 2.32).

Amounts written back	**Rand**
Product Jax (1)	1 200 000

(1) 1 200 × [3 000 – 2 000] = 1 200 000

❑ QUESTION IAS 2.3

Unique Ltd entered into the following inventory transactions during April 20.6:

April

1	Inventory on hand: 20 units	– 14 at R180 each – 6 at R200 each
5	Purchased 60 units at R300 each	
10	Purchased 35 units at R400 each	
11	Sold 30 units	
15	Purchased 40 units at R500 each	
19	Sold 50 units	
22	Purchased 100 units at R400 each	
30	Sold 60 units	

The selling price during April amounted to R600 per unit.

Unique Ltd uses a perpetual inventory system. On 30 April 20.6 it was determined that the normal selling price of the units had dropped to R500 per unit because a competitor had entered the market. Normal selling expenses amount to R100 per unit.

Required

a. Calculate the cost of sales in the statement of profit or loss and other comprehensive income for April and the value of inventory on hand at 30 April 20.6 using each of the following cost formulas:
   i. FIFO (first-in, first-out); and
   ii. Weighted average cost method.
b. Present the above information in the statement of profit or loss and other comprehensive income of Unique Ltd for the month ended April 20.6 in compliance with the requirements of International Financial Reporting Standards (IFRS). Ignore taxation.

❖ **Suggested solution IAS 2.3**

a. Cost of inventory and inventory on hand

i. FIFO method

Cost of sales (calc 1)	**Rand**
Cost of inventory sold	48 220
11 April 20.6	6 720
19 April 20.6	15 000
30 April 20.6	26 500
Inventory written down to net realisable value (1)	1 500
Cost of inventory	49 720

Closing inventory	**Rand**
Net realisable value (2)	46 000

(1) 47 500 (calc 1) – 46 000 = 1 500
(2) 115 × (500 – 100) = 46 000

ii. Weighted average cost method

Cost of sales (calc 2)	**Rand**
11 April 20.6	9 330
19 April 20.6	18 550
30 April 20.6	23 280
Cost of inventory sold	51 160

	Rand
Closing inventory	
Cost price (calc 2)	44 560

b. Disclosure

UNIQUE LTD
EXTRACT FROM THE STATEMENT OF PROFIT OR LOSS AND OTHER COMPREHENSIVE INCOME FOR THE MONTH ENDED 30 APRIL 20.6

	FIFO Rand	**Weighted average** Rand
Revenue (1)	84 000	84 000
Cost of sales	(49 720)	(51 160)
Gross profit	34 280	32 840

(1) (30 + 50 + 60) × R600 = R84 000

Calculations

1. FIFO cost formula

		Number of units	Price p.u. Rand	Total Rand
1 April	Balance	14	180	2 520
	Balance	6	200	1 200
5 April	Purchases	60	300	18 000
10 April	Purchases	35	400	14 000
11 April	Sales	(30)		(6 720)
	Sales	14	180	2 520
	Sales	6	200	1 200
	Sales	10	300	3 000
15 April	Purchases	40	500	20 000
19 April	Sales	(50)	300	(15 000)
22 April	Purchases	100	400	40 000
30 April	Sales	(60)		(26 500)
	Sales	35	400	14 000
	Sales	25	500	12 500
Total		115		47 500

2. Weighted average cost formula

		Number of units	Price p.u. Rand	Total Rand
1 April	Balance	14	180	2 520
	Balance	6	200	1 200
5 April	Purchases	60	300	18 000
10 April	Purchases	35	400	14 000
	Balance (1)	115	311	35 720
11 April	Sales	(30)	311	(9 330)
	Balance	85		26 390
15 April	Purchases	40	500	20 000
	Balance (2)	125	371	46 390
19 April	Sales	(50)	371	(18 550)
	Balance	75		27 840
22 April	Purchases	100	400	40 000
	Balance (3)	175	388	67 840
30 April	Sales	(60)	388	(23 280)
		115		44 560

(1) 35 720 / 115 = 311
(2) 46 390 / 125 = 371
(3) 67 840 / 175 = 388

❑ QUESTION IAS 2.4

Action Ltd, which was incorporated on 1 January 20.3, manufactures product 'Power' for the building industry. Action Ltd has a reporting date of 31 December.

The following information is provided:

- Normal capacity of plant – 25 000 units
- Market demand per annum – 18 000 units

- Various fixed costs incurred:

Year	20.5 Rand
Total	136 000
Insurance – factory plant and equipment	6 000
Selling expenses	18 000
Depreciation – factory	80 000
Depreciation – offices	10 000
Auditors' remuneration	16 000
Insurance – delivery vehicles	6 000

- Fixed production overheads have increased annually at the same rate as variable costs.
- Variable costs included in closing inventory at 31 December are as follows:

Year	20.5	20.4	20.3
Variable costs	R87 120	R77 000	R60 000

- The following inventory was on hand at 31 December:

Year	20.5	20.4	20.3
Units	6 600	7 000	6 000

- All sales are on credit.

Required

Calculate the value of inventory of Action Ltd for the reporting dates 31 December 20.3 to 20.5 in accordance with the requirements of International Financial Reporting Standards (IFRS).

❖ **Suggested solution IAS 2.4**

Fixed production overheads – 20.5	**Rand**
Insurance – factory plant and equipment	6 000
Depreciation – factory	80 000
	86 000

Increase in variable costs	**20.5**	**20.4**	**20.3**
Variable cost per unit (1)	R13,20	R11,00	R10,00
% increase (2)	20%	10%	–

(1) 87 120 / 6 600 = 13,20; 77 000 / 7 000 = 11,00; 60 000 / 6 000 = 10,00
(2) (11,00 – 10,00) / 10,00 × 100 = 10%; (13,20 – 11,00) / 11,00 × 100 = 20%

Units produced	**20.5**	**20.4**	**20.3**
Opening inventory	(7 000)	(6 000)	–
Sales	18 000	18 000	18 000
Closing inventory	6 600	7 000	6 000
Production	17 600	19 000	24 000

Fixed production overheads for 20.3 to 20.5	**Rand**
20.5 (as calculated)	86 000
20.4 (20% increase – 86 000 / 120 × 100)	71 667
20.3 (10% increase – 71 667 / 110 × 100)	65 152

Fixed production overheads to be included for 20.3 to 20.5	**Rand**
20.5 (86 000 / 25 000) × 6 600	22 704
20.4 (71 667 / 25 000) × 7 000	20 067
20.3 (65 152 / 25 000) × 6 000	15 636

Value of inventory, including fixed production overheads at 31 December

	20.5 Rand	**20.4 Rand**	**20.3 Rand**
Variable costs allocated	87 120	77 000	60 000
Fixed production overheads allocated	22 704	20 067	15 636
Total	109 824	97 067	75 636

❑ QUESTION IAS 2.5

The following information has been extracted from the trial balance of Tech Ltd, a manufacturer with a reporting date of 31 December 20.6:

	Rand Dr/(Cr)
Sales	(800 000)
Opening inventory	
Finished goods	80 000
Work in progress	30 000
Raw materials	50 000
Purchase of raw materials	180 000
Variable production costs	
Labour and overheads	120 000
Fixed production overheads	100 000

Additional information

1. During the year there was an abnormal spillage of raw materials of R20 000.
2. Fixed production overheads are allocated at R2 per unit based on a normal capacity of 50 000 units. The actual production for 20.6 was 40 000 units.

3. Closing inventory is as follows:

	Cost Rand	Net realisable value Rand
Raw materials	30 000	30 000
Work in progress	50 000	40 000
Finished goods	40 000	60 000

4. Other closing inventory is as follows:

	Cost Rand
Stationery	10 000
Packaging materials	15 000

The net realisable value of the above is more than cost.

Tech Ltd uses the first-in, first-out method to value inventory.

Required

Present and disclose all matters related to inventories in the financial statements of Tech Ltd for the reporting period ended 31 December 20.6 in compliance with the requirements of International Financial Reporting Standards (IFRS). Ignore taxation.

❖ **Suggested solution IAS 2.5**

Presentation and disclosure

TECH LTD
EXTRACT FROM THE STATEMENT OF FINANCIAL POSITION AS AT 31 DECEMBER 20.6

	Note	Rand
ASSETS		
Current assets		
Inventory	2	145 000

TECH LTD
EXTRACT FROM THE STATEMENT OF PROFIT OR LOSS AND OTHER COMPREHENSIVE INCOME FOR THE YEAR ENDED 31 DECEMBER 20.6

	Rand
Revenue	800 000
Cost of sales (calc 4)	(440 000)
Gross profit	360 000

TECH LTD
NOTES FOR THE YEAR ENDED 31 DECEMBER 20.6

1. Accounting policy

1.1 Inventory

Inventory is valued at the lower of cost and net realisable value. Cost is assigned using the first-in, first-out cost formula.

2. Inventory	**Rand**
Consumable goods	25 000
Raw materials	30 000
Work in progress (calc 2)	50 000
Finished goods	40 000
	145 000

Calculations

1. Raw materials	**Rand**
Opening inventory	50 000
Purchases	180 000
Write off of abnormal spillage	(20 000)
Closing inventory	(30 000)
Transferred to work in progress	180 000

2. Work in progress	**Rand**
Opening inventory	30 000
Raw materials (calc 1)	180 000
Variable production overheads	120 000
Fixed production overheads (1)	80 000
Closing inventory (2)	(50 000)
Transferred to finished goods	360 000

(1) 40 000 × 2,00 = 80 000

(2) No adjustment is made for the net realisable value of work in progress as the finished goods in which they will be incorporated are expected to be sold at or above cost based on the comparison of cost and net realisable value of finished goods at 31 December 20.6 (refer to IAS 2.32).

3. Finished goods	**Rand**
Opening inventory	80 000
Transferred from work in progress	360 000
Closing inventory	(40 000)
Cost of finished goods	400 000

4. Cost of sales

	Rand
Cost of finished goods (calc 3)	400 000
Raw material abnormal spillage	20 000
Under recovery of fixed production overheads (3)	20 000
	440 000

(3) 100 000 – 80 000 = 20 000

❑ QUESTION IAS 2.6

Dumela Ltd purchases computer equipment. Some of this equipment is sold to customers as part of stand-alone computer installations, while the other computer equipment is installed by Dumela Ltd in a specific manufacturing plant.

Dumela Ltd currently uses the same cost formulas to value its entire computer inventory.

Required

Discuss, in terms of IAS 2, whether it will be allowed to value the stand-alone computer equipment differently from the computer equipment used in the manufacturing plant.

❖ Suggested solution IAS 2.6

Paragraph 25 of IAS 2 requires that either one of two cost formulas (FIFO or weighted average) be used to value inventories which have a similar nature and use to an entity.

Paragraphs 25 and 26 of IAS 2 state that where items of inventory have a different nature or use to the entity, different cost formulas may be justified. However, a difference in geographical location of inventories is, by itself, not sufficient to justify the use of different cost formulas (not applicable in this case).

Dumela Ltd, therefore, could apply one cost formula to the computer equipment sold as stand-alone computer equipment to customers and another cost formula to the computer equipment installed in the manufacturing plant. This treatment is allowed since the computer equipment has a different use in each case.

❑ QUESTION IAS 2.7

Zela Ltd was incorporated on 3 January 20.2.

The following information was extracted from the financial records of Zela Ltd for the reporting date 31 December 20.2:

- **Joint products**

  Total manufacturing cost (material, labour and overheads) to produce 15 000 kg of finished goods Joint Product 1 (JP1) and Joint Product 2 (JP2) amounted to R150 000.

The 15 000 kg of finished goods represents 5 000 kg of JP1 and 10 000 kg of JP2. The net realisable values of both products are in excess of their cost.

At 31 December 20.2, there are 1 000 kg of JP1 and 2 000 kg of JP2 on hand.

- **By-product**

  Product Y and by-product YY are produced during the manufacturing process of Product Y.

  By-product YY can be sold for R3 per unit while Product Y can be sold for R30 per unit.

  The total cost of manufacture of Product Y is R25 per unit.

  At 31 December 20.2, there are 10 000 units of Product Y and 100 units of by-product YY on hand.

Required

Calculate the value of the inventory items on hand as at 31 December 20.2 of Zela Ltd in accordance with the requirements of International Financial Reporting Standards (IFRS).

❖ **Suggested solution IAS 2.7**

Joint products	**Rand**
JP1 (1)	10 000
JP2 (2)	20 000
	30 000

(1) (5 000 / 15 000 × 150 000) × 1 000 / 5 000 = 10 000
(2) (10 000 / 15 000 × 150 000) × 2 000 / 10 000 = 20 000

Primary product	**Rand**
Y (1)	249 700

(1) 10 000 × 25 = 250 000 – (100 × 3) = 249 700

By-product	**Rand**
YY (1)	300

(1) 100 × 3 = 300

❑ QUESTION IAS 2.8

Babe Ltd began operations on 5 January 20.4. The following costs were incurred during the year ended 31 December 20.4:

	Rand
Raw materials purchased	125 000
Direct labour	300 000
Variable production overheads (administrative: 20%; manufacturing: 80%)	250 000
Fixed production overheads	500 000

The level of normal production was expected to be 100 000 units for the year ended 31 December 20.4, whereas the actual level of production was 80 000 units for this period.

Of the raw materials, 80% have been used in the manufacturing process during the year. Work in progress represents 20% of the total manufacturing costs at 31 December 20.4.

As at 31 December 20.4, 60% of those goods that were finished were sold at cost plus a 10% mark-up.

At year end it was apparent that the entire balance of finished goods could be sold for R400 000, the entire balance of work in progress could be sold for R220 000 (assuming that the work in progress will be completed at a further cost of R50 000 and selling costs of R5 000 will be incurred), and the entire inventory of raw materials could be sold 'as is' for R26 000 (no further costs will be incurred).

Required

a. Calculate the cost per class of inventory at 31 December 20.4 so as to comply with the requirements of International Financial Reporting Standards (IFRS).
b. Calculate the net realisable values per class of inventory at 31 December 20.4 so as to comply with the requirements of International Financial Reporting Standards (IFRS).
c. Prepare the notes related to all matters of inventories in the financial statements of Babe Ltd for the year ended 31 December 20.4 so as to comply with the requirements of International Financial Reporting Standards (IFRS). Ignore taxation.

❖ Suggested solution IAS 2.8

a. Cost per class of inventory

	Rand
Raw materials at 31 December 20.4	
Raw material purchased	125 000
Transfer to work in progress (1)	(100 000)
Closing inventory	25 000

(1) 125 000 × 80% = 100 000

Total cost of manufacturing at 31 December 20.4	
Raw materials used	100 000
Direct labour	300 000
Variable production overheads (1)	200 000
Fixed production overheads (2)	400 000
Total cost of manufacturing	1 000 000

(1) 250 000 × 80% = 200 000
(2) 500 000/100 000 × 80 000 = 400 000

	Rand
Work in progress at 31 December 20.4	
Closing inventory (1)	200 000

(1) 1 000 000 × 20% = 200 000

Finished goods at 31 December 20.4	
Goods finished during 20.4 (1)	800 000
Goods already sold (2)	(480 000)
Closing inventory	320 000

(1) 1 000 000 × 80% = 800 000
(2) 800 000 × 60% = 480 000

b. **Net realisable value per inventory class**

	Rand
Raw materials	26 000
Work in progress (1)	165 000
Finished goods	400 000

(1) 220 000 – 50 000 – 5 000 = 165 000

c. **BABE LTD**
NOTES FOR THE YEAR ENDED 31 DECEMBER 20.4

1. **Accounting policies**

1.1 **Inventories**

Inventory is measured at the lower of cost and net realisable value using the weighted average cost formula.

2. **Inventories**

	20.4 Rand
Raw materials	25 000
Work in progress (1)	165 000
Finished goods	320 000
	510 000

(1) Work in progress is valued at net replacement value.

❑ QUESTION IAS 2.9

Pices Ltd has the sole right to distribute a certain product in Gauteng. The product is purchased from the manufacturer and sold at a mark-up of 25% on the cost of the purchase before any discounts are taken into account.

Pices Ltd always pays the manufacturer 10 days after the receipt of the product, because they are then entitled to a 5% settlement discount.

A large customer placed an order for products to the value of R100 000 (sales price) with Pices Ltd. Pices Ltd purchased the products from the manufacturer and delivered them to the customer.

Required

a. Prepare the journal entries for the purchase and sale transactions in the records of Pices Ltd if the customer pays cash on the date of delivery and a cash discount of 10% is given.
b. Prepare the journal entries for the sale transaction in the records of Pices Ltd if the customer usually pays 10 days after the product is delivered to the customer and a settlement discount of 10% is given. Ignore taxation.

❖ **Suggested solution IAS 2.9**

a. Purchase transaction

	Rand Dr/(Cr)
Inventory (P or L) (1)	76 000
Creditor (SFPos)	(80 000)
Allowance for settlement discount (SFPos)	4 000
Creditor (SFPos)	80 000
Bank (SFPos)	(76 000)
Allowance for settlement discount (SFPos)	(4 000)

(1) 100 000 × 100 / 125 = 80 000
80 000 × 95% = 76 000

Sale transaction

	Rand Dr/(Cr)
Bank (SFPos) (2)	90 000
Revenue (P or L)	(90 000)
Cost of sales (P or L)	76 000
Inventory (SFPos)	(76 000)

(2) 100 000 × 90% = 90 000

b. Sale transaction

	Rand Dr/(Cr)
Debtor (SFPos) (3)	100 000
Revenue (P or L)	(90 000)
Allowance for settlement discount (SFPos)	(10 000)
Bank (SFPos)	90 000
Debtor (SFPos)	(100 000)
Allowance for settlement discount (SFPos)	10 000
Cost of sales (P or L)	76 000
Inventory (SFPos)	(76 000)

(3) 100 000 × 90% = 90 000

❑ QUESTION IAS 2.10

The following information is available in respect of Dolo Ltd, a manufacturing concern:

Calculation of historical cost of manufactured inventory – per unit	**Rand**
Raw materials (1 kg per unit)	625
Labour	225
Variable overheads	350
Fixed overheads	200
	1 400

Additional information

1. More competitors have entered the market resulting in the selling price being reduced by R500 to R2 000. The R2 000 represents the average price at which finished goods can be sold.

2. Delivery costs of products sold amount to 20% of the selling price.

3. Commission payable on sales is calculated at 15% of the selling price.

Required

Calculate the net realisable value per unit of inventory of Dolo Ltd in accordance with the requirements of International Financial Reporting Standards (IFRS).

❑ QUESTION IAS 2.11

Daisy Ltd manufactures and sells a specific product. Purchases of raw materials are done every Monday and amount to 15 000 tons per week. The supplier's price for the raw materials was R1 000 per ton for the first semester of 20.5, but it increased on 1 July 20.5 to R1 500 per ton and then stayed constant until 1 February 20.6, after which the price decreased to R1 300 per ton. Additional customs tax of R100 per ton and transport costs to the company's factory of R200 per ton are also paid.

The following production information is available for the reporting date 31 December 20.5:

• Normal capacity per week	15 000 ton
• Variable production overheads	R250 per ton
• Fixed production overheads based on the normal capacity of the facility	R300 000 per week

There is no loss in tonnage during the production process.

The finished goods are marketed at R2 400 per ton. Costs to sell amounted to R30 000 per week and delivery costs amounted to R70 per ton.

There was no inventory on hand at the beginning of the year, but at 31 December 20.5 there were 50 000 tons of raw materials and 2 000 tons of finished goods on hand. It is expected that the costs to sell and deliver as mentioned above will still be valid for 20.6.

Required

a. Calculate the value of finished goods, closing inventory at 31 December 20.5 so as to comply with the requirements of International Financial Reporting Standards (IFRS).
b. Calculate the value of raw materials, closing inventory at 31 December 20.5 so as to comply with the requirements of International Financial Reporting Standards (IFRS).
c. Indicate if your answer in b. will be influenced if the sales price of the finished goods decreased to R2 300 per ton due to the decrease in the cost of raw materials.

❑ QUESTION IAS 2.12

Egoli Ltd has its head office in Gauteng and owns a factory in Mpumalanga. The company manufactures a product known as 'Gold Star' at the factory in Mpumalanga as there is surplus labour available. The raw materials are transported to Mpumalanga from Gauteng. A small quantity of the product is sold in Mpumalanga while the remainder is sent to Gauteng for sale.

The following information was obtained from the factory's records on 31 December 20.6:

	Rand Dr/(Cr)
Sales – 80 units 'Gold Star'	(2 000)
Machinery – at cost	110 000
Purchased on 30 June 20.4	60 000
Purchased on 30 June 20.6	50 000
Accumulated depreciation – 31 December 20.5	(18 000)
Loan (concluded to purchase machinery on 30 June 20.6, bearing interest at 10% per annum, repayable in full on 30 June 20.9)	(50 000)
Interest paid on loan	2 000
Salaries and wages for production	250 000
Transport costs for 2 000 units of 'Gold Star' to Gauteng	28 000
Administrative expenses paid	40 000

On 31 December 20.6 the following information was extracted from the accounting records of Egoli Ltd:

	Rand
Sales – 1 600 units 'Gold Star'	700 000
Cash	500 000
Credit	200 000
Raw materials for 2 800 units sent to Mpumalanga for production	56 000
Transport costs of the above 2 800 units	5 000
Administrative expenses paid	12 000

Additional information

1. There were only finished units of 'Gold Star' on hand at Egoli Ltd's head office on 31 December 20.6. Only raw material inventory is on hand in Mpumalanga. There were no inventory shortages, work in progress at the beginning or end of the year or opening inventory of raw materials and finished goods.

2. One unit of raw material is used to produce one unit of 'Gold Star'.

3. Machinery is depreciated using the straight-line method at 20% per annum.

Required

a. Calculate the value of the closing inventory of Egoli Ltd at 31 December 20.6 in compliance with the requirements of International Financial Reporting Standards (IFRS).
b. Calculate the profit or loss before tax of Egoli Ltd for the year ended 31 December 20.6 in compliance with the requirements of International Financial Reporting Standards (IFRS).

❑ QUESTION IAS 2.13

Bleshoender Ltd was incorporated on 15 December 20.0. The accountant has requested your assistance with the calculation and disclosure of inventory in the financial statements for the year ended 31 December 20.1.

The company manufactures and sells poultry feed. Three basic raw materials, namely bone meal, maize meal and a growth stimulant, are mixed in a predetermined ratio and are prepacked in 10 kg bags. No loss in kilograms occurs during the process.

The following information is available:

		Rand
Purchases:	Bone meal	13 515
	Maize meal	16 350
	Growth stimulants	11 630
	10 kg bags	1 790
Total variable production overheads		8 400
Total fixed production overheads		6 375
Distribution costs		3 000

Additional information

1. Closing inventory at 31 December 20.1 is as follows:

Bone meal	450 kg
Maize meal	750 kg
Growth stimulants	300 kg
Finished products	100 bags

   There is no work in progress closing inventory.

2. The normal capacity for the plant for the period under review is 850 bags.

3. The bone meal, maize meal, growth stimulants and finished products are valued on the FIFO basis and the 10 kg bags on the weighted average basis.

4. During the year the bags of feed were sold at R100 per bag. Due to the drought and the resulting shortage of maize, it is anticipated that the cost per bag, as well as the selling price per bag, will increase by at least R20 per bag.

5. During the inventory count on 31 December 20.1 it was discovered that the closing inventory of growth stimulants had been damaged and is no longer suitable for the manufacturing of feed. A local farmer undertook to buy the damaged growth stimulant at R3,00 per kg. Bleshoender Ltd is responsible for the delivery costs which are estimated to be R270 in total.

6. The current tax rate is 27%. Assume that all costs are tax deductible.

The accountant of Bleshoender Ltd has prepared the following schedule giving details of the purchases:

PURCHASES OF INVENTORY

Bone meal				**Rand**
1.	17/09/20.1	300 kg ×	R5,00 =	1 500,00
2.	25/10/20.1	600 kg ×	R5,25 =	3 150,00
3.	15/11/20.1	900 kg ×	R5,30 =	4 770,00
4.	01/12/20.1	450 kg ×	R5,40 =	2 430,00
5.	20/12/20.1	300 kg ×	R5,55 =	1 665,00
		2 550 kg ×	*R5,30 =	13 515,00

Maize meal				**Rand**
1.	18/09/20.1	500 kg ×	R3,50 =	1 750,00
2.	20/10/20.1	1 000 kg ×	R3,75 =	3 750,00
3.	17/11/20.1	1 500 kg ×	R3,90 =	5 850,00
4.	15/12/20.1	1 250 kg ×	R4,00 =	5 000,00
		4 250 kg ×	*R3,85 =	16 350,00

Growth stimulant				**Rand**
1.	17/09/20.1	200 kg ×	R7,00 =	1 400,00
2.	01/11/20.1	800 kg ×	R7,10 =	5 680,00
3.	17/12/20.1	700 kg ×	R6,50 =	4 550,00
		1 700 kg ×	*R6,84 =	11 630,00

10 kg bags				**Rand**
1.	25/09/20.1	300 ×	R1,70 =	510,00
2.	13/10/20.1	500 ×	R1,80 =	900,00
3.	30/11/20.1	200 ×	R1,90 =	380,00
		1 000 ×	*R1,79 =	1 790,00

* Average price per kg

Required

a. Present and disclose inventory and all matters relating to inventory in the financial statements of Bleshoender Ltd for the year ended 31 December 20.1 so as to comply with the requirements of International Financial Reporting Standards (IFRS).

b. Assume Bleshoender Ltd has two branches, one in East London and another in Nelspruit. At financial year end, each branch has unsold inventory on hand. The inventory on hand at the East London branch is valued on the weighted average basis while that at the Nelspruit branch is valued on the first-in, first-out basis.

Is the use of these different methods of valuation permitted in terms of IAS 2?

IAS 7

Statement of cash flows

❑ QUESTIONS AND SOLUTIONS

IAS 7.1	Statement of cash flows – revaluation of land, replacement and scrapping of property, plant and equipment, bank overdraft and share transactions
IAS 7.2	Consolidated statement of cash flows – indirect method, sale of property, plant and equipment
IAS 7.3	Consolidated statement of cash flows with acquisition of subsidiary
IAS 7.4	Consolidated statement of cash flows with equity accounting
IAS 7.5	Statement of cash flows – sundry transactions
IAS 7.6	Statement of cash flows – financial instruments: discussion

❑ QUESTIONS

IAS 7.7	Statement of cash flows – issue and redemption of shares
IAS 7.8	Statement of cash flows – sundry aspects – indirect method
IAS 7.9	Statement of cash flows – equity accounting
IAS 7.10	Consolidated statement of cash flows – indirect method
IAS 7.11	Consolidated statement of cash flows with purchase of subsidiary
IAS 7.12	Consolidated statement of cash flows with sale of subsidiary*

* *This question is not in the textbook, but is available in the electronic guide for lecturers containing the suggested solutions for questions without answers.*

Note: In all consolidation questions in this chapter, it is assumed that non-controlling interest is measured at the non-controlling interest's proportionate share of the acquiree's identifiable net assets.

❑ QUESTION IAS 7.1

You are provided with the following information in respect of Hagar Ltd:

HAGAR LTD
STATEMENT OF FINANCIAL POSITION AS AT 31 DECEMBER 20.5

	Note	20.5 Rand	20.4 Rand
ASSETS			
Non-current assets		521 000	258 000
Property, plant and equipment	5	500 000	250 000
Intangible assets		11 000	–
Financial asset at fair value through other comprehensive income – unlisted shares		6 000	4 000
Investment in subsidiary at cost		4 000	4 000
Current assets		399 500	308 000
Inventories		170 000	140 000
Trade and other receivables		214 000	150 000
Financial assets at fair value through profit or loss – held for trading		10 500	8 000
Cash and cash equivalents		5 000	10 000
Total assets		920 500	566 000
EQUITY AND LIABILITIES			
Total equity		488 140	240 000
Share capital	2	300 000	150 000
Retained earnings		172 760	85 000
Other components of equity		15 380	5 000
Total liabilities		432 360	326 000
Non-current liabilities		251 760	235 000
Long-term borrowings	4	250 000	235 000
Deferred tax		1 760	–
Current liabilities		180 600	91 000
Trade and other payables		103 000	71 000
Current portion of long-term borrowings		10 000	10 000
Current tax payable		47 600	–
Bank overdraft		20 000	10 000
Total equity and liabilities		920 500	566 000

HAGAR LTD
STATEMENT OF PROFIT OR LOSS AND OTHER COMPREHENSIVE INCOME FOR THE YEAR ENDED 31 DECEMBER 20.5

	Note	Rand	
Revenue		1 500 000	
Cost of sales		(1 000 000)	
Gross profit		500 000	
Other income	8	5 500	
Other expenses		(300 000)	
Finance costs		(30 000)	
Profit before tax	7	175 500	
Income tax expense	9	(47 740)	
Profit for the year		127 760	
Other comprehensive income			
Items that will not be reclassified to profit or loss			
Property revaluation		8 650	
Gain on property valuation			10 000
Tax expense			(1 350)
Share investment at fair value through other comprehensive income		1 730	
Gains arising during the year			2 000
Tax expense			(270)
Total comprehensive income for the year		138 140	

HAGAR LTD
STATEMENT OF CHANGES IN EQUITY FOR THE YEAR ENDED 31 DECEMBER 20.5

	A Rand	B Rand	C Rand	D Rand	E Rand
Balance at 1 January 20.5	150 000	5 000	–	85 000	240 000
Changes in equity for 20.5					
Total comprehensive income for the year	–	8 650	1 730	127 760	138 140
Profit for the year	–	–	–	127 760	127 760
Other comprehensive income	–	8 650	1 730	–	10 380
Dividends	–	–	–	(40 000)	(40 000)
Issue of share capital	150 000	–	–	–	150 000
Balance 31 December 20.5	300 000	13 650	1 730	172 760	488 140

A = Share capital
B = Revaluation surplus
C = Mark-to-market reserve
D = Retained earnings
E = Total equity

HAGAR LTD
EXTRACT FROM THE NOTES FOR THE YEAR ENDED 31 DECEMBER 20.5

2. **Share capital**	**20.5 Rand**	**20.4 Rand**
Ordinary shares		
Authorised and issued – 200 000 shares	300 000	150 000
	300 000	150 000

4. **Long-term borrowings**	**20.5 Rand**	**20.4 Rand**
B Bank – secured by a first bond over land and buildings – repayable at R10 000 per annum	150 000	160 000
X Bank – unsecured – repayable on 1 January 20.8	100 000	75 000
	250 000	235 000

5. **Property, plant and equipment**	**Land Rand**	**Machinery and equipment Rand**	**Vehicles Rand**	**Total Rand**
Carrying amount at 1 January 20.5	150 000	50 000	50 000	250 000
Gross carrying amount/cost	150 000	80 000	75 000	305 000
Accumulated depreciation	–	(30 000)	(25 000)	(55 000)
Depreciation for the year	–	(38 000)	(5 000)	(43 000)
Revaluation	10 000	–	–	10 000
Additions	105 000	163 000	–	268 000
Replacements	–	20 000	–	20 000
Scrapping of assets	–	(5 000)	–	(5 000)
Carrying amount at 31 December 20.5	265 000	190 000	45 000	500 000
Gross carrying amount/cost	265 000	255 000	75 000	595 000
Accumulated depreciation	–	(65 000)	(30 000)	(95 000)

7. **Profit before tax**	**20.5 Rand**
Profit before tax is shown after taking the following into account:	
Depreciation	43 000
Loss on scrapping of machinery	5 000

8. **Other income**	**20.5 Rand**
Included in other income are the following:	
Investment income – dividends received	5 000
Fair value adjustment – held for trading investment	500

9. Income tax expense	**20.5 Rand**
The income tax expense comprises the following:	
Current tax	47 600
Deferred tax	140

Additional information

1. Included in trade and other payables is an amount of R2 000 (20.4: R2 000) being dividends payable to shareholders. This is the outstanding amount in respect of ordinary dividends.
2. The company purchased additional land and machinery during the year thereby increasing the capacity of the company. A machine with a carrying amount of R5 000, on which R3 000 depreciation has been written off, was scrapped during the year and replaced by a similar machine at a cost of R20 000.
3. A patent to manufacture equipment for aircrafts was acquired on 30 December 20.5 and therefore no amortisation was necessary.
4. Included in trade and other receivables is an amount of R4 000 (20.4: RNil) related to prepaid expenses.
5. A normal SA tax rate of 27% and a CGT rate of 13,5% are assumed.
6. The bank overdraft is repayable on demand and forms an integral part of Hagar Ltd's cash management activities. The bank balance often fluctuates from being positive to overdrawn.

Required

Prepare the statement of cash flows, using the direct method, of Hagar Ltd for the year ended 31 December 20.5 in accordance with the requirements of International Financial Reporting Standards (IFRS). Ignore comparative amounts.

❖ **Suggested solution IAS 7.1**

HAGAR LTD
STATEMENT OF CASH FLOWS FOR THE YEAR ENDED 31 DECEMBER 20.5

	Note	Rand
Cash flows from operating activities		119 000
Cash receipts from customers (calc 1)		1 440 000
Cash paid to suppliers and employees (calc 2)		(1 254 000)
Cash generated from operations	1	186 000
Dividends received*		5 000
Interest paid		(30 000)
Dividends paid** (calc 3)		(40 000)
Purchase of shares held at fair value through profit or loss*** (calc 4)		(2 000)

	Note	Rand
Cash flows from investing activities		(299 000)
Purchase of property, plant and equipment	2	(288 000)
Additions to property, plant and equipment		(268 000)
Replacement of property, plant and equipment		(20 000)
Purchase of patents and trademarks (1)		(11 000)
Cash flows from financing activities		165 000
Proceeds from long-term borrowings (calc 6)	3	25 000
Repayment of long-term borrowings (calc 6)	3	(10 000)
Proceeds from issue of shares (calc 5)		150 000
Net decrease in cash and cash equivalents		(15 000)
Cash and cash equivalents at beginning of year	4	–
Cash and cash equivalents at end of year	4	(15 000)

* Could also be classified as investing activities, but is classified consistently as operating activities in this chapter.

** Could also be classified as financing activities, but is classified consistently as operating activities in this chapter.

*** In compliance with IAS 7.14(g) and .15 and .16(d).

(1) 11 000 – 0 = 11 000

HAGAR LTD
NOTES FOR THE YEAR ENDED 31 DECEMBER 20.5

1. Reconciliation of cash generated from operations and profit before tax (not required by IAS 7)

	Rand
Profit before tax	175 500
Adjustments	
Investment income	(5 000)
Fair value adjustment – Held for trading investment	(500)
Interest paid	30 000
Loss on scrapping of assets	5 000
Depreciation	43 000
Profit before changes in working capital	248 000
Changes in working capital	(62 000)
Increase in trade and other receivables (1)	(64 000)
Increase in inventories (calc 2)	(30 000)
Increase in trade and other payables (calc 2)	32 000
Cash generated from operations	186 000

(1) 214 000 – 150 000 = 64 000

2. Purchases of property, plant and equipment

	Rand
Additions to land and buildings	105 000
Additions to machinery and equipment	163 000
Replacement of machinery and equipment	20 000
	288 000

3. Increase in long-term borrowings

	Rand
Loans raised (calc 6)	25 000
Loans repaid (calc 6)	(10 000)
	15 000

4. Reconciliation of liabilities arising from financing and other activities

	20.4 Rand	Cash flows Rand	Non-cash changes* Rand	20.5 Rand
Financing activities				
Long-term borrowings	235 000			250 000
Current portion of long-term borrowings	10 000			10 000
Total long-term borrowings (1)	245 000	15 000	–	260 000
Other activities				
Cash and cash equivalents (other than bank overdraft)	(10 000)	5 000		(5 000)
Bank overdraft (IAS 7.8) (2)	10 000	10 000	–	20 000
Cash and cash equivalents	–	15 000	–	15 000

* Included for illustration purposes only

(1) See note 3.
(2) IAS 7.44E requires separate disclosure of changes in assets and liabilities classified in financing activities (i.e., long-term borrowings) from changes in other assets and liabilities included in other categories (i.e., bank overdraft).

Calculations

1. Cash receipts from customers

	Rand
Revenue	1 500 000
Increase in trade and other receivables (1)	(60 000)
	1 440 000

(1) (214 000 – 4 000) – 150 000 = 60 000

2. Cash paid to suppliers and employees

	Rand
Cost of sales	1 000 000
Increase in inventories (1)	30 000
Increase in trade and other payables (2)	(32 000)
Other costs paid in cash	256 000
Other expenses per statement of profit or loss and other comprehensive income	300 000
Non-cash items:	
Loss on scrapping of assets	(5 000)
Depreciation (3)	(43 000)
Prepaid expenses (4)	4 000
	1 254 000

(1) 170 000 – 140 000 = 30 000
(2) (103 000 – 2 000) – (71 000 – 2 000) = 32 000
(3) 38 000 + 5 000 = 43 000
(4) 4 000 – 0 = 4 000

3. Dividends paid

	Rand
Amounts unpaid at beginning of year	2 000
Amounts debited against retained earnings	40 000
Amounts unpaid at end of year	(2 000)
	40 000

4. Purchase of shares held at fair value through profit or loss – listed

	Rand
Opening balance	8 000
Fair value adjustment	500
Closing balance	(10 500)
Purchases	2 000

Purchase of shares at fair value through other comprehensive income – unlisted

	Rand
Opening balance	4 000
Mark-to-market reserve	2 000
Closing balance	(6 000)
Purchases	–

5. Proceeds on issue of shares

	Rand
Shares issued (1)	150 000

(1) 300 000 – 150 000 = 150 000

6. Movement in long-term borrowings

	Rand
Opening balance (1)	245 000
Movements	15 000
Loans raised (2)	25 000
Loans repaid (3)	(10 000)
Closing balance (4)	260 000

(1) 235 000 + 10 000 = 245 000
(2) 100 000 – 75 000 = 25 000
(3) 160 000 – 150 000 = 10 000
(4) 250 000 + 10 000 = 260 000

❑ QUESTION IAS 7.2

The following information is obtained from Strike It Rich Ltd at 31 December 20.14:

STRIKE IT RICH LTD GROUP
CONSOLIDATED STATEMENT OF FINANCIAL POSITION AS AT 31 DECEMBER 20.14

	20.14 Rand	20.13 Rand
ASSETS		
Non-current assets	234 995 000	216 580 000
Property, plant and equipment	234 995 000	216 580 000
Current assets	112 870 000	89 444 000
Inventories	41 000 000	45 000 000
Trade and other receivables	38 020 000	28 000 000
Financial assets held at fair value through profit or loss – held for trading	750 000	340 000
Cash and cash equivalents	33 100 000	16 104 000
Total assets	347 865 000	306 024 000
EQUITY AND LIABILITIES		
Total equity	190 321 000	145 600 000
Equity attributable to owners of the parent	185 821 000	142 100 000
Share capital	100 000 000	100 000 000
Retained earnings	84 696 000	41 000 000
Other components of equity	1 125 000	1 100 000
Non-controlling interest	4 500 000	3 500 000
Total liabilities	157 544 000	160 424 000
Non-current liabilities	112 169 000	113 354 000
Long-term borrowings	112 140 000	113 354 000
Deferred tax	29 000	–
Current liabilities	45 375 000	47 070 000
Trade and other payables	23 361 000	28 626 000
Current tax payable	18 800 000	15 030 000
Shareholders for dividends	2 000 000	2 200 000
Current portion of long-term borrowings	1 214 000	1 214 000
Total equity and liabilities	347 865 000	306 024 000

STRIKE IT RICH LTD GROUP
CONSOLIDATED STATEMENT OF PROFIT OR LOSS AND OTHER COMPREHENSIVE INCOME FOR THE YEAR ENDED 31 DECEMBER 20.14

	Rand
Revenue	438 580 000
Cost of sales	(258 150 000)
Gross profit	180 430 000
Other income	315 000
Other expenses	(115 360 000)
Finance costs	(310 000)
Profit before tax	65 075 000
Income tax expense	(18 829 000)
Profit for the year	46 246 000
Other comprehensive income	–
Total comprehensive income for the year	46 246 000
Profit attributable to:	
Owners of the parent	45 021 000
Non-controlling interest	1 225 000
	46 246 000
Total comprehensive income attributable to:	
Owners of the parent	45 021 000
Non-controlling interest	1 225 000
	46 246 000

STRIKE IT RICH LTD GROUP
EXTRACT FROM THE CONSOLIDATED STATEMENT OF CHANGES IN EQUITY FOR THE YEAR ENDED 31 DECEMBER 20.14

	A Rand	B Rand	C Rand	D Rand	E Rand
Balance at 1 Jan 20.14	100 000 000	1 100 000	41 000 000	3 500 000	145 600 000
Changes in equity for 20.14					
Total comprehensive income for the year	–	–	45 021 000	1 225 000	46 246 000
Dividends – ordinary shares	–	–	(1 300 000)	(225 000)	(1 525 000)
Transfer to asset replacement reserve	–	25 000	(25 000)	–	–
Balance at 31 Dec 20.14	100 000 000	1 125 000	84 696 000	4 500 000	190 321 000

A = **Share capital**
B = **Asset replacement reserve**
C = **Retained earnings**
D = **Non-controlling interest**
E = **Total equity**

Additional information

1. Included in profit before tax is the profit made on the expropriation of land of a subsidiary in which Strike It Rich Ltd has an 80% interest. This land had a cost (carrying amount) of R100 000 at 1 January 20.14. The other investment in land was made to expand future operations.
2. The carrying amount of motor vehicles sold during the year was R10 000 at 1 January 20.14.
3. The carrying amount of equipment sold during the year was R750 000. Plant and equipment was only acquired to maintain present production capacity.
4. Other expenses consist of the following:

	Rand
Depreciation – vehicles	1 314 000
– plant and equipment	13 996 000
Sundry expenses	100 000 000
Loss on sale of equipment	50 000

5. Other income consists of the following:

	Rand
Fair value adjustment – held for trading investments	100 000
Investment income – listed investment: dividends received	85 000
Profit on sale of vehicle	5 000
Profit on expropriation of land	125 000

6. Property, plant and equipment is made up as follows:

	20.14 Rand	20.13 Rand
Land and buildings	180 000 000	150 000 000
Plant and equipment	49 739 000	60 000 000
Vehicles	5 256 000	6 580 000

The tax bases are equal to the carrying amounts of the property, plant and equipment.

7. The income tax expense in the statement of profit or loss and other comprehensive income consists of the following:

	Rand
Current tax	18 800 000
Deferred tax	29 000
	18 829 000

A tax rate of 29% is assumed.

Required

Prepare the consolidated statement of cash flows, using the indirect method, of the Strike It Rich Ltd Group as it would appear in the published consolidated financial statements at 31 December 20.14. Ignore comparative amounts. Your answer must comply with the requirements of International Financial Reporting Standards (IFRS).

❖ **Suggested solution IAS 7.2**

STRIKE IT RICH LTD GROUP
CONSOLIDATED STATEMENT OF CASH FLOWS FOR THE YEAR ENDED 31 DECEMBER 20.14

	Note	Rand
Cash flows from operating activities		51 855 000
Profit before tax		65 075 000
Adjustments		
Profit on expropriation of land		(125 000)
Depreciation (1)		15 310 000
Loss on sale of equipment		50 000
Fair value adjustment – held for trading investments		(100 000)
Dividends received		(85 000)
Interest paid		310 000
Profit on sale of vehicle		(5 000)
		80 430 000
Decrease in inventories (2)		4 000 000
Increase in trade and other receivables (3)		(10 020 000)
Decrease in trade and other payables (4)		(5 265 000)
Cash generated from operations		69 145 000
Interest paid		(310 000)
Dividends received		85 000
Income taxes paid (calc 4)		(15 030 000)
Dividends paid (5)		(1 725 000)
Purchases of financial assets held at fair value through profit or loss (6)		(310 000)
Cash flows from investing activities		(33 645 000)
Purchase of property, plant and equipment		(34 585 000)
Replacement of plant and equipment (calc 2)		(4 485 000)
Additions to land and buildings (calc 1)		(30 100 000)
Proceeds on sale of property, plant and equipment (7)		940 000
Cash flows from financing activities		
Payment of long-term borrowings (8)	1	(1 214 000)
Net increase in cash and cash equivalents		16 996 000
Cash and cash equivalents at beginning of year		16 104 000
Cash and cash equivalents at end of year		33 100 000

(1) 1 314 000 + 13 996 000 = 15 310 000
(2) 45 000 000 – 41 000 000 = 4 000 000
(3) 38 020 000 – 28 000 000 = 10 020 000
(4) 23 361 000 – 28 626 000 = 5 265 000
(5) 1 500 000 (calc 5) + 225 000 (calc 6) = 1 725 000
(6) 750 000 – 340 000 – 100 000 = 310 000
(7) 700 000 (calc 2) + 15 000 (calc 3) + 225 000 (calc 1) = 940 000
(8) (112 140 000 + 1 214 000) – (113 354 000 + 1 214 000) = 1 214 000

STRIKE IT RICH LTD GROUP
NOTES FOR THE YEAR ENDED 31 DECEMBER 20.14

1. Reconciliation of liabilities arising from financing activities

	20.13 Rand	Cash flows Rand	Non-cash changes* Rand	20.14 Rand
Long-term borrowings	113 354 000			112 140 000
Current portion of long-term borrowings	1 214 000			1 214 000
Total long-term borrowings	114 568 000	(1 214 000)	–	113 354 000

* Included for illustration purposes only.

Calculations

1. Land

	Rand
Balance 1 January 20.14	150 000 000
Carrying amount of land expropriated	(100 000)
	149 900 000
Balance 31 December 20.14	(180 000 000)
Land purchased for expansion	(30 100 000)
Proceeds on expropriation of land (1)	225 000

(1) 100 000 + 125 000 = 225 000

2. Plant and equipment

	Rand
Balance 1 January 20.14	60 000 000
Carrying amount of equipment sold	(750 000)
	59 250 000
Depreciation	(13 996 000)
	45 254 000
Balance 31 December 20.14	(49 739 000)
Purchased for purposes of replacement	(4 485 000)
Proceeds on sale (1)	700 000

(1) 750 000 – 50 000 = 700 000

3. Vehicles

	Rand
Balance 1 January 20.14	6 580 000
Carrying amount of vehicles sold	(10 000)
Depreciation	(1 314 000)
Balance 31 December 20.14	5 256 000
Proceeds on sale (1)	15 000

(1) 10 000 + 5 000 = 15 000

4. Income taxes paid

	Rand
Amounts unpaid at beginning of year	15 030 000
Amounts debited to the statement of profit or loss and other comprehensive income – current tax	18 829 000
Amounts unpaid at end of year (1)	(18 829 000)
Cash amounts paid	15 030 000

(1) 18 800 000 + 29 000 = 18 829 000

5. Dividends paid

	Rand
Amounts unpaid at beginning of year	2 200 000
Amounts debited against retained earnings	1 300 000
Amounts unpaid at end of year	(2 000 000)
Cash amounts paid	1 500 000

6. Dividend paid to non-controlling shareholders

	Rand
Balance 1 January 20.14	3 500 000
Share of profit	1 225 000
	4 725 000
Balance 31 December 20.14	(4 500 000)
Dividend paid to non-controlling shareholders	225 000

❑ QUESTION IAS 7.3

Dukki Ltd acquired 80% of the shares in Pompies Ltd for R420 000 on 31 March 20.5 when Pompies Ltd's assets and liabilities, fairly valued, were as follows:

	Rand
Land and buildings	400 000
Plant and equipment	50 000
Vehicles	30 000
Current assets	100 000
Trade and other receivables	50 000
Inventories	40 000
Cash	10 000
Trade payables	(45 000)
Long-term borrowings – X Bank	(105 000)
Net assets at acquisition	430 000

After the consolidated financial statements for the year ended 31 December 20.5 had been prepared, you were approached to assist the company in preparing the consolidated statement of cash flows.

The following abridged information was presented to you:

DUKKI LTD GROUP
CONSOLIDATED STATEMENT OF FINANCIAL POSITION AS AT 31 DECEMBER 20.5

	20.5 Rand	20.4 Rand
ASSETS		
Non-current assets	271 902 000	240 980 000
Property, plant and equipment	258 826 000	225 980 000
Goodwill	76 000	–
Share investment at fair value through other comprehensive income	10 000 000	15 000 000
Deferred tax	3 000 000	–
Current assets	184 390 000	116 400 000
Inventories	52 310 000	64 104 000
Trade and other receivables	83 410 000	42 130 000
Cash and cash equivalents	48 670 000	10 166 000
Total assets	456 292 000	357 380 000
EQUITY AND LIABILITIES		
Total equity	236 505 000	178 590 000
Equity attributable to owners of the parent	236 138 000	178 590 000
Share capital	50 000 000	50 000 000
Retained earnings	186 138 000	124 340 000
Other components of equity	–	4 250 000
Non-controlling interest	367 000	–
Total liabilities	219 787 000	178 790 000
Non-current liabilities	149 990 000	120 750 000
Long-term borrowings	149 990 000	120 000 000
Deferred tax	–	750 000
Current liabilities	69 797 000	58 040 000
Trade and other payables	22 797 000	6 740 000
Current tax payable	3 000 000	7 300 000
Current portion of long-term borrowings	41 000 000	40 000 000
Short-term borrowings	3 000 000	4 000 000
Total equity and liabilities	456 292 000	357 380 000

DUKKI LTD GROUP
CONSOLIDATED STATEMENT OF PROFIT OR LOSS AND OTHER COMPREHENSIVE INCOME FOR THE YEAR ENDED 31 DECEMBER 20.5

	Rand
Revenue	471 270 000
Cost of sales	(167 544 000)
Gross profit	303 726 000
Other income	406 000
Other expenses	(215 448 000)
Profit before tax	88 684 000
Income tax expense	(26 605 000)
Profit for the year	62 079 000

	Rand
Other comprehensive loss	
Items that will not be reclassified to profit or loss	
Share investment at fair value through other comprehensive income	(4 250 000)
Loss made during the year	(5 000 000)
Tax saving	750 000
Total comprehensive income for the year	57 829 000
Profit attributable to:	
Owners of the parent	61 798 000
Non-controlling interest	281 000
	62 079 000
Total comprehensive income attributable to:	
Owners of the parent	57 548 000
Non-controlling interest	281 000
	57 829 000

DUKKI LTD GROUP
EXTRACT FROM THE CONSOLIDATED STATEMENT OF CHANGES IN EQUITY FOR THE YEAR ENDED 31 DECEMBER 20.5

	A Rand	B Rand	C Rand	D Rand	E Rand
Balance at 1 Jan 20.5	50 000 000	4 250 000	124 340 000	–	178 590 000
Changes in equity for 20.5					
Total comprehensive income for the year	–	(4 250 000)	61 798 000	281 000	57 829 000
Profit for the year	–	–	61 798 000	281 000	62 079 000
Other comprehensive loss	–	(4 250 000)			(4 250 000)
Non-controlling interest at acquisition	–	–	–	86 000	86 000
Balance at 31 Dec 20.5	50 000 000	–	186 138 000	367 000	236 505 000

A = **Share capital**
B = **Mark-to-market reserve**
C = **Retained earnings**
D = **Non-controlling interest**
E = **Total equity**

Additional information

1. Depreciation for the year

	20.5 Rand
Plant and equipment	12 000 000
Vehicles	234 000
	12 234 000

2. Other expenses

   Interest paid of R5 200 000 is included in other expenses. An unrealised foreign exchange loss of R10 000 000 on the loan from X Bank is also included in other expenses.

3. No dividends were declared or paid during the past two years.

4. Land and buildings were acquired to facilitate growth.

5. Long-term borrowings consist of the following:

	20.5 Rand	20.4 Rand
X Bank (including subsidiary)	109 990 000	–
Y Bank	40 000 000	120 000 000

6. The current portion of long-term borrowings consist of the following:

	20.5 Rand	20.4 Rand
X Bank	1 000 000	–
Y Bank	40 000 000	40 000 000

7. Property, plant and equipment are made up as follows:

	20.5 Rand	20.4 Rand
Land and buildings	210 000 000	165 000 000
Plant and equipment	48 050 000	60 000 000
Vehicles	776 000	980 000

8. The fair value of the share investment at fair value through other comprehensive income decreased by R5 000 000 on 31 December 20.5.

9. Assume a tax rate of 30% and a CGT rate of 15%.

10. Other income consists of rent received.

11. Income tax expense consists of:

	20.5 Rand
Current tax	29 605 000
Deferred tax	(3 000 000)
	26 605 000

Required

Prepare the consolidated statement of cash flows, using the direct method, of the Dukki Ltd Group for the year ended 31 December 20.5 in accordance with the requirements of International Financial Reporting Standards (IFRS). Ignore comparative amounts.

❖ **Suggested solution IAS 7.3**

DUKKI LTD GROUP
CONSOLIDATED STATEMENT OF CASH FLOWS FOR THE YEAR ENDED 31 DECEMBER 20.5

	Note	Rand	
Cash flows from operating activities			63 629 000
Cash receipts from customers (calc 5)		430 446 000	
Cash paid to suppliers and employees (calc 6)		(327 712 000)	
Cash generated from operations	1	102 734 000	
Interest paid		(5 200 000)	
Income taxes paid (calc 4)		(33 905 000)	
Cash flows from investing activities			(45 010 000)
Additions to property, plant and equipment (calc 1 & 2)	3	(44 600 000)	
Acquisition of interest in subsidiary	2	(410 000)	
Cash flows from financing activities			19 885 000
Proceeds from long-term borrowings (calc 3)	4	100 885 000	
Repayment of long-term borrowings (calc 3)	4	(80 000 000)	
Payment of short-term borrowings (calc 7)	4	(1 000 000)	
Net increase in cash and cash equivalents			38 504 000
Cash and cash equivalents at beginning of year			10 166 000
Cash and cash equivalents at end of year			48 670 000

DUKKI LTD GROUP
NOTES FOR THE YEAR ENDED 31 DECEMBER 20.5

1. Reconciliation of cash generated from operations and profit before tax (not required by IAS 7)

	Rand	
Profit before tax		88 684 000
Adjustments		
Depreciation		12 234 000
Unrealised currency loss		10 000 000
Interest paid		5 200 000
Profit before changes in working capital		116 118 000
Changes in working capital		(13 384 000)
Decrease in inventories (calc 6)	11 834 000	
Increase in trade and other receivables (calc 5)	(41 230 000)	
Increase in trade and other payables (calc 6)	16 012 000	
Cash generated from operations		102 734 000

2. Acquisition of interest in subsidiary

During the year the group acquired an 80% interest in subsidiary Pompies Ltd. The fair value of assets acquired, and liabilities assumed were as follows:

	Rand
Property, plant and equipment	480 000
Inventories	40 000
Trade and other receivables	50 000
Cash and cash equivalents	10 000
Trade and other payables	(45 000)
Long-term borrowings	(105 000)
Net assets acquired	430 000
Non-controlling interest (20%)	(86 000)
Goodwill at acquisition (1)	76 000
Total consideration	420 000
Less: Cash and cash equivalents of subsidiary	(10 000)
Net cash outflow	410 000

(1) 420 000 – (430 000 × 80%) = 76 000

3. Purchase of property, plant and equipment

	Rand
Additions to land and buildings (calc 1 & 2)	44 600 000

4. Reconciliation of liabilities arising from financing activities

	20.4	Cash flows	Non-cash changes		20.5
			A	B	
	Rand	Rand	Rand	Rand	Rand
Long-term borrowings	120 000 000				149 990 000
Current portion of long-term borrowings	40 000 000				41 000 000
Total long-term borrowings	160 000 000	20 885 000	105 000	10 000 000	190 990 000
Short-term borrowings	4 000 000	(1 000 000)	–	–	3 000 000
	164 000 000	19 885 000	105 000	10 000 000	193 990 000

A = Acquisition
B = Exchange differences

Calculations

1. Land and buildings

	Rand
Balance 1 January 20.5	165 000 000
Acquisition of Pompies Ltd	400 000
	165 400 000
Balance 31 December 20.5	(210 000 000)
Purchase of land and buildings	44 600 000

2. Other assets

	A Rand	B Rand
Balance 1 January 20.5	60 000 000	980 000
Acquisition of Pompies Ltd	50 000	30 000
	60 050 000	1 010 000
Depreciation	(12 000 000)	(234 000)
Balance 31 December 20.5	48 050 000	776 000

A = Plant and equipment
B = Vehicles

3. Long-term borrowings

	X Bank Rand	Y Bank Rand
Balance 1 January 20.5 (1)	–	160 000 000
Acquisition of Pompies Ltd	105 000	–
Loans acquired	100 885 000	–
Loans repaid	–	(80 000 000)
Unrealised exchange loss	10 000 000	–
Balance 31 December 20.5 (2) (3)	110 990 000	80 000 000

(1) 120 000 000 + 40 000 000 = 160 000 000
(2) 40 000 000 + 40 000 000 = 80 000 000
(3) 109 990 000 + 1 000 000 = 110 990 000

4. Income taxes paid

	Rand
Amounts unpaid at beginning of year (1)	8 050 000
Amounts debited to the statement of profit or loss and other comprehensive income (2)	25 855 000
Amounts unpaid at end of year (3)	–
Cash amounts paid	33 905 000

(1) 7 300 000 + 750 000 = 8 050 000
(2) 26 605 000 – 750 000 = 25 855 000
(3) 3 000 000   3 000 000 – 0

5. Cash receipts from customers

	Rand
Revenue	471 270 000
Increase in trade and other receivables (1)	(41 230 000)
Other income – rent received	406 000
	430 446 000

(1) (83 410 000 – 50 000) – 42 130 000 = 41 230 000

6.	**Cash paid to suppliers and employees**	**Rand**
	Cost of sales	167 544 000
	Decrease in inventory (1)	(11 834 000)
	Increase in trade and other payables (2)	(16 012 000)
	Other costs paid in cash	188 014 000
	Other expenses per statement of profit or loss and other comprehensive income	215 448 000
	Non-cash items	
	Depreciation	(12 234 000)
	Foreign exchange loss	(10 000 000)
	Interest paid shown separately	(5 200 000)
		327 712 000

(1) (52 310 000 – 40 000) – 64 104 000 = 11 834 000
(2) (22 797 000 – 45 000) – 6 740 000 = 16 012 000

7.	**Short-term borrowings**	**Rand**
	Balance 1 January 20.5	4 000 000
	Loans repaid	(1 000 000)
	Balance 31 December 20.5	3 000 000

8.	**Share investment at fair value through other comprehensive income**	**Rand**
	Balance 1 January 20.5	15 000 000
	Fair value adjustment	(5 000 000)
	Balance 31 December 20.5	10 000 000

❑ QUESTION IAS 7.4

Rocval Ltd approached you to assist in the preparation of a statement of cash flows for the group. The following abridged information was obtained from the group's financial statements at 30 June 20.5:

ROCVAL LTD GROUP
CONSOLIDATED STATEMENT OF FINANCIAL POSITION AS AT 30 JUNE 20.5

	20.5 Rand	**20.4 Rand**
ASSETS		
Non-current assets	213 543 000	191 403 000
Property, plant and equipment	183 000 000	163 000 000
Investments in associates	30 543 000	28 403 000
Current assets	85 410 000	132 400 000
Inventories	43 210 000	50 300 000
Trade and other receivables	21 400 000	47 700 000
Cash and cash equivalents	20 800 000	34 400 000
Total assets	298 953 000	323 803 000

EQUITY AND LIABILITIES

	20.5 Rand	20.4 Rand
Total equity	144 961 000	126 811 000
Equity attributable to owners of the parent	136 756 000	120 308 000
Share capital	45 000 000	45 000 000
Retained earnings	91 756 000	75 308 000
Non-controlling interest	8 205 000	6 503 000
Total liabilities	153 992 000	196 992 000
Non-current liabilities	123 207 000	125 807 000
Long-term borrowings	107 906 000	112 402 000
Deferred tax	15 301 000	13 405 000
Current liabilities	30 785 000	71 185 000
Trade and other payables	12 202 000	34 100 000
Current tax payable	8 050 000	30 135 000
Shareholders for dividends	3 193 000	–
Current portion of long-term borrowings	4 496 000	4 496 000
Short-term borrowings	2 844 000	2 454 000
Total equity and liabilities	298 953 000	323 803 000

ROCVAL LTD GROUP

CONSOLIDATED STATEMENT OF PROFIT OR LOSS AND OTHER COMPREHENSIVE INCOME FOR THE YEAR ENDED 30 JUNE 20.5

	Rand
Revenue	376 000 000
Cost of sales	(200 000 000)
Gross profit	176 000 000
Other income	134 000
Other expenses	(142 324 000)
Share of profit of associates	2 270 000
Dividends received	130 000
Retained equity profit of associates	2 140 000
Profit before tax	36 080 000
Income tax expense	(10 785 000)
Profit for the year	25 295 000
Other comprehensive income	–
Total comprehensive income for the year	25 295 000
Profit attributable to:	
Owners of the parent	23 361 000
Non-controlling interest	1 934 000
	25 295 000
Total comprehensive income attributable to:	
Owners of the parent	23 361 000
Non-controlling interest	1 934 000
	25 295 000

ROCVAL LTD GROUP
CONSOLIDATED STATEMENT OF CHANGES IN EQUITY FOR THE YEAR ENDED 30 JUNE 20.5

	A Rand	B Rand	C Rand	D Rand
Balance at 1 July 20.4	45 000 000	75 308 000	6 503 000	126 811 000
Changes in equity for 20.5				
Profit/total comprehensive income for the year	–	23 361 000	1 934 000	25 295 000
Dividends	–	(6 913 000)	(232 000)	(7 145 000)
Balance at 30 June 20.5	45 000 000	91 756 000	8 205 000	144 961 000

A = **Share capital**
B = **Retained earnings**
C = **Non-controlling interest**
D = **Total equity**

Additional information

1. Property, plant and equipment consist only of plant and equipment. The proceeds on disposal of plant and equipment amounted to R43 000. It is estimated that R31 000 000 of the plant and equipment purchases were for the expansion of operations.
2. Depreciation for the year amounted to R34 050 000 and the profit on sale of plant and equipment was R11 000. Both amounts have been included in other expenses.
3. Interest paid for the year amounted to R11 000 and is included in other expenses.
4. The income tax expense in the consolidated statement of profit or loss and other comprehensive income consists of the following:

	20.5 Rand
Current tax	8 889 000
Deferred tax	1 896 000

5. Other income consists of interest received from the bank and debtors.

Required

Prepare the consolidated statement of cash flows, using the direct method, of the Rocval Ltd Group for the year ended 30 June 20.5 in accordance with the requirements of International Financial Reporting Standards (IFRS). Ignore comparative amounts.

❖ **Suggested solution IAS 7.4**

ROCVAL LTD GROUP
CONSOLIDATED STATEMENT OF CASH FLOWS FOR THE YEAR ENDED 30 JUNE 20.5

	Note	Rand
Cash flows from operating activities		44 545 000
Cash receipts from customers (calc 4)		402 300 000
Cash paid to suppliers and employees (calc 5)		(323 082 000)
Cash generated from operations	1	79 218 000
Dividends received		130 000
Interest received		134 000
Interest paid		(11 000)
Income taxes paid (calc 2)		(30 974 000)
Dividends paid (calc 3)		(3 952 000)
Cash flows from investing activities		(54 039 000)
Purchase of property, plant and equipment (calc 1)		(54 082 000)
Replacements of property, plant and equipment		(23 082 000)
Additions to property, plant and equipment		(31 000 000)
Proceeds on sale of property, plant and equipment		43 000
Cash flows from financing activities		(4 106 000)
Repayment of long-term borrowings (calc 6)	2	(4 496 000)
Proceeds from short-term borrowings (calc 7)	2	390 000
Net decrease in cash and cash equivalents		(13 600 000)
Cash and cash equivalents at beginning of year		34 400 000
Cash and cash equivalents at end of year		20 800 000

ROCVAL LTD GROUP
NOTES FOR THE YEAR ENDED 30 JUNE 20.5

1. Reconciliation of cash generated from operations and profit before tax (not required by IAS 7)

	Rand
Profit before tax	36 080 000
Adjustments	
Depreciation	34 050 000
Gain on sale of property, plant and equipment	(11 000)
Dividends received	(130 000)
Interest received	(134 000)
Interest paid	11 000
Retained equity profit of associates	(2 140 000)
Profit before changes in working capital	67 726 000
Changes in working capital	11 492 000
Decrease in inventories (calc 5)	7 090 000
Decrease in trade and other receivables (calc 4)	26 300 000
Decrease in trade and other payables (calc 5)	(21 898 000)
Cash generated from operations	79 218 000

2. **Reconciliation of liabilities arising from financing activities**

	20.4	Cash flows	Non-cash changes*	20.5
	Rand	Rand	Rand	Rand
Long-term borrowings	112 402 000			107 906 000
Current portion of long-term borrowings	4 496 000			4 496 000
Total long-term borrowings	116 898 000	(4 496 000)	–	112 402 000
Short-term borrowings	2 454 000	390 000	–	2 844 000
	119 352 000	(4 106 000)	–	115 246 000

* Included for illustration purposes only

Calculations

1. **Property, plant and equipment purchased**

	Rand
Carrying amount 1 July 20.4	163 000 000
Carrying amount of property, plant and equipment sold (1)	(32 000)
Depreciation	(34 050 000)
	128 918 000
Carrying amount 30 June 20.5	(183 000 000)
Increase in property, plant and equipment	(54 082 000)
For expansion of activities	31 000 000
Replacement of property, plant and equipment	(23 082 000)

(1) 43 000 – 11 000 = 32 000

2. **Income taxes paid**

	Rand
Amounts unpaid at beginning of year (1)	43 540 000
Amounts debited to the statement of profit or loss and other comprehensive income	10 785 000
Amounts unpaid at end of year (2)	(23 351 000)
Cash amounts paid	30 974 000

(1) 30 135 000 + 13 405 000 = 43 540 000
(2) 8 050 000 + 15 301 000 = 23 351 000

3. **Dividends paid**

	Rand
Amounts unpaid at beginning of year	–
Amounts debited to retained earnings	6 913 000
Amounts unpaid at end of year	(3 193 000)
Cash amounts paid	3 720 000
Dividend paid to non-controlling interest (1)	232 000
Total dividends paid	3 952 000

(1) 6 503 000 + 1 934 000 – 8 205 000 = 232 000

4. Cash receipts from customers

	Rand
Revenue	376 000 000
Decrease in trade and other receivables (1)	26 300 000
	402 300 000

(1) 47 700 000 – 21 400 000 = 26 300 000

5. Cash paid to suppliers and employees

	Rand
Cost of sales	200 000 000
Decrease in inventories (1)	(7 090 000)
Decrease in trade and other payables (2)	21 898 000
Other costs paid in cash	108 274 000
Other expenses per statement of profit or loss and other comprehensive income	142 324 000
Non-cash items	
Depreciation	(34 050 000)
Gain on sale of plant and equipment	11 000
Interest paid shown separately	(11 000)
	323 082 000

(1) 43 210 000 – 50 300 000 = 7 090 000
(2) 34 100 000 – 12 202 000 = 21 898 000

6. Long-term borrowings

	Rand
Balance 1 July 20.4 (1)	116 898 000
Loans repaid	(4 496 000)
Balance 30 June 20.5 (2)	112 402 000

(1) 112 402 000 + 4 496 000 = 116 898 000
(2) 107 906 000 + 4 496 000 = 112 402 000

7. Short-term borrowings

	Rand
Balance 1 July 20.4	2 454 000
Loans raised	390 000
Balance 30 June 20.5	2 844 000

❑ **QUESTION IAS 7.5**

You are provided with the following abridged financial statements:

MIRAGE LTD
STATEMENT OF FINANCIAL POSITION AS AT 31 DECEMBER 20.9

	20.9 Rand	20.8 Rand
ASSETS		
Non-current assets	514 000	369 550
Property, plant and equipment	514 000	310 000
Deferred tax	–	15 500
Investment in subsidiary at cost	–	44 050
Current assets	474 660	309 400
Inventories	16 900	4 000
Trade and other receivables	386 000	175 000
Financial asset held at fair value through profit or loss – Held for trading	16 400	39 400
Cash and cash equivalents	55 360	91 000
Total assets	988 660	678 950
EQUITY AND LIABILITIES		
Total equity	626 910	248 500
Share capital	200 000	100 000
Retained earnings	326 910	78 500
Other components of equity	100 000	70 000
Total liabilities	361 750	430 450
Non-current liabilities	204 500	310 000
Long-term borrowings	200 000	310 000
Deferred tax	4 500	–
Current liabilities	157 250	120 450
Trade and other payables	29 090	73 620
Dividends payable	50 000	30 000
Current portion of long-term borrowings	50 460	–
Current tax payable	27 700	16 830
Total equity and liabilities	988 660	678 950

MIRAGE LTD
STATEMENT OF PROFIT OR LOSS AND OTHER COMPREHENSIVE INCOME FOR THE YEAR ENDED 31 DECEMBER 20.9

	Rand
Revenue	665 000
Cost of sales	(276 000)
Gross profit	389 000
Other income	222 910
Other expenses	(73 000)
Finance costs	(88 660)
Profit before tax	450 250
Income tax expense	(121 840)
Profit for the year	328 410

	Rand
Other comprehensive income	–
Total comprehensive income for the year	328 410

MIRAGE LTD
STATEMENT OF CHANGES IN EQUITY FOR THE YEAR ENDED 31 DECEMBER 20.9

	A Rand	B Rand	C Rand	D Rand
Balance at 1 January 20.9	100 000	70 000	78 500	248 500
Changes in equity for 20.9				
Profit/total comprehensive income for the year	–	–	328 410	328 410
Dividends	–	–	(50 000)	(50 000)
Redeemable debentures converted into shares	100 000	–	–	100 000
Transfer to asset replacement reserve	–	30 000	(30 000)	–
Balance at 31 December 20.9	200 000	100 000	326 910	626 910

A = Share capital – ordinary
B = Asset replacement reserve
C = Retained earnings
D = Total equity

Additional information

1. Mirage Ltd makes deliveries on behalf of customers, and its property, plant and equipment consists only of delivery vehicles.
2. No delivery vehicles were disposed of during the past year. The delivery vehicles that were bought for replacement purposes were bought at the end of the current year in terms of an instalment credit agreement. A deposit of R55 000 was paid in cash and the remaining amount will be paid with interest over a period of four years.
3. The current portion of long-term borrowings relates to the current portion of the instalment credit agreement.
4. Debentures of R200 000 were redeemed at par and the remainder was converted into ordinary share capital.
5. Cost of sales includes an amount of R68 000 in respect of depreciation on the delivery vehicles.
6. Included in profit before tax are the following income and expenses:

	Rand
Investment income – dividends received	44 100
Gain on sale of subsidiary	178 810
Fair value adjustment – held for trading investment	(23 000)
Other costs paid in cash	(50 000)

7. The income tax expense in the statement of profit or loss and other comprehensive income consists of the following:

	Rand
Current tax	101 840
Deferred tax	20 000

8. Long-term borrowings are made up as follows:

	20.9 Rand	20.8 Rand
Instalment credit agreement liability	125 000	–
Bank loan	75 000	10 000
Redeemable debentures	–	300 000

Required

Prepare the statement of cash flows of Mirage Ltd, using the direct method, for the year ended 31 December 20.9 in accordance with the requirements of International Financial Reporting Standards (IFRS). Ignore comparative amounts.

❖ **Suggested solution IAS 7.5**

MIRAGE LTD
STATEMENT OF CASH FLOWS FOR THE YEAR ENDED 31 DECEMBER 20.9

	Note	Rand
Cash flows from operating activities		(26 960)
Cash receipts from customers (calc 1)		454 000
Cash paid to suppliers and employees (calc 2)		(315 430)
Cash generated from operations	1	138 570
Interest paid		(88 660)
Dividends received		44 100
Income taxes paid (calc 3)		(90 970)
Dividends paid (calc 4)		(30 000)
Cash flows from investing activities		167 860
Proceeds on sale of subsidiary (1)		222 860
Purchase of vehicles		
Replacement of vehicles (given)		(55 000)
Cash flows from financing activities		(176 540)
Redemption of debentures	3	(200 000)
Proceeds from long-term borrowings (2)	3	65 000
Repayment of long-term borrowings (calc 6)	3	(41 540)
Net decrease in cash and cash equivalents		(35 640)
Cash and cash equivalents at beginning of year		91 000
Cash and cash equivalents at end of year		55 360

(1) 44 050 + 178 810 = 222 860
(2) 75 000 – 10 000 = 65 000

MIRAGE LTD
NOTES FOR THE YEAR ENDED 31 DECEMBER 20.9

1. Reconciliation of cash generated from operations and profit before tax (not required by IAS 7)

	Rand
Profit before tax	450 250
Adjustments	
Interest paid	88 660
Dividends received	(44 100)
Fair value adjustment – held for trading investment	23 000
Gain on sale of subsidiary	(178 810)
Depreciation	68 000
Profit before changes in working capital	407 000
Changes in working capital	(268 430)
Increase in trade and other receivables (calc 1)	(211 000)
Increase in inventories (calc 2)	(12 900)
Decrease in trade and other payables (calc 2)	(44 530)
Cash generated from operations	138 570

2. Non-cash investments and financing activities

- At the end of the current year, delivery vehicles to the value of R272 000 were purchased in terms of an instalment credit agreement of which R217 000 was financed.
- During the year, debentures to the value of R100 000 were converted at par into ordinary share capital.

3. Reconciliation of liabilities arising from financing activities

	20.8	Cash flows	Non-cash changes		20.9
			A	B	
	Rand	Rand	Rand	Rand	Rand
Long-term borrowings	310 000				200 000
Current portion of long-term borrowings	–				50 460
Total long-term borrowings (1)	310 000	(176 540)	217 000	(100 000)	250 460

A = **New instalment credit agreement**
B = **Conversion of debentures**

(1) See calculation 6 for the amount of R217 000.

Calculations

1. Cash receipts from customers

	Rand
Revenue	665 000
Increase in trade and other receivables (1)	(211 000)
	454 000

(1) 386 000 – 175 000 = 211 000

2. Cash paid to suppliers and employees

	Rand
Cost of sales	276 000
Non-cash item – depreciation	(68 000)
Increase in inventories (1)	12 900
Decrease in trade and other payables (2)	44 530
Other costs paid in cash	50 000
Other income per statement of profit or loss and other comprehensive income	(222 910)
Other expenses per statement of profit or loss and other comprehensive income	73 000
Non-cash items:	
Fair value adjustment – held for trading investment	(23 000)
Investing activity:	
Gain on sale of subsidiary	178 810
Disclosed separately:	
Dividends received	44 100
	315 430

(1) 16 900 – 4 000 = 12 900
(2) 73 620 – 29 090 = 44 530

3. Income taxes paid

	Rand
Amounts unpaid at beginning of year (1)	1 330
Amounts debited to the statement of profit or loss and other comprehensive income	121 840
Amounts unpaid at end of year (2)	(32 200)
Cash amounts paid	90 970

(1) 16 830 – 15 500 = 1 330
(2) 27 700 + 4 500 = 32 200

4. Dividends paid

	Rand
Amounts unpaid at beginning of year	30 000
Amounts debited against retained earnings	50 000
Amounts unpaid at end of year	(50 000)
Cash amounts paid	30 000

5. Delivery vehicles

	Rand
Carrying amount	
Opening balance (given)	310 000
Depreciation (given)	(68 000)
Purchases (cash deposit of R55 000 included)	272 000
Closing balance (given)	514 000

6. Repayment of long-term borrowings

	Rand
Gross purchases	272 000
Cash deposit	(55 000)
Total liability in respect of instalment credit agreement	217 000
Outstanding liability in respect of instalment credit agreement	
Short-term	(50 460)
Long-term	(125 000)
Capital amount redeemed in cash	41 540

❑ QUESTION IAS 7.6

The following transactions pertain to Alpha Ltd:

Transaction 1

On 1 January 20.0 Alpha Ltd purchased 6 000 10% R200 debentures at R190 each. Transaction costs amounted to R5 000. Interest is payable annually on 31 December. The debentures are accounted for as financial assets at amortised cost and are redeemable at par on 31 December 20.2.

Transaction 2

On 1 January 20.0 Alpha Ltd acquired 5 000 ordinary shares on the JSE Ltd for R50 000 with related transaction costs of R2 000. The fair value of the investment is R70 000 at 31 December 20.0. The shares are accounted for as financial assets at fair value through other comprehensive income.

Transaction 3

On 2 January 20.0 Alpha Ltd purchased 40 all share index (ALSI) futures for speculative purposes when the ALSI was 2 400. Transaction costs amounted to R1 000 and the margin deposit was R50 000. Alpha Ltd sold the futures on 15 August 20.1. The mark-to-market ALSI is 2 650 at 31 December 20.0 and 2 740 at 15 August 20.1. Each index point trades at R10. The mark-to-market adjustment is settled daily. The futures are accounted for as financial assets at fair value through profit or loss.

Transaction 4

On 1 August 20.0 Alpha Ltd purchased inventories of $100 000 from a US supplier. The inventory was shipped free on board (FOB) on the same day. On the same day Alpha Ltd took out a three-month forward exchange contract (FEC). On 1 November 20.0 Alpha Ltd took out a new three-month FEC. The creditor was settled on 31 January 20.1. Alpha Ltd does not apply hedge accounting. The following exchange rates apply:

	Spot rate	Forward rate
1 August 20.0	$1 = R4,68	$1 = R5,00
1 November 20.0	$1 = R5,45	$1 = R6,00
31 December 20.0	$1 = R6,25	$1 = R6,50*
31 January 20.1	$1 = R6,10	

* One-month forward rate

Required

In accordance with the requirements of International Financial Reporting Standards (IFRS), discuss how each of the above-mentioned transactions will be treated in Alpha Ltd's statement of cash flows for all financial years concerned. Alpha Ltd's year-end is 31 December. Assume that all the hedging criteria apply where applicable.

Recommendation: *First perform the journal entries of complex transactions for all years concerned to establish what the transactions' impact on the statement of cash flows will be.*

❖ **Suggested solution IAS 7.6**

	Rand Dr/(Cr)
Transaction 1	
1 January 20.0	
Investment – debentures (at amortised cost) (SFPos) (1)	1 145 000
Bank	(1 145 000)
31 December 20.0	
Investment – debentures (at amortised cost) (SFPos)	16 314
Bank (2)	120 000
Interest received (P or L) (3)	(136 314)
31 December 20.1	
Investment – debentures (at amortised cost) (SFPos)	18 256
Bank (2)	120 000
Interest received (P or L) (4)	(138 256)
31 December 20.2	
Investment – debentures (at amortised cost) (SFPos)	20 430
Bank (2)	120 000
Interest received (P or L) (5)	(140 430)
Bank (6)	1 200 000
Investment – debentures (at amortised cost) (SFPos)	(1 200 000)

(1) (6 000 × 190) + 5 000 = 1 145 000
(2) 6 000 × 200 × 10% = 120 000
(3) n = 3, FV = 1 200 000, PV = – 1 145 000, PMT = 120 000. Thus i = 11,90515686
1 145 000 × 11,90515686% = 136 314
(4) (1 145 000 + 16 314) × 11,90515686% = 138 256
(5) (1 145 000 + 16 314 + 18 256) × 11,90515686% = 140 430
(6) 6 000 × 200 = 1 200 000

Discussion of influence on the statement of cash flows

Financial year ended 31 December 20.0

- An investment in debentures of R1 145 000 will be shown as a cash outflow in the cash flows from investing activities section.
- Interest received (cash inflow) of R120 000 will be shown after a non-cash adjustment of R16 314, as part of cash flows from operating activities or investing activities provided that the classification is consistent from one period to the next.

- Remember to adjust for the non-cash movement of R16 314 in the 'Investment – debentures' account when this statement of financial position account is analysed for purposes of identifying other cash movements in debentures.

Financial year ended 31 December 20.1

- Interest received of R120 000 will be shown as a cash inflow, after a non-cash adjustment of R18 256, as part of cash flows from operating activities or investing activities as determined in 20.0.
- Remember to adjust for the non-cash movement of R18 256 in the 'Investment – debentures' account when this statement of financial position account is analysed for purposes of identifying other cash movements in debentures.

Financial year ended 31 December 20.2

- Interest received of R120 000 will be shown as a cash inflow, after a non-cash adjustment of R20 430, as part of cash flows from operating activities or investing activities as determined in 20.0.
- Remember to adjust for the non-cash movement of R20 430 in the 'Investment – debentures' account when this statement of financial position account is analysed for purposes of identifying other cash movements in debentures.
- Redemption of debentures will be shown in the cash flows from investing activities section of the statement of cash flows to the value of R1 200 000 (cash inflow).

Transaction 2	**Rand Dr/(Cr)**
1 January 20.0	
Investment – shares (at fair value through OCI) (1)	52 000
Bank	(52 000)
31 December 20.0	
Investment – shares (at fair value through OCI) (2)	18 000
Fair value adjustment* (OCI)	(18 000)

* Before closing off to mark-to-market reserve in equity.

(1) 50 000 + 2 000 = 52 000
(2) 70 000 – 52 000 = 18 000

Discussion of influence on statement of cash flows

Financial year ended 31 December 20.0

- An investment in shares of R52 000 (cash outflow) will be shown as part of cash flows from investing activities.
- The fair value adjustment of R18 000 will not affect the calculation of cash generated from operations, as it is not included in profit or loss for the year but is included in other comprehensive income.
- Remember the non-cash movement of R18 000 in the 'Investment – shares' account when this statement of financial position account is analysed for purposes of identifying other cash movements in shares.

Transaction 3

	Rand Dr/(Cr)
2 January 20.0	
Margin deposit (SFPos)	50 000
Transaction costs / Loss on futures (P or L)	1 000
Bank	(51 000)
31 December 20.0	
Bank (1)	100 000
Profit on futures (P or L)	(100 000)
15 August 20.1	
Bank (2)	36 000
Profit on futures (P or L)	(36 000)
Bank	50 000
Margin deposit (SFPos)	(50 000)

(1) (2 650 – 2 400) × R10 × 40 = 100 000
(2) (2 740 – 2 650) × R10 × 40 = 36 000

Note: Cash flows on SAFEX take place daily – each day's profit/(loss) on the mark-to-market index is settled the next day. A debtor/creditor will therefore be created at 31 December 20.0 (year-end) for the amount payable on the next day.

Discussion of influence on the statement of cash flows

Financial year ended 31 December 20.0

- The margin deposit of R50 000 will be shown as a cash outflow from operating activities as part of changes in debtors in the 'cash receipts from customers' line item (IAS 7.15).
- Since the net profit on futures of R99 000 (R100 000 – R1 000) is of a cash nature, no adjustment for non-cash items is necessary to profit before tax for this item.
- The profit/(loss) on the last day's trading for which a debtor/creditor has been created (see the note above) shall be shown as a non-cash adjustment to profit before tax, while the amount will also be included in the normal working capital adjustments.

Financial year ended 31 December 20.1

- The repayment of the margin deposit of R50 000 must be shown as a cash inflow from operating activities as part of changes in debtors in the 'cash receipts from customers' line item (IAS 7.15).
- Profit before tax is not adjusted for the non-cash items since the total profit on futures of R36 000 is of a cash nature.

Transaction 4	**Rand Dr/(Cr)**
1 August 20.0	
Inventory (SFPos) (1)	468 000
Trade and other payables (SFPos)	(468 000)
1 November 20.0	
Bank (2)	45 000
Foreign exchange gain (P or L)	(45 000)
31 December 20.0	
Foreign exchange loss (P or L) (3)	157 000
Trade and other payables (SFPos)	(157 000)
FEC asset (SFPos) (4)	50 000
Foreign exchange gain (P or L)	(50 000)
31 January 20.1	
Trade and other payables (SFPos) (5)	15 000
Foreign exchange gain (P or L)	(15 000)
Trade and other payables (SFPos) (6)	610 000
Foreign exchange loss (P or L) (8)	40 000
FEC asset (SFPos)	(50 000)
Bank (7)	(600 000)

(1) 100 000 × 4,68 = 468 000
(2) 100 000 × (5,45 – 5,00) = 45 000
(3) 100 000 × (6,25 – 4,68) = 157 000
(4) 100 000 × (6,50 – 6,00) = 50 000
(5) 100 000 × (6,25 – 6,10) = 15 000
(6) 100 000 × 6,10 = 610 000
(7) 100 000 × 6,00 = 600 000
(8) 100 000 × (6,50 – 6,10) = 40 000

Discussion of influence on the statement of cash flows

Financial year ended 31 December 20.0

- The purchase of the inventory and the related creditor will form part of the normal working capital movements.
- Profit before tax will be adjusted for a non-cash item: a foreign exchange loss of R157 000. No adjustment is needed for the foreign exchange gain of R45 000 since it is entirely of a cash nature.
- The FEC asset is of a non-cash nature and will be disclosed separately in the notes to the statement of cash flows. Profit before tax will be adjusted for a non-cash item: a foreign exchange gain of R50 000.

Financial year ended 31 December 20.1

- The creditor will form part of the normal working capital movements. The creditor is paid an amount of R610 000 in cash (R6,10 × R100 000). Remember to adjust for the non-cash movement of R15 000 in the 'Creditors' account when this statement of financial position account is analysed for purposes of identifying other cash movements in 'Creditors'.
- Profit before tax will be adjusted for two non-cash items: foreign exchange gain of R15 000 and a foreign exchange loss of R40 000.

- The net gain on the FEC of R10 000 [(6,10 – 6,00) × R100 000] will be reflected as part of working capital movements and represents cash inflow.
- The total cash flow for the year is therefore R600 000 and will be included as part of cash generated from operations.

❑ QUESTION IAS 7.7

You are in charge of the audit of Lugdienste Ltd and are presented with the following:

LUGDIENSTE LTD
STATEMENT OF FINANCIAL POSITION AS AT 31 DECEMBER 20.2

	Note	20.2 Rand	20.1 Rand
ASSETS			
Non-current assets		147 400 000	110 000 000
Property, plant and equipment	1, 3	126 500 000	100 000 000
Share investment at fair value through other comprehensive income	4	20 900 000	10 000 000
Current assets		124 700 000	91 000 000
Inventories	1, 4	60 600 000	50 000 000
Trade and other receivables	1	50 100 000	30 000 000
Cash and cash equivalents		14 000 000	11 000 000
Total assets		272 100 000	201 000 000
EQUITY AND LIABILITIES			
Total equity		104 342 000	69 710 000
Share capital	1	71 050 000	58 600 000
Retained earnings		18 476 000	250 000
Other components of equity		14 816 000	10 860 000
Total liabilities		167 758 000	131 290 000
Non-current liabilities		112 384 000	97 040 000
Long-term borrowings	2	111 600 000	96 900 000
Deferred tax		784 000	140 000
Current liabilities		55 374 000	34 250 000
Trade and other payables	1	11 800 000	600 000
Current tax payable		9 324 000	10 000 000
Shareholders for dividends		2 100 000	500 000
Short-term borrowings		32 150 000	23 150 000
Total equity and liabilities		272 100 000	201 000 000

LUGDIENSTE LTD
STATEMENT OF CHANGES IN EQUITY FOR THE YEAR ENDED 31 DECEMBER 20.2

	A Rand	B Rand	C Rand	D Rand	E Rand
Balance at 1 Jan 20.2	58 600 000	10 000 000	860 000	250 000	69 710 000
Changes in equity for 20.2					
Profit/total comprehensive income for the year	–	2 236 000	1 720 000	24 226 000	28 182 000
Dividends	–	–	–	(6 000 000)	(6 000 000)
Issue of share capital	12 450 000	–	–	–	12 450 000
Balance at 31 Dec 20.2	71 050 000	12 236 000	2 580 000	18 476 000	104 342 000

A = **Share capital**
B = **Revaluation surplus**
C = **Mark-to-market reserve**
D = **Retained earnings**
E = **Total equity**

Further investigation revealed the following information:

1. On 1 January 20.2, Lugdienste Ltd issued ordinary shares, for which the new shareholders transferred the following consideration:

	Rand
Land and buildings	1 500 000
Inventories	2 100 000
Trade and other receivables	1 900 000
Trade and other payables	(2 700 000)
	2 800 000

2. Long-term borrowings consist of:

	20.2 Rand	20.1 Rand
10% compulsory redeemable preference shares	5 600 000	6 400 000
Bank loans	106 000 000	90 500 000
	111 600 000	96 900 000

During 20.2, 400 000 10% compulsory redeemable preference shares of R2 each were redeemed at par in cash, partly from profits and partly by the issue of ordinary shares. A third issue of ordinary shares also took place. The effective interest rate of the preference shares in accordance with IFRS 9 is 10%.

3. During 20.2, equipment with a carrying amount of R3 200 000 was sold for R3 650 000 and was replaced with new equipment. The new equipment was purchased for cash.

4. On 31 December 20.2 Lugdienste Ltd purchased ordinary shares in Lugdinamika Ltd, to be held as an investment and paid for it as follows:

	Rand
Equipment at carrying amount	6 100 000
Inventories	2 800 000
	8 900 000

The directors of Lugdienste Ltd designated the investment as a financial asset at fair value through other comprehensive income together with shares held in an unlisted investment in Jule (Pty) Ltd with a directors' valuation of R12 000 at 31 December 20.2. This approximates the fair value of the investment. The original cost price of the investment in Jule (Pty) Ltd was R9 000.

5. An abridged statement of profit or loss and other comprehensive income of Lugdienste Ltd for the year ended 31 December 20.2 is as follows:

LUGDIENSTE LTD
STATEMENT OF PROFIT OR LOSS AND OTHER COMPREHENSIVE INCOME FOR THE YEAR ENDED 31 DECEMBER 20.2

		Rand
Revenue		123 500 000
Cost of sales		(54 300 000)
Gross profit		69 200 000
Other income		700 000
Other expenses		(30 200 000)
Finance costs (including preference dividends)		(6 150 000)
Profit before tax		33 550 000
Income tax expense		(9 324 000)
Profit for the year		24 226 000
Other comprehensive income		
Items that will not be reclassified to profit or loss		
Property revaluation		2 236 000
Gain on revaluation of land	2 600 000	
Tax expense	(364 000)	
Share investment at fair value through OCI		1 720 000
Gains arising during the year	2 000 000	
Tax expense	(280 000)	
Total comprehensive income for the year		28 182 000

6. Other income consists of:

	Rand
Dividends received	250 000
Profit on sale of equipment	450 000

7. Other expenses include the following:

	Rand
Directors' remuneration	4 000 000
Depreciation – equipment	10 400 000

8. Assume a tax rate of 28% and a CGT rate of 14%.

Required

Prepare the statement of cash flows of Lugdienste Ltd, using the direct method, for the year ended 31 December 20.2 so as to comply with the requirements of International Financial Reporting Standards (IFRS). Ignore comparative amounts.

❑ QUESTION IAS 7.8

The following balances of Kudu Ltd at 31 December 20.2 and 20.3 are available:

	20.3 Rand Dr/(Cr)	20.2 Rand Dr/(Cr)
Share capital – ordinary shares	(140 000)	(140 000)
Asset replacement reserve	(30 000)	(30 000)
12% compulsory redeemable preference shares of R1 each	(15 000)	(25 000)
Deferred tax	(900)	–
Cash at bank	3 900	–
Bank overdraft	–	(11 000)
Retained earnings	(354 100)	(311 000)
Trade and other receivables	150 000	180 000
Trade and other payables	(18 800)	(60 990)
Intangible assets	24 000	25 000
Machinery – at cost	50 625	50 625
Furniture – at cost	19 500	18 000
Current tax asset	46 001	6 000
Accumulated depreciation		
– machinery	(20 250)	(10 125)
– furniture	(13 601)	(13 200)
Inventories	245 625	281 690
Financial assets held at fair value through profit or loss		
– held for trading investment	53 000	40 000

The following information was taken from the statement of profit or loss and other comprehensive income and the statement of changes in equity:

	20.3 Rand	20.2 Rand
Tax provided – current	14 400	111 000
– deferred	900	–
Dividends provided and paid	20 000	20 000
Amortisation of intangible assets	1 000	–
Interest paid	5 000	4 000
Investment income – dividends received	(8 500)	(7 500)
Fair value adjustment – held for trading investment	(3 000)	–

Additional information

1. On 1 July 20.3, 10 000 compulsory redeemable preference shares were redeemed at an amount of R10 000 cash. The redemption was done from cash funds that the company had at its disposal. The effective interest rate on the compulsory redeemable preference shares, calculated in terms of IFRS 9, is 12%.
2. The following are the movements in respect of furniture:
   - Furniture to the value of R5 500 was purchased to maintain current capacity. An amount of R3 000 owed in respect of the purchase of furniture is included in trade and other payables.
   - Furniture with a cost price of R3 200 was sold for R8 000 on the same day it was acquired, as management realised that they will not use the furniture and they could realise a gain through sale.
   - Furniture with a carrying amount of R1 (cost – R800) was scrapped during the year.
3. No machinery was purchased or sold during the year.
4. Investment income receivable of R1 500 (20.2: R1 000) is included in trade and other receivables.
5. The bank overdraft is repayable on demand and forms an integral part of Kudu Ltd's cash management activities.

Required

Prepare the statement of cash flows, using the indirect method, of Kudu Ltd for the year ended 31 December 20.3 so as to comply with the requirements of International Financial Reporting Standards (IFRS). Comparative amounts are not required.

❑ QUESTION IAS 7.9

The following abridged information is available for Tackle Ltd:

TACKLE LTD
STATEMENT OF FINANCIAL POSITION AS AT 31 DECEMBER 20.8

	20.8 Rand	20.7 Rand
ASSETS		
Non-current assets	546 200	457 700
Property, plant and equipment	453 200	405 200
Investments in associates	93 000	52 500
Current assets	49 800	34 700
Inventories	16 000	15 800
Trade and other receivables	33 800	18 900
Total assets	596 000	492 400
EQUITY AND LIABILITIES		
Total equity	383 000	239 500
Share capital	29 000	13 000
Retained earnings	307 500	180 000
Other components of equity	46 500	46 500

	20.8 Rand	20.7 Rand
Total liabilities	213 000	252 900
Non-current liabilities	177 000	182 000
Long-term borrowings	177 000	182 000
Current liabilities	36 000	70 900
Trade and other payables	7 500	17 900
Current tax payable	7 000	12 000
Shareholders for dividends	4 000	3 000
Current portion of long-term borrowings	5 000	3 000
Bank overdraft	12 500	35 000
Total equity and liabilities	596 000	492 400

TACKLE LTD
STATEMENT OF PROFIT OR LOSS AND OTHER COMPREHENSIVE INCOME FOR THE YEAR ENDED 31 DECEMBER 20.8

	Rand
Revenue	550 000
Cost of sales	(300 000)
Gross profit	250 000
Other expenses	(99 000)
Share of profit of associates	54 500
Dividends received	14 000
Retained equity profit of associates	40 500
Profit before tax	205 500
Income tax expense	(57 450)
Profit for the year	148 050
Other comprehensive income	–
Total comprehensive income for the year	148 050

TACKLE LTD
STATEMENT OF CHANGES IN EQUITY FOR THE YEAR ENDED 31 DECEMBER 20.8

	A Rand	B Rand	C Rand	D Rand
Balance at 1 January 20.8	13 000	46 500	180 000	239 500
Changes in equity for 20.8				
Profit/total comprehensive income for the year	–	–	148 050	148 050
Dividends	–	–	(20 550)	(20 550)
Issue of share capital	16 000	–	–	16 000
Balance at 31 December 20.8	29 000	46 500	307 500	383 000

A = **Share capital**
B = **Revaluation surplus**
C = **Retained earnings**
D = **Total equity**

Additional information

1. Profit before tax is stated after taking the following into account:

	Rand
Interest paid	18 000
Depreciation on machinery and equipment	58 000
Profit on sale of machinery and equipment	1 500

2. During the year machinery and equipment were purchased for R12 500 to replace machinery and equipment with a carrying amount of R2 500, which were sold.

3. Property, plant and equipment consist of the following:

	20.8 Rand	20.7 Rand
Land at cost	296 500	296 500
Machinery and equipment at carrying amount	156 700	108 700

4. The bank overdraft is repayable on demand and forms an integral part of Tackle Ltd's cash management activities.

Required

Prepare the statement of cash flows, using the direct method, of Tackle Ltd for the year ended 31 December 20.8 in accordance with the requirements of International Financial Reporting Standards (IFRS). Comparative amounts are not required.

❑ QUESTION IAS 7.10

The consolidated trial balances of the Konsol Ltd Group at 31 December 20.2 and 20.3 are available:

	20.3 Rand	20.2 Rand
Credits		
Share capital	145 000	115 000
Revaluation surplus	126 000	–
Asset replacement reserve	50 000	30 000
Mark-to-market reserve	12 750	–
Retained earnings	391 612	397 563
Non-controlling interest	34 820	36 900
Long-term borrowings	426 800	300 000
Deferred tax	56 250	–
Trade and other payables	618 800	660 990
Bank overdraft	44 900	2 100
Shareholders for dividends	18 000	8 000
Current tax payable	42 973	148 000
	1 967 905	1 698 553

	20.3 Rand	20.2 Rand
Debits		
Property, plant and equipment at carrying amount	825 000	635 500
Goodwill at carrying amount	11 000	12 000
Share investment at fair value through other comprehensive income	385 000	180 000
Inventories	440 000	800 000
Trade and other receivables	306 905	71 053
	1 967 905	1 698 553

The abridged consolidated statement of profit or loss and other comprehensive income and statement of changes in equity of the Konsol Ltd Group for the year ended 31 December 20.3 are as follows:

CONSOLIDATED STATEMENT OF PROFIT OR LOSS AND OTHER COMPREHENSIVE INCOME FOR THE YEAR ENDED 31 DECEMBER 20.3

	Rand
Revenue	872 930
Cost of sales	(600 000)
Gross profit	272 930
Other income	95 870
Other expenses	(113 100)
Finance costs	(14 830)
Profit before tax	240 870
Income tax expense	(72 561)
Profit for the year	168 309
Other comprehensive income	
Items that will not be reclassified to profit or loss	
Property revaluation	126 000
Gain on property revaluation	180 000
Tax expense	(54 000)
Share investment at fair value through other comprehensive income	12 750
Gains arising during the year	15 000
Tax expense	(2 250)
Total comprehensive income for the year	307 059
Profit attributable to:	
Owners of the parent	159 909
Non-controlling interest	8 400
	168 309
Total comprehensive income attributable to:	
Owners of the parent	298 659
Non-controlling interest	8 400
	307 059

EXTRACTS FROM THE CONSOLIDATED STATEMENT OF CHANGES IN EQUITY FOR THE YEAR ENDED 31 DECEMBER 20.3

	A Rand	B Rand	C Rand	D Rand	E Rand	F Rand	G Rand
Balance at 1 Jan 20.3	115 000	–	30 000	–	397 563	36 900	579 463
Changes in equity for 20.3							
Total comprehensive income for the year	–	126 000	–	12 750	159 909	8 400	307 059
Profit for the year	–	–	–	–	159 909	8400	168 309
Other comprehensive income	–	126 000	–	12 750	–	–	138 750
Dividends	–	–	–	–	(145 860)	(10 480)	(156 340)
Issue of share capital	30 000	–	–	–	–	–	30 000
Transfer to asset replacement reserve	–	–	20 000	–	(20 000)	–	–
Balance at 31 Dec 20.3	145 000	126 000	50 000	12 750	391 612	34 820	760 182

A = **Share capital**
B = **Revaluation surplus**
C = **Asset replacement reserve**
D = **Mark-to-market reserve**
E = **Retained earnings**
F = **Non-controlling interest**
G = **Total equity**

Additional information

1. No property, plant and equipment were sold during the year. All the additions to property, plant and equipment were in respect of delivery vehicles to enable the group to be in the position to expand its operating activities.

2. After negotiations with the bank, the directors of Konsol Ltd managed to acquire an increase in the long-term borrowings of R200 000.

3. Other expenses consist of the following:

	Rand
Depreciation	87 100
Auditors' remuneration	25 000
Impairment of goodwill	1 000

4. Assume a 30% tax rate and a 15% CGT rate.

5. Other income consists of rent received.

6. The bank overdraft is repayable on demand and forms an integral part of Konsol Ltd Group's cash management activities.

Required

Prepare the consolidated statement of cash flows, using the indirect method, of the Konsol Ltd Group for the year ended 31 December 20.3 in accordance with the requirements of International Financial Reporting Standards (IFRS). Comparative amounts are not required.

❑ QUESTION IAS 7.11

The following consolidated information of the Buffelbed Ltd Group is presented to you:

BUFFELBED LTD GROUP
CONSOLIDATED STATEMENT OF FINANCIAL POSITION AS AT 31 DECEMBER 20.3

	20.3 Rand	20.2 Rand
ASSETS		
Non-current assets	136 750	138 400
Property, plant and equipment	135 000	138 400
Goodwill – Kalfie Ltd at carrying amount	1 750	–
Current assets	227 580	227 910
Inventories	40 200	40 660
Trade and other receivables	187 180	187 150
Cash and cash equivalents	200	100
Total assets	364 330	366 310
EQUITY AND LIABILITIES		
Total equity	131 870	59 550
Equity attributable to owners of the parent	75 850	35 650
Share capital	30 000	10 000
Retained earnings	33 250	25 650
Other components equity	12 600	–
Non-controlling interest	56 020	23 900
Total liabilities	232 460	306 760
Non-current liabilities	111 910	152 500
Long-term borrowings	106 510	152 500
Deferred tax	5 400	–
Current liabilities	120 550	154 260
Trade and other payables	100 800	81 090
Current tax payable	3 800	8 070
Shareholders for dividends	11 000	–
Bank overdraft	4 950	65 100
Total equity and liabilities	364 330	366 310

BUFFELBED LTD GROUP
CONSOLIDATED STATEMENT OF PROFIT OR LOSS AND OTHER COMPREHENSIVE INCOME FOR THE YEAR ENDED 31 DECEMBER 20.3

		Rand
Revenue		690 000
Cost of sales		(315 000)
Gross profit		375 000
Other expenses		(341 786)
Profit before tax		33 214
Income tax expense		(9 964)
Profit for the year		23 250
Other comprehensive income		
Items that will not be reclassified to profit or loss		
Property revaluation		12 600
Gain on property revaluation		18 000
Tax expense		(5 400)
Total comprehensive income for the year		35 850
Profit attributable to:		
Owners of the parent		18 600
Non-controlling interest		4 650
		23 250
Total comprehensive income attributable to:		
Owners of the parent		31 200
Non-controlling interest		4 650
		35 850

BUFFELBED LTD GROUP
EXTRACTS FROM THE CONSOLIDATED STATEMENT OF CHANGES IN EQUITY FOR THE YEAR ENDED 31 DECEMBER 20.3

	A Rand	B Rand	C Rand	D Rand	E Rand
Balance at 1 Jan 20.3	10 000	–	25 650	23 900	59 550
Changes in equity for 20.3					
Total comprehensive income for the year	–	12 600	18 600	4 650	35 850
Profit for the year	–	–	18 600	4 650	23 250
Other comprehensive income	–	12 600	–	–	12 600
Dividends	–	–	(11 000)	–	(11 000)
Acquisition of a subsidiary	–	–	–	27 470	27 470
Issue of share capital	20 000	–	–	–	20 000
Balance at 31 Dec 20.3	30 000	12 600	33 250	56 020	131 870

A = **Share capital**
B = **Revaluation surplus**
C = **Retained earnings**
D = **Non-controlling interest**
E = **Total equity**

Additional information

1. The bank overdraft is repayable on demand and forms an integral part of Buffelbed Ltd Group's cash management activities.

2. Buffelbed Ltd acquired an 80% holding in Kalfie Ltd on 1 July 20.3 to expand the group's manufacturing capacity. The company's assets are fairly valued. This was the only subsidiary purchased during the year and no subsidiaries were sold during the year.

KALFIE LTD
STATEMENT OF FINANCIAL POSITION AS AT 1 JULY 20.3

	Rand
ASSETS	
Non-current assets	
Property, plant and equipment	80 000
Current assets	
Inventories	57 350
	137 350
EQUITY AND LIABILITIES	
Total equity	
Share capital	40 000
Retained earnings	97 350
	137 350

3. No property, plant and equipment were purchased by the group during the year.

4. The property, plant and equipment that were sold during the year, were sold at carrying amount.

5. Included in other expenses are the following disclosable items:

	Rand
Impairment of goodwill	250
Auditors' remuneration	38 000
Net finance costs	44 800
Finance costs	45 050
Non-taxable interest received	(250)
Depreciation – property, plant and equipment	19 020

6. Assume a tax rate of 30%.

Required

Prepare the consolidated statement of cash flows, using the direct method, of the Buffelbed Ltd Group for the year ended 31 December 20.3 in accordance with the requirements of International Financial Reporting Standards (IFRS). Comparative amounts are not required.

IAS 8

Accounting policies, changes in accounting estimates and errors

---

❑ **QUESTIONS AND SOLUTIONS**

IAS 8.1	Evaluation of accounting policy notes: discussion
IAS 8.2	Change in accounting estimate – method of depreciation, without tax: calculations, correcting journals and disclosure notes
IAS 8.3	Change in accounting estimate – method of depreciation, with tax: calculations, journals and discussion of disclosure
IAS 8.4	Prior period error with taxation: preparation of financial statements and notes
IAS 8.5	Change in accounting estimate (residual value) and prior period error with tax: preparation of financial statements and notes
IAS 8.6	Change in accounting policy of inventory (prospectively and retrospectively) (voluntary): preparation of financial statements and notes

❑ **QUESTIONS**

IAS 8.7	Drafting of accounting policy notes: discussion
IAS 8.8	Change in accounting estimate – useful life with tax: preparation of financial statements and notes
IAS 8.9	Prior period error with tax: correcting journal entries and preparation of financial statements and notes
IAS 8.10	Evaluation of accounting policies: discussion
IAS 8.11	Change in accounting policy of inventory (voluntary): preparation of financial statements and notes
IAS 8.12	Change in accounting policy (limited retrospective application) (voluntary) and prior period error: preparation of financial statements and notes
IAS 8.13	Prior period error: journal entries and note disclosures
IAS 8.14[#]	Change in accounting policy (in terms of standard on borrowing costs (IAS 23)): preparation of note disclosures
IAS 8.15[@]	Change in accounting estimate (repayment of government grant i.t.o. IAS 20): preparation of financial statements and notes

[@] *This question contains topics or principles that were not included in the ITC syllabus of SAICA at the time of publishing this book, but might still be included in university syllabi.*

[#] *This question contains topics or principles that were at an awareness level of proficiency in the ITC syllabus of SAICA, at the time of publishing this book.*

❑ QUESTION IAS 8.1

The following notes regarding accounting policy were prepared for inclusion in the financial statements of a company:

1. Investment property

Investment property is accounted for on the fair value model.

2. Revenue

Revenue consists of goods invoiced to customers.

3. Leased assets

Lease agreements are capitalised.

4. Unlisted investments

The unlisted investments of the company represent long-term investments and are carried at fair value.

5. Finance charges on instalment credit purchases

Finance charges on instalment credit purchases of plant and equipment are written off over the period of the agreement on a straight-line basis.

Required

Suggest improvements to the proposed accounting policy notes in the interest of good disclosure and reporting practice according to the requirements of IAS 8. You are not required to rewrite the notes.

❖ Suggested solution IAS 8.1

1. Investment property

- Suggested improvements:
  - Mention the fact that investment property consists of land and buildings held to earn rental income or for capital appreciation, or both.
  - Fair value gains or losses are recognised in profit or loss.
  - The fair value is determined at reporting date by an independent sworn appraiser based on market evidence of the most recent prices obtained in arm's-length transactions of similar properties in the same area.

2. Revenue

- Suggested improvements:
  - Mention that revenue is measured at the consideration the entity is expected to be entitled to.
  - The fact that VAT is excluded.
  - The fact that revenue is recognised when control of the goods is transferred to the buyer.
  - Any other relevant principles in IFRS 15 applicable to the entity should be mentioned.

3. Leased assets

- Suggested improvements:
  - Indication of the treatment of short-term leases and leases for which the underlying assets are of low value.
  - That the asset is capitalised at the present value of the future lease payments, and a corresponding liability is raised.
  - The method which is used for recognition of finance costs over the term of the lease agreement (effective interest method).
  - Indication of methods and rates of depreciation applied to allocate the cost of such assets (this could, however, be included under the property, plant and equipment accounting policy note).

4. Unlisted investments

- Suggested improvement:
  - Also indicate how gains/losses on fair value adjustments should be treated (e.g. mark-to-market reserve).

5. Finance charges on instalment credit purchases

- The straight-line write-off of finance costs is not related to the capital balance of the outstanding liability and is therefore not in accordance with the matching concept.

- Suggested improvement:
  - The policy should state that finance charges are recognised according to the effective interest method.

❑ QUESTION IAS 8.2

After the financial statements for 20.4 had been prepared, Vink Ltd changed its method of depreciating machinery. The previous pattern of depreciation differed from the actual pattern of economic benefits derived from the depreciable assets. As a result, the reducing balance method at 20% p.a. will be applied in future instead of the straight-line method over five years as in the past.

A summary of the machinery account at 30 June 20.3, the previous financial year-end of the company, is as follows:

	Rand
Carrying amount of machinery	400 000
Cost	800 000
Accumulated depreciation	(400 000)

No machinery has been purchased or disposed of during the year ended 30 June 20.4.

Ignore all tax implications.

Required

a. Calculate the following amounts resulting from the change in accounting estimate for inclusion in the financial statements of Vink Ltd for the year ended 30 June 20.4:
- Depreciation for the current year.
- Depreciation for 20.5 and 20.6.

b. Journalise all necessary adjustments to account for the change in accounting estimate in 20.4.

c. Assume the amounts involved in the change in accounting estimate to be material, and disclose these in terms of the requirements of IAS 8 *Accounting Policies, Errors and Changes in Accounting Estimates*. Accounting policy notes are not required.

❖ **Suggested solution IAS 8.2**

In terms of IAS 16.61, a change in the depreciation method for property, plant and equipment resulting from a change in the expected pattern of economic benefits from these assets is not classified as a change in accounting policy, but as a change in accounting estimate.

a. Depreciation

	Rand
Carrying amount – 30 June 20.3	400 000
Depreciation 20.4 – new (1)	(80 000)
Carrying amount – 30 June 20.4	320 000
Depreciation 20.5 – new (2)	(64 000)
Carrying amount – 30 June 20.5	256 000
Depreciation 20.6 – new (3)	(51 200)
Carrying amount – 30 June 20.6	204 800

(1) 400 000 × 20% = 80 000
(2) 320 000 × 20% = 64 000
(3) 256 000 × 20% = 51 200

- Current year's depreciation = R80 000
- Depreciation for 20.5 = R64 000
- Depreciation for 20.6 = R51 200

b. Correcting journal entries

Correcting journal entries is necessary as the depreciation for 20.4 was calculated by applying the straight-line method instead of the reducing balance method. The correcting journal is as follows:

	Rand Dr/(Cr)
Accumulated depreciation – machinery (SFPos)	80 000
Depreciation (P or L) (1)	(80 000)
Adjustment of depreciation written off in 20.4	

(1) (800 000 × 20%) – (400 000 × 20%) = 80 000

c. **Disclosure**

VINK LTD
NOTES FOR THE YEAR ENDED 30 JUNE 20.4

6. **Profit before tax**

Profit before tax is stated after taking into account the following:

	Rand
Expenses:	
Depreciation	80 000

Change in accounting estimate:
The depreciation method of machinery changed from the straight-line method to the reducing balance method. This resulted in a decrease in depreciation for the current year of R80 000 (1) and a cumulative increase in future periods of R80 000 (2).

(1) [(800 000 × 20%) (old method) – 80 000 (new method)] = 80 000 decrease
(2) Future depreciation (old method) 240 000 – future depreciation (new method) 320 000 = 80 000 increase

❑ QUESTION IAS 8.3

Records of the property, plant and equipment of Reier Ltd showed the following at 1 July 20.6:

	Rand
Machinery at cost	600 000
Accumulated depreciation	(292 800)
	307 200

In the past the company accounted for depreciation at 20% per annum using the reducing balance method. However, at a meeting of the board of directors during 20.7 it was decided that from the beginning of the year ending 30 June 20.7, machinery would be depreciated on the straight-line method as it better reflects the economic benefits from the machinery. The total useful life of the machinery had originally been estimated as seven years. (It may be assumed that this estimate is still correct.) No depreciation charge has been accounted for in the current year.

The South African Revenue Service allows a wear-and-tear allowance of 20% using the reducing balance method. Tax rates for the past five years have remained unchanged at 28%. The company will earn sufficient taxable income in future to justify the creation of a debit balance on the deferred tax account should it be necessary.

Required

a. Calculate the following amounts for inclusion in the financial statements of Reier Ltd for the year ended 30 June:
   - Depreciation for the current year (20.7).
   - Depreciation for 20.8 and 20.9.

b. Journalise all necessary adjustments to account for the change in accounting estimate in 20.7.

c. Discuss the disclosure requirements relating to the above change in accounting estimate so as to comply with the requirements of IAS 8 *Accounting Policies, Errors and Changes in Accounting Estimates.*

❖ **Suggested solution IAS 8.3**

Calculations

	Carrying amount Rand	**Tax base Rand**	**Temporary difference Rand**	**Deferred tax Rand**	**Profit or loss Rand**	
Reducing balance method – old						
Cost – 1 July 20.3	600 000	600 000				
Depreciation 20.4 (1)	(120 000)	–				
Wear-and-tear allowance (1)	–	(120 000)				
30 June 20.4	480 000	480 000				
Depreciation 20.5 (2)	(96 000)	–				
Wear-and-tear allowance (2)	–	(96 000)				
30 June 20.5	384 000	384 000				
Depreciation 20.6 (3)	(76 800)	–				
Wear-and-tear allowance (3)	–	(76 800)				
30 June 20.6	307 200	307 200				
Straight-line method – new						
Depreciation 20.7 (4)	(76 800)	–				
Wear-and-tear allowance (5)	–	(61 440)				
30 June 20.7	230 400	245 760	(15 360)	(4 301)	4 301 cr	
Depreciation 20.8 (6)	(76 800)	–				
Wear-and-tear allowance (7)	–	(49 152)				
30 June 20.8	153 600	196 608	(43 008)	(12 042)	7 741 cr	(8)

(1) 600 000 × 20% = 120 000
(2) 480 000 × 20% = 96 000
(3) 384 000 × 20% = 76 800
(4) 307 200/(7 – 3) = 76 800
(5) 307 200 × 20% = 61 440
(6) 307 200/4 = 76 800
(7) 245 760 × 20% = 49 152
(8) 12 042 – 4 301 = 7 741

a. Depreciation

	Rand
• Depreciation for current year (20.7)	76 800
• Depreciation per year for 20.8 to 20.9	76 800

b. Journal entries

	Rand Dr/(Cr)
20.7	
Depreciation (P or L)	76 800

	Rand Dr/(Cr)
Accumulated depreciation – machinery (SFPos)	(76 800)
Deferred tax (SFPos) (9)	4 301
Income tax expense (P or L)	(4 301)
20.8 (only for illustrative purposes)	
Depreciation (P or L)	76 800
Accumulated depreciation – machinery (SFPos)	(76 800)
Deferred tax (SFPos) (10)	7 741
Income tax expense (P or L)	(7 741)

(9) 15 360 × 28% = 4 301
(10) (43 008 – 15 360) × 28% = 7 741

c. **Disclosure requirements**

In terms of IAS 8.39 the nature (change in depreciation method) and amount (increase in depreciation in current year of R15 360) of a change in an accounting estimate should be disclosed, including the cumulative effect of the change on future periods (cumulative decrease in depreciation in future periods of R15 360).

❑ QUESTION IAS 8.4

The following are the statements of comprehensive income of Aaskamp Ltd for the years ended 31 December:

	20.8 Rand	20.7 Rand
Revenue	79 500	52 400
Cost of sales	(39 000)	(26 000)
Gross profit	40 500	26 400
Other expenses	(500)	(400)
Profit before tax	40 000	26 000
Income tax expense (current tax only)	(12 000)	(7 800)
Profit for the year	28 000	18 200
Other comprehensive income	–	–
Total comprehensive income for the year	28 000	18 200

Included in profit before tax for 20.8 is an amount of R7 500 (20.7 – R10 000), which represents the profit before tax of a division of Aaskamp Ltd.

When Aaskamp Ltd's tax calculations for 20.8 and 20.7 were prepared, the inexperienced accountant did not take into account any temporary differences and non-taxable/non-deductible differences relating to the division. However, **after** the statement of profit or loss and other comprehensive income for 20.8 had been prepared, it came to light that the taxable temporary differences of the division amounted to R17 000 (20.7 – R14 000) and non-taxable items of the division amounted to R12 500 (20.7 – R14 000).

Apart from the above it was also established that temporary differences occurred for the first time in 20.7.

The South African Revenue Service had already assessed the company on R26 000 for 20.7. The company applied for a reassessment, which was granted. The tax rate for the past two years has remained constant at 30%.

Aaskamp Ltd paid a dividend of R10 000 for 20.8 and for 20.7. The retained earnings on 1 January 20.7 amounted to R17 000.

Required

Prepare the statement of profit or loss and other comprehensive income and statement of changes in equity (retained earnings only) of Aaskamp Ltd for the year ended 31 December 20.8 in accordance with the requirements of International Financial Reporting Standards (IFRS). The only notes required are those concerning the rectification of the prior period error and tax.

❖ **Suggested solution IAS 8.4**

AASKAMP LTD
STATEMENT OF PROFIT OR LOSS AND OTHER COMPREHENSIVE INCOME FOR THE YEAR ENDED 31 DECEMBER 20.8

	Note	20.8 Rand	20.7 Rand
Revenue		79 500	52 400
Cost of sales		(39 000)	(26 000)
Gross profit		40 500	26 400
Other expenses		(500)	(400)
Profit before tax		40 000	26 000
Income tax expense	1	(8 250)	(3 600)
Profit for the year		31 750	22 400
Other comprehensive income		–	–
Total comprehensive income for the year		31 750	22 400

AASKAMP LTD
STATEMENT OF CHANGES IN EQUITY FOR THE YEAR ENDED 31 DECEMBER 20.8

	Note	Retained earnings Rand
Balance at 1 January 20.7		17 000
Changes in equity for 20.7		
Total comprehensive income for the year – restated	2	22 400
Profit for the year – restated		22 400
Other comprehensive income		–
Dividends		(10 000)
Balance at 31 December 20.7 – restated		29 400
Changes in equity for 20.8		
Total comprehensive income for the year		31 750
Profit for the year		31 750
Other comprehensive income		–
Dividends paid		(10 000)
Balance at 31 December 20.8		51 150

AASKAMP LTD
NOTES FOR THE YEAR ENDED 31 DECEMBER 20.8

1. Income tax expense

	20.8 Rand	20.7 Rand
Major components of tax expense		
Current tax expense: current year	2 550	–
Deferred tax expense: current year	5 700	3 600
Tax expense	8 250	3 600

Tax rate reconciliation	%	%
Statutory tax rate	30	30
Decrease attributable to:		
Non-taxable items (1)	(9)	(16)
Effective tax rate (2)	21	14

(1) (12 500 × 30%)/40 000 × 100 = 9; (14 000 × 30%)/26 000 × 100 = 16
(2) 8 250/40 000 × 100 = 21; 3 600/26 000 × 100 = 14

2. Correction of prior period error

A correction of the tax calculation in respect of 20.7 was made due to the fact that temporary differences and non-taxable income were previously ignored in the tax calculation. Comparative amounts have been appropriately restated. The effect of the adjustment on the 20.7 results is as follows:

	20.7 Rand
Decrease in income tax expense	4 200
Increase in profit for the year	4 200
Increase in deferred tax liability	3 600
Decrease in current tax payable to the South African Revenue Service	(7 800)
Increase in equity	4 200
Increase in basic earnings per share	xx
Increase in diluted earnings per share	xx

Calculations

Current tax of Aaskamp Ltd after correction	20.8 Rand	20.7 Rand
Profit before tax	40 000	26 000
Taxable temporary differences	(17 000)	(14 000)
Non-taxable items	(12 500)	(14 000)
Taxable income/(tax loss)	10 500	(2 000)
Tax loss brought forward	(2 000)	–
Taxable income/(tax loss)	8 500	(2 000)
Current tax @ 30%	2 550	Nil

Temporary differences after correction	**20.8 Rand**	**20.7 Rand**
Cumulative taxable temporary differences (1)	31 000	14 000
Tax loss	–	(2 000)
	31 000	12 000
Deferred tax liability (30%)	9 300	3 600
Movement in profit or loss (2)	5 700	3 600

(1) 17 000 + 14 000 = 31 000
(2) 9 300 – 3 600 = 5 700

Total income tax expense after correction

	20.8 Rand	**20.7 Rand**
Current tax	2 550	–
Deferred tax – current year	5 700	3 600
Total income tax expense	8 250	3 600

Correcting journal entries

	Rand Dr/(Cr)
20.7	
Current tax payable to SARS (SFPos)	7 800
Income tax expense (P or L)	(7 800)
Income tax expense (P or L)	3 600
Deferred tax (SFPos)	(3 600)

Correction of error

	Rand
Current tax as shown previously (20.7)	7 800
Current tax as revised	–
Current tax written back (credit income tax expense)	7 800
Deferred tax (debit income tax expense)	(3 600)
Net credit against income tax expense in profit or loss	4 200

❑ QUESTION IAS 8.5

The following are the abridged trial balances of Stressed Eric Ltd for the years ended 30 June 20.5 and 20.6:

	20.6 Rand Dr/(Cr)	20.5 Rand Dr/(Cr)
Share capital	(10 000)	(10 000)
Net current assets	40 000	6 000
Other expenses	80 000	50 000
Depreciation (straight-line method @ 20% per annum)	16 000	16 000
Electricity expense	15 000	–
Machinery		
Cost	90 000	90 000
Accumulated depreciation	(56 000)	(40 000)
Income tax expense	15 600	9 600
Dividends paid	5 000	5 000
Retained earnings at beginning of year	(54 400)	(35 000)
Profit on disposal of land (not taxable)	(10 000)	–
Gross profit	(150 000)	(100 000)

After the trial balance had been prepared as at 30 June 20.6, the board of directors re-estimated the residual value of machinery to be R7 000. The original residual value was R10 000. No machinery has been purchased or disposed of since 20.4. The South African Revenue Service allows a wear-and-tear deduction of 20% per annum, straight-line, not allocated on a pro rata basis for parts of the year.

The electricity expense of R15 000 which relates to 20.5 (per the trial balance) was paid during 20.6. The expense arose in 20.6 only after the auditors found an underpayment of electricity expense relating to 20.5. The expense was never recorded in 20.5. Assume that the amount is material. The South African Revenue Service agreed to reopen the 20.5 tax assessment.

The following information is available:

	20.6	20.5
Revenue (excluding VAT)	R300 000	R200 000
Gross profit percentage on sales	50%	50%

The tax rate has remained unchanged at 30% for the past three years. Ignore capital gains tax.

Required

Prepare the statement of profit or loss and other comprehensive income and statement of changes in equity (retained earnings only) of Stressed Eric Ltd for the year ended 30 June 20.6 in accordance with the requirements of International Financial Reporting Standards (IFRS). The only notes required are those relating to the change in accounting estimate and the prior period error.

❖ **Suggested solution IAS 8.5**

STRESSED ERIC LTD
STATEMENT OF PROFIT OR LOSS AND OTHER COMPREHENSIVE INCOME FOR THE YEAR ENDED 30 JUNE 20.6

	Note	20.6 Rand	20.5 Rand
Revenue		300 000	200 000
Cost of sales		(150 000)	(100 000)
Gross profit (1)		150 000	100 000
Other income		10 000	–
Other expenses (calc 3)		(97 200)	(81 000)
Profit before tax	6	62 800	19 000
Income tax expense (calc 4)		(15 240)	(5 100)
Profit for the year		47 560	13 900
Other comprehensive income		–	–
Total comprehensive income for the year		47 560	13 900

(1) 300 000 × 50% = 150 000; 200 000 × 50% = 100 000

STRESSED ERIC LTD
STATEMENT OF CHANGES IN EQUITY FOR THE YEAR ENDED 30 JUNE 20.6

	Note	Retained earnings Rand
Balance at 1 July 20.4		35 000
Changes in equity for 20.5		
Total comprehensive income for the year – restated	7	13 900
Profit for the year		13 900
Other comprehensive income		–
Dividends		(5 000)
Balance at 30 June 20.5 – restated		43 900
Changes in equity for 20.6		
Total comprehensive income for the year		47 560
Profit for the year		47 560
Other comprehensive income		–
Dividends		(5 000)
Balance at 30 June 20.6		86 460

STRESSED ERIC LTD
NOTES FOR THE YEAR ENDED 30 JUNE 20.6

6. **Profit before tax**

The profit before tax is stated after taking into account the following:

	20.6 Rand	20.5 Rand
Expenses		
Depreciation	17 200	16 000

Change in estimate

During the year the residual value was changed. This change in estimate resulted in an increase in depreciation in the current year of R1 200 (1). The cumulative effect of this change on future periods will be an increase in depreciation of R1 800 (2).

(1) 17 200 – 16 000 = 1 200
(2) 10 000 old residual value – 7 000 new residual value – 1 200 (1)

7. **Correction of prior period error**

Electricity was underpaid during 20.5. The resulting outstanding electricity payment was made during 20.6, after which the comparative amounts have been appropriately restated. The effect of the adjustment on the 20.5 results is as follows:

	20.5 **Rand**
Increase in other expenses	15 000
Decrease in income tax expense	(4 500)
Decrease in profit for the year	10 500
Increase in electricity payable	15 000
Decrease in current tax payable	(4 500)
Decrease in equity	10 500
Decrease in basic earnings per share	xx
Decrease in diluted earnings per share	xx

Calculations

1. **Change in accounting estimate**

	20.6
Accumulated depreciation on 30 June 20.5	40 000
Thus: Expired useful life (1) on 30 June 20.5	2,5 years
Remaining useful life on 1 July 20.5 (5 years total – 2,5 years expired)	2,5 years
	Rand
Carrying amount of machinery on 30 June 20.5 (2)	50 000
Revised residual value	7 000
Thus revised depreciation for 20.6 (3)	17 200
Carrying amount on 30 June 20.6 (4)	32 800

(1) 40 000/16 000 = 2,5 years
(2) 90 000 – 40 000 = 50 000
(3) (50 000 – 7 000)/2,5 years = 17 200
(4) 50 000 – 17 200 = 32 800

2. Correcting journal entries

	Rand Dr/(Cr)
Depreciation (P or L) (5)	1 200
Accumulated depreciation – machinery (SFPos) (20.6)	(1 200)
Deferred tax (SFPos) (20.6)	360
Income tax expense (P or L)	(360)
Other expenses (P or L) (20.5)	15 000
Electricity payable/Accrued expenses (SFPos)	(15 000)
Current tax payable to SARS (SFPos)	4 500
Income tax expense (P or L) (20.5)	(4 500)

(5) 17 200 – 16 000 = 1 200

3. Other expenses

	20.6 Rand	20.5 Rand
Other expenses per trial balance (given)	80 000	50 000
Depreciation		
Old residual value	–	16 000
New residual value	17 200	–
Prior period error	–	15 000
Other expenses	97 200	81 000

4. Income tax expense

	20.6 Rand	20.5 Rand
Given	15 600	9 600
Correction in deferred tax movement (calc 5)	(360)	–
Prior period error (6)	–	(4 500)
	15 240	5 100

(6) 15 000 × 30% = 4 500

5. Deferred tax

	CA Rand	TB Rand	TD Rand	DT Rand Dr/(Cr)	P or L Rand Dr/(Cr)
After correction					
20.5 Machinery (7)	50 000	36 000	14 000	(4 200)	4 200
20.6 Machinery (8)	32 800	18 000	14 800	(4 440)	5 640

(7) 90 000 – (90 000 × 20% × 3) = 36 000
(8) 90 000 – (90 000 × 20% × 4) = 18 000

	CA Rand	TB Rand	TD Rand	DT Rand Dr/(Cr)	P or L Rand Dr/(Cr)
Before correction					
20.5 Machinery	50 000	36 000	14 000	(4 200)	4 200
20.6 Machinery	34 000	18 000	16 000	(4 800)	6 000

Thus correction in movement in deferred tax (9) = 360 cr

(9) 6 000 – 5 640 = 360

CA	=	**Carrying amount**
TB	=	**Tax base**
TD	=	**Temporary difference**
DT	=	**Deferred tax balance**
P or L	=	**Movement in profit or loss**

❑ QUESTION IAS 8.6

The following information relating to Galaxy Ltd is available:

- Revenue for 20.7 amounted to R564 000 (20.6 – R315 000).
- Purchases of inventories for the two years were as follows:
  - R303 000 (20.7)
  - R182 500 (20.6)
- Other expenses
  - R100 000 (20.7)
  - R78 000 (20.6)
- Profit before tax for 20.7 amounted to R182 000 (20.6 – R62 000).
- Retained earnings at the end of 20.7 amounted to R76 700. No dividends have been paid in the last few years.
- The tax rate has remained unchanged at 30% for the past four years. Taxable income was the same as profit before tax for the past four years, except for a penalty of R2 000 which was paid to the local government in 20.7. The South African Revenue Service did not allow this penalty as a deduction.

The purchase prices of inventories have recently been very volatile and after taking into account the above information, the directors decided to change the basis for valuing inventories from the first-in, first-out method (FIFO) to the weighted average cost method, as it would result in more stable inventory values.

A summary of closing inventories is provided:

	20.4 **Rand**	**20.5** **Rand**	**20.6** **Rand**	**20.7** **Rand**
On the first-in, first-out method	18 000	19 500	27 000	48 000
On the weighted average cost method	19 000	22 900	34 800	51 000
	1 000	3 400	7 800	3 000

The South African Revenue Service will only accept the new inventory values from 31 December 20.7 onwards.

Required

a. Prepare the statement of profit or loss and other comprehensive income (with notes) and statement of changes in equity (retained earnings only) of Galaxy Ltd for the year ended 31 December 20.7 applying the new method of inventory valuation so as to comply with the requirements of International Financial Reporting Standards (IFRS).
b. Prepare the statement of profit or loss and other comprehensive income, statement of changes in equity (retained earnings only) and note on change in accounting policy if the weighted average cost of inventory could not be determined at the end of 20.4 and 20.5.
c. Prepare the statement of profit or loss and other comprehensive income, statement of changes in equity (retained earnings only) and note on change in accounting policy if the weighted average cost of inventory could not be determined at the end of 20.6, 20.5 and 20.4.

❖ **Suggested solution IAS 8.6**

a. **GALAXY LTD**
STATEMENT OF PROFIT OR LOSS AND OTHER COMPREHENSIVE INCOME FOR THE YEAR ENDED 31 DECEMBER 20.7

	Note	20.7 Rand	20.6 Rand
Revenue		564 000	315 000
Cost of sales (1)		(286 800)	(170 600)
Gross profit		277 200	144 400
Other expenses		(100 000)	(78 000)
Profit before tax		177 200	66 400
Income tax expense (2)	3	(53 760)	(19 920)
Profit for the year		123 440	46 480
Other comprehensive income		–	–
Total comprehensive income for the year		123 440	46 480

(1) 34 800 + 303 000 – 51 000 = 286 800; 22 900 + 182 500 – 34 800 = 170 600
(2) 56 100 (calc 4) – 2 340 (calc 3) = 53 760; 18 600 (calc 4) + 1 320 (calc 3) = 19 920

GALAXY LTD
STATEMENT OF CHANGES IN EQUITY FOR THE YEAR ENDED 31 DECEMBER 20.7

	Note	Retained earnings/ (accumulated loss) Rand
Balance at 1 January 20.6 (calc 5)		(93 500)
Change in accounting policy	4	2 380
Restated balance		(91 120)
Changes in equity for 20.6		
Total comprehensive income for the year (restated)	4	46 480
Profit for the year		46 480
Other comprehensive income		–
Balance at 31 December 20.6 (restated)		(44 640)

	Note	Retained earnings/ (accumulated loss) Rand
Changes in equity for 20.7		
Total comprehensive income for the year		123 440
Profit for the year		123 440
Other comprehensive income		–
Balance at 31 December 20.7 (3)		78 800

(3) 76 700 + 2 100 (calc 1) = 78 800

GALAXY LTD
NOTES FOR THE YEAR ENDED 31 DECEMBER 20.7

1. Accounting policy

1.1 Inventories

Inventories are valued at the lower of cost and net realisable value on the weighted average cost method.

1.2 Deferred tax

Deferred tax is provided for on temporary differences according to the reporting date balance liability method.

1.3 Revenue

Revenue consists of net invoiced sales and is measured at the amount of consideration the entity is expected to be entitled to, excluding VAT. Revenue is recognised when control of the goods is transferred to the customer.

3. Income tax expense

	20.7 Rand	20.6 Rand
Major components of tax expense:		
Current tax expense: current year (calc 4)	56 100	18 600
Deferred tax expense: current year (calc 3)	(2 340)	1 320
	53 760	19 920

Tax rate reconciliation	**20.7 %**	**20.6 %**
Statutory tax rate	30,00	30,00
Non-deductible items (4)	0,34	–
Effective tax rate (5)	30,34	30,00

(4) (2 000 × 30%)/177 200 × 100 = 0,34%

(5) 53 760/177 200 × 100 = 30,34%

4. Change in accounting policy

During the year the company changed its accounting policy for the valuation of inventories from the first-in, first-out method of valuation to the weighted average cost method as it results in more stable inventory values given the recent volatile inventory prices.

The change in policy has been accounted for retrospectively and the comparative amounts have been appropriately restated. The effect of this change in accounting policy is as follows:

	20.7 Rand	**20.6 Rand**	**20.5 Rand**
(Increase)/decrease in cost of sales	(4 800)	4 400	
Decrease/(increase) in income tax expense	1 440	(1 320)	
(Decrease)/increase in profit for the year	(3 360)	3 080	
Increase in inventory	3 000	7 800	3 400
Increase in deferred tax liability	–	(2 340)	(1 020)
Increase in current tax payable	(900)	–	–
Increase in equity	2 100	5 460	2 380
Adjustment against retained earnings at the end of 20.5			2 380
(Decrease)/increase in basic earnings per share	(xx)	xx	
(Decrease)/increase in diluted earnings per share	(xx)	xx	

Calculations

1. Inventories

	20.7 SFPos Rand	**P or L Rand**	**20.6 SFPos Rand**	**P or L Rand**	**20.5 SFPos Rand**
Old method	(48 000)		(27 000)		(19 500)
New method	51 000		34 800		22 900
Increase in equity	3 000		7 800		3 400
Increase/(decrease) in profit for the year		(4 800) (2)		4 400 (1)	
Tax effect @ 30%	(900)	1 440	(2 340)	(1 320)	(1 020)
After tax	2 100	(3 360)	5 460	3 080	2 380

(1) 7 800 – 3 400 = 4 400
(2) 3 000 – 7 800 = (4 800)

2. Reconstruction of the statement of profit or loss and other comprehensive income according to the 'old' method to determine 20.6 figures

	20.7 Rand	20.6 Rand
Profit before tax	182 000	62 000
Income tax expense (3)	(55 200)	(18 600)
Profit after tax	126 800	43 400

(3) 62 000 × 30% = 18 600; (182 000 + 2 000) × 30% = 55 200

3. Deferred tax

	CA Rand	TB Rand	TD Rand	DT Rand Dr/(Cr)	P or L Rand Dr/(Cr)
20.5	22 900	19 500	3 400	(1 020)	1 020
20.6	34 800	27 000	7 800	(2 340)	1 320
20.7	51 000	51 000	–	–	(2 340)

4. Tax calculation

		20.7 Rand	20.6 Rand
Profit before tax – old		182 000	62 000
Opening inventory:	old (previously deducted, now added back)	27 000	19 500
	New	(34 800)	(22 900)
Closing inventory:	old (previously added, now deducted)	(48 000)	(27 000)
	New	51 000	34 800
Profit before tax after change in accounting policy		177 200	66 400
Non-deductible expense			
Penalty		2 000	
Temporary differences		7 800	(4 400)
Opening inventory:	new (accounting)	34 800	22 900
	old (taxation)	(27 000)	(19 500)
Closing inventory (4):	new (accounting)	(51 000)	(34 800)
	old (taxation)	51 000	27 000
Taxable income		187 000	62 000
Current tax @ 30%		56 100	18 600

(4) The closing inventory in 20.7 causes no temporary differences since the South African Revenue Service has accepted the new valuation method.

5. Reconstruction of statement of changes in equity according to the 'old' method to determine 20.6 and 20.5 figures

	Retained earnings/ (accumulated loss) Rand
Balance at 31 December 20.7 (given)	76 700
Profit/total comprehensive income for the year (calc 2)	(126 800)
Balance at 31 December 20.6	(50 100)
Profit/total comprehensive income for the year (calc 2)	(43 400)
Balance at 31 December 20.5	(93 500)

b. As new inventory values are not available for 20.4 and 20.5, it is impossible to calculate the effect of the change in policy on 20.6 (opening inventory for 20.6 not determinable). As a result, the change in accounting policy should be accounted for retrospectively from 20.7 onwards, resulting in an adjustment to the opening balance of retained earnings. Comparative amounts will not be restated.

GALAXY LTD
STATEMENT OF PROFIT OR LOSS AND OTHER COMPREHENSIVE INCOME FOR THE YEAR ENDED 31 DECEMBER 20.7

	20.7 Rand	20.6 Rand
Revenue	564 000	315 000
Cost of sales (1)	(286 800)	(175 000)
Gross profit	277 200	140 000
Other expenses	(100 000)	(78 000)
Profit before tax	177 200	62 000
Income tax expense (2)	(53 760)	(18 600)
Profit for the year	123 440	43 400
Other comprehensive income	–	–
Total comprehensive income for the year	123 440	43 400

(1) 34 800 + 303 000 – 51 000 = 286 800; 19 500 + 182 500 – 27 000 = 175 000
(2) (177 200 + 2 000) × 30% = 53 760; 62 000 × 30% = 18 600

GALAXY LTD
STATEMENT OF CHANGES IN EQUITY FOR THE YEAR ENDED 31 DECEMBER 20.7

	Notes	Retained earnings/ (accumulated loss) Rand
Balance at 1 January 20.6 (refer to part a)		(93 500)
Changes in equity for 20.6		
Total comprehensive income for the year		43 400
Profit for the year		43 400
Other comprehensive income		–
Balance at 31 December 20.6		(50 100)
Change in accounting policy (1)	4	5 460
Restated balance		(44 640)
Changes in equity for 20.7		
Total comprehensive income for the year		123 440
Profit for the year		123 440
Other comprehensive income		–
Balance at 31 December 20.7		78 800

(1) 7 800 × 70% = 5 460

GALAXY LTD
NOTES FOR THE YEAR ENDED 31 DECEMBER 20.7

4. Change in accounting policy

During the year, the company changed its accounting policy for the valuation of inventories from the first-in, first-out method of valuation to the weighted average cost method as it would result in more stable inventory values in view of recent volatile inventory prices.

Full retrospective application of the change was not possible as the company was not able to determine the new value of inventory at the end of 20.4 and 20.5 due to deficient costing systems. As a result, the change has been accounted for retrospectively from the beginning of 20.7 with an adjustment of R5 460 against the opening balance of retained earnings. The effect of the change in accounting policy is as follows:

	20.7 Rand	20.6 Rand
Increase in cost of sales	(4 800)	
Decrease in income tax expense	1 440	
Decrease in profit for the year	(3 360)	
Increase in inventory	3 000	7 800
Increase in deferred tax liability	–	(2 340)
Increase in current tax payable	(900)	–
Increase in equity	2 100	5 460
Adjustment against retained earnings at the end of 20.6		5 460
Decrease in basic earnings per share	xx	xx
Decrease in diluted earnings per share	xx	xx

c. As new inventory values are not available for 20.4, 20.5 and 20.6, it is impossible to calculate the cumulative effect of the change at the beginning of 20.7. As a result, the new policy is applied prospectively from the earliest date practicable (which will be the end of 20.7).

GALAXY LTD
STATEMENT OF PROFIT OR LOSS AND OTHER COMPREHENSIVE INCOME FOR THE YEAR ENDED 31 DECEMBER 20.7

	20.7 Rand	20.6 Rand
Revenue	564 000	315 000
Cost of sales (1)	(279 000)	(175 000)
Gross profit	285 000	140 000
Other expenses	(100 000)	(78 000)
Profit before tax	185 000	62 000
Income tax expense (2)	(56 100)	(18 600)
Profit for the year	128 900	43 400
Other comprehensive income	–	–
Total comprehensive income for the year	128 900	43 400

(1) 27 000 + 303 000 – 51 000 = 279 000
(2) (185 000 + 2 000) × 30% = 56 100; 62 000 × 30% = 18 600

GALAXY LTD
STATEMENT OF CHANGES IN EQUITY FOR THE YEAR ENDED 31 DECEMBER 20.7

	Retained earnings/ (accumulated loss) Rand
Balance at 1 January 20.6 (refer to part a)	(93 500)
Changes in equity for 20.6	
Total comprehensive income for the year	43 400
Profit for the year	43 400
Other comprehensive income	–
Balance at 31 December 20.6	(50 100)
Changes in equity for 20.7	
Total comprehensive income for the year	128 900
Profit for the year	128 900
Other comprehensive income	–
Balance at 31 December 20.7	78 800

GALAXY LTD
NOTES FOR THE YEAR ENDED 31 DECEMBER 20.7

4. **Change in accounting policy**

During the year the company changed its accounting policy for the valuation of inventories from the first-in, first-out method of valuation to the weighted average cost method as it will result in more stable inventory values in view of recent volatile inventory prices.

The change in policy could not be accounted for retrospectively, as it was not possible to determine the cumulative effect of the change at the beginning of 20.7, due to deficient costing systems. As a result, the change in accounting policy was accounted for prospectively by adjusting the closing inventory for 20.7. The effect of the change in accounting policy is as follows:

	20.7 Rand
Decrease in cost of sales	3 000
Increase in income tax expense	(900)
Increase in profit for the year	2 100
Increase in inventory	3 000
Increase in current tax payable	(900)
Increase in equity	2 100
Increase in basic earnings per share	xx
Increase in diluted earnings per share	xx

❑ QUESTION IAS 8.7

The following information is available:

Property, plant and equipment

Plant and machinery are not revalued annually, but are shown at historical cost.
- Depreciation is recognised on the straight-line method.
- The depreciation rate is 15% per annum.
- The useful life of the assets is revised annually. Depreciation rates are adjusted where deemed necessary.

Vehicles are shown at historical cost.
- Depreciation is recognised using the sum-of-the-digits method.
- Depreciation is calculated over five years.
- Estimated physical wear and obsolescence is taken into account in determining the useful life of the vehicles.
- The expected scrap value is taken into account in determining the depreciation charge.

Inventories

Inventories consist of finished goods, raw materials, consumables and work in progress.

Inventories are valued at cost or net realisable value, whichever is the lower.

The following accounting bases are used in the valuation:

- **Finished goods** – shown at direct manufacturing cost and an applicable portion of manufacturing overheads on the first-in, first-out basis.
- **Raw materials** – shown at actual historical purchase price on a first-in, first-out basis.
- **Consumables** – shown at actual cost on a first-in, first-out basis.
- **Work in progress** – shown at direct manufacturing cost and an applicable portion of manufacturing overheads on a first-in, first-out basis.

Specific provision is made for obsolete and slow-moving inventories if necessary.

The allocation of production overheads is based on the capacity of the facilities.

The historical cost of inventories includes all costs of bringing them to their current location and condition.

Revenue

Revenue:
- includes the amount invoiced to customers;
- excludes VAT;
- excludes sales of associated companies.

Intragroup transactions are eliminated.

Deferred tax

Deferred tax is calculated by applying the rate of tax to temporary differences which arise as differences between the tax base of an asset or liability and its carrying amount in the statement of financial position.

Required

Prepare the accounting policy notes (where applicable) dealing with the above-mentioned matters in accordance with the requirements of IAS 8.

❑ QUESTION IAS 8.8

The following items were taken from the trial balance of Parfait Ltd for the year ended 28 February 20.4:

	Rand
Sales	500 000
Cost of sales	180 000
Other expenses (not specified)	120 000
Loss on disposal of vehicle (tax deductible)	30 000
Depreciation – machinery	30 000
Net profit from inventory damaged by flood (taxable)	10 000
(Cost of inventory – R50 000; insurance claim – R60 000)	
Loss due to expropriation of inventories by the government (tax deductible)	12 000
Machinery at cost	150 000
Accumulated depreciation – machinery (28 February 20.4)	60 000

Additional information

1. The useful life of machinery was originally estimated to be five years from date of purchase. Owing to technological changes, the remaining useful life as at 28 February 20.3 is estimated to be only two years. The change in useful life has yet to be reflected in the trial balance. The machinery has no residual value.

2. The company tax rate is 28%, and the South African Revenue Service is prepared to allow the additional wear and tear needed to write off the value of the machinery over the remaining useful life. There are no other non-deductible/non-taxable items.

Required

Prepare the statement of profit or loss and other comprehensive income of Parfait Ltd for the year ended 28 February 20.4 so as to comply with the requirements of International Financial Reporting Standards (IFRS). Only the note on profit before tax is required.

❑ QUESTION IAS 8.9

The following is a list of items in the statement of profit or loss and other comprehensive income of Gunter (Pty) Ltd for the year ended 30 June 20.2 and 20.1:

	20.2 Rand	**20.1 Rand**
Revenue	4 800 000	3 950 000
Profit before tax	540 000	330 000
Retained earnings – beginning of year	?	35 600

During the current year, Gunter (Pty) Ltd converted from a CC to a company after your client obtained a majority interest. As a result of the conversion the audit was moved from the previous accounting officer to your firm of registered accountants and auditors.

During the course of the audit the following information regarding the previous and the current year was obtained:

1. The revenue figures above include dividend income of R100 000 (20.1 – R50 000). The gross profit percentage of the company has remained constant at 50% during the last five years. Other expenses for 20.2 amounted to R1 910 000 (20.1 – R1 670 000) before taking into account any adjustments relating to the details below.

2. Delivery vehicles purchased on 1 July 20.0 under an instalment sales agreement (ISA) were recorded as follows:

Details of agreement	**Rand**
Cash price (VAT excluded)	250 000
VAT at 14%	35 000
Finance charges	148 000
Contract liability	433 000

The term of the ISA is 48 months.

Journal entries:	**20.2 Rand Dr/(Cr)**	**20.1 Rand Dr/(Cr)**
Vehicles	–	433 000
ISA liability	–	(433 000)
ISA liability (1)	108 250	108 250
Bank	(108 250)	(108 250)
Depreciation at 20% (2)	86 600	86 600
Accumulated depreciation	(86 600)	(86 600)
Income tax expense (P or L) (3)	6 495	6 495
Deferred tax (SFPos)	(6 495)	(6 495)

(1) 433 000 × 12/48 = 108 250
(2) 433 000 × 20% = 86 600
(3) [(433 000 × 25%) – (433 000 × 20%)] × 30% = 6 495

3. Other information

- VAT can be claimed as an input credit.
- The estimated useful life of each vehicle is five years.
- The tax rate is 30%.
- The company obtained a directive from the South African Revenue Service to claim wear and tear on the straight-line basis over four years.
- Any corrective action regarding the South African Revenue Service has already been approved and accepted. Prior years' assessments will therefore be reopened.

- Apart from the temporary differences and non-taxable/non-deductible items arising from the above information, there are no other such differences.

4. Finance charges per the ISA are recognised on the effective interest method for accounting and tax purposes. The following figures represent the capital outstanding in respect of the ISA at 30 June of each year and should be accepted as correct:

	Rand
20.1	227 680
20.2	168 280
20.3	93 680

Required

a. Prepare the adjusting journal entries.
b. Prepare the statement of profit or loss and other comprehensive income and statement of changes in equity (retained earnings only) of Gunter (Pty) Ltd for the year ended 30 June 20.2 so as to comply with the requirements of International Financial Reporting Standards (IFRS). Only the note regarding the adjustment needs to be shown. Accounting policy notes are not required.

❑ QUESTION IAS 8.10

Critically evaluate the following comments made by Pistol Pete, the financial director of Sampras Ltd, for the financial year ended 31 December 20.1 with reference to the requirements of International Financial Reporting Standards (IFRS) and Interpretations of IFRS:

- 'We completed our plant last year after five years of construction. Fortunately we were able to capitalise the borrowing costs incurred. The plant is used in the production of our new product, a very durable tennis ball which is baked in the sun for two years. We finance all our activities in a debt–equity ratio of 60% debt to 40% equity. The finance charges relating to the tennis balls had a negative impact on this year's profit or loss, since the tennis balls manufactured during the first year still need one year's ageing. No products were sold during the current year.'

- 'The board of directors decided to revalue the plant every second year at its net replacement value. Since our other products are manufactured with outdated machinery, we have decided not to revalue machinery.'

- 'We have 1 000 of our tennis racquet units on hand at reporting date. The cost price of the items is R1 000 and the net realisable value is R2 000. A decision was taken at the previous management meeting to carry these items at net realisable value in the statement of financial position.'

❑ QUESTION IAS 8.11

Extra Ltd is a specialised engineering company involved in various projects. During the year the company decided to change the accounting policy for the valuation of inventory from the first-in, first-out method to the weighted average method as a result of inventory price fluctuations over the last few months and because the new method will result in more stable inventory values. The company's financial year ends on 31 December.

The following is the abridged statement of profit or loss and other comprehensive income of Extra Ltd for the year ended 31 December (before the change in inventory valuation was taken into account):

	20.8 **Rand**	**20.7** **Rand**
Profit before tax	140 000	141 000
Income tax expense – current	(42 000)	(44 100)
Profit for the year	98 000	96 900
Dividends paid	10 000	5 000

Additional information

1. The following information is relevant regarding the change in accounting policy i.r.o. inventory:

Inventory (closing)	**20.8** **Rand**	**20.7** **Rand**	**20.6** **Rand**
Weighted average (new method)	110 000	140 000	120 000
First-in, first-out (old method)	90 000	130 000	130 000

The South African Revenue Service will only accept the new inventory valuation method from 31 December 20.8.

2. Included in profit before tax for 20.8 is the following:

   A loss of R6 500 (net of insurance proceeds) resulting from flooding of one of the plants due to severe rainstorms. The proceeds from the insurance claim amounted to R13 500.

3. Revenue for 20.8 amounted to R800 000 and R650 000 for 20.7. The gross profit percentage (before the change in accounting policy) is 50% (20.7 – 60%).

4. Included in profit for 20.7 is a gain of R15 000 relating to the sale of land. The profit is of a capital nature.

5. Assume that, unless otherwise specified, all income and expenses are taxable and deductible respectively. The tax rate was 30% for 20.8 and 35% for 20.7 and 20.6. Ignore capital gains tax.

6. Retained earnings at the beginning of the year amounted to:

	Rand
20.7	12 000
20.8	103 900

Required

Prepare the statement of profit or loss and other comprehensive income and statement of changes in equity (retained earnings only) of Extra Ltd for the year ended 31 December 20.8 so as to comply with the requirements of International Financial Reporting Standards (IFRS). Only the following notes should be provided:

- Profit before tax
- Change in accounting policy
- Income tax expense

❑ QUESTION IAS 8.12

The abridged pro forma statement of profit or loss and other comprehensive income of Sabre Ltd for the year ended 30 June 20.8 is as follows:

	20.8 Rand	20.7 Rand
Revenue	800 000	700 000
Cost of sales	(650 000)	(565 000)
Gross profit	150 000	135 000
Other expenses	(30 000)	(25 000)
Profit on sale of share investment (not taxable)	–	15 000
Dividends received – Sword (Pty) Ltd	9 000	9 000
Profit before tax	129 000	134 000
Income tax expense (current)	?	(33 000)
Profit for the year		101 000
Other comprehensive income	–	–
Total comprehensive income for the year	?	101 000

Additional information

The following issues have **not yet been accounted for** in the above statement of profit or loss and other comprehensive income of Sabre Ltd:

1. On 30 June 20.8, after completing the pro forma financial statements, the board of directors decided to change the accounting policy with respect to the inventory valuation from the weighted average basis to the first-in, first-out (FIFO) basis as inventory prices have recently increased significantly. Inventories are valued as follows using both methods:

	Weighted average (old method) Rand	FIFO (new method) Rand
30 June 20.8	700 000	800 000
30 June 20.7	600 000	680 000
30 June 20.6	500 000	Cannot be determined

2. The South African Revenue Service is prepared to accept the new valuation of closing inventory as at 30 June 20.8 for tax purposes.

3. On 30 April 20.8 the company disposed of land realising a capital profit of R14 000. This amount is not taxable.

4. On 28 February 20.8 the company suffered material flood damage in respect of inventory to the amount of R100 000. The company was not insured for this type of risk. This amount is deductible for tax purposes.

5. A batch of sales invoices with a total value of R24 000 was not processed in 20.7 – this is regarded as material. However, the cost of sales associated with these invoices was taken into account. The South African Revenue Service reopened the 20.7 assessment as a result of this error.

6. Dividends paid for the year ended 30 June 20.8 amounted to R30 000 (20.7: R30 000).

7. The ruling tax rate for the last three years was 30%. There are no other temporary or non-taxable/non-deductible differences apart from those evident from the question. You may ignore any other form of tax, including capital gains tax.

8. Retained earnings are as follows on the dates indicated:

	Rand
30 June 20.6	51 000
30 June 20.7	122 000

Required

Prepare the statement of profit or loss and other comprehensive income and statement of changes in equity (retained earnings only) of Sabre Ltd for the year ended 30 June 20.8. Notes to the statement of profit or loss and other comprehensive income and statement of changes in equity are also required, excluding accounting policy notes. Your answer must comply with the requirements of International Financial Reporting Standards (IFRS) in so far as the information allows you to do so. Assume that all amounts are material.

❑ QUESTION IAS 8.13

Krazy Krys Ltd is a public company listed on the JSE Ltd. Krazy Krys Ltd imports and sells eccentric toys such as jumping castles for adults and miniature poker sets for children.

Krazy Krys Ltd leases a low-value asset under a lease agreement with the following terms (the company elected, in terms of IFRS 16, not to capitalise the contract):

Lease term:	10 years (1 August 20.0 – 31 July 20.10)	
Lease payments:	First 12 months:	R200 per month
	1 August 20.1 – 31 July 20.6:	R150 per month
	1 August 20.6 – 31 July 20.10:	R100 per month

All lease payments are payable monthly in arrears and include VAT at 14%.

Krazy Krys Ltd accounted for the lease as follows:

Financial year ended 31 December 20.0:	**Rand Dr/(Cr)**
Lease expense (P or L)	1 000
Bank	(1 000)
Lease payments: R200 × 5 months	

You may assume an unchanged normal tax rate of 29%. No journal entries relating to taxation have been processed by Krazy Krys Ltd. All lease instalments were paid timeously. Assume that all amounts are material.

Required

a. Provide **adjusting** journal entries (you may ignore current tax implications) for the financial year ended 31 December 20.0. You may not reverse or re-record any journal entries that were posted by Krazy Krys Ltd.
b. Provide **originating** journal entries (you may ignore current tax implications) for the financial year ended 31 December 20.1.
c. Disclose all relevant notes pertaining to the above-mentioned information for the financial year ended 31 December 20.1 if it is assumed that the error in 20.0 was never corrected during 20.0. You may ignore current tax implications. Your answer must comply with the requirements of International Financial Reporting Standards (IFRS).

❑ QUESTION IAS 8.14[#]

Traders Ltd is currently in the process of erecting various plants across the country to manufacture its products. The costs incurred to erect the plants, which take a substantial period of time to erect, are financed through loans.

In accordance with Traders Ltd's accounting policy, borrowing costs on qualifying assets have always been expensed as incurred. However, the auditors of Traders Ltd recently informed management that IAS 23 *Borrowing costs* was revised during the year and that in future all borrowing costs on qualifying assets must be capitalised against the asset.

The auditors informed management that the effective date of the revised standard is 1 January 20.9. The transitional provisions of the standard state that an entity must capitalise borrowing costs on all qualifying assets for which the commencement date for capitalisation is on or after the effective date of the standard.

However, the transitional provisions of the standard do provide that an entity may designate any date before the standard's effective date as its own effective date. If an entity designates an earlier date, the borrowing costs on all qualifying assets for which the commencement date for capitalisation is on or after the entity's own effective date, must be capitalised.

The auditor explained that this means that in future only borrowing costs on new qualifying assets will be capitalised and that no retrospective restatement will occur.

Management informed its auditors that borrowing costs on qualifying plant that will be erected from 1 January 20.8 will be capitalised.

Details in respect of qualifying plant for the years ended 31 December 20.7 and 20.8 are as follows:

	Plant A	Plant B
Commencement date for the capitalisation of borrowing costs	1 July 20.7	1 March 20.8
Completion date of the erection of plant	31 December 20.7	30 November 20.8
Total cost of plant	R2 million	R3,6 million
Borrowing costs incurred which qualify for capitalisation	R358 500	R450 000

Plant is accounted for in accordance with the cost model and is depreciated straight-line over the estimated useful life of five years, with no material residual value.

The South African Revenue Service allows pre-production interest as a once-off deduction as soon as the asset is brought into use. Wear and tear is allowed over a period of three years, not allocated on a pro-rata basis for parts of the year. Accept a tax rate of 28%.

Required

Prepare the note to the annual financial statements of Traders Ltd for the year ended 31 December 20.8 in accordance with IAS 8.

❑ QUESTION IAS 8.15@

On 1 July 20.6 Adams Ltd received a grant of R1,5 million from the local government for the purchase of machinery of R4,5 million, purchased on the same day.

The requirements of the grant stipulate that Adams Ltd must utilise the machinery in the manufacturing of blankets for the Department of Social Services. From 1 July 20.6, Adams Ltd must manufacture 5 000 blankets per month for the next five years. At the end of the five years the machinery will no longer be usable.

A pro-rata amount of the grant must be repaid at the end of each year if the required annual production is not delivered. This amount will be calculated based on the ratio of the number of uncompleted blankets to the total number of blankets to be produced over the five-year period.

Adams Ltd accounts for machinery on the cost model and it is depreciated in accordance with the production unit method.

The South African Revenue Service allows machinery to be written off over three years and you must assume that the government grant is taxable. The tax rate for the past few years has remained unchanged at 28%. Assume that there will be sufficient future taxable income for the recognition of any deferred tax assets.

Adams Ltd manufactured the following number of blankets for the respective years:

Year ended 30 June	**Number of blankets**
20.7	60 000
20.8	60 000
20.9	45 000

On 30 June 20.9 Adams Ltd repaid the required amount to the local government.

You can assume a profit before tax, after taking the above information into account, of R1 million for each of the respective years.

Required

a. Disclose the matter above in the notes to the statement of profit or loss and other comprehensive income of Adams Ltd for the year ended 30 June 20.9, in accordance with the requirements of International Financial Reporting Standards (IFRS), if the government grant is **offset against the carrying amount of the asset**. Comparative amounts are not required.

b. Disclose the matter above in the notes to the statement of profit or loss and other comprehensive income of Adams Ltd for the year ended 30 June 20.9, in accordance with the requirements of International Financial Reporting Standards (IFRS), if the government grant is **recognised as deferred income**. Comparative amounts are not required.

IAS 10

Events after the reporting period

❑ QUESTIONS AND SOLUTIONS

IAS 10.1	Various events after the reporting period: identification, discussion of impact on financial statements, presentation and disclosure
IAS 10.2	Various events after the reporting period: identification, discussion of impact on financial statements, presentation and disclosure
IAS 10.3	Various events after the reporting period: discussion, presentation and disclosure

❑ QUESTIONS

IAS 10.4	Various events after the reporting period: identification, discussion of impact on financial statements
IAS 10.5	Adjusting event after the reporting period: discussion of accounting treatment and impact on financial statements
IAS 10.6	Various events after the reporting period: commentary and disclosure
IAS 10.7	Various non-adjusting events after the reporting period: discussion on accounting treatment in financial statements
IAS 10.8	Dividends and going concern basis: discussion and disclosure

❑ QUESTION IAS 10.1

The financial statements of Matthews Ltd for the year ended 31 December 20.1 were presented to the board of directors on 30 March 20.2 for authorisation for issue. You are the accountant of the company. The following events have taken place since the reporting date:

1. During January 20.2 a bomb exploded at one of Matthews Ltd's branches. Damage amounted to R200 000, R80 000 of which was for damage to inventory. The company's insurance policy does not cover such occurrences and the claim was repudiated by the insurance company. A contract was concluded with Regmaak Ltd on 1 March 20.2 to repair the damage to the building at a cost of R120 000. This will be financed out of surplus cash funds.

2. Jolo Ltd, a customer of the company, was placed in liquidation by its creditors on 15 January 20.2. Jolo Ltd owes Matthews Ltd an amount of R40 000, which was included in receivables at the reporting date. Jolo Ltd's liquidator notified all creditors on 15 March 20.2 that the estimated liquidation dividend would be 20 cents in the rand.

3. A rights issue of shares was made on 1 February 20.2 to finance the acquisition and furnishing of office buildings. The full issuance of R1 200 000 (at R12 per share) was taken up by shareholders. The directors concluded an 'option to purchase' in respect of office buildings during October 20.1. The rights issue was approved by the directors on 15 November 20.1.

4. On 15 January 20.2 a competitor sued Matthews Ltd for an infringement of a patent. Matthews Ltd appointed attorneys to defend the action. To date legal costs have already amounted to R10 000. It is not possible to determine the costs to defend the case or its outcome. It may be assumed that the alleged infringement took place during 20.1 or earlier.

5. The market value of a listed share investment decreased to R150 000 on 31 March 20.2. On the reporting date the investment was shown at R300 000, which represented the market value at that date. The investment is classified as a financial asset at fair value through profit or loss.

6. An invoice dated 27 December 20.1 for R60 000 was received from Owe Ltd and included in creditors on the reporting date. Inventories listed on the invoice were delivered on 4 January 20.2 and are included in the inventory figure at R60 000 on the reporting date. A positive creditors' circularisation was carried out and Owe Ltd positively confirmed the amount outstanding at 31 December 20.1. However, Matthews Ltd discovered during January 20.2 that the invoice from Owe Ltd contained a calculation error and the correct amount for the inventories should in fact be R80 000. Owe Ltd is not yet aware of this error.

Additional information

Authorised share capital	**Rand**
1 000 000 ordinary shares	1 000 000
Issued share capital	
600 000 ordinary shares issued at R1 each	600 000

Purchase price and furnishing costs of office buildings (see point 3) are estimated by the board of directors at R1 200 000

Assume a tax rate of 27% and that 80% of capital gains are taxed. You can also assume that Matthews Ltd had a deferred tax liability balance as at 31 December 20.1.

Required

a. Classify each of the events after the reporting date as either adjusting or non-adjusting events.
b. Briefly discuss the effect of the above-mentioned events on the financial statements as at 31 December 20.1.
c. Provide an extract from the financial statements of Matthews Ltd as at 31 December 20.1, presenting and disclosing the results of the discussion in b. above to ensure compliance with the requirements of International Financial Reporting Standards (IFRS).

Assume that all amounts are material and that the company is a going concern notwithstanding the effect of the above-mentioned events on the financial statements.

❖ **Suggested solution IAS 10.1**

1.a. Classification: non-adjusting event.

b. Discussion

Although Matthews Ltd did not have insurance cover at the reporting date, the loss should not be taken into account for the year ended 31 December 20.1 as no loss had been incurred on that date. The bomb explosion at the branch is not indicative of conditions that existed at the reporting date, and therefore the amounts in the financial statements should not be updated to reflect the impact of this occurrence (IAS 10.10). Both the loss of inventory and damage to buildings shall be disclosed by way of a note to the financial statements, as non-disclosure of the events will affect the ability of users to make proper evaluations and decisions, since the amounts involved are material (IAS 10.21).

c. Disclosure

MATTHEWS LTD
NOTES FOR THE YEAR ENDED 31 DECEMBER 20.1

14. Events after the reporting date

During January 20.2 a bomb exploded at one of the branches of the company. Inventory amounting to R80 000 was destroyed. Damage to buildings amounted to R120 000.

15. Contracts for capital expenditure

A contract was concluded with Regmaak Ltd to repair the damage (see note 14) to the buildings for R120 000. Surplus cash funds will be utilised to finance the cost of the repairs.

2.a. Classification: adjusting event.

b. Discussion

The event indicates that an asset was impaired at the reporting date (see IAS 10.9(b)(i)).

The applicable loss is calculated by taking into account the estimated liquidation dividend [thus R40 000 – (20% × R40 000)]. Adjustments to the amounts in the financial statements are required if events which took place after the reporting date provide further evidence of conditions that existed at the reporting date (IAS 10.8).

The financial statements should be adjusted and normal disclosure requirements will apply. Receivables are reduced by R32 000 (80% × R40 000) and the allowance for credit losses is increased by the same amount. This will result in a R32 000 reduction in profit before tax, a R8 640 (R32 000 × 27%) reduction in income tax expense and a R8 640 decrease in the deferred tax liability in the statement of financial position, provided that the tax authorities will only give a tax deduction for the allowance for credit losses relating to this debtor, once the loss is actually incurred (i.e. during 20.2).

c. Disclosure

MATTHEWS LTD
STATEMENT OF FINANCIAL POSITION AS AT 31 DECEMBER 20.1

	Rand
ASSETS	
Current assets	
Trade receivables (xx xxx – 32 000)	xx xxx
EQUITY AND LIABILITIES	
Total equity	
Retained earnings (xx xxx – 23 360 (2))	xx xxx
Non-current liabilities	
Deferred tax liability (xx xxx – 8 640 (1))	xx xxx

MATTHEWS LTD
STATEMENT OF PROFIT OR LOSS AND OTHER COMPREHENSIVE INCOME FOR THE YEAR ENDED 31 DECEMBER 20.1

	Rand
Revenue	xx xxx
Other expenses (xx xxx + 32 000)	(xx xxx)
Profit before tax (xx xxx – 32 000)	xx xxx
Income tax expense (xx xxx – 8 640 (1))	(xx xxx)
Profit for the year (xx xxx – 23 360 (2))	xx xxx
Other comprehensive income	–
Total comprehensive income for the year	xx xxx

(1) 32 000 × 27% = 8 640
(2) 32 000 – 8 640 = 23 360

3.a. Classification: non-adjusting event.

b. Discussion

Although the directors of Matthews Ltd approved the rights issue on 15 November 20.1, the transaction only took place on 1 February 20.2. The amounts in the financial statements will not be adjusted as the event does not relate to conditions existing at the reporting date (IAS 10.10).

The price paid for the option, if any, should be capitalised as part of the purchase price of the office buildings and does not influence the financial statements as at 31 December 20.1.

However, in view of the importance of the matter (rights issue), a note will be included to the financial statements in which the matter is explained to enable users to evaluate the financial statements properly and to enable them to make informed decisions (IAS 10.21). IAS 10 further specifically requires disclosure regarding major ordinary share transactions after the reporting period (IAS 10.22(f)).

The total amount or estimated amount of capital expenditure on contracts will be explained by way of a note to the financial statements. The source from which the expenditure will be financed must also be disclosed.

c. Disclosure

MATTHEWS LTD
NOTES FOR THE YEAR ENDED 31 DECEMBER 20.1

2. Share capital	**Rand**
Authorised	
1 000 000 ordinary shares	1 000 000
Issued	
600 000 ordinary shares issued at R1 each	600 000

A rights issue of 100 000 shares issued at R12 per share was made on 1 February 20.2. The issue was fully subscribed.

15. Contracts for capital expenditure

The directors concluded an 'option to purchase' an office building during October 20.1 for the acquisition of office buildings. The proceeds of the rights issue will be used to finance the purchase and to furnish the office buildings (see note 2). The directors estimate that the cost of purchase and furnishing will amount to R1 200 000.

4.a. Classification: non-adjusting event.

b. Discussion

As the available information is vague and the outcome and costs of the case cannot be determined, only the existence and nature of the possible obligation must be disclosed as a contingent liability (IAS 37.10 – see definition of contingent liability).

The nature of the contingent liability, namely possible infringement of a competitor's patent, and the fact that the outcome and costs of the case cannot be determined must be disclosed in the financial statements by way of a note (IAS 10.21). No specific mention of the R10 000 legal costs incurred after the reporting period is necessary.

c. **Disclosure**

MATTHEWS LTD
NOTES FOR THE YEAR ENDED 31 DECEMBER 20.1

14. **Contingent liability**

The company is a defendant in a lawsuit with a competitor, the outcome and costs of which cannot be determined at present. The plaintiff alleges infringement of a patent held by him.

5.a. **Classification:** non-adjusting event.

b. **Discussion**

As a reduction in the market value of the listed investment took place after the reporting date, the amounts in the financial statements will not be adjusted (IAS 10.10). In terms of IFRS 9 *Financial Instruments* the company is obliged to account for such investments at market value if classified at fair value through profit or loss.

If a non-adjusting event such as an abnormally large change in asset prices after the reporting date is of such importance (IAS 10.22(g)) that non-disclosure would affect the ability of users to make proper evaluations and decisions, the nature of the event as well as an estimate of its financial effect, or a statement that such an estimate cannot be made, must be disclosed in a note to the financial statements (IAS 10.21).

c. **Disclosure**

MATTHEWS LTD
NOTES FOR THE YEAR ENDED 31 DECEMBER 20.1

14. **Events after the reporting date**

At the end of March 20.2 the market value of a listed investment with a carrying amount of R300 000 decreased to R150 000. This will result in a decrease in profit before tax of R150 000 during the next financial year.

6.a. **Classification:** adjusting event.

b. **Discussion**

As both Matthews Ltd and Owe Ltd accounted for the transaction in December 20.1, the delivery date is not relevant. The error made by Owe Ltd will not be to Matthews Ltd's advantage from a legal point of view. Owe Ltd will accordingly invoice Matthews Ltd for the difference as soon as they discover the error. Whether Matthews Ltd points out the error to Owe Ltd or conceals it, the additional liability of R20 000 and increase in inventory must be recognised in the financial statements.

The amounts in the financial statements must be adjusted for events occurring after the reporting date which provide further evidence of conditions that existed at the reporting date (IAS 10.8). Both creditors and closing inventory will increase by R20 000. The net effect on profit before tax in the statement of profit or loss and other comprehensive income is nil as there is an increase in both purchases and closing inventory.

c. **Disclosure**

MATTHEWS LTD
STATEMENT OF FINANCIAL POSITION AS AT 31 DECEMBER 20.1

	Rand
ASSETS	
Current assets	
Inventories (xx xxx + 20 000)	xx xxx
EQUITY AND LIABILITIES	
Current liabilities	
Trade and other payables (xx xxx + 20 000)	xx xxx

In each of the above-mentioned cases and in addition to the given disclosure, the date must be disclosed when the financial statements were authorised for issue and who gave such authorisation. If any party has the power to amend the financial statements after issue date, this fact must also be disclosed (IAS 10.17).

❑ QUESTION IAS 10.2

The financial statements of Mossie Ltd for the year ended 31 December 20.3 were presented to the board of directors for authorisation for issue on 20 March 20.4. You are the accountant of the company. The following events occurred after the reporting date:

1. Owing to the current economic recession and to increased competition, the selling price of Mossie Ltd's main product was considerably reduced on 15 February 20.4. The lower selling price will cause a 15% decrease in gross profit in respect of the main product. It is estimated that profit before tax for the year ended 31 December 20.4 will decrease by R500 000.

2. The board of directors decided to declare an additional ordinary dividend of R20 000 on 15 February 20.4. The dividends will be paid on 5 April 20.4.

3. Dik Daan Ltd, a debtor, sent a letter to all their creditors on 18 March 20.4 stating that they were terminating their business, owing to financial difficulties. They suggested an offer of compromise of 20 cents in the rand. A statement of assets and liabilities supported by an auditors' certificate was attached to the letter. The amount owing by Dik Daan Ltd to Mossie Ltd amounts to R20 000 and is included in receivables at the reporting date. Assume that all the transactions with Dik Daan Ltd were conducted in the normal course of business.

4. During February 20.4 a fire broke out in a warehouse, and inventory amounting to R60 000 was destroyed. Mossie Ltd was not insured. Assume that the loss resulting from the fire damage will be deductible for tax purposes.

5. On 15 January 20.4 a customer sued Mossie Ltd for failing to meet specifications on certain goods supplied. The case was taken to court and judgment has not yet been passed. The attorneys of Mossie Ltd notified the financial director that the company will probably lose the case and that compensation (which is tax deductible) of approximately R100 000 will likely be payable before the end of 20.4. The inventory was delivered to the customer during the year ended 31 December 20.3.

6. The research department of Mossie Ltd developed a product during November 20.3 which will make an exceptional contribution to profits in future.

Assume a normal tax rate of 27% and that 80% of capital gains are taxed. Ignore all other forms of taxation. You can also assume that Mossie Ltd had a deferred tax liability balance as at 31 December 20.3.

Required

a. Identify in each case whether an adjusting or non-adjusting event took place.
b. Briefly discuss the effect of each event on the financial statements as at 31 December 20.3.
c. Provide an extract from the financial statements of Mossie Ltd as at 31 December 20.3, presenting and disclosing the results of the discussion in b. above to ensure compliance with the requirements of International Financial Reporting Standards (IFRS).

Assume that all amounts are material and that the company is a going concern, notwithstanding the effect of the above events on the financial statements.

❖ **Suggested solution IAS 10.2**

1.a. Classification: non-adjusting event.

b. Discussion

The information provided indicates lower profits in the forthcoming financial year. If these are material this must be disclosed in the directors' report.

c. Disclosure

MOSSIE LTD
DIRECTORS' REPORT FOR THE YEAR ENDED
31 DECEMBER 20.3

The selling price of the company's main product was substantially reduced in 20.4 due to the present economic recession and stronger competition. The reduced selling price will result in an estimated decrease in the total comprehensive income for the year ended 20.4 of R365 000 (R500 000 before tax).

2.a. Classification: non-adjusting event.

b. Discussion

IAS 10.13 stipulates that a dividend declared after the reporting date but before the financial statements were authorised for issue will not be recognised as a liability at the reporting date. IAS 1 requires such a declaration after the reporting date to be disclosed in the notes to the financial statements.

c. Disclosure

MOSSIE LTD
NOTES FOR THE YEAR ENDED 31 DECEMBER 20.3

15. Events after the reporting date

An additional dividend of R20 000 was declared on 15 February 20.4 and will be paid on 5 April 20.4.

3.a. Classification: adjusting event.

b. Discussion

The fact that Dik Daan Ltd notified their creditors in writing that they were experiencing financial difficulties emphasises the fact that creditors should expect losses and indicates that an asset was impaired at the reporting date (see IAS 10.9(b)). This is confirmed by the auditors' certificate, and legal action will not lead to increased recovery per rand. It is therefore reasonable to take the estimated recoverable amount of the debt of Dik Daan Ltd into account when calculating the carrying amount of receivables. The amounts in the financial statements will have to be adjusted and normal disclosure requirements will apply (IAS 10.8).

The allowance for credit losses and profit before tax will decrease by R16 000 (R20 000 × 80c). The income tax expense and the deferred tax liability in the statement of financial position will decrease by R4 320 (R16 000 × 27%), provided that the tax authorities will only give a tax deduction for the allowance for credit losses relating to this debtor, once the loss is actually incurred (i.e. during 20.4).

c. Disclosure

MOSSIE LTD
STATEMENT OF FINANCIAL POSITION AS AT 31 DECEMBER 20.3

	Rand
ASSETS	
Current assets	
Trade receivables (xx xxx – 16 000)	xx xxx
EQUITY AND LIABILITIES	
Total equity	
Retained earnings (xx xxx – 11 680 (2))	xx xxx
Non-current liabilities	
Deferred tax liability (xx xxx – 4 320 (1))	xx xxx

MOSSIE LTD
STATEMENT OF PROFIT OR LOSS AND OTHER COMPREHENSIVE INCOME FOR THE YEAR ENDED 31 DECEMBER 20.3

	Rand
Revenue	xx xxx
Other expenses (xx xxx + 16 000)	(xx xxx)
Profit before tax (xx xxx – 16 000)	xx xxx
Income tax expense (xx xxx – 4 320 (1))	(xx xxx)
Profit for the year (xx xxx – 11 680 (2))	xx xxx
Other comprehensive income	–
Total comprehensive income for the year	xx xxx

(1) 16 000 × 27% = 4 320
(2) 16 000 – 4 320 = 11 680

4.a. **Classification:** non-adjusting event.

b. **Discussion**

Although Mossie Ltd was not insured at the reporting date, the amounts in the financial statements for the year ended 31 December 20.3 must not be adjusted for the loss (IAS 10.10). The cause of the loss was the fire, which only took place during February 20.4 and therefore does not provide additional evidence of conditions that existed at the reporting date.

The loss of inventory must nevertheless be disclosed by way of a note to the financial statements to enable users to make proper evaluations and decisions, since the amounts involved are material (IAS 10.21).

c. **Disclosure**

MOSSIE LTD
NOTES FOR THE YEAR ENDED 31 DECEMBER 20.3

12. Events after the reporting date

During February 20.4 a fire in a warehouse destroyed inventory valued at R60 000. The loss is tax deductible.

5.a. **Classification:** adjusting event.

b. **Discussion**

A present obligation exists at the reporting date arising from a past obligating event, the settlement of which is expected to result in an outflow of resources embodying economic benefits, and a reliable estimate of the amount of the loss can be made. Since there is uncertainty attached to the amount and/or timing of the compensation to be paid, this amount would have had to be accounted for as a provision at year-end. Recognition of the provision will result in an increase in liabilities in the statement of financial position and an increase in expenses in the statement of profit or loss and other comprehensive income.

Disclosure of the provision must be done according to the requirements of IAS 37.

c. Disclosure

MOSSIE LTD
STATEMENT OF FINANCIAL POSITION AS AT 31 DECEMBER 20.3

	Note	Rand
EQUITY AND LIABILITIES		
Total equity		
Retained earnings (xx xxx – 73 000 (2))		xx xxx
Non-current liabilities		
Deferred tax (xx xxx – 27 000 (1))		xx xxx
Current liabilities		
Short-term provisions (xx xxx + 100 000)	12	xx xxx

MOSSIE LTD
STATEMENT OF PROFIT OR LOSS AND OTHER COMPREHENSIVE INCOME FOR THE YEAR ENDED 31 DECEMBER 20.3

	Rand
Revenue	xx xxx
Other expenses (xx xxx + 100 000)	(xx xxx)
Profit before tax (xx xxx – 100 000)	xx xxx
Income tax expense (xx xxx – 27 000 (1))	(xx xxx)
Profit for the year (xx xxx – 73 000 (2))	xx xxx
Other comprehensive income	–
Total comprehensive income for the year	xx xxx

(1) 100 000 × 27% = 27 000
(2) 100 000 – 27 000 = 73 000

MOSSIE LTD
NOTES FOR THE YEAR ENDED 31 DECEMBER 20.3

12. Short-term provisions

	Rand
Carrying amount at 31 December 20.2	xx xxx
Additional provision for indemnity (xx xxx + 100 000)	xx xxx
Carrying amount at 31 December 20.3	xx xxx

The company is a defendant in a court case with a customer of which the result will probably favour the customer. The probable indemnity claim will amount to R100 000.

6.a. Classification: does not constitute an event after the reporting date.

b. Discussion

Because no transaction has taken place, the development has no effect on the items at the reporting date. No note is required. The directors shall, however, disclose the item in the directors' report for the benefit of potential investors and current shareholders. However, the directors may prefer not to mention this fact for strategic reasons.

c. Disclosure

No disclosure is required.

In each of the above-mentioned cases and in addition to the given disclosure, the date must be disclosed when the financial statements were authorised for issue and who gave such authorisation. If any party has the power to amend the financial statements after issue date, this fact must also be disclosed (IAS 10.17).

❑ QUESTION IAS 10.3

Gimli Ltd's financial statements for the year ended 31 December 20.4 were presented to the board of directors for authorisation for issue on 20 March 20.5. The following events took place after the reporting date:

1. During the auditors' execution of the debtors' circularisation on 2 January 20.5, it was discovered that an error had been made on one of the invoices sent out. The sale transaction was recorded as R870 000 but should have been only R780 000.

2. On 4 February 20.5 Gimli Ltd received notice from Fargon (Pty) Ltd that a dividend of 10 cents per ordinary share was declared and authorised at the annual general meeting held on 31 January 20.5 to shareholders registered on 31 December 20.4. Gimli Ltd has owned 150 000 ordinary shares in Fargon (Pty) Ltd for the past three years, representing 3% of Fargon (Pty) Ltd's issued share capital.

3. On 25 February 20.5 a material design defect was discovered in one of the company's new vehicles. Production of the vehicle had commenced on 1 October 20.4 and considerable costs will have to be incurred to correct the defect. The following estimates have been made:

	Rand
Cost to repair defects in closing inventory	150 000
Cost related to defects in units sold	
• To recover	45 000
• To repair	295 000
Cost to recover and repair units manufactured in 20.5	135 000

Additional information

1. Assume a normal tax rate of 27% and that 80% of capital gains are taxed.
2. Assume that all amounts are material and that the company is a going concern notwithstanding the effect of the above events on the financial statements.

Required

Briefly discuss how the events in each of the above cases will affect the financial statements. Also prepare extracts from the financial statements of Gimli Ltd as at 31 December 20.4 to present and disclose the relevant items to ensure compliance with the requirements of International Financial Reporting Standards (IFRS).

❖ **Suggested solution IAS 10.3**

1. **Discussion**

This represents an event after the reporting date providing additional information about the value of assets (receivables) at the reporting date. The error must be corrected by adjusting the financial statements. IAS 8.41 also requires current period errors discovered in that period to be corrected before the financial statements are authorised for issue.

Disclosure

GIMLI LTD
STATEMENT OF FINANCIAL POSITION AS AT 31 DECEMBER 20.4

	Rand
ASSETS	
Current assets	
Trade receivables (xx xxx – 90 000 (1))	xx xxx
EQUITY AND LIABILITIES	
Total equity	
Retained earnings (xx xxx – 65 700 (3))	xx xxx
Non-current liabilities	
Deferred tax (xx xxx – 24 300 (2))	xx xxx

GIMLI LTD
STATEMENT OF PROFIT OR LOSS AND OTHER COMPREHENSIVE INCOME FOR THE YEAR ENDED 31 DECEMBER 20.4

	Rand
Revenue (xx xxx – 90 000)	xx xxx
Profit before tax (xx xxx – 90 000 (1))	xx xxx
Income tax expense (xx xxx – 24 300 (2))	(xx xxx)
Profit for the year (xx xxx – 65 700 (3))	xx xxx
Other comprehensive income	–
Total comprehensive income for the year	xx xxx

(1) 870 000 – 780 000 = 90 000
(2) 90 000 × 27% = 24 300
(3) 90 000 – 24 300 = 65 700

2. **Discussion**

The declaration of dividends occurred after the reporting date. It is therefore not an event that provides additional evidence of a condition that existed on the reporting date, but rather one that arose after the reporting date. Financial statements must not be adjusted for dividends declared after the reporting date (IAS 10.13). The matter must be disclosed in the note 'Events after the reporting date' if the non-disclosure will affect the ability of the users of the financial statements to make proper evaluations and decisions (IAS 10.21).

Disclosure

GIMLI LTD
NOTES FOR THE YEAR ENDED 31 DECEMBER 20.4

14. Events after the reporting date

Fargon (Pty) Ltd declared a dividend of 10 cent per share on 31 January 20.5 to shareholders registered on 31 December 20.4. Gimli Ltd is entitled to dividends of R15 000, which will increase profit for the 20.5 year by the same amount.

3. **Discussion**

Unsold inventory on hand: IAS 2.30 requires that in determining the net realisable value of inventory on hand, the most reliable evidence at the time the estimates are made must be taken into account. These estimates take into consideration fluctuations in price or costs directly relating to events that occurred after the end of the period to the extent that such events confirm conditions existing at the reporting date. These inventory items have an inherent defect, which means that they cannot be sold in their present condition and this condition existed at the reporting date.

IAS 2 states further that the cost of inventories may not be recoverable if the estimated costs of completion or the estimated costs to be incurred to make the sale, have increased. Clearly, additional costs will have to be incurred to make the unsold inventory saleable, thus in determining the net realisable value of inventory, the selling price will need to be reduced by the repair costs to be incurred in the next financial year to make the unsold inventory saleable. This 'reduced' selling price will then be compared to the cost price at which the inventory is presently valued in the statement of financial position, and a write-down to net realisable value may be necessary at the reporting date. The event may then be an adjusting event if the inventory on hand needs to be written down to its net realisable value, which requires the amounts in the financial statements to be adjusted (IAS 10.8).

Units sold during the year under review: The financial statements must be adjusted for the additional costs to be incurred to recall and repair these units (R45 000 + R295 000 = R340 000). Thus a provision to repair inventory sold of R340 000 must be recognised at the reporting date because a current obligation exists, and it is probable that an outflow of economic benefits will occur to settle the obligation and the amount can be reliably determined.

Repair costs for 20.5: The costs to repair inventory actually manufactured in 20.5 must not be recognised in the financial statements for 20.4. Disclosure, however, must be made of the nature and estimated financial effect by way of a note to the financial statements if the user's ability to make proper evaluations or decisions will be affected (IAS 10.21).

Disclosure

GIMLI LTD
STATEMENT OF FINANCIAL POSITION AS AT 31 DECEMBER 20.4

	Rand
ASSETS	
Current assets	
Inventories (xx xxx – any write down to NRV that may be needed)	xx xxx
EQUITY AND LIABILITIES	
Total equity	
Retained earnings (xx xxx – 248 200 (2))	xx xxx
Non-current liabilities	
Deferred tax (xx xxx – 91 800 (1))	xx xxx
Current liabilities	
Short-term provisions	340 000

GIMLI LTD
STATEMENT OF PROFIT OR LOSS AND OTHER COMPREHENSIVE INCOME FOR THE YEAR ENDED 31 DECEMBER 20.4

	Note	Rand
Profit before tax (xx xxx – 45 000 – 295 000 – any write-down to NRV that may be needed)	4	xx xxx
Income tax expense (xx xxx – 91 800 (1))		(xx xxx)
Profit for the year (xx xxx – 248 200 (2))		xx xxx
Other comprehensive income		–
Total comprehensive income for the year		xx xxx

(1) (45 000 + 295 000) × 27% = 91 800
(2) 45 000 + 295 000 – 91 800 = 248 200

GIMLI LTD
NOTES FOR THE YEAR ENDED 31 DECEMBER 20.4

4. Profit before tax

Profit before tax is stated after taking the following into account:

Costs provided for in respect of the rectification of a material design defect amounted to R340 000 (see note 12).

12. Events after the reporting date

Costs of R135 000 will be incurred during 20.5 to rectify a material design defect for goods manufactured in 20.5 (see note 4).

In each of the above-mentioned cases and in addition to the given disclosure, the date must be disclosed when the financial statements were authorised for issue and who gave such authorisation. If any party has the power to amend the financial statements after issue date, this fact must also be disclosed (IAS 10.17).

❑ QUESTION IAS 10.4

The financial statements of Penari Ltd are in the process of being finalised for the year ended 31 March 20.2. Penari Ltd would like to present the financial statements for authorisation for issue on 10 June 20.2. Uncertainty still exists on the following matters:

1. Penari Ltd determined during May 20.2 that a debtor, IOU Ltd, which owed an amount of R20 000 to Penari Ltd at 31 March 20.2, is currently experiencing financial difficulties and will probably not be able to settle its debt. After further investigation it came to light that the problem had already existed for the past six months, but as Penari Ltd was unaware of this, the company continued granting credit to IOU Ltd. The result is that an amount of R35 000 was owed by IOU Ltd as at 31 May 20.2.

2. Owing to a cloud burst during the first week in April 20.2, the basement level of Penari Ltd's premises was flooded, resulting in the total destruction of the inventory stored there. The cost of this inventory, amounting to R75 000, is included in the inventories figure in the financial statements at 31 March 20.2. Penari Ltd was not insured.

3. A claim amounting to R150 000 was instituted against Penari Ltd on 1 March 20.2 arising from the terms of a product guarantee given by Penari Ltd on its products. On 10 June 20.2 it is still not certain if the claim will be successful and the extent of the costs are also uncertain.

4. Penari Ltd has a debtor, Dot Ltd, which owed the company R55 000 as at 31 March 20.2. During April 20.2 Dot Ltd's premises were destroyed by a fire, including all the assets and the accounting records. Dot Ltd was not insured and it appears that the company will not be able to settle any of its debts. At the time of the fire the outstanding amount according to Penari Ltd's records was R64 000.

5. On 31 March 20.2 Penari Ltd had 800 'Item 4' inventory units on hand at a total cost of R16 000. During April 20.2 Penari Ltd determined that half of the 'Item 4' inventory units on hand at 31 March 20.2 had a defect due to a manufacturing error resulting from a problem encountered with Machine 1. The defective items can be sold for R5 each and the costs to repair the machine will be R15 000.

Ignore all forms of taxation.

Required

a. State, in each of the above cases, whether an adjusting or non-adjusting event occurred.
b. Briefly discuss how each event will affect the financial statements for the year ended 31 March 20.2.

Give reasons for the answers in a. and b. above for each of the cases discussed. It is not necessary to give the disclosure concerning the date the financial statements were authorised for issue and who gave the authorisation, as required by IAS 10. Your solution must comply with the requirements of International Financial Reporting Standards (IFRS).

❑ QUESTION IAS 10.5

Park Developers Ltd concentrates on township development. During the past few years it has been selling township property to the public.

During the financial year ended 31 December 20.7, legal action was instituted against the company for the return of payments made in connection with property sold in unproclaimed townships. Court cases are pending. The company has rejected any liability for the amount claimed. After year-end, but before finalising the financial statements, a court order instructed the company to repay an amount of R8,4 million to buyers. In addition, as a result of the court order, an amount of R4,2 million included in receivables, will not be collected.

The cost of sales of these stands was R1,5 million for land and R2,1 million for development costs.

The company proposes to disclose the above matter in a note explaining that a contingent liability exists for the possible repayment that may be required of amounts received for stands in unproclaimed townships. The directors propose to refer to the court order and to the effect that it will have on the statement of profit or loss and other comprehensive income and statement of financial position, in the directors' report under the heading 'Events after the reporting date'.

Required

a. Briefly discuss the proposed treatment of the court order by the company in terms of the requirements of International Financial Reporting Standards (IFRS).
b. Briefly describe what effect the court order will have on the financial statements of the company as at 31 December 20.7. The company makes full provision for development costs when the first stand is sold, but it has agreed to change the balance at year-end so that the provision for development costs only applies to stands sold. Your solution must comply with the requirements of International Financial Reporting Standards (IFRS).

❑ QUESTION IAS 10.6

Vespa Ltd is a listed company whose financial statements were authorised for issue on 2 October 20.7. The following note has been extracted from the financial statements of the company for the year ended 30 June 20.7:

VESPA LTD
NOTES FOR THE YEAR ENDED 30 JUNE 20.7

17. Events after the reporting date

17.1 On 15 August 20.7 the shareholders approved a change of the company's name to Baby Equip Ltd. This name is more descriptive of the business of the group which has expanded considerably during the past few years. The change does not indicate a change in the ownership or management of the group. The board of directors is confident that the new name will lead to a considerable improvement in the company's business image.

17.2 An intrinsic defect was discovered in one of the company's products on 30 September 20.7. Due to a guarantee provided to customers on the products sold, the sold units will have to be recalled and recovered in order to correct it. Inventory on hand will also have to be corrected.

Additional information

1. Assume a normal tax rate of 27% and that 80% of capital gains are taxed.
2. Assume that all amounts involved are material and that the company is a going concern irrespective of the effect of the above-mentioned on the financial statements.

Required

Comment on the acceptability of the note in view of International Financial Reporting Standards (IFRS). Indicate how each of the above-mentioned matters shall be disclosed in the financial statements of the company in order to comply with the requirements of International Financial Reporting Standards (IFRS) if the following is assumed:

	Rand
• Cost to rectify closing inventory	30 000
• Cost to recover defective units sold in 20.7	10 000
• Cost to repair defective units sold in 20.7	60 000
• Cost to recover and repair defective units manufactured in 20.8	150 000

It is not necessary to give the disclosure concerning the date the financial statements were authorised for issue and who gave that authorisation, as required by IAS 10.

❑ QUESTION IAS 10.7

The following information pertaining to two companies, unrelated to each other, is available:

1. Fly Construction Ltd is a Durban-based company currently involved in a construction project in a foreign country. The multi-million rand project involves a hotel and convention centre for an international group of hoteliers.

After the reporting date but prior to the authorisation of the financial statements for issue, the company received the news that, as a result of a bloodless *coup d'état*, all construction work has ceased. As a precautionary measure, the American embassy in that country advised foreigners to leave. Fly Construction Ltd's technical and supervisory staffs were all evacuated.

Total construction costs incurred up to the date of the evacuation amounted to R11,0 million of which R9,5 million was incurred up to the reporting date. A R2,0 million progress payment due at year-end is still outstanding.

2. During the current financial year under review, Play Galore Ltd completed a housing development project consisting of 2 000 units for Blacksburgh Inc, an American company engaged in a mining venture in Iceland.

   Shortly afterwards, a hurricane caused extensive damage to these houses, which resulted in considerable loss to Blacksburgh Inc. The company contended that Play Galore Ltd had not taken into account the adverse weather conditions normally experienced in the region in the design and construction of the houses.

   Blacksburgh Inc indicated that it will take civil action in both the American and South African courts claiming R20 million.

   Play Galore Ltd's legal advisors are of the opinion that any case against the company to be heard in the South African courts will fail, but are not able to express an opinion on the outcome of the case if it is heard in America as they lack sufficient information on the plaintiff's case.

   On the date the directors authorised the financial statements for issue, no case had been filed nor had legal proceedings commenced in either country.

Required

Discuss how Fly Construction Ltd and Play Galore Ltd must deal with the above matters in their financial statements so as to comply with the requirements of International Financial Reporting Standards (IFRS). Commence your answer with a brief analysis of all the facts and issues involved. Assume that all amounts involved are material and that the involved companies are going concerns irrespective of the effect of the above-mentioned on their financial statements. Ignore all forms of taxation.

(Natal Centre for Professional Accounting Education CC – adapted)

❑ QUESTION IAS 10.8

1. The financial statements of Kheela Ltd for the year ended 31 December 20.2 are in the process of being finalised. On 15 February 20.3 the directors decided to declare an additional ordinary dividend of R30 000, which was authorised by the shareholders on 18 February 20.3. The ordinary dividend will be paid on 15 March 20.3 to all ordinary shareholders registered on 31 December 20.2. On 3 March 20.3 the financial statements were authorised for issue by the directors. There are no preference shares in issue.

Required

Disclose the above-mentioned information in the financial statements of Kheela Ltd for the year ended 31 December 20.2 in accordance with the requirements of International Financial Reporting Standards (IFRS).

2. On 28 February 20.3 the factory of Kheela Ltd was destroyed in a fire, which was caused by a short circuit in the electricity supply to the factory. Kheela Ltd did not have any insurance cover, and the directors therefore have no choice but to cease operations and to liquidate the company.

Required

Discuss how Kheela Ltd shall deal with the above matter in its financial statements for the year ended 31 December 20.2 in order to comply with the requirements of International Financial Reporting Standards (IFRS).

IAS 12 & *FRP 1*

Income taxes

❑ QUESTIONS AND SOLUTIONS

IAS 12.1@	Calculating current tax and deferred tax, preparing tax rate reconciliation and FRP 1 discussion
IAS 12.2	Impact of change in tax rate on deferred tax calculation: journal entries
IAS 12.3	Capital profit on sale of asset, decrease in tax rate and other temporary differences: presentation and disclosure
IAS 12.4@	Tax presentation and disclosure in financial statements and FRP 1
IAS 12.5	Deductible temporary differences and the recognition of deferred tax asset: presentation and disclosure
IAS 12.6	Tax loss and change in tax rate: presentation and disclosure
IAS 12.7	Sale of asset, tax loss and change in tax rate: presentation and disclosure
IAS 12.8	Tax loss: presentation and disclosure
IAS 12.9	Capital gains tax, tax loss and change in tax rate: presentation and disclosure
IAS 12.10@	Calculation of a deferred tax liability in different situations if asset is accounted for in accordance with cost model or revaluation model

❑ QUESTIONS

IAS 12.11	Integrated question including wear and tear allowances, allowances for credit losses, capital gains, etc.: calculations, presentation and disclosure
IAS 12.12	Decrease in tax rate, tax loss and capital gains tax: calculations, presentation and disclosure
IAS 12.13	Unutilised tax loss and other temporary differences: calculations, presentation and disclosure
IAS 12.14	Deferred tax asset, tax loss and other temporary differences: presentation and disclosure
IAS 12.15	Foreign tax, tax loss, change in tax rate, under provision of tax and other temporary differences: presentation and disclosure
IAS 12.16*	Temporary differences – presentation and disclosure
IAS 12.17*	Temporary differences – presentation and disclosure
IAS 12.18*	Temporary differences – presentation and disclosure
IAS 12.19@*	Deferred tax disclosure of revalued assets

@ *These questions contain topics or principles that were not included in the ITC syllabus of SAICA at the time of publishing this book, but might still be included in university syllabi.*

* *These questions are not in the textbook, but are available in the electronic guide for lecturers containing the suggested solutions for questions without answers.*

❑ QUESTION IAS 12.1[@]

The accountant of Uno Ltd prepared separate accounting profit and taxable income calculations for the year ended 31 December 20.3:

	Notes	Accounting profit Rand	Taxable income Rand
Gross profit		475 000	475 000
Other expenses		(200 000)	(200 000)
Other income		100 000	100 000
Dividends received		40 000	–
Donations		(20 000)	–
Office building	1		
Depreciation		(10 000)	–
Manufacturing plant	2		
Depreciation		(60 000)	–
Wear-and-tear allowance		–	(85 000)
Gain on sale of land		110 000	–
Rental received for the year (operating lease)		120 000	120 000
Rental received in advance		–	10 000
VAT penalty		(5 000)	–
		550 000	420 000

Additional information

1. The original cost of the office building was R200 000 and the building is depreciated at 5% per annum using the straight-line method. On 31 December 20.3, the carrying amount was R150 000. No tax allowances are given on this building.

2. Information on the manufacturing plant is as follows:

Carrying amount at 31 December 20.3	R140 000
Tax base at 31 December 20.3	R115 000

3. Assume that the residual value, useful life and depreciation method of all assets were reviewed at each financial year end and that there were no changes.

4. Assume a tax rate of 27%. Ignore capital gains tax.

5. There was no balance on the deferred tax liability account at 31 December 20.2.

Required

a. Prepare a reconciliation between accounting profit and taxable income by differentiating between temporary differences, non-taxable items and non-deductible items for tax purposes.
b. Calculate and journalise the transfer to or from the deferred tax account at 31 December 20.3.
c. Calculate the income tax expense for the year ended 31 December 20.3.
d. Prepare the tax rate reconciliation for the year ended 31 December 20.3.

e. Assume that on 1 February 20.4 the Minister of Finance announces a change in the corporate tax rate from 28% to 27% in the Budget Speech. The change is effective for entities with a year of assessment ending on or after 1 March 20.5. No other significant changes in the tax laws are announced in the Budget Speech.

Assume that the financial statements for 20.3 are approved for issue on 15 February 20.4.

Discuss, with reasons, what the effect of the reduction in the tax rate has on the financial statements for the year ended 31 December 20.3.

Your solution must comply with the requirements of International Financial Reporting Standards (IFRS).

❖ **Suggested solution IAS 12.1**

a. Reconciliation

	Rand
Profit before tax (given)	550 000
Less: Non-taxable items	
Dividends received	(40 000)
Profit on sale of land	(110 000)
Add: Non-deductible items	
Donations	20 000
Depreciation on office buildings	10 000
VAT penalty	5 000
Profit before tax adjusted for non-taxable and non-deductible items	435 000
Temporary differences	(15 000)
Add: Depreciation: manufacturing plant	60 000
Rent received in advance (taxed in year of cash receipt)	10 000
Less: Wear-and-tear allowance: manufacturing plant	(85 000)
Taxable income	420 000
Current tax @ 27%	113 400

b. Temporary differences

	CA Rand	TB Rand	TD Rand	DTL Rand (Dr)/Cr	P or L Rand Dr/(Cr)
20.2 (given)	–	–	Nil	Nil	
20.3					
Office building (1)	150 000	–	150 000	exempt	
Manufacturing plant	140 000	115 000	25 000	6 750	
Rental received in advance (2)	(10 000)	–	(10 000)	(2 700)	
				4 050	4 050

CA = **Carrying amount**
TB = **Tax base**
TD = **Temporary difference**
DTL = **Deferred tax liability**
P or L = **Profit or loss (movement)**

(1) The temporary difference arises from the initial recognition of the asset (carrying amount = R200 000 and tax base = RNil) and accounting profit and tax profit are not affected at initial recognition. In terms of IAS 12.15(b) this temporary difference is then exempt from deferred tax.
(2) The tax base of income received in advance is the carrying amount less amounts not taxable in future. As the amount was taxed in the current year when received in cash, the full amount will not be taxable in future. The tax base of the rental received in advance is therefore RNil (10 000 – 10 000).

Transfer to deferred tax liability account	**Rand**
Transfer (1)	4 050

(1) 4 050 (20.3) – 0 (20.2) = 4 050 movement for the year

Journal	**Rand Dr/(Cr)**
Deferred tax expense (P or L)	4 050
Deferred tax (SFPos)	(4 050)

c. Income tax expense as calculated for the profit or loss section of the statement of profit or loss and other comprehensive income

	Rand
Current tax expense (refer a)	113 400
Deferred tax expense (refer b)	4 050
Total income tax expense	117 450

d. Tax rate reconciliation

	%
Applicable (statutory) tax rate	27,00
Non-taxable items	
Dividends received (1)	(1,96)
Capital profit (2)	(5,40)
Non-deductible expenditure	
Donations (3)	0,98
Depreciation on office buildings (4)	0,49
Penalty (5)	0,25
Average effective tax rate (6)	21,35

(1) (40 000 × 27%)/550 000 × 100 = 1,96
(2) (110 000 × 27%)/550 000 × 100 = 5,40
(3) (20 000 × 27%)/550 000 × 100 = 0,98
(4) (10 000 × 27%)/550 000 × 100 = 0,49
(5) (5 000 × 27%)/550 000 × 100 = 0,25
(6) 117 450/550 000 × 100 = 21,35

OR

	Rand
Accounting profit before tax	550 000
Tax at applicable (statutory) tax rate of 27% (1)	148 500
Non-taxable items	
Dividends received (2)	(10 800)
Capital profit (3)	(29 700)
Non-deductible expenditure	
Donations (4)	5 400
Depreciation on office buildings (5)	2 700
Penalty (6)	1 350
Income tax expense	117 450

(1) 550 000 × 27% = 148 500
(2) 40 000 × 27% = 10 800
(3) 110 000 × 27% = 29 700
(4) 20 000 × 27% = 5 400
(5) 10 000 × 27% = 2 700
(6) 5 000 × 27% = 1 350

e. In terms of IAS 12.46, current tax assets and liabilities are measured at the amounts that are expected to be paid to or recovered from the tax authorities, using rates that have been enacted or substantially enacted at the **reporting date**.

In terms of IAS 12.47, deferred tax assets and liabilities are measured at tax rates that are expected to apply to the period when the asset is realised or the liability is settled, based on the tax rates that have been enacted or substantially enacted by the **reporting date**.

In terms of FRP 1, changes in tax rates should be regarded as substantially enacted from the time they are announced in terms of the Minister of Finance's budget speech, provided that the change in tax rate is not inextricably linked to other changes in the tax laws.

In this question the change in tax rate can therefore be regarded as substantially enacted from 1 February 20.4.

Owing to the fact that the change in the tax rate was not substantially enacted at the 31 December 20.3 year end, the deferred and current tax liabilities for the year ended 31 December 20.3 will still be based on 28%.

However, due to the fact that the substantive enactment (1 February 20.4) occurs prior to the publication of the financial statements (15 February 20.4), this would constitute a non-adjusting event after the reporting period and disclosure should be provided in a note in terms of IAS 10. The note will stipulate that any deferred tax balance will reduce in future as a result of the change in corporate tax rate from 28% to 27%.

❑ QUESTION IAS 12.2

The information given below is in respect of a manufacturing company:

	20.3	20.2	20.1
Purchase price – plant (1 January)	–	R500 000	R200 000
Depreciation – straight-line method	20%	20%	20%
Applicable tax rate	30%	45%	40%

The South African Revenue Service grants a wear-and-tear allowance on plant over four years (25% per year) with no apportionment on a time basis.

The company earned taxable income in all three years.

Assume that the residual value, useful life and depreciation method of the plant were reviewed at each financial year-end and that there were no changes.

Required

Calculate and journalise the transfers to and from the deferred tax account for the years ended 31 December 20.1 to 20.3.

Your solution must comply with the requirements of International Financial Reporting Standards (IFRS).

❖ Suggested solution IAS 12.2

1. Calculations

	CA Rand	TB Rand	TD Rand	DTL Rand (Dr)/Cr	P or L Rand Dr/(Cr)
20.0					
Cumulative temporary differences			–	–	
20.1					
New plant – 31 December (1)	160 000	150 000	10 000		
Cumulative temporary differences @ 40% (2)			10 000	4 000	4 000
20.2					
Rate change 40% – 45% (3)				500	500
Adjusted opening balance				4 500	
New plant – 31 December (4)	400 000	375 000	25 000		
Old plant – 31 December (5)	120 000	100 000	20 000		
Cumulative temporary differences @ 45% (6)			45 000	20 250	15 750
20.3					
Rate change 45% – 30% (7)				(6 750)	(6 750)
Adjusted opening balance				13 500	
Plant – 31 December (8)	380 000	300 000	80 000		
Cumulative temporary differences @ 30% (9)			80 000	24 000	10 500

CA	=	**Carrying amount**
TB	=	**Tax base**
TD	=	**Temporary difference**
DTL	=	**Deferred tax liability**
P or L	=	**Profit or loss (movement)**

(1) 200 000 × 80% = 160 000; 200 000 × 75% = 150 000
(2) 4 000 (DTL 20.1) – 0 (DTL 20.0) = 4 000 movement
(3) ((45 – 40)/40) × 4 000 = 500
(4) 500 000 × 80% = 400 000; 500 000 × 75% = 375 000
(5) 200 000 × 60% = 120 000; 200 000 × 50% = 100 000
(6) 20 250 – 4 500 = 15 750
(7) ((45 – 30)/45) × 20 250 = 6 750
(8) (200 000 × 40%) + (500 000 × 60%) = 380 000;
(200 000 × 25%) + (500 000 × 50%) = 300 000
(9) 24 000 – 13 500 = 10 500

2. Journals

	20.1 Rand Dr/(Cr)	**20.2 Rand Dr/(Cr)**	**20.3 Rand Dr/(Cr)**
31 December			
Deferred tax expense (P or L)	4 000	15 750	10 500
Deferred tax (SFPos)	(4 000)	(15 750)	(10 500)
1 January			
Deferred tax expense/(income) (P or L)	–	500	(6 750)
Deferred tax (SFPos)	–	(500)	6 750

❑ QUESTION IAS 12.3

PART I

Manuf Ltd bought a manufacturing plant on 1 January 20.2 and put it into production immediately. The cost price of the plant was R500 000 and its useful life is five years. Manuf Ltd decided to depreciate it over five years using the straight-line method, with no residual value.

The South African Revenue Service allows wear and tear on the following basis:

50% in the 1st year
30% in the 2nd year
20% in the 3rd year

On 31 December 20.5 Manuf Ltd sold the plant for R100 000.

The profit before tax for 20.4 was R120 000 and for 20.5, R150 000. The tax rate was constant at 27% for the years 20.2 to 20.5.

The company's financial year-end is 31 December.

Assume that the residual value, useful life and depreciation method of the manufacturing plant were reviewed at each financial year end and that there were no changes.

Assume that for the year ended 31 December 20.4, provisional tax amounting to R27 000 was paid to SARS and for the year ended 31 December 20.5, R90 000.

Ignore capital gains tax.

Required

a. Calculate the temporary differences and deferred tax asset/liability for the years 20.2 to 20.5, clearly indicating the debits and credits on the deferred tax asset/liability account in the statement of financial position.
b. Calculate the taxable income and current tax expense for 20.4 and 20.5.
c. Disclose the relevant information in the annual financial statements of Manuf Ltd for the year ended 31 December 20.5 in accordance with the requirements of International Financial Reporting Standards (IFRS).

PART II

Engine Ltd bought machinery to the value of R250 000 on 1 January 20.6 and put it into production immediately. The machinery was depreciated over five years using the straight-line method to the residual value of R50 000. The South African Revenue Service allows wear and tear on this machinery at 20% per annum on the straight-line method.

Engine Ltd sold the machinery on 31 December 20.7 for R270 000.

The profit before tax for 20.6 was R100 000 and for 20.7, R120 000. The tax rate was 28% in 20.6 and decreased to 27% in 20.7.

The company's financial year-end is 31 December.

Assume that the residual value, useful life and depreciation method of the manufacturing plant were reviewed at each financial year end and that there were no changes.

Ignore capital gains tax.

Required

a. Calculate the temporary differences and deferred tax asset/liability for the years 20.6 and 20.7, clearly indicating the debits and credits on the deferred tax asset/liability account in the statement of financial position.
b. Calculate the taxable income and income tax expense for 20.6 and 20.7.
c. Disclose the relevant information in the annual financial statements of Engine Ltd for the year ended 31 December 20.7, in accordance with the requirements of International Financial Reporting Standards (IFRS).

❖ **Suggested solution IAS 12.3**

PART I

a. Deferred tax

	CA Rand	TB Rand	TD Rand	DTL Rand (Dr)/Cr	P or L Rand Dr/(Cr)
31 December 20.2	400 000	250 000	150 000	40 500	40 500
31 December 20.3 (1)	300 000	100 000	200 000	54 000	13 500
31 December 20.4 (2)	200 000	–	200 000	54 000	–
31 December 20.5 (3)	–	–	–	–	(54 000)

CA = Carrying amount
TB = Tax base
TD = Temporary difference
DTL = Deferred tax liability
P or L = Profit or loss (movement)

(1) 54 000 – 40 500 = 13 500
(2) 54 000 – 54 000 = 0
(3) 0 – 54 000 = (54 000)

b. Taxable income and current income tax expense

	20.5 Rand	20.4 Rand
Profit before tax	150 000	120 000
Profit on sale for accounting purposes (1)	–	–
Depreciation for accounting purposes	100 000	100 000
Recoupment for tax purposes (2)	100 000	–
Wear-and-tear allowance for tax purposes	–	(100 000)
Taxable income	350 000	120 000
Current tax at 27%	94 500	32 400

(1) 100 000 selling price – 100 000 carrying amount = RNil
(2) 100 000 selling price – 0 tax base = 100 000

c. Disclosure

MANUF LTD
STATEMENT OF FINANCIAL POSITION AS AT 31 DECEMBER 20.5

	Note	20.5 Rand	20.4 Rand
EQUITY AND LIABILITIES			
Non-current liabilities			
Deferred tax liability	2	–	54 000
Current liabilities			
The South African Revenue Service (1)		4 500	5 400

(1) 20.4: 32 400 (part b) – 27 000 (provisional tax) = 5 400
20.5: 94 500 (part b) – 90 000 (provisional tax) = 4 500

MANUF LTD
STATEMENT OF PROFIT OR LOSS AND OTHER COMPREHENSIVE INCOME FOR THE YEAR ENDED 31 DECEMBER 20.5

	Note	20.5 Rand	20.4 Rand
Profit before tax		150 000	120 000
Income tax expense	3	(40 500)	(32 400)
Profit for the year		109 500	87 600
Other comprehensive income		–	–
Total comprehensive income for the year		109 500	87 600

MANUF LTD
NOTES FOR THE YEAR ENDED 31 DECEMBER 20.5

2. **Deferred tax liability**	20.5 Rand	20.4 Rand
Analysis of temporary differences		
Capital allowances in respect of plant	–	54 000

3. **Income tax expense**	20.5 Rand	20.4 Rand
Major components of tax expense		
Current tax	94 500	32 400
Deferred tax	(54 000)	–
	40 500	32 400

Note: A tax rate reconciliation is not required, due to the fact that the average effective tax rate and the statutory tax rate are the same.

PART II

a. **Deferred tax**	**CA Rand**	**TB Rand**	**TD Rand**	**DTL Rand (Dr)/Cr**	**P or L Rand Dr/(Cr)**
31 Dec 20.6 (1)	210 000	200 000	10 000	2 800	2 800
20.7 Rate change 28% – 27% (2)				(100)	(100)
				2 700	
31 Dec 20.7	–	–	–	–	(2 700)

(1) 250 000 – ((250 000 – 50 000) × 20%) = 210 000; 250 000 – (250 000 × 20%) = 200 000

(2) ((28 – 27)/28) × 2 800 = 100

CA	=	**Carrying amount**
TB	=	**Tax base**
TD	=	**Temporary difference**
DTL	=	**Deferred tax liability**
P or L	=	**Profit or loss (movement)**

b. Taxable income and income tax expense

	20.7 Rand	20.6 Rand
Taxable income		
Profit before tax	120 000	100 000
Less: non-taxable items		
Capital profit on sale of machinery (3)	(20 000)	–
Temporary differences	10 000	(10 000)
Depreciation	40 000	40 000
Gain on sale of machinery (4)	(80 000)	–
Wear-and-tear allowance	(50 000)	(50 000)
Recoupment (5)	100 000	–
Taxable income	110 000	90 000
Current tax @ 27% (20.6: 28%)	29 700	25 200
Total income tax expense	26 900	28 000
Current tax expense	29 700	25 200
Deferred tax expense relating to the origination and (reversal) of temporary differences	(2 700)	2 800
Deferred tax income resulting from the reduction in tax rate	(100)	–

(3) 270 000 – 250 000 = 20 000
(4) 250 000 – (2 × 40 000) = 170 000 – 250 000 = 80 000
(5) 250 000 – (2 × 50 000) = 150 000 – 250 000 (max) = 100 000

c. Disclosure

ENGINE LTD
STATEMENT OF FINANCIAL POSITION AS AT 31 DECEMBER 20.7

	Note	20.7 Rand	20.6 Rand
EQUITY AND LIABILITIES			
Non-current liabilities			
Deferred tax	2	–	2 800

ENGINE LTD
STATEMENT OF PROFIT OR LOSS AND OTHER COMPREHENSIVE INCOME FOR THE YEAR ENDED 31 DECEMBER 20.7

	Note	20.7 Rand	20.6 Rand
Profit before tax		120 000	100 000
Income tax expense	3	(26 900)	(28 000)
Profit for the year		93 100	72 000
Other comprehensive income		–	–
Total comprehensive income for the year		93 100	72 000

ENGINE LTD
NOTES FOR THE YEAR ENDED 31 DECEMBER 20.7

2. Deferred tax liability

	20.7 Rand	20.6 Rand
Analysis of temporary differences		
Capital allowances in respect of machinery	–	2 800

3. Income tax expense

	20.7 Rand	20.6 Rand
Major components of tax expense		
Current tax	29 700	25 200
Deferred tax: current year	(2 700)	2 800
: rate change	(100)	–
	26 900	28 000

Reconciliation of tax expense and accounting profit

	20.7 %	20.6 %
Applicable (statutory) tax rate	27,00	28,00
Tax effect of income not taxable (1)	(4,50)	–
Reduction in opening deferred tax resulting from reduction in tax rate (2)	(0,08)	–
Average effective tax rate (3)	22,42	28,00

The authorities reduced the tax rate during the current year to 27% (20.6: 28%).

(1) (20 000 × 27%)/120 000 × 100 = 4,50%
(2) 100/120 000 × 100 = 0,08%
(3) 26 900/120 000 × 100 = 22,42%
28 000/100 000 × 100 = 28%

OR

	20.7 Rand	20.6 Rand
Accounting profit before tax	120 000	100 000
Tax at applicable (statutory) rate (1)	32 400	28 000
Tax effect of income not taxable (2)	(5 400)	–
Reduction in opening deferred tax resulting from reduction in tax rate	(100)	–
Income tax expense	26 900	28 000

The authorities reduced the tax rate during the current year to 27% (20.6: 28%).

(1) 120 000 × 27% = 32 400; 100 000 × 28% = 28 000
(2) 20 000 × 27% = 5 400

❑ QUESTION IAS 12.4@

The financial year of Mom Ltd, a manufacturer, ends on 28 February. The following information for the year ended 28 February 20.2 is available:

	Rand
Profit before depreciation	300 000
Dividends paid	11 520
Retained earnings at beginning of year	115 320
Plant	
Carrying amount – 1 March 20.1	350 000
Tax base – 1 March 20.1	250 000
Purchase price of new plant – 2 March 20.1	80 000
Depreciation	86 000
Tax allowances for 20.2	
Wear-and-tear allowance	82 000

Additional information

1. Issued share capital – 1 000 000 ordinary shares issued at 50c each (listed on the JSE Ltd).
2. The deferred tax liability on 1 March 20.1 was R28 000 and originated from temporary differences on the plant. The tax rate for 20.2 is 27% (20.1: 28%).
3. Assume that the residual value, useful life and depreciation method of the plant were reviewed at each financial year end and that there were no changes. Depreciation is provided using the reducing balance method.
4. Assume that for the year ended 28 February 20.2, provisional tax amounting to R54 000 was paid.

Required

a. Prepare an extract from the statement of profit or loss and other comprehensive income for the year ended 28 February 20.2 and an extract from the statement of financial position as at that date of Mom Ltd in accordance with the requirements of International Financial Reporting Standards (IFRS). Comparative amounts and disclosure of earnings and dividend per share are not required. The extract must be as complete as the given information will allow.

b. Assume that on 15 February 20.2, the Minister of Finance in the Budget Statement announces a change in the corporate tax rate from 28% to 27%. This change is effective for entities with a year of assessment ending on or after 1 May 20.2. No other significant changes in tax laws are expected.

   Discuss and state at which tax rates the current tax and deferred tax balances will be measured in the following circumstances:

   1. Mom Ltd has a year-end of 31 January 20.2.
   2. Mom Ltd has a year-end of 28 February 20.2.
   3. Mom Ltd has a year-end of 31 March 20.2.
   4. Mom Ltd has a year-end of 31 May 20.2.

❖ **Suggested solution IAS 12.4**

a. Disclosure

MOM LTD
STATEMENT OF FINANCIAL POSITION AS AT 28 FEBRUARY 20.2

	Note	Rand
ASSETS		
Non-current assets		
Property, plant and equipment	4	344 000
EQUITY AND LIABILITIES		
Total equity		761 020
Share capital		500 000
Retained earnings (1)		261 020
Non-current liabilities		
Deferred tax	3	25 920
Current liabilities		
Tax owing (2)		4 860

(1) 157 220 – 11 520 + 115 320 = 261 020
(2) 58 860 (calc a) – 54 000 = 4 860

MOM LTD
STATEMENT OF PROFIT OR LOSS AND OTHER COMPREHENSIVE INCOME FOR THE YEAR ENDED 28 FEBRUARY 20.2

	Note	Rand
Profit before tax	5	214 000
Income tax expense	6	(56 780)
Profit for the year		157 220
Other comprehensive income		–
Total comprehensive income for the year		157 220

MOM LTD
NOTES FOR THE YEAR ENDED 28 FEBRUARY 20.2

1. Accounting policies

The financial statements are prepared on the historical cost basis and comply with the requirements of International Financial Reporting Standards (IFRS). They incorporate the following principal accounting policies which are consistent with those of the previous year, unless otherwise stated:

1.1 Deferred tax

Deferred tax is provided for on all temporary differences, according to the reporting date liability method.

1.2 Property, plant and equipment

Plant is stated at cost less accumulated depreciation.

Depreciation on plant is provided for on the reducing balance method over the expected useful life of assets.

3. Deferred tax

	Rand
Analysis of temporary differences	
Accelerated wear-and-tear for tax purposes – plant	25 920

4. Property, plant and equipment

	Plant Rand
Cost	xxx
Accumulated depreciation	xxx
Carrying amount beginning of year	350 000
Additions	80 000
Depreciation	(86 000)
Carrying amount end of year	344 000
Cost	xxx
Accumulated depreciation	xxx

5. Profit before tax

Profit before tax is stated after taking the following, inter alia, into account:

Expenses	**Rand**
Depreciation	86 000

6. Income tax expense

	Rand
Major components of tax expense	
Current tax (calc a)	58 860
Deferred tax : current year	(1 080)
: decrease in tax rate	(1 000)
	56 780

Tax rate reconciliation	**%**
Applicable (statutory) tax rate	27,00
Tax effect on opening deferred tax resulting from reduction in tax rate (1)	(0,47)
Average effective tax rate (2)	26,53

The authorities reduced the tax rate during the current year to 27%.

(1) 1 000/214 000 × 100 = 0,47%
(2) 56 780/214 000 × 100 = 26,53%

OR

	Rand
Accounting profit before tax	214 000
Tax at applicable tax rate of 27% (1)	57 780
Tax effect on opening deferred tax resulting from reduction in tax rate (2)	(1 000)
Income tax expense	56 780

The authorities reduced the tax rate during the current year to 27%.

(1) 214 000 × 27% = 57 780
(2) Calc b

Calculations

a. Taxable income

	20.2 Rand
Profit before tax (1)	214 000
Depreciation for accounting purposes	86 000
Wear-and-tear allowance for tax purposes	(82 000)
Taxable income	218 000
Current tax at 27%	58 860

(1) 300 000 – 86 000 = 214 000

b. Deferred tax

	CA Rand	TB Rand	TD Rand	DTL Rand (Dr)/Cr	P or L Rand Dr/(Cr)
28 Feb 20.1 Plant	350 000	250 000	100 000	28 000	
1 Mar 20.1 Rate change 28% – 27% (1)				(1 000)	(1 000)
Adjusted balance				27 000	
28 Feb 20.2 Plant (2)(3)	344 000	248 000	96 000	25 920	(1 080)

CA = Carrying amount
TB = Tax base
TD = Temporary differences
DTL = Deferred tax liability
P or L = Profit or loss (movement)

(1) ((27 – 28)/28) × 28 000 = 1 000
(2) 350 000 + 80 000 – 86 000 = 344 000; 250 000 + 80 000 – 82 000 = 248 000
(3) 96 000 × 27% = 25 920

PART B

b.1	Current tax	– 28%
	Deferred tax	– 28%
b.2	Current tax	– 28%
	Deferred tax	– 27%
b.3	Current tax	– 28%
	Deferred tax	– 27%
b.4	Current tax	– 27%
	Deferred tax	– 27%

Discussion

In terms of IAS 12.46, current tax assets and liabilities are measured at the amounts that are expected to be paid to or recovered from the tax authorities, using rates that have been enacted or substantially enacted at the **reporting date**.

In terms of IAS 12.47, deferred tax assets and liabilities are measured at tax rates that are expected to apply to the period when the asset is realised or the liability is settled, based on the tax rates that have been enacted or substantially enacted by the **reporting date**.

In terms of FRP 1, changes in tax rates should be regarded as substantially enacted from the time they are announced in terms of the Minister of Finance's budget speech, provided that the change in tax rates is not inextricably linked to other changes in the tax laws.

In this question the changes in tax rate can therefore be regarded as substantially enacted from 15 February 20.2.

For financial years ending before 15 February 20.2, the tax rate applicable when calculating current tax and deferred tax will be 28%.

For financial years ending on or after 15 February 20.2 and before 1 May 20.2, current tax will be calculated at 28% whereas deferred tax will be calculated at 27%.

For financial years ending on or after 1 May 20.2, current tax and deferred tax will be calculated at 27%.

❑ QUESTION IAS 12.5

PART I

Ben Ltd made a profit before tax of R314 700 for the year ended 31 December 20.5. The accountant is busy with the tax calculation and has established the following:

- There is a net deductible temporary difference of R68 000 for the year (movement), consisting of the following:

	Rand
Depreciable assets	(5 000)
Current liabilities for which related expenses will be deductible for tax purposes on a cash basis (provision for guarantee claims)	73 000

- Ben Ltd received dividends of R188 000 which have been included in the above-mentioned profit before tax.
- Expenses of R5 300, which have been included in the above-mentioned profit before tax, are not deductible for tax purposes.
- The balance of the deferred tax account on 31 December 20.4 is a credit of R5 400.
- Assume a tax rate of 27%.

Required

Show how income taxes will be presented in the statement of profit or loss and other comprehensive income (profit or loss section) and prepare accompanying notes of Ben Ltd for the year ended 31 December 20.5, in accordance with the requirements of International Financial Reporting Standards (IFRS), if:

a. Ben Ltd is certain that there is assurance beyond a reasonable doubt that there will be sufficient taxable profit in the future to realise the tax benefit.
b. Ben Ltd is not certain that there is assurance beyond a reasonable doubt that there will be sufficient taxable profit in the future to realise the tax benefit.

Comparative amounts are not required.

PART II

Ben Ltd prepared the following tax calculation for the year ended 31 December 20.6:

	Rand
Accounting profit	425 000
Dividends received	(150 000)
	275 000
Taxable temporary differences	(80 000)
Taxable income	195 000

Refer to Part I b. of this question for the amounts of the previous year and assume that the tax rate is still 27%.

Required

Show how income taxes will be presented in the statement of profit or loss and other comprehensive income (profit or loss section) and prepare accompanying notes of Ben Ltd for the year ended 31 December 20.6, in accordance with the requirements of International Financial Reporting Standards (IFRS). Comparative amounts are not required.

❖ **Suggested solution IAS 12.5**

PART I

Calculations

Current tax

	Rand
Accounting profit	314 700
Dividends received	(188 000)
Non-deductible expenditure	5 300
Taxable profit before taking temporary differences into account	132 000
Deductible temporary differences	68 000
Taxable income	200 000
Current tax @ 27%	54 000

Deferred tax account

		a Rand	b Rand
1 Jan 20.5	Balance	5 400	5 400
31 Dec 20.5	Deductible temporary differences (1)	(18 360)	(5 400)
	Balance	(12 960)	Nil

(1) 68 000 × 27% = 18 360;
In situation b the debit entry is limited to the available credit so as not to create a debit balance.

Disclosure

BEN LTD
STATEMENT OF PROFIT OR LOSS AND OTHER COMPREHENSIVE INCOME FOR THE YEAR ENDED 31 DECEMBER 20.5

	Note	a Rand	b Rand
Profit before tax		314 700	314 700
Income tax expense	3	(35 640)	(48 600)
Profit for the year		279 060	266 100
Other comprehensive income		–	–
Total comprehensive income for the year		279 060	266 100

BEN LTD
NOTES FOR THE YEAR ENDED 31 DECEMBER 20.5

3. Income tax expense	**a Rand**	**b Rand**
Major components of tax expense		
Current tax	54 000	54 000
Deferred tax	(18 360)	(5 400)
	35 640	48 600

Tax rate reconciliation	**%**	**%**
Applicable (statutory) tax rate	27,00	27,00
Tax effect of income not taxable		
Dividends received (1)	(16,13)	(16,13)
Tax effect of expenses not deductible (2)	0,45	0,45
Unprovided temporary differences (3)	–	4,12
Average effective tax rate (4)	11,32	15,44

(1) (188 000 × 27%)/314 700 × 100 = 16,13
(2) (5 300 × 27%)/314 700 × 100 = 0,45
(3) (68 000 – 20 000) = 48 000; (48 000 × 27%)/314 700 × 100 = 4,12
(4) 35 640/314 700 × 100 = 11,32 (rounded down)
48 600/314 700 × 100 = 15,44

OR

	a Rand	**b Rand**
Accounting profit before tax (1)	314 700	314 700
Tax at applicable (statutory) tax rate of 27% (2)	84 969	84 969
Income not taxable – dividends (3)	(50 760)	(50 760)
Expenses not deductible (4)	1 431	1 431
Unprovided temporary differences (5)	–	12 960
Income tax expense	35 640	48 600

(1) Amount per statement of profit or loss and other comprehensive income
(2) 314 700 × 27% = 84 969
(3) 188 000 × 27% = 50 760
(4) 5 300 × 27% = 1 431
(5) 68 000 – 20 000 = 48 000; 48 000 × 27% = 12 960

PART II

Calculations

Deferred tax	**Temporary differences Rand**	**Deferred tax liability Rand (Dr)/Cr**	**Profit or loss Rand Dr/(Cr)**
20.4 Balance (1)	20 000	5 400	
20.5 (2)	(20 000)	–	(5 400)
20.6 (3)	32 000	8 640	8 640

(1) 5 400/0,27 = 20 000
(2) 68 000 – 48 000 not recognised = 20 000
(3) (48 000) not recognised previous year + 80 000 = 32 000

Disclosure

BEN LTD
STATEMENT OF PROFIT OR LOSS AND OTHER COMPREHENSIVE INCOME FOR THE YEAR ENDED 31 DECEMBER 20.6

	Note	**Rand**
Profit before tax		425 000
Income tax expense	3	(61 290)
Profit for the year		363 710
Other comprehensive income		–
Total comprehensive income for the year		363 710

BEN LTD
NOTES FOR THE YEAR ENDED 31 DECEMBER 20.6

3. Income tax expense	**Rand**
Major components of tax expense	
Current tax (1)	52 650
Deferred tax	8 640
	61 290

(1) 195 000 × 27% = 52 650

Tax rate reconciliation	**%**
Applicable (statutory) tax rate	27,00
Dividends received not taxable (1)	(9,53)
Previous year's unprovided temporary differences (2)	(3,05)
Average effective tax rate (3)	14,42

(1) (150 000 × 27%)/425 000 × 100 = 9,53%
(2) (48 000 × 27%)/425 000 × 100 = 3,05%
(3) 61 290/425 000 × 100 = 14,42%

OR

	Rand
Accounting profit before tax	425 000
Tax at applicable (statutory) tax rate of 27% (1)	114 750
Dividends received not taxable (2)	(40 500)
Previous year's unprovided temporary differences (3)	(12 960)
Income tax expense	61 290

(1) 425 000 × 27% = 114 750
(2) 150 000 × 27% = 40 500
(3) 48 000 × 27% = 12 960

❑ QUESTION IAS 12.6

Difir Ltd has the following property, plant and equipment on 31 December 20.4:

	Cost Rand	Accumulated depreciation Rand	Carrying amount Rand	Tax base Rand
Machinery	900 000	180 000	720 000	450 000
Land	500 000	–	500 000	Nil
Buildings	1 500 000	300 000	1 200 000	Nil

Machinery is depreciated over five years using the straight-line method.

Land is not depreciated.

Buildings, comprising the office buildings of the company, are depreciated over 25 years using the straight-line method.

The office buildings comply with the definition of commercial buildings in terms of the Income Tax Act and the buildings therefore qualify i.t.o. section 13*quin* for a 5% tax allowance per year.

On machinery, a wear-and-tear allowance on the 50/30/20 basis is allowed. The machinery was bought on 1 January 20.4.

Difir Ltd had an assessed loss on 31 December 20.4 of R175 000. The tax rate for 20.4 was 28%, and for 20.5 and 20.6 it was 27%.

Accounting profit before tax was R300 000 for the 20.5 financial year and R400 000 for 20.6. Difir Ltd received dividends of R80 000 (included in the profit) and paid dividends of R60 000 during 20.5. During 20.6 dividends of R100 000 were received and no dividends were paid.

There are no other items causing temporary or other differences except those arising from the information given.

Assume that the residual value, useful life and depreciation method of all assets were reviewed at each financial year end and that there were no changes.

No provisional tax was paid for either 20.5 or 20.6.

Required

Prepare an extract from the statement of profit or loss and other comprehensive income of Difir Ltd for the year ended 31 December 20.6 and an extract from the statement of financial position as at that date. Also prepare all the relevant tax notes that will accompany the financial statements of Difir Ltd for the year ended 31 December 20.6. Your answer must be in accordance with the requirements of International Financial Reporting Standards (IFRS). Accounting policy notes are not required.

❖ **Suggested solution IAS 12.6**

Calculations

1. Current tax calculation

	20.6 Rand	20.5 Rand
Accounting profit	400 000	300 000
Tax effect of items not taxable for tax purposes		
Dividends received	(100 000)	(80 000)
	300 000	220 000
Temporary differences	(15 000)	(105 000)
Depreciation: office buildings (1)	60 000	60 000
Depreciation: machinery	180 000	180 000
Wear-and-tear allowance	(180 000)	(270 000)
Building allowance (2)	(75 000)	(75 000)
	285 000	115 000
Assessed loss utilised	(60 000)	(175 000)
Taxable income/(unutilised tax loss)	225 000	(60 000)
Current tax payable @ 27%	60 750	–

(1) 1 500 000/25 = 60 000
(2) 1 500 000 × 5% = 75 000

2. Deferred tax

	CA Rand	TB Rand	TD Rand	DTL Rand (Dr)/Cr	P or L Rand Dr/(Cr)
31 December 20.4					
Machinery (1)	720 000	450 000	270 000	75 600	
Office buildings (2)	1 200 000	1 125 000	75 000	21 000	
Land	500 000	–	500 000	Exempt	
Unutilised tax loss	–	(175 000)	(175 000)	(49 000)	
				47 600	
1 January 20.5					
Rate change					
(28% – 27%) (3)				(1 700)	(1 700)
Adjusted balance				45 900	
31 December 20.5				105 300	59 400
Machinery (4)	540 000	180 000	360 000	97 200	
Office buildings (5)	1 140 000	1 050 000	90 000	24 300	
Land	500 000	–	500 000	Exempt	
Unutilised tax loss	–	(60 000)	(60 000)	(16 200)	
31 December 20.6				125 550	20 250
Machinery (6)	360 000	–	360 000	97 200	
Office buildings (7)	1 080 000	975 000	105 000	28 350	
Land	500 000	–	500 000	Exempt	
Unutilised tax loss	–	–	–	–	

CA = Carrying amount
TB = Tax base
TD = Temporary difference
DTL = Deferred tax liability
P or L = Profit or loss (movement)

(1) 900 000/2 = 450 000
(2) 300 000/60 000 = 5 years; 1 500 000 – (1 500 000 × 5% × 5 years) = 1 125 000
(3) ((28 – 27)/28) × 47 600 = 1 700
(4) 720 000 – 180 000 (calc 1) = 540 000; 900 000 × 20% = 180 000
(5) 1 200 000 – 60 000 (calc 1) = 1 140 000
1 125 000 – 75 000 (calc 1) = 1 050 000
(6) 540 000 – 180 000 (calc 1) = 360 000
(7) 1 140 000 – 60 000 (calc 1) = 1 080 000
1 050 000 – 75 000 (calc 1) = 975 000

Disclosure

DIFIR LTD
STATEMENT OF FINANCIAL POSITION AS AT 31 DECEMBER 20.6

	Note	20.6 Rand	20.5 Rand
EQUITY AND LIABILITIES			
Non-current liabilities			
Deferred tax	2	125 550	105 300
Current liabilities			
South African Revenue Service		60 750	

DIFIR LTD
STATEMENT OF PROFIT OR LOSS AND OTHER COMPREHENSIVE INCOME FOR THE YEAR ENDED 31 DECEMBER 20.6

	Note	20.6 Rand	20.5 Rand
Profit before tax		400 000	300 000
Income tax expense	3	(81 000)	(57 700)
Profit for the year		319 000	242 300
Other comprehensive income		–	–
Total comprehensive income for the year		319 000	242 300

DIFIR LTD
NOTES FOR THE YEAR ENDED 31 DECEMBER 20.6

2. **Deferred tax**

	20.6 Rand	20.5 Rand
Analysis of temporary differences		
Accelerated wear-and-tear allowances for tax purposes (1) (2)	125 550	121 500
Unutilised tax loss (3)	–	(16 200)
	125 550	105 300

(1) 97 200 (calc 2) + 24 300 (calc 2) = 121 500
(2) 97 200 (calc 2) + 28 350 (calc 2) = 125 550
(3) 60 000 (calc 1) × 27% = 16 200

3. **Income tax expense**

	20.6 Rand	20.5 Rand
Major components of tax expense		
Current tax (calc 1)	60 750	–
Deferred tax : current year (calc 2)	20 250	59 400
: rate change (calc 2)	–	(1 700)
	81 000	57 700

Tax rate reconciliation	**20.6** **%**	**20.5** **%**
Applicable (statutory) tax rate	27,00	27,00
Tax rate change (1)	–	(0,57)
Tax effect of income not taxable		
Dividends received (2)	(6,75)	(7,20)
Average effective tax rate (3)	20,25	19,23

(1) (1 700/300 000) × 100 = 0,57
(2) (100 000 × 27%)/400 000 × 100 = 6,75; (80 000 × 27%)/300 000 × 100 = 7,20
(3) (81 000/400 000) × 100 = 20,25; (57 700/300 000) × 100 = 19,23

OR

	20.6 **Rand**	**20.5** **Rand**
Accounting profit before tax (1)	400 000	300 000
Tax at applicable (statutory) rate of 27% (2)	108 000	81 000
Income not taxable – dividends (3)	(27 000)	(21 600)
Tax rate change	–	(1 700)
Income tax expense (4)	81 000	57 700

(1) Amount per statement of profit or loss and other comprehensive income
(2) 400 000 × 27% = 108 000; 300 000 × 27% = 81 000
(3) 100 000 × 27% = 27 000; 80 000 × 27% = 21 600
(4) Amount per income tax expense note

❑ QUESTION IAS 12.7

The following information regarding Supa Ltd is available on 1 January 20.3:

	Rand
Plant and equipment	300 000

The plant and equipment had a cost price of R1 000 000 and is written off over 10 years using the straight-line method. The tax base on 1 January 20.3 was RNil.

On 1 July 20.3, new plant and equipment with a cost price of R10 000 000 were available for use as intended by management. This plant will also be depreciated on the same basis as the original plant. The South African Revenue Service will allow a wear-and-tear allowance at 20% per annum on cost, regardless of how long the plant was in use for any specific year.

The original plant and equipment were withdrawn from production on 30 September 20.3 and sold for R350 000.

For the tax year ended 31 December 20.2, Supa Ltd had an assessed loss of R250 000. The tax rate for 20.2 and 20.3 was 28% and for 20.4 it is 27%.

Assume that the residual value, useful life and depreciation method of all plant and equipment were reviewed at each financial year end and that there were no changes.

Profit before tax and depreciation amounted to R3 500 000 for 20.4 and R1 500 000 for 20.3. None of the above information has been taken into account in determining the profit before tax and depreciation.

Profit before tax and depreciation includes the following items:

	20.4 Rand	20.3 Rand
Dividends received	100 000	50 000
Fines paid	10 000	–

There are no other temporary differences other than those apparent from the information provided.

The credit balance on deferred tax on 31 December 20.1 amounted to R14 000.

For the year ended 31 December 20.4, provisional tax amounting to R180 000 was paid. No provisional tax was paid for the year ended 31 December 20.3.

Ignore capital gains tax.

Required

Prepare extracts of the statement of financial position and the statement of profit or loss and other comprehensive income, as well as all the relevant tax notes to accompany the financial statements of Supa Ltd for the financial year ended 31 December 20.4, in accordance with the requirements of International Financial Reporting Standards (IFRS). Accounting policy notes are not required.

❖ **Suggested solution IAS 12.7**

Calculations

1. Profit before tax

	20.4 Rand	20.3 Rand
Profit before depreciation (given)	3 500 000	1 500 000
Depreciation for accounting purposes (1)	(1 000 000)	(575 000)
Gain on sale of plant (2)	–	125 000
Profit before tax	2 500 000	1 050 000

(1) 1 000 000 × 10% × 9/12 = 75 000; 10 000 000 × 10% × 6/12 = 500 000; 75 000 + 500 000 = 575 000

(2) 350 000 – (300 000 – 75 000) = 125 000

2. Current tax

	20.4 Rand	20.3 Rand
Profit before tax	2 500 000	1 050 000
Items (not taxable)/not deductible for tax purposes		
Dividends received	(100 000)	(50 000)
Fines paid	10 000	–
Temporary differences	(1 000 000)	(1 200 000)
Depreciation	1 000 000	575 000
Wear-and-tear allowance	(2 000 000)	(2 000 000)
Gain on sale of plant	–	(125 000)
Recoupment of wear and tear (3)	–	350 000
Taxable income/(tax loss)	1 410 000	(200 000)
Assessed loss utilised	(450 000)	(250 000)
Taxable income/(unused tax loss)	960 000	(450 000)
Current tax (4)	259 200	–

(3) 350 000 – 0 = 350 000
(4) 960 000 × 27% = 259 200

3. Deferred tax

	CA R'000	TB R'000	TD R'000	DTL R'000 (Dr)/Cr	P or L R'000 Dr/(Cr)
31 December 20.1 (given)				14,0	
31 December 20.2					
Assets – plant and machinery	300	–	300	84,0	
Unutilised tax loss	–	(250)	(250)	(70,0)	
Balance/movement				14,0	–
31 December 20.3					
Assets – plant and machinery (1)	9 500	8 000	1 500	420,0	
Unutilised tax loss	–	(450)	(450)	(126,0)	
Balance/movement				294,0	280,0
1 January 20.4					
Rate change 28% – 27% (2)				(10,5)	(10,5)
Adjusted balance				283,5	
31 December 20.4					
Assets – plant and machinery (3)	8 500	6 000	2 500	675,0	391,5

CA = **Carrying amount**
TB = **Tax base**
TD = **Temporary differences**
DTL = **Deferred tax liability**
P or L = **Profit or loss (movement)**

(1) 10 000 000 – 500 000 = 9 500 000; 10 000 000 – 2 000 000 = 8 000 000
(2) [(28 – 27)/28] × 294 000 = 10 500
(3) 9 500 000 – 1 000 000 = 8 500 000; 8 000 000 – 2 000 000 = 6 000 000

Disclosure

SUPA LTD
STATEMENT OF FINANCIAL POSITION AS AT 31 DECEMBER 20.4

	Note	20.4 Rand	20.3 Rand
EQUITY AND LIABILITIES			
Non-current liabilities			
Deferred tax	2	675 000	294 000
Current liabilities			
Tax owing (1)		79 200	–

(1) 259 200 (calc 2) – 180 000 = 79 200

SUPA LTD
STATEMENT OF PROFIT OR LOSS AND OTHER COMPREHENSIVE INCOME FOR THE YEAR ENDED 31 DECEMBER 20.4

	Note	20.4 Rand	20.3 Rand
Profit before tax		2 500 000	1 050 000
Income tax expense	3	(640 200)	(280 000)
Profit for the year		1 859 800	770 000
Other comprehensive income		–	–
Total comprehensive income for the year		1 859 800	770 000

SUPA LTD
NOTES FOR THE YEAR ENDED 31 DECEMBER 20.4

2. Deferred tax

	20.4 Rand	20.3 Rand
Analysis of temporary differences		
Accelerated wear-and-tear allowance for tax purposes (calc 3)	675 000	420 000
Unutilised tax loss (calc 3)	–	(126 000)
	675 000	294 000

3. Income tax expense

	20.4 Rand	20.3 Rand
Major components of tax expense		
Current tax	259 200	–
Deferred tax : current year	391 500	280 000
: rate change	(10 500)	–
	640 200	280 000

Tax rate reconciliation	**20.4 %**	**20.3 %**
Applicable (statutory) tax rate	27,00	28,00
Tax effect of income not taxable		
Dividends received (1)	(1,08)	(1,33)
Tax effect of expenses not deductible		
Fines paid (2)	0,11	–
Rate change (3)	(0,42)	–
Average effective tax rate (4)	25,61	26,67

The authorities reduced the applicable tax rate during the current year to 27% (20.3: 28%).

(1) (100 000 × 27%)/2 500 000 × 100 = 1,08
(50 000 × 28%)/1 050 000 × 100 = 1,33
(2) (10 000 × 27%)/2 500 000 × 100 = 0,11
(3) 10 500/2 500 000 × 100 = 0.42
(4) 640 200/2 500 000 × 100 = 25,61
280 000/1 050 000 × 100 = 26,67

OR

	20.4 Rand	**20.3 Rand**
Accounting profit before tax	2 500 000	1 050 000
Tax at applicable (statutory) rate of 27% (20.3: 28%)	675 000	294 000
Tax effect of income not taxable		
Dividends received (5)	(27 000)	(14 000)
Tax effect of expenses not deductible		
Fines (6)	2 700	–
Rate change	(10 500)	–
Income tax expense	640 200	280 000

The authorities reduced the applicable tax rate during the current year to 27% (20.3: 28%).

(5) 100 000 × 27% = 27 000; 50 000 × 28% = 14 000
(6) 10 000 × 27% = 2 700

❑ QUESTION IAS 12.8

A company provides for deferred tax, and the tax rate for 20.1 and 20.2 was 27%. According to the company's statement of financial position, the deferred tax liability at the end of 20.1 amounted to R4 725 after taking into account the effect of any tax loss at the end of 20.1.

Situation 20.2	**I Rand**	**II Rand**	**III Rand**	**IV Rand**	**V Rand**
Profit/(loss) per financial statements	24 000	6 000	22 000	40 000	(15 000)
(Taxable)/deductible temporary differences	(8 000)	4 000	(9 000)	(17 500)	(8 750)
(Income not taxable)/expenses not deductible	(6 000)	(30 000)	(8 000)	10 000	10 000
Taxable profit/(tax loss) for the year	10 000	(20 000)	5 000	32 500	(13 750)
Tax loss end of 20.1	–	(2 000)	(13 000)	(21 250)	(7 500)
Tax loss end of 20.2		(22 000)	(8 000)		(21 250)
Taxable profit for 20.2	10 000			11 250	

Required

a. Calculate the deferred tax income or expense for 20.2 for each of the above situations as well as the deferred tax asset or liability. Assume that the tax loss in the previous year was debited against the deferred tax account and that there is certainty beyond any reasonable doubt that there will be sufficient taxable profit in future (all calculations to be done to the nearest rand).

b. Explain how the answer in situation II would have been different had there been no certainty at the end of 20.2 about future taxable profit.

Your solution must comply with the requirements of International Financial Reporting Standards (IFRS).

❖ **Suggested solution IAS 12.8**

a. Deferred tax account

Situation	**I Rand**	**II Rand**	**III Rand**	**IV Rand**	**V Rand**
Net opening deferred tax liability	4 725	4 725	4 725	4 725	4 725
Net closing deferred tax liability/ (asset)	6 885	(1 755)	8 505	15 188	3 375
Deferred tax liability i.r.o. temporary differences (1)	6 885	4 185	10 665	15 188	9 113
Deferred tax asset for tax loss at year end @ 30%	–	(5 940)	(2 160)	–	(5 738)
Deferred tax (income)/expense (2)	2 160	(6 480)	3 780	10 463	(1 350)

(1) 4 725 + (8 000 × 27%) = 6 885;
[4 725 + (2 000 × 27%)] – (4 000 × 27%) = 4 185;
[4 725 + (13 000 × 27%)] + (9 000 × 27%) = 10 665;
[4 725 + (21 250 × 27%)] + (17 500 × 27%) = 15 188;
[4 725 + (7 500 × 27%)] + (8 750 × 27%) = 9 113

(2) 8 000 × 27% = 2 160 or 6 885 – 4 725 = 2 160
(4 000 × 27%) + (20 000 × 27%) = 6 480; or 1 755 + 4 725 = 6 480
(9 000 × 27%) + (5 000 × 27%) = 3 780; or 8 505 – 4 725 = 3 780
(17 500 × 27%) + (21 250 × 27%) = 10 463; or 15 188 – 4 725 = 10 463
(8 750 × 27%) – (13 750 × 27%) = 1 350; or 3 375 – 4 725 = 1 350

b. The company will have to decide in terms of IAS 12.33–.35 whether to recognise a deferred tax asset or not. If there is no certainty about future taxable profits, no deferred tax asset (debit balance) will be recognised.

Situation	**I**	**II**	**III**	**IV**	**V**
	Rand	**Rand**	**Rand**	**Rand**	**Rand**
Net opening deferred tax liability	4 725	4 725	4 725	4 725	4 725
Net closing deferred tax liability	6 885	–	8 505	15 188	3 375
Deferred tax liability due to temporary differences	6 885	4 185	10 665	15 188	9 113
Deferred tax asset for tax loss (3)	–	(4 185)	(2 160)	–	(5 738)
Deferred tax (income)/expense	2 160	(4 725)	3 780	10 463	(1 350)

(3) For case II there is a debit of R1 755 (5 940 (refer a.) – 4 185) unrecognised against deferred tax, as the creation of a debit balance is not allowed.

Note: South African tax law is such that tax losses (in the case of a going concern) can be set off against future taxable income arising from the subsequent reversal of credit balances on deferred tax.

❑ QUESTION IAS 12.9

The following information is presented to you:	**Rand**
Tax base of machinery – 1 January 20.1	160 000
Machinery at cost – 1 January 20.1	500 000
Accumulated depreciation – 1 January 20.1	187 500
Purchase of new machine – 30 June 20.2	160 000
Details of machine sold	
Proceeds on 30 June 20.3	230 000
Cost price	220 000
Accumulated depreciation – 1 January 20.3	110 000
Tax base – 30 June 20.3	40 550

The company qualifies for the following wear-and-tear allowances:

- R32 000 for 20.1
- R113 600 for 20.2
- R30 380 for 20.3

The tax rate was 40% for 20.1 and 20.2 and 48% for 20.3.

Profit before tax (before taking into account depreciation and profit on sale of asset) and taxable profit (before taking into account wear-and-tear allowances and recoupment) are as follows:

- R200 000 for 20.1
- R100 000 for 20.2
- R350 000 for 20.3

Depreciation is recognised over eight years using the straight-line method.

Assume that the residual value, useful life and depreciation method of all machinery were reviewed at each financial year end and that there were no changes.

For the year ended 31 December 20.3, provisional tax amounting to R150 000 was paid. No provisional tax was paid for the year ended 31 December 20.2

Ignore capital gains tax.

Required

a. Calculate the transfers to and from the deferred tax account for the years 20.1 to 20.3. All calculations are to be done to the nearest rand.

b. Show how the relevant items will be presented and disclosed in the statement of profit or loss and other comprehensive income for the year ended 31 December 20.3 and in the statement of financial position as at that date, in accordance with the requirements of International Financial Reporting Standards (IFRS). Give only the tax note(s) that will accompany the profit or loss section of the statement of profit or loss and other comprehensive income.

c. Assume that 80% of all capital gains are taxable, and disclose the income tax expense note for the year ended 31 December 20.3. Comparative amounts are not required.

❖ **Suggested solution IAS 12.9**

Calculations

1. Machinery

Carrying amount	**20.3 Rand**	**20.2 Rand**	**20.1 Rand**
Cost price – opening balance	660 000	500 000	500 000
Purchase of assets	–	160 000	–
Realisation of assets	(220 000)	–	–
Cost price – end of year	440 000	660 000	500 000
Accumulated depreciation	(267 500)	(322 500)	(250 000)
Opening balance	322 500	250 000	187 500
Depreciation (1)	68 750	72 500	62 500
Realisation (2)	(123 750)	–	–
Carrying amount – end of year	172 500	337 500	250 000

(1) 500 000/8 = 62 500
500 000/8 + (160 000/8 × 6/12) = 72 500
(660 000 – 220 000)/8 + (220 000/8 × 6/12) = 68 750
(2) 110 000 + (220 000/8 × 6/12) = 123 750

Tax base	**20.3 Rand**	**20.2 Rand**	**20.1 Rand**
Cost price – opening balance	660 000	500 000	500 000
Purchase of assets	–	160 000	–
Realisation of assets	(220 000)	–	–
Cost price – end of year	440 000	660 000	500 000
Accumulated wear-and-tear allowances	(336 530)	(485 600)	(372 000)
Opening balance (3)	485 600	372 000	340 000
Wear-and-tear allowance – current period (given)	30 380	113 600	32 000
Wear-and-tear allowances recouped (4)	(179 450)	–	–
Tax base	103 470	174 400	128 000

(3) 500 000 – 160 000 = 340 000
(4) 220 000 (limited to original cost price) – 40 550 = 179 450

2. **Deferred tax**

	Carrying amount Rand	**Tax base Rand**	**Temporary difference Rand**
20.1 Machinery	250 000	128 000	122 000
Deferred tax balance on 31 Dec 20.1 (taxable temporary differences): 40% × 122 000			48 800
20.2 Machinery	337 500	174 400	163 100
Assessed loss (calc 4)	–	(13 600)	(13 600)
			149 500
Deferred tax balance on 31 Dec 20.2 (taxable temporary differences): 40% × 149 500			59 800
20.3 Machinery	172 500	103 470	69 030
Deferred tax balance on 31 Dec 20.3 (taxable temporary differences): 48% × 69 030			33 134

3. **Profit before tax**

	20.3 Rand	**20.2 Rand**
Profit before depreciation and profit on sale	350 000	100 000
Depreciation (calc 1)	(68 750)	(72 500)
Profit on sale (1)	133 750	–
	415 000	27 500

(1) 230 000 – (220 000 – 123 750) = 133 750

4. Taxable profit and current tax expense/(income)

	20.3 Rand	20.2 Rand	20.1 Rand
Taxable profit before wear-and-tear allowance and recoupment	350 000	100 000	200 000
Wear-and-tear allowance (given)	(30 380)	(113 600)	(32 000)
Recoupment of wear-and-tear allowance (calc 1)	179 450	–	–
	499 070	(13 600)	168 000
Assessed loss utilised	(13 600)	–	–
Taxable profit/(tax loss)	485 470	(13 600)	168 000
Applicable tax rate	48%	40%	40%
Current tax expense	233 026	–	67 200

a. Transfers to and from the deferred tax account

	Rand
1 Jan 20.1 Balance (credit) (1)	61 000
Movement for the year i.r.o. machinery: transfer from	(12 200)
1 Jan 20.2 Balance (calc 2)	48 800
Movement for the year i.r.o. machinery: transfer to (2)	16 440
Tax loss: Transfer from (3)	(5 440)
1 Jan 20.3 Balance (calc 2)	59 800
Rate adjustment: transfer to (4)	11 960
Movement for the year i.r.o. machinery: transfer from (5)	(45 154)
Tax loss utilised: transfer to (6)	6 528
Balance (calc 2)	33 134

(1) [(500 000 – 187 500) – 160 000] × 40% = 61 000
(2) (122 000 – 163 100) × 40% = 16 440
(3) 40% × 13 600 = 5 440
(4) ((48 – 40)/40) × 59 800 = 11 960, or 59 800 × 8/40 = 11 960
(5) (163 100 – 69 030) × 48% = 45 154
(6) 48% × 13 600 = 6 528

b. Disclosure

COMPANY NAME
STATEMENT OF FINANCIAL POSITION AS AT 31 DECEMBER 20.3

	20.3 Rand	20.2 Rand
ASSETS		
Non-current assets		
Property, plant and equipment	172 500	337 500
EQUITY AND LIABILITIES		
Non-current liabilities		
Deferred tax	33 134	59 800
Current liabilities		
Tax owing (1)	83 026	–

(1) 233 026 (calc 4) – 150 000 (given) = 83 026

COMPANY NAME
STATEMENT OF PROFIT OR LOSS AND OTHER COMPREHENSIVE INCOME FOR THE YEAR ENDED 31 DECEMBER 20.3

	Note	20.3 Rand	20.2 Rand
Profit before tax		415 000	27 500
Income tax expense	2	(206 360)	(11 000)
Profit for the year		208 640	16 500
Other comprehensive income		–	–
Total comprehensive income for the year		208 640	16 500

COMPANY NAME
NOTES FOR THE YEAR ENDED 31 DECEMBER 20.3

2. Income tax expense

	20.3 Rand	20.2 Rand
Major components of tax expense		
Current tax	233 026	–
Deferred tax : current year (1)	(38 626)	11 000
: rate change	11 960	–
	206 360	11 000

(1) 16 440 – 5 440 = 11 000; 45 154 – 6 528 = 38 626

Tax rate reconciliation

	20.3 %	20.2 %
Applicable (statutory) tax rate	48,0	40,0
Non-taxable profit on sale of property, plant and equipment (1)	(1,2)	–
Increase in tax rate (2)	2,9	–
Average effective tax rate (3)	49,7	40,0

The authorities increased the standard tax rate during the current year to 48% (20.2: 40%).

(1) ((230 000 – 220 000) × 48%)/415 000 × 100 = 1,2
(2) 11 960/415 000 × 100 = 2,9
(3) 206 360/415 000 × 100 = 49,7; 11 000/27 500 × 100 = 40,0

OR

	20.3 Rand	20.2 Rand
Accounting profit before tax	415 000	27 500
Tax at applicable (statutory) tax rate (1)	199 200	11 000
Non- taxable profit on sale of property, plant and equipment (2)	(4 800)	–
Increase in tax rate (3)	11 960	–
Income tax expense	206 360	11 000

The authorities increased the applicable tax rate during the current year to 48% (20.2: 40%).

(1) 415 000 × 48% = 199 200; 27 500 × 40% = 11 000
(2) (230 000 – 220 000) × 48% = 4 800
(3) 59 800 (calc 2) × 8/40 = 11 960

c. Current tax calculation for 20.3

		Rand
Profit before tax		415 000
Non-taxable differences		
20% of capital profit on machine (1)		(2 000)
		413 000
Temporary differences		94 070
Depreciation	68 750	
Wear-and-tear allowance	(30 380)	
Profit on sale (income nature) (2)	(123 750)	
Recoupment of wear-and-tear allowances	179 450	
Taxable income before utilisation of losses		507 070
Tax loss utilised		(13 600)
Taxable income		493 470
Current tax @ 48%		236 866

(1) (230 000 – 220 000) × 20% = 2 000
(2) 220 000 – (220 000 – 123 750) = 123 750

COMPANY NAME
NOTES FOR THE YEAR ENDED 31 DECEMBER 20.3

2. Income tax expense

	20.3 Rand
Major components of tax expense	
Current tax	236 866
Deferred tax : current year	(38 626)
: rate change	11 960
	210 200

Tax rate reconciliation	**%**
Applicable (statutory) tax rate	48,0
20% of capital profit on sale of machine (1)	(0,2)
Increase in tax rate	2,9
Average effective tax rate (2)	50,7

The authorities increased the applicable tax rate during the current year to 48% (20.2: 40%).

(1) (10 000 × 20% × 48%)/415 000 × 100 = 0,2
(2) 210 200/415 000 × 100 = 50,7

OR

	Rand
Accounting profit before tax	415 000
Tax at applicable (statutory) tax rate	199 200
20% of capital profit on sale of machine (1)	(960)
Increase in tax rate	11 960
Income tax expense	210 200

The authorities increased the applicable tax rate during the current year to 48% (20.2: 40%).

(1) 10 000 × 20% × 48% = 960

❑ QUESTION IAS 12.10@

The directors of Fairness Ltd approached you as their auditor for advice on the application of IAS 12.

The following financial information is provided:

Cost of asset	R1 000
Carrying amount	R800
Useful life of asset	5 years
Tax rate	27%
Cumulative wear-and-tear allowances for tax purposes	R350

The intention is to use the asset in the production of income for at least five years.

Assume that the residual value, useful life and depreciation method of the asset were reviewed at each financial year end and that there were no changes.

Required

a. The directors want to know what the deferred tax asset or liability will be in the following circumstances:
   1. Given the above information.
   2. The cumulative wear-and-tear allowances for tax purposes are RNil as the South African Revenue Service does not grant any allowances on this asset.
   3. The company wants to sell the asset without further use.

b. The directors subsequently revalued the asset to net replacement cost of R1 200. No equivalent adjustment is made for tax purposes. Given the above information, the directors want to know what the deferred tax asset or liability will be in the following circumstances:
   1. Sale proceeds in excess of cost will not be taxable and the company expects to recover the carrying amount of the asset through use.
   2. Sale proceeds in excess of cost will not be taxable and the company expects to recover the carrying amount by selling the asset immediately.
   3. 80% of capital gains are taxable and the company expects to recover the carrying amount of the asset through use.

4. 80% of capital gains are taxable and the company expects to recover the carrying amount by selling the asset immediately.

All calculations are to be done to the nearest rand.

❖ **Suggested solution IAS 12.10@**

a1. Tax base of asset = 1 000 – 350 = 650
Taxable temporary difference = 800 – 650 = 150
Deferred tax liability = 150 × 27% = 41

a2. Deferred tax liability = 0
No deferred tax liability will be raised, because it results from the initial recognition of the asset [IAS 12.15(b)].

a3. Tax base of asset = 1 000 – 350 = 650
Taxable temporary difference = 800 – 650 = 150
Deferred tax liability = 150 × 27% = 41

b1. Tax base of asset = 1 000 – 350 = 650
Taxable temporary difference = 1 200 – 650 = 550
Deferred tax liability = 550 × 27% = 149

b2. If a decision has already been taken to sell the asset at the time of revaluation, deferred tax is only provided for on the revaluation surplus up to cost price. The total surplus is R400 (1 200 – 800) but only R200 (1 000 – 800) will be taxable. The existing deferred tax liability on this asset will reverse on sale of the asset.

Tax base of asset = 1 000 – 350 = 650
Taxable temporary difference = 1 000 – 650 = 350
Deferred tax liability = 350 × 27% = 95

b3. Tax base of asset = 1 000 – 350 = 650
Taxable temporary difference = 1 200 – 650 = 550
Deferred tax liability = 550 × 27% = 149

b4. The proceeds on sale in excess of the cost, R200 (R1 200 – R1 000), will be taxed at effectively 21,6% (80% × 27%). The cumulative wear-and-tear allowances for tax purposes of R350 will be included in the taxable profit and taxed at 27%.

The tax base of the asset = 1 000 – 350 = 650
Taxable temporary difference = 1 200 – 650 = 550
Deferred tax liability = [(80% × 27%) × (1 200 – 1 000)] + [27% × (550 – 200)]
= (21,6% × 200) + (27% × 350)
= 43 + 95
= 138

❑ QUESTION IAS 12.11

Mickey Ltd is a manufacturing company. The following information is available for the year ended 31 December 20.9:

Extract from the trial balance	**Rand Dr/(Cr)**
Profit or loss items	
Depreciation for accounting purposes	67 250
Office buildings	11 000
Factory buildings	25 000
Machinery	31 250
Lease expense of low-value asset	5 000
Impairment loss in respect of receivables	7 000
Allowance for credit losses – adjustment	10 000
– 20.8 allowance	(5 000)
– 20.9 allowance	15 000
Traffic fines	5 000
Dividends received	(30 000)
Gain on sale of vehicle	(17 000)
Rental received (operating lease)	(6 000)
Statement of financial position items	
Rental received in advance (taxable in year of receipt 20.9)	(2 000)
Allowance for credit losses	(15 000)
Office buildings	89 000
Factory buildings	100 000
Machinery	48 750

Additional information

1. The accounting profit before tax for the year ended 31 December 20.9, after taking into account the above items per the trial balance, amounted to R178 000.

2. The South African Revenue Service allows a building allowance of R37 500 on the factory buildings and a wear-and-tear allowance of R50 000 on the machinery. There is no deduction in respect of the office buildings. The tax base of the factory buildings on 31 December 20.9 is R75 000 and the tax base of the machinery on 31 December 20.9 is R11 250.

3. The lease expense of low value asset is the equalised amount in respect of a 10-year lease contract which commenced on 1 January 20.9. The conditions of the contract are as follows:

	Rand
Lease premium paid on 1 January 20.9	10 000
Lease instalments	
Year 1 to 5 – R2 000 per year for five years	10 000
Year 6 to 10 – R6 000 per year for five years	30 000
Total cost of the lease	50 000
Recognised annually in profit or loss (R50 000/10 years)	5 000

The South African Revenue Service allows the lease premium as a deduction over the lease period (straight-line) and the instalments are deductible once they are paid.

4. The impairment loss in respect of receivables is as a result of the liquidation of a debtor and the South African Revenue Service is satisfied that the debt is not collectible.

5. A list of the debtors included in the allowance for credit losses was submitted to the South African Revenue Service and 25% of the list will be allowed as a deduction.

6. A vehicle with a carrying amount of R15 000 (original cost of R25 000) was sold on 1 January 20.9 for R32 000. The tax base of the vehicle on 1 January 20.9 was R10 000.

7. Assume that the residual value, useful life and depreciation method of all assets were reviewed at each financial year end and that there were no changes.

8. On 31 December 20.8, the deferred tax account had a credit balance of R8 775.

9. The tax rate was 27% for the past two years. There are no other temporary differences other than those which are apparent from the given information.

10. 80% of capital gains are taxable.

Required

a. Calculate the following:
   i. The current tax expense for the year ended 31 December 20.9;
   ii. The deferred tax expense (movement on the deferred tax balance) for the year ended 31 December 20.9.

b. Show how income taxes will be presented in the profit or loss section of the statement of profit or loss and other comprehensive income and disclose notes thereto for the year ended 31 December 20.9, in accordance with the requirements of International Financial Reporting Standards (IFRS). Ignore comparative amounts.

All calculations are to be done to the nearest rand.

❑ QUESTION IAS 12.12

Due to technological changes in the manufacturing process and small changes in its products, Chemisycs Ltd decided to replace its plant, which is less than two years old, with a more modern plant.

Details regarding the old plant are as follows:	**Rand**
Original cost	450 000
Accumulated depreciation up to 31 December 20.2	(67 500)
	382 500
Tax base	
on 31 December 20.2	270 000
on 30 June 20.3	180 000

Additional information

1. Depreciation is written off on the old plant at 15% per annum using the straight-line method. Wear and tear was allowed on this plant on a 40/20/20/20 basis in terms of section 12C.
2. On 30 June 20.3, the old plant was withdrawn from the production process and was sold for R461 000. On 1 July 20.3, the new plant with a cost price of R800 000 was brought into use (also the day it was available for use).
3. The directors decided to depreciate the newly acquired plant over four years using the straight-line method.
4. The South African Revenue Service will allow wear and tear on the new plant on a 40/20/20/20 basis in terms of section 12C. This allowance is not apportioned on a pro-rata basis for periods shorter than a year.
5. On 31 December 20.2 the company had an assessed loss of R10 000.
6. The company had a profit of R1 000 000 for the year ended 31 December 20.3 before taking the above into account.
7. The residual value, useful life and depreciation method of the newly acquired plant were reviewed at 31 December 20.3, but there were no changes.
8. The tax rate for 20.2 was 28% and for 20.3 it is 27%.
9. There are no other temporary differences other than those mentioned above.
10. Ignore capital gains tax.

Required

a. Calculate the current tax expense of Chemisycs Ltd for the year ended 31 December 20.3.
b. Calculate the amount which will be transferred to/from the deferred tax account for the year ended 31 December 20.3.
c. Prepare the relevant tax notes that will accompany the profit or loss section of the statement of profit or loss and other comprehensive income and the statement of financial position of Chemisycs Ltd for the year ended 31 December 20.3, in accordance with the requirements of International Financial Reporting Standards (IFRS). Ignore comparative amounts and deem all amounts to be material.
d. Assume that 80% of all capital gains are taxable, and prepare the income tax expense note that will accompany the statement of profit or loss and other comprehensive income for the year ended 31 December 20.3.

❑ QUESTION IAS 12.13

Toktokkie Ltd was incorporated on 1 July 20.4. The accounting profit before tax for the year ended 30 June 20.6 amounted to R220 000 and the accounting loss before tax for the year ended 30 June 20.5 amounted to R40 000.

The following items were taken into account in the calculation of accounting profit/loss before tax:

	20.6 Rand	20.5 Rand
Depreciation		
Office buildings	5 000	5 000
Plant and machinery	15 000	15 000
Dividends received	20 000	–

Additional information

1. During June 20.6, an operating lease instalment amounting to R12 000 was received in respect of July 20.6. This amount is taxable in the tax year ended 30 June 20.6.

2. The assessment for the 20.5 tax year showed an assessed loss of R80 000. This agreed with the records of the company.

3. The company operates in a risky industrial sector and at this early date of the company's existence there is no certainty of future taxable income against which tax losses can be utilised.

4. For the 20.5 tax year, temporary differences consisted of taxable temporary differences on the plant amounting to R45 000, before taking into account the assessed loss. The cost price of the plant was R150 000 on 1 July 20.4 and depreciation amounting to R15 000 was recognised for 20.5. The South African Revenue Service grants a wear-and-tear allowance in terms of section 12C on a 40/20/20/20 basis.

5. The carrying amount of the office building amounted to R270 000 on 30 June 20.5.

6. The tax rate for both years is 27%. There are no other temporary differences or non-taxable/non-deductible differences except for those apparent from the given information.

7. Assume that the residual value, useful life and depreciation method of all assets were reviewed at each financial year end and that there were no changes.

8. The office building does not qualify for any tax allowances as it was not new and unused when purchased.

9. No provisional tax has been paid in either 20.5 or 20.6.

Required

a. Calculate the major components of the income tax expense for 20.5 and 20.6.

b. Present income taxes in the profit or loss section of the statement of profit or loss and other comprehensive income for the year ended 30 June 20.6 and in the statement of financial position as at that date, in accordance with the requirements of International Financial Reporting Standards (IFRS). (Also prepare the relevant tax notes that will accompany the financial statements for the year ended 30 June 20.6). Comparative amounts are not required. The accounting policy note is not required

c. Assume exactly the same information as for part b, except that the profit before tax for the year ended 30 June 20.6 amounted to R90 000. Prepare the relevant tax notes that will accompany the financial statements of Toktokkie Ltd for the year ended 30 June 20.6 in accordance with the requirements of International Financial Reporting Standards (IFRS). (The accounting policy note is not required).

❑ QUESTION IAS 12.14

The following information regarding the listed companies mentioned below for the year ended 31 December 20.4 is available:

	Aura Ltd Rand	**Bona Ltd Rand**	**Ceaza Ltd Rand**	**Duka Ltd Rand**
Profit for the period before tax and before accounting for the following:	50 000	70 000	12 000	20 000
Depreciation	–	10 000	7 000	6 000
Legal costs	–	4 000	4 000	–
Dividends received	5 000	12 000	–	–
Profit on sale of buildings	–	21 000	–	–
Wear-and-tear allowance	–	14 000	10 000	12 000
Assessed loss brought forward from 20.3	16 000	–	–	30 000
Carrying amount and tax base of property, plant and equipment at 31 December 20.3	–	540 000	320 000	330 000

Additional information

1. The profit on sale of buildings resulted from the sale of buildings on 1 January 20.4. Current tax payable thereon amounts to R4 500. The cost and value of land are RNil. The tax base and carrying amount of the buildings amounted to R85 000 on 31 December 20.3.

2. The legal fees are not deductible for tax purposes.

3. The tax rate is 27%. Ignore capital gains tax.

4. The companies are deemed to be going concerns and there is reasonable assurance that sufficient future taxable profit will be earned to utilise the deferred tax assets, as tax planning opportunities are available that will create taxable profits in future.

5. Except for Aura Ltd and Duka Ltd, no other company had temporary differences at 31 December 20.3. Both Aura Ltd and Duka Ltd's temporary differences resulted only from the assessed losses.

Required

Prepare an extract of the statements of profit or loss and other comprehensive income of all the above companies, as well as the tax notes that will accompany the financial statements of the above companies for the year ended 31 December 20.4. Your answer must comply with the requirements of International Financial Reporting Standards (IFRS). Accounting policy notes and comparative amounts are not required.

❑ QUESTION IAS 12.15

The accountant of Taksi Ltd prepared the following tax calculation for the year ended 31 December 20.3:

Taxable income from SA sources	**Rand**
Profit before tax	500 000
Tax loss 20.2	(10 000)
Depreciation on property, plant and equipment	70 000
Wear-and-tear allowances on property, plant and equipment	(55 000)
Gain on the sale of vacant land	(50 000)
Companies Act penalties	15 000
Dividends received from subsidiary	(60 000)
Taxable income	410 000

Taxable income from foreign sources

Gross foreign income	100 000
Foreign tax paid	35 000

Additional information

1. The deferred tax balance at 31 December 20.2 amounts to R12 860 after taking into account the effect of the R10 000 calculated tax loss for 20.2. (Refer point 6 below.)

2. After the above tax calculation was performed, the tax assessment for 20.2 was received. The assessment showed a taxable profit of R2 000. The difference between the tax provision for 20.2 and the actual assessment resulted from departmental policy applied by the South African Revenue Service in respect of differences other than temporary differences. This was accepted by Taksi Ltd after enquiries had been made.

3. Included in profit before tax is a gain of R50 000 attributable to the sale of vacant land on 1 January 20.3, which was accounted for as an investment property using the cost model. The original cost of the vacant land was R800 000 and the land was sold for R850 000.

4. The directors of Taksi Ltd declared an interim dividend of R100 000 on 15 December 20.3.

5. The carrying amount and tax base of the depreciable property, plant and equipment of Taksi Ltd amounted to R1 000 000 and R944 000 respectively on 31 December 20.2.

6. The tax rate for 20.2 was 28% and for 20.3 it is 27%. Ignore capital gains tax.

7. Assume that the residual value, useful life and depreciation method of all assets were reviewed at each financial year end and that there were no changes.

Required

Prepare the profit or loss section of the statement of profit or loss and other comprehensive income of Taksi Ltd for the year ended 31 December 20.3 and disclose the income tax expense note thereto so as to comply with the requirements of International Financial Reporting Standards (IFRS). Ignore comparative amounts.

IAS 16 & IFRIC 1

Property, plant and equipment

❑ QUESTIONS AND SOLUTIONS

IAS 16.1	Determination of cost and carrying amount
IAS 16.2	Determination of cost on exchange transactions
IAS 16.3	Determination of cost, depreciable amount and depreciation
IAS 16.4	Accounting for various categories of assets
IAS 16.5	Self-constructed asset
IAS 16.6	Change in useful life and residual value
IAS 16.7	Subsequent expenditure on tangible assets – theory
IAS 16.8	Major inspection and overhaul costs
IAS 16.9	Accounting for components and derecognition
IAS 16.10@	Revaluations of depreciable assets, with deferred tax
IAS 16.11@	Decision to revalue depreciable assets (consecutive years and two methods to account for accumulated depreciation)
IAS 16.12	Revaluation of land – capital gains tax, theory
IAS 16.13@	Revaluation of depreciable asset with residual value above cost and deferred tax

❑ QUESTIONS

IAS 16.14	Reassessment of depreciation methods, useful life and residual value
IAS 16.15	Reassessment of residual value to greater than carrying amount
IAS 16.16	Accounting for components, derecognition and subsequent expenditure
IAS 16.17	Accounting and disclosure – various asset classes
IAS 16.18@	Various matters regarding revaluations
IAS 16.19@	Decrease in replacement cost of depreciable asset and change in useful life*
IAS 16.20	Revaluations of land and capital gains tax*
IAS 16.21	Plant with related long-term liability (IFRIC 1)*

** These questions are not in the textbook, but are available in the electronic guide for lecturers containing the suggested solutions for questions without answers.*

@ These questions contain topics or principles that were not included in the ITC syllabus of SAICA at the time of publishing this book, but might still be included in university syllabi.

❑ QUESTION IAS 16.1

Sandton Ltd purchased a machine on 1 January 20.3. The following details are applicable:

	Note	Rand
Purchase price	1	100 000
Delivery costs		3 000
Installation costs		6 000
General administrative costs	2	1 000
Costs of testing	3	5 000
Pre-production costs	4	2 000
Initial operating losses	5	10 000
		127 000

Additional information

1. The purchase price of R100 000 is only payable on 31 December 20.3. The supplier of the machine does not usually allow credit for the purchase of similar machines.

2. The administrative costs are of a general and indirect nature.

3. The costs of testing comprise costs incurred to produce samples while testing whether the machine is functioning properly. Samples were sold at net proceeds of R500.

4. The pre-production costs were necessary to bring the machine to the condition necessary to be able to operate in the manner intended by management.

5. The initial operating losses are attributable to the initial production of small quantities.

6. The asset was ready for use on 3 January 20.3 and immediately put to use.

7. The current interest rate is 14% per annum and the company does not follow a policy of capitalising borrowing costs.

8. The machine will be depreciated using the straight-line method over eight years, taking into account a residual value of R7 000.

9. Assume that a liability exists to dismantle and remove the machine at the end of its useful life at a cost of R3 500 (discounted present value equals R1 700).

10. Ignore VAT.

Required

a. Calculate the cost at which the asset will be recognised.
b. Calculate the carrying amount of the asset on 31 December 20.3.

Your answer must comply with the requirements of International Financial Reporting Standards (IFRS).

❖ **Suggested solution IAS 16.1**

a. Determination of cost price

	Rand
Purchase price (1)	87 719
Delivery costs	3 000
Installation costs	6 000
General administrative costs	–
Costs of testing (2)	–
Pre-production costs (3)	2 000
Initial operating losses (4)	–
Cost to dismantle and remove the machine (5)	1 700
	100 419

(1) 100 000 × 1/1,14 = 87 719 (refer to IAS 16.23) or with a financial calculator: FV = 100 000; n = 1; i = 14; calculate PV = 87 719
(2) Refer to IAS 16.20A
(3) Refer to IAS 16.16(b)
(4) Refer to IAS 16.20(b)
(5) Refer to IAS 16.16(c)

b. Carrying amount

	Rand
Cost	100 419
Depreciation (1)	(11 677)
	88 742

(1) (100 419 – 7 000)/8 = 11 677

❑ **QUESTION IAS 16.2**

Soapy Ltd manufactures soap products. During the year the company acquired four items of property, plant and equipment by means of exchange transactions. You can assume that the requirements of IFRS 5 were never met and that the assets given up were therefore never classified as 'held for sale' in terms of IFRS 5.

Machine X102

This machine, with a fair value of R15 200, was acquired on 31 July 20.4 for the exchange of a vehicle. The fair value of the vehicle was R15 000. The vehicle had a cost of R32 000 and accumulated depreciation of R18 000 at the time of the exchange transaction. The fair value of both these assets was clearly evident, as there is an active second-hand market for them. Installation costs amounted to R1 000.

Machine RX23

This machine was acquired on 31 October 20.4 for the exchange of a similar machine with a fair value of R26 000. The machine given up had a cost of R40 000 and accumulated depreciation of R20 000 at the time of the exchange transaction. The machine received was used in a similar business of soap manufacturing and will be used for the same purpose as the machine given up. The only reason for the exchange transaction is that the factory manager prefers the colour of the machine received.

Machine ZZ

This machine was acquired on 1 December 20.4 for the exchange of machine ZA. Machine ZA had a carrying amount of R19 000 (cost of R30 000 and accumulated depreciation of R11 000) at the time of the exchange transaction. The fair value of neither machine is reliably measurable.

Delivery vehicle

A delivery vehicle was acquired on 31 December 20.4 for the exchange of specialised equipment. The fair value of the delivery vehicle is R35 000 and there is an active second-hand market for delivery vehicles. The carrying amount of the specialised equipment given up was R28 000 (cost of R39 000 and accumulated depreciation of R11 000). There is no active second-hand market for this specialised equipment. However, the financial accountant used valuation techniques to estimate the fair value of the equipment at R33 000.

Required

Prepare the journal entries at the date of the exchange transactions to comply with the requirements of International Financial Reporting Standards (IFRS).

❖ **Suggested solution IAS 16.2**

Journals

	Rand Dr/(Cr)
31 July 20.4 (Machine X102)	
Machine – cost (1)	15 000
Accumulated depreciation – vehicles	18 000
Cost – vehicles	(32 000)
Profit on exchange of assets (P or L)	(1 000)
Exchange of vehicle for machine	
Machine – cost	1 000
Bank	(1 000)
Installation costs	
31 October 20.4 (Machine RX23)	
New machine – cost (2)	20 000
Old machine – cost	(40 000)
Old machine – accumulated depreciation	20 000
Exchange of machines	

1 December 20.4 (Machine ZZ)

New machine – cost (3)	19 000
Old machine – cost	(30 000)
Old machine – accumulated depreciation	11 000
Exchange of machines	

31 December 20.4 (Delivery vehicle)

Delivery vehicle – cost (4)	35 000
Equipment – cost	(39 000)
Equipment – accumulated depreciation	11 000
Profit on exchange of assets (P or L)	(7 000)
Exchange of specialised equipment for delivery vehicle	

(1) In terms of IAS 16.6, the cost of an asset can be the fair value of the asset given up. IAS 16.24 requires that the cost of an asset acquired in an exchange transaction is measured at fair value, but does not indicate whether the fair value of the asset acquired or given up should be used. However, the Standard often refers (paragraphs 24 and 26) to the fair value of the asset given up and accordingly this is used. When taking the definition of 'fair value' into account, the fair value of the asset given up would not differ materially from the fair value of the asset acquired.

(2) This exchange transaction lacks commercial substance as described in IAS 16.24. The transaction does not meet the requirements of commercial substance as listed in IAS 16.25. The cost of the machine received is then measured at the carrying amount of the machine given up.

(3) As the fair value of neither the asset received nor the asset given up is reliably measurable, the cost of the machine received is measured at the carrying amount of the machine given up in accordance with IAS 16.24.

(4) As the fair value of the delivery vehicle is more clearly evident, the cost of the delivery vehicle is measured at its own (asset received) fair value in accordance with IAS 16.26.

❑ QUESTION IAS 16.3

Wood Ltd commenced in 20.4 with the manufacturing of wood products at a new plant. The plant was purchased on 1 January 20.4 for R700 000. During January 20.4, some equipment was installed and other equipment was modified. Installation and modification costs incurred amounted to R130 000. For security reasons a fence was erected at the plant at a cost of R20 000. The plant was ready for use on 1 February 20.4. An opening function was held in the plant on 15 February 20.4 at a cost of R50 000 in order to entertain customers and to introduce the new products to be manufactured at this plant. Production only commenced on 1 March 20.4.

The plant has a useful life of 10 years and the residual value was estimated at R200 000. Expected scrapping costs amount to R140 000 (discounted present value of scrapping costs equals R100 000). Assume that the provision for the scrapping costs will be raised in accordance with IAS 37.

At the end of August 20.4 heavy rain caused severe damage to the houses of the employees in the region. Management granted special leave to all the employees of the plant to attend to the repair of their houses. The plant stood idle during September 20.4.
The company's year-end is 31 December.

Required

a. Calculate the cost of the plant.
b. Calculate the depreciable amount of the plant.
c. Calculate depreciation for the year ended 31 December 20.4.
d. Calculate the carrying amount of the plant on 31 December 20.4.

Your answer must comply with the requirements of International Financial Reporting Standards (IFRS).

❖ **Suggested solution IAS 16.3**

a. Cost

	Rand
Purchase price	700 000
Installation and modification	130 000
Fence (1)	20 000
Opening function (2)	–
Scrapping costs (3)	100 000
Cost	950 000

(1) Refer to IAS 16.11
(2) Refer to IAS 16.19
(3) Refer to IAS 16.16(c)

b. Depreciable amount

	Rand
Cost	950 000
Residual value	(200 000)
	750 000

c. Depreciation

	Rand
Depreciation for the year (1)	68 750

(1) 750 000/10 × 11/12 = 68 750 (refer to IAS 16.55). Depreciation of an asset begins when it is available for use (1 February 20.4). Depreciation does not cease when the asset becomes idle (September 20.4).

d. Carrying amount

	Rand
Cost	950 000
Accumulated depreciation	(68 750)
Carrying amount at 31 December 20.4	881 250

❑ QUESTION IAS 16.4

The register of property, plant and equipment of Dijkman (Pty) Ltd is presented to you. As the accountant you are required to prepare all the entries and calculations, and satisfy all disclosure requirements, regarding property, plant and equipment in the financial statements of the company for the financial year ended 30 June 20.5.

A summary of the register of property, plant and equipment at 1 July 20.4 is as follows:

		Rand
Furniture		
Cost		22 000
Accumulated depreciation		8 000
Motor vehicles		
Cost		60 000
Accumulated depreciation		31 000
Machinery		
Cost		96 000
	Machine A	15 000
	Machine B	63 000
	Machine C	18 000
Accumulated depreciation		10 000
	Machine A	7 000
	Machine B	–
	Machine C	3 000
Land		
Cost		150 000

Additional information

1. The following rates and methods of depreciation are applicable:
   - Property, plant and equipment are accounted for on the cost model.
   - Land – no depreciation.
   - Furniture – 10% straight line.
   - Motor vehicles – 20% straight line.
   - Machinery – 20% diminishing balance method.
   - Capitalised leased machinery – 20% diminishing balance method.
   - The assets have insignificant residual values.

2. On 31 December 20.4, a delivery vehicle with an original cost of R18 000 was sold for R7 500 and this amount was credited to the motor vehicle account. On 1 July 20.4 the accumulated depreciation of the vehicle amounted to R11 000. Assume that the requirements of IFRS 5 were never met and that the asset was therefore never classified as 'held for sale' in terms of IFRS 5.

3. Machine B was obtained and put into operation on 30 June 20.4, and is held in terms of a lease agreement. Right-of-use assets are not presented separately from other assets in the statement of financial position.

4. Land consists of stand no. 65, Industria, and was purchased in 20.0. The board of directors estimated the current fair value of the property to be R200 000 at 30 June 20.5. The land is not classified as an investment property.

5. The current fair value of the other assets does not differ materially from their carrying amounts.

6. No other transactions relating to property, plant and equipment took place during the year.

Required

a. Prepare all the journal entries necessary for the financial year ended 30 June 20.5 regarding property, plant and equipment in compliance with requirements of International Financial Reporting Standards (IFRS).
b. Disclose the property, plant and equipment in the statement of financial position and accompanying notes (including profit before tax) of Dijkman (Pty) Ltd for the year ended 30 June 20.5 so as to comply with the requirements of International Financial Reporting Standards (IFRS). Ignore comparative amounts. Ignore the note on the preparation of the financial statements and compliance with International Financial Reporting Standards (IFRS).

❖ **Suggested solution IAS 16.4**

a. Journal entries

	Rand Dr/(Cr)
Depreciation (1)	2 200
Accumulated depreciation – furniture	(2 200)
Depreciation (2)	10 200
Accumulated depreciation – motor vehicles	(10 200)
Depreciation (3)	4 600
Accumulated depreciation – machinery	(4 600)
Depreciation (4)	12 600
Accumulated depreciation – capitalised leased machinery	(12 600)
Being depreciation provided for the year	
Accumulated depreciation – motor vehicles (5)	12 800
Bank	7 500
Motor vehicles at cost	(18 000)
Gain on disposal of motor vehicles (P or L) (6)	(2 300)
Being gain on disposal of motor vehicles	

(1) 22 000 × 10% = 2 200
(2) [(60 000 – 18 000) × 20%] + (18 000 × 20% × 6/12) = 10 200
(3) (96 000 – 63 000 – 10 000) × 20% = 4 600
(4) 63 000 × 20% = 12 600
(5) 11 000 + (18 000 × 20% × 6/12) = 12 800
(6) 7 500 – (18 000 – 12 800) = 2 300

b. Disclosure

DIJKMAN (PTY) LTD
STATEMENT OF FINANCIAL POSITION AS AT 30 JUNE 20.5

	Note	Rand
ASSETS		
Non-current assets		
Property, plant and equipment	2	244 200

DIJKMAN (PTY) LTD
NOTES FOR THE YEAR ENDED 30 JUNE 20.5

1. Accounting policy

1.1 Property, plant and equipment

Property, plant and equipment are stated at cost less accumulated depreciation, except for land, which is not depreciated, and which is carried at cost. The remaining assets are depreciated according to the following rates and methods:

- Furniture at 10% according to the straight-line method.
- Motor vehicles at 20% according to the straight-line method.
- Machinery at 20% according to the diminishing balance method.

Rates are considered appropriate to reduce carrying amounts of the assets to estimated residual values over their expected useful lives.

2. Property, plant and equipment

	A Rand	B Rand	C Rand
Carrying amount at 1 July 20.4:	150 000	14 000	29 000
Cost	150 000	22 000	60 000
Accumulated depreciation	–	(8 000)	(31 000)
Movement during the year:			
Depreciation	–	(2 200)	(10 200)
Disposal	–	–	(5 200)
Carrying amount at 30 June 20.5:	150 000	11 800	13 600
Cost	150 000	22 000	42 000
Accumulated depreciation (1)	–	(10 200)	(28 400)

	D Rand	E Rand	Total Rand
Carrying amount at 1 July 20.4:	63 000	23 000	279 000
Cost	63 000	33 000	328 000
Accumulated depreciation	–	(10 000)	(49 000)
Movement during the year:			
Depreciation	(12 600)	(4 600)	(29 600)
Disposal	–	–	(5 200)
Carrying amount at 30 June 20.5:	50 400	18 400	244 200
Cost	63 000	33 000	310 000
Accumulated depreciation (1)	(12 600)	(14 600)	(65 800)

A	=	**Land**
B	=	**Furniture**
C	=	**Motor vehicles**
D	=	**Machinery – leased**
E	=	**Machinery – other**

On 30 June 20.5 the fair value (2) of the land was estimated at R200 000.

(1) For C: 31 000 + 10 200 – 12 800 = 28 400
(2) Refer to IAS 16.79(d)

3. Profit before tax

Profit before tax is stated after taking the following into account:

	Rand
Income	
Gain on disposal of motor vehicle	2 300
Proceeds (1)	7 500
Carrying amount of vehicle sold	(5 200)

(1) Refer to IAS 16.74(d)

	Rand
Expenses	
Depreciation*	29 600

* IAS 16 does not require depreciation to be split into the separate classes of assets. Furthermore, IAS 16 does not require separate disclosure of amounts capitalised as part of the cost of other assets (e.g. depreciation on machinery that can be part of the cost of inventory). Refer to IAS 16.75(a).

❑ QUESTION IAS 16.5

Gaba Ltd is a company which presses motor vehicle bodies. During the year crane A was withdrawn from production and used to establish an additional production line X.

The cost of this production line was as follows:

	Rand
Direct material	500 000
Direct costs of employee benefits (per IAS 19)	200 000
Directly allocated overheads	50 000
	750 000

This production line was completed on 1 January 20.5 and immediately put into operation.

As the accountant of Gaba Ltd, you found that, during the financial year ended 28 February 20.5, crane A had been used for six months of the year to establish production line X. No depreciation has as yet been capitalised to the cost of this production line.

Depreciation on machinery is provided for at 20% per annum on the straight-line method.

The following balances appeared in the financial records of Gaba Ltd at 28 February 20.5:

	Rand	
Machinery, at cost	?	
Production line X		?
Crane A		80 000
Other machinery		420 000
Depreciation for the year		
Furniture and equipment	20 000	
Motor vehicles	42 000	
Machinery	?	

Required

a. Calculate the cost of production line X.
b. Show the amount and how depreciation will be calculated and disclosed in the note on profit before tax of Gaba Ltd for the year ended 28 February 20.5 in accordance with the requirements of International Financial Reporting Standards (IFRS). The accounting policy note and comparative amounts are not required.

❖ **Suggested solution IAS 16.5**

a. Cost of production line X

	Rand
Direct costs (refer to IAS 16.16(b) and IAS 16.17(a))	750 000
Depreciation on crane A capitalised (1)	8 000
Total cost of production line	758 000

(1) $80\ 000 \times 20\% \times 6/12 = 8\ 000$

b. Disclosure

GABA LTD
NOTES FOR THE YEAR ENDED 28 FEBRUARY 20.5

10. Profit before tax

Profit before tax is shown after taking into account the following:

	Rand
Expenses	
Depreciation*	179 267

* IAS 16 does not require separate disclosure of the amount capitalised (refer to IAS 16.75(a)).

Calculations

Depreciation on machinery	**Rand**
Production line X (1)	25 267
Crane A (2)	8 000
Other machinery (3)	84 000
	117 267

(1) 758 000 × 20% × 2/12 = 25 267
(2) 80 000 × 20% = 16 000 × 6/12 = 8 000
(3) 420 000 × 20% = 84 000

Total depreciation expense	**Rand**
Furniture and equipment	20 000
Motor vehicles	42 000
Machinery	117 267
	179 267

❑ QUESTION IAS 16.6

Budweizer Ltd purchased machinery for its brewery on 1 January 20.0 at a cost of R696 000. At the time it was estimated that the machinery had a useful life of 10 years and a residual value of R16 000.

Depreciation has been provided for, for the past seven years, using the straight-line method. At each of the previous year ends the useful life and residual value were reviewed, and management found that the initial estimates were still applicable. In 20.7, a re-evaluation showed that the machinery actually had a total useful life of 15 years with a residual value of R12 000.

Required

a. Calculate and prepare the journal entries to account for depreciation for the year ended 31 December 20.7. Assume that Budweizer Ltd uses the reallocation method to account for changes in estimates.
b. Discuss the disclosure requirements.

Your answer must comply with the requirements of International Financial Reporting Standards (IFRS).

❖ Suggested solution IAS 16.6

a. Journal entries		**Rand Dr/(Cr)**
20.7	Depreciation (P or L) (1)	26 000
	Accumulated depreciation – machinery	(26 000)

(1) Depreciation on old basis = (696 000 – 16 000)/10 = 68 000
Carrying amount after seven years = 696 000 – (7 × 68 000) = 220 000
New revised depreciation = (220 000 – 12 000)/(15 – 7) = 26 000

b. Discussion

The re-evaluation of the useful life and residual value represents a change in estimate and therefore the nature, amount and cumulative effect on future periods shall be shown in terms of IAS 8.39 as it is material. The amount of the change will be the difference between depreciation based on the previous estimate of useful life and residual value (R68 000) and the depreciation based on the new estimate (R26 000); in other words, a decrease in depreciation and an increase in profit of R42 000. It would also result in a cumulative increase in depreciation in future periods of R46 000 (2).

		Rand
(2)	Depreciable amount end 20.7 using 'old' estimates (3)	136 000
	Depreciable amount end 20.7 using 'new' estimates (3)	182 000
	Increase in future depreciation	46 000

(3) (696 000 – 16 000) / 10 × 2 = 136 000; (220 000 – 12 000) / 8 × 7 = 182 000

❑ QUESTION IAS 16.7

The information contained in the register of property, plant and equipment of Compal Ltd in respect of machinery for the year ended 31 December 20.8 is as follows:

	Cost	Accumulated depreciation 31 Dec 20.7	Carrying amount
	Rand	Rand	Rand
Machine 1	125 000	(40 000)	85 000
Machine 2	520 000	(160 000)	360 000

Additional information

1. The company provides for depreciation on machinery at 20% per year on the diminishing balance method.

2. The company incurred the following expenditure in connection with assets for the year ended 31 December 20.8:

   - **Machine 1** – the directors of the company approved a modification (which included the replacements of parts) of the machine which has resulted in increased capacity of the machine. The machine can now produce on average 20% more than prior to the modification. To date the machine has maintained its original capacity. The modification was performed on 1 January 20.8 at a cost of R75 000.
   - **Machine 2** – this machine was overhauled and serviced during January 20.8. Compal Ltd did not initially account for the major overhaul costs as a separate component of the asset. The machine originally had an output of 310 000 units per annum and this has reduced to 270 000 units per annum over time. The output has increased to 300 000 units per annum as a result of the overhaul. The costs incurred for the overhaul amounted to R66 000.

3. The effect of the expenditure has not been accounted for in the register of property, plant and equipment. No further transactions relating to property, plant and equipment have taken place during the current year.

Required

Discuss how this expenditure should be recognised in the financial statements of Compal Ltd for the year ended 31 December 20.8 so as to comply with the requirements of International Financial Reporting Standards (IFRS).

❖ **Suggested solution IAS 16.7**

Machine 1:

The cost of an item of property, plant and equipment shall be recognised as an asset if, and only if:

- it is probable that future economic benefits associated with the item will flow to the entity; and
- the cost of the item can be measured reliably (refer to IAS 16.7).

This recognition principle applies to initial and subsequent recognition of assets.

Compal Ltd shall evaluate under this recognition principle all its property, plant and equipment costs at the time they are incurred. These costs include costs incurred initially to acquire or construct an item of property, plant and equipment and costs incurred subsequently to add to, replace parts of, or service it (i.e. the cost of the modification).

Under the recognition principle in IAS 16.7, Compal Ltd recognises the modification costs of the item in the carrying amount of an item of property, plant and equipment when the cost is incurred and the recognition criteria are met. It would seem from the increased capacity that the recognition criteria have been met.

The carrying amount of any parts that are replaced is derecognised in accordance with the derecognition requirements of IAS 16.

If, under the recognition principle in IAS 16.7, Compal Ltd recognises in the carrying amount of an item of property, plant and equipment the cost of a replacement for part of the item, then it derecognises the carrying amount of the replaced part regardless of whether the replaced part had been depreciated separately.

If it is not practicable for Compal Ltd to determine the carrying amount of the replaced part, it may use the cost of the replacement as an indication of what the cost of the replaced part was at the time it was acquired or constructed.

Compal Ltd shall therefore capitalise the modification costs to property, plant and equipment and shall derecognise the carrying amount of any parts replaced during the modification.

Machine 2:

The cost of an item of property, plant and equipment shall be recognised as an asset if, and only if:

- it is probable that future economic benefits associated with the item will flow to the entity; and
- the cost of the item can be measured reliably (refer to IAS 16.7).

This recognition principle applies to initial and subsequent recognition of assets.

Compal Ltd will evaluate under this recognition principle all the costs of its property, plant and equipment costs at the time they are incurred. These costs include costs incurred initially to acquire or construct an item of property, plant and equipment, and costs incurred subsequently to add to, replace part of or service it (i.e. the cost of the major overhaul).

A condition of continuing to operate an item of property, plant and equipment may be performing regular major overhauls regardless of whether parts of the item are replaced. When each major overhaul is performed, its cost is recognised in the carrying amount of the item of property, plant and equipment as a replacement if the recognition criteria are satisfied.

It would seem from the increased capacity, if compared to capacity before the overhaul, that the recognition criteria are met. All relevant factors will, however, be considered. The fact that the new output of 300 000 is still below the original output of 310 000 would not influence the recognition provided that the recognition criteria are met.

It would seem that the recognition criteria are met as the output increased from 270 000 units per annum to 300 000 units per annum over time.

Any remaining carrying amount of the cost of the previous overhaul (as distinct from physical parts) is derecognised. This occurs regardless of whether the cost of the previous overhaul was identified in the transaction in which the item was acquired or constructed. If necessary, the estimated cost of a future similar overhaul may be used as an indication of what the cost of the existing overhaul component was when the item was acquired or constructed.

Thus, the fact that the overhaul was not initially treated as a separate component would not influence the recognition.

IAS 16 requires each part of an item of property, plant and equipment with a cost that is significant in relation to the total cost of the item to be depreciated separately. The overhaul costs might therefore be treated as a separate component from now on.

Compal Ltd shall therefore capitalise the overhaul costs to property, plant and equipment and shall derecognise any carrying amount of any previous overhaul component. Any carrying amount of parts replaced during the overhaul shall also be derecognised.

❑ QUESTION IAS 16.8

On 1 January 20.1, Hopper Ltd bought an aeroplane with a useful life of 20 years for R850 000. As this aeroplane had to be inspected and overhauled every three years at a cost of approximately R150 000 per inspection, it was decided at date of acquisition to identify and depreciate these expected costs as a separate component. On 31 December 20.3 the plane was inspected and overhauled for the first time at a cost of R152 000.

Required

Disclose the above information in the notes of Hopper Ltd for the year ended 31 December 20.4 so as to comply with the requirements of International Financial Reporting Standards (IFRS). Ignore accounting policy notes and all tax implications.

❖ **Suggested solution IAS 16.8**

HOPPER LTD
NOTES FOR THE YEAR ENDED 31 DECEMBER 20.4

2. Property, plant and equipment	**20.4 Rand**	**20.3 Rand**
Aeroplane		
Carrying amount at beginning of year	747 000	680 000
Cost	852 000	850 000
Accumulated depreciation (1)	(105 000)	(170 000)
Depreciation (2)	(85 667)	(85 000)
Capitalisation of inspection costs	–	152 000
Carrying amount at end of year	661 333	747 000
Cost (3)	852 000	852 000
Accumulated depreciation (4)	(190 667)	(105 000)

(1) [(850 000 – 150 000) × 2/20] + (150 000 × 2/3) = 170 000
(2) (850 000 – 150 000)/20 + (150 000/3) = 85 000 and
(700 000/20) + (152 000/3) = 85 667
(3) 850 000 – 150 000 + 152 000 = 852 000
(4) 170 000 + 85 000 – 150 000 = 105 000 and
105 000 + 85 667 = 190 667

3. Profit before tax	**20.4 Rand**	**20.3 Rand**
Profit before tax is shown after taking into account the following:		
Expenses		
Depreciation (1)	85 667	85 000

(1) (850 000 – 150 000)/20 + (150 000/3) = 85 000 and
(700 000/20) + (152 000/3) = 85 667

❑ **QUESTION IAS 16.9**

Green Ltd is a manufacturing company and is manufacturing rugby balls for Bok Ltd. Green Ltd uses machine Super 00, purchased on 1 January 20.1 for R1 000 000, for the manufacturing of the rugby balls.

Machine Super 00 comprises three components. Details of the components are as follows:

Component	**Cost Rand**	**Useful life Years**	**Residual value Rand**
Super 1	500 000	5	40 000
Super 2	300 000	4	Insignificant
Super 3	200 000	2	Insignificant
Total	1 000 000		

The components can function independently, but are used as a unit. Components are independently replaced at the end of their useful life.

On 30 September 20.2, part 22 of component Super 2 broke down unexpectedly. The part was replaced at a cost of R110 000. Management estimated that the original cost of part 22 was R100 000.

On 31 December 20.2, at the end of its useful life, component Super 3 was replaced at a cost of R210 000.

Costs of day-to-day servicing of the machine amounted to R45 000 during 20.2 (20.1: R42 000).

During 20.2 the useful life and residual value of the components were reassessed and they were considered not to have changed.

Required

Prepare the journal entries necessary to account for all aspects of property, plant and equipment for the years ended 31 December 20.1 and 20.2. (Journal entries must be provided for each component.) Your solution must comply with the requirements of International Financial Reporting Standards (IFRS).

❖ **Suggested solution IAS 16.9**

Journal entries (Note 1)

	Components			Total
	Super 1 Rand Dr/(Cr)	Super 2 Rand Dr/(Cr)	Super 3 Rand Dr/(Cr)	Rand Dr/(Cr)
1 January 20.1				
Property, plant and equipment – cost	500 000	300 000	200 000	1 000 000
Bank	(500 000)	(300 000)	(200 000)	(1 000 000)
Purchase of machine Super 00				
31 December 20.1				
Depreciation (P or L) (1) (2) (3)	92 000	75 000	100 000	267 000
Accumulated depreciation – plant & equipment	(92 000)	(75 000)	(100 000)	(267 000)
Depreciation for the year				
Repair and maintenance costs (P or L)				42 000
Bank				(42 000)
Cost of day-to-day servicing				
30 September 20.2				
Depreciation (P or L) (4)		18 750		18 750
Accumulated depreciation – plant & equipment		(18 750)		(18 750)
Depreciation of part 22				
Write-off of replaced part 22 (P or L) (5)		56 250		56 250
Accumulated depreciation – plant & equipment (6)		43 750		43 750
Property, plant and equipment – cost		(100 000)		(100 000)
Write-off of replaced part 22				

	Components Super 1 Rand Dr/(Cr)	Super 2 Rand Dr/(Cr)	Super 3 Rand Dr/(Cr)	Total Rand Dr/(Cr)
Property, plant and equipment – cost		110 000		110 000
Bank		(110 000)		(110 000)
Capitalising of new part				
31 December 20.2				
Depreciation (P or L) (7)	92 000	62 222	100 000	254 222
Accumulated depreciation – plant & equipment	(92 000)	(62 222)	(100 000)	(254 222)
Depreciation for the year				
Property, plant and equipment – cost			210 000	210 000
Bank			(210 000)	(210 000)
Capitalising of new part				
Repair and maintenance costs (P or L)				45 000
Bank				(45 000)
Cost of day-to-day servicing				

(1) (500 000 – 40 000)/5 = 92 000
(2) 300 000/4 = 75 000
(3) 200 000/2 = 100 000
(4) 100 000/4 × 9/12 = 18 750
(5) 100 000 – 43 750 = 56 250 (refer to IAS 16.13, .70)
(6) 100 000 × 21/48 months = 43 750
(7) [(300 000 – 100 000)/4] + (110 000 × 3/27 remaining months) = 62 222 (refer to note 2).

Notes:

1. The components should be split in the register of property, plant and equipment in order to calculate the relevant amounts in the journals. In this question, separate journal entries were used just to illustrate the principle. Although depreciation is separately calculated for each component, the whole machine will be combined with other machinery and be presented as one class of assets.

2. The new part will also be replaced with the rest of component Super 2 at the end of its useful life of four years. Only 27 months remain and depreciation is calculated over the remaining useful life. The total depreciation of component Super 2 for 20.2 amounted to R80 972 (8).

(8) 18 750 + 62 222 = 80 972 or
(300 000/4 × 9/12) + (200 000/4 × 3/12) + (110 000 × 3/27) = 80 972

❑ QUESTION IAS 16.10@

Bolton Ltd manufactures and markets product Z. Several machines are used to produce the components of product Z. On 1 January 20.2 the directors decided that, due to the substantial increase in gross replacement costs, machinery will be shown at net replacement cost. The replacement cost will be determined annually by an independent sworn appraiser with reference to observable prices in an active market. The following information is available:

Machinery	**S** **Rand**	**T** **Rand**	**O** **Rand**	**P** **Rand**
Cost	105 000	40 000	40 000	87 500
Accumulated depreciation – 1 January 20.2	(60 000)	(10 000)	(15 000)	(35 000)
Carrying amounts – 1 January 20.2	45 000	30 000	25 000	52 500
Tax base – 1 January 20.2	30 000	20 000	17 500	26 250
Gross replacement cost – 1 January 20.2	157 500	48 000	56 000	131 250
Original useful life in years	7	4	8	5
Remaining useful life in years – 1 January 20.2	3	3	5	3

Additional information

1. Depreciation is provided for according to the straight-line method, and residual values are insignificant.

2. The South African Revenue Service grants a 20% wear-and-tear allowance on machinery according to the diminishing balance method for 20.2.

3. Temporary differences are the result of differences between the carrying amounts and the tax bases of machinery. The tax rate was 28% for 20.1 and 20.2.

4. Transfers are made annually from the revaluation surplus to retained earnings, representing the realised portion of the revaluation.
5. Revaluations are performed at the beginning of the financial year. On revaluation, accumulated depreciation is set off against the gross carrying amounts.

6. The profit for the year, after taking into account the information above, is R450 000 and the balance of retained earnings on 31 December 20.1 is R760 000. Other comprehensive income is presented gross of any related taxation in the statement of profit or loss and other comprehensive income.

Required

a. Prepare the following notes of Bolton Ltd for the year ended 31 December 20.2 in accordance with the requirements of International Financial Reporting Standards (IFRS):
   - Accounting policy for property, plant and equipment
   - Property, plant and equipment
   - Deferred tax asset/liability
   - Profit before tax

b. Prepare the statement of profit or loss and other comprehensive income of Bolton Ltd for the year ended 31 December 20.2 in accordance with the requirements of International Financial Reporting Standards (IFRS).

c. Prepare the statement of changes in equity of Bolton Ltd for the year ended 31 December 20.2 in accordance with the requirements of International Financial Reporting Standards (IFRS).

Comparative amounts are not required. Ignore the note on the preparation of the financial statements and compliance with the requirements of International Financial Reporting Standards (IFRS).

❖ **Suggested solution IAS 16.10@**

a. **BOLTON LTD**
NOTES FOR THE YEAR ENDED 31 DECEMBER 20.2

1. Accounting policy

1.1 Property, plant and equipment

Machinery is shown at net replacement cost less accumulated depreciation. Revaluation surpluses are regarded as realised as the relevant assets are used. Depreciation on machinery is written off over the estimated useful lives of the assets using the straight-line method. The revaluation of property, plant and equipment represents a change in accounting policy as machinery was previously shown at historical cost. This change was necessitated by the substantial increase in gross replacement costs of machinery.

Note: This change in accounting policy shall, in terms of IAS 8.17, only be treated as a revaluation in accordance with IAS 16 and the normal requirements for the change in accounting policy of IAS 8 are thus not applicable.

2. Property, plant and equipment

Machinery	**Rand**
Cost	272 500
Accumulated depreciation	(120 000)
Carrying amount at 31 December 20.1	152 500
Revaluation (calc 1)	64 750
Depreciation (calc 2)	(67 750)
Carrying amount at 31 December 20.2	149 500
Revalued cost (gross carrying amount)	217 250
Accumulated depreciation	(67 750)

Machinery is revalued annually on 1 January by an independent sworn appraiser on a gross replacement cost basis, with reference to observable prices in an active market.

	Rand
Carrying amount if carried at cost model (1)	105 000

(1) 152 500 – 47 500 = 105 000

3. Deferred tax

	Rand
Accelerated wear and tear for tax purposes (1)	8 400
Revaluation after deduction of related depreciation (2)	12 460
	20 860

(1) (105 000 – 75 000) × 28% = 8 400
(2) (149 500 – 105 000) × 28% = 12 460

4. Profit before tax

Profit before tax is stated after taking the following into account:

	Rand
Expenses	
Depreciation (calc 2)	67 750

b. **BOLTON LTD**
STATEMENT OF PROFIT OR LOSS AND OTHER COMPREHENSIVE INCOME FOR THE YEAR ENDED 31 DECEMBER 20.2

	Rand
Profit for the year	450 000
Other comprehensive income	
Items that will not be reclassified to profit or loss	
Machinery revaluation	46 620
Gain on revaluation of machinery	64 750
Tax expense	(18 130)
Total comprehensive income for the year	496 620

c. **BOLTON LTD**
STATEMENT OF CHANGES IN EQUITY FOR THE YEAR ENDED 31 DECEMBER 20.2

	Retained earnings Rand	Revaluation surplus Rand	Total Rand
Balance at 1 January 20.2	760 000	–	760 000
Changes in equity for 20.2			
Total comprehensive income for the year	450 000	46 620	496 620
Profit for the year	450 000	–	450 000
Other comprehensive income	–	46 620	46 620
Transfer to retained earnings (1)	14 580	(14 580)	–
Balance at 31 December 20.2	1 224 580	32 040	1 256 620

(1) [67 750 (calc 2) – 47 500 (calc 2)] × 72% = 14 580 or (16 200 (calc 1)/3) + (4 320 (calc 1)/3) + (7 200 (calc 1)/5) + (18 900 (calc 1)/3) = 14 580

Calculations

1. Net replacement cost at 1 January 20.2 and revaluation surplus

	A	B	C	D	E
	Rand	**Rand**	**Rand**	**Rand**	**Rand**
Machine S (1)	67 500	45 000	22 500	16 200	6 300
Machine T (2)	36 000	30 000	6 000	4 320	1 680
Machine O (3)	35 000	25 000	10 000	7 200	2 800
Machine P (4)	78 750	52 500	26 250	18 900	7 350
	217 250	152 500	64 750	46 620	18 130

(1) 157 500 × 3/7 = 67 500
(2) 48 000 × 3/4 = 36 000
(3) 56 000 × 5/8 = 35 000
(4) 131 250 × 3/5 = 78 750

A = Net replacement cost on 1 January 20.2
B = Carrying amount on 1 January 20.2
C = Revaluation surplus before tax
D = Revaluation surplus after tax (72%)
E = Deferred tax liability (28%)

2. Depreciation

	A	B
	Rand	**Rand**
Machine S (1)	22 500	15 000
Machine T (2)	12 000	10 000
Machine O (3)	7 000	5 000
Machine P (4)	26 250	17 500
	67 750	47 500

(1) 1/3 × 67 500 or 157 500/7 = 22 500; 1/3 × 45 000 or 105 000/7 = 15 000
(2) 1/3 × 36 000 or 48 000/4 = 12 000; 1/3 × 30 000 or 40 000/4 = 10 000
(3) 1/5 × 35 000 or 56 000/8 = 7 000; 1/5 × 25 000 or 40 000/8 = 5 000
(4) 1/3 × 78 750 or 131 250/5 = 26 250; 1/3 × 52 500 or 87 500/5 = 17 500

A = On revaluation
B = On carrying amount (cost)

3. Deferred tax asset/liability

Machinery	**CA**	**TB**	**TD**	**DTL**
	Rand	**Rand**	**Rand**	**Rand (Dr)/Cr**
Balance at beginning of year	152 500	93 750	58 750	16 450
Revaluation (calc 1)	64 750	–	64 750	18 130
Wear and tear (1)/ depreciation (calc 2)	(67 750)	(18 750)	(49 000)	(13 720)
Balance at end of year	149 500	75 000	74 500	20 860

(1) 93 750 × 20% = 18 750

CA	=	**Carrying amount**
TB	=	**Tax base**
TD	=	**Temporary difference**
DTL	=	**Deferred tax liability**

❑ QUESTION IAS 16.11[@]

On 1 January 20.0, Charlie Ltd purchased plant at a cost of R120 000. The estimated useful life of the plant was 10 years with an insignificant residual value. Assume that it is company policy to revalue plant annually, to carry the plant at net replacement cost, and to realise revaluation surpluses while the relevant assets are used.

The gross replacement cost at 31 December 20.0 amounted to R130 000. It increases annually on 31 December by R10 000. Plant is revalued annually by an independent sworn appraiser on a gross replacement cost basis, with reference to observable prices in an active market. Depreciation for each year is based on the gross replacement cost at the end of that specific year. Assume that the residual value and useful life of the plant did not change over the years.

Revaluation surplus balances are realised to retained earnings over the remaining useful life of the plant. Assume a tax rate of 29%. A 12% wear-and-tear allowance per annum on the straight-line method is granted by the South African Revenue Service.

Required

a. Calculate the annual depreciation and carrying amounts based on replacement costs for the years 20.0 to 20.3.
b. Calculate the current tax payable for 20.0 to 20.3 (assume a profit before depreciation of R80 000 per annum).
c. Calculate the deferred tax asset/liability for 20.0 to 20.3. Assume that Charlie Ltd has no intention to recover the carrying amount of the plant through sale.
d. Calculate profit after tax for 20.0 to 20.3.
e. Prepare the journal entries required to account for the depreciation, revaluation of plant, deferred tax and transfers to reserves from 20.0 to 20.3 using both methods (IAS 16.35) to account for accumulated depreciation. Journal narrations are not required.
f. Prepare the note regarding property, plant and equipment for 20.0 to 20.3 using both methods (IAS 16.35) to account for accumulated depreciation.

Your answer must comply with the requirements of International Financial Reporting Standards (IFRS).

❖ Suggested solution IAS 16.11[@]

a. Calculation of annual depreciation and carrying amounts

	20.0 Rand	**20.1 Rand**	**20.2 Rand**	**20.3 Rand**
Gross replacement cost	130 000	140 000	150 000	160 000
Depreciation (10%)	13 000	14 000	15 000	16 000
Historical cost	12 000	12 000	12 000	12 000
Revaluation surplus	1 000	2 000	3 000	4 000
Accumulated depreciation*	(13 000)	(28 000)	(45 000)	(64 000)
Net replacement cost	117 000	112 000	105 000	96 000

* These amounts do not appear in the statements, but are provided so that the net replacement cost can be calculated.

13 000 × 1 = 13 000
14 000 × 2 = 28 000
15 000 × 3 = 45 000
16 000 × 4 = 64 000

The net replacement costs can also be calculated as follows at 31 December:

20.0	9/10 × 130 000 = 117 000
20.1	8/10 × 140 000 = 112 000
20.2	7/10 × 150 000 = 105 000
20.3	6/10 × 160 000 = 96 000

Calculations: revaluation surplus

	20.0 Rand	**20.1 Rand**	**20.2 Rand**	**20.3 Rand**
Plant at valuation				
End of year	117 000	112 000	105 000	96 000
Depreciation for the year	13 000	14 000	15 000	16 000
Plant at valuation				
Beginning of year	130 000	126 000	120 000	112 000
Carrying amount	(120 000)	(117 000)	(112 000)	(105 000)
Revaluation of plant				
Beginning of year	10 000	9 000	8 000	7 000
Historical carrying amounts	(108 000)	(96 000)	(84 000)	(72 000)
Revaluation carrying amounts	117 000	112 000	105 000	96 000
Revaluation surplus	9 000	16 000	21 000	24 000
Less deferred tax (29%)	(2 610)	(4 640)	(6 090)	(6 960)
Revaluation surplus balance	6 390	11 360	14 910	17 040

OR

	20.0 Rand	**20.1 Rand**	**20.2 Rand**	**20.3 Rand**
Opening balance	–	6 390	11 360	14 910
Revaluation for the year	10 000	9 000	8 000	7 000
Deferred tax (29%)	(2 900)	(2 610)	(2 320)	(2 030)
Transfer to retained earnings	(710)	(1 420)	(2 130)	(2 840)
Revaluation surplus balance	6 390	11 360	14 910	17 040

b. Current tax expense

	20.0 to 20.3 Rand
Profit before depreciation	80 000
Tax allowance	
Wear and tear (12%) (1)	(14 400)
Taxable income	65 600
Current tax (29%)	19 024

(1) 120 000 × 12% = 14 400

c. Deferred tax asset/liability

	CA Rand	TB Rand	TD Rand	DTL Rand (Dr)/Cr	P or L Rand Dr/(Cr)
Cost – 1 January 20.0	120 000	120 000	–	–	
Wear-and-tear allowance/ depreciation (P or L)	(13 000)	(14 400)	1 400	406	406
Revaluation (OCI)	10 000	–	10 000	2 900	
31 December 20.0 – balances	117 000	105 600	11 400	3 306	
Wear-and-tear allowance/ depreciation (P or L)	(14 000)	(14 400)	400	116	116
Revaluation (OCI)	9 000	–	9 000	2 610	
31 December 20.1 – balances	112 000	91 200	20 800	6 032	
Wear-and-tear allowance/ depreciation (P or L)	(15 000)	(14 400)	(600)	(174)	(174)
Revaluation (OCI)	8 000	–	8 000	2 320	
31 December 20.2 – balances	105 000	76 800	28 200	8 178	
Wear-and-tear allowance/ depreciation (P or L)	(16 000)	(14 400)	(1 600)	(464)	(464)
Revaluation (OCI)	7 000	–	7 000	2 030	
31 December 20.3 – balances	96 000	62 400	33 600	9 744	

Deferred tax	**20.0 Rand**	**20.1 Rand**	**20.2 Rand**	**20.3 Rand**
(Asset)/liability	3 306	6 032	8 178	9 744

CA = Carrying amount
TB = Tax base
TD = Temporary difference
DTL = Deferred tax liability
P or L = Profit or loss (movement)

d. Profit after tax for the years ended 31 December

	20.0 Rand	**20.1 Rand**	**20.2 Rand**	**20.3 Rand**
Profit before depreciation	80 000	80 000	80 000	80 000
Depreciation	(13 000)	(14 000)	(15 000)	(16 000)
Historical cost	12 000	12 000	12 000	12 000
Revaluation surplus	1 000	2 000	3 000	4 000
Profit before tax	67 000	66 000	65 000	64 000
Income tax expense	(19 430)	(19 140)	(18 850)	(18 560)
Current	19 024	19 024	19 024	19 024
Deferred	406	116	(174)	(464)
Profit after tax	47 570	46 860	46 150	45 440

e. Journals

Method 1: To adjust accumulated depreciation proportionately (IAS 16.35(a))

	20.0 Rand Dr/(Cr)	20.1 Rand Dr/(Cr)	20.2 Rand Dr/(Cr)	20.3 Rand Dr/(Cr)
Plant at valuation	130 000	10 000	10 000	10 000
Plant at cost	(120 000)	–	–	–
Accumulated depreciation (1)	–	(1 000)	(2 000)	(3 000)
Gain on revaluation (OCI)	(10 000)	(9 000)	(8 000)	(7 000)
Income tax on items in OCI	2 900	2 610	2 320	2 030
Deferred tax asset/liability (SFPos)	(2 900)	(2 610)	(2 320)	(2 030)

(1) (14 000 × 2) – (14 000 + 13 000) = 1 000;
(15 000 × 3) – (14 000 + 14 000 + 15 000) = 2 000;
(16 000 × 4) – [(15 000 × 3) + 16 000)] = 3 000

Method 2: To set off accumulated depreciation against the gross carrying amount (IAS 16.35(b))

	20.0 Rand Dr/(Cr)	20.1 Rand Dr/(Cr)	20.2 Rand Dr/(Cr)	20.3 Rand Dr/(Cr)
Accumulated depreciation	–	13 000	14 000	15 000
Plant at valuation (1)	130 000	(4 000)	(6 000)	(8 000)
Plant at cost	(120 000)	–	–	–
Gain on revaluation (OCI)	(10 000)	(9 000)	(8 000)	(7 000)
Income tax on items in OCI	2 900	2 610	2 320	2 030
Deferred tax asset/liability (SFPos)	(2 900)	(2 610)	(2 320)	(2 030)

For methods 1 and 2:

	20.0 Rand Dr/(Cr)	20.1 Rand Dr/(Cr)	20.2 Rand Dr/(Cr)	20.3 Rand Dr/(Cr)
Depreciation (P or L)	13 000	14 000	15 000	16 000
Accumulated depreciation	(13 000)	(14 000)	(15 000)	(16 000)
Income tax expense (P or L)	406	116	(174)	(464)
Deferred tax liability (SFPos)	(406)	(116)	174	464
Revaluation surplus (equity) (2)	710	1 420	2 130	2 840
Retained earnings (note 1)	(710)	(1 420)	(2 130)	(2 840)

(1) 130 000 – 126 000 = 4 000; 126 000 – 120 000 = 6 000; 120 000 – 112 000 = 8 000
(2) (13 000 – 12 000) × 71% = 710; (14 000 – 12 000) × 71% = 1 420;
(15 000 – 12 000) × 71% = 2 130; (16 000 – 12 000) × 71% = 2 840

f. Method 1

To adjust accumulated depreciation proportionately – IAS 16.35(a).

Plant	**20.0 Rand**	**20.1 Rand**	**20.2 Rand**	**20.3 Rand**
Carrying amount at beginning of year	–	117 000	112 000	105 000
Revalued cost	–	130 000	140 000	150 000
Accumulated depreciation	–	(13 000)	(28 000)	(45 000)
Movements for the year:				
Additions	120 000	–	–	–
Revaluation	10 000	9 000	8 000	7 000
Depreciation (part a.)	(13 000)	(14 000)	(15 000)	(16 000)
Carrying amount at end of year (part a.)	117 000	112 000	105 000	96 000
Revalued cost	130 000	140 000	150 000	160 000
Accumulated depreciation	(13 000)	(28 000)	(45 000)	(64 000)

Plant is revalued annually on 31 December by an independent sworn appraiser on a gross replacement cost basis, with reference to observable prices in an active market. If plant was carried at cost less accumulated depreciation, the carrying amount would have been as follows:

	20.0 Rand	**20.1 Rand**	**20.2 Rand**	**20.3 Rand**
Carrying amount (1)	108 000	96 000	84 000	72 000

(1) Annual depreciation based on cost: 120 000/10 = 12 000
Carrying amount 20.0: 120 000 – 12 000 = 108 000 and then annually less 12 000

Method 2

To set off accumulated depreciation against the gross carrying amount – IAS 16.35(b).

Plant	**20.0 Rand**	**20.1 Rand**	**20.2 Rand**	**20.3 Rand**
Carrying amount at beginning of year	–	117 000	112 000	105 000
Revalued cost	–	130 000	126 000	120 000
Accumulated depreciation	–	(13 000)	(14 000)	(15 000)
Movements for the year:				
Additions	120 000	–	–	–
Revaluation	10 000	9 000	8 000	7 000
Depreciation (part a.)	(13 000)	(14 000)	(15 000)	(16 000)
Carrying amount at end of year (part a.)	117 000	112 000	105 000	96 000
Revalued cost	130 000	126 000	120 000	112 000
Accumulated depreciation	(13 000)	(14 000)	(15 000)	(16 000)

Plant is revalued annually on 31 December by an independent sworn appraiser on a gross replacement cost basis, with reference to observable prices in an active market. If plant was carried at cost less accumulated depreciation, the carrying amount would have been as follows:

	20.0 Rand	20.1 Rand	20.2 Rand	20.3 Rand
Carrying amount (1)	108 000	96 000	84 000	72 000

(1) Annual depreciation based on cost: 120 000/10 = 12 000
Carrying amount 20.0: 120 000 – 12 000 = 108 000 and then annually less 12 000

❑ QUESTION IAS 16.12

Zozo Ltd owns land with a cost of R800 000. This land was carried at cost in the financial statements of previous years. The directors are, however, of the opinion that the statement of financial position will reflect more relevant information if the land is revalued, and therefore decided that this will be done from the current financial year onwards. An independent sworn appraiser determined that the fair value of the land amounted to R1 000 000 on 1 January 20.5. Assume a tax rate of 30%.

Required

a. Discuss whether or not deferred tax must be raised on the revaluation surplus of R200 000, if capital gains are **not taxed.**
b. Discuss whether or not deferred tax must be raised on the revaluation surplus of R200 000, if 66.6% of capital gains **are taxed.**

Note: If you conclude that deferred tax must be raised in any of the scenarios above, also briefly address the recognition and measurement thereof. Your solution must comply with the requirements of International Financial Reporting Standards (IFRS).

❖ Suggested solution IAS 16.12

a. Land is regarded as a non-depreciable asset, as it has an unlimited useful life. Land will therefore never be consumed, and will be carried in the statement of financial position until it is eventually sold. This implies that the carrying amount of land can only be recovered by selling it. Consequently, the deferred tax relating to the land will reflect the tax consequences of selling the land. As capital gains (according to the question) are not taxed, the revaluation surplus will never result in any current tax, and therefore no deferred tax will be raised on the revaluation surplus.

b. Similar to scenario a., it is necessary to determine what the tax consequences will be if the land is sold. If it is assumed that the land was purchased subsequent to 1 October 2001 (when capital gains tax was introduced) the total revaluation surplus of R200 000 will be regarded as a taxable capital gain if the land was sold on 1 January 20.5 for R1 000 000. Only 66.6% of this capital gain will, however, be included in taxable income, as only 66.6% of the capital gain will be taxed. The potential current tax thus amounts to R200 000 × 66.6% × 30% = R40 000, but this tax will only become payable once the land is actually sold. For accounting purposes this amount is, however, immediately raised as deferred tax in order to match the tax consequence with the revaluation gain in the current year. The deferred tax account will be credited with R40 000, while the revaluation surplus (through other comprehensive income) will be debited with the same amount. Note that the deferred tax follows the gain, and therefore goes to other comprehensive income and not through profit or loss.

Note: Even though the deferred tax on the revaluation is based on the tax consequences as if the land was to be sold, the land is not 'held for sale' and thus IFRS 5 is not applicable.

❑ QUESTION IAS 16.13@

Clever Ltd decided to revalue its specialised item of plant on 31 December 20.3. Details of the plant on 31 December 20.3 were as follows:

	Rand
Cost (1 January 20.1)	100 000
Carrying amount	70 000
Tax base	40 000

The net replacement cost of the plant was determined to be R130 000 with a residual value of R110 000 on 31 December 20.3. The plant will be used for another two years before being sold at the expected residual value. The tax rate is 30%, and 66.6% of capital gains is taxable.

Required

Calculate the revaluation surplus and the balance of deferred tax at 31 December 20.3. Your answer must comply with the requirements of International Financial Reporting Standards (IFRS).

❖ Suggested solution IAS 16.13@

The revaluation surplus is R43 002 (1) and the balance of deferred tax is R25 998.

(1) 60 000 – 16 998 = 43 002

Calculations

Revaluation surplus and deferred tax

	A **Rand**	**B** **Rand**	**C** **Rand**	**D** **Rand**	**E** **Rand**
Carrying amount					
31 December 20.3	70 000	70 000	40 000	30 000	9 000
Revaluation (1) (2)	60 000	–	–	60 000	16 998
Balance after revaluation (3)	130 000	70 000	40 000	90 000	25 998

A = **Carrying amount – revalued**
B = **Carrying amount – cost**
C = **Tax base**
D = **Temporary differences**
E = **Deferred tax liability**

(1) 130 000 – 70 000 = 60 000
(2) 25 998 – 9 000 = 16 998
(3) The fact that the asset will be used until the end of its useful life and then sold at its residual value (deemed selling price on disposal date) results in the balance of deferred tax to be calculated as follows to reflect the possible future tax implications of the plant:
The value from 110 000 (residual value) to 130 000 (valuation) will be recovered through use, and deferred tax is at 30% because the asset will still be used until the end of its useful life. The deferred tax on this will be (130 000 – 110 000) × 30% = 6 000.
The value from 100 000 (cost) to 110 000 (residual value) will be recovered through sale because the residual value is the deemed selling price and will be taxed at the capital gains tax rate of 66.6% × 30%. The deferred tax on this will be (110 000 – 100 000) × 66.6% × 30% = 1 998.
The value from 40 000 (tax base) to 100 000 (cost) will be recovered through sale (which represents the recoupment of the capital allowances when the asset is sold at its residual value) and will be taxed at a rate of 30%. The deferred tax on this will be (100 000 – 40 000) × 30% = 18 000.
The total deferred tax balance at the end of 20.3 is thus: 6 000 + 1 998 + 18 000 = 25 998.

❑ QUESTION IAS 16.14

The following is included in the property, plant and equipment of All Africa Ltd:

Printing equipment with an estimated useful life of six years and an insignificant residual value was purchased at a cost of R300 000 in January 20.6. At the first three year ends, the useful life, pattern of use and residual values of the equipment were reviewed, and management found that the initial estimates were still applicable.

Case 1

The equipment was written off in the first three years for financial reporting purposes using the sum of the digits method. In 20.9 the company decided to change the method for providing for depreciation to the straight-line method. The useful life of the equipment is estimated as originally envisaged.

Case 2

The equipment was depreciated for the first three years using the straight-line method. In 20.9 the company estimated that the remaining useful life will be two years with a residual value of R20 000.

Required

For both cases, calculate the effect of the change, and disclose the note on profit before tax of All Africa Ltd for the year ended 31 December 20.9 so as to comply with the requirements of International Financial Reporting Standards (IFRS). Assume that All Africa Ltd uses the reallocation method to account for changes in estimates.

❑ QUESTION IAS 16.15

On 1 January 20.1, Ship Ltd acquired an oil tanker at a cost of R10 000 000. The company initially decided to replace the oil tanker once it became 10 years old and depreciated it on the straight-line method over the useful life to its residual value.

Owing to inflation the residual value is expected to increase annually.

Details of the oil tanker's estimated useful life at the beginning of each year and its expected residual value are as follows:

Year	**Remaining useful life**	**Residual value Rand**
20.1	10 years	8 000 000
20.2	8 years	9 000 000
20.3	7 years	9 500 000
20.4	6 years	9 750 000

Required

a. Calculate the depreciation for the years ending 31 December 20.1 to 20.4 and the carrying amount of the oil tanker at each year end.
b. Prepare the note on profit before tax of Ship Ltd for the year ended 31 December 20.2 so as to comply with the requirements of International Financial Reporting Standards (IFRS).

❑ QUESTION IAS 16.16

Furnace
Beta Ltd operates a furnace, purchased on 1 January 20.1 at a cost R18 000 000 in cash. Included in this amount was R4 000 000 in respect of the lining of the furnace. The expected useful life of the furnace is 20 years and it is expected to produce products constantly over this time. The residual value of this asset is insignificant. Relining of the furnace is expected to be required every five years and consequently the lining was replaced on 1 January 20.6 at a cost of R4 500 000 in cash.

Aircraft
On 1 January 20.5, Beta Ltd purchased a small aircraft at a cost of R1 850 000 in order to undertake business trips. The useful life of the aircraft is 15 years. However, the useful life of the aircraft's seats (cost R300 000) and the galley (cost R250 000) is only five years. The residual value of the galley is estimated at R20 000. No other component had a significant residual value. Depreciation is calculated on the straight-line basis over the expected useful life.

Major inspections of the aircraft shall be performed after every 500 hours of flight at an expected cost of R150 000 per inspection.

On 31 December 20.5, 300 hours of flight had been undertaken. By 30 June 20.6, 500 hours of flight would have been undertaken, but for practical reasons management decided to perform the inspection on 1 June 20.6 after 450 hours of flight at a cost of R145 000. On 31 December 20.6, another 200 hours of flight had been undertaken since the inspection on 1 June 20.6.

On 31 August 20.6, bad weather caused the aircraft to be damaged during landing. The left wing was replaced at a cost of R220 000 paid in cash. The wing was initially not treated as a separate component and the cost thereof was not specified separately when the aircraft was acquired. Management estimated that the initial cost attributed to the wing amounted to R200 000.

Additional information

Day-to-day servicing (cost of material and labour) of the furnace and the aircraft for the years ended 31 December 20.6 and 31 December 20.5 was as follows:

	20.6 **Rand**	**20.5** **Rand**
Furnace	50 000	48 000
Aircraft	33 000	27 000

Required

Prepare the note on property, plant and equipment of Beta Ltd for the year ended 31 December 20.6 so as to comply with the requirements of International Financial Reporting Standards (IFRS).

❑ QUESTION IAS 16.17

The following balances are taken from the financial statements of Arend Ltd for the year ended 31 December 20.3:

	Cost **Rand**	**Accumulated depreciation** **Rand**	**Carrying amount** **Rand**
Catering equipment	400 000	120 000	280 000
Office equipment	120 000	80 000	40 000
Hotel furniture	800 000	520 000	280 000
Garden furniture	60 000	40 000	20 000
Vehicles	380 000	280 000	100 000
Land and hotel buildings (separable)	1 000 000	240 000	760 000
Capitalised leased assets:			
Catering equipment	120 000	80 000	40 000

Additional information

1. Depreciation rates and methods:
   - Catering equipment – 20% p.a. straight line.
   - Office equipment – 10% p.a. diminishing balance.
   - Hotel furniture – 15% p.a. diminishing balance.
   - Garden furniture – 10% p.a. straight line.
   - Vehicles – 20% p.a. straight line.
   - Hotel buildings – 2% p.a. straight line.
   - Capitalised leased assets:
     - Catering equipment – sum of the digits method over the term of the lease.

The catering equipment held under a lease agreement (recognised as a right-of-use asset) has a useful life which differs from that of the purchased equipment, and a different depreciation method is therefore used.

2. The catering equipment held under lease agreement was obtained on 1 January 20.0 and the lease agreement covers the period from date of acquisition to 31 December 20.8.

3. Catering equipment (not leased) was sold on 1 July 20.4 for R2 000. The cost and accumulated depreciation at 31 December 20.3 was R10 000 and R6 000 respectively.

4. On 31 December 20.4, certain items of the hotel furniture were withdrawn from use and are standing idle. However, they have been kept as management is uncertain of their future use. The cost and accumulated depreciation at 31 December 20.3 was R80 000 and R50 000 respectively.

5. The proceeds from the sale of vehicles on 1 October 20.4 was R3 000. The cost and accumulated depreciation at 31 December 20.3 was R6 000 and R4 000 respectively.

6. The land component of land and hotel buildings represents 22% of the total cost. The land and hotel buildings are situated on the farm Keurboomsriver and comprise a hotel, outbuildings and land, measuring 11,143 hectares in the district of Plettenberg Bay. The land and hotel buildings were purchased some time ago.

7. The following assets were purchased for cash during the year:
   - Microwave oven – 1 April 20.4 = R25 000
   - Word processor – 1 July 20.4 = R30 000
   - Dishwasher – 1 September 20.4 = R12 000
   - Delivery vehicle – 1 October 20.4 = R22 000

8. There were no further transactions involving property, plant and equipment during the year under review.
9. Assume that all purchases and sales were for cash.
10. Right-of-use assets are not presented separately from property, plant and equipment in the statement of financial position.
11. Assume that the requirements of IFRS 5 were not met until the date of the sale and that the assets were never classified as 'held for sale'.

Required

a. Prepare all the journal entries required to account for the transactions (including cash transactions) for the year ended 31 December 20.4. Ignore taxation.
b. Disclose all property, plant and equipment and relevant items in the financial statements of Arend Ltd for the year ended 31 December 20.4 so as to comply with the requirements of International Financial Reporting Standards (IFRS). Comparative amounts are not required. Ignore the note on the preparation of the financial statements and compliance with International Financial Reporting Standards (IFRS). Ignore the disclosure requirements of IFRS 5.

❑ QUESTION IAS 16.18@

The following information relates to plant of Eagle Ltd, a listed company which manufactures and markets a number of products. Manufacturing is carried out in two different plants and the useful life of each of the plants is different. The plants will be valued annually from 20.5 at replacement cost by an independent sworn appraiser with reference to observable prices in an active market.

Plant	**Diamond Rand**	**Sapphire Rand**
Historical cost	200 000	150 000
Accumulated depreciation – 1 January 20.5	(39 000)	(54 000)
Carrying amount – 1 January 20.5	161 000	96 000
Gross replacement cost – 31 December 20.5	250 000	137 500
Depreciation rate (straight-line)	15%	12%

The tax rate was 30% for 20.4 and 20.5. Ignore capital gains tax.

The revaluation surplus is realised to retained earnings over the remaining useful life of the underlying asset. The decrease in the replacement cost of Sapphire is permanent.

The accumulated depreciation is adjusted in proportion at the time of the valuation. Depreciation shall be based on the gross replacement cost at the end of the year.

The profit for the year after taking the above information into account is R300 000 and the balance of retained earnings on 1 January 20.5 is R275 000.

Required

a. Prepare all the journal entries to account for the transactions relating to plants for the year ended 31 December 20.5. (Account for each plant separately.) Journal narrations are not required.
b. Prepare the statement of profit or loss and other comprehensive income of Eagle Ltd for the year ended 31 December 20.5 in accordance with the requirements of International Financial Reporting Standards (IFRS).
c. Prepare the statement of changes in equity of Eagle Ltd for the year ended 31 December 20.5 so as to comply with the requirements of International Financial Reporting Standards (IFRS).
d. Prepare the following notes of Eagle Ltd for the year ended 31 December 20.5 so as to comply with the requirements of International Financial Reporting Standards (IFRS):
   - Property, plant and equipment.
   - Profit before tax.

IAS 19

Employee benefits

❑ QUESTIONS AND SOLUTIONS

IAS 19.1	Short-term and termination benefits, bonus: disclosure of profit before tax note with no comparative amounts
IAS 19.2	Defined contribution plan, no tax implications: disclosure of relevant notes with comparative amounts
IAS 19.3	Employee benefits, accumulating, non-vesting leave, bonus, annual salary increase, deferred tax implications: calculation of monthly cost to company; monthly journal entries to account for employee benefits and settlement of liabilities; calculation of total annual employee cost; calculation of leave pay accrual if accumulated leave was to be paid (instead of used)
IAS 19.4@	Defined benefit plan, interest, past service cost, no tax implications: calculation of actuarial gains or losses (no asset ceiling); presentation of actuarial gains or losses in financial statements (no asset ceiling); disclosure of relevant notes (no asset ceiling); calculation of actuarial gains or losses (asset ceiling); disclosure of net defined benefit asset (asset ceiling)
IAS 19.5@	Other long-term benefits, interest, actuarial gains and losses, current and deferred tax implications: disclosure of relevant amounts and notes in the statement of financial position
IAS 19.6	Leave liability, accumulating, vesting leave with limit on days to be carried forward, no tax implications: calculation of leave accrual at beginning of year; journal entries to account for leave for full year
IAS 19.7@	Defined benefit plan, interest, past service costs, no asset ceiling, deferred tax implications: disclosure of specific notes; calculation and journalising of deferred tax; preparation of statement of profit or loss and other comprehensive income and statement of changes in equity with comparative amounts

❑ QUESTIONS

IAS 19.8	Defined contribution plan, no tax implications: disclosure of relevant amounts and notes in the statement of financial position with no comparative amounts
IAS 19.9	Short-term benefits, defined contribution plan, vacation leave, accumulating sick leave: disclosure of profit before tax note with no comparative amounts
IAS 19.10@	Other long-term benefits, current and deferred tax implications: disclosure of relevant amounts and notes in the statement of financial position

@ *These questions contain topics or principles that were not included in the ITC syllabus of SAICA at the time of publishing this book, but might still be included in university syllabi.*

❑ QUESTION IAS 19.1

The following is an extract from the trial balance of Florida Ltd for the year ended 31 December 20.1:

	Note	Rand
Salaries paid in cash	1	1 615 000
Vacation leave compensation paid	2	35 000

Additional information

1. Owing to cash flow problems experienced during December 20.0, Florida Ltd paid the December 20.0 salaries, amounting to R95 000, only in January 20.1.

2. Each employee is entitled to 18 working days' paid vacation leave per year. Five days may be carried forward to the following year, after which it lapses without payment. Thirteen days may not be carried forward and are paid out if not used in the current year.

   During the year, R35 000 was paid out in respect of current year's vacation leave that was not used. It is expected that four of the unused five days' leave will be taken in the following year, amounting to an additional R28 000.

3. During December 20.1 the services of four part-time employees were terminated before the normal retirement date. The company drafted a detailed formal plan according to which an amount of R50 000 would be paid to each of the employees during February 20.2. The plan was announced before year end and thereby created a valid expectation for those affected that the amounts would be paid.

4. Florida Ltd's bonus policy provides for a bonus of 8% of profit for the year, payable to the employees during February of the following calendar year. The profit for the year ended 31 December 20.1, after the bonus payment of 8% and all other provisions, amounts to R966 000.

Required

Disclose the 'profit before tax' note of Florida Ltd for the year ended 31 December 20.1 in accordance with the requirements of International Financial Reporting Standards (IFRS).

Comparative amounts are not required.

❖ **Suggested solution IAS 19.1**

FLORIDA LTD
NOTES FOR THE YEAR ENDED 31 DECEMBER 20.1

1. Profit before tax

	20.1 Rand
Profit before tax is stated after taking the following into account:	
Employee benefits expense	1 867 000
Short-term employee benefits (1)	1 667 000
Termination benefits (5)	200 000

(1) 1 520 000 (2) + 63 000 (3) + 84 000 (4) = 1 667 000
(2) 1 615 000 – 95 000 = 1 520 000
(3) 35 000 + 28 000 = 63 000
(4) 966 000 / 92% × 8% = 84 000
(5) 50 000 × 4 = 200 000 (IAS 19.165)

❑ **QUESTION IAS 19.2**

All the employees of Atlanta Ltd belong to a funded provident fund (the Atlanta Provident Fund), which is classified as a defined contribution plan.

The following information relates to this plan:

	20.1 Rand	20.0 Rand
Gross salaries paid	2 860 000	2 600 000
Additional contributions by employer		
Retired employees	20 000	–
Current employees	30 000	–

Atlanta Ltd and all employees each contribute 7,5% of gross salaries to the provident fund.

Ignore all tax implications.

Required

Disclose the above-mentioned information in the notes of Atlanta Ltd for the year ended 31 December 20.1 in accordance with the requirements of International Financial Reporting Standards (IFRS).

❖ **Suggested solution IAS 19.2**

ATLANTA LTD
NOTES FOR THE YEAR ENDED 31 DECEMBER 20.1

1. Accounting policy

1.1 Post-employment benefits cost

Contributions to the Atlanta Provident Fund, a defined contribution plan, are recognised as an expense in profit or loss when employees have rendered services entitling them to the contributions.

1. Profit before tax	**20.1 Rand**	**20.0 Rand**
Profit before tax is stated after taking the following into account (IAS 19. 25 & 53):		
Employee benefits expense	3 124 500	2 795 000
Short-term employee benefits	2 860 000	2 600 000
Defined contribution plan expense (1) (2)	264 500	195 000

(1) 20.1: (2 860 000 × 7,5%) + 20 000 + 30 000 = 264 500;
20.0: 2 600 000 × 7,5% = 195 000

(2) Only the employer's contribution. The employee's contribution forms part of the gross salaries paid and is already included under short-term employee benefits.

❑ **QUESTION IAS 19.3**

Benjamin Ltd has 10 employees, all earning a gross salary of R20 000 per month. All the employees belong to a funded provident fund (defined contribution plan) and contribute 7,5% of their gross salary to the fund. Benjamin Ltd contributes the same amount to the fund. An employee's salary slip is as follows:

Employee: Mrs Lucky	**Rand**
Gross salary	20 000
Deductions	
PAYE	(4 000)
Provident fund (7,5%)	(1 500)
Other sundry statutory deductions	(400)
Net salary (paid into Mrs Lucky's account)	14 100

The net salaries are paid at the end of each month, while the deductions and contributions are paid at the beginning of the following month. In addition to the entity's contributions to the provident fund, Benjamin Ltd also incurs other sundry statutory costs of R1 000 per employee per month.

Each employee is entitled to 20 working days' paid vacation leave per year. A maximum of five days may be carried forward to the following year, after which it lapses with payment. At 31 December 20.8, each employee had four days unused leave and the directors expect that all four days will be taken as leave during the next financial year. All salary costs are expected to increase by 10% in the next financial year.

Although Benjamin Ltd is not contractually obliged to pay any bonuses to the employees, the directors decided to pay each employee a bonus of R5 000, based on their services rendered during the current year. During the last week of December 20.8, the directors sent an internal memo to this effect to all employees. The bonuses will be paid in the second week of January 20.9.

The tax rate is 28%. Assume that all salary costs paid in cash by Benjamin Ltd are deductible for tax purposes when the cash is paid. Assume that there are 20 working days per month. Assume that there have been no resignations and appointments during 20.8 and 20.9.

Required

a. Calculate the total monthly cost to the company (excluding bonuses) per employee of Benjamin Ltd.
b. Prepare the journal entries (including cash payments and deferred tax, but not current tax) for December 20.8 to account for all employee benefits of Benjamin Ltd.
c. Prepare the journal entries for January 20.9 to account for all the payments made in respect of the employee deductions and Benjamin Ltd's contributions.
d. Calculate the total expense for employee benefits of Benjamin Ltd for the year ended 31 December 20.8.
e. Indicate what the amount of the leave pay accrual in part b would have been if it was expected that the four unused leave days as at 31 December 20.8 would be paid out in cash during December 20.9 (the employer's contributions and other costs would normally not be made).

Your solution should be in accordance with the requirements of International Financial Reporting Standards (IFRS). Clearly show all calculations and work to the nearest rand. Assume all amounts to be material.

❖ **Suggested solution IAS 19.3**

a. Total monthly cost to company

	Rand
Gross salaries	20 000
Employer's contribution to provident fund (1)	1 500
Other statutory employer's costs	1 000
Total	22 500

(1) 20 000 × 7,5% = 1 500

b. Journal entries

	Rand Dr/(Cr)
December 20.8	
Short-term employee benefits: Gross salaries (P or L) (1)	200 000
SARS: PAYE payable (SFPos) (2)	(40 000)
Provident fund: Employees' contribution payable (SFPos) (3)	(15 000)
Other payables: Employees' deductions payable (SFPos) (4)	(4 000)
Bank (net salaries) (5)	(141 000)
Recording of monthly gross salaries	
Short-term employee benefits: Employer's costs (P or L) (6)	10 000
Other payables: Employer's costs payable (SFPos)	(10 000)
Recording of salary costs of employer	

	Rand Dr/(Cr)
Post-employment benefits: Defined contribution plan (P or L) (3)	15 000
Provident fund: Employer's contribution payable (SFPos)	(15 000)
Recording of employer's contribution to provident fund	
Short-term employee benefits: Additional leave compensation (P or L)	49 500
Leave pay accrual (SFPos) (7)	(49 500)
Recording of leave pay accrual	
Deferred tax asset (SFPos) (8)	13 860
Income tax expense (P or L)	(13 860)
Recording of deferred tax on leave pay accrual	
Short-term employee benefits: Bonuses (P or L)	50 000
Creditors: Bonuses payable (SFPos) (9)	(50 000)
Recording of bonuses payable	
Deferred tax asset (SFPos) (10)	14 000
Income tax expense (P or L)	(14 000)
Recording of deferred tax on bonuses payable	

(1) 10 × 20 000 = 200 000
(2) 10 × 4 000 = 40 000
(3) 10 × 20 000 × 7,5% = 15 000
(4) 10 × 400 = 4 000
(5) 10 × 14 100 = 141 000
(6) 10 × 1 000 = 10 000
(7) 10 × 4 × (22 500 × 1,1) (part a.) / 20 working days per month = 49 500
The leave pay accrual is based on the total cost to the company as the employer will still need to make its contributions while the employee is on leave. The measurement of the leave pay accrual also needs to reflect the increased salary as the amount that will be paid when the employee is on leave, will be based on the increased salary.
(8) 49 500 × 28% = 13 860. The carrying amount of the leave pay accrual is R49 500 and the tax base is RNil.
(9) 10 × 5 000 = 50 000
(10) 50 000 × 28% = 14 000. The carrying amount of the bonuses payable is R50 000, and the tax base is RNil.

c. **Journal entries**

	Dr/(Cr) Rand
January 20.9	
SARS: PAYE payable (SFPos)	40 000
Provident fund: Employees' contribution payable (SFPos)	15 000
Other payables: Employees' deductions payable (SFPos)	4 000
Bank	(59 000)
Payment of employees' deductions	
Other payables: Employer's costs payable (SFPos)	10 000
Provident fund: Employer's contribution payable (SFPos)	15 000
Bank	(25 000)
Payment of employer's contributions and costs	

	Dr/(Cr) Rand
Creditors: Bonuses payable (SFPos)	50 000
Bank	(50 000)
Payment of bonuses	

d. Total expense for employee benefits

	Rand
Gross salaries (see b.)	200 000
Employer's contribution to provident fund (see b.)	15 000
Other statutory employer's costs (see b.)	10 000
Total monthly payments	225 000
Annual equivalent (1)	2 700 000
Additional leave compensation (see b.)	49 500
Bonuses (see b.)	50 000
Total	2 799 500

(1) 225 000 × 12 = 2 700 000

e. Leave pay accrual – to be paid in cash

The measurement of the leave pay accrual will still reflect the increased salary as the amount that will be paid in future when the employee is on leave, will be based on the increased salary. However, the leave pay accrual is now based on the basic gross salary per employee (rather than on the total cost to company) as the employer will probably not need to make contributions to the provident fund and incur the other costs (depending on the specific leave terms agreed with employees).

Leave pay accrual to be paid in cash: 10 × 4 × (20 000 × 1,1) / 20 working days per month = 44 000.

❑ QUESTION IAS 19.4@

All the employees of Colorado Ltd are members of a funded pension fund (the Colorado Pension Fund), which is classified as a defined benefit plan. The fund is governed by the South African Pension Fund Act, 1956 (as amended).

The following information relates to the plan:

	20.2 Rand	20.1 Rand	20.0 Rand
Present value of the defined benefit obligation at the end of the year	1 850 000	1 700 000	1 600 000
Fair value of the plan assets at the end of the year	1 820 000	1 600 000	1 550 000
Current service costs	310 000	280 000	270 000
Contributions paid by Colorado Ltd to the fund (at 8% of gross salaries)	310 000	250 000	170 000
Benefits paid out by the fund to retired employees	360 000	400 000	340 000

At 31 December 20.2 the plan assets consist of the following:

- Land and buildings in the Johannesburg central business district (CBD) with a fair value of R1 200 000 (20.1: R1 000 000) occupied and used by Colorado Ltd.
- Equity instruments in Colorado Ltd with a fair value of R300 000 (20.1: R200 000).
- Various items of artwork valued at R320 000 (20.1: R400 000).

On 1 January 20.1, Colorado Ltd made amendments to the pension fund to increase certain benefits. The past service costs resulting from the increased benefits amounted to R60 000.

Additional information

	20.2	**20.1**	**20.0**
Discount rate at beginning of year	13,5%	14,0%	12,9%
Expected increase in salaries (for 20.3: 7%)	8,0%	10,0%	10,0%

An actuary, who is of the opinion that the plan is in a sound financial position, performed the relevant valuations on 31 December 20.2. The actuarial valuations will be performed again on 31 December 20.3.

Assume all transactions occur at year-end.

Required

a. Calculate the net actuarial gains or losses that should be recognised in the financial statements of Colorado Ltd for the years ended 31 December 20.2 and 20.1 in accordance with the requirements of International Financial Reporting Standards (IFRS).

b. Present the actuarial gains or losses, that should be recognised by Colorado Ltd for the year ended 31 December 20.2, in the financial statements in accordance with the requirements of International Financial Reporting Standards (IFRS).

c. Disclose the following notes of Colorado Ltd for the year ended 31 December 20.2 in accordance with the requirements of International Financial Reporting Standards (IFRS):
   - Profit before tax
   - Post-employment benefits
   - Characteristics of defined benefit plan

d. Calculate the net actuarial gains or losses to be recognised in the financial statements of Colorado Ltd for the years ended 31 December 20.2 and 20.1 in accordance with the requirements of International Financial Reporting Standards (IFRS) based on the following assumptions at 31 December 20.2:
   - The information that relates to the plan (current and prior years) remains the same, except that the fair value of the equity instruments in Colorado Ltd is R450 000 (20.1: R350 000), resulting in a total fair value of the plan assets of R1 970 000 (20.1: R1 750 000). The fair value of the total plan assets on 31 December 20.0 remained unchanged at R1 550 000; and
   - The present value of available future refunds from the plan and reductions in future contributions to the plan (asset ceiling) is R80 000 (20.1: R70 000).

e. Disclose the net defined benefit asset (based on the assumptions listed in d. above) in accordance with the requirements of International Financial Reporting Standards (IFRS) on the face of the statement of financial position of Colorado Ltd as at 31 December 20.2.

Note: Ignore the disclosure requirements of IAS 19 regarding sensitivity analyses of actuarial assumptions and other matters affecting the amount, timing and uncertainty of future cash flows (IAS 19.145-147). Also, ignore any normal or deferred taxation implications.

❖ **Suggested solution IAS 19.4@**

a. Actuarial gain on defined benefit obligation

	20.2 Rand	20.1 Rand
Benefit obligation – beginning of year	1 700 000	1 600 000
Current service costs	310 000	280 000
Past service costs	–	60 000
Interest expense (1)	229 500	224 000
Benefits paid out of the fund	(360 000)	(400 000)
∴ Actuarial gain	(29 500)	(64 000)
Benefit obligation – end of year	1 850 000	1 700 000

(1) 20.2: 1 700 000 × 13,5% = 229 500; 20.1: 1 600 000 × 14% = 224 000

Actuarial gain on plan assets

	20.2 Rand	20.1 Rand
Plan assets – beginning of year	1 600 000	1 550 000
Interest income (2)	216 000	217 000
Contributions paid into fund	310 000	250 000
Benefits paid out of the fund	(360 000)	(400 000)
∴ Actuarial gain/(loss)	54 000	(17 000)
Plan assets – end of year	1 820 000	1 600 000

(2) 20.2: 1 600 000 × 13.5% = 216 000; 20.1: 1 550 000 × 14% = 217 000

Net actuarial gain or loss

	20.2 Rand	20.1 Rand
Actuarial gain on defined benefit obligation	29 500	64 000
Actuarial gain/(loss) on plan assets	54 000	(17 000)
Net actuarial gain (remeasurement of the net defined benefit liability)	83 500	47 000

b. COLORADO LTD
STATEMENT OF PROFIT OR LOSS AND OTHER COMPREHENSIVE INCOME FOR THE YEAR ENDED 31 DECEMBER 20.2

	20.2 Rand	20.1 Rand
Other comprehensive income		
Items that will not be reclassified to profit or loss		
Remeasurement of the net defined benefit liability	83 500	47 000
Total other comprehensive income	83 500	47 000
Attributable to:*		
Owners of the parent	83 500	47 000
Non-controlling interest	–	–
	83 500	47 000

* If consolidated financial statements

c. COLORADO LTD
NOTES FOR THE YEAR ENDED 31 DECEMBER 20.2

1. Profit before tax

	20.2 Rand	20.1 Rand
Profit before tax is stated after taking the following into account:		
Employee benefits expense		
Short-term employee benefits (1)	3 875 000	3 125 000
Defined benefit cost	323 500	347 000
Service costs (2)	310 000	340 000
Net interest on net defined benefit liability (3)	13 500	7 000

(1) 20.2: 310 000 / 8% = 3 875 000; 20.1: 250 000 / 8% = 3 125 000
(2) 20.2: Current service cost 310 000;
20.1: Current service cost 280 000 + past service cost 60 000 = 340 000
(3) 20.2: 229 500 – 216 000 = 13 500; 20.1: 224 000 – 217 000 = 7 000

2. Post-employment benefits

2.1 Net defined benefit liability

	20.2 Rand	20.1 Rand
Present value of the defined benefit obligation	1 850 000	1 700 000
Fair value of the plan assets	(1 820 000)	(1 600 000)
Net defined benefit liability (IAS 19.63 & .140)	30 000	100 000

2.2 Reconciliation from the opening balance to closing balance of the net defined benefit liability (IAS 19.140)

	20.2 Rand	20.1 Rand
Opening balance of net defined benefit liability (4)	100 000	50 000
Defined benefit cost (through profit or loss)	323 500	347 000
Contributions paid into the fund	(310 000)	(250 000)
Remeasurement of the net defined benefit liability (through OCI)	(83 500)	(47 000)
Closing balance of net defined benefit liability	30 000	100 000

(4) 20.1 opening balance: 1 600 000 – 1 550 000 = 50 000

2.3 Reconciliation from the opening to closing balances of the present value of defined benefit obligation (IAS 19.140)

	20.2 Rand	20.1 Rand
Present value of defined benefit obligation at 1 January	1 700 000	1 600 000
Current service costs	310 000	280 000
Past service costs	–	60 000
Interest expense	229 500	224 000
Benefits paid	(360 000)	(400 000)
Actuarial gain	(29 500)	(64 000)
Present value of defined benefit obligation at 31 December	1 850 000	1 700 000

2.4 Reconciliation from the opening to closing balances of the fair value of plan assets (IAS 19.140)

	20.2 Rand	20.1 Rand
Fair value of plan assets at 1 January	1 600 000	1 550 000
Interest income	216 000	217 000
Contributions paid	310 000	250 000
Benefits paid	(360 000)	(400 000)
Actuarial gain/(loss)	54 000	(17 000)
Fair value of plan assets at 31 December	1 820 000	1 600 000

3. Characteristics of defined benefit plan (IAS 19.139 & .142-144)

The Colorado Pension Fund, which is governed by the South African Pension Fund Act, 1956 (as amended), is a final salary defined benefit plan for employees, to which no minimum funding requirements relate. All the employees are members of the pension fund. Trustees of the Colorado Pension Fund govern the plan.

The plan assets consist of the following:

	20.2 Rand	%	20.1 Rand	%
Land and buildings in the Johannesburg CBD (occupied and used by Colorado Ltd)	1 200 000	66	1 000 000	63
Equity instruments issued by Colorado Ltd	300 000	16	200 000	12
Various items of artwork	320 000	18	400 000	25
	1 820 000	100	1 600 000	100

Risks relating to these assets could include property market risk, as the most significant portion of assets consists of land and buildings. These assets run the risk of devaluation due to market changes. Being situated in the Johannesburg CBD could pose further risks (for example devaluation or direct damage due to riots/protests/vandalism in the proximity of the buildings). The fair value of artwork is dependent on fashion and personal preferences and therefore market risk relating to artwork also prevails (IAS 19.139b).

Actuarial valuations are performed annually. The most recent actuarial valuation was performed on 31 December 20.2, while the next valuation will be performed on 31 December 20.3. The actuary is of the opinion that the plan is in a sound financial position.

The principal actuarial assumptions at the reporting date (expressed as weighted averages) are:

	20.2 %	20.1 %
Discount rate	13,5	14,0
Expected increase in salaries (7% for 20.3)	8,0	10,0

Amendments to the fund to increase certain benefits occurred in 20.1. No amendments, curtailments or settlements took place in 20.2 (IAS 19.139c).

d. Net actuarial gain or loss

Actuarial gain on the plan assets	**20.2 Rand**	**20.1 Rand**
Plan assets – beginning of year	1 750 000	1 550 000
Interest income (1)	236 250	217 000
Contributions paid into fund	310 000	250 000
Benefits paid out of the fund	(360 000)	(400 000)
∴ Actuarial gain	33 750	133 000
Plan assets – end of year	1 970 000	1 750 000

(1) 20.2: 1 750 000 × 13.5% = 236 250; 20.1: 1 550 000 × 14% = 217 000

Effect of the asset ceiling	**20.2 Rand**	**20.1 Rand**
Surplus of the defined benefit plan asset (2)	120 000	50 000
Asset ceiling	80 000	70 000
Lower of the surplus and the asset ceiling (3)	80 000	50 000

(2) 20.2: 1 970 000 – 1 850 000 = 120 000
20.1: 1 750 000 – 1 700 000 = 50 000

(3) The net defined benefit plan asset should be measured at the lower of the surplus of the defined benefit plan asset and the asset ceiling. In 20.1, the surplus is the lower amount and consequently no adjustment needs to be made in 20.1 (the net defined benefit plan asset is already measured at the lower amount). The effect of the asset ceiling in 20.1 is thus RNil.

Net actuarial gain or loss

	20.2 Rand	**20.1 Rand**
Actuarial gain on defined benefit obligation (see a.)	29 500	64 000
Actuarial gain on plan assets	33 750	133 000
Remeasurement as a result of the asset ceiling (4)	(40 000)	–
Net actuarial gain (remeasurement of the net defined benefit asset)	23 250	197 000

(4) 120 000 – 80 000 = 40 000
IAS 19.126: Interest on the effect of the asset ceiling is part of the total change in the effect of the asset ceiling and is determined by multiplying the effect of the asset ceiling by the discount rate specified in IAS 19.83 (both as determined at the start of the annual reporting period). The difference between that amount (R0 × 13.5% = R0 interest for 20.2 as a result of the asset ceiling opening balance of R0) and the total change in the effect of the asset ceiling (R0 to R40 000) is included in the remeasurement of the net defined benefit plan asset.

e. **COLORADO LTD**
STATEMENT OF FINANCIAL POSITION AS AT 31 DECEMBER 20.2

	Note	**20.2 Rand**	**20.1 Rand**
ASSETS			
Non-current assets			
Defined benefit plan asset	xx	80 000	50 000

❑ QUESTION IAS 19.5@

All employees of Christopher Ltd qualify for long-service leave in terms of the current personnel policy. Every employee is therefore entitled to long-term compensated absences that relate to the number of years in service.

The following information relates to the Christopher Ltd long service leave fund:

	20.2	**20.1**
Discount rate – beginning of year	13%	12,5%
Current service costs	170 000	160 000
Benefits paid out by the fund	193 000	214 000
Contributions paid by Christopher Ltd to the fund	110 000	96 000
Fair value of plan assets – beginning of year	1 400 000	1 260 000
Present value of obligation – beginning of year	1 500 000	1 200 000
Present value of increased benefits on 1 January 20.1 (past service costs)	–	30 000

Actuarial valuations of the Christopher Ltd long service leave fund are performed annually. The most recent valuation was performed on 31 December 20.2. On this date the present value of the obligation amounted to R1 600 000 and the fair value of the plan assets to R1 490 000. The actuary is of the opinion that the fund is in a sound financial position.

Assume all transactions occur at year-end.

Christopher Ltd's profit before tax for the year ended 31 December 20.2, before taking into account any of the above-mentioned expenses, amounts to R2 400 000 (20.1: R1 900 000). Assume a tax rate of 28%. The company will be profitable and taxable in the foreseeable future.

Required

Disclose the above-mentioned information in the financial statements of Christopher Ltd for the year ended 31 December 20.2 in accordance with the requirements of International Financial Reporting Standards (IFRS).

Note: A statement of profit or loss and other comprehensive income, statement of changes in equity and a statement of cash flows are not required.

❖ **Suggested solution IAS 19.5@**

CHRISTOPHER LTD
STATEMENT OF FINANCIAL POSITION AS AT 31 DECEMBER 20.2

	Note	20.2 Rand	20.1 Rand
ASSETS			
Non-current assets			
Deferred tax (calc 4)	4	30 800	28 000
EQUITY AND LIABILITIES			
Non-current liabilities			
Long-term employee benefit liability (1) (calc 4)		110 000	100 000

(1) No further disclosures in the notes are required for 'other long-term employee benefits' (IAS 19.158).

CHRISTOPHER LTD
NOTES FOR THE YEAR ENDED 31 DECEMBER 20.2

1. Accounting policy

The financial statements are prepared on the historical cost basis in accordance with the requirements of International Financial Reporting Standards (IFRS). The following are the principal accounting policies.

1.1 Long-term employee benefit expense

Actuarial gains and losses, as well as past service costs, are recognised in profit or loss.

1.2 Deferred tax

Deferred tax is calculated on all temporary differences.

2. Profit before tax

	20.2 Rand	20.1 Rand
Included in profit before tax are the following:		
Employee benefits expense		
Long-service leave compensation (2) (calc 2)	120 000	256 000

(2) No further disclosure regarding the make-up of this amount is required for 'other long-term employee benefits' (IAS 19.158).

3. Income tax expense

	20.2 Rand	20.1 Rand
Major categories of tax expense		
Current tax expense (calc 3)	641 200	505 120
Deferred tax expense – current year (calc 4)	(2 800)	(44 800)
	638 400	460 320

4. Deferred tax

	20.2 Rand	20.1 Rand
Long-service leave compensation liability (calc 4)	30 800	28 000

A deferred tax asset has been provided because it is expected that the company will carry on generating taxable profit in the foreseeable future, against which deductible temporary differences can be set off.

Calculations

1. Actuarial gains/losses

On the plan assets	20.2 Rand	20.1 Rand
Balance at beginning of year	1 400 000	1 260 000
Interest income (3)	182 000	157 500
Benefits paid	(193 000)	(214 000)
Contributions paid in	110 000	96 000
∴ Actuarial gain/(loss)	(9 000)	100 500
Balance at end of year	1 490 000	1 400 000

(3) 20.2: 1 400 000 × 13% = 182 000; 20.1: 1 260 000 × 12.5% = 157 500

On the obligation

Balance at beginning of year	1 500 000	1 200 000
Interest expense (4)	195 000	150 000
Current service costs	170 000	160 000
Past service costs (IAS 19.156(a))	–	30 000
Benefits paid	(193 000)	(214 000)
∴ Actuarial (gain)/loss	(72 000)	174 000
Balance at end of year	1 600 000	1 500 000

On plan assets – gain/(loss)	(9 000)	100 500
On obligation – gain/(loss)	72 000	(174 000)
To recognise in profit or loss – gain/(loss)	63 000	(73 500)

(4) 20.2: 1 500 000 × 13% = 195 000; 20.1: 1 200 000 × 12.5% = 150 000

2. Long-service leave compensation (P or L)	**20.2 Rand**	**20.1 Rand**
Current service costs	170 000	160 000
Past service costs	–	30 000
Interest expense	195 000	150 000
Interest income	(182 000)	(157 500)
Actuarial (gain)/loss (calc 1)	(63 000)	73 500
	120 000	256 000

3. Income tax calculation	**20.2 Rand**	**20.1 Rand**
Profit before tax (given)	2 400 000	1 900 000
Long-service leave compensation	(120 000)	(256 000)
Profit before tax – final	2 280 000	1 644 000
Temporary differences	10 000	160 000
Long-service leave compensation (calc 2)	120 000	256 000
Contributions paid	(110 000)	(96 000)
Taxable income	2 290 000	1 804 000
Current tax at 28%	641 200	505 120

4. Deferred tax	**Carrying amount Rand**	**Tax base Rand**	**Temporary Difference Rand**	**Deferred tax Rand**
20.0				
Long-term benefit asset (1 200 000 – 1 260 000)	60 000	–	60 000	(16 800) L
20.1				
Movement (in P or L)				44 800
Long-term benefit liability (1 500 000 – 1 400 000)	(100 000)	–	(100 000)	28 000 A
20.2				
Movement (in P or L)				2 800
Long-term benefit liability (1 600 000 – 1 490 000)	(110 000)	–	(110 000)	30 800 A

❑ QUESTION IAS 19.6

Connecticut Ltd grants paid annual leave to all employees. All employees are entitled to 24 days leave per year which accrues to them evenly throughout the year. Eight of these leave days can be accumulated and carried forward indefinitely. If an employee has more than eight unused leave days left at the end of a financial year, the extra days are paid out in cash. All such cash payments take place in December.

Connecticut Ltd's total labour force consists of 40 employees. During the year, 5% of employees did not use their leave benefits at all, 70% used 10 days, 15% used 15 days and 5% used 20 days. Further, one employee took 36 days' leave while another took 28 days. These two employees both had enough accumulated leave from prior years to be able to take this leave. Leave taken is firstly accounted for against the current year's leave entitlement and then against accumulated entitlements that arose in the past. Assume that there have been no resignations and appointments during 20.0 and 20.1.

The leave pay accrual is created proportionately in relation to the average daily salary per employee expected to be paid as a result of the unused entitlement. Salary increases are effective from 1 January of every year and amount to a consistent 7% per year.

On 31 December 20.0 the accumulated number of leave days amounted to 176 (after payment of all days exceeding the eight days allowed to be carried forward) and the average annual salary per employee R120 000 (before the 20.1 increases became effective).

All accumulated leave is payable in full in cash if an employee were to terminate his service.

The daily cost of leave taken is equal to the daily average salary per employee (rounded off to the nearest rand).

Assume that all employees take their leave during July every year, when it is a quiet period from a business perspective.

Assume that all transactions take place at the end of the month.

Use 360 days per year for the purpose of calculations. Round off all amounts to the nearest rand.

Required

a. Determine the amount of the leave pay accrual of Connecticut Ltd as at 31 December 20.0.
b. Provide the full year's journal entries (in chronological sequence) in relation to annual leave (including cash transactions but excluding any tax and closing entries) of Connecticut Ltd for the year ended 31 December 20.1.

Your solution must comply with the requirements of International Financial Reporting Standards (IFRS).

❖ **Suggested solution IAS 19.6**

a. In terms of IAS 19.16 an entity shall measure the expected cost of accumulating compensated absences as the additional amount the entity expects to pay as a result of the unused entitlement. This implies that the measurement of the leave pay accrual needs to reflect the increased salaries.

Expected salary for 20.1: R120 000 × 1.07 = R128 400
Per day: R128 400 / 360 = R357 per day
Thus, leave pay accrual on 31 December 20.0 is R357 × 176 days = R62 832

b.

	Rand Dr/(Cr)
January 20.1	
Leave compensation (P or L) (2)	28 560
Leave pay accrual (SFPos)	(28 560)

	Rand Dr/(Cr)
February 20.1	
Leave compensation (P or L) (2)	28 560
Leave pay accrual (SFPos)	(28 560)
March 20.1	
Leave compensation (P or L) (2)	28 560
Leave pay accrual (SFPos)	(28 560)
April 20.1	
Leave compensation (P or L) (2)	28 560
Leave pay accrual (SFPos)	(28 560)
May 20.1	
Leave compensation (P or L) (2)	28 560
Leave pay accrual (SFPos)	(28 560)
June 20.1	
Leave compensation (P or L) (2)	28 560
Leave pay accrual (SFPos)	(28 560)
July 20.1	
Leave compensation (P or L) (2)	28 560
Leave pay accrual (SFPos)	(28 560)
Leave pay accrual (SFPos) (3)	169 218
Bank	(169 218)
August 20.1	
Leave compensation (P or L) (2)	28 560
Leave pay accrual (SFPos)	(28 560)
September 20.1	
Leave compensation (P or L) (2)	28 560
Leave pay accrual (SFPos)	(28 560)
October 20.1	
Leave compensation (P or L) (2)	28 560
Leave pay accrual (SFPos)	(28 560)
November 20.1	
Leave compensation (P or L) (2)	28 560
Leave pay accrual (SFPos)	(28 560)
December 20.1	
Leave compensation (P or L) (2)	28 560
Leave pay accrual (SFPos)	(28 560)
Leave pay accrual (SFPos) (4)	73 542
Bank	(73 542)
Leave compensation (P or L) (9)	11 400
Leave pay accrual (SFPos)	(11 400)

(1)	(120 000 × 1,07) / 360 = 357 per day			
(2)	357 (1) × (24 / 12) × 40 = 28 560 per month			
(3)	5% × 40 × 0	=	0	
	70% × 40 × 10	=	280	
	15% × 40 × 15	=	90	
	5% × 40 × 20	=	40	
	1 × 28	=	28	
	1 × 36	=	36	
			474	days × 357 (1) = 169 218 – leave taken

(4)	5% × 40 × (24 – 0 – 8)	=	32	
	70% × 40 × (24 – 10 – 8)	=	168	
	15% × 40 × (24 – 15 – 8)	=	6	
	5% × 40 × (24 – 20 – 4)	=	0	} None that has to be paid
	1 × (24 – 24)	=	0	
	1 × (24 – 24)	=	0	
			206	days × 357(1) = 73 542 – leave paid

(5) 176 + (2 × 12 × 40) – 474 – 206 = 456 days unused leave – 31 December 20.1

(6) Leave pay accrual 31 December 20.1: 456 (5) × [(128 400 (a) × 1,07) / 360] = 174 192

(7) Total leave pay accrual created 20.1: 28 560 (2) × 12 = 342 720

(8) Total leave payment/utilisation 20.1: 169 218 (3) + 73 542 (4) = 242 760

(9) Adjustment to leave pay accrual:

Leave pay accrual 31 December 20.0 (from a.)	62 832
Leave pay accrual created (7)	342 720
Leave pay accrual utilised (8)	(242 760)
Leave pay accrual 31 December 20.1 (6)	(174 192)
	11 400

Proof: During the year the leave pay accrual was based on R357 per day. Thus, the balance was 456 days × R357 = R162 792. However, the leave pay accrual is now to be based on the expected increased salary cost of R382 per day. Thus, the balance should be 456 days × R382 = R174 192. The adjustment is: 174 192 – 162 792 = 11 400.

❑ QUESTION IAS 19.7@

All the employees of Utah Ltd are members of the Utah Pension Fund, a defined benefit plan. The following information relates to the Pension Fund:

	20.6 Rand	**20.5 Rand**
Fair value of plan assets at 31 December	5 010 000	4 590 000
Present value of obligation at 31 December	5 540 000	4 990 000
Contributions paid	387 000	372 000
Current service costs	341 000	316 000
Discount rate at beginning of the year	10,7%	11,0%

On 1 January 20.5 the present value of the obligation amounted to R4 110 000 and the fair value of the plan assets to R3 970 000. On 31 December 20.6, benefits amounting to R319 700 (20.5: R300 670) were paid. Assume that all transactions occur at year-end.

During January 20.5 certain benefits were increased and the necessary amendments were made to the Utah Pension Fund. These amendments resulted in past service costs amounting to R360 000.

Actuarial valuations of the Utah Pension Fund are made annually using the projected unit credit method. On 31 December 20.4 cumulative actuarial gains amounting to R88 400 (before tax) had been included in retained earnings.

Utah Ltd's profit for the year, after taking into account all the above-mentioned information, amounts to R9 300 000 for the year ended 31 December 20.6 (20.5: R8 550 000). Assume a tax rate of 28%.

Required

a. Disclose the following notes in the financial statements of Utah Ltd for the year ended 31 December 20.6:
   - Profit before tax
   - Post-employment benefits

   Notes regarding accounting policy and characteristics of the defined benefit plan are not required.
b. Calculate deferred tax relating to the defined benefit plan of Utah Ltd and provide the journal entries for the deferred tax for the year ended 31 December 20.6 and 20.5.
c. Prepare the statement of profit or loss and other comprehensive income and the statement of changes in equity of Utah Ltd for the year ended 31 December 20.6.

Your answer should comply with the requirements of International Financial Reporting Standards (IFRS).

❖ **Suggested solution IAS 19.7@**

a. **UTAH LTD**
NOTES FOR THE YEAR ENDED 31 DECEMBER 20.6

1. **Profit before tax**

	20.6 Rand	20.5 Rand
Included in profit before tax are the following:		
Employee benefits expense		
Defined benefit costs	383 800	691 400
Service costs (1)	341 000	676 000
Net interest on net defined benefit liability (2)	42 800	15 400

(1) 20.5: Current service cost 316 000 + past service cost 360 000 = 676 000
(2) 20.5: (4 110 000 × 11% = 452 100) – (3 970 000 × 11% = 436 700) = 15 400
20.6: (4 990 000 × 10,7% = 533 930) – (4 590 000 × 10,7% = 491 130) = 42 800

2. **Post-employment benefits**

2.1 **Net defined benefit liability**

	20.6 Rand	20.5 Rand
Present value of the defined benefit obligation	5 540 000	4 990 000
Fair value of the plan assets	(5 010 000)	(4 590 000)
	530 000	400 000

2.2 Reconciliation from the opening balance to closing balance of the net defined benefit liability (IAS 19.140)

	20.6 Rand	20.5 Rand
Opening balance of net defined benefit liability (3)	400 000	140 000
Defined benefit cost (through profit or loss)	383 800	691 400
Contributions paid into the fund	(387 000)	(372 000)
Remeasurement of the net defined benefit liability (through OCI) (4)	133 200	(59 400)
Closing balance of net defined benefit liability	530 000	400 000

(3) 20.5: 4 110 000 – 3 970 000 = 140 000
(4) 20.5: 52 570 loss + 111 970 gain = 59 400 gain
20.6: 5 230 gain + 138 430 loss = 133 200 loss (also see notes 2.3 and 2.4)

2.3 Reconciliation of opening and closing balances of present value of defined benefit obligation (IAS 19.140)

	20.6 Rand	20.5 Rand
Present value of obligation at 1 January	4 990 000	4 110 000
Interest expense (2)	533 930	452 100
Current service costs	341 000	316 000
Past service costs – increased benefits	–	360 000
Benefits paid	(319 700)	(300 670)
Actuarial (gain)/loss	(5 230)	52 570
Present value of obligation at 31 December	5 540 000	4 990 000

2.4 Reconciliation of opening and closing balances of fair value of plan assets (IAS 19.140)

	20.6 Rand	20.5 Rand
Fair value of plan assets at 1 January	4 590 000	3 970 000
Interest income (2)	491 130	436 700
Contributions paid	387 000	372 000
Benefits paid	(319 700)	(300 670)
Actuarial gain/(loss)	(138 430)	111 970
Fair value of plan assets at 31 December	5 010 000	4 590 000

b. Calculation of deferred tax

Defined benefit plan	**Carrying amount Rand Dr/(Cr)**	**Tax base Rand**	**Temporary difference Rand**	**Deferred tax Rand Dr/(Cr)**	**Movement Rand Dr/(Cr)**
Balance 20.4 (3)	(140 000)	–	(140 000)	39 200	
Profit or loss:					
Employee benefit expense (see a.)	(691 400)				
Contributions	372 000		(319 400)	89 432	(89 432)
Other comprehensive income:					
Actuarial gain/loss (4)	59 400		59 400	(16 632)	16 632
Balance 20.5 (see note 2.1)	(400 000)	–	(400 000)	112 000	
Profit or loss:					
Employee benefit expense (see a.)	(383 800)				
Contributions	387 000		3 200	(896)	896
Other comprehensive income:					
Actuarial gain/(loss) (4)	(133 200)		(133 200)	37 296	(37 296)
Balance 20.6 (see note 2.1)	(530 000)	–	(530 000)	148 400	

Journal entries

	Dr/(Cr) Rand
20.5	
Deferred tax asset (SFPos)	72 800
Tax expense (OCI)	16 632
Income tax expense (P or L)	(89 432)
20.6	
Deferred tax asset (SFPos)	36 400
Income tax expense (P or L)	896
Tax expense (OCI)	(37 296)

c. UTAH LTD

STATEMENT OF PROFIT OR LOSS AND OTHER COMPREHENSIVE INCOME FOR THE YEAR ENDED 31 DECEMBER 20.6

	20.6 Rand	**20.5 Rand**
Profit for the year	9 300 000	8 550 000
Other comprehensive income		
Items that will not be reclassified to profit or loss	(95 904)	42 768
Actuarial gains/(losses) on defined benefit plans (4)	(133 200)	59 400
Tax expense (see b.)	37 296	(16 632)
Total comprehensive income for the year	9 204 096	8 592 768

UTAH LTD
STATEMENT OF CHANGES IN EQUITY FOR THE YEAR ENDED 31 DECEMBER 20.6

	Retained earnings Rand
Balance at 1 January 20.5	xxx
Changes in equity for 20.5	
Profit/Total comprehensive income for the year	8 592 768
Balance at 31 December 20.5	xxx
Changes in equity for 20.6	
Profit/Total comprehensive income for the year	9 204 096
Balance at 31 December 20.6	xxx

❑ QUESTION IAS 19.8

Nevada Ltd's labour force consists mainly of employees in training. The expected service term of employees is therefore limited to the training period, which ranges from two to five years, after which staff members normally resign to take up more permanent employment elsewhere. Owing to the temporary nature of the labour force, Nevada Ltd has adopted a policy whereby employees contribute to an independent defined contribution plan, the Nevada Provident Fund. Nevada Ltd's contribution is 14% of gross pensionable remuneration. Gross remuneration to employees for the year ended 31 December 20.1 amounted to R22 680 000. Payments made to the contribution plan amounted to R2 853 900 of which R200 000 relates to 20.0. All employees are members of the fund.

Required

Disclose the information in the statement of financial position and notes of Nevada Ltd for the year ended 31 December 20.1 in accordance with the requirements of International Financial Reporting Standards (IFRS). Ignore comparative amounts and any tax implications.

❑ QUESTION IAS 19.9

The following information relates to Iowa Ltd's employee benefits for the year ended 31 December 20.1:

1. Salaries and bonuses (a 13th cheque) paid, amounted to R5 500 000. The R5 500 000 included an amount of R40 000 outstanding at 31 December 20.0.

2. Contributions to the Iowa Provident Fund amounted to 8% of the annual salaries and bonuses.

3. Employees are obliged to take their 28 days' vacation leave during each year. Seven days may be paid out if not used in the current year. The company expects, based on past experience, which is expected to continue, that an average of three days will be paid out during January of the next year. The vacation leave accrual will be based on 360 working days and on salaries, including bonuses.

4. Each employee is entitled to 30 days' sick leave per annum. Sick leave can be accumulated for one year. At the end of the second year, sick leave (for years one and two) lapses with payment and the cycle starts again the following year. The current sick leave cycle ended on 31 December 20.1. Sick leave payments are made annually on 31 December.

   Past experience indicated that employees earning 70% of the total salaries (excluding bonuses, paid vacation leave and contributions to the provident fund) use five days, 20% use 16 days and 10% use 35 days. Sick leave is firstly taken from the previous year's balance brought forward, and thereafter from the current year's entitlement. All sick leave shortages are offset against annual vacation leave. Assume that there have been no resignations and appointments during 20.0 and 20.1. The total value of sick leave (salary on which the sick leave accrual was based) for the year ended 31 December 20.0 amounted to R380 000 per month. The value of the sick leave is based on salaries only (excluding bonuses, paid vacation leave and contributions to the provident fund). Salaries increased in 20.1, after the financial statements of 20.0 were approved.

Required

Disclose the profit before tax note in the financial statements of Iowa Ltd for the year ended 31 December 20.1 in accordance with the requirements of International Financial Reporting Standards (IFRS). Comparative amounts are not required.

Use 360 working days in your calculations. Round off all amounts to the nearest rand.

❑ QUESTION IAS 19.10@

All the employees of Mississippi Ltd are entitled to disability leave. These long-term employee benefits are split between permanent and temporary disability. Permanent disability benefits are paid from the date of disability to the date of retirement and are based on 105% of the final annual salaries. Temporary disability benefits are paid from the date of temporary disability to the date when the service is resumed and are based on 98% of the final annual salaries. No normal salaries will be payable for the period of disability. Salaries will probably increase with 8% (compound) on 1 January each year.

The following information relates to disability benefits;

	20.2	**20.1**	**20.0**
Discount rate	13,5%	15%	14%
Final annual salaries			
– Permanently disabled employees	R151 632	R140 400	R130 000
– Temporarily disabled employees	R79 000	R75 600	R70 000
Expected number of years' disability benefits outstanding on 31 December			
– Permanently disabled employees	1 year	2 years	3 years
– Temporarily disabled employees	1 year	2 years	3 years

Assume that disability starts at the beginning of a year. Assume that all payments are made at the end of the year. The profit before tax of Mississippi Ltd, before taking into account the above-mentioned expenses, amounted to R1 769 602 for the year ended 31 December 20.2 (20.1: R1 470 000). Assume a tax rate of 27%. The company will be profitable in the foreseeable future.

Required

Disclose the above information in the statement of financial position and notes of Mississippi Ltd for the year ended 31 December 20.2 in accordance with the requirements of International Financial Reporting Standards (IFRS). Round off all amounts to the nearest rand.

The following are **not** required:

- Note on compliance with International Financial Reporting Standards (IFRS).
- Note on deferred tax.
- Accounting policy note.

IAS 20 & SIC 10

Accounting for government grants and disclosure of government assistance

---

❑ QUESTIONS AND SOLUTIONS

IAS 20.1@	Grants related to assets, no deferred tax: journal entries
IAS 20.2@	Grants related to assets, including deferred tax: journal entries and deferred tax calculations
IAS 20.3@	Grants related to income where expenses are a constant amount each year, including deferred tax: journal entries
IAS 20.4@	Grants related to income where expenses vary over time, including deferred tax: journal entries and deferred tax calculations
IAS 20.5@	Discussion of government grants and disclosure of government assistance in terms of IAS 20 and SIC 10: discussion and application of theory

❑ QUESTIONS

IAS 20.6@	Repayment of grant related to assets, including deferred tax: journal entries and deferred tax calculations
IAS 20.7@	Repayment of grant related to assets, including deferred tax: disclosure and taxation consequences
IAS 20.8@	Repayment of grant relating to income for varying amounts of expenses, including deferred tax: journal entries
IAS 20.9@	Waiving of a loan provided by government: journal entries
IAS 20.10@	Non-monetary government grant: journal entries

@ These questions contain topics or principles that were not included in the ITC syllabus of SAICA at the time of publishing this book, but might still be included in university syllabi.
Please note: the whole IAS 20 is not included in the ITC syllabus of SAICA.

❑ QUESTION IAS 20.1@

Housing Ltd erected a number of houses for its employees at a cost of R1 000 000, which was settled on 1 January 20.0 in cash. These buildings, which have a useful life of 10 years, were completed and put into use on 1 January 20.0.

Housing Ltd received a government grant of R100 000 on 1 January 20.0, since the national government regards it as a priority to provide houses for all its citizens.

Assume a profit before tax prior to the above transactions of R500 000.

Ignore tax.

Required

a. Prepare the journal entries (cash transactions included) for the year ended 31 December 20.0 in respect of the above transactions if it is assumed that the government grant is presented in the statement of financial position as deferred income.
b. Prepare the journal entries (cash transactions included) for the year ended 31 December 20.0 in respect of the above transactions if it is assumed that the government grant is presented in the statement of financial position by deducting the government grant from the carrying amount of the asset.

Your solution must comply with the requirements of International Financial Reporting Standards (IFRS).

❖ Suggested solution IAS 20.1@

a. Journal entries on:

	Rand Dr/(Cr)
1 January 20.0	
Buildings – cost	1 000 000
Bank	(1 000 000)
Bank	100 000
Deferred income (SFPos)	(100 000)
31 December 20.0	
Depreciation	100 000
Accumulated depreciation on buildings	(100 000)
Deferred income (SFPos)	10 000
Deferred income amortised (P or L)	(10 000)

b. Journal entries on:

	Rand Dr/(Cr)
1 January 20.0	
Buildings – cost	1 000 000
Bank	(1 000 000)
Bank	100 000
Buildings – cost	(100 000)

	Rand Dr/(Cr)
31 December 20.0	
Depreciation (1)	90 000
Accumulated depreciation on buildings	(90 000)

(1) 900 000/10 = 90 000

☐ QUESTION IAS 20.2@

Builders Ltd erected a number of houses at a cost of R4 000 000, which was settled on 1 January 20.0 in cash. These buildings, which have a useful life of 10 years, were completed and put into use on 1 January 20.0.

Builders Ltd received a government grant of R1 000 000 on 1 January 20.0, since it is important for the national government to provide houses for all citizens.

Assume that this government grant complies with the definition of gross income and is fully taxable when received. An income tax allowance of 10% per annum on the straight-line method is allowed on the total cost of all houses.

Assume a profit before tax prior to accounting for the above transactions of R1,5 million.

Assume a tax rate of 27%.

Assume that there will be sufficient other future taxable income and that deferred tax assets can be recognised.

Required

a. Prepare the journal entries (cash transactions included) for the year ended 31 December 20.0 in respect of the above transactions if it is assumed that the government grant is presented in the statement of financial position as deferred income.
b. Prepare the journal entries (cash transactions included) for the year ended 31 December 20.0 in respect of the above transactions if it is assumed that the government grant is presented in the statement of financial position by deducting the government grant from the carrying amount of the asset.

Your solution must comply with the requirements of International Financial Reporting Standards (IFRS).

❖ Suggested solution IAS 20.2@

a. Journal entries on:

	Rand Dr/(Cr)
1 January 20.0	
Buildings – cost	4 000 000
Bank	(4 000 000)
Bank	1 000 000
Deferred income (SFPos)	(1 000 000)

	Rand Dr/(Cr)
31 December 20.0	
Depreciation (1)	400 000
Accumulated depreciation on buildings	(400 000)
Deferred income (SFPos) (2)	100 000
Amortisation of government grant (P or L)	(100 000)
Income tax expense (P or L) (calc 1)	567 000
South African Revenue Service/tax payable	(567 000)
Deferred tax (SFPos) (calc 1 and/or 2)	243 000
Income tax expense (P or L)	(243 000)

(1) 4 000 000/10 years = 400 000
(2) 1 000 000/10 years = 100 000

Calculations

1. Normal tax calculation (and test in respect of deferred tax)

	Rand
Profit before tax (given)	1 500 000
Depreciation	(400 000)
Government grant related to buildings amortised	100 000
Accounting profit before tax according to profit or loss	1 200 000
Temporary differences	900 000
Government grant received	1 000 000
Government grant amortised	(100 000)
Depreciation (4 000 000/10 years)	400 000
Wear-and-tear allowance (4 000 000/10 years)	(400 000)
Taxable income	2 100 000

Current tax at 27% = 2 100 000 × 27% = 567 000 debit in P or L
Deferred tax at 27% = 900 000 × 27% = 243 000 credit in P or L

2. Deferred tax calculation

	Carrying amount (CA) Rand	Tax base (TB) Rand	Temporary differences Rand	Deferred tax SFPos Rand
31 December 19.9	–	–	–	–
31 December 20.0				
Deferred income (1) (2)	(900 000)	–	(900 000)	243 000 Asset
Buildings (3) (4)	3 600 000	3 600 000	–	–
				243 000 Asset

(1) 1 000 000 – 100 000 = 900 000
(2) 900 000 × 27% = 243 000
(3) 4 000 000 – 400 000 = 3 600 000 CA
(4) 4 000 000 – 400 000 = 3 600 000 TB

The deferred income is a negative asset. In terms of IAS 12.8, deferred income is deemed to be revenue received in advance for the purpose of calculating deferred tax. The tax base of revenue received in advance is its carrying amount less any amount of the revenue that will not be taxable in future. The deferred income is not taxable in future, because the government grant received has already been fully taxed during the year of assessment ended 31 December 20.0.

Thus the movement in deferred tax allocated to profit or loss for the year ended 31 December 20.0 is R243 000 (movement from RNil to R243 000) as a credit amount.

Tax base on 31 December 20.0 = 900 000 – 900 000 (not taxable in future, because already taxed in the year of assessment ended 31 December 20.0) = RNil.

b. Journal entries on:

	Rand Dr/(Cr)
1 January 20.0	
Buildings – cost	4 000 000
Bank	(4 000 000)
Bank	1 000 000
Buildings – cost	(1 000 000)
31 December 20.0	
Depreciation (1)	300 000
Accumulated depreciation on buildings	(300 000)
Income tax expense (calc 1)	567 000
South African Revenue Service/tax payable	(567 000)
Deferred tax (SFPos) (calc 2)	243 000
Income tax expense (P or L)	(243 000)

(1) (4 000 000 – 1 000 000)/10 years = 300 000

Calculations

1. Normal tax calculation (and test in respect of deferred tax)

	Rand
Profit before tax (given)	1 500 000
Depreciation	(300 000)
Accounting profit before tax	1 200 000
Temporary differences	900 000
Government grant received	1 000 000
Depreciation	300 000
Wear-and-tear allowance (4 000 000 × 10% or 4 000 000/10 years)	(400 000)
Taxable income	2 100 000

Current tax = 2 100 000 × 27% = 567 000 debit in P or L
Deferred tax = 900 000 × 27% = 243 000 credit in P or L

2. Deferred tax calculation

	Carrying amount Rand	Tax base Rand	Temporary differences Rand	Deferred tax in SFPos Rand
31 December 19.9	–	–	–	–
31 December 20.0				
Buildings (1) (2)	2 700 000	3 600 000	(900 000)	243 000 Asset
Buildings	3 600 000	3 600 000	–	–
Government grant	(900 000)	–	(900 000)	243 000 Asset

(1) 4 000 000 – 1 000 000 – 300 000 = 2 700 000
(2) 4 000 000 – 400 000 = 3 600 000

Thus movement in deferred tax in profit or loss for the year ended 31 December 20.0 is R243 000 (movement from RNil to R243 000) as a credit amount.

❑ QUESTION IAS 20.3@

Distributors Ltd provides medical services in remote areas in KwaZulu-Natal. They receive a government grant every year in respect of these medical services provided in that specific year, since the government wishes to provide medical services to all residents of South Africa.

Distributors Ltd spent R500 000 in respect of the provision of medical services in remote areas in KwaZulu-Natal during the year ended 31 December 20.1.

Distributors Ltd collected R10 000 during the year from the inhabitants of the remote areas in KwaZulu-Natal and received a R400 000 grant on 1 January 20.1 from the provincial government in that province.

Assume a tax rate of 27%. Distributors Ltd has no other income or expenses. Assume also that there will be sufficient other taxable income in future periods and that deferred tax assets can be recognised. The grants received from the government are taxable when received.

Required

a. Prepare the journal entries (cash transactions included) for the year ended 31 December 20.1 in respect of the above transactions if it is assumed that the government grant is presented as other income in the statement of profit or loss and other comprehensive income.
b. Prepare the journal entries (cash transactions included) for the year ended 31 December 20.1 in respect of the above transactions if it is assumed that the government grant is deducted from the related expense, in the statement of profit or loss and other comprehensive income.

Your solution must comply with the requirements of International Financial Reporting Standards (IFRS).

❖ **Suggested solution IAS 20.3@**

a. Journal entries for the year ended 31 December 20.1

	Rand Dr/(Cr)
Medical costs incurred (P or L)	500 000
Bank	(500 000)
Bank	10 000
Income from provision of medical services (P or L)	(10 000)
Bank	400 000
Government grant in respect of provision of medical services (P or L)	(400 000)
Deferred tax (SFPos) (1) (2)	24 300
Income tax expense (P or L)	(24 300)

(1) 500 000 – 400 000 – 10 000 = 90 000 unused tax loss
(2) 90 000 × 27% = 24 300

b. Journal entries for the year ended 31 December 20.1

	Rand Dr/(Cr)
Medical costs incurred (P or L)	500 000
Bank	(500 000)
Bank	10 000
Income from provision of medical services (P or L)	(10 000)
Bank	400 000
Medical costs incurred (P or L)	(400 000)
Deferred tax (SFPos) (1) (2)	24 300
Income tax expense (P or L)	(24 300)

(1) 500 000 – 400 000 – 10 000 = 90 000 unused tax loss
(2) 90 000 × 27% = 24 300

❑ **QUESTION IAS 20.4@**

Helping Hand Ltd decided to participate in the national government's drive towards the alleviation of unemployment in the rural areas. The government agreed to subsidise 15 employees' total cost of employment for a four-year period.

Helping Hand Ltd employed 15 employees on 1 January 20.4 at a total annual cost of R450 000. It is expected that their total remuneration cost shall increase at 7,5% per year. A grant, received from the national government on 1 January 20.4 for the four year period, amounted to R2 million.

Assume a tax rate of 28%. The grant is taxable in full when received in cash. Assume a profit before tax, before the above information has been accounted for, of R750 000 for each of the four years. There are no temporary differences other than any arising from the information provided. Assume that there will be sufficient future taxable income and that deferred tax assets can be recognised.

Required

Prepare the journal entries (cash transactions included) for each of the four years ended 31 December 20.7 to account for the above information in accordance with the requirements of International Financial Reporting Standards (IFRS) assuming that the government grant is deducted from the related expense in the statement of profit or loss and other comprehensive income.

❖ **Suggested solution IAS 20.4@**

Journal entries:

	20.4 Rand Dr/(Cr)	**20.5 Rand Dr/(Cr)**	**20.6 Rand Dr/(Cr)**	**20.7 Rand Dr/(Cr)**
Bank	2 000 000	–	–	–
Deferred income (SFPos)	(2 000 000)	–	–	–
Salaries (P or L) (calc 1)	450 000	483 750	520 031	559 034
Bank	(450 000)	(483 750)	(520 031)	(559 034)
Deferred income (SFPos)	447 135	480 670	516 720	555 475
Salaries (P or L) (calc 2)	(447 135)	(480 670)	(516 720)	(555 475)
Current tax expense (P or L) (calc 3)	644 000	74 550	64 391	53 470
Current tax owing (SFPos)	(644 000)	(74 550)	(64 391)	(53 470)
Deferred tax (SFPos) (calc 4)	434 802	(134 587)	(144 682)	(155 533)
Deferred tax expense (P or L)	(434 802)	134 587	144 682	155 533

Calculations

1. Calculation of salary cost over four-year period

		Rand
31 December 20.4	given	450 000
31 December 20.5	450 000 × 107.5%	483 750
31 December 20.6	483 750 × 107.5%	520 031
31 December 20.7	520 031 × 107.5%	559 034
		2 012 815

2. Calculation of amortisation of grant over four-year period

		Rand
31 December 20.4	2 000 000 × 450 000/2 012 815	447 135
31 December 20.5	2 000 000 × 483 750/2 012 815	480 670
31 December 20.6	2 000 000 × 520 031/2 012 815	516 720
31 December 20.7	2 000 000 × 559 034/2 012 815	555 475
		2 000 000

3. Current tax calculation

	20.4 Rand	20.5 Rand	20.6 Rand	20.7 Rand
Profit before tax (given)	750 000	750 000	750 000	750 000
Staff costs (calc 1)	(450 000)	(483 750)	(520 031)	(559 034)
Grant amortised (calc 2)	447 135	480 670	516 720	555 475
Accounting profit before tax	747 135	746 920	746 689	746 441
Temporary differences	1 552 865	(480 670)	(516 720)	(555 475)
Grant amortised	(447 135)	(480 670)	(516 720)	(555 475)
Grant received in cash	2 000 000	–	–	–
Taxable income	2 300 000	266 250	229 969	190 966
Current tax at 28%	644 000	74 550	64 391	53 470

4. Deferred tax calculation

	CA Rand	TB Rand	TD Rand	DT (28%) Rand Dr/(Cr)	P or L Rand (Dr)/Cr
31 December 20.3					
Deferred income	–	–	–	–	–
31 December 20.4					
Deferred income (1)	1 552 865	–	1 552 865	434 802	434 802
31 December 20.5					
Deferred income (2)	1 072 195	–	1 072 195	300 215	(134 587)
31 December 20.6					
Deferred income (3)	555 475	–	555 475	155 533	(144 682)
31 December 20.7					
Deferred income (4)	–	–	–	–	(155 533)

CA = Carrying amount
TB = Tax base
TD = Temporary difference
DT = Deferred tax (SFPos)
P or L = Profit or loss (movement)

(1) 2 000 000 – 447 135 (calc 2) = 1 552 865
(2) 1 552 865 – 480 670 (calc 2) = 1 072 195
(3) 1 072 195 – 516 720 (calc 2) = 555 475
(4) 555 475 – 555 475 (calc 2) = Nil

TB of deferred income = CA of liability less amount of this liability not taxable in future. Since the whole R2 million was taxed on receipt, no amount will be taxed in the future.

❑ QUESTION IAS 20.5@

The national government of South Africa has embarked on a policy of developing certain rural areas.

Help U Ltd manufactures precast concrete walls that can be used in the construction of houses that will significantly reduce their construction time. Help U Ltd has agreed to build a new factory in one of these rural areas and the national government has agreed to provide the following assistance:

- The immediate write-off of all capital expenses for tax purposes and a reduced corporate tax rate in terms of recently legislated reforms to the tax legislation;
- Assistance in the form of an annual grant of 50% of the total staff cost of employees during the first five years provided that they are drawn from the rural area in which the factory will be set up;
- The awarding of an interest-free loan of R5 million, which will not be repayable, to provide immediate financial support;
- Improvements to and provision of the road and rail infrastructure as well as water reticulation and electricity that will also benefit the people living in the area; and
- A R10 million grant related to the construction of the factory building and the purchase of specialised plant and equipment.

In addition to this, the national government has also agreed to purchase 80% of the precast concrete walls, manufactured by Help U Ltd, for the first 10 years. The terms of purchase will be the same as those of other customers of Help U Ltd.

A government organisation based in Sweden has also undertaken to provide free technical advice to Help U Ltd related to the material composition of these precast concrete walls.

Required

Identify and explain whether or not the types of government assistance provided to Help U Ltd are government assistance and government grants in accordance with IAS 20 *Accounting for government grants and disclosures of government assistance* and SIC 10 *Government assistance – no specific relation to operating activities.*

❖ Suggested solution IAS 20.5@

Government assistance is defined as action taken by the government to provide an economic benefit to an entity provided it meets certain criteria. Government assistance excludes any benefits provided indirectly through action affecting general trading conditions, such as the provision of infrastructure in development areas (IAS 20.03).

Government grants are defined as government assistance involving the transfer of resources to an entity in return for a past or future compliance with certain conditions relating to the operating activities of the entity. Grants exclude any government assistance that cannot reasonably have a value placed upon them and any transactions with government that cannot be distinguished from the normal trading transactions of the entity (IAS 20.03).

Government is defined as any government, government agency and similar body that may be national, international or local (IAS 20.03).

SIC 10.01 deals with the issue of government assistance to entities aimed at the encouragement or long-term support of business activities either in certain regions or industry sectors. The conditions to receive such assistance may not be specifically related to the operating activities of the entity (per definition of government grants in IAS 20.03). An example of such assistance provided for by SIC 10 is where an entity starts or continues to run its business in an under-developed area.

SIC 10 concedes that government assistance to an entity meets the definition of government grants in IAS 20 even if there are no conditions specifically relating to the operating activities of the entity other than the requirement to operate in certain regions or sectors of industry.

SIC 10 further states that the general requirement to operate in a certain region or industry section in order to qualify for the government assistance constitutes such a condition envisaged in IAS 20.03. Therefore such assistance falls within the definition of government grants.

IAS 20.02(b) scopes out any government assistance provided to an entity in the form of benefits arising in determining taxable income such as accelerated wear-and-tear allowances and reduced tax rates.

IAS 20 further defines two types of government grants as either:

- grants related to assets: grants whose primary condition for qualifying for the grant requires that the entity must purchase, construct or otherwise acquire a long-term asset. Subsidiary conditions may also be attached to such grants restricting the type of asset or location of the asset acquired.
- grants related to income: grants other than those related to assets.

Since the government assistance provided to Help U Ltd is not provided specifically in respect of its operating activities but rather because it has decided to locate a new factory in a development area, the government assistance provided meets the criteria for government assistance of SIC 10.

In order to determine whether or not the government assistance is assistance and a government grant in terms of IAS 20, the definitions and criteria above will now be applied to each form of assistance provided:

1. Immediate write-off of all capital expenditure and a reduced corporate tax rate

Specifically scoped out of IAS 20 and therefore this is not government assistance per IAS 20.

2. Annual grant of 50% of salary cost

This is government assistance since action has been taken by the government to provide an economic benefit to the entity provided it meets certain conditions. This is further refined as a government grant since it involves the transfer of resources to Help U Ltd by the government in return for compliance with the condition that the employees are drawn from the rural area in which the factory will be set up. This is also further refined as an income-based grant since it does not relate to the construction or acquisition of a long-term asset.

3. Interest-free loan

This is government assistance since action has been taken by the government to provide an economic benefit to the entity provided it meets certain conditions. This is further refined as a government grant since it involves the transfer of resources to Help U Ltd by the government in return for compliance with the condition that the entity will open a new factory in the rural area. This is further refined as an income-based grant since it does not relate to the construction or acquisition of a long-term asset.

4. Improvements to infrastructure

This is not government assistance per definition of IAS 20 as it is specifically excluded from the definition. The infrastructure will provide an economic benefit to the entity but also to the general public in the rural area and therefore it is not specific to the entity.

5. Grant in respect of construction of factory and purchase of specialised equipment

This is government assistance since action has been taken by the government to provide economic benefits to the entity provided it meets certain conditions. This is also further refined as a government grant since it involves the transfer of resources to Help U Ltd by the government in return for compliance with the condition that the company constructs a factory in the rural area. Further refinement of this grant is that it is an asset-based grant since the primary condition for qualifying for this grant is that the entity will construct a factory and acquire specialised plant which are long-term assets.

6. Purchase of 80% of production by government

This is government assistance since it is action taken by the government to provide an economic benefit specific to the entity by it agreeing to purchase 80% of the production of Help U Ltd for the first 10 years on the same terms as other customers. However, it is not a government grant as transactions with government which cannot be distinguished from the normal trading transactions of an entity are excluded from government grants per definition.

7. Technical assistance provided by Swedish government agency

This is government assistance since it is action taken by a foreign/international government body to provide an economic benefit specific to the entity in the form of free technical assistance. However, it is not a government grant as it is government assistance which cannot reasonably have a value placed on it and is therefore excluded from government grants per definition.

❑ QUESTION IAS 20.6[@]

Bricks Ltd erected a recreation centre for its employees drawn from underdeveloped rural areas at a cost of R2,5 million, which was paid for on 1 January 20.0 in cash. The recreation centre has an estimated useful life of 10 years, and was completed and put into use on 1 January 20.0.

Bricks Ltd received a government grant of R1 800 000 on 1 January 20.0 in cash. The provision of such facilities to employees meets the government strategy to take care of the physical wellbeing of its citizens in rural areas.

A tax allowance of 15% per annum on the straight-line method is allowed on the total cost of this recreation centre.

However, on 1 January 20.2 the national government decided that R400 000 of the government grant received on 1 January 20.0 must be paid back immediately since Bricks Ltd did not meet all of the conditions of the government grant.

Assume a profit before tax prior to the above transactions of R500 000 for the years ended 31 December 20.0 to 31 December 20.2.

Assume a tax rate of 28%.

Assume that Bricks Ltd will have future taxable income and that any debit balances on deferred tax can be recognised.

Required

a. Prepare the journal entries (cash transactions included) for the years ended 31 December 20.0 to 31 December 20.2 in respect of the above transactions if it is assumed that the government grant is treated as deferred income; and
   i. the government grant is taxable when received in cash and any repayment is tax deductible when paid in cash; and
   ii. the government grant is not taxable and any repayment is not tax deductible.
b. Prepare the journal entries (cash transactions included) for the years ended 31 December 20.0 to 31 December 20.2 in respect of the above transactions if it is assumed that the government grant is deducted from the carrying amount of the asset; and
   i. the government grant is taxable when received in cash and any repayment is tax deductible when paid in cash; and
   ii. the government grant is not taxable and any repayment is not tax deductible.

Your solution must comply with the requirements of International Financial Reporting Standards (IFRS).

❑ QUESTION IAS 20.7@

Use the information provided in Question IAS 20.6 to prepare the notes to the annual financial statements of Bricks Ltd for the years ended 31 December 20.0 to 31 December 20.2 for each of the scenarios.

Your solution must comply with the requirements of International Financial Reporting Standards (IFRS). Total columns in the notes are not required.

Assume all amounts are material.

❑ QUESTION IAS 20.8[@]

Grants Ltd was approached by the government to participate in its programme relating to the alleviation of unemployment in the rural areas. Consequently, Grants Ltd employed 50 additional employees at a total salary cost for the year ended 30 June 20.1 of R650 000. The employees were appointed on 1 July 20.0.

The agreement between Grants Ltd and the government stated that:
- 50 additional employees would be employed for at least a five-year period during which time they would be trained as part of the factory staff;
- a total grant of R3,7 million would be received from the government;
- the salaries of these employees would increase at 7,5% per year over the five-year period; and
- should any of these employees be dismissed or leave before the end of five years, 1/50 (per employee) of the total grant would be repayable immediately to the government.

The tax rate is 28%. The grant received is taxable in full in the year received in cash. Any repayments will be tax deductible in the year in which they are paid back.

The grant was received on 1 July 20.0.

Assume that there will be sufficient other taxable income in the future and that deferred tax assets can be recognised.

Required

a. Prepare the journal entries (cash transactions included) for the year ended 30 June 20.1 if it is assumed that the government grant is deducted from the related expense in the statement of profit or loss and other comprehensive income.
b. Prepare the journal entries (cash transactions included) for the year ended 30 June 20.4 assuming that 10 of the 50 employees were dismissed. Assume that the government grant is deducted from the related expense in the statement of profit or loss and other comprehensive income.

Your solution to both (a) and (b) must comply with the requirements of International Financial Reporting Standards (IFRS).

❑ QUESTION IAS 20.9[@]

Cement Ltd erects low-cost housing. The provision of housing to all residents of South Africa is a priority for the South African government. The government provided a loan of R20 000 000 at a market-related rate of 10% per annum to Cement Ltd on 1 January 20.1. Interest on this loan is payable half-yearly in arrears.

The loan agreement provides that the repayment of the loan will be waived by the South African government on the date of completion of the project.

The housing project was completed on 30 June 20.1 and the total cost of R30 000 000 was settled in cash on 30 June 20.1.

The useful life of the housing units is 20 years, commencing on 1 July 20.1.

Government grants are deducted from the carrying amount of the asset.

Ignore the tax implications.

Required

Prepare the journal entries (cash transactions included) for the year ended 31 December 20.1 to account for the above transactions in accordance with the requirements of International Financial Reporting Standards (IFRS).

❑ QUESTION IAS 20.10@

Break and Build Ltd erects low-cost houses. The provincial government of Gauteng decided on 1 January 20.1 to donate land with a fair value of R5 000 000 to Break and Build Ltd for the erection of such houses.

Break and Build Ltd received the land and the accompanying registration certificates on 1 February 20.1. Break and Build Ltd paid transfer taxes and professional fees of R50 000 related to the land received on this date. The erection of the low-cost houses commenced on 1 March 20.1 and had not been completed at year end. The total costs incurred during the period 1 March 20.1 to 31 December 20.1 amounts to R800 000. This cost was settled in cash.

It is the policy of Break and Build Ltd to treat government grants as deferred income and to account for non-monetary assets at fair value.

Assume a tax rate of 28%.

Required

Prepare the journal entries (cash transactions included) for the year ended 31 December 20.1 to account for the above transactions in accordance with the requirements of International Financial Reporting Standards (IFRS).

IAS 21 & SIC 7

The effects of changes in foreign exchange rates

❑ QUESTIONS AND SOLUTIONS

IAS 21.1	Functional and presentation currency: discussion
IAS 21.2	Export sale of goods with resulting foreign debtor: journal entries
IAS 21.3	Imports of inventory with various resulting foreign creditors: journal entries
IAS 21.4	Foreign currency loan, illustrating two alternative solutions: one where accrued interest is capitalised to the loan account, and the other where accrued interest is accounted for separate from the loan account: journal entries
IAS 21.5[@]	Imports with and without forward exchange contracts, illustrating accounting both with and without fair value hedging principles (IFRS 9): journal entries
IAS 21.6[@]	Imports, illustrating accounting both with cash flow and fair value hedging principles (IFRS 9) and without hedge accounting: journal entries and presentation
IAS 21.7	Equal and opposite forward exchange contracts, without hedge accounting, and financial risk disclosures (IFRS 7): journal entries, presentation and disclosure
IAS 21.8	Foreign subsidiary: translation of results and discussion

❑ QUESTIONS

IAS 21.9	Import of a machine without a forward exchange contract, including deferred tax on machine: journal entries
IAS 21.10	Import of a machine, funded with a short-term foreign loan, and a forward exchange contract on the loan, including the impact of deferred tax: calculations
IAS 21.11	Foreign currency loan with renewable forward cover on the capital portion: journal entries
IAS 21.12	Consolidation of foreign subsidiary: presentation

❑ ADDITIONAL QUESTIONS: HEDGE ACCOUNTING (IFRS 9)[@]

IAS 21.13[@]	Qualifying hedging criteria and hedge effectiveness: discussion and calculations
IAS 21.14[@]	Import of a machine with a cash flow hedge by way of a forward exchange contract: journal entries
IAS 21.15[@]	Import of inventory where only one leg of the transaction is hedged: journal entries
IAS 21.16[@]	Import of inventory under cash flow and fair value hedges with a variety of forward exchange contracts: journal entries

Note:	Assume that all entities in the questions to this chapter do not apply hedge accounting, unless stated otherwise. Ignore the effect of the time value of money on all forward contracts.

[@] *These questions contain topics or principles that were not included in the ITC syllabus of SAICA at the time of publishing this book, but might still be included in university syllabi.*

❑ QUESTION IAS 21.1

A 'Perky & Central' coffee shop was recently opened in Melrose Arch by Mr Bing. It is the first of what he hopes will be many such outlets on the African continent. It forms part of the Perky & Central group of coffee shops that was founded in New York, USA, in the late 1990s by a group of friends.

Perky & Central SA (Pty) Ltd (hereafter 'Perky & Central SA') has been incorporated as a private company in South Africa and is wholly owned by Central Perk Incorporated (hereafter 'Central Perk'), a company incorporated in the USA, which is also the holding company for the remainder of the group.

The Central Perk group reports under International Financial Reporting Standards (IFRS). International (i.e. non-American) companies are required to submit their financial statements, presented in US dollars (USD), to Central Perk on a quarterly basis. While Perky & Central SA attracts more American clientele than the average coffee shop in the area, all customers are billed in South African rand (ZAR) for products purchased.

Perky & Central SA is required to pay a substantial USD management fee to Central Perk on a monthly basis. This fee covers the right to trade under the Perky & Central brand in South Africa as well as support received from permanent Central Perk baristas (expert coffee makers) who travel between international coffee shops to ensure that the coffee is being roasted correctly and that the coffee being prepared locally is of the same quality as that which is prepared at its flagship outlet in New York.

Perky & Central SA imports all coffee beans, cream, and bottled water used to prepare the coffee directly from Central Perk to ensure the quality and taste of each cup of coffee will be on a par with what customers have come to expect from the established brand. Freshly baked goods and milk are purchased locally from approved suppliers.

Two coffee machines had to be imported from Italy, at a cost of euro 48 000 each before Perky & Central SA could open.

Central Perk has shared the group's logo and coffee cup design with a South African supplier, that manufactures the coffee cups and lids in its factory in Woodmead. Shop fittings and furniture were sourced from a company in the Eastern Cape, South Africa.

Perky & Central employs local South Africans to run the coffee shop and remuneration is paid in ZAR.

Required

Recommend, with reasons, which currency Perky & Central SA (Pty) Ltd should use as their functional currency, and as their presentation currency.

❖ Suggested solution IAS 21.1

An entity's 'functional currency' is defined as the currency of the primary economic environment in which the entity operates (IAS 21.8). The primary economic environment in which an entity operates is normally the one in which it primarily generates and expends cash (IAS 21.9).

IAS 21.9 lists the following additional factors that an entity should consider to determine an entity's primary economic environment and functional currency:

i) It is the currency that mainly influences sales prices for goods and services (this will often be the currency in which sales prices for its goods and services are denominated and settled);
ii) It is the currency of the country whose competitive forces and regulations mainly determine the sales prices of its goods and services; and
iii) It is the currency that mainly influences labour, material and other costs of providing goods or services (this will often be the currency in which such costs are denominated and settled).

Perky & Central SA's primary economic environment appears to be South Africa, based on the following facts:

- The company's business is to sell coffee from its coffee shop based in Melrose Arch where all customers buy coffee and other products in South African rand (ZAR).
- Even though Perky & Central SA attracts more American clientele than the average coffee shop in Melrose Arch, all customers are invoiced in ZAR for products purchased.
- As the coffee shop is based in Melrose Arch, the competitive forces in South Africa will establish how much a cup of coffee can be sold for. The price cannot be set in US dollars (USD) and translated as Perky & Central SA could price themselves out of the market using such a pricing strategy.
- All shop fittings, labour, milk and consumables are purchased locally in ZAR, with the only exceptions being the coffee beans, cream and water imported from the USA, and the coffee machines imported from Italy.
- The cost of labour will be influenced by South African market forces as all employees would be hired in South Africa with the exception of the baristas included in the management fee.

Perky & Central SA will thus use ZAR as its functional currency.

An entity's 'presentation currency' is the currency in which the financial statements are presented (IAS 21.8). An entity may present its financial statements in any currency (IAS 21.38).

Perky & Central SA is a private company with one shareholder, being its US-based holding company (Central Perk Incorporated). Perky & Central SA are required to submit their financial statements, presented in USD, to Central Perk on a quarterly basis.

It is therefore recommended that Perky & Central SA use USD as their presentation currency, as it will provide more meaningful results for its holding company and will likely result in a more efficient quarterly and year-end reporting process. Perky & Central SA may also present results in ZAR (in addition to those submitted to Central Perk Incorporated) for internal reporting purposes.

❑ QUESTION IAS 21.2

Makeself Ltd manufactures African decor locally and markets the products abroad. The company's year-end is 31 December. Makeself Ltd sold African decor to the value of R10 000 to Importing USA Inc on 7 August 20.2. No forward exchange contract (FEC) was taken out. The transaction was invoiced in dollars at the spot rate ruling on transaction date. Makeself Ltd uses the South African rand (R) as its functional and presentation currency.

The relevant exchange rates are as follows:

7 August 20.2	R1,25 = \$1
12 November 20.2	R1,00 = \$1
31 December 20.2	R0,85 = \$1
31 December 20.3	R1,60 = \$1
16 July 20.4	R1,30 = \$1
31 December 20.4	R0,56 = \$1

Required

Journalise all the relevant transactions (without journal narrations) assuming that payment by Importing USA Inc took place on the following dates:

a. 12 November 20.2
b. 31 December 20.3
c. 16 July 20.4

Your solution must comply with the requirements of International Financial Reporting Standards (IFRS). Ignore taxation.

❖ Suggested solution IAS 21.2

	20.2 Rand Dr/(Cr)	20.3 Rand Dr/(Cr)	20.4 Rand Dr/(Cr)
a. Payment on 12 November 20.2			
7 August 20.2			
Receivables (1)	10 000		
Sales (P or L)	(10 000)		
12 November 20.2			
Foreign exchange loss (P or L) (2)	2 000		
Bank (3)	8 000		
Receivables	(10 000)		
b. Payment on 31 December 20.3			
7 August 20.2			
Receivables (1)	10 000		
Sales (P or L)	(10 000)		
31 December 20.2			
Foreign exchange loss (P or L) (4)	3 200		
Receivables	(3 200)		

	20.2 Rand Dr/(Cr)	20.3 Rand Dr/(Cr)	20.4 Rand Dr/(Cr)
31 December 20.3			
Receivables		6 000	
Foreign exchange gain (P or L) (5)		(6 000)	
Bank (6)		12 800	
Receivables (7)		(12 800)	

c. **Payment on 16 July 20.4**

	20.2 Rand Dr/(Cr)	20.3 Rand Dr/(Cr)	20.4 Rand Dr/(Cr)
7 August 20.2			
Receivables (1)	10 000		
Sales (P or L)	(10 000)		
31 December 20.2 / 20.3			
Foreign exchange loss/(gain) (P or L) (20.2: (4); 20.3: (5))	3 200	(6 000)	
Receivables	(3 200)	6 000	
16 July 20.4			
Foreign exchange loss (P or L) (8)			2 400
Bank (9)			10 400
Receivables (7)			(12 800)

(1) Invoiced price R10 000; equivalent to \$8 000 (R10 000/1,25 = \$8 000).
Note: The dollar equivalent sales price is required in order to calculate foreign exchange gains and losses after the transaction date.
(2) \$8 000 × (1,25 – 1,00) = R2 000
(3) \$8 000 × 1 = R8 000. Cash is recorded at the spot exchange rate on the payment date.
(4) \$8 000 × (1,25 – 0,85) = R3 200 foreign exchange loss between transaction date and 31 December 20.2.
(5) \$8 000 × (1,60 – 0,85) = R6 000 foreign exchange gain between 31 December 20.2 and 31 December 20.3.
(6) \$8 000 × 1,60 = R12 800
(7) R10 000 – R3 200 + R6 000 = R12 800. Cash is recorded at the spot exchange rate on the payment date.
(8) \$8 000 × (1,60 – 1,30) = R2 400 foreign exchange loss between 31 December 20.3 and 16 July 20.4.
(9) \$8 000 × 1,30 = R10 400. Cash is recorded at the spot exchange rate on the payment date.

Note: Once the debtor is settled and derecognised, there are no foreign exchange movements recorded after the settlement date.

❑ QUESTION IAS 21.3

South African Importing Ltd purchases certain products on foreign markets. Assume that the purchase dates represent the dates on which the entity is irrevocably committed to the transactions. These products are then sold to wholesalers on the local market. No forward cover was taken out. The company's financial year ends on 31 December. You may assume that the effect of time value of money is insignificant. South African Importing Ltd uses the South African rand (R) as its functional and presentation currency.

The following transactions in respect of imported products were entered into:

	Purchase	Payment to creditor	Closing inventory
Product **Zaza** from Alabama Inc			
12 July 20.2 (purchase date)	$6 000		
31 December 20.2		$3 600	Nil
12 August 20.3		$2 400	Nil
Product **Xaxa** from American Textiles Inc			
15 September 20.2 (purchase date)	$8 000		
20 November 20.2		$8 000	–
31 December 20.2		–	$6 400
31 December 20.3		–	Nil
Product **Quqa** from USA Exporters Inc			
16 October 20.2 (purchase date)	$10 000		
31 December 20.2		–	$3 500
12 August 20.3		$4 000	–
31 December 20.3		–	$2 000
12 September 20.4		$6 000	–
31 December 20.4		–	Nil

The relevant exchange rates are as follows:

12 July 20.2	R1 = $1,25
15 September 20.2	R1 = $1,15
16 October 20.2	R1 = $1,80
20 November 20.2	R1 = $1,00
31 December 20.2	R1 = $1,00
12 August 20.3	R1 = $1,20
31 December 20.3	R1 = $0,95
12 September 20.4	R1 = $1,20
31 December 20.4	R1 = $0,80

Required

Journalise all of the above transactions (including cash transactions) for the years 20.2 to 20.4 to ensure compliance with the requirements of International Financial Reporting Standards (IFRS). Journal narrations are not required. Ignore taxation.

❖ **Suggested solution IAS 21.3**

Journals – Product Zaza	**20.2 Rand Dr/(Cr)**	**20.3 Rand Dr/(Cr)**
Inventory (1)	4 800	–
Creditor – Alabama Inc	(4 800)	–
Cost of sales (P or L) (2)	4 800	–
Inventory	(4 800)	–
Foreign exchange loss/(gain) (P or L) (3)	1 200	(400)
Creditor	(1 200)	400

Journals – Product Zaza	**20.2 Rand Dr/(Cr)**	**20.3 Rand Dr/(Cr)**
Creditor	3 600	2 000
Bank (4)	(3 600)	(2 000)

(1) $6 000/1,25 = R4 800 recorded at spot on the transaction date.
(2) As there is no inventory remaining at 31 December 20.2, all inventory has been sold and is recorded as cost of sales at spot on transaction date (historic cost).
(3) ($6 000/1) – R4 800 = R1 200 foreign exchange loss on creditor between acquisition date and 31 December 20.2;
$6 000 – $3 600 payment = $2 400 remaining creditor balance;
($2 400/1,20) – ($2 400/1) = R400 foreign exchange gain on unpaid portion of creditor balance remaining between 31 December 20.2 and payment date.
(4) $3 600/1 = R3 600; $2 400/1,20 = R2 000 cash payments recorded at spot on the payment dates.

Journals – Product Xaxa	**20.2 Rand Dr/(Cr)**	**20.3 Rand Dr/(Cr)**
Inventory (1)	6 957	–
Creditor – American Textiles Inc	(6 957)	–
Foreign exchange loss (P or L) (2)	1 043	–
Creditor	(1 043)	–
Creditor	8 000	–
Bank (3)	(8 000)	–
Cost of sales (P or L) (4)	1 391	5 566
Inventory	(1 391)	(5 566)

(1) $8 000/1,15 = R6 957 recorded at spot on the transaction date.
(2) ($8 000/1,00) – R6 957 = R1 043 foreign exchange loss on creditor between acquisition date and 20 November 20.2. No additional foreign exchange gains or losses are recognised as the creditor has been settled in full on 20 November 20.2.
(3) $8 000/1,00 = R8 000 cash payment recorded at spot on the payment date.
(4) R6 957 × 20% = R1 391 ($8 000 – $6 400 closing inventory = $1 600 sold in 20.2, thus recognise $1 600/$8 000 = 20% as cost of sales at historic cost);
R6 957 × 80% = R5 566 ($8 000 – $0 closing inventory = $8 000 sold, 20% already recognised in 20.2, recognise remaining 80% as cost of sales at historic cost).

Journals – Product Quqa	**20.2 Rand Dr/(Cr)**	**20.3 Rand Dr/(Cr)**	**20.4 Rand Dr/(Cr)**
Inventory (1)	5 555	–	–
Creditor – USA Exporters Inc	(5 555)	–	–
Foreign exchange loss (P or L) (2)	4 445		
Creditor	(4 445)		
Creditor (3)	–	667	1 316
Foreign exchange gain (P or L)	–	(667)	(1 316)
Foreign exchange loss (P or L) (4)		316	–
Creditor		(316)	–
Creditor (5)	–	3 333	5 000
Bank	–	(3 333)	(5 000)
Cost of sales (P or L) (6)	3 611	833	1 111
Inventory	(3 611)	(833)	(1 111)

(1) $10 000/1,80 = R5 555 recorded at spot on the transaction date.
(2) ($10 000/1) – 5 555 = 4 445 foreign exchange loss on creditor between acquisition date and 31 December 20.2 on full balance as no payments have been made in 20.2.
(3) ($4 000/1,20) – ($4 000/1) = R667; ($6 000/1,2) – ($6 000/0,95) = R1 316 foreign exchange gains on portion of creditor paid between the year-end and the payment date.
(4) $10 000 - $4 000 = $6 000 remaining creditor balances.
($6 000/0,95) – ($6 000/1) = R316 foreign exchange loss on creditor balance between 31 December 20.2 and 31 December 20.3 that remained outstanding for the full financial year.
(5) $4 000/1,2 = R3 333; $6 000/1,2 = R5 000 cash payments recorded at spot on the payment dates.
(6) 5 555 × 65% = R3 611 ($10 000 – $3 500 closing inventory = $6 500 sold in 20.2, thus recognise 65% as cost of sales in 20.2 at historic cost);
5 555 × 15% = R833 ($10 000 – $2 000 closing inventory = $8 000 sold, 65% was already recognised in 20.2, thus recognise the additional 15% as cost of sales in 20.3 at historic cost);
5 555 × 20% = R1 111 ($10 000 – $0 closing inventory = $10 000 sold, 80% already cumulatively recognised 20.2 and 20.3, thus recognise the remaining 20% as cost of sales at historic cost in 20.4).

❑ QUESTION IAS 21.4

Manufacturers Ltd is a manufacturing entity with a financial year ending on 31 December. Manufacturers Ltd uses the South African rand (R) as its functional and presentation currency. The board of directors decided to obtain a foreign loan to improve the company's liquidity. The necessary statutory requirements were adhered to and the loan was obtained from European Borrowers Bank Ltd.

The loan was approved on 1 January 20.2 and the money was deposited into the bank account of Manufacturers Ltd on the same date.

An extract from the agreement entered into with the bank reads as follows:

1. The amount of the loan is FC 1 000 000.
2. Interest is charged on the outstanding loan amount at a market-related rate of 10% per annum.
3. The loan is repayable at FC 147 950 per annum in advance with the first payment due on 1 January 20.2.
4. No forward cover was taken out.
5. The relevant exchange rates are as follows:

1 January 20.2	FC 1 = R0,85
31 December 20.2/1 January 20.3	FC 1 = R1,00
31 December 20.3/1 January 20.4	FC 1 = R0,65
31 December 20.4	FC 1 = R0,55

6. The changes in the exchange rates occurred evenly during each period.

Required

Journalise the above transactions (including cash transactions) for the three years ended 31 December 20.2, 20.3 and 20.4 to ensure compliance with the requirements of International Financial Reporting Standards (IFRS). Journal narrations are not required. Ignore taxation.

❖ **Suggested solution IAS 21.4**

Alternative solution 1: ***All payments and interest charged to loan account and a single foreign exchange gain or loss is calculated per annum***

Journals

	20.2 Rand Dr/(Cr)	**20.3 Rand Dr/(Cr)**	**20.4 Rand Dr/(Cr)**
Bank (1)	850 000	–	–
Long-term loan	(850 000)	–	–
Long-term loan (2)	125 758	147 950	96 168
Bank	(125 758)	(147 950)	(96 168)
Interest expense (P or L) (3)	78 815	65 118	43 217
Long-term loan	(78 815)	(65 118)	(43 217)
Foreign exchange (gain)/ loss (P or L) (calc 1)	134 198	(290 070)	(75 630)
Long-term loan	(134 198)	290 070	75 630

(1) FC 1 000 000 × 0,85 = R850 000; Loan recorded at spot rate on day 1.
(2) Payments recorded at spot rate on the payment dates (calc 1).
(3) Record interest expense at the average exchange rates for the year (calc 1 & 2).

Calculations

1. Loan

	FC	**Rate**	**Rand**
1 January 20.2	1 000 000	0,85	850 000
1 January 20.2 – payment (1)	(147 950)	0,85	(125 758)
Balance – 1 January 20.3 (after payment)	852 050	0,85	724 242
Add: Interest expense at 10% recognised in profit or loss for the year (2)	85 205	0,925	78 815
31 December 20.2 – exchange difference (balancing)	–		134 198
Balance – 31 December 20.2	937 255	1,00	937 255
1 January 20.3 – payment (3)	(147 950)	1,00	(147 950)
Balance – 1 January 20.3 (after payment)	789 305	1,00	789 305
Add: Interest expense at 10% recognised in profit or loss for the year (4)	78 931	0,825	65 118
31 December 20.3 – exchange difference (balancing)	–		(290 070)
Balance – 31 December 20.3	868 236	0,65	564 353
1 January 20.4 – payment (5)	(147 950)	0,65	(96 168)
Balance – 1 January 20.4 (after payment)	720 286	0,65	468 186
Add: Interest expense at 10% recognised in profit or loss for the year (6)	72 029	0,60	43 217
31 December 20.4 – exchange difference (balancing)	–		(75 630)
Balance – 31 December 20.4	792 315	0,55	435 773

(1) FC 147 950 × 0,85 = R125 758 at spot on the payment date.
(2) FC 852 050 × 10% × 0,925 = R78 815 at average exchange rate for 20.2.
(3) FC 147 950 × 1,00 = R147 950 at spot on the payment date.
(4) FC 789 305 × 10% × 0,825 = R65 118 at average exchange rate for 20.3.
(5) FC 147 950 × 0,65 = R96 168 at spot on the payment date.
(6) FC 720 286 × 10% × 0,60 = R43 217 at average exchange rate for 20.4.

2. Average exchange rates for recording interest expenses at, as rates occurred evenly during each period

(0,85 + 1,00)/2 = 0,925 average exchange rate for 20.2.
(1,00 + 0,65)/2 = 0,825 average exchange rate for 20.3.
(0,65 + 0,55)/2 = 0,600 average exchange rate for 20.4.

<u>Alternative solution 2:</u> Interest payments charged to accrued interest, with multiple foreign exchange gains or losses calculated per annum

Journals

	20.2 Rand Dr/(Cr)	**20.3 Rand Dr/(Cr)**	**20.4 Rand Dr/(Cr)**
Bank (calc 1)	850 000	–	–
Long-term loan	(850 000)	–	–
Foreign exchange loss (P or L) (calc 1)	127 808	(276 257)	(72 029)
Long-term loan	(127 808)	276 257	72 029
Long-term loan (calc 1)	125 758	62 745	44 863
Accrued interest (calc 1)	–	85 205	51 305
Bank (1)(2)(3)	(125 758)	(147 950)	(96 168)
Interest expense (P or L) (calc 1)	78 815	85 205	51 305
Accrued interest	(78 815)	(85 205)	(51 305)
Foreign exchange loss/(gain) (P or L) (calc 1)	6 390	(13 813)	(3 601)
Accrued interest	(6 390)	13 813	3 601

(1) FC 147 950 × 0,85 = R125 758 at spot rate on the payment date.
(2) FC 147 950 × 1,00 = R147 950 at spot rate on the payment date.
(3) FC 147 950 × 0,65 = R96 168 at spot rate on the payment date.

Calculations

1. Loan	**FC**	**Rate**	**Rand**
1 January 20.2	1 000 000	0,85	850 000
1 January 20.2 – principal repayment (1)	(147 950)	0,85	(125 758)
31 December 20.2 – exchange difference (balancing)	–		127 808
Balance – 31 December 20.2	852 050	1,00	852 050
1 January 20.3 – principal repayment (3)	(62 745)	1,00	(62 745)
31 December 20.3 – exchange difference (balancing)	–		(276 257)
Balance – 31 December 20.3	789 305	0,65	513 048
1 January 20.4 – principal repayment (5)	(69 020)	0,65	(44 863)
31 December 20.4 – exchange difference (balancing)	–		(72 029)
Balance – 31 December 20.4	720 286	0,55	396 157

Accrued interest

	FC	Rate	Rand
Add: Interest expense at 10% recognised in profit or loss for the year (2)	85 205	0,925	78 815
31 December 20.2 – exchange difference (balancing)	–		6 390
Balance – 31 December 20.2	85 205	1,00	85 205
1 January 20.3 – interest payment	(85 205)	1,00	(85 205)
Add: Interest expense at 10% recognised in profit or loss for the year (4)	78 931	0,825	65 118
31 December 20.3 – exchange difference (balancing)	–		(13 813)
Balance – 31 December 20.3	78 931	0,65	51 305
1 January 20.4 – interest payment	(78 931)	0,65	(51 305)
Add: Interest expense at 10% recognised in profit or loss for the year (6)	72 029	0,60	43 217
31 December 20.4 – exchange difference (balancing)	–		(3 601)
Balance – 31 December 20.4	72 029	0,55	39 616

(1) FC 147 950 × 0,85 = R125 758 at spot on the payment date.
(2) FC 852 050 × 10% = FC 85 205× 0,925 = R78 815 at average exchange rate for 20.2.
(3) FC 147 950 – FC 85 205 = FC 62 745 × 1,00 = R62 745 at spot on the payment date.
(4) FC 789 305 × 10% = FC 78 931× 0,825 = R65 118 at average exchange rate for 20.3.
(5) FC 147 950 – FC 78 931 = FC 69 020 × 0,65 = R44 863 at spot on the payment date.
(6) FC 720 286 × 10% = FC 72 029 × 0,60 = R43 217 at average exchange rate for 20.4.

2. Average exchange rates for recording interest expenses at, as rates occurred evenly during each period

(0,85 + 1,00)/2 = 0,925 average exchange rate for 20.2.
(1,00 + 0,65)/2 = 0,825 average exchange rate for 20.3.
(0,65 + 0,55)/2 = 0,600 average exchange rate for 20.4.

❑ QUESTION IAS 21.5@

On 1 May 20.1 Pine Ltd purchased goods from Oak Ltd, a company in England. The invoice was for £10 000, and the account was settled on 31 July 20.1. The financial year-end of Pine Ltd is 30 June. Pine Ltd uses the South African rand (R) as its functional and presentation currency.

Exchange rates are as follows:

Date	£1 = Rand
1 May 20.1	
Spot rate	4,40
Forward rate for forward exchange contract (FEC) maturing on 31 Jul 20.1	4,46
Forward rate for FEC maturing on 1 June 20.1	4,42
1 June 20.1	
Spot rate	4,45
Forward rate for FEC maturing on 31 July 20.1	4,50

Date	£1 = Rand
30 June 20.1	
Spot rate	4,41
Forward rate for FEC maturing on 31 July 20.1	4,48
31 July 20.1	
Spot rate	4,52

Required

Prepare all the journal entries (including cash transactions) pertaining to the above transaction, to ensure compliance with the requirements of International Financial Reporting Standards (IFRS) assuming the following:

a. No forward exchange contract (FEC) was taken out.
b. An FEC was taken out for the period 1 May 20.1 to 31 July 20.1.
c. An FEC was taken out for the period 1 June 20.1 to 31 July 20.1.
d. An FEC was taken out for the period 1 May 20.1 to 1 June 20.1. At that date the cover was 'rolled forward'/renewed to 31 July 20.1.
e. An FEC was taken out for the period 1 May 20.1 to 31 July 20.1. For this part, assume that the company applies fair value hedge accounting to the foreign exchange risk of recognised liabilities, i.e. the liability is the hedged item. You may assume that the hedging criteria per IFRS 9.6.4.1 have been complied with.

All FECs are net settled on the maturity date. Show journal narrations. Ignore taxation.

❖ **Suggested solution IAS 21.5@**

a. No FEC was taken out

	Rand Dr/(Cr)
1 May 20.1	
Inventory (1)	44 000
Payables	(44 000)
Purchase of inventory for £10 000	
30 June 20.1	
Foreign exchange difference (loss) (P or L) (2)	100
Payables	(100)
Exchange loss on translation of creditor at year-end	
31 July 20.1	
Foreign exchange difference (loss) (P or L) (3)	1 100
Payables	(1 100)
Exchange loss on translation of creditor at payment date	
Payables (4)	45 200
Bank (5)	(45 200)
Settlement of foreign creditor	

b. An FEC was taken out for the period 1 May 20.1 to 31 July 20.1

	Rand Dr/(Cr)
1 May 20.1	
Inventory (1)	44 000
Payables	(44 000)
Purchase of inventory for £10 000	
30 June 20.1	
Foreign exchange difference (loss) (P or L) (2)	100
Payables	(100)
Exchange loss on translation of creditor at year-end	
Forward exchange contract (asset)	200
Foreign exchange difference (gain) (P or L) (6)	(200)
Raise forward exchange contract asset at year-end	
31 July 20.1	
Foreign exchange difference (loss) (P or L) (3)	1 100
Payables	(1 100)
Exchange loss on translation of creditor at payment date	
Forward exchange contract (asset)	400
Foreign exchange difference (gain) (P or L) (7)	(400)
Restatement of FEC at settlement date	
Payables (4)	45 200
Forward exchange contract (asset) (200 + 400)	(600)
Bank (8)	(44 600)
Settlement of creditor and net settlement of FEC	

c. An FEC was taken out for the period 1 June 20.1 to 31 July 20.1

	Rand Dr/(Cr)
1 May 20.1	
Inventory (1)	44 000
Payables	(44 000)
Purchase of inventory for £10 000	
1 June 20.1	
No transaction	
30 June 20.1	
Foreign exchange difference (loss) (P or L) (2)	100
Payables	(100)
Exchange loss on translation of creditor at year-end	
Foreign exchange difference (loss) (P or L) (9)	200
Forward exchange contract (liability)	(200)
Raise forward exchange contract liability at year-end	
31 July 20.1	
Foreign exchange difference (loss) (P or L) (3)	1 100
Payables	(1 100)
Exchange loss on translation of creditor at payment date	

	Rand Dr/(Cr)
Forward exchange contract (liability)	200
Forward exchange contract (asset)	200
Foreign exchange difference (gain) (P or L) (7)	(400)
Restatement of FEC at settlement date	
Payables (4)	45 200
Forward exchange contract (asset)	(200)
Bank (10)	(45 000)
Settlement of creditor and net settlement of FEC	

d. An FEC was taken out for the period 1 May 20.1 to 1 June 20.1. At that date the cover was 'rolled forward' to 31 July 20.1

	Rand Dr/(Cr)
1 May 20.1	
Inventory (1)	44 000
Payables	(44 000)
Purchase of inventory for £10 000	
1 June 20.1	
Bank	300
Foreign exchange difference (gain) (P or L) (11)	(300)
Gain realised and net settled on renewal of first FEC	
30 June 20.1	
Foreign exchange difference (loss) (P or L) (2)	100
Payables	(100)
Exchange loss on translation of creditor	
Foreign exchange difference (loss) (P or L) (9)	200
Forward exchange contract (liability)	(200)
Forward exchange contract liability raised on second FEC at year-end	
31 July 20.1	
Foreign exchange difference (loss) (P or L) (3)	1 100
Payables	(1 100)
Restatement of creditor at payment date	
Forward exchange contract (liability)	200
Forward exchange contract (asset)	200
Foreign exchange difference (gain) (P or L) (7)	(400)
Restatement of FEC on settlement date	
Payables (4)	45 200
Forward exchange contract (asset)	(200)
Bank (10)	(45 000)
Settlement of creditor and net settlement of FEC	

e. An FEC was taken out for the period 1 May 20.1 to 31 July 20.1 and the company applies fair value hedging

The journal entries will be exactly the same as for part b of the question if the company elected to apply hedge accounting.

(1) £10 000 × 4,40 = 44 000 inventory and payables recorded at spot on transaction date.
(2) £10 000 × (4,41 – 4,40) = 100 remeasure payables to year-end spot rate.
(3) £10 000 × (4,52 – 4,41) = 1 100 remeasure payables to settlement date spot rate.
(4) 44 000 + 100 + 1 100 = 45 200 OR £10 000 × 4,52 = R45 200
(5) £10 000 × 4,52 = 45 200 cash transaction recorded at spot on the payment date.
(6) £10 000 × (4,48 – 4,46) = 200 gain between FEC contract rate, and the contract rate that can be realised on a one-month FEC maturing on 31 July 20.1, at 30 June 20.1.
(7) £10 000 × (4,52 – 4,48) = 400 gain on FEC measured at the difference between last measurement rate (at 30 June 20.1) and the spot rate on the maturity/settlement date.
(8) £10 000 × 4,46 = 44 600 net cash flow at the FEC rate on settlement date.
(9) £10 000 × (4,48 – 4,50) = 200 loss between FEC contract rate, and the contract rate that can be realised on a one-month FEC maturing on 31 July 20.1, at 30 June 20.1.
(10) £10 000 × 4,50 = 45 000 net cash flow at the FEC rate on settlement date.
(11) £10 000 × (4,45 – 4,42) = 300 gain realised between FEC contract rate and the spot rate on the date cover is rolled forward.

❑ QUESTION IAS 21.6@

A machine to the value of FC 1 000 was ordered on 1 January 20.1 in terms of a non-cancellable order when the spot rate was R1 = FC 0,51. Forward cover was immediately taken out at R1 = FC 0,50 for six months in view of the expected delivery of the machine on 30 September 20.1. It was the intention of the entity to roll the cover forward to 30 September 20.1. The first forward exchange contract expired on 30 June 20.1 when the spot rate was R1 = FC 0,41. A new contract was concluded at R1 = FC 0,40 for a further seven months.

The company's reporting date is 30 September. At this date the spot rate is R1 = FC 0,33 and forward exchange contracts with maturity dates on 31 January 20.2 are trading at R1 = FC 0,38. The creditor is paid on 31 January 20.2 when the spot rate is R1 = FC 0,32.

The company has chosen to apply hedge accounting. All the hedging criteria per IFRS 9.6.4.1 have been met. The company accounts for a hedge of foreign exchange risk of a firm commitment as a cash flow hedge.

On 1 January 20.1 the company designated the FEC as the hedging instrument and any firm commitment or foreign creditor that arises as a result of the transaction as the hedged item. The renewal of the forward cover is part of, and consistent with, the company's documented risk management objectives. The company uses the South African rand (R) as its functional and presentation currency.

Required

a. Provide the applicable journal entries for the year ended 30 September 20.1, if delivery of the machine took place on 30 September 20.1 to ensure compliance with the requirements of International Financial Reporting Standards (IFRS). Your answer should deal specifically with hedging in terms of IFRS 9.
b. Also provide the journal entries for the settlement date of 31 January 20.2.
c. Present the movement in the cash flow hedge reserve for 20.1 in the statement of profit or loss and other comprehensive income.
d. For this part, assume that the company chose not to apply hedge accounting as defined. Provide the applicable journal entries for the year ended 30 September 20.1, if delivery of the machine took place on 30 September 20.1 to ensure compliance with the requirements of International Financial Reporting Standards (IFRS).

Ignore taxation.

❖ Suggested solution IAS 21.6[@]

		Rand Dr/(Cr)
a.	**1 January 20.1**	
	No transaction accounted for; FEC with RNil fair value is taken out at no cost.	
	30 June 20.1	
	Bank	439
	Cash flow hedge reserve (OCI) (1)(2)	(439)
	Gain on expiry of FEC, deferred as this is a cash flow hedge	
	30 September 20.1	
	Forward exchange contract (asset) (3)	132
	Cash flow hedge reserve (OCI) (4)	(132)
	Recognise forward exchange contract asset at year-end. Exchange gain is deferred as this is a cash flow hedge up to this point	
	Machine (5)	3 030
	Creditor	(3 030)
	Machine physically delivered and taken up as property, plant and equipment (PPE)	
	Cash flow hedge reserve (equity) (6)	571
	Machine	(571)
	Adjust carrying amount of machine with hedging gains	
b.	**31 January 20.2**	
	Foreign exchange loss (P or L)	95
	Creditor (7)	(95)
	Restate creditor to spot rate at settlement date	
	Forward exchange contract (asset) (8)	493
	Foreign exchange gain (P or L)	(493)
	Restatement of FEC at settlement date	
	Creditor	3 125
	Forward exchange contract (asset) (9)	(625)
	Bank (10)	(2 500)
	Settlement of creditor and net settlement of derivative (FEC)	

(1) (FC1 000/0,41) – (FC1 000/0,50) = R439 gain between first FEC contract rate and the spot rate on the maturity date of the FEC.

(2) Effective part of hedge limited to: (FC1 000/0,51) – (FC1 000/0,41) = R478.

(3) (FC1 000/0,38) – (FC1 000/0,40) = R132 gain between second FEC contract rate, and the contract rate that can be realised at 30 September 20.1 on a similar instrument maturing on 31 January 20.2.

(4) Effective part of hedge (cumulative) limited to the lower of:
(FC1 000/0,51) – (FC1 000/0,33) = R1 070, or
R439 + R132 = R571
Movement in cash flow hedge reserve therefore: R571 (lower of the two) less R439 (previous balance) = R132.

(5) FC1 000/0,33 = R3 030 asset and creditor recorded at spot exchange rate on the transaction date.

(6) R439 + R132 = R571 transfer hedging gains from equity to machine on transaction date.
(7) (FC1 000/0,32) – R3 030 = R95 foreign exchange loss on creditor between transaction date spot rate and settlement date spot rate.
(8) (FC1 000/0,38) – (FC1 000/0,32) = R493 gain on second FEC; difference between spot rate on maturity and the rate used on 30 September 20.1.
(9) R132 + R493 = R625.
(10) FC1 000/0,40 = R2 500 net settlement of FEC.

c. Disclosure

COMPANY NAME
EXTRACT FROM STATEMENT OF PROFIT OR LOSS AND OTHER COMPREHENSIVE INCOME
FOR THE YEAR ENDED 30 SEPTEMBER 20.1

	20.1
	Rand
Profit for the year	xx
Other comprehensive income	
Items that may not subsequently be reclassified to profit or loss	
Gains on cash flow hedge	571
Total comprehensive income for the year	xx

Note: The adjustment of the initial cost of the machine with the R571 cash flow hedge reserve is not a reclassification adjustment and therefore does not flow through other comprehensive income (see IFRS 9.6.5.11(d)(i)).

	Rand
	Dr/(Cr)
d. 1 January 20.1	
No transaction accounted for; FEC with RNil fair value is taken out at no cost	
30 June 20.1	
Bank	439
Foreign exchange gain (P or L) (1)	(439)
Recognise exchange gain on expiry of first FEC	
30 September 20.1	
Forward exchange contract (asset)	132
Foreign exchange gain (P or L) (2)	(132)
Recognise gain on second FEC at year-end	
Machine (3)	3 030
Creditor	(3 030)
Machine physically delivered and taken up as PPE	

(1) (FC1 000/0,41) – (FC1 000/0,50) = R439 gain between first FEC contract rate and the spot rate on the maturity date of the FEC.

(2) (FC1 000/0,38) – (FC1 000/0,40) = R132 gain between second FEC contract rate, and the contract rate that can be realised at 30 September 20.1 on a similar instrument maturing on 31 January 20.2.

(3) FC1 000/0,33 = R3 030 asset and creditor recorded at the spot rate on transaction date.

Note: The journal entries on the creditor settlement date will be exactly the same as for part b of the question if the company elected not to apply hedge accounting.

❑ QUESTION IAS 21.7

Martin Ltd obtained a short-term loan amounting to £500 000 on 1 September 20.4. The amount is repayable on 30 June 20.5 and the company immediately took out forward cover at a discount of R0,04 for the full term. The spot rate on 1 September 20.4 was £1 = R4,50 and consequently the forward rate contracted at was £1 = R4,46 (R4,50 less R0,04 discount).

The continued improvement of the rand against the pound sterling resulted in the company deciding that forward cover was unnecessary. In view of this, the company took out an equal but opposite forward cover contract on 1 January 20.5 for a term of six months. This was acquired at a discount of R0,07. The spot rate on that date amounted to £1 = R4,38 and consequently the forward rate was £1 = R4,31 (R4,38 less R0,07 discount).

On 31 March 20.5, the financial reporting date, the spot rate amounted to £1 = R4,25 and forward exchange contracts maturing on 30 June 20.5 traded at £1 = R4,20. Ignore the effect of the time value of money on the short-term loan and FECs. The loan was granted on market-related terms. The company chooses not to apply hedge accounting. Martin Ltd uses the South African rand (R) as its functional and presentation currency.

Required

a. Provide the applicable journal entries (including cash transactions) for the financial year ended 31 March 20.5 so as to comply with the requirements of International Financial Reporting Standards (IFRS). Ignore journal narrations.

b. Briefly list the presentation and disclosure requirements of International Financial Reporting Standards (IFRS) which result from the above transactions, without preparing the actual notes. Ignore accounting policies.

Ignore taxation.

❖ Suggested solution IAS 21.7

a. Journal entries

	Rand Dr/(Cr)
1 September 20.4	
Bank	2 250 000
Short-term loan (1)	(2 250 000)
31 March 20.5	
Short-term loan (2)	125 000
Foreign exchange gain (P or L)	(125 000)
Foreign exchange loss (P or L) (3)	130 000
Forward exchange contract (liability)	(130 000)

	Rand Dr/(Cr)
Forward exchange contract (asset)	55 000
Foreign exchange gain (P or L) (4)	(55 000)

(1) £500 000 × 4,50 = R2 250 000 loan recognised at spot rate on transaction date.
(2) £500 000 × (4,50 – 4,25) = R125 000 remeasure loan to spot rate at year-end.
(3) £500 000 × (4,46 – 4,20) = R130 000 loss on first FEC between contractual forward rate, and the forward rate that can be realised on a similar instrument maturing on 30 June 20.5, measured at 31 March 20.5. It is a loss, as the FEC would be to buy dollars in order to settle the loan balance in the future.
(4) £500 000 × (4,20 – 4,31) = R55 000 gain on second FEC between contractual forward rate, and the forward rate that can be realised on a similar instrument maturing on 30 June 20.5, at 31 March 20.5. It is a gain, as the FEC would be to sell dollars to offset the impact of the first FEC.

As hedge accounting is not applied, the forward contracts are held-for-trading financial instruments (derivatives) and are consequently classified in the 'at fair value through profit or loss' category (see IFRS 9).

b. Disclosure requirements

- The short-term loan is included on the face of the statement of financial position under current liabilities, in the line item 'financial liabilities'.
- The first FEC (R130 000) is included on the face of the statement of financial position under current liabilities, in the line item 'financial liabilities'.
- The second FEC (R55 000) is included on the face of the statement of financial position under current assets, in the line item 'financial assets'.
- The net foreign exchange gains of R50 000 (R125 000 – R130 000 + R55 000) are included on the face of the statement of profit or loss and other comprehensive income in the 'other income' line item.
- The note to financial liabilities will show the short-term loan of R2 125 000 (R2 250 000 – R125 000) as part of 'financial liabilities measured at amortised cost' (IFRS 7.8(g)).
- The short-term loan will be included in the entity's UK pound analysis of concentration of currency risk (IFRS 7.34(a); B8).
- The entity will include the short-term loan in the appropriate time band in the analysis of concentration of interest rate risk (IFRS 7.34(a); B8).
- The entity will include the short-term loan in the appropriate time band in the analysis of concentration of liquidity risk (IFRS 7.34(a), B8, 39(a), B11).
- The forward cover contract liability of R130 000 will be shown as part of 'financial liabilities at fair value through profit or loss – held for trading' in the note to the financial liability line item (IFRS 7.8(e)).
- The entity will include the forward exchange contract (liability) in the appropriate time band in the analysis of concentration of liquidity risk (IFRS 7.34(a), B8, 39(a), B11).
- The note to financial assets will show the forward exchange contract (asset) of R55 000 as part of 'financial assets at fair value through profit or loss – mandatorily measured as such' (IFRS 7.8(a)).

- The profit before tax note will show separately net gains on financial liabilities measured at amortised cost of R125 000, net losses on financial liabilities at fair value through profit or loss (held for trading) of R130 000 and net gains on financial assets at fair value through profit or loss (mandatorily measured as such) of R55 000 (IFRS 7.20(a)).

❑ QUESTION IAS 21.8

Disvest Ltd is a South African company with the South African rand as its functional and presentation currency. On 1 October 20.4, Disvest Ltd formed a company, Searching Inc, in the USA and took up all the issued shares. Searching Inc has the US dollar as its functional currency. The following list of balances was extracted from the records of the foreign company at 30 September 20.5:

	Dr $	Cr $
Trade and other payables		48 000
Trade receivables	83 000	
Other expenses	87 000	
Bank	44 500	
Depreciation	15 400	
Dividends (paid 30 June 20.5)	40 000	
Property, plant and equipment at cost (1 October 20.4)	84 000	
Accumulated depreciation – property, plant and equipment		15 400
Long-term loan (obtained 30 April 20.5)		75 000
Interest on long-term loan (incurred evenly)	4 500	
Cost of sales	320 000	
Sales		500 000
Share capital		100 000
Closing inventory at cost	60 000	
	738 400	738 400

Additional information

1. Searching Inc's business is not seasonal and activities commenced immediately after incorporation.

2. Closing inventory was purchased evenly during the last three months of the financial year.

3. The long-term loan is repayable in dollars to an American bank on 30 June 20.10.

4. The spot rates were as follows:

1 October 20.4	$1 = R1,50
30 September 20.5	$1 = R1,38

   The rand weakened gradually/evenly against the dollar during the year.

5. Ignore taxation.

Required

a. Translate the trial balance of Searching Inc to rand.
b. Discuss how the gain or loss on translation will be accounted for in the consolidated financial statements of Disvest Ltd.

Your solution must comply with the requirements of International Financial Reporting Standards (IFRS).

❖ **Suggested solution IAS 21.8**

a. Translation

	$ Dr/(Cr)	Rate	Rand Dr/(Cr)
Trade and other payables (1)	(48 000)	1,38	(66 240)
Trade receivables (1)	83 000	1,38	114 540
Other expenses (2)	87 000	1,44	125 280
Bank (1)	44 500	1,38	61 410
Depreciation (2)	15 400	1,44	22 176
Dividends (3)	40 000	1,41	56 400
Property, plant and equipment – cost (1)	84 000	1,38	115 920
Property, plant and equipment – accumulated depreciation (1)	(15 400)	1,38	(21 252)
Long-term loan (1)	(75 000)	1,38	(103 500)
Interest paid (4)	4 500	1,43	6 435
Cost of sales (2)	320 000	1,44	460 800
Sales (2)	(500 000)	1,44	(720 000)
Share capital (5)	(100 000)	1,50	(150 000)
Inventory	60 000	1,38	82 800
Exchange differences (balancing)			15 231
			Nil

(1) Assets and liabilities are translated at the spot rate at year-end (1,38).
(2) Income and expenses incurred evenly during the full financial year are translated at the average rate: (1,50 + 1,38)/2 = 1,44.
(3) Dividends are translated at the spot rate on the transaction date:
1,50 – [(1,50 – 1,38) × 9/12] = 1,41.
Note: as the rand weakened gradually/evenly against the dollar during the year, the movement in the exchange rate is apportioned by 9/12 months to get the spot rate on 30 June 20.5.
(4) Interest paid is translated at the average exchange rate over the last six months of the year, as the loan was only incurred on 30 April 20.5:
[1,38 + (1,50 – 1,38) × 5/12] /2 = 1,43.
(5) Equity is translated at the spot exchange rate at the beginning of the year (1,50).

b. Exchange gain/loss on translation

The exchange gain on translation should be taken to equity via other comprehensive income (foreign currency translation reserve) and should not be accounted for through profit or loss.

❑ QUESTION IAS 21.9

On 1 November 20.1, Zozo Ltd acquired a machine for $100 000 for manufacturing purposes. The machine was put into use immediately. Payment of the purchase price will take place on 15 October 20.2. Depreciation is written off at 20% per annum according to the straight-line method. Wear and tear is allowed at 10% per annum on the reducing balance method and is weighted on a time proportional basis. The tax rate is 27%. The company's reporting date is 31 December. Zozo Ltd uses the South African rand (R) as its functional and presentation currency.

Applicable exchange rates are as follows:

1 November 20.1	R1 = $1,30
31 December 20.1	R1 = $1,28
15 October 20.2	R1 = $1,05

Required

Show the journal entries for 20.1 and 20.2 to ensure compliance with the requirements of International Financial Reporting Standards (IFRS). Journal narrations are not required. Ignore current tax.

❑ QUESTION IAS 21.10

Valuta Ltd purchased certain manufacturing machinery during the year ended 31 December 20.8 for $500 000 from the US. Freight and clearing charges in respect of this transaction amounted to R75 000 and non-refundable import taxes amounted to R100 000.

The order for the machinery was placed on 15 January 20.8 and the machinery was sent free on board (FOB) from New York on 1 February 20.8. It was cleared in Cape Town on 2 May 20.8 and available for use by Valuta Ltd on 1 June 20.8. Depreciation on machinery is written off at 15% per annum on cost on a straight-line basis. For tax purposes a wear-and-tear allowance of 20% per annum, which is unapportioned (i.e. not calculated pro rata) for the year, is applicable.

The purchase was financed via a short-term loan for the same amount from the transaction date. The foreign loan carries interest at 15% per annum (market related) and both the full principal debt and the accrued interest are repayable on 30 June 20.9.

Forward cover was initially not obtained. On 1 September 20.8, the company decided, based on advice given by its bankers, to acquire forward cover in respect of the $500 000 debt in order to economically hedge itself against changes in the fair value of the principal component of the debt. A forward rate of $1 = R2,30 was quoted.

The financial statements for the year ended 31 December 20.8 were finalised on 14 March 20.9. Valuta Ltd uses the South African rand (R) as its functional and presentation currency.

Applicable foreign exchange spot rates are as follows:

	\$1 = R
15 January 20.8	2,00
1 February 20.8	1,98
2 May 20.8	2,10
1 June 20.8	2,15
1 September 20.8	2,20
31 December 20.8	2,18
14 March 20.9	2,50
Average rate: 1 February 20.8 – 31 December 20.8	2,05

On 31 December 20.8, the forward rate on similar forward exchange contracts as the one concluded on 1 September 20.8 was \$1 = R2,32. The tax rate is 27%.

Required

State at what amounts the following items will be shown in the financial statements of Valuta Ltd for the year ended 31 December 20.8:

a. Machinery and depreciation
b. Current liabilities related to the purchase transaction
c. Asset/liability related to the forward exchange contract
d. Foreign exchange differences
e. Interest expense
f. Deferred tax balance

Your answer must comply with the requirements of International Financial Reporting Standards (IFRS). Ignore current tax.

❑ QUESTION IAS 21.11

Betha Ltd, a South African company, concluded the following foreign exchange transactions:

- On 30 June 20.0, a loan of \$10 000 was incurred. The capital is repayable on 31 December 20.1. The loan carries interest at a market-related rate of 10% per annum. Interest is payable six-monthly in arrears.
- An FEC for \$10 000 was concluded on the same day and is renewable on a six-monthly basis. The FEC has not been designated as a hedging instrument for changes in the fair value of the capital of the loan.

Betha Ltd uses the South African rand (R) as its functional and presentation currency.

Additional information

1. The year-end of Betha Ltd is 31 December.

2. The applicable exchange rates are as follows (changes in exchange rates occurred evenly during the periods):

	Spot rate	Forward rate (six months forward)
	$1 = R	$1 = R
30 June 20.0	11.36	10.87
31 December 20.0	10.75	10.53
30 June 20.1	12.20	11.63
31 December 20.1	11.76	N/A

Required
Prepare the journal entries for the years 20.0 and 20.1 to ensure compliance with the requirements of International Financial Reporting Standards (IFRS). Journal narrations are not required. Ignore taxation.

❑ QUESTION IAS 21.12

On 1 January 20.1, Geelbek Ltd acquired an 80% share in Panvis Inc, an American company. Panvis Inc manufactures and markets corn alkaline throughout the US. Panvis Inc operates independently from Geelbek Ltd except that Geelbek Ltd now and then imports corn alkaline from Panvis Inc to sell in South Africa. Geelbek Ltd uses the South African rand (R) as its functional and presentation currency. Panvis Inc uses the American dollar ($) as its functional and presentation currency.

The following trial balance of Panvis Inc is available at 30 June 20.1:

	$ Dr	$ Cr
Share capital		10 000
Retained earnings – 1 Jan 20.1		20 000
Long-term loan		20 000
Trade and other payables		15 000
Property, plant and equipment	20 000	
Inventory (evenly purchased from 1 Jan 20.1 – 30 Jun 20.1)	25 000	
Trade receivables	38 000	
Bank	2 000	
Sales		120 000
Cost of sales	60 000	
Expenses	30 000	
Depreciation	10 000	
	185 000	185 000

Additional information

1. All income and expense items were incurred evenly during the period 1 January 20.1 to 30 June 20.1.

2. Panvis Inc purchased all its property, plant and equipment on 1 January 20.0 on which date the long-term loan was granted.

3. The following exchange rates are applicable:

1 January 20.0	R2,00 = $1
1 January 20.1	R2,40 = $1
30 June 20.1	R2,90 = $1
Weighted average 1 January 20.1 – 30 June 20.1	R2,63 = $1

4. The trial balance of Geelbek Ltd at 30 June 20.1 is as follows:

	Rand Dr/(Cr)
Share capital	(20 000)
Retained earnings – 1 July 20.0	(80 000)
Investment in Panvis Inc (at cost)	57 600
Other investments	200 000
Bank (overdraft)	(37 600)
Long-term liabilities	(100 000)
Dividend income	(45 000)
Interest paid	25 000
	Nil

The dividend income was earned from other investments and not from the investment in Panvis Inc.

5. It is the policy of the group to measure any non-controlling interest at acquisition date at the non-controlling interest's proportionate share of the acquiree's identifiable net assets.

Required

Prepare the consolidated financial statements of the Geelbek Ltd Group for the year ended 30 June 20.1 to ensure compliance with the requirements of International Financial Reporting Standards (IFRS). Ignore taxation. Notes and comparative amounts are not required.

❑ QUESTION IAS 21.13[@]

Ace Ltd bought inventory of Foreign Currency (FC) 50 000 on credit on 1 January 20.0 when the spot rate was FC1 = R2,80. The creditor will be paid on 30 June 20.0.

A FEC maturing on 30 June 20.0 is obtained on 1 January 20.0 at a forward exchange rate of FC1 = R3,00.

The spot rate at reporting date, 28 February 20.0, is FC1 = R2,82 and the forward rate for delivery four months after that date is FC1 = R3,02.

The decision to hedge the import was unanimously taken at a meeting of the board of directors, and the resolution was minuted as such.

Ace Ltd uses the South African rand (R) as its functional and presentation currency.

Required

a. Discuss whether Ace Ltd is allowed to apply hedge accounting in terms of IFRS 9.
b. At 30 June 20.0 the chief executive officer of Ace Ltd asked you for a quantitative indication of how effective the hedge actually was. Calculate hedge effectiveness if the spot rate at 30 June 20.0 was:
   - FC 1 = R3,03
   - FC 1 = R3,90

❑ QUESTION IAS 21.14@

Bee-bee Ltd ordered a machine from the US for $40 000 on 1 February 20.3 in terms of a non-cancellable order. The machine was shipped FOB on 1 May 20.3 (transaction date). It arrived in South Africa on 15 June 20.3 and was available for use on 1 July 20.3.

The creditor is payable on 1 June 20.3. On 1 February 20.3 a four-month FEC was taken out for the full amount payable.

Bee-bee Ltd has a 31 March year-end. Machinery is written off on a straight-line basis over three years.

The applicable foreign exchange rates were as follows:

Date	**Spot rate $1 = R**	**Forward rate $1 = R**
1 February 20.3	7,00	7,03 (4 months)
31 March 20.3	7,10	7,14 (2 months)
1 May 20.3	7,20	7,22 (1 month)
1 June 20.3	7,25	

The entity applies cash flow hedge accounting to the foreign currency risk of firm commitments and fair value hedge accounting to recognised liabilities. Bee-bee Ltd uses the South African rand (R) as its functional and presentation currency.

Required

Prepare the journal entries for Bee-bee Ltd for the years ended 31 March 20.3 and 31 March 20.4 to account for the above-mentioned information.

Ignore taxation.

❑ QUESTION IAS 21.15@

On 15 September 20.2, SA Ltd received inventory from Germany with an invoice value of €200 000. The irrevocable order was placed on 30 June 20.2 and the goods were shipped FOB on 31 July 20.2. The entity elected not to apply hedge accounting. SA Ltd uses the South African rand (R) as its functional and presentation currency.

Applicable spot exchange rates at 31 July 20.2 are as follows: R1 = $0,48 and $1 = €3,11.

SA Ltd decided to hedge only the rand/dollar leg of the transaction on 31 August 20.2 at a cover discount of $0,02. Applicable spot exchange rates at 31 August 20.2 are as follows: R1 = $0,46 and $1 = €3,07.

Settlement took place on 28 February 20.3 when the relevant spot exchange rates were as follows: R1 = \$0,38 and \$1 = €2,86.

Assume that all the inventories had been sold by the reporting date, 31 March 20.3.

Required

Provide the applicable journal entries, including cash transactions, from 30 June 20.2 to 31 March 20.3 to ensure compliance with the requirements of International Financial Reporting Standards (IFRS). Journal narrations are not required. Ignore taxation.

❑ QUESTION IAS 21.16[@]

Alfa Ltd imported inventory to the value of \$10 000 from the US during the year ended 28 February 20.2. Goods were shipped 'free on board' (FOB) on 1 October 20.1 (transaction date).

The company adds 40% to the cost price of inventory to determine the selling price. On 28 February 20.2, 65% of the imported inventory was still on hand, but by 28 February 20.3 all imported inventory had been sold. All goods were sold on credit to customers.

Applicable exchange rates (spot rates) are as follows:

	\$1 = R
1 March 20.1	3,15
30 April 20.1	2,95
31 August 20.1	3,00
1 October 20.1	3,05
30 October 20.1	2,90
30 November 20.1	2,65
28 February 20.2	2,90
31 March 20.2	3,28
1 May 20.2	2,90
28 February 20.3	3,10

The company accounts for hedges of the changes in fair value of recognised liabilities as a result of changes in foreign exchange rates as fair value hedges. You may assume that the hedging criteria per IFRS 9.6.4.1 have been complied with. Ignore taxation. Alfa Ltd uses the South African rand (R) as its functional and presentation currency.

Required

Journal narrations are not required for the following parts, and your solutions must comply with the requirements of International Financial Reporting Standards (IFRS).

a. Prepare the journal entries for the two years until 28 February 20.3 if the transaction had not been covered. The foreign creditor was paid on 1 May 20.2.

b. Prepare the journal entries for the two years until 28 February 20.3 if a forward exchange contract was taken out on 1 October 20.1 to cover the transaction at a forward rate of \$1 = R3,25, and it was renewed on 31 March 20.2 at a forward rate of \$1 = 3,30. On 28 February 20.2, the forward rate on similar FECs was \$1 = R3,27. The creditor was paid on the expiry date of the second FEC, namely 1 May 20.2.

c. Provide the journal entries for the year ended 28 February 20.2 if an FEC was taken out on 30 April 20.1 in anticipation of the highly probable purchase transaction on 1 October 20.1 at a forward rate of $1 = R3,00. On 1 October 20.1, the forward rate on similar FECs was $1 = R3,10. The foreign creditor was paid on 30 October 20.1, the expiry date of the FEC.

d. Provide the journal entries for the year ended 28 February 20.2 if an FEC was already taken out on 1 March 20.1 in anticipation of the purchase transaction at a forward rate of $1 = R3,20. The FEC was renewed on 31 August 20.1 at $1 = R3,12. The renewal of the forward cover is part of, and consistent with, the company's documented risk management objectives. On 1 October 20.1 the FEC rate on similar FECs is $1 = R3,10. The foreign creditor was paid on 30 October 20.1, the expiry date of the FEC.

e. Provide the journal entries for the year to 28 February 20.2 if an FEC which expires on 31 March 20.2 (the day on which the foreign creditor must be paid) was taken out on 1 October 20.1 at a forward rate of $1 = R3,25. However, on 30 November 20.1 a decision was taken to immediately settle the creditor, and an equal and opposite FEC which also expires on 31 March 20.2 was taken out at $1 = R2,75. On 28 February 20.2 the forward rate on similar FECs, in respect of both the original FEC and the equal and opposite FEC, is $1 = R3,27.

IAS 23

Borrowing costs

❑ **QUESTIONS AND SOLUTIONS**

❑ **QUESTIONS**

 # These questions contain topics or principles that were at an awareness level of proficiency in the ITC syllabus of SAICA, at the time of publishing this book.

❑ QUESTION IAS 23.1#

You have recently been appointed as the accountant of Asterix Ltd. The company is currently in the process of constructing a new manufacturing plant and the financial director approached you for advice regarding the application of IAS 23.

You obtained the following information:

1. The board of directors appointed a committee to research the project. The committee estimated that it would take 20 months to complete the construction of the plant.

2. Construction of the plant commenced on 12 June 20.1.

3. Expenditure associated with the project has already been correctly capitalised to the cost of the plant, but no borrowing costs have been capitalised to date.

4. The project is financed as follows:
   - Use of a general overdraft facility at an interest rate of 24% per annum until 31 October 20.1.
   - The issue of debentures on 1 November 20.1 at an interest rate of 12% per annum, redeemable at a premium of 5%. These debentures will be issued specifically to finance the project.

5. The company's reporting date is 31 October 20.1.

Required

Advise the financial director of Asterix Ltd on the following:

a. Whether the interest paid on the overdraft facility for the period 12 June 20.1 to 31 October 20.1 should be capitalised to the plant.
b. Whether the interest paid on the debentures as well as the premium on future redemption, should be capitalised to the plant.

Justify your answer with reference to International Financial Reporting Standards (IFRS).

❖ Suggested solution IAS 23.1#

a. Comments – Overdraft facility

Borrowing costs that are directly attributable to the acquisition, construction or production of a qualifying asset, must be capitalised to the cost of that asset (IAS 23.8). The manufacturing plant is a qualifying asset since it is an asset that will necessarily take a substantial period of time (i.e. 20 months) to get ready for its intended use (IAS 23.5 and .7).

The borrowing costs that are directly attributable to the construction of the plant are those borrowing costs that would have been avoided if the expenditure on the qualifying asset had not been incurred (IAS 23.10).

Where funds are borrowed generally, as is the case with the overdraft facility, the borrowing costs capitalised are calculated by applying the capitalisation rate to the expenditures on that asset, while the amount of borrowing costs capitalised during a period must be limited to the amount of borrowing costs actually incurred during that period (IAS 23.14).

Therefore, the interest paid on the overdraft facility should be capitalised to the cost of the manufacturing plant, but subject to the requirements above.

b. Comments – Debentures

Where funds are borrowed specifically for the purpose of obtaining a qualifying asset, as is the case with the issue of the debentures, the actual borrowing costs incurred during the period less any investment income on the temporary investment of those funds, should be capitalised (IAS 23.12).

In terms of IAS 23.6(a), any interest calculated in accordance with the effective interest method of IFRS 9 can be capitalised as borrowing costs. Effective interest in terms of IFRS 9 includes all fees, transaction costs, premiums and discounts. Therefore the effective interest calculated on the debentures (taking into account the payment based on the coupon rate as well as the redemption of the debentures at a premium of 5%), should be capitalised to the cost of the manufacturing plant.

❑ QUESTION IAS 23.2#

On 1 January 20.10, an entity obtained a loan of R2 million to specifically fund the construction of a qualifying asset.

Expenditure in respect of the asset was incurred evenly during each of the following periods:

	Rand
1 March 20.10 – 31 May 20.10	200 000
1 June 20.10 – 31 August 20.10	400 000
1 September 20.10 – 30 November 20.10	1 400 000
	2 000 000

Interest incurred in respect of the specific loan was as follows:

	Rand
1 January 20.10 – 28 February 20.10	40 000
1 March 20.10 – 30 November 20.10	180 000
1 December 20.10 – 31 December 20.10	20 000
	240 000

Interest income earned from the temporary investment of surplus funds obtained from the specific loan, was as follows:

	Rand
1 January 20.10 – 28 February 20.10	13 333
1 March 20.10 – 30 November 20.10	84 000
1 December 20.10 – 31 December 20.10	–
	97 333

Additional information

1. The activities necessary to prepare the asset for its intended use commenced on 1 March 20.10, while substantially all these activities were complete on 1 December 20.10.

2. The asset was available for use as intended by management on 31 December 20.10.

3. The entity has a 31 December reporting date.

Required

Calculate the amount of borrowing costs to be capitalised for the year ended 31 December 20.10 in accordance with International Financial Reporting Standards (IFRS).

❖ **Suggested solution IAS 23.2#**

Borrowing costs capitalised for the year ended 31 December 20.10

	Rand
Interest incurred on specific loan (1 Mar 20.10 – 30 Nov 20.10)	180 000
Interest income earned (1 Mar 20.10 – 30 Nov 20.10)	(84 000)
Borrowing costs capitalised	96 000

❑ QUESTION IAS 23.3#

Dam Ltd is currently busy with the construction of a catchment dam, which is a qualifying asset for the purposes of IAS 23. The following information relates to this project:

Commencement date	1 July 20.3
Balance at 1 January 20.4	
Costs capitalised to date (excluding borrowing costs)	R2 500 000
Borrowing costs capitalised to date	R90 000
Financing available	
Debentures @ 16% per annum	R4 000 000
Bank overdraft @ 17% – 19% per annum	R3 000 000
General loan @ 20% per annum (from 15 August 20.4)	R1 500 000

None of the available financing is considered to be specific to this project.

Borrowing costs are capitalised quarterly for accounting purposes. The following capitalisation rates are available:

1 January 20.4 – 31 March 20.4	16,43% per annum
1 April 20.4 – 30 June 20.4	17,29% per annum
1 July 20.4 – 30 September 20.4	17,55% per annum
1 October 20.4 – 31 December 20.4	17,76% per annum

During the current financial year, project costs were incurred evenly over the following periods:

	Rand
1 January 20.4 – 31 March 20.4	1 500 000
1 April 20.4 – 30 June 20.4	1 700 000
1 July 20.4 – 30 September 20.4	2 000 000
1 October 20.4 – 15 December 20.4	1 200 000

The project was completed on 15 December 20.4.

Required

Calculate the amount of borrowing costs that should be capitalised for the year ended 31 December 20.4, in accordance with International Financial Reporting Standards (IFRS). Round all calculations to the nearest rand.

❖ **Suggested solution IAS 23.3#**

Borrowing costs capitalised

Carrying amount	**Rand**		**Interest Rand**
Opening balance (1)	2 590 000	× 16,43% × 3/12	106 384
Project costs	1 500 000	× 50% × 16,43% × 3/12	30 806
Borrowing costs	137 190		137 190
	4 227 190	× 17,29% × 3/12	182 720
Project costs	1 700 000	× 50% × 17,29% × 3/12	36 741
Borrowing costs	219 461		219 461
	6 146 651	× 17,55% × 3/12	269 684
Project costs	2 000 000	× 50% × 17,55% × 3/12	43 875
Borrowing costs	313 559		313 559
	8 460 210	× 17,76% × 2½/12	313 028
Project costs	1 200 000	× 50% × 17,76% × 2½/12	22 200
Borrowing costs	335 228		335 228
	9 995 438		
Borrowing costs to be capitalised for 20.4			1 005 438

(1) 2 500 000 + 90 000 = 2 590 000

❑ **QUESTION IAS 23.4#**

Talita Ltd commenced with the construction of a new warehouse on 1 January 20.5. The following relevant information is available:

Estimated cost of the warehouse	R4 000 000
Estimated period of construction	16 months

Expenditure in respect of the project was incurred evenly during each of the following months:

	Rand
January 20.5	80 000
February 20.5	30 000
March 20.5	60 000
April 20.5	50 000
December 20.5	200 000

On 30 April 20.5, active development of the warehouse was suspended. Construction only resumed on 1 December 20.5.

From 1 January 20.5 up to 31 March 20.5, the project was primarily financed with a bank overdraft facility at an interest rate of 15% per annum, which was specifically obtained for the project. Assume that interest incurred in respect of the bank overdraft facility amounted to R3 438 for the period 1 January 20.5 to 31 March 20.5. The balance of the bank overdraft facility was R170 000 on 1 April 20.5.

On 1 April 20.5, the full balance of the bank overdraft facility was repaid from the general borrowings of the company. From that date onwards, the project was also financed by means of the general borrowings of the company. Assume a capitalisation rate of 17% per annum. Borrowing costs are capitalised on an annual basis for accounting purposes.

The total interest expense of Talita Ltd amounted to R1 374 567 for the year ended 31 December 20.5.

Required

Disclose the following notes to the financial statements of Talita Ltd for the year ended 31 December 20.5, in accordance with International Financial Reporting Standards (IFRS):

- Property, plant and equipment
- Finance costs

Accounting policy notes and comparative amounts are not required. Round all calculations to the nearest rand.

❖ **Suggested solution IAS 23.4#**

Disclosure

TALITA LTD
NOTES FOR THE YEAR ENDED 31 DECEMBER 20.5

1. Property, plant and equipment

	Rand
Building under construction	
Carrying amount beginning of the year	–
Cost	–
Accumulated depreciation	–
Additions (1)	420 000
Borrowing costs capitalised (calc 2)	10 734
Carrying amount end of the year	430 734
Cost	430 734
Accumulated depreciation	–

(1) 80 000 + 30 000 + 60 000 + 50 000 + 200 000 = 420 000

4. Finance costs

	Rand
Finance costs incurred (given)	1 374 567
Capitalised (calc 2)	(10 734)
	1 363 833

The capitalisation rate used for the capitalisation of borrowing costs was 15% per annum for specific borrowings and 17% per annum for general borrowings.

Calculations

1. Amount utilised from general borrowings

	Rand
Bank overdraft repaid on 1 April 20.5 (given)	170 000
Expenditure incurred during April 20.5	50 000
Balance on 30 April 20.5	220 000
Expenditure incurred during December 20.5	200 000
Balance on 31 December 20.5	420 000

Borrowing costs to be capitalised in respect of general borrowings

	Rand
1 Apr 20.5 – 30 Apr 20.5 [(170 000 + 220 000)/2 × 17% × 1/12]	2 763
1 Dec 20.5 – 31 Dec 20.5 [(220 000 + 420 000)/2 × 17% × 1/12]	4 533
	7 296

Note: Capitalisation of borrowing costs should be suspended during extended periods where active development is suspended (IAS 23.20). Consequently, no borrowing costs should be capitalised from May 20.5 to November 20.5.

2. Borrowing costs capitalised

	Rand
Interest paid on bank overdraft (given)	3 438
Interest on general pool of funds (calc 1)	7 296
Borrowing costs capitalised	10 734

❑ QUESTION IAS 23.5#

The following sequence of events relating to Atlantic Ltd took place during the year ended 31 December 20.5:

15 January
Atlantic Ltd purchased a piece of land on the West Coast for R2 million on 15 January 20.5, using a mortgage bond that carries interest at 18% per annum. When the land was purchased, the directors had no formal plans relating to the use of this land but after extensive market research the directors decided to build luxury townhouses on the property.

28 February
The directors approached architects to draw up the necessary plans as well as town planners to assist with the necessary rezoning applications.

30 April
Building commenced on this date and the builders worked hard to finish the buildings in time for the summer season.

31 October
All major buildings and townhouses were completed and ready for occupation. Only 25 of the 100 townhouses were sold by this date.

15 December
A large company bought 50 of the townhouses for their staff.

31 December
The remaining 25 townhouses are unsold but the directors are confident that they will be sold in the new financial year.

Additional information

1. Building costs of R4 million in respect of the townhouses were incurred evenly over the construction period of 30 April 20.5 to 31 October 20.5. These costs were financed by means of general borrowings of the entity.

2. During the year ended 31 December 20.5, borrowing costs of R500 000 were incurred in respect of the general borrowings of the entity at an average borrowing rate of 15% per annum.

3. Borrowing costs are capitalised annually for accounting purposes.

Required

a. Briefly discuss the relevant dates for the commencement and cessation of the capitalisation of borrowing costs, in accordance with International Financial Reporting Standards (IFRS).
b. Calculate the amount of borrowing costs to be capitalised for the year ended 31 December 20.5, in accordance with International Financial Reporting Standards (IFRS).
c. The directors only want to capitalise the borrowing costs incurred in respect of the townhouses (buildings) and not the borrowing costs incurred in respect of the land. Advise the directors in accordance with International Financial Reporting Standards (IFRS) of the acceptability, or not, of the above treatment.

❑ QUESTION IAS 23.6#

JR Ltd commenced with the construction of a new office building, known as the Dallas project, during the 20.5 financial year. The building is intended to be used as the administrative head office of the company.

The following information relates to the Dallas project:

- Land was purchased on 1 January 20.2 for R500 000. The purchase of the land was financed by means of a mortgage bond that was obtained on the same day from Pleasure Bank, at an interest rate of 12% per annum. The following interest was incurred in respect of this loan:

	Rand
1 January 20.5 – 31 January 20.5	5 000
1 February 20.5 – 31 December 20.5	55 000
	60 000
1 January 20.6 – 31 March 20.6	12 000
1 April 20.6 – 31 December 20.6	36 000
	48 000

- The construction of the office building was undertaken internally and commenced on 1 February 20.5.

- Klippe Kou Bank granted a mortgage bond of R1 500 000, which was taken up in full on 1 February 20.5, specifically for the construction of the office building. The loan bears interest at 20% per annum. The following interest was incurred in respect of this loan:

	Rand
1 February 20.5 – 31 December 20.5	275 000
1 January 20.6 – 31 March 20.6	75 000
1 April 20.6 – 31 December 20.6	225 000
	300 000

The funds obtained from the mortgage bond were invested at Maksimallie Bank on 1 February 20.5, at an interest rate of 1% per month. The following interest was earned in respect of the temporary investment of the surplus funds from the loan:

	Rand
1 February 20.5 – 31 July 20.5	72 000
1 August 20.5 – 31 December 20.5	26 250
	98 250
1 January 20.6 – 31 January 20.6	750

- The cost and completion dates of the office building are as follows:

	Costs Rand	Completion date
Phase 1	600 000	31 July 20.5
Phase 2	900 000	31 January 20.6
Phase 3	150 000	31 March 20.6

Phases 2 and 3 will only commence on completion of phases 1 and 2 respectively. The asset can only be put into use on completion of phase 3.

Expenditure within each phase is incurred evenly and paid for immediately.

Any expenditure in respect of the project that exceeds external financing, is financed from surplus cash funds of the company.

Additional information

1. JR Ltd did not incur any other borrowing costs, except for those mentioned above.

2. The office building was available for use as intended by management on 1 April 20.6 and was also taken into use on that date. Office buildings are depreciated over 10 years according to the straight-line method. Assume that there is no building allowance in respect of the office building for tax purposes, as it was erected before new tax legislation came into effect.

3. Assume that JR Ltd does not carry on a 'trade' for tax purposes before the office building is taken into use, and that pre-production interest is therefore deferred in accordance with section 11A and only allowed as a tax deduction when the office building is taken into use.

4. Assume a tax rate of 27% and that there will be sufficient future taxable profit against which any deductible temporary differences can be utilised. On 1 January 20.5, the balance on the deferred tax account was RNil.

5. Assume a profit before tax of R1 000 000 for both years before taking the above-mentioned information into account.

Required

a. Calculate the cumulative borrowing costs that must be capitalised in respect of the land and office building for the years ended 31 December 20.5 and 31 December 20.6, in accordance with International Financial Reporting Standards (IFRS).
b. Calculate the carrying amount of the land and office building (Dallas project) to be included in the financial statements of JR Ltd for the years ended 31 December 20.5 and 31 December 20.6, in accordance with International Financial Reporting Standards (IFRS).
c. Disclose the following notes to the financial statements of JR Ltd for the year ended 31 December 20.6, in accordance with International Financial Reporting Standards (IFRS):
   - Finance costs
   - Income tax expense

IAS 24

Related party disclosures

❑ QUESTIONS AND SOLUTIONS

❑ QUESTIONS

❑ QUESTION IAS 24.1

Asort Ltd's group structure includes various entities and management are concerned about the implications that the disclosure requirements of the standard on related parties (IAS 24) might have on their annual financial reporting.

Required

Explain how the disclosure requirements of IAS 24 address the qualitative characteristics of faithful representation and comparability as set out in the Conceptual Framework for Financial Reporting (2010).

❖ Suggested solution IAS 24.1

Faithful representation

Financial statements must be a faithful representation of that which they purport to represent. This implies that financial statements are a representation of transactions which are entered into with independent parties under normal business conditions.

Transactions between related parties, however, are frequently entered into under conditions which do not normally apply in the free market. Therefore, these transactions would compromise the reliability of the financial statements in general. Good examples of related party transactions are free management services delivered to a subsidiary by its parent and an advertising campaign which benefits all the companies in a group, but the cost of which is carried by only one of the companies in the group.

The scope of IAS 24 covers the identification and disclosure of these related party transactions, and the application of this standard will therefore ultimately improve the faithful representation and therefore also the usefulness of financial statements, because due to this disclosure the users of financial statements then have the necessary information for decision-making at their disposal.

Comparability

According to the Conceptual Framework, users of financial statements must be able to compare the financial statements of different entities in order to evaluate their relative financial position, performance and changes in financial position (economic resources of the entity and claims against the entity). The financial statements of related parties, which include related party transactions of a material nature, will not be comparable to those of entities whose financial statements do not include such transactions. The reason for this is that transactions between related parties are frequently entered into under conditions which do not normally apply in the free market.

The scope of IAS 24 covers the identification and disclosure of these related party transactions and the application of IAS 24 will therefore ultimately improve the comparability, faithful representation and therefore also the usefulness of financial statements.

❑ QUESTION IAS 24.2

Mr Smith holds 11% of the issued ordinary share capital and of the voting rights of Devlop Ltd. His five-year-old son holds 40% of the voting rights as he has inherited shares from his late uncle who was a shareholder of Devlop Ltd.

Required

a. Discuss whether Mr Smith is a related party of Devlop Ltd.
b. How would your answer in a. change if Mr Smith's son was 25 years old?

❖ Suggested solution IAS 24.2

a. Mr Smith's son is a party that is related to Devlop Ltd, as his son owns an interest in the entity that gives him significant influence over Devlop Ltd (par (a)(ii) of the definition of a related party in IAS 24). Note that IAS 28.5 assumes that a party exercises significant influence over an entity if it owns more than 20% of the voting power of the entity.

A close family member of the five-year-old son would also be a related party of Devlop Ltd in accordance with par (a) of the definition of a related party in IAS 24. The question therefore is whether Mr Smith is a close family member of his five-year-old son. IAS 24 defines a close member of family as those persons that may be expected to influence or to be influenced by that person in their dealings with the reporting entity.

One can reasonably assume that Mr Smith will influence his five-year-old son and as such Mr Smith is also a related party of Devlop Ltd.

b. Mr Smith's son will still be a related party of Devlop Ltd as he has significant influence over Devlop Ltd. Mr Smith will only be a related party if he can influence his son in his dealings with Devlop Ltd, or vice versa. Although his son is not a minor, they will probably still influence one another. Mr Smith is therefore still a related party of Devlop Ltd.

❑ QUESTION IAS 24.3

The following related party transaction occurred between Bubble Bath Ltd and its parent, Soap Suds Ltd, for the financial year ended 31 December 20.9:

- Bubble Bath Ltd borrowed an amount of R275 000 as a medium-term loan from Clean Bank on 31 December 20.9. The bank was not willing to grant the loan unless Soap Suds Ltd signed as guarantor in respect of the loan. The loan is repayable in 24 monthly instalments, starting on 31 January 20.10. The market-related interest rate on this loan is 20% per annum compounded monthly. Soap Suds Ltd does not make use of debt in the financing of its operations.

Required

a. Discuss whether or not the above-mentioned related party transaction requires disclosure in the consolidated financial statements of the group.
b. Discuss whether or not the above-mentioned related party transaction requires disclosure in the separate financial statements of the parent, Soap Suds Ltd.

❖ **Suggested solution IAS 24.3**

a. According to IAS 24.3, disclosure of intragroup-related party transactions, including commitments, are required in consolidated financial statements, even though such transactions are eliminated in the preparation of consolidated financial statements.

b. According to IAS 24.3, disclosure of intragroup-related party transactions, including commitments, are specifically also required in separate financial statements of a parent. This matter therefore requires disclosure in the separate financial statements of Soap Suds Ltd.

❑ **QUESTION IAS 24.4**

Saafaa Ltd is the reporting entity and manufactures soccer balls. Mr Zakumi is the managing director of Saafaa Ltd and he controls Vuvuzela Ltd. Mr Zakumi is married to Mrs Zakumi. Mr Zakumi is also a director of Rugby Ltd.

Saafaa Ltd is a subsidiary of Fiifaa Ltd. Fiifaa Ltd also controls Itali Ltd through its 75% interest in the ordinary shares of Itali Ltd.

Saafaa Ltd owns 90% of the ordinary shares of Jerseys Ltd, a company that manufactures soccer jerseys. Saafaa Ltd also has significant influence over Baggs Ltd, a company that manufactures sports bags.

All the employees of Saafaa Ltd are members of the Bafaan Pension Fund and members of the Soccas Trade Union.

Required

Indicate which of the parties are related to Saafaa Ltd and which are not.

❖ **Suggested solution IAS 24.4**

The following persons are related to Saafaa Ltd:

- Mr Zakumi as a member of the key management personnel of Saafaa Ltd (definition of related party, par (a)(iii))
- Mrs Zakumi as a close member of family of Mr Zakumi (par (a))

The following entities are related to Saafaa Ltd:

- Vuvuzela Ltd as it is controlled by Mr Zakumi (identified in par (a) as a member of the key management personnel of Saafaa Ltd) (par (b)(vi))
- Fiifaa Ltd as the parent of Saafaa Ltd (par (b)(i))
- Itali Ltd as a fellow subsidiary in the same group (par (b)(i))
- Jersey Ltd as a subsidiary of Saafaa Ltd (par (b)(i))
- Baggs Ltd as an associate of Saafaa Ltd (par (b)(ii))
- Bafaan Pension Plan as the post-employment benefit plan for the benefit of the employees of Saafaa Ltd (par (b)(v))

The following entities are not related to Saafaa Ltd:

- Rugby Ltd – the fact that Mr Zakumi is a member of the key management personnel of both entities does not on its own cause Rugby Ltd to be a related party (par 11(a))
- Soccas Trade Union, simply by virtue of its normal dealings with Saafaa Ltd (par 11(c)(ii))

❑ QUESTION IAS 24.5

Mr White is the senior manager in charge of the purchasing department of Red Ltd, a company that makes significant purchases. Mr White arranges the purchase of a material amount of inventory from Blue Ltd, a company which he controls.

Required

Discuss whether Mr White and Blue Ltd are related parties of Red Ltd.

❑ QUESTION IAS 24.6

Approximately 90% of the employees of a gold-mining company, Black Hole Ltd, are members of the industry trade union, MUNSA. During the past financial year MUNSA, under the leadership of Mr PM Mokgaba, was able to negotiate a 25% increase in the basic wage rate of its union members, with a two-year backdated effect. Mr Mokgaba is also a director of Black Hole Ltd.

Required

Discuss whether Mr Mokgaba and MUNSA are related parties of Black Hole Ltd.

❑ QUESTION IAS 24.7

The following information has been extracted from the financial statements of Romulus Ltd and Remus Ltd for the year ended 31 December 20.8:

	Romulus Ltd Rand	**Remus Ltd Rand**
Revenue	15 000	12 000
Cost of sales	(12 000)	(10 000)
Gross profit	3 000	2 000
Other expense	(1 000)	(800)
Profit before tax	2 000	1 200

The following information has been brought to your attention by the senior accountant of Romulus Ltd, Mrs Wolf:

- Mr Fox is an executive director of Romulus Ltd and a non-executive director of Remus Ltd. His brother, Mr Jackal, is the executive director of Remus Ltd.
- Remus Ltd purchases inventory from Romulus Ltd. The normal pricing policy of Romulus is to add a 50% mark-up to its cost price in order to calculate the selling price. Inventory sold to Remus Ltd is, however, sold at a mark-up of 10% on cost price. Goods at a cost price of R1,5 million were sold to Remus Ltd during the year ended 31 December 20.8. Remus Ltd owes Romulus Ltd R500 000 on 31 December 20.8 for these purchases.
- Remus Ltd provides administrative services to the branches of Romulus Ltd. According to the administrative manager of Remus Ltd, the cost of these services, if billed in the open market, would amount to R200 000. No entries were accounted for in the records of either company in respect of these transactions as it was agreed upon between the companies that the service would be provided free of charge.

Required

a. Discuss whether Remus Ltd is a related party of Romulus Ltd.
b. If one assumes that Remus Ltd is related party of Romulus Ltd, disclose the relevant note in the financial statements of Romulus Ltd for the year ended 31 December 20.8 in respect of the related party transactions, so as to comply with the requirements of International Financial Reporting Standards (IFRS).

❑ QUESTION IAS 24.8

Mr Binocular is the controlling shareholder of Birds Ltd. He also holds 40% of the ordinary shares of Antelope Ltd, giving him significant influence over the company. Mr Binocular is a director of Wildlife Ltd.

Birds Ltd has joint control over Kingfisher Ltd and Barbet Ltd. Kingfisher Ltd is the parent of Canary Ltd.

Birds Ltd also controls Eagle Ltd and has significant influence over Pigeon Ltd. Pigeon Ltd controls Penguin Ltd.

Required

a. Identify the related parties of Birds Ltd.
b. Indicate whether Barbet Ltd is a related party of Kingfisher Ltd.
c. Indicate whether Pigeon Ltd is a related party of Kingfisher Ltd.

❑ QUESTION IAS 24.9

The South African (SA) Department of Education is controlled by the SA government. Mrs Creeley is the MEC (Member of the Executive Committee) for the Department of Education. Mrs Creeley owns 100% of the share capital of Stationary (Pty) Ltd.

The SA government has significant influence over South African Airways (Pty) Ltd. South African Airways (Pty) Ltd controls SA Travel (Pty) Ltd and has significant influence over Fly Kooler (Pty) Ltd. The SA government also has joint control of SA Training (Pty) Ltd.

During the past financial year there were material transactions between the Department of Education and Stationary (Pty) Ltd, South African Airways (Pty) Ltd, SA Travel (Pty) Ltd, SA Training (Pty) Ltd and Fly Kooler (Pty) Ltd.

Required

a. In terms of IAS 24.25, identify the related parties of the Department of Education that will be exempt from the disclosure requirements of IAS 24.18.
b. Name the minimum disclosure requirements stated in IAS 24.26 that the reporting entity must adhere to if that entity were to be exempt from the disclosure requirements of IAS 24.18.
c. Indicate which entity or entities are not exempt in terms of IAS 24.25 and therefore have to disclose all information in accordance with IAS 24.18, as well as which entity or entities are not subject to the disclosure requirements of IAS 24 at all.

IAS 27

Separate financial statements

Note: As this chapter and the chapter on IFRS 10 both deal with consolidations, the questions on these two chapters are integrated and such questions are presented as part of the chapter on IFRS 10.

IAS 28 & IFRS 12

Investments in associates

Note:	This chapter deals only with investments in associates. Investments in joint ventures are dealt with in the chapter on IFRS 11.

❑ QUESTIONS AND SOLUTIONS

IAS 28.1	Basic set of financial statements based on the equity method
IAS 28.2	Basic set of financial statements based on the equity method
IAS 28.3	Piecemeal acquisition of a holding in an associate
IAS 28.4	Associate with other post-acquisition reserves and post-acquisition losses
IAS 28.5	Associate with significant post-acquisition losses

❑ QUESTIONS

IAS 28.6	An associate with intragroup transactions
IAS 28.7	An associate with other post-acquisition reserves
IAS 28.8[@]	Associates in a vertical group
IAS 28.9	Associate with intragroup transactions
IAS 28.10	Associate with intragroup transactions

[@] *This question contains topics or principles that were not included in the ITC syllabus of SAICA at the time of publishing this book, but might still be included in university syllabi.*

❑ QUESTION IAS 28.1

Hommel Ltd acquired 70 000 of the issued ordinary shares of Abel (Pty) Ltd on 1 January 20.1 for R100 000. Abel (Pty) Ltd is unlisted and operates in the textile industry. The acquisition of the shares enables Hommel Ltd to exercise significant influence over the policy-making decisions of Abel (Pty) Ltd. At the date of acquisition the abridged statement of financial position of Abel (Pty) Ltd was as follows:

ABEL (PTY) LTD
STATEMENT OF FINANCIAL POSITION AS AT 1 JANUARY 20.1

	Rand
ASSETS	
Current assets	400 000
Total assets	400 000
EQUITY AND LIABILITIES	
Total equity	400 000
Share capital (280 000 shares)	280 000
Retained earnings	120 000
Total equity and liabilities	400 000

After completion of the purchase transaction Hommel Ltd's statement of financial position was as follows:

HOMMEL LTD
STATEMENT OF FINANCIAL POSITION AS AT 1 JANUARY 20.1

	Rand
ASSETS	
Non-current assets	
Investment in associate	100 000
Current assets	500 000
Total assets	600 000
EQUITY AND LIABILITIES	
Total equity	600 000
Share capital	360 000
Retained earnings	240 000
Total equity and liabilities	600 000

The reporting date ends on 31 December each year. The revenue of Hommel Ltd for 20.1 amounted to R253 500, while cost of sales, other expenses and tax amounted to R55 000, R37 500 and R45 080 respectively. A dividend of R40 000 was paid at year end.

The profit after tax of Abel (Pty) Ltd for 20.1 (from rental income) amounted to R43 200 (after tax of R16 800). A dividend of R16 000 was paid on 30 September 20.1.

Required

a. Prepare the statement of profit or loss and other comprehensive income, statement of financial position, as well as the statement of changes in equity, in which the investment in Abel (Pty) Ltd is accounted for by using the equity method, of Hommel Ltd for the year ended 31 December 20.1.

b. Provide the relevant notes to the financial statements of Hommel Ltd for the year ended 31 December 20.1 in as far as this relates to the investment in associate.

Your solution must comply with the requirements of International Financial Reporting Standards (IFRS). Comparative amounts are not required.

❖ **Suggested solution IAS 28.1**

HOMMEL LTD
STATEMENT OF FINANCIAL POSITION AS AT 31 DECEMBER 20.1

	Note	Rand
ASSETS		
Non-current assets		
Investment in associate	3	106 800
Current assets (1)		579 920
Total assets		686 720
EQUITY AND LIABILITIES		
Total equity		686 720
Share capital		360 000
Retained earnings		326 720
Total equity and liabilities		686 720

(1) Balancing figure

HOMMEL LTD
STATEMENT OF PROFIT OR LOSS AND OTHER COMPREHENSIVE INCOME FOR THE YEAR ENDED 31 DECEMBER 20.1

	Note	Rand
Revenue		253 500
Cost of sales		(55 000)
Gross profit		198 500
Other expenses		(37 500)
Share of profit of associate (2)	2	10 800
Profit before tax		171 800
Income tax expense		(45 080)
Profit for the year		126 720
Other comprehensive income		–
Total comprehensive income for the year		126 720

(2) 43 200 × 25% = 10 800 or
[(43 200 – 16 000) × 25%] + (16 000 × 25%) (dividend) = 10 800

HOMMEL LTD
STATEMENT OF CHANGES IN EQUITY FOR THE YEAR ENDED 31 DECEMBER 20.1

	Share capital Rand	Retained earnings Rand	Total Rand
Balance at 1 January 20.1	360 000	240 000	600 000
Changes in equity for 20.1			
Total comprehensive income for the year	–	126 720	126 720
Dividend	–	(40 000)	(40 000)
Balance at 31 December 20.1	360 000	326 720	686 720

HOMMEL LTD
NOTES FOR THE YEAR ENDED 31 DECEMBER 20.1

1. Accounting policy

1.1 Investments in associates

Investments in associates are accounted for by using the equity method.

2. Share of profit of associate

Share of profit of associate consists of the following items:	Rand
Dividend received (IFRS 12.B12(a))	4 000
Retained equity profit	6 800
	10 800

3. Investment in associate

Hommel Ltd holds 70 000 ordinary shares (25% interest) in Abel (Pty) Ltd, an unlisted company in the textiles industry (IFRS 12.21(a)).

	Rand
Carrying amount of the investment:	
Cost price of investment	100 000
Retained earnings since acquisition (1)	6 800
	106 800

(1) (43 200 – 16 000) × 25% = 6 800

(Note: IFRS 12.21(b)(ii) and.B12(b) require the disclosure of summarised financial information of associates. IFRS 12.21(a)(iii) requires disclosure of the associate's principal place of business and IFRS 12.21(b)(iii) requires the disclosure of the fair value of the investment).

❑ QUESTION IAS 28.2

The following are the trial balances of Hans Ltd and Aap Ltd as at 31 December 20.4:

	Hans Ltd Rand Dr/(Cr)	Aap Ltd Rand Dr/(Cr)
Share capital (100 000/10 000 shares)	(100 000)	(10 000)
Retained earnings – 1 January 20.4	(50 000)	(15 000)
Sales	(600 000)	(200 000)
Dividend from Aap Ltd	(5 000)	–
Current liabilities	(37 000)	(5 000)
Loan from Hans Ltd (non-current liability)	–	(20 000)
Cost of sales	300 000	100 000
Other expenses	150 000	50 000
Income tax expense	45 000	15 000
Land and buildings (separable)	47 000	–
Investment in Aap Ltd at cost price	4 500	–
Loan to Aap Ltd	20 000	–
Current assets	185 500	65 000
Dividend	40 000	20 000

Hans Ltd acquired 25% of the issued ordinary share capital of Aap Ltd, a manufacturing concern, on 1 January 20.1, when the latter's accumulated loss amounted to R2 000. Aap Ltd's assets were considered to be fairly valued. Hans Ltd significantly influences the operating and financial decisions of Aap Ltd.

The trial balances do not take the relationship between Hans Ltd and Aap Ltd into account.

On 31 December 20.4, Aap Ltd's shares traded on the JSE Ltd at R5,00 per share.

Required

a. Prepare the statement of profit or loss and other comprehensive income, statement of financial position and statement of changes in equity, in which the investment in Aap Ltd is accounted for by using the equity method, of Hans Ltd for the year ended 31 December 20.4.
b. Provide the relevant notes to the financial statements of Hans Ltd for the year ended 31 December 20.4 in so far this relates to the investment in associate.

Your solution must comply with the requirements of International Financial Reporting Standards (IFRS). An accounting policy note is not required. Comparative amounts are not required.

❖ **Suggested solution IAS 28.2**

HANS LTD
STATEMENT OF FINANCIAL POSITION AS AT 31 DECEMBER 20.4

	Notes	Rand
ASSETS		
Non-current assets		79 500
Property, plant and equipment		47 000
Investment in associate	2	12 500
Loan to Aap Ltd	2	20 000
Current assets		185 500
Total assets		265 000
EQUITY AND LIABILITIES		
Total equity		228 000
Share capital		100 000
Retained earnings		128 000
Current liabilities		37 000
Total equity and liabilities		265 000

HANS LTD
STATEMENT OF PROFIT OR LOSS AND OTHER COMPREHENSIVE INCOME FOR THE YEAR ENDED 31 DECEMBER 20.4

	Note	Rand
Revenue		600 000
Cost of sales		(300 000)
Gross profit		300 000
Other expenses		(150 000)
Share of profit of associate (1)	1	8 750
Profit before tax		158 750
Income tax expense		(45 000)
Profit for the year		113 750
Other comprehensive income		–
Total comprehensive income for the year		113 750

(1) (25% × 20 000) (dividend) + [25% × (200 000 – 100 000 – 50 000 – 15 000 – 20 000)] = 8 750 or [25% × (200 000 – 100 000 – 50 000 – 15 000)] = 8 750

HANS LTD
STATEMENT OF CHANGES IN EQUITY FOR THE YEAR ENDED 31 DECEMBER 20.4

	Share capital Rand	Retained earnings Rand	Total Rand
Balance at 1 January 20.4 (2)	100 000	54 250	154 250
Changes in equity for 20.4			
Total comprehensive income for the year	–	113 750	113 750
Dividend	–	(40 000)	(40 000)
Balance at 31 December 20.4	100 000	128 000	228 000

(2) 50 000 (Hans Ltd) + (25% × 17 000 post-acquisition (Aap Ltd)) = 54 250

HANS LTD
NOTES FOR THE YEAR ENDED 31 DECEMBER 20.4

1. **Share of profit of associate**

	Rand
Share of profit of associate consists of the following items:	
• Dividend received (IFRS 12.B12(a))	5 000
• Retained equity profit	3 750
	8 750

2. **Investment in associate**

Hans Ltd holds 2 500 ordinary shares (25% interest) in Aap Ltd, a listed manufacturing company (IFRS 12.21(a)).

	Rand
Carrying amount of the investment	
Cost price of investment	4 500
Retained earnings since acquisition (3)	8 000
	12 500
Fair value of investment (IFRS 12.21(b)(iii)) (4)	12 500

(3) 25% × (15 000 + 2 000) + (200 000 – 100 000 – 50 000 – 15 000 – 20 000) × 25% = 8 000
(4) 25% × 10 000 × 5,00 = 12 500

Summarised financial information of Aap Ltd (IFRS 12. B12(b))	**Rand**
Current assets	65 000
Non-current assets	–
Current liabilities	5 000
Non-current liabilities	20 000
Revenue	200 000
Profit for the year	35 000

(Note: IFRS 12.21(a)(iii) requires disclosure of the associate's principal place of business and IFRS 12.21(b)(iii) requires the disclosure of the fair value of the investment).

❑ QUESTION IAS 28.3

Alex Ltd acquired a 10% interest in the share capital of Beer Ltd on incorporation of the company on 1 January 20.1 for R40 000. On 1 January 20.6, Alex Ltd acquired a further 5% interest in Beer Ltd for R50 000. On this date the fair value of a 15% share in the net assets amounted to R135 000. It is the policy of Alex Ltd to recognise fair value adjustments in respect of share investments through profit or loss in the statement of profit or loss and other comprehensive income. Alex Ltd has exercised significant influence over the financial and operating policies of Beer Ltd since 1 January 20.6. The abridged statements of profit or loss and other comprehensive income of the two companies are as follows:

STATEMENTS OF PROFIT OR LOSS AND OTHER COMPREHENSIVE INCOME FOR THE YEAR ENDED 30 JUNE 20.6

	Alex Ltd Rand	Beer Ltd Rand
Profit before tax	363 000	666 600
Income tax expense	(163 000)	(366 600)
Profit for the year	200 000	300 000
Other comprehensive income	–	–
Total comprehensive income for the year	200 000	300 000

Additional information

	Rand	Rand
Retained earnings at beginning of year	700 000	600 000
Dividend paid at year end	30 000	10 000
Fair value adjustment (included in profit before tax)	50 000	–

Assume that the income of both companies was earned evenly throughout the year.

The investment is not impaired.

Required

Prepare the statement of profit or loss and other comprehensive income and statement of changes in equity (only a column for retained earnings) of Alex Ltd for the year ended 30 June 20.6 in which the investment in Beer Ltd is accounted for by using the equity method. Show how the investment in associate should be disclosed in the statement of financial position at 30 June 20.6. Your solution must comply with the requirements of International Financial Reporting Standards (IFRS). Comparative amounts are not required.

❖ **Suggested solution IAS 28.3**

ALEX LTD
STATEMENT OF FINANCIAL POSITION AS AT 30 JUNE 20.6

ASSETS	**Rand**
Non-current assets	
Investment in associate (1) (2)	161 000

(1) 15% × [(6/12 × 300 000) – 10 000] = 21 000
(2) 90 000 (fair value of 10% interest) + 50 000 (cost price) + 21 000 (since acquisition reserves) = 161 000

ALEX LTD
STATEMENT OF PROFIT OR LOSS AND OTHER COMPREHENSIVE INCOME FOR THE YEAR ENDED 30 JUNE 20.6

	Rand
Revenue	xxx xxx
Cost of sales	(xxx xxx)
Gross profit	xxx xxx
Other expenses	(xxx xxx)
Share of profit of associate (3)	22 500
Profit before tax (4)	384 000
Income tax expense	(163 000)
Profit for the year	221 000
Other comprehensive income	–
Total comprehensive income for the year	221 000

(3) 15% × [(6/12 × 300 000) – 10 000] = 21 000 + (15% × 10 000 dividend) = 22 500 or [15% × (300 000 × 6/12)] = 22 500
(4) 363 000 – (15% × 10 000 dividend received) + 22 500 = 384 000

ALEX LTD
STATEMENT OF CHANGES IN EQUITY FOR THE YEAR ENDED 30 JUNE 20.6

	Retained earnings Rand
Balance at 1 July 20.5	700 000
Changes in equity for 20.6	
Total comprehensive income for the year	221 000
Dividend	(30 000)
Balance at 30 June 20.6	891 000

❑ QUESTION IAS 28.4

Ans Ltd, a listed company, acquired 25% of the ordinary shares of Bat Ltd, a company in the food industry, on 1 January 20.1 for R12 500 when the net assets of Bat Ltd were considered to be fairly valued. At this time the owners' equity of Bat Ltd was as follows:

	Rand
20 000 ordinary shares	20 000
Retained earnings	30 000
	50 000

The abridged financial statements of Ans Ltd and Bat Ltd for the year ended 31 December 20.5 were as follows:

STATEMENT OF FINANCIAL POSITION AS AT 31 DECEMBER 20.5

	Ans Ltd Rand	Bat Ltd Rand
ASSETS		
Non-current assets	81 500	50 000
Property, plant and equipment	60 000	50 000
Investment in Bat Ltd	21 500	–
Shares at cost price	12 500	–
Loan	9 000	–
Current assets	48 500	14 000
Inventory	20 000	7 000
Trade receivables	28 500	7 000
Total assets	130 000	64 000
EQUITY AND LIABILITIES		
Total equity	120 000	19 000
Share capital	20 000	20 000
Revaluation surplus	20 000	5 000
Retained earnings	80 000	(6 000)
Current liabilities	10 000	45 000
Trade and other payables	10 000	36 000
Loan – Ans Ltd	–	9 000
Total equity and liabilities	130 000	64 000

STATEMENT OF PROFIT OR LOSS AND OTHER COMPREHENSIVE INCOME FOR THE YEAR ENDED 31 DECEMBER 20.5

	Ans Ltd Rand	Bat Ltd Rand
Revenue	150 000	100 000
Cost of sales	(70 000)	(80 000)
Gross profit	80 000	20 000
Other expenses	(50 000)	(50 000)
Profit/(loss) before tax	30 000	(30 000)
Income tax (expense)/income	(12 000)	9 000
Profit/(loss) for the year	18 000	(21 000)
Other comprehensive income		
Items that will not be reclassified to profit or loss		
Gain on revaluation of property, plant and equipment	–	5 000
Total comprehensive income/(loss) for the year	18 000	(16 000)

STATEMENT OF CHANGES IN EQUITY FOR THE YEAR ENDED 31 DECEMBER 20.5

	Retained earnings/ (accumulated loss) Ans Ltd Rand	Retained earnings/ (accumulated loss) Bat Ltd Rand	Revaluation surplus Bat Ltd Rand
Balance at 1 January 20.5	64 000	15 000	–
Changes in equity for 20.5			
Total comprehensive income/(loss) for the year	18 000	(21 000)	5 000
Dividends paid	(2 000)	–	–
Balance at 31 December 20.5	80 000	(6 000)	5 000

Additional information

The investment in Bat Ltd is not impaired.

Required

Prepare the statement of profit or loss and other comprehensive income, statement of changes in equity and statement of financial position of Ans Ltd for the year ended 31 December 20.5 in which the investment in Bat Ltd is accounted for by using the equity method. Your solution must comply with the requirements of International Financial Reporting Standards (IFRS). Disclose only the notes to the statement of profit or loss and other comprehensive income and statement of financial position in respect of the investment in the associate. Comparative amounts are not required.

❖ **Suggested solution IAS 28.4**

ANS LTD
STATEMENT OF FINANCIAL POSITION AS AT 31 DECEMBER 20.5

	Note	Rand
ASSETS		
Non-current assets		73 750
Property, plant and equipment		60 000
Investment in associate	2	4 750
Loan to associate		9 000
Current assets		48 500
Inventory		20 000
Trade receivables		28 500
Total assets		122 250
EQUITY AND LIABILITIES		
Total equity		112 250
Share capital		20 000
Revaluation surplus		21 250
Retained earnings		71 000
Current liabilities		
Trade and other payables		10 000
Total equity and liabilities		122 250

ANS LTD
STATEMENT OF PROFIT OR LOSS AND OTHER COMPREHENSIVE INCOME FOR THE YEAR ENDED 31 DECEMBER 20.5

	Note	Rand
Revenue		150 000
Cost of sales		(70 000)
Gross profit		80 000
Other expenses		(50 000)
Share of loss of associate (1)	1	(5 250)
Profit before tax		24 750
Income tax expense		(12 000)
Profit for the year		12 750
Other comprehensive income		
Items that will not be reclassified to profit or loss		
Gain on revaluation of property, plant and equipment (2)		1 250
Total comprehensive income for the year		14 000

(1) (– 21 000 × 25%) = – 5 250
(2) 5 000 × 25% = 1 250

ANS LTD
STATEMENT OF CHANGES IN EQUITY FOR THE YEAR ENDED 31 DECEMBER 20.5

	Share capital Rand	Revaluation surplus Rand	Retained earnings Rand	Total Rand
Balance at 1 January 20.5 (3)	20 000	20 000	60 250	100 250
Changes in equity for 20.5				
Total comprehensive income for the year	–	1 250	12 750	14 000
Dividend	–	–	(2 000)	(2 000)
Balance at 31 December 20.5	20 000	21 250	71 000	112 250

(3) 64 000 + [25% × (15 000 – 30 000)] = 60 250

ANS LTD
NOTES FOR THE YEAR ENDED 31 DECEMBER 20.5

1. Share of loss of associate

	Rand
Share of loss of associate consists of the following items:	
Retained equity loss	(5 250)

2. Investment in associate

Ans Ltd holds a 25% interest in the ordinary shares of Bat Ltd, an unlisted company in the food industry (IFRS 12.21(a)).

	Rand
Carrying amount of the investment:	
Cost price of investment	12 500
Accumulated loss since acquisition (4)	(9 000)
Revaluation surplus since acquisition (5)	1 250
	4 750

(4) (15 000 – 30 000) × 25% + (– 21 000 × 25%) = – 9 000
(5) 5 000 × 25% = 1 250

Summarised financial information of Bat Ltd
(IFRS 12. B12(b))

	Rand
Current assets	14 000
Non-current assets	50 000
Current liabilities	45 000
Non-current liabilities	–
Revenue	100 000
Loss for the year	(21 000)
Other comprehensive income	5 000
Total comprehensive loss	(16 000)

(Note: IFRS 12.21(a)(iii) requires disclosure of the associate's principal place of business and IFRS 12.21(b)(iii) requires the disclosure of the fair value of the investment).

❑ QUESTION IAS 28.5

See Ltd acquired a 35% interest in Sand Ltd, a listed company in the financial sector, for R45 000 on 1 January 20.2. Since that date See Ltd has exercised significant influence over the financial and operating decisions of Sand Ltd. On 1 January 20.2, Sand Ltd had 50 000 issued ordinary shares (R50 000) and retained earnings of R70 000.

The following statements of profit or loss and other comprehensive income and statements of changes in equity of See Ltd and Sand Ltd are available for the years ended 31 December 20.2 and 31 December 20.3. This information does not yet take the relationship between See Ltd and Sand Ltd into account.

STATEMENTS OF PROFIT OR LOSS AND OTHER COMPREHENSIVE INCOME FOR THE YEAR ENDED 31 DECEMBER 20.2 AND 20.3

	See Ltd 20.3 Rand	See Ltd 20.2 Rand	Sand Ltd 20.3 Rand	Sand Ltd 20.2 Rand
Revenue	200 000	300 000	190 000	150 000
Cost of sales	(100 000)	(150 000)	(95 000)	(275 000)
Gross profit/(loss)	100 000	150 000	95 000	(125 000)
Other expenses	(20 000)	(40 000)	(30 000)	(55 000)
Profit/(loss) before tax	80 000	110 000	65 000	(180 000)
Income tax (expense)/income	(30 000)	(45 000)	(20 000)	30 000
Profit/(loss) for the year	50 000	65 000	45 000	(150 000)
Other comprehensive income	–	–	–	–
Total comprehensive income/(loss) for the year	50 000	65 000	45 000	(150 000)
Market value per share as at 31 December	1,50	1,35	1,40	1,25

STATEMENTS OF CHANGES IN EQUITY FOR THE YEAR ENDED 31 DECEMBER 20.2 AND 20.3

	Retained earnings/(accumulated loss)	
	See Ltd Rand	Sand Ltd Rand
Balance at 1 January 20.2	200 000	70 000
Changes in equity for 20.2		
Total comprehensive income/(loss) for the year	65 000	(150 000)
Balance at 1 January 20.3	265 000	(80 000)
Changes in equity for 20.3		
Total comprehensive income for the year	50 000	45 000
Balance at 31 December 20.3	315 000	(35 000)

Required

a. Provide the journal entries for the years ended 31 December 20.2 and 20.3 in order to account for the investment in Sand Ltd in accordance with the equity method.
b. Prepare the statement of profit or loss and other comprehensive income of See Ltd for the year ended 31 December 20.3 in which the investment in Sand Ltd is accounted for in accordance with the equity method, together with the relevant notes. Your solution must comply with the requirements of International Financial Reporting Standards (IFRS).
c. Show how the note 'Investment in associate' should be disclosed in the financial statements of See Ltd at 31 December 20.3.

❖ **Suggested solution IAS 28.5**

a. Journal entries

	Rand Dr/(Cr)
20.2	
Share of loss of associate (P or L) (1)	45 000
Investment in associate (SFPos)	(45 000)
20.3	
Investment in associate (SFPos) (2)	8 250
Share of profit of associate (P or L)	(8 250)

(1) 150 000 × 35% = 52 500 limited to cost price of investment = 45 000
(2) 45 000 × 35% = 15 750 – 7 500 (unrecognised loss) = 8 250

b. Statement of profit or loss and other comprehensive income

SEE LTD
STATEMENT OF PROFIT OR LOSS AND OTHER COMPREHENSIVE INCOME FOR THE YEAR ENDED 31 DECEMBER 20.3

	Note	20.3 Rand	20.2 Rand
Revenue		200 000	300 000
Cost of sales		(100 000)	(150 000)
Gross profit		100 000	150 000
Other expenses		(20 000)	(40 000)
Share of profit/(loss) of associate	1	8 250	(45 000)
Profit before tax		88 250	65 000
Income tax expense		(30 000)	(45 000)
Profit for the year		58 250	20 000
Other comprehensive income		–	–
Total comprehensive income for the year		58 250	20 000

c. **Disclosure**

SEE LTD
NOTES FOR THE YEAR ENDED 31 DECEMBER 20.3

1. **Share of profit/(loss) of associate**

	20.3 Rand	20.2 Rand
Share of profit/(loss) of associate consists of the following:		
Retained equity profit/(loss)	8 250	(45 000)

2. **Investment in associate**

17 500 ordinary shares (35%) in Sand Ltd, a listed company in the financial sector (IFRS 12.21(a)).

	20.3 Rand	20.2 Rand
Carrying amount of investment		
Cost price of investment	45 000	45 000
Accumulated loss since acquisition (3)	(36 750)	(45 000)
	8 250	–
Unrecognised attributable loss of associate	–	7 500
Fair value of the investment (IFRS 12.21(b)(iii)) (4)	24 500	21 875

(3) (– 150 000 × 35%) + (45 000 × 35%) = – 36 750
(4) 17 500 × 1,40 = 24 500; 17 500 × 1,25 = 21 875

(Note: IFRS 12.21(b)(ii) and.B12(b) also require the disclosure of summarised financial information of associates). IFRS 12.21(a)(iii) requires disclosure of the associate's principal place of business and IFRS 12.21(b)(iii) requires the disclosure of the fair value of the investment).

❑ **QUESTION IAS 28.6**

Hen Ltd acquired a 25% interest (150 000 ordinary shares) in the share capital of Ann Ltd, a company in the retail industry, on 1 January 20.1 for R195 000. Hen Ltd accounts for its interest in Ann Ltd in accordance with the equity method. Both companies are listed.

On 1 January 20.1, the issued share capital of Ann Ltd comprises 600 000 ordinary shares amounting to R600 000 and Ann Ltd had retained earnings of R120 000, with no other reserves. The net assets of Ann Ltd were fairly valued at this time.

The share capital of Hen Ltd, which has remained unchanged since acquisition, comprises 1 000 000 ordinary shares amounting to R1 000 000, and 200 000 10% preference shares with a nominal value of R1 each.

The investment is not impaired as at 31 December.

The following are the statements of profit or loss and other comprehensive income and the statements of changes in equity of Hen Ltd and Ann Ltd for the years ended 31 December 20.2 and 20.1 without taking into account the relationship between the two companies:

STATEMENTS OF PROFIT OR LOSS AND OTHER COMPREHENSIVE INCOME FOR THE YEARS ENDED 31 DECEMBER 20.2 AND 20.1

	Hen Ltd 20.2 Rand	Hen Ltd 20.1 Rand	Ann Ltd 20.2 Rand	Ann Ltd 20.1 Rand
Revenue	1 800 000	1 400 000	1 200 000	800 000
Cost of sales	(900 000)	(800 000)	(900 000)	(500 000)
Gross profit	900 000	600 000	300 000	300 000
Other expenses	(680 000)	(435 000)	(124 828)	(213 793)
Dividend received – Ann Ltd	12 500	10 000	–	–
Profit before tax	232 500	175 000	175 172	86 207
Income tax expense	(84 000)	(63 000)	(65 172)	(36 207)
Profit for the year	148 500	112 000	110 000	50 000
Other comprehensive income	–	–	–	–
Total comprehensive income for the year	148 500	112 000	110 000	50 000
Market value per share at 31 December	2,00	1,80	1,70	1,55

STATEMENTS OF CHANGES IN EQUITY FOR THE YEAR ENDED 31 DECEMBER 20.2

	Retained earnings Hen Ltd Rand	Retained earnings Ann Ltd Rand
Balance at 1 January 20.1	210 500	120 000
Changes in equity for 20.1		
Total comprehensive income for the year	112 000	50 000
Dividend	(70 000)	(40 000)
Balance at 1 January 20.2	252 500	130 000
Changes in equity for 20.2		
Total comprehensive income for the year	148 500	110 000
Dividend	(80 000)	(50 000)
Balance at 31 December 20.2	321 000	190 000

Additional information

1. During the year ended 31 December 20.2, Hen Ltd started selling inventory to Ann Ltd at cost price plus 25%. Total sales to Ann Ltd amounted to R80 000 for the year. Included in the closing inventory of Ann Ltd on 31 December 20.2, is inventory of R40 000 purchased from Hen Ltd.

2. Assume a tax rate of 27% for both years.

Required

a. Prepare the journal entries in respect of the elimination of the unrealised profit for the year ended 31 December 20.2.
b. Prepare the statement of profit or loss and other comprehensive income and statement of changes in equity (only a column for retained earnings) of Hen Ltd for the year ended 31 December 20.2, in which the investment in Ann Ltd is accounted for by using the equity method, together with the relevant notes. Your solution must comply with the requirements of International Financial Reporting Standards (IFRS).
c. Show how the note 'Investment in associate' should be disclosed in the financial statements of Hen Ltd at 31 December 20.2.

❑ QUESTION IAS 28.7

Alf Ltd acquired a 40% holding in Brom Ltd on 1 January 20.0 for R35 000. At that date Brom Ltd had 50 000 issued ordinary shares amounting to R50 000 and retained earnings of R30 000. At that date there were no other reserves.

The investment is not impaired.

At 31 December 20.6, Brom Ltd's shareholders' equity comprised the following:

	Rand
Ordinary shares	50 000
Retained earnings	75 000
Surplus on revaluation of land and buildings	40 000
	165 000

The statements of profit or loss and other comprehensive income of the companies for the year ended 31 December 20.6 are as follows:

	Alf Ltd Rand	**Brom Ltd Rand**
Revenue	200 000	50 000
Cost of sales	(80 000)	(15 000)
Gross profit	120 000	35 000
Other expenses	(40 000)	(10 000)
Dividend received	4 000	–
Profit before tax	84 000	25 000
Income tax expense	(40 000)	(5 000)
Profit for the year	44 000	20 000
Other comprehensive income	–	–
Total comprehensive income for the year	44 000	20 000

Additional information

	Alf Ltd Rand	Brom Ltd Rand
Retained earnings at beginning of year	113 000	65 000
Ordinary dividend paid	(12 000)	(10 000)

Required

a. Prepare Alf Ltd's statement of profit or loss and other comprehensive income for the year ended 31 December 20.6 in which the investment in Brom Ltd is accounted for by using the equity method. Your solution must comply with the requirements of International Financial Reporting Standards (IFRS). No notes are required. Comparative amounts are not required.

b. Calculate the carrying amount of the following item in the statement of financial position of Alf Ltd as at 31 December 20.6:
   - Investment in associate.

❑ QUESTION IAS 28.8@

On 1 March 20.4, Stein Ltd acquired 30% of the shares of Tollie Ltd for R60 000. On 1 June 20.4, Tollie Ltd acquired 40% of the equity shares of Reg Ltd for R30 000. The following information in respect of the companies is available for the years ended as indicated:

	Stein Ltd 28 Feb 20.5 Rand	Tollie Ltd 28 Feb 20.5 Rand	Reg Ltd 28 Feb 20.5 Rand
Revenue	50 000	40 000	30 000
Profit before tax	*28 000	*24 000	16 000
Income tax expense	10 000	8 000	6 000
Dividends paid at year end	12 000	9 000	5 000
Retained earnings (opening balance)	80 000	90 000	80 000
Cost of sales	10 000	8 000	6 000

* Excluding dividends received from associates.

Additional information

1. Profit before tax is earned evenly throughout the periods except for a non-taxable profit of R4 000 earned by Tollie Ltd on 18 October 20.4. Tollie Ltd earned this profit by selling land to Stein Ltd for an amount of R36 000. (The R4 000 gain is included in the R24 000 profit.)

2. The respective shareholdings enable the investors to significantly influence decisions of the investees.

3. You may assume that the investments were made at net asset value, i.e. no goodwill is included in the investments.

Required

a. Prepare the statement of profit or loss and other comprehensive income of Stein Ltd for the year ended 28 February 20.5 in which investments in associates are accounted for by using the equity method in accordance with the requirements of International Financial Reporting Standards (IFRS). No notes are required. Comparative amounts are not required.

b. Show how the 'Investment in associate' should be reflected in the statement of financial position of Stein Ltd as at 28 February 20.5.

❑ QUESTION IAS 28.9

You are presented with the following trial balances at 31 December 20.7 of the companies in the Alfa Ltd group:

	Alfa Ltd Rand Dr/(Cr)	Ceta Ltd Rand Dr/(Cr)
Gross profit	(317 000)	(64 000)
Other expenses	270 700	36 000
Interest received from Ceta Ltd	(3 600)	–
Income tax expense	15 000	9 800
Damage caused by earthquake on 31 October – not tax deductible	–	7 500
Dividend paid on 31 December	4 000	–
Ordinary share capital (140 000 / 10 000 shares)	(140 000)	(10 000)
Retained earnings – 1 January	(75 000)	(10 000)
Plant and equipment – carrying amount	25 000	16 000
Investments:		
Ceta Ltd – at cost price	8 000	–
Loan: Alfa Ltd/Ceta Ltd	20 000	(20 000)
Deferred tax	(1 400)	(600)
Trade receivables (debtors)	162 900	18 700
Inventory	250 000	34 000
Trade and other payables (creditors)	(218 600)	(17 400)
	Nil	Nil

Additional information

1. On 2 January 20.5, Alfa Ltd acquired 40% of the issued share capital of Ceta Ltd when the retained earnings of Ceta Ltd amounted to R9 250. At that stage all the assets and liabilities of Ceta Ltd were deemed to be valued fairly. Since 2 January 20.5, Alfa Ltd has exercised significant influence over the financial and operating decisions of Ceta Ltd. The investment is accounted for in accordance with the equity method.

2. Alfa Ltd also lent Ceta Ltd R20 000 on 2 January 20.5. The loan is repayable on 30 June 20.8.

3. The investment is not impaired.

4. Since 2 January 20.5, Alfa Ltd has been selling inventories to Ceta Ltd at a profit of 50% on the cost price. Included in the inventories of Ceta Ltd on 31 December 20.6 is R1 500 in respect of such inventories at the cost price for Ceta Ltd. Included in the inventories of Ceta Ltd on 31 December 20.7 is R2 700 in respect of such inventories at the cost price for Ceta Ltd. Total sales of Alfa Ltd to Ceta Ltd amounted to R10 000 during 20.7.

5. Assume a tax rate of 30%.

Required

Prepare the statement of profit or loss and other comprehensive income and the statement of changes in equity of the Alfa Ltd Group for the year ended 31 December 20.7 as well as the statement of financial position at that date, so as to comply with the requirements of International Financial Reporting Standards (IFRS).

Comparative amounts and notes to the financial statements are not required.

❑ QUESTION IAS 28.10

The following financial statements were presented to you:

STATEMENTS OF FINANCIAL POSITION AS AT 31 DECEMBER 20.4

	Maan Ltd Rand	Sat Ltd Rand
ASSETS		
Non-current assets	11 080 000	400 000
Property, plant and equipment	10 800 000	400 000
Investment in Sat Ltd	40 000	–
Other listed investments	240 000	–
Current assets	2 250 000	215 600
Inventory	88 000	120 000
Trade receivables	162 000	55 000
Bank	2 000 000	40 600
Total assets	13 330 000	615 600
EQUITY AND LIABILITIES		
Total equity	11 330 000	615 600
Share capital – 8 000 000 / 100 000 shares	8 000 000	100 000
Preference shares	1 000 000	–
Retained earnings	2 330 000	515 600
Non-current liabilities		
Deferred tax	200 000	–
Current liabilities		
Trade and other payables	1 800 000	–
Total equity and liabilities	13 330 000	615 600

STATEMENTS OF PROFIT OR LOSS AND OTHER COMPREHENSIVE INCOME FOR THE YEAR ENDED 31 DECEMBER 20.4

	Maan Ltd Rand	Sat Ltd Rand
Profit before dividends	985 000	251 600
Dividend received	74 720	–
Profit before tax	1 059 720	251 600
Income tax expense	(300 720)	(68 000)
Profit for the year	759 000	183 600
Other comprehensive income	–	–
Total comprehensive income for the year	759 000	183 600

STATEMENTS OF CHANGES IN EQUITY FOR THE YEAR ENDED 31 DECEMBER 20.4

	Retained earnings	
	Maan Ltd Rand	Sat Ltd Rand
Balance at 1 January 20.4	1 730 000	342 000
Changes in equity for 20.4		
Total comprehensive income for the year	759 000	183 600
Preference dividend	(120 000)	–
Ordinary dividend – 31 December 20.4	(39 000)	(10 000)
Balance at 31 December 20.4	2 330 000	515 600

Additional information

1. Maan Ltd bought 40 000 ordinary shares in Sat Ltd on 1 March 20.1 for R40 000. On this date, Sat Ltd had retained earnings of R25 000. There were no other reserves. Since this date, Maan Ltd has exercised significant influence over the financial and operating decisions of Sat Ltd, and consequently accounted for the investment in accordance with the equity method.

2. Since acquiring its interest in Sat Ltd, Sat Ltd sells certain inventory items to Maan Ltd at cost price plus 30%. Included in the inventory of Maan Ltd at 31 December 20.3 and 31 December 20.4 are inventory acquired from Sat Ltd to the value of R26 000 and R19 500 respectively.

3. The investment in associate is not impaired.

4. Assume a tax rate of 30%.

Required

Prepare the statement of profit or loss and other comprehensive income and statement of changes in equity (retained earnings column only) of the Maan Ltd Group for the year ended 31 December 20.4 as well as the statement of financial position on this date, using the equity method. Your solution must comply with the requirements of International Financial Reporting Standards (IFRS).

Notes to the financial statements and comparative amounts are not required.

IAS 32

Financial instruments: presentation

Note:	As this chapter and the chapter on IFRS 9 both deal with financial instruments, the questions on these two chapters are integrated and such questions are presented as part of the chapter on IFRS 9.

IAS 33 & Circular 1/2021

Earnings, headline earnings and dividend per share

❑ QUESTIONS AND SOLUTIONS

IAS 33.1@	Theory and disclosure
IAS 33.2@	Share issue, preference dividend and loss situations
IAS 33.3@	Capitalisation issue and share split
IAS 33.4@	Contingently issuable shares
IAS 33.5@	Calculation and disclosure of basic and headline earnings; including a capitalisation issue
IAS 33.6@	Discontinued operations – basic and diluted earnings per share
IAS 33.7@	Headline earnings – theory

❑ QUESTIONS

IAS 33.8@	Preference shares and dilution
IAS 33.9@	Capitalisation, share split and loss situation
IAS 33.10@	Rights issue with bonus element

@ *These questions contain topics or principles that were not included in the ITC syllabus of SAICA at the time of publishing this book, but might still be included in university syllabi.*
Please note: the whole IAS 33 is not included in the ITC syllabus of SAICA.

Note:	In all questions in this chapter, it is assumed that the entity presents all items of income and expense recognised in a period in a single statement of profit or loss and other comprehensive income [IAS 1.81(a)].

❑ QUESTION IAS 33.1@

Answer the following questions:

a. Clearly explain what is meant by 'basic earnings'.

b. Clearly explain what is meant by 'basic earnings per share'.

c. Clearly explain what is meant by 'dividend per share'.

d. Clearly state to which companies IAS 33 is applicable.

e. List cases when the comparative amounts of basic earnings per share in the current year are restated.

f. i. When is it not necessary to disclose diluted earnings per share?
   ii. What is the position in the calculation of diluted earnings per share if one of the potential dilutions leads to an increase in earnings per share?

g. Explain how financial managers of listed companies are able to manipulate earnings to reflect earnings per share lower than they would have been otherwise.

h. Explain briefly what is meant by 'headline earnings per share' according to Circular 1/2021.

❖ Suggested solution IAS 33.1@

a. Basic earnings are amounts attributable to ordinary equity holders (owners) of the parent entity in respect of:
   i. profit or loss from continuing operations attributable to the parent entity; and
   ii. profit or loss attributable to the parent entity,
   and are the amounts in (i) and (ii) adjusted for the after-tax amounts of preference dividends, differences arising on the settlement of preference shares, and other similar effects of preference shares classified as equity (IAS 33.12).

b. Basic earnings per share shall be calculated for profit or loss attributable to ordinary equity holders (owners) of the parent entity and, if presented, profit or loss from continuing operations attributable to those equity holders. Basic earnings per share shall be calculated by dividing profit or loss attributable to ordinary equity holders of the parent entity (the numerator) by the weighted average number of ordinary shares outstanding (the denominator) during the period (IAS 33.9-10). Basic earnings per share are presented for each class of ordinary share that has a different right to share in profit for the year (IAS 33.66).

c. Dividend per share (IAS 1) refers to the dividends declared to ordinary equity holders (owners) of the parent for the year divided by the specific number of ordinary shares in issue at the date of each dividend declaration.

d. Companies (IAS 33.2-3):
- whose ordinary shares or potential ordinary shares are traded in a public market;
- that file or are in the process of filing, their financial statements with a securities commission or other regulatory organisation for the purpose of issuing ordinary shares in a public market; or
- which otherwise choose to disclose earnings per share.

e. Comparative amounts to be restated for the following (IAS 33.64):
- Capitalisation issue
- A bonus element as part of a share issue (for example, a rights issue at less than market value)
- A share split
- A reverse share split (share consolidation)
- The effect of errors and adjustments resulting from changes in accounting policies restated retrospectively.

f. i. A potential increase in earnings (anti-dilution) is not disclosed.
ii. If a potential dilution leads to an increase in basic earnings per share, its effect is ignored in calculating diluted earnings per share.

g. Timing of transactions
- Large (material) orders for sales received before year end but delayed and only delivered after year end.
- The date of certifying contracts in progress is scheduled just after year end.
- Consumables are not included as inventories anymore, for example stationery and petrol.
- Repairs and maintenance of property, plant and equipment can be performed in the current year instead of deferring it.

Estimation of figures
- Quantities of inventories, for example game, scrap and coal, can be estimated at lower levels.
- The estimated useful life of assets can be shortened.
- The estimation of unsaleable inventories included in trading inventories can be increased.

Reclassification of items
- Certain improvements or replacement of machinery is classified as repairs and maintenance.
- The allocation of overheads to inventories could be changed by decreasing the overheads included in closing inventories.

h. 'Headline earnings' refers to an additional earnings number which is permitted by IAS 33. The starting point is earnings as determined in IAS 33, *excluding* 'separately identifiable re-measurements' (as defined), net of related tax (both current and deferred) and non-controlling interest, *other than* re-measurements specifically included in headline earnings ('included re-measurements', as defined) (Circular 1/2021 (par. 14)). The general purpose of disclosing headline earnings is to reflect more closely maintainable earnings, which will be more comparative from year to year and possibly also between different entities.

❑ QUESTION IAS 33.2@

Since incorporation, Duiker Ltd has had an authorised share capital of 5 000 000 ordinary shares and 500 000 8% non-cumulative preference shares with a nominal value of R2,00 each. The issued share capital was as follows:

Ordinary shares

Issued at incorporation	2 500 000 at R2,00 each
30 June 20.5	1 000 000 at R3,50 each
31 December 20.6	1 000 000 at R4,00 each

Preference shares (8% non-cumulative)

Issued at incorporation	200 000 at R2,00 each
31 December 20.6	50 000 at R2,00 each

The profit/(loss) for the year amounted to R750 000 and (R115 000) for the years ended 30 June 20.7 and 30 June 20.6 respectively. The company has paid preference dividends every year since incorporation except for the year ended 30 June 20.6.

Required

Show how the earnings per share must be disclosed in the financial statements of Duiker Ltd for the year ended 30 June 20.7 so as to comply with the requirements of International Financial Reporting Standards (IFRS).

❖ Suggested solution IAS 33.2@

Calculations

Basic earnings/(loss)	**20.7 Rand**	**20.6 Rand**
Profit/(loss) for the year	750 000	(115 000)
Preference dividend (1)	(36 000)	–
	714 000	(115 000)
Basic earnings/(loss) per share (2)	0,18	(0,03)

Equity shares	**20.7 Shares**	**20.6 Shares**
Issued to 30 June 20.5	3 500 000	3 500 000
Issued on 31 December 20.6 (3)	500 000	–
	4 000 000	3 500 000

(1) (400 000 × 8%) + (100 000 × 8% × 6/12) = 36 000
(2) 714 000/4 000 000 = 0,18; (115 000)/3 500 000 = (0,03)
(3) 1 000 000 × 6/12 = 500 000

Disclosure

DUIKER LTD
STATEMENT OF PROFIT OR LOSS AND OTHER COMPREHENSIVE INCOME FOR THE YEAR ENDED 30 JUNE 20.7

	Note	20.7 Rand	20.6 Rand
Total comprehensive income for the year		750 000	(115 000)
Basic earnings/(loss) per share for profit attributable to ordinary equity holders	8	0,18	(0,03)

DUIKER LTD
NOTES FOR THE YEAR ENDED 30 JUNE 20.7

8. Earnings per share

Reconciliation of numerator used for basic earnings per share	**20.7 Rand**	**20.6 Rand**
Profit for the year attributable to equity holders	750 000	(115 000)
Dividend on non-cumulative preference shares	(36 000)	–
Numerator for basic earnings	714 000	(115 000)

	20.7	**20.6**
Weighted average number of ordinary shares used for basic earnings per share	4 000 000	3 500 000

❑ **QUESTION IAS 33.3@**

Bok Ltd has had an issued ordinary share capital of R500 000 since incorporation. Assume that Bok Ltd has been incorporated under the previous Companies Act and is authorised to issue par value shares. On 1 January 20.2 the company made a capitalisation issue of one share for every five shares held. On 1 January 20.3 a special resolution was passed according to which the nominal (par) value of the ordinary shares was to be reduced from R2 per share to 50c per share.

The profit for the year ended 30 June 20.3 amounted to R360 000 (20.2 – R276 000). No dividends were declared during the years ended 30 June 20.2 and 30 June 20.3.

Required

Calculate the earnings per share for the years ended 30 June 20.3 and 30 June 20.2 so as to comply with the requirements of International Financial Reporting Standards (IFRS).

❖ Suggested solution IAS 33.3@

Calculations

Equity shares	**20.3**	**20.2**
Original issue (1)	250 000	250 000
Capitalisation issue (2)	50 000	50 000
	300 000	300 000

	20.3 **Rand**	**20.2** **Rand**
Change in nominal value (3)	1 200 000	1 200 000
Basic earnings	360 000	276 000
Basic earnings per share (4)	0,30	0,23

(1) 500 000/2 = 250 000
(2) 250 000/5 × 1 = 50 000
(3) 300 000 × 2,00/0,50 = 1 200 000
(4) 360 000/1 200 000 = 0,30; 276 000/1 200 000 = 0,23

❑ QUESTION IAS 33.4@

Ribbok Ltd, a company with a financial year end of 31 December, entered into an agreement on 1 April 20.4 with senior management in terms of which 20 000 shares will be issued to them at no cost if the market price of the company's shares exceeds R50,00 per share on 31 December 20.7. Assume that the market price of the shares was as follows on the following dates:

	Rand
31 December 20.4	55,00
31 December 20.5	49,80
31 December 20.6	59,00

Required

Briefly discuss the effect of the contingently issuable shares on the diluted earnings per share for the various years.

❖ Suggested solution IAS 33.4@

20.4 As the share price exceeds R50,00, the weighted average number of shares for diluted earnings per share purposes will increase with 15 000 shares (9/12 × 20 000). Note that the shares are weighted as the contract was entered into on 1 April 20.4.

20.5 As the share price does not exceed R50,00, the contingently issuable shares will have no effect on diluted earnings per share. The 20.4 diluted earnings per share number is not restated.

20.6 As the share price exceeds R50,00, the weighted average number of shares for diluted earnings per share purposes will increase with 20 000 shares. The 20.5 diluted earnings per share number is not restated.

❑ QUESTION IAS 33.5@

The following is an extract from the consolidated statement of profit or loss and other comprehensive income of the Standard Ltd Group for the year ended 31 December 20.6:

	Rand
Profit before tax	300 000
Income tax expense	(80 000)
Profit for the year	220 000
Profit attributable to:	
Owners of the parent	196 000
Non-controlling interest	24 000
	220 000

Additional information

1. Profit before tax is calculated after taking into account the following:

	Rand
Income	
Gain on sale of factory building (non-controlling interest – R14 000) (The gain of R100 000 represents a recoupment of wear-and-tear allowances for tax purposes)	100 000
Fair value adjustment on investment property – land	10 000
Profit on expropriation of land	100 000
Expenses	
Goodwill – impairment loss	20 000
Reorganisation costs provided with downscaling of entity	30 000
Depreciation	30 000
Allowance for credit losses	20 000

2. The tax rate is 30%. The inclusion rate for capital gains tax is 50%.
3. Ordinary dividends amounting to R20 000 were paid on 30 November 20.6 by Standard Ltd.
4. At the beginning of the year Standard Ltd only had 150 000 ordinary shares in issue. On 1 July 20.6 the parent had a one for three capitalisation issue.

Required

a. Calculate and disclose basic earnings per share.
b. Calculate the headline earnings per share for the group and disclose this in the consolidated financial statements of the Standard Ltd Group for the year ended 31 December 20.6.

Your answer must comply with the requirements of International Financial Reporting Standards (IFRS).

❖ **Suggested solution IAS 33.5@**

Calculations

a. Basic earnings per share

Weighted average number of shares in issue

Opening balance	150 000
Capitalisation issue (1)	50 000
Weighted average	200 000

	Rand
Basic earnings per share (2)	0,98

(1) 150 000/3 = 50 000
(2) 196 000/200 000 = 0,98

Disclosure

STANDARD LTD GROUP
CONSOLIDATED STATEMENT OF PROFIT OR LOSS AND OTHER COMPREHENSIVE INCOME FOR THE YEAR ENDED 31 DECEMBER 20.6

	Notes	**Rand**
Profit for the year		220 000
Profit attributable to:		
Owners of the parent		196 000
Non-controlling interest		24 000
		220 000
Basic earnings per share for profit attributable to ordinary equity holders of the parent	11	0,98

b. Headline earnings per share (3)

(3) 66 500/200 000 = 0,33

STANDARD LTD GROUP
NOTES FOR THE YEAR ENDED 31 DECEMBER 20.6

11. Headline earnings per share

	Rand
Headline earnings per share	0,33

Reconciliation of earnings with headline earnings – 20.6

	Gross	Tax	Non-controlling interest	Net
	Rand	**Rand**	**Rand**	**Rand**
Basic earnings (IAS 33 earnings)				196 000
Gain on sale of factory building (IAS 16) (1)	(100 000)	30 000	14 000	(56 000)
Fair value adjustment on investment property – land (IAS 40) (2)	(10 000)	1 500	–	(8 500)
Gain on expropriation of land (3)	(100 000)	15 000	–	(85 000)
Impairment of goodwill (IAS 36)	20 000	–	–	20 000
Headline earnings				66 500
Weighted average number of ordinary shares used for basic and headline earnings per share				200 000

(1) 100 000 – (100 000 × 30%) = 70 000 less non-controlling interest 14 000 = 56 000
(2) 10 000 – (10 000 × 50% × 30%) = 8 500
(3) 100 000 – (100 000 × 50% × 30%) = 85 000

❑ QUESTION IAS 33.6@

Steenbok Ltd's profit for the year amounts to R6 200. This includes an after-tax operating loss attributable to discontinued operations of R15 000.

The company's share capital at the beginning of the year consisted of 300 000 ordinary shares. Three years ago, 30 000 4% cumulative preference shares with a nominal value of R1 each, convertible after five years into an equal number of ordinary shares at the option of Steenbok Ltd, were issued. Simultaneously, 100 000 compulsory convertible debentures were issued that are to be converted into an equal number of ordinary shares after seven years (the interest expense on the debentures amounted to R10 000 in the current year).

A preference dividend of R3 600 was declared during the current financial year.

Assume a tax rate of 27%.

Required

Calculate the basic earnings per share and diluted earnings per share which must be disclosed in the financial statements of Steenbok Ltd, so as to comply with the requirements of International Financial Reporting Standards (IFRS).

❖ Suggested solution IAS 33.6@

	Rand
Basic earnings per share	
Profit from continuing operations (calc 1 – 3)	0,05
Loss from discontinued operations (1)	(0,04)
Profit for the year	0,01

Diluted earnings per share

Profit from continuing operations (calc 4)	0,05
Loss from discontinued operations (2)	(0,03)
Profit for the year	0,02

(1) 15 000/400 000 = 0,04
(2) 15 000/430 000 = 0,03

Calculations

1. Basic earnings

	Rand
Profit for the year	6 200
Cumulative preference dividend (1)	(1 200)
Basic earnings – profit for the year	5 000
Loss from discontinued operations	15 000
Basic earnings – profit from continuing operations	20 000

(1) 30 000 × 4% = 1 200

2. Weighted average number of ordinary shares

	Shares
In issue at the beginning of the year	300 000
To be issued upon conversion of debentures (conversion mandatory) (IAS 33.23)	100 000
	400 000

3. Basic earnings per share

	Rand
For profit from continuing operations (2)	0,05
For profit for the year (3)	0,01

(2) 20 000/400 000 = 0,05
(3) 5 000/400 000 = 0,01

4. Test for dilution

	Rand
Basic earnings – profit from continuing operations	20 000
Dividend saving (4)	1 200
	21 200

(4) 30 000 × 4% = 1 200

	Shares
Number of ordinary shares used for basic earnings per share	400 000
Convertible preference shares	30 000
	430 000

	Rand
∴ Potential diluted earnings per share for profit from continuing operations (5)	0,05

(5) 21 200/430 000 = 0,05

5. Diluted earnings per share – profit for the year

	Rand
Basic earnings – profit for the year	5 000
Dividend saving	1 200
	6 200
Diluted earnings per share – profit for the year (6)	0,02

(6) 6 200/430 000 = 0,02 (rounded up in order to balance with the total of continuing and discontinued operations)

Note: The diluted earnings per share for profit for the year (1,44 cents) is higher than the basic earnings per share for profit for the year (1,25 cents). However, as the convertible preference shares cause dilution in respect of the earnings per share for profit from **continuing** operations, these preference shares must be included in the calculation of all diluted earnings per share amounts.

❑ QUESTION IAS 33.7@

The following is an extract from the statement of profit or loss and other comprehensive income of the Gideon Ltd Group for the year ended 31 December 20.9:

	Rand
Profit before tax	5 000 000
Income tax expense	(1 416 667)
Profit for the year	3 583 333
Profit attributable to:	
Owners of the parent	3 083 333
Non-controlling interest	500 000
	3 583 333

Additional information

Profit before tax is calculated after taking into account the following:

		Rand
1.	Realised gain on the disposal of a subsidiary	(1 000 000)
2.	Reversal of a write-down of inventory to net realisable value	(50 000)
3.	A decrease in the deferred tax balance (contra to profit or loss) due to a change in the tax rate	(83 333)
4.	Depreciation on plant	60 000
5.	Disposal of a manufacturing segment (which meets the definition of a discontinued operation)	
	5.1 Trading loss incurred during 20.9	100 000
	5.2 Realised loss on disposal of the disposal group constituting the discontinued operation	75 000
6.	Foreign exchange profit on re-measuring a debtor to the closing rate	(25 000)
7.	Impairment loss on a financial asset measured at amortised cost	(55 000)
8.	Transaction cost with business combination	(20 000)

Required

Determine, with reference to Circular 1/2021, if the above items should be included or excluded in the computation of headline earnings. Present your answer in the following format:

Item	*Applicable IFRS*	*Included/ Excluded*	*Reason*

❖ **Suggested solution IAS 33.7@**

Item	*Applicable IFRS*	*Included/ Excluded*	*Reason*
1	IFRS 10	Excluded	Remeasurement of an asset
2	IAS 2	Included	Remeasurement: relates to normal operating/trading activities of the entity
3	IAS 12	Included	Remeasurement: relates to normal operating/trading activities of the entity
4	IAS 16	Included	Remeasurement: relates to the usage of a non-current asset, which is an operating/trading activity of the entity
5.1	IFRS 5	Included	Not a remeasurement
5.2	IFRS 5	Excluded	Not part of the normal operating/trading activities of the entity
6	IAS 21	Included	Remeasurement on foreign exchange movements on monetary asset relates to operating/trading activities of the entity
7	IFRS 9	Included	Remeasurement following adjustment to a financial instrument due to application of IFRS 9
8	IFRS 3	Included	Remeasurement: relates to normal operating profit or loss of the entity

❑ **QUESTION IAS 33.8@**

The following information of Never-Never Ltd for the year ended 31 December 20.9 is available:

	20.9 Rand	**20.8 Rand**
Profit before tax	101 389	29 167
Income tax expense	(28 389)	(8 167)
Profit for the year	73 000	21 000

Additional information

1. The capital structure of Never-Never Ltd was as follows at 31 December 20.8 (no new shares or debentures were issued during 20.8):

	Rand
Ordinary shares (50 000 shares issued at R6 each)	300 000
11% preference shares (nominal value of R1 each)	30 000
15% convertible debentures (nominal value of R1 each)	100 000

2. All debentures are convertible on 1 July 20.9 at the option of Never-Never Ltd on the following basis: one ordinary share will be issued for every two debentures held and interest on debentures will only accumulate until 30 June 20.9. The convertible debentures were issued on 1 July 20.6. Similar debentures without conversion rights bear interest at 17% per annum.

3. Preference dividends for the years ended 31 December 20.9 and 31 December 20.8 were paid on 31 December 20.9.

4. Assume a tax rate of 27%.

Required

a. Calculate the earnings per share of Never-Never Ltd for the year ended 31 December 20.9.
b. Show how it must be disclosed in the financial statements, so as to comply with the requirements of International Financial Reporting Standards (IFRS).

❑ QUESTION IAS 33.9[@]

Mars Ltd, a company listed on the JSE Ltd in 20.2, had the following capital structure at 28 February 20.5:

Ordinary shares of R1 each – R800 000. Assume that Mars Ltd has been incorporated under the previous Companies Act and is authorised to issue par value shares.

On 31 August 20.5 the company had a capitalisation issue from retained earnings of one ordinary share for every eight held.

On 31 August 20.6 a special resolution was passed splitting the nominal value of ordinary shares to R0,50 per share in order to improve the marketability of the shares.

The abridged consolidated statement of profit or loss and other comprehensive income of the Mars Ltd Group for the year ended 28 February is as follows:

	20.7 Rand	20.6 Rand
Profit/(loss) before tax	(160 000)	263 889
Income tax expense	–	(73 889)
Profit/(loss) for the year	(160 000)	190 000

	20.7 Rand	20.6 Rand
Profit/(loss) attributable to:		
Owners of the parent	(163 000)	162 000
Non-controlling interest	3 000	28 000
	(160 000)	190 000

Ordinary dividends amounting to R50 000 were paid by Mars Ltd on 28 February 20.6.

Required

a. Calculate the basic earnings per share and dividend per share (consolidated).
b. Show how they must be disclosed in the consolidated statement of profit or loss and other comprehensive income and statement of changes in equity of the Mars Ltd Group for the year ended 28 February 20.7, so as to comply with the requirements of International Financial Reporting Standards (IFRS).

❑ QUESTION IAS 33.10@

Klipspringer Ltd's profit for the years ended 31 March 20.7 and 31 March 20.8 amounted to R180 000 and R253 750 respectively.

The issued share capital of the company consisted of:

	20.8 Rand	20.7 Rand
Ordinary shares – 31 March		
(20.8: 337 500 shares; 20.7: 225 000 shares)	337 500	225 000
12% preference shares	100 000	100 000

On 30 September 20.7, Klipspringer Ltd had a rights issue of one share for every two previously held.

Before the announcement of the rights issue the shares traded on the JSE Ltd at R1,80 per share. To ensure that all shares were taken up during the rights issue, the shares were offered to intended shareholders at R1,25 each.

Required

Calculate the basic earnings per share of Klipspringer Ltd for the years ended 31 March 20.8 and 31 March 20.7. Your answer must comply with the requirements of International Financial Reporting Standards (IFRS).

IAS 34

Interim financial reporting

❑ **QUESTIONS AND SOLUTIONS**

❑ **QUESTION**

@ *These questions contain topics or principles that were not included in the ITC syllabus of SAICA at the time of publishing this book, but might still be included in university syllabi.*
Please note: the whole IAS 34 is not included in the ITC syllabus of SAICA.

☐ QUESTION IAS 34.1[@]

Alpha Ltd has a financial year end of 31 December and presents interim financial reports half-yearly.

Required

Which financial reports will Alpha Ltd present in its interim financial report as at 30 June 20.1?

❖ Suggested solution IAS 34.1[@]

IAS 34.20

Statement of financial position As at 30 June 20.1	**Comparative amounts** As at 31 December 20.0
Statement of profit or loss and other comprehensive income 6 months ended 30 June 20.1	6 months ended 30 June 20.0
Statement of cash flows 6 months ended 30 June 20.1	6 months ended 30 June 20.0
Statement of changes in equity 6 months ended 30 June 20.1	6 months ended 30 June 20.0

☐ QUESTION IAS 34.2[@]

Beta Ltd incurred the following expenses during 20.2:

- On 1 January 20.2 a R36 000 upfront payment for the 20.2 annual advertising campaign was made.
- A payment of R60 000 for employee training was made on 1 February 20.2. This training will be provided over a period of two years.
- Year-end bonuses of R48 000 were to be paid on 31 December 20.2. Should an employee resign before 31 December 20.2, he is still entitled to a pro rata bonus (this is stipulated in the employment contract).

In addition to the above expenses, a fire destroyed a machine on 1 May 20.2. The machine had a cost price of R400 000 and accumulated depreciation of R144 000 at 1 January 20.2. The depreciation on the machine and the loss has yet to be accounted for. Machinery is depreciated at 25% per annum on cost.

The company's year-end is 31 December.

Required

Journalise all relevant transactions (journal narrations are not required) for interim reporting purposes for the six months ended 30 June 20.2.

❖ Suggested solution IAS 34.2[@]

	Rand Dr/(Cr)
30 June 20.2	
Advertising cost (P or L) (1)	18 000
Advertising paid in advance (SFPos)	18 000
Bank	(36 000)
Employee training (P or L) (2)	12 500
Employee training paid in advance (SFPos)	47 500
Bank	(60 000)
Employee benefit costs (P or L) (3)	24 000
Bonus accrual (SFPos)	(24 000)
Depreciation (P or L) (4)	33 333
Machinery: Accumulated depreciation (SFPos)	(33 333)
Machinery: Accumulated depreciation (SFPos) (5)	177 333
Machinery written-off / scrapped (P or L) (6)	222 667
Machinery: Cost (SFPos)	(400 000)

(1) 36 000 × 6 / 12 months = 18 000
(2) 60 000 × 5 / 24 months = 12 500
(3) 48 000 × 6 / 12 months = 24 000
(4) 400 000 / 4 years × 4 / 12 months = 33 333 depreciation 1 January 20.2 to 1 May 20.2
(5) 144 000 1 January 20.2 accumulated depreciation + 33 333 (4) = 177 333
(6) 400 000 cost – 177 333 (5) = 222 667

❑ QUESTION IAS 34.3[@]

Delta Ltd is a manufacturing entity with a year end of 31 December. The company had an assessed loss of R200 000 for the year ended 31 December 20.2. No deferred tax asset has been recognised for the assessed loss. Delta Ltd reports on 30 June 20.3 on the interim results for the six months then ended.

For the first six months of the 20.3 financial year the company earned R500 000 taxable income and expects to earn R600 000 taxable income in the remaining six months. A tax rate of 27% is applicable in the jurisdiction in which Delta Ltd operates.

Required

Calculate the income tax expense to be reported in the interim report for the six months ended 30 June 20.3. Your answer must comply with the requirements of International Financial Reporting Standards (IFRS).

❖ Suggested solution IAS 34.3@

Tax expense for the interim report shall be:

[(500 000 + 600 000) – 200 000 assessed loss] × 27% = 243 000 expected total tax expense for 20.2
(243 000 / 1 100 000) = 22.0909% average annual effective tax rate
22.0909% × 500 000 = 110 454

See IAS 34 Illustrative Examples B12 to B22.

❑ QUESTION IAS 34.4@

Total Onslaught Ltd is engaged in the manufacturing and renting of gas-filled air balloons. The following represents the unaudited trial balances for each quarter forming part of the interim period starting on 1 July 20.1 and ending on 31 December 20.1.

	Note	First quarter Rand Dr/(Cr)	Second quarter Rand Dr/(Cr)
Revenue	1	(250 000)	(600 000)
Distribution costs		8 000	34 000
Administrative expenses		15 000	50 000
Other expenses		18 000	65 000
Cost of sales	2	83 250	300 000
Finance costs		10 500	10 500
Insurance expenses	3	14 000	6 000
Maintenance costs	4	20 000	1 000
Property, plant and equipment	5	750 000	800 000
Accumulated depreciation on property, plant and equipment as at 30 June 20.1		(150 000)	(150 000)
Inventory		419 500	400 000
Trade receivables		351 750	550 000
Trade and other payables		(250 000)	(513 250)
Listed investment	6	–	90 000
Bank balance		85 000	163 000
Long-term borrowings		(300 000)	(300 000)
Share capital	7	(500 000)	(500 000)
Retained earnings – 30 June/30 September		(325 000)	(406 250)
		Nil	Nil

Additional information and notes

1. Revenue would normally be earned evenly throughout the year, but as Christmas and the December holidays fall in the second quarter, the sales during that quarter are higher than those in the other quarters of the year.

2. Cost of sales amount to 33,3% of the selling price. In the second quarter obsolete inventory to the amount of R100 000 was written off. Had this write-down taken place at year end, it would have been regarded as separately disclosable once it exceeded R250 000. Historic records have, however, shown that in the past such write-downs during interim periods have never exceeded R75 000. The write-down has already been correctly accounted for.

3. The insurance costs incurred in the first quarter relate to the period 1 July 20.1 to 30 June 20.2. This is for the annual insurance. The insurance costs incurred in the second quarter relate to the Christmas season, when the risks of injury and claims against the company are much higher.

4. Maintenance of air balloons usually amounts to R1 000 per quarter, but during the first quarter all balloons are checked and re-gassed for the Christmas period that lies ahead.

5. Depreciation on plant and equipment still has to be recognised at 20% per annum on cost using the straight-line method. A new machine was bought on 1 November 20.1 to refill the balloons more quickly with gas. No machines were disposed of during the period.

6. The listed investment (classified as a fair value through profit or loss financial asset) had a market value of R85 000 at close of business on 31 December 20.1.

7. The issued share capital of 500 000 ordinary shares remained unchanged. An interim dividend of 5c per share was declared on 15 December 20.1 and has yet to be accounted for.

8. The average effective tax rate for the full year is estimated to be 25% of the pre-tax profit for the year.

9. A claim for damages to the amount of R50 000 was lodged against the company during June 20.1. At the end of December 20.1, the legal advisors of the company were of the opinion that the claim would be successful and that the company would have to pay the R50 000. This event was disclosed as a contingent liability in the notes to the statement of financial position as at 30 June 20.1.

10. It is the company's policy to prepare condensed interim financial statements. The omission of any line items on the face of these financial statements is regarded as misleading. The accounting policies followed by the company in the preparation of interim financial reports are consistent with that used to prepare the most recent annual financial statements.

Required

Prepare the interim financial statements (excluding a statement of cash flows) with accompanying notes for the six-month interim period ended 31 December 20.1. Your answer must comply with the requirements of IAS 34.

IAS 36

Impairment of assets

❑ QUESTIONS AND SOLUTIONS

IAS 36.1	Calculation of fair value less costs of disposal and disclosure of impairment loss in profit before tax note
IAS 36.2	Change in useful life of asset due to impairment: calculation of impairment loss
IAS 36.3	Basic calculation of value in use needed for calculating impairment loss
IAS 36.4	Identifying the cash-generating unit of an impaired machine and recognition of impairment loss: discussion
IAS 36.5	Allocation of impairment loss to assets in the cash generating unit: calculation
IAS 36.6@	Impairment of a revalued asset with a subsequent reversal of impairment loss: journal entries
IAS 36.7	Impairment of a cash-generating unit with a subsequent reversal of impairment loss: calculations
IAS 36.8	Allocation of reversal of impairment loss to assets in a cash-generating unit: calculations

❑ QUESTIONS

IAS 36.9	Impairment loss for cash-generating unit: calculation
IAS 36.10	Indication of impairment of machine and change in useful life of machine: disclosure and discussion
IAS 36.11	Impairment and subsequent reversal of impairment loss for individual assets: disclosure
IAS 36.12	Compensation for impairment, etc.: disclosure in profit before tax note
IAS 36.13	Allocation of impairment loss to assets in cash-generating unit: calculation
IAS 36.14	Corporate assets that can/cannot be allocated to cash-generating unit under review: calculations
IAS 36.15	Impairment against goodwill, with non-controlling interest at proportional interest and fair value: calculations
IAS 36.16	Impairment testing when goodwill cannot be allocated to individual cash-generating units and allocation and reallocation of impairment loss for cash-generating unit: calculations
IAS 36.17	Cash generating units with goodwill: disclosure in profit before tax note

@ *This question contains topics or principles that were not included in the ITC syllabus of SAICA at the time of publishing this book, but might still be included in university syllabi.*

❑ QUESTION IAS 36.1

Sipho Ltd is a manufacturing company that owns several machines. At the end of the current year, two of these machines were damaged, but are still in working order. The useful lives and pattern of use of the machines were not influenced by the damage. The carrying amounts of the machines on 31 December 20.4 were as follows:

	Rand
Machine 1	500 000
Machine 2	380 000

Machine 1 can at this stage be disposed of for R490 000, in an orderly transaction between market participants. In order to sell the machine, it has to be serviced and tuned at a cost of R10 000. Direct selling expenses of R5 000 would also have to be incurred. Management determined the value in use of the machine to be R488 000 using an appropriate discount rate of 10%.

Machine 2 can at this stage be disposed of for R380 000, in an orderly transaction between market participants. Direct selling expenses of R5 000 would also have to be incurred. Management determined the value in use of the machine to be R390 000 using an appropriate discount rate of 10%.

Required

Prepare the profit before tax note that will accompany the financial statements of Sipho Ltd for the year ended 31 December 20.4, so as to comply with the requirements of International Financial Reporting Standards (IFRS). Comparative amounts and an accounting policy note are not required.

❖ Suggested solution IAS 36.1

SIPHO LTD
NOTES FOR THE YEAR ENDED 31 DECEMBER 20.4

2. Profit before tax

Included in profit before tax are, inter alia, the following items:

	Rand
Expenses	
Impairment loss on machine (calc 1)	12 000
(included in cost of sales line item)	

Machine 1, a manufacturing machine belongs to the manufacturing segment. The impairment loss is due to physical damage to the asset. Machine 1's recoverable amount of R488 000 is its value in use, which was calculated by using a discount rate of 10%.

(**Note:** The above narrative information can be presented here or as part of the property, plant and equipment note.)

Calculations

1. Machine 1

1.1 Recoverable amount	**Rand**
Fair value less costs of disposal:	
Selling price	490 000
Cost to bring asset into condition for sale (IAS 36.28)	(10 000)
Selling expenses	(5 000)
Fair value less costs of disposal	475 000
Value in use	488 000
Recoverable amount (higher of the two amounts above)	488 000

1.2 Impairment loss

Carrying amount	500 000
Recoverable amount (calc 1.1)	(488 000)
Impairment loss	12 000

2. Machine 2

2.1 Determination of the recoverable amount	**Rand**
Fair value less costs of disposal:	
Selling price	380 000
Selling expenses	(5 000)
Fair value less costs of disposal	375 000
Value in use	390 000
Recoverable amount (higher of the two amounts above)	390 000

2.2 Determination of the impairment loss

Carrying amount	380 000
Recoverable amount (calc 2.1)	(390 000)
Impairment loss	–

There is no impairment loss as the recoverable amount is higher than the carrying amount.

❑ QUESTION IAS 36.2

Bloo Ltd is a manufacturing company and owns various items of machinery. At the end of the current year, one of these machines was damaged, but it is still in working order. The machine was acquired on 1 January 20.2 at a cost of R900 000. Depreciation was calculated using the straight-line method over the expected useful life of 10 years. Due to the damage the useful life of the machine was reviewed, and management estimated that the remaining useful life of the machine is now only three years from 31 December 20.4.

Management determined the fair value less costs of disposal to be R530 000 and the value in use of the machine to be R525 000 using an appropriate discount rate of 10%.

Ignore any tax implications.

Required

Calculate the impairment loss to be recognised by Bloo Ltd for the year ended 31 December 20.4 so as to comply with the requirements of International Financial Reporting Standards (IFRS).

❖ Suggested solution IAS 36.2

Impairment loss to be recognised by Bloo Ltd for the year ended 31 December 20.4:

	Rand
Carrying amount of machine (calc 1)	630 000
Recoverable amount of machine (calc 2)	(530 000)
Impairment loss	100 000

Calculations

1. Carrying amount of machine	**Rand**
Cost	900 000
Accumulated depreciation – 31 December 20.4 (1)	(270 000)
Carrying amount – 31 December 20.4	630 000

(1) 900 000/10 × 3 years (1 January 20.2 – 31 December 20.4) = 270 000

(**Note**: Depreciation for 20.4 is not based on the revised useful life, seeing as the useful life was revised due to physical damage to the asset (impairment indicator) which only occurred **at year-end**).

2. Recoverable amount of machine	**Rand**
Fair value less costs of disposal	530 000
Value in use	525 000
Recoverable amount (higher of the two amounts above)	530 000

❑ QUESTION IAS 36.3

Bravo Ltd is a manufacturing company that owns various items of machinery. As a result of new technology in the manufacturing industry, Bravo Ltd now expects to earn less revenue from two items of machinery. The carrying amounts of the two items on 31 December 20.4 were as follows:

	Rand
Machine ABC	850 000
Machine XYZ	750 000

Management determined the fair value less costs of disposal of machine ABC to be R800 000 and that of machine XYZ to be R740 000 on 31 December 20.4.

Bravo Ltd is of the opinion that machine ABC will generate net cash inflows of R210 000 per annum over the next five years and this was confirmed in the most recent cash flow budget of management. Machine ABC can be disposed of for a net amount of R15 000 at the end of its useful life.

The budgeted net cash inflows for the next five years from machine XYZ (that occur at the end of each year), are as follows:

	Rand
20.5	190 000
20.6	195 000
20.7	205 000
20.8	200 000
20.9	180 000

An appropriate after-tax discount rate is 7,3%. The tax rate is 27%.

Required

Calculate the impairment loss to be recognised by Bravo Ltd for the year ended 31 December 20.4 so as to comply with the requirements of International Financial Reporting Standards (IFRS).

❖ Suggested solution IAS 36.3

Impairment loss to be recognised by Bravo Ltd for the year ended 31 December 20.4:

	Rand
Machine ABC (calc 1.3)	44 621
Machine XYZ (calc 2.3)	10 000
Total	54 621

Calculations

1. Machine ABC

1.1 Value in use

	Rand
Net cash inflows per annum	R210 000
Period over which inflow will occur	5 years
Expected net cash inflow at disposal	R15 000
Pre-tax discount rate (7,3%/0,73)	10%

Present value of cash generated via usage

PMT = 210 000; n = 5 years; i = 10%
PV = R796 065

Present value of cash generated through sale

FV = 15 000; n = 5 years; i = 10%
PV = R9 314

Total value in use is therefore: R796 065 + R9 314 = R805 379

1.2 Recoverable amount

	Rand
Fair value less costs of disposal (given)	800 000
Value in use (calc 1.1)	805 379
Recoverable amount (higher of the two amounts above)	805 379

1.3 Impairment loss

Carrying amount (given)	850 000
Recoverable amount (calc 1.2)	(805 379)
Impairment loss	44 621

2. Machine XYZ

2.1 Value in use

CFi	0	:	0
	1	:	190 000
	2	:	195 000
	3	:	205 000
	4	:	200 000
	5	:	180 000
	i	=	10 (7,3/0,73)
∴	NPV	=	736 272

2.2 Recoverable amount

	Rand
Fair value less costs of disposal (given)	740 000
Value in use (calc 2.1)	736 272
Recoverable amount (higher of the two amounts above)	740 000

2.3 Impairment loss

	Rand
Carrying amount (given)	750 000
Recoverable amount (calc 2.2)	(740 000)
Impairment loss	10 000

❑ **QUESTION IAS 36.4**

The following information on the property, plant and equipment of Zoom Ltd is presented to you:

A machine has suffered physical damage but is still working, although not as well as it used to. The fair value less costs of disposal of the machine is less than its carrying amount. The value in use of the machine cannot be determined independently of the value in use of other assets. The smallest identifiable group of assets that includes the machine and generates cash inflows that are largely independent of the cash inflows from other assets is the production line to which the machine belongs. The value in use of the production line shows that the production line, taken as a whole, is not impaired.

Required

Identify the machine's cash-generating unit and discuss whether an impairment loss must be recognised in respect of the machine if:

a. the entity has no intention of replacing the machine;
b. the entity will sell the machine and replace it.

❖ **Suggested solution IAS 36.4**

a. There is an indication that the machine may be impaired (suffered physical damage) and therefore the recoverable amount of the machine must be calculated.

The recoverable amount of the machine alone cannot be calculated due to the following (IAS 36.67):

i) The machine does not generate cash inflows from continuing use that are largely independent of those from other assets.

ii) The fair value less costs of disposal of the machine can be determined, but the value in use of the machine cannot be estimated to be close to its fair value less costs of disposal due to the fact that the entity is still going to use the machine and the future cash flows from continuing use can therefore not be estimated to be negligible.

The recoverable amount of the machine alone can therefore not be determined.

The recoverable amount of the cash-generating unit (production line) to which that asset belongs must therefore be determined (IAS 36.66).

The question stipulates that the production line as a whole is not impaired.

Due to the fact that no impairment loss is recognised in respect of the production line, no impairment loss will be recognised in respect of the machinery (IAS 36.107(b)).

However, the entity may need to reassess the depreciation period or the depreciation method for the machine. A shorter depreciation period or an accelerated depreciation method could perhaps be required to reflect the expected remaining useful life of the machine or the pattern in which economic benefits are consumed by the entity (refer to IAS 36.17).

b. There is an indication that the machine may be impaired (have suffered physical damage) and therefore the recoverable amount of the machine must be calculated.

The recoverable amount of the machine alone can be calculated due to the fact that the fair value less costs of disposal of the machine can be determined and the value in use of the machine can be estimated to be close to its fair value less costs of disposal. This is because the value in use of the machinery will consist mainly of the net disposal proceeds, as the future cash flows from continuing use of the machinery are negligible (IAS 36.67(a)).

The recoverable amount of the machine is therefore its fair value less costs of disposal.

Since the machine's fair value less costs of disposal is less than its carrying amount, an impairment loss is recognised.

❑ QUESTION IAS 36.5

The following information is available for cash-generating unit Z:

1. **Cash-generating unit Z consists of the following:**

	Carrying amount Rand	Fair value less costs of disposal Rand
Asset A	15 000	12 000
Asset B	10 000	5 000
Asset C	4 000	2 000
Goodwill	1 000	–
	30 000	

2. The recoverable amount of cash-generating unit Z amounts to R20 000.

Required

Calculate the carrying amounts of the assets after impairment was taken into account, as well as the impairment loss that will be recognised per asset. Your answer must comply with the requirements of International Financial Reporting Standards (IFRS).

❖ **Suggested solution IAS 36.5**

Carrying amounts of the assets after impairment was taken into account, as well as the impairment loss that will be recognised per asset:

	Carrying amount Rand	Impairment loss Rand
Asset A (1)	12 000	3 000
Asset B (2)(4)	5 715	4 285
Asset C (3)(5)	2 285	1 715
Goodwill (calc 2)	–	1 000
		10 000

(1) 15 000 – 12 000 = 3 000
(2) 6 897 (calc 2) – 1 182 (calc 3) = 5 715
(3) 2 758 (calc 2) – 473 (calc 3) = 2 285
(4) 3 103 (calc 2) + 1 182 (calc 3) = 4 285
(5) 1 242 (calc 2) + 473 (calc 3) = 1 715

Calculations

Note:

Due to the fact that cash-generating unit (CGU) Z is a CGU to which goodwill has been allocated, it has to be tested for impairment at least annually.

If goodwill was not allocated to CGU Z, CGU Z would have been tested for impairment in the following circumstances (ignore the effect of corporate assets):

- When there is an indication at reporting date that the CGU may be impaired; or
- When there is an indication at reporting date that asset A, asset B or asset C may be impaired, but the recoverable amount of the individual asset cannot be determined. The CGU to which that individual asset belongs (i.e. CGU Z) should then be tested for impairment.

1. Impairment loss of cash-generating unit Z

	Rand
Carrying amount (given)	30 000
Recoverable amount (given)	20 000
Impairment loss	10 000

2. Allocation of impairment loss of cash-generating unit Z (IAS 36.104)

	Carrying amount before Rand	Allocation Rand	Carrying amount after Rand
Impairment loss (calc 1)		10 000	
Goodwill	1 000	(1 000)	–
		9 000	
Asset A (1)	15 000	4 655	10 345
Asset B (2)	10 000	3 103	6 897
Asset C (3)	4 000	1 242	2 758
	29 000	–	

(1) 15 000 / 29 000 × 9 000 = 4 655

(2) 10 000 / 29 000 × 9 000 = 3 103
(3) 4 000 / 29 000 × 9 000 = 1 242

3. Reallocation of impairment loss (limitation in terms of IAS 36.105)

The adjusted carrying amount of asset A amounts to R10 345 which is less than the fair value less costs of disposal of R12 000.

R1 655 (1) of the impairment loss must therefore be reallocated to asset B and asset C:
Asset B = R1 182 (3)
Asset C = R473 (4)

(1) 12 000 – 10 345 = 1 655
(2) 6 897 (calc 2) + 2 758 (calc 2) = 9 655
(3) 6 897/9 655 (2) × 1 655 = 1 182; or 10 000/14 000 × 1 655 = 1 182
(4) 2 758/9 655 (2) × 1 655 = 473; or 4 000/14 000 × 1 655 = 473

❑ QUESTION IAS 36.6@

It is the accounting policy of Red Ltd to revalue its assets every three years at the end of the year. At revaluation the accumulated depreciation is eliminated against the gross carrying amount of the asset. Depreciation for each financial year is calculated on the most recent revalued amount. The revaluation surplus is realised as the assets are used.

On 1 January 20.1, Red Ltd purchased a plant at a cost of R100 000. Depreciation is calculated using the straight-line method over the expected useful life of 10 years. At the end of 20.3 the net replacement cost of this plant amounted to R71 750.

At the end of 20.4 there were indications that the plant was impaired. The recoverable amount was determined to be R58 000.

At the end of 20.5 the circumstances that led to the impairment in 20.4 no longer existed and the recoverable amount of the plant was determined as R51 000.

The South African Revenue Service allows a wear-and-tear allowance of 10% per annum without any adjustments for impairment losses. The tax rate is 27%.

Required

Prepare all the journal entries for the plant of Red Ltd for the years ended 31 December 20.3, 31 December 20.4 and 31 December 20.5 so as to comply with the requirements of International Financial Reporting Standards (IFRS). Journal narrations are not required.

❖ **Suggested solution IAS 36.6@**

Red Ltd
Journal entries for the year ended 31 December 20.3

	Rand Dr/(Cr)
Plant at cost	(100 000)*
Plant at valuation (1)	82 000*
Accumulated depreciation: plant (2)	20 000
Gain on revaluation (OCI) (3)	(2 000)

* These amounts can also be journalised on a net basis.

Income tax on gain on revaluation in OCI (OCI) (4)	540
Deferred tax (SFPos)	(540)
Depreciation (P or L) (5)	10 250
Accumulated depreciation: Plant	(10 250)
Deferred tax (SFPos) (6)	67
Income tax expense (P or L)	(67)
Revaluation reserve (equity) (7)	183
Retained earnings	(183)

(1) 71 750/7 × 8 = 82 000
(2) 100 000/10 × 2 = 20 000
(3) 82 000 – 80 000 = 2 000
(4) 2 000 × 27% = 540
(5) 82 000/8 = 10 250
(6) 473 (calc 1) – 540 (4) = 67
(7) (2 000 – 540)/8 = 183; or (10 250 – 10 000) × 73% = 183

Red Ltd
Journal entries for the year ended 31 December 20.4

	Rand Dr/(Cr)
Depreciation (P or L)	10 250
Accumulated depreciation: plant	(10 250)
Revaluation reserve (equity)	183
Retained earnings	(183)
Loss on revaluation (OCI) (2)	1 500
Impairment loss (P or L) (3)	2 000
Accumulated depreciation and impairment losses: Plant (1)	(3 500)
Deferred tax (SFPos)	405
Income tax on loss on revaluation in OCI (OCI) (4)	(405)
Deferred tax (SFPos) (5)	608
Income tax expense (P or L)	(608)

(1) 58 000 – [82 000 – (10 250 × 2)] = 3 500
(2) 2 000/8 × 6 = 1 500
(3) 3 500 – 1 500 = 2 000
(4) 1 500 × 27% = 405
(5) [(540 (calc 1) + 473 (calc 1) – 405 (4)] = 608

Red Ltd
Journal entries for the year ended 31 December 20.5

	Rand Dr/(Cr)
Depreciation (P or L) (1)	9 667
Accumulated depreciation and impairment losses: Plant	(9 667)
Accumulated depreciation and impairment losses: Plant (2)	2 667
Reversal of impairment loss (P or L)	(2 000)
Gain on revaluation (OCI) (3)	(667)
Income tax on gain on revaluation in OCI (OCI) (4)	180
Deferred tax (SFPos)	(180)
Income tax expense (P or L) (5)	630
Deferred tax (SFPos)	(630)

(1) 58 000/6 = 9 667
(2) Lower of R51 000 (recoverable amount) and R51 250 (82 000/8 × 5)
(58 000 – 9 667) – 51 000 = 2 667
(3) 2 667 – 2 000 = 667
(4) 667 × 27% = 180
(5) [(540 (calc 1) + 270 (calc 1)) – 180 (4)] = 630

Calculations

1. Deferred tax	**CA**	**TB**	**TD**	**DT @ 27%**
	Rand	**Rand**	**Rand**	**Rand**
31 December 20.3 (1)(2)	71 750	70 000	1 750	473
31 December 20.4 (1)(3)	58 000	60 000	(2 000)	(540)
31 December 20.5 (1)(4)	51 000	50 000	1 000	270

CA = Carrying amount
TB = Tax base
TD = Temporary differences
DT = Deferred tax (SFPos)

(1) Given
(2) 100 000 × 70% = 70 000
(3) 100 000 × 60% = 60 000
(4) 100 000 × 50% = 50 000

❑ QUESTION IAS 36.7

On 1 January 20.1, Big Picture Ltd acquired all the net assets of Outthere Ltd which operates in three different continents. The purchase price of R20 million could be allocated as follows:

	Purchase price	Carrying amount of assets	Goodwill
	Rand	Rand	Rand
Europe	10 000 000	7 000 000	3 000 000
Asia	4 000 000	3 000 000	1 000 000
Africa	6 000 000	4 000 000	2 000 000
	20 000 000	14 000 000	6 000 000

During 20.4 there was a severe drought throughout Africa and the production of the African cash-generating unit decreased by 70%. Management determined the recoverable amount of the African operations to be R1 500 000 on 31 December 20.4. Accumulated impairment losses in respect of goodwill of the African operations amounted to R800 000 on 31 December 20.3.

By 20.7 the region had had adequate rainfall to relieve the drought conditions, and it is estimated that production would again increase with approximately 50%.

All assets are written off over a period of 10 years on a straight-line basis.

Required

a. Calculate the impairment loss for the Africa continent for the year ended 31 December 20.4 and indicate how it will be allocated.
b. Calculate the reversal of the impairment loss for the Africa continent for the year ended 31 December 20.7 if the recoverable amount is R1 600 000.
c. Calculate the reversal of the impairment loss for the Africa continent for the year ended 31 December 20.7 if the recoverable amount is R1 000 000.

Your solution must comply with the requirements of International Financial Reporting Standards (IFRS).

❖ Suggested solution IAS 36.7

a. Impairment loss for the Africa continent for the year ended 31 December 20.4 and allocation thereof

	Total	Carrying amount of assets	Goodwill
	Rand	Rand	Rand
Purchase price – 1 Jan 20.1	6 000 000	4 000 000	2 000 000
Accumulated depreciation/amortisation (1)	(1 600 000)	(1 600 000)	–
Accumulated impairment losses (given)	(800 000)	–	(800 000)
Carrying amount – 31 Dec 20.4	3 600 000	2 400 000	1 200 000
Recoverable amount (given)	(1 500 000)		
Impairment loss	2 100 000	(900 000)	(1 200 000)
Carrying amount after loss – 31 Dec 20.4		1 500 000	–

(1) 4 000 000/10 × 4 = 1 600 000

b. Reversal of the impairment loss for the Africa continent for the year ended 31 December 20.7 if the recoverable amount is R1 600 000

	Rand
Carrying amount on 31 Dec 20.7 (1)	750 000
Carrying amount on 31 Dec 20.7 if no impairment took place in 20.4 (2)	1 200 000
Recoverable amount on 31 Dec 20.7 (given)	1 600 000
Reversal of impairment loss:	
Lower of:	
Recoverable amount (R1 600 000); and	
Carrying amount (unadjusted) (R1 200 000)	1 200 000
Carrying amount (adjusted)	(750 000)
Reversal	450 000

(1) 1 500 000/6 × 3 = 750 000
(2) 4 000 000/10 × 3 = 1 200 000

c. Reversal of the impairment loss for the Africa continent for the year ended 31 December 20.7 if the recoverable amount is R1 000 000

	Rand
Lower of:	
Recoverable amount (R1 000 000); and	
Carrying amount (unadjusted) (R1 200 000 (part b))	1 000 000
Carrying amount (adjusted) (part b)	(750 000)
Reversal	250 000

❑ QUESTION IAS 36.8

Cash-generating unit Z consists of assets A, B and C:

	Asset A Rand	Asset B Rand	Asset C Rand
Carrying amount – 31 December 20.1	20 000	30 000	25 000
Impairment loss – 31 December 20.1	(2 500)	(7 500)	(5 000)
Remaining useful life – five years	17 500	22 500	20 000
Depreciation 20.2	(3 500)	(4 500)	(4 000)
Carrying amount – 31 December 20.2	14 000	18 000	16 000
Recoverable amount – 31 December 20.2	–	22 000	23 000
Carrying amount of Z – 31 December 20.2			48 000
Recoverable amount of Z – 31 December 20.2			57 000
Possible reversal			9 000

Required

Calculate the carrying amounts of the assets of cash-generating unit Z after the reversal of the impairment loss, as well as the reversal of impairment loss that will be recognised per asset. Your answer must comply with the requirements of International Financial Reporting Standards (IFRS).

❖ **Suggested solution IAS 36.8**

Carrying amounts of the assets of cash-generating unit Z after the reversal of the impairment loss, as well as the reversal of impairment loss that will be recognised per asset

	Carrying amount	Reversal of impairment loss
	Rand	Rand
Asset A (1)	16 000	2 000
Asset B (2)(3)	21 706	3 706
Asset C (4)(5)	19 294	3 294
		9 000

(1) 14 000 – 16 000 = 2 000
(2) 21 375 (calc 2) + 331 (calc 3) = 21 706
(3) 3 375 (calc 1) + 331 (calc 3) = 3 706
(4) 19 000 (calc 2) + 294 (calc 3) = 19 294
(5) 3 000 (calc 1) + 294 (calc 3) = 3 294

Calculations

1. Allocation of reversal

Asset A: 14/48 (1) × 9 000 = 2 625
Asset B: 18/48 (1) × 9 000 = 3 375
Asset C: 16/48 (1) × 9 000 = 3 000

(1) 14 000 + 18 000 + 16 000 = 48 000

2. Carrying amounts after allocation of reversal

Asset A: 14 000 + 2 625 (calc 1) = 16 625
Asset B: 18 000 + 3 375 (calc 1) = 21 375
Asset C: 16 000 + 3 000 (calc 1) = 19 000

3. Limit of adjusted carrying amount (IAS 36.123)

	Asset A	Asset B	Asset C
	Rand	Rand	Rand
Carrying amount on 31 December 20.1	20 000	30 000	25 000
Depreciation	(4 000)	(6 000)	(5 000)
Carrying amount on 31 December 20.2 if no impairment loss was recognised on 31 December 20.1	16 000	24 000	20 000
Recoverable amount	–	22 000	23 000
Limit	16 000	22 000	20 000

Excess in respect of asset A: 16 625 (calc 2) – 16 000 = 625

Reallocate to asset B and asset C.
Asset B: R331 (2)
Asset C: R294 (3)

(1) 21 375 (calc 2) + 19 000 (calc 2) = 40 375
(2) 18/(18 + 16) × 625 = 331; or 21 375/40 375 (1) × 625 = 331
(3) 16/(18 + 16) × 625 = 294; or 19 000/40 375 (1) × 625 = 294

❑ QUESTION IAS 36.9

On 1 January 20.2, Power Ltd purchased all the net assets of Flower Ltd for R5 000. At that date the fair value of Flower Ltd amounted to R4 000, which could be allocated as follows:

	Rand
Cut flower division	2 500
Pot-plant division	1 500

Goodwill is allocated to each cash-generating unit pro rata on the basis of the carrying amounts of the assets in the cash-generating units.

For the year ended 31 December 20.2 the cut flower division and the pot-plant division were not impaired.

During December 20.3 the pot-plant division incurred significant losses due to plant diseases.

On 31 December 20.3 the carrying amounts of the identifiable net assets of the divisions are as follows:

	Rand
Cut flower division	2 000
Pot-plant division	400

On 31 December 20.3 the value in use of the pot-plant division amounted to R400 and the fair value less costs of disposal amounted to R200. On 31 December 20.3 the value in use of the cut flower division amounted to R2 700 and the fair value less costs of disposal amounted to R2 800. During the year ended 31 December 20.3, no impairment losses have been recognised in respect of the cut flower division or the pot-plant division.

Required

Calculate the impairment loss that Power Ltd will recognise in profit or loss for the year ended 31 December 20.3, so as to comply with the requirements of International Financial Reporting Standards (IFRS).

❑ QUESTION IAS 36.10

Kima Ltd is a manufacturer of several household products. A machine that is used in one of the product lines was physically damaged during the year ended 30 June 20.7. The machine is still working although not as well as it used to. The value in use of the machine cannot be determined independently from the value in use of other assets. The smallest identifiable group of assets that includes the machine and generates cash inflows that are largely independent of cash inflows from other assets is the Vera production line to which the machine belongs.

The management of Kima Ltd decided not to replace the machine after considering the following:

Damaged machine on 30 June 20.7	**Rand**
Fair value less costs of disposal	20 000
Historical cost	90 000
Accumulated depreciation (three years)	(27 000)
Carrying amount	63 000

Vera production line on 30 June 20.7	**Rand**
Fair value less costs of disposal (plant and machinery)	1 200 000
Value in use	1 700 000
Historical cost	1 500 000
Accumulated depreciation (three years)	(450 000)
Carrying amount	1 050 000

A discount rate of 15% was used to extrapolate the short-term forecasts of management. This rate does not exceed the long-term average growth rate for the market to which the product line was allocated.

Management decided that the remaining useful life of the damaged machine will be three years **from 1 July 20.6**. This change in the useful life is not as a result of the damage caused to the machine and has not yet been accounted for in the information supplied above.

Required

a. Disclose the above information in the notes of Kima Ltd for the year ended 30 June 20.7. Notes on accounting policies and comparative amounts are not required.
b. Discuss, with reasons, if an impairment loss in respect of the machine would have been recognised for the year ended 30 June 20.7, if at 30 June 20.7 management reflected a commitment to replace the machine and to sell it in the near future, and cash flows from the continuing use of the machine until its disposal were estimated to be negligible.

Your solution must comply with the requirements of International Financial Reporting Standards (IFRS).

❑ QUESTION IAS 36.11

On 28 February 20.8, Monty Ltd did an evaluation in order to determine whether there are any indications that any of its assets had undergone impairment. The result of the evaluation is as follows:

- Machine X has been negatively influenced by technological changes. New-generation machinery has become available for the same purpose for which machine X is used and this would force Monty Ltd to replace machine X within the near future in order to remain competitive. The quoted amount receivable from the sale of machine X in an orderly transaction between market participants is R600 000 and the costs of disposal are R50 000. The value in use amounts to R300 000. The carrying amount of the asset on 28 February 20.8 (before considering the impairment) was as follows:

	Rand
Historical cost	4 000 000
Accumulated depreciation (20% p.a. straight-line)	(2 400 000)
Carrying amount	1 600 000

- On 28 February 20.6 an impairment loss amounting to R300 000 was recognised for machine Y. The actual cash flows for the year ended 28 February 20.8 were materially higher that those previously estimated, before the effect of discounting. The major competitor for the product manufactured by machine Y left South Africa during 20.7, therefore resulting in the increased cash flows. It is expected that this trend will continue. On 28 February 20.8 the recoverable amount, based on the value in use, was calculated as R525 000. The discount rate is 14% per annum and this is the same rate that was used in previous years.

  The following information relates to machine Y:

Historical cost (available for use on 1 March 20.5)	R1 000 000
Depreciation (straight-line)	20% p.a.

Additional information

- Machine X and machine Y are part of the assets of the manufacturing segment.
- Impairment losses in excess of R100 000 (recognised or reversed) are seen to be material for disclosure purposes.
- The current tax rate is 27%.

Required

a. Disclose the above information in the profit before tax note and the property, plant and equipment note of Monty Ltd for the year ended 28 February 20.8 so as to comply with the requirements of International Financial Reporting Standards (IFRS).
b. Calculate the deferred tax asset/liability on 28 February 20.8 originating from the machinery. The South African Revenue Service allows wear and tear on machinery at 33,33% per annum on a straight-line basis.

❑ QUESTION IAS 36.12

Nubake Ltd is a company which owns several bakeries and supermarkets which form the basis for the company's segment reporting. On 30 December 20.1 a short circuit in one of the bakeries caused damage to an oven, with a carrying amount of R180 000. The oven could still be used, but only for eight hours per day and not 12 hours per day as in the past.

It is estimated that the oven will be in use for another four years, after which it will be sold for R10 000. The net cash inflow per annum generated by using the oven will amount to R50 000. If the oven were to be sold on 31 December 20.1 in an orderly transaction between market participants, the selling price would have amounted to R150 000.

The company's insurers indicated on 31 December 20.1 that R20 000 would be paid out in connection with the damage (assume that the amount accrues on 31 December 20.1). Nubake Ltd plans to use this money in the next financial year to repair the oven. Once this has been done, the oven's production capacity will exceed the original capacity determined when it was brought into use for the first time. Consequently, the annual net cash inflow generated by the oven will increase to R80 000. Its useful life and scrap value will, however, not be affected.

A discount rate of 10% before tax is regarded as appropriate. The company's financial year ends on 31 December 20.1.

Required

a. Calculate the impairment loss, if any, for the year ended 31 December 20.1. Your solution must comply with the requirements of International Financial Reporting Standards (IFRS).
b. Prepare the profit before tax note for the year ended 31 December 20.1. Assume that all amounts are material. Your solution must comply with the requirements of International Financial Reporting Standards (IFRS).

❑ QUESTION IAS 36.13

Problem Ltd has various cash-generating units. The plastic cash-generating unit has a recoverable amount of R650 000 and consists of the following assets:

	Rand
Equipment	270 000
Factory building	300 000
Motor vehicles	150 000
Goodwill allocated	50 000
Total carrying amount at 31 December 20.5	770 000

The fair value less costs of disposal of certain individual assets of the plastic cash-generating unit could be obtained at 31 December 20.5 and were as follows:

	Rand
Factory building	250 000
Motor vehicles	140 000

Required

Calculate the carrying amount of each individual asset belonging to the plastic cash-generating unit of Problem Ltd on 31 December 20.5 after the impairment has been taken into account. Your answer must comply with the requirements of International Financial Reporting Standards (IFRS).

❑ QUESTION IAS 36.14

Boom Ltd has three cash-generating units – XX, YY and ZZ. The two corporate assets are the head-office building and the centralised data processor. The head-office building supports all three cash-generating units, but the centralised data processor supports only XX and YY on a 50:50 ratio. The head-office building cannot be allocated to the relevant cash-generating units. The carrying amounts of the cash-generating units/assets of Boom Ltd at 31 December 20.5 were as follows:

	Rand
Cash-generating unit XX	500 000
Cash-generating unit YY	300 000
Cash-generating unit ZZ	400 000
Head-office building	105 000
Centralised data-processor	280 000

The recoverable amounts of the cash-generating units of Boom Ltd at 31 December 20.5 were as follows:

	Rand
Cash-generating unit XX	630 000
Cash-generating unit YY	420 000
Cash-generating unit ZZ	490 000
Total	1 540 000

Assume that at 31 December 20.5 there are indications of impairment for cash-generating unit XX and cash-generating unit ZZ.

Required

Calculate the total impairment loss to be allocated to the assets of Boom Ltd for the year ended 31 December 20.5 so as to comply with the requirements of International Financial Reporting Standards (IFRS).

❑ QUESTION IAS 36.15

Green Ltd acquired a 75% ownership interest in Gold Ltd for R900 000 on 1 January 20.7. On that date, Gold Ltd's identifiable net assets had a fair value of R1 100 000. The assets of Gold Ltd together are the smallest group of assets that generate cash inflows that are largely independent of the cash inflows from other assets or groups of assets. You can also assume that Gold Ltd is a stand-alone cash-generating unit.

On 31 December 20.7 the carrying amount of the consolidated identifiable net assets of Gold Ltd amounted to R820 000. The recoverable amount of the cash-generating unit, Gold Ltd, was R790 000.

Required

a. Calculate the impairment loss to be allocated to the assets of Gold Ltd for the year ended 31 December 20.7 so as to comply with the requirements of International Financial Reporting Standards (IFRS). Assume that Green Ltd elected to measure the non-controlling interest in the ordinary shares of Gold Ltd at its proportional interest in the fair value of the identifiable net assets of Gold Ltd.
b. Calculate the impairment loss to be allocated to the assets of Gold Ltd for the year ended 31 December 20.7 so as to comply with the requirements of International Financial Reporting Standards (IFRS). Assume that Green Ltd elected to measure the non-controlling interest in the ordinary shares of Gold Ltd at its fair value of R287 500.

❑ QUESTION IAS 36.16

On 1 January 20.0 Hotshot Ltd acquired 100% of the net assets of Gigo Ltd for R200 000 (known as the Gigo division once acquired by Hotshot Ltd). The Gigo division's operations consist of three shops, which can each be regarded as a separate cash-generating unit. The individual assets of the branches do not generate cash flows that are independent of those from the other assets of the branch. The fair values of the net assets of the different shops on the date of acquisition were as follows:

	Rand
Pretoria branch	50 000
Johannesburg branch	100 000
Springs branch	25 000

The goodwill arising on acquisition could not be allocated between the different shops.

The accumulated impairment loss in respect of goodwill amounted to R7 500 on 31 December 20.1.

On 31 December 20.2 there were indications that the Johannesburg branch might be impaired. On 31 December 20.2 the net assets of the different shops were as follows:

	Carrying amount Rand
Pretoria branch	60 000
Johannesburg branch*	130 000
Springs branch	28 000

* The net assets of the Johannesburg branch are made up as follows:

	Carrying amount Rand	Fair value less costs of disposal Rand
Building	60 000	50 000
Equipment	30 000	28 000
Vehicle	40 000	22 000

On 31 December 20.2 the value in use of the Johannesburg branch amounted to R110 000, while that of the Gigo division amounted to R200 000. The fair value less costs of disposal of the Johannesburg branch amounted to R100 000 and that of the Gigo division to R205 000.

Required

a. Calculate the total impairment loss that will be recognised in the statement of profit or loss and other comprehensive income of Hotshot Ltd for the year ended 31 December 20.2. Your answer must comply with the requirements of International Financial Reporting Standards (IFRS).
b. Calculate the impairment loss to be allocated to each of the assets of the Johannesburg branch for the year ended 31 December 20.2. Also calculate the final carrying amount of each asset of the Johannesburg branch at 31 December 20.2. Your answer must comply with the requirements of International Financial Reporting Standards (IFRS).

❑ QUESTION IAS 36.17

Happy Ltd is a company that runs two production lines, A and B. Since the beginning of the current year, the profits from production line B declined considerably as the competition cut their selling prices.

The non-current assets of Happy Ltd comprised the following at 31 October 20.9:

	Cost Rand	Accumulated depreciation Rand	Carrying amount Rand
Plant and machinery	23 100 000	8 200 000	14 900 000
Furniture and fittings	4 900 000	2 400 000	2 500 000
Goodwill	4 100 000	–	4 100 000

Production line B represents a cash-generating unit. The carrying amounts of the non-current assets of production line B at 31 October 20.9 amounts to the following:

	Cost Rand	Accumulated depreciation Rand	Carrying amount Rand
Plant and machinery	9 600 000	3 200 000	6 400 000
Furniture and fittings	2 300 000	1 100 000	1 200 000

The fair value (based on quoted market prices) less costs of disposal of the furniture and fittings of production line B amounts to R950 000 as at 31 October 20.9, and 40% of the goodwill of Happy Ltd can be allocated to production line B.

At 31 October 20.9 the fair value less costs of disposal of production line B amounts to R5 600 000.

The net cash flow expected from production line B in future is as follows:

	Sales	Cost of sales	Directly attributable costs
	Rand	**Rand**	**Rand**
20.10	18 000 000	12 400 000	3 600 000
20.11	19 400 000	12 900 000	3 900 000
20.12	20 200 000	13 200 000	4 100 000
20.13	16 100 000	12 100 000	3 200 000
20.14	8 200 000	6 600 000	1 800 000

At the end of 20.14 it should be possible to sell the plant and machinery, and the furniture and fittings of production line B for R500 028 (net) after deducting all costs of disposal.

An appropriate after-tax discount rate is 13,14% and the tax rate is 27%.

Assume that up to the year ended 31 October 20.8, none of the cash-generating units have been impaired.

Also assume that for the year ended 31 October 20.9, the recoverable amount of production line A exceeds the carrying amount.

Required

Disclose the impairment loss in the 'profit before tax' note that will accompany the financial statements of Happy Ltd for the year ended 31 October 20.9 in accordance with the requirements of International Financial Reporting Standards (IFRS). Comparative amounts are not required.

IAS 37 & IFRIC 1

Provisions, contingent liabilities and contingent assets

❑ QUESTIONS AND SOLUTIONS

IAS 37.1	Recognition of provisions: discussion
IAS 37.2	Recognition of provisions linked to Conceptual Framework and disclosure: discussion and disclosure
IAS 37.3	Recognition of provision and contingent asset: discussion and disclosure
IAS 37.4	Measurement of provision: journal entries, presentation of an extract of the statement of financial position and note disclosure
IAS 37.5	Recognition of future cost as provision: discussion

❑ QUESTIONS

IAS 37.6	Measurement of provision with deferred tax consequences: journal entries
IAS 37.7	Recognition of restructuring provision: discussion
IAS 37.8	Recognition and measurement of sundry provisions: discussion
IAS 37.9	Recognition of provisions: discussion, extract of the statement of financial position and note disclosure with comparative amounts
IAS 37.10	Sundry provisions with measurement: journal entries, presentation of an extract of the statement of financial position and note disclosure
IAS 37.11	Recognition and measurement of onerous contracts and provision: discussion
IAS 37.12	Initial and subsequent measurement of provision for rehabilitation cost (IFRIC 1) with deferred tax consequences: journal entries, extract of the statement of financial position and note disclosure
IAS 37.13	Recognition of provision: discussion

❑ QUESTION IAS 37.1

The following provisions have been included in the financial statements of Provider Ltd as at 31 December 20.8:

		Rand
a.	Provision for repair costs for sales under warranty	250 000
b.	Provision for repairs and maintenance of plant and machinery	75 000
c.	Provision for expected operating losses to be incurred in a trade show scheduled for March 20.9	35 000
d.	Provision for the dismantling and selling of non-current assets classified as held for sale	15 000
e.	Provision for severance pay to employees in a discontinued operation	50 000
f.	Provision for relocating and retraining staff affected by the restructuring programme	60 000

Required

Discuss with brief reasons, in each of the above cases, whether a provision must be recognised at 31 December 20.8 so as to comply with the requirements of International Financial Reporting Standards (IFRS). Assume all amounts to be material.

❖ Suggested solution IAS 37.1

a. The company has a present legal obligation as a result of past events, i.e. in terms of the sales agreement the company is obliged to repair or replace any item sold under warranty. If the amount of R250 000 is a reliable estimate of the obligation, then such a provision will be raised in order to comply with IAS 37.

b. There is no legal or constructive obligation to incur future repairs and maintenance costs on plant and machinery. In terms of IAS 37.14(a), a provision shall only be raised for a current obligation arising from a past event. A provision in this case shall not be raised as these costs relate to repairs and maintenance that will be incurred in the future. In some circumstances an entity may be under a constructive or legal obligation to maintain its assets to a specified level of performance to be able to operate them. Even in these circumstances the accounting treatment is not to recognise a provision. Any commitments to maintain the asset will be recognised as a liability when the expenditure has been incurred.

c. IAS 37.63 clearly states that provisions shall not be raised for future operating losses. The recognition criteria of a provision require a legal or constructive present obligation resulting from a past event which leaves the company with no realistic alternative other than to settle the obligation. In this case, future operating losses, which are outflows of economic benefits, will not be recognised as the event creating the obligation has not occurred. Even if operating losses are expected, management generally retains the discretion to change the activities, for example to dispose of or restructure the operation. Therefore, in terms of IAS 37, a provision will not be raised.

It could be argued that, if a contract had been signed in 20.8, the company is legally committed to participate in the trade show leaving the company with no realistic alternative but to incur the losses. In this case, it could be argued that the obligation has arisen as a result of a past event, i.e. a contract concluded in 20.8, and therefore a provision must be raised. Such a contract could be an onerous one.

d. No legal or constructive obligation arose when the assets were classified as held for sale. The future dismantling and selling costs are used in the measurement of the non-current assets held for sale since non-current assets held for sale are measured at the lower of carrying amount and fair value less costs to sell, therefore no such provision can be raised.

e. In terms of IAS 37.80, costs for severance pay to employees directly resulting from a restructuring are included in the restructuring provision as it is considered to be a direct expenditure arising from the restructuring, since it is necessarily entailed by the restructuring and not associated with the ongoing activities of the entity. A provision may only be made if an entity has a detailed formal plan and has raised valid expectations in those affected.

f. A provision for relocating and retraining staff could qualify as costs that are associated with the ongoing activities of the entity. These costs are not included in a restructuring provision. IAS 37.81 specifically *excludes* them from a restructuring provision.

❑ QUESTION IAS 37.2

Upstage Ltd manufactures a brand of quality watches. The company sells these watches to the general public via retail outlets. All watches are sold with a one-year warranty.

At 31 December 20.8 the warranty ledger account showed the following:

	Rand
Balance on 31 December 20.7	25 000
Repairs done to watches sold under warranty in 20.7	(20 000)
Warranty provision for 20.8	45 000
Balance on 31 December 20.8	50 000

The accountant has calculated the following warranty provisions for 20.8:

		Rand
a.	Provision calculated on the basis of the expected value of the cost of repairs where 25% of items sold will be returned with defects	25 000
b.	Provision calculated on the basis of the expected value of the cost of repairs where 75% of items sold will be returned with defects	45 000

Based on the company's past experience, approximately 25% of its goods sold are returned with defects. However, the company decided to be prudent and made a provision based on 75% of goods sold being returned with defects, hence a provision for expected repair costs of R45 000 has been raised.

By the end of 20.8 the warranties for all watches sold in 20.7 had elapsed and no further costs are expected to be incurred in respect of these sales.

Consider all amounts to be material.

Required

a. Comment, with reference to the Conceptual Framework and IAS 37 *Provisions, Contingent Liabilities and Contingent Assets*, on the decision taken by the company in raising a provision of R45 000. Should you disagree with the provision raised, recommend a suitable provision.
b. Disclose all relevant information in respect of the suggested suitable provision above in the short-term provision note of Upstage Ltd for the year ended 31 December 20.8. No comparative amounts are required.

The answer must comply with the requirements of International Financial Reporting Standards (IFRS).

❖ **Suggested solution IAS 37.2**

a. Discussion

Chapter 3 of the Conceptual Framework (2018) does not include prudence or conservatism as an aspect of faithful representation because including either would be inconsistent with neutrality. Also, in terms of IAS 37, a provision should be measured at the best estimate of the expenditure required to settle the present obligation. The best estimate is the amount an entity would rationally pay to settle the liability and can be based on previous experiences with similar transactions. Based on past experience it is estimated that 25% of the goods sold will be returned with defects. The fact that repairs amounting to only R20 000 were done in the previous year serves as further proof that a provision in excess of R25 000 would be excessive. Consequently, it would be an unrealistic and excessive estimate to provide for 75% of goods sold being returned with defects. The provision raised should only be R25 000.

b. Disclosure

UPSTAGE LTD
NOTES FOR THE YEAR ENDED 31 DECEMBER 20.8

10. Short-term provisions	**Rand**
Warranty provision	
Balance on 31 December 20.7	25 000
Costs incurred in respect of 20.7 sales	(20 000)
Unused amount transferred to profit or loss	(5 000)
Provision for 20.8	25 000
Balance on 31 December 20.8	25 000

A provision of R25 000 has been recognised for expected warranty claims in respect of products sold during the current financial year. It is expected that all of this expenditure will be incurred in the next financial year.

❑ QUESTION IAS 37.3

The following information relates to Compu Ltd:

1. During 20.3, Compu Ltd started to manufacture and sell computers. All computers are equipped with B20 microchips. In November 20.3 a new microchip, the B40, which can store double the information that the B20 can, was introduced to the market. During a management meeting held on 30 November 20.3 it was decided that in future only the new B40 microchip would be used, and that all the B20 microchips in computers already sold before 1 December 20.3 would be replaced free of charge with the new B40 during 20.4. This was announced through advertisements in the media during December 20.3. Management has estimated that 75% of the approximately 3 000 customers who purchased a computer would act on these advertisements. These estimates are based on past experience of a similar type of transaction. The cost to replace a single microchip will amount to approximately R250.

2. A claim of R50 000 was instituted by Compu Ltd against Future Ltd on 3 September 20.3 on the grounds of infringement of a trademark. At the financial year end, Compu Ltd's legal advisors are of the opinion that the claim would probably succeed, but are not virtually certain about its outcome.

Required

a. Discuss whether a provision should be recognised in the financial statements of Compu Ltd for the year ended 31 December 20.3.
b. Discuss whether a contingent asset should be recognised in the financial statements of Compu Ltd for the year ended 31 December 20.3.
c. Prepare the 'short-term provisions' as well as 'contingent assets' notes in respect of the information in the question for Compu Ltd for the year ended 31 December 20.3 so as to comply with the requirements of International Financial Reporting Standards (IFRS). All amounts are material.

❖ Suggested solution IAS 37.3

a. Discussion – provision

A provision is recognised provided that there is an obligation at the reporting date that arises from a past event and it is probable that an outflow of economic benefits will be required and a reliable estimate can be made of the amount (IAS 37.14).

The past event was the decision taken by management to replace the B20 microchips with the B40. With the announcement of management's decision in the media, a present constructive obligation has arisen because there are valid expectations with the owners of these computers – that B20 microchips will be replaced with B40 microchips. Compu Ltd indicated with a specific current decision and statement that they accept the responsibility to replace the B20 chip with a B40.

It is probable that there will be an outflow of economic resources since management has estimated that about 75% of its customers will respond to the advertisements. This means that there will be an outflow of economic resources as the company will have to purchase the B40 microchips and utilise its economic resources to pay for them.

The amount can be reliably estimated since management has estimated that of the 3 000 customers affected, about 75% will respond to the advertisement. The cost of the component is known, so the provision can be reliably measured. The use of an estimate does not undermine the reliability of the measurement (IAS 37.25). The estimates are based on past experience of a similar type of offer made to customers.

A provision is recognised at 31 December 20.3 for R562 500 (3 000 × 75% × R250).

b. Discussion – contingent asset

A contingent asset is a possible asset that arises from past events and whose existence will be confirmed only by the occurrence or non-occurrence of one or more uncertain future events not wholly within the control of the entity (IAS 37.10). IAS 37.31 states clearly that an entity shall not recognise a contingent asset.

The legal claim will be the past event from which the contingent asset arises. The outcome of the claim will only be established in future once the case has been heard in a court of law.

Because the inflow of economic benefits is probable but not virtually certain, no asset is recognised, but disclosure in a note is required (IAS 37.34).

c. Disclosure

COMPU LTD
NOTES FOR THE YEAR ENDED 31 DECEMBER 20.3

1. Short-term provision

	20.3 Rand
Provision for replacement costs	
Balance on 31 December 20.2	–
Provision made during the year	562 500
Balance on 31 December 20.3	562 500

The provision has been made for the estimated cost of the replacement of the B20 microchip with the B40 microchip in computers sold before 1 December 20.3. It is anticipated that these costs will be incurred during 20.4.

2. Contingent asset

A claim for the infringement of a trademark was instituted against a company during the year. According to the company's legal advisors it is probable that the claim will be successful but the realisation of income is not virtually certain. If the claim was to be successful, Compu Ltd will receive R50 000 before tax.

❑ QUESTION IAS 37.4

Medgars Ltd, a retail store, has a policy of refunding the purchases of dissatisfied customers, even though it is under no legal obligation to do so. Its policy of refunds is generally known to its customers. According to Medgars Ltd's refunding policy, customers may return purchased goods within three months of the date of purchase provided that they still have their price tickets attached.

Previous experience shows that 10% of goods sold are returned in the month following the month of sale, 5% in the second month and 2% in the third month after the sale.

Actual refunds amounted to R34 000 during 20.3 and R30 000 during 20.2. The balance on the provision for refunds account amounted to R36 500 on 1 January 20.2.

The following sales figures are available:	20.3 Rand	20.2 Rand
October	120 000	110 000
November	130 000	130 000
December	150 000	140 000

Assume that the effect of discounting is immaterial.

Required

a. Prepare the journal entries to account for the above information related to the provision for refunds for the year ended 31 December 20.3.

b. Prepare an extract of the statement of financial position as well as the 'short-term provisions' note to the financial statements of Medgars Ltd for the year ended 31 December 20.3 to reflect the information provided in the question. Your answer must comply with the requirements of International Financial Reporting Standards (IFRS).

❖ Suggested solution IAS 37.4

a. Journal entries

	20.3 Rand Dr/(Cr)
31 December 20.3	
Provision for refunds (SFPos)	34 000
Bank (SFPos)	(34 000)
Amounts used during the year	
Provision for refunds (1) (SFPos)	1 100
Provision for refunds – adjustment (P or L)	(1 100)
Unused amounts reversed during the year	
Provision for refunds – adjustment (P or L)	37 000
Provision for refunds (2) (SFPos)	(37 000)
Additional provision made during the year	

(1) (110 000 × 2%) + (130 000 × 5%) + (140 000 × 10%) + (130 000 × 2%) + (140 000 × 5%) + (140 000 × 2%) – 34 000 = 1 100

(2) (120 000 × 2%) + (130 000 × 5%) + (150 000 × 10%) + (130 000 × 2%) + (150 000 × 5%) + (150 000 × 2%) = 37 000

b. Disclosure

MEDGARS LTD
EXTRACT FROM THE STATEMENT OF FINANCIAL POSITION AS AT 31 DECEMBER 20.3

EQUITY AND LIABILITIES	**Note**	**20.3 Rand**	**20.2 Rand**
Current liabilities			
Short-term provisions	12	37 000	35 100

MEDGARS LTD
NOTES FOR THE YEAR ENDED 31 DECEMBER 20.3

12. Short-term provisions

Provision for refunds	**20.3 Rand**	**20.2 Rand**
Balance at beginning of year	35 100	36 500
Amounts used during the year	(34 000)	(30 000)
Unused amounts reversed during the year	(1 100)	(6 500)
Additional provision made during the year	37 000	35 100
Balance at end of year	37 000	35 100

Provision has been made for estimated refunds to customers for goods purchased which are expected to be incurred during the first three months of the new financial year.

❑ QUESTION IAS 37.5

Natco Products Ltd is faced with stiff competition in the chemical industry. In an attempt to exploit a new market the company decided to produce a new chemical, Natco3, which is superior to the previous chemicals produced. Before finalising the financial statements for the year ended 31 December 20.8, the following matters require consideration:

1. During 20.8 the company purchased specialised plant and machinery to produce Natco3. Owing to the high acidic content in this new product, the company expects to replace component parts of the plant at regular intervals. The directors have provided an amount of R10 000 per month to cover the estimated costs of replacing the component parts of the new plant. No replacements were required during the 20.8 year but the directors believe that the provision should remain in the financial statements as the component parts would have to be replaced in the 20.9 financial year.

2. The directors realised that the production of the new product Natco3 contaminated the land on which the factory is situated. Since incorporation, the company has always maintained a policy of cleaning up any contamination caused by its manufacturing process. No clean-up procedures have been initiated in 20.8, but the company has made a provision of R250 000, the expected cost of a clean-up process that may be required in the future.

Assume that the effect of discounting is immaterial.

Required

Draft a letter to the financial director of Natco Products Ltd in which you review the acceptability of the accounting treatment of the above provisions based on International Financial Reporting Standards (IFRS).

❖ **Suggested solution IAS 37.5**

Att: Financial Director
Natco Products Ltd
P.O. Box 123
Durban 4000

Dear Sir

Following our discussion concerning certain provisions, we report as follows on our findings and recommendations:

In considering whether an entity should recognise a provision, it is important to assess whether a legal or a constructive obligation exists as a result of a past event. The mere intention or necessity to incur expenditure relating to the future is not sufficient to give rise to an obligation. Therefore, if an entity decides to incur specific capital expenditure, a repair or a replacement in the future, the decision in itself does not create an obligation. An obligation would only arise when the refurbishment or replacement has been performed and the entity is obliged to pay a third party for the work undertaken. Natco Products Ltd has no present legal or constructive obligation as the company could decide to avoid replacing the component parts of the new plant. Only those obligations existing independently of Natco Products Ltd's future actions may be recognised as provisions (IAS 37.19). The replacement provision does not comply with this requirement and therefore no provision for the replacement cost of components should be recognised at 31 December 20.8.

In 20.8 Natco Products Ltd had not initiated a clean-up process. Although Natco Products Ltd has no legal obligation it does have a constructive obligation to clean up any contamination caused by its manufacturing process because of its published policy, past actions and concern for its reputation. In these circumstances a provision of R250 000, the expected cost of a clean-up process, could be raised which will be in compliance with IAS 37.

Yours sincerely
A. Consultant

Note: Determining whether a constructive obligation exists is often more difficult than identifying a legal obligation and in most cases judgment will be required, depending on the circumstances of each case, to determine whether or not a constructive obligation exists.

❑ QUESTION IAS 37.6

Mad Max Ltd is a listed company that sources and sells old comic books. They use their website, madmax.com, in a similar way to ebay.com. Individuals log onto the website and are able to sell to or purchase classic collections of comic books from Mad Max Ltd.

On 31 December 20.5, Mad Max Ltd raised a justified provision for an obligation towards the South African government for a future charity initiative. Mad Max Ltd had committed themselves on 31 December 20.5 to contribute to a charity initiative called Mad Gov. Mad Gov will work on the same principle as madmax.com, since old *Government Gazettes* will be auctioned on a website called madgov.com. The proceeds of this initiative will be donated to a charity of the government's choice. Mad Max Ltd will pay over the agreed amount of R10 000 000 on 31 December 20.10. You may assume that the time value of money is material and that a nominal after-tax discount rate of 10% was applicable in 20.5 as well as 20.6.

Mad Max Ltd processed the following journals on 31 December 20.5 to account for the provision:

	Rand Dr/(Cr)
Other expenses (P or L)	10 000 000
Provision (SFPos)	(10 000 000)
Recognition of provision payable in 20.10	
Deferred tax (SFPos)	2 800 000
Income tax expense (P or L)	(2 800 000)
Recognition of deferred tax on provision raised @ 28%	

Assume that the tax rate remained unchanged at 28%. The South African Revenue Service will allow a deduction for the provision on a cash basis.

Required

a. Supply the adjusting journal entries to account for the provision and deferred tax implications for the year ended 31 December 20.5.
b. Supply the journal entries to account for the provision and deferred tax implications for the year ended 31 December 20.6. Note: For this part the originating entries are required, not the adjusting entries.

Note: Round off to the nearest rand.

The solution must comply with the requirements of International Financial Reporting Standards (IFRS).

❑ QUESTION IAS 37.7

Lion Ltd manufactures computers for both local and export markets. Faced with stiff competition in the local market, the company decided to restructure its activities by downsizing its local market and allocating more of its resources to the export of computers to surrounding Southern African countries.

On 1 December 20.8 the board of directors decided to restructure its activities as from 31 March 20.9. A detailed plan was drafted by 31 December 20.8 on which day a public announcement was made as to the restructuring intentions of the company. Lion Ltd's creditors, employees and customers were also informed of the restructuring plan by letters on the day the public announcement was made.

At 31 December 20.8, provisions for the following costs were included in the trial balance of the company:

	Rand
Dismantling costs of assets to be sold	20 000
Profit to be made on sale of assets	(10 000)
Employee severance packages to be paid to employees affected by the restructuring	85 000
Future operating losses for months January 20.9 – March 20.9 on computers manufactured for the local market	25 000
Penalty payable on early termination of short-term lease	20 000
Retraining and relocating continuing staff	15 000
Marketing and investment in new systems and distribution networks for the Southern African region	25 000
Total amount provided in respect of the restructuring	180 000

Required

Advise Lion Ltd in terms of the requirements of International Financial Reporting Standards (IFRS) whether a provision for the above costs is allowable for inclusion in the financial statements at 31 December 20.8. State the reasons for your conclusions. Ignore all tax implications and consider all amounts to be material.

❑ QUESTION IAS 37.8

The financial statements of Saheli Ltd are in the process of being finalised for the year ended 31 December 20.8. The following matters require consideration in response to the raising of provisions per IAS 37:

1. Saheli Ltd is a manufacturer of desktop inkjet printers. These printers are sold with a warranty whereby the manufacturer is obliged to repair or replace the printers that fail within the warranty period. Based on the company's past experience and future expectations it is estimated that 80% of its printers sold will have no defects, 15% will have minor defects and 5% will have major defects. If minor defects were detected in all products sold, repair costs of R1 million would result. If major defects were detected in all products sold then repair costs of R3 million would result. No entries have been made for this as the accountant is unsure of how to calculate an appropriate provision.

2. In response to changes in legislation introduced in the income tax system, Saheli Ltd is required to retrain a large proportion of its administrative and sales workforce. If adequate retraining is not given to its employees then Saheli Ltd will not be able to continue selling its products and continue its business. As the company will not be able to avoid this expenditure, a provision of R250 000 has been made in respect of future training costs.

3. In January 20.8, Saheli Ltd reviewed its insurance arrangements for its liability in respect of accidents sustained by customers in its chain of retail outlets. The company pays insurance premiums of R20 000 per month to cover customer claims. The directors decided that, based on past experience, the cost of these accidents is approximately R150 000 per annum. Therefore, instead of continuing its policy with an insurance company, Saheli Ltd decided to self-insure. A provision of R12 500 per month was made to carry the risk of Saheli Ltd paying for any customer claims. Two accidents have been reported in the company's retail outlets in the Gauteng area and claims of R80 000 have been received. The final outcome of these claims by customers will be decided during the court hearing scheduled for February 20.9.

Required

In respect of each of the above situations, briefly discuss whether a provision must be raised for the financial year ending on 31 December 20.8, in accordance with the requirements of International Financial Reporting Standards (IFRS).

❑ QUESTION IAS 37.9

After a wedding on 17 September 20.0, two people died, possibly as a result of food poisoning from products sold by Cater Ltd. Legal proceedings have been instituted against Cater Ltd seeking damages, but the company disputes liability.

Up to 31 December 20.0, Cater Ltd's lawyers advised that it is probable that the entity would be found liable, but they could not give any estimate on the amount that it would be liable for.

On 30 November 20.1 the entity's lawyers advise that owing to developments in the case it is probable that the entity would be found liable for R300 000. The case will only be heard during June 20.2.

Assume that the effect of discounting is immaterial.

Required

a. Discuss the accounting recognition of the above matter in the financial statements of Cater Ltd for the years ended 31 December 20.0 and 31 December 20.1.
b. Disclose the above information in an extract of the statement of financial position and prepare the 'short-term provisions' as well as the 'contingent liabilities' notes (where applicable) to the financial statements of Cater Ltd for the year ended 31 December 20.0 and 31 December 20.1.

The solution must comply with the requirements of International Financial Reporting Standards (IFRS).

❑ QUESTION IAS 37.10

The following information relates to the operations of Platinum Ltd, a mining company, for the year ended 31 December 20.5:

1. Platinum Ltd damaged the environment when it commenced mining operations on 1 January 20.5. It is estimated that this damage will cost R5 000 000 to repair at the end of the mining operations on 31 December 20.15. At 31 December 20.5 a discount rate of 15% before tax was considered to be appropriate.

   Environmental legislation requires that damage to the environment must be repaired at the end of the mining operation.

2. Under new legislation the company is required to fit filters on all its heavy equipment before 30 April 20.6. On 31 December 20.5 the company has not yet done so, but has budgeted an amount of R200 000 for the fitting of the filters.

3. On 12 December 20.5 the board of directors decided to close down a division during 20.6. They made an announcement on 20 December 20.5 in the press concerning their decision and released a formal business plan.

   Some of this division's personnel will leave the services of Platinum Ltd on 31 March 20.6, for which they will receive ex-gratia payments amounting to R600 000 in total. Other personnel will be relocated to other divisions, which will cost the company R120 000 in re-establishment costs.

Required

a. Prepare the journal entries, where applicable, to account for the above transactions in the records of Platinum Ltd for the year ended 31 December 20.5.
b. Disclose the above information in an extract of the statement of financial position and prepare the notes relating to provisions in the financial statements of Platinum Ltd for the year ended 31 December 20.5.

The solution must comply with the requirements of International Financial Reporting Standards (IFRS).

❑ QUESTION IAS 37.11

Potter Ltd, an equipment and furniture manufacturing company, has a head office in Johannesburg and branches in Durban, Cape Town and Bloemfontein. The year end of the company is 31 December and the annual financial statements for the year ended 31 December 20.8 are currently being finalised. The following problems have been identified and the company has requested your advice:

Electricity agreement
On 1 January 20.2 Potter Ltd entered into an agreement with Harry Ltd for the acquisition of electricity for use in their factory for a period of eight years. Owing to several reasons, the board of directors decided on 31 October 20.8 to move the factory to a smallholding outside Bloemfontein. During December 20.8 the factory was moved to the new premises and, consequently, Potter Ltd no longer required the use of the electricity.

The terms of the agreement with Harry Ltd state that early termination of the agreement would result in a penalty payment of 75% of the remaining electricity payments, payable two months after the termination of the agreement. This agreement would have terminated on 31 December 20.9. All the payments for the year ended 31 December 20.8 have been paid. The electricity payments are R1 000 000 a year, payable in arrears.

Assume that the effect of discounting is immaterial.

Repair of machinery
The Bloemfontein branch uses three identical machines in the manufacturing process. One of them was accidentally dropped while being moved from the one factory to the other, and was badly damaged. The machine was not insured against damage caused by being moved.

During January 20.9 the machine was repaired at a cost of R150 000. The financial manager considers creating a provision for the cost of repairing the machine in the financial year ended 31 December 20.8. He argues that since the damage was caused by an accident that took place during the moving between factories, the cost must be accounted for in the year the moving took place. A contract has already been entered into with Wolf Ltd for the repair of the machine on 20 December 20.8 and it will therefore be prudent to make a provision on 31 December 20.8.

Required

Write a report to the financial manager of Potter Ltd in which you discuss the accounting recognition, measurement and disclosure of the above-mentioned issues for the year ended 31 December 20.8 in accordance with the requirements of International Financial Reporting Standards (IFRS).

❑ QUESTION IAS 37.12

Brilliant Cut Ltd is a diamond mining company with a 31 December year end. Environmental legislation provides for the rehabilitation of the environment to its original condition after the abandonment of the mining operations.

Brilliant Cut Ltd erected the Alpha diamond mining plant at a cost of R20 000 000.

On 1 January 20.2 (the day on which Brilliant Cut Ltd started with mining activities at its Alpha plant) it was established that it would cost approximately R15 000 000 (at future prices) to rehabilitate the environment after 20 years when the plant is abandoned.

The actual cost for the rehabilitation of the environment in December 20.21 (i.e. 20 years after mining activities started) amounted to R16 500 000.

Additional information

The rehabilitation cost is tax deductible when it is actually paid in 20.21. The tax rate has remained unchanged at 30%.

The company will earn sufficient taxable income in the future to justify the recognition of a debit balance on the deferred tax account should it be necessary.

A nominal after-tax discount rate was 10,5% for the financial years ended 31 December 20.2 to 31 December 20.3. During 20.4 the suitable after-tax discount rate changed to 8,4% and it remained unchanged until 20.21.

The South African Revenue Service allows a wear-and-tear allowance of 5% per annum on the plant. The company depreciates the plant over its useful life of 20 years and there is no residual value.

Required

a. Prepare the journal entries for the financial years ended 31 December 20.2, 20.3, 20.4 and 20.21. Include the journal entries for the provision for environmental costs, depreciation on the plant and deferred tax.
b. Prepare an extract of the statement of financial position of Brilliant Cut Ltd for the year ended 31 December 20.21 to reflect the above transaction.
c. Prepare the following note to the financial statements for the year ended 31 December 20.21:
   - Provision for environmental costs (no comparative amounts are required)

The solution must comply with the requirements of International Financial Reporting Standards (IFRS).

❑ QUESTION IAS 37.13

Indwe Pharmaceuticals Ltd is a company that specialises in research and development of animal medication. The company is based in the Eastern Cape, with its major customers being pig farmers around the province.

Early in 20.5, the Eastern Cape faced an outbreak of a disease that decreased the iron reserves in piglets when they were born. This disease resulted in a large number of piglets dying within the first two to three weeks of birth. In response to the outbreak, Indwe Pharmaceuticals Ltd started its research on a medicine that would provide immunity to piglets suffering from this disease, and by August 20.5 the company's researchers had found a vaccination that was believed to be able to provide the required immunity.

The vaccination was sold to a number of farmers in the area. Indwe Pharmaceuticals Ltd published a leaflet in the vaccination box that stated that the vaccination had no negative side effects.

In November 20.5, a number of farmers brought a civil lawsuit against the company, claiming for damages for severe side effects that the piglets had developed since being vaccinated. At the year end (31 December 20.5) of Indwe Pharmaceuticals Ltd, the court case had not yet been finalised.

On 28 December 20.5 after an extensive consultation process with the company's lawyers and experts on animal medicine, the CEO of Indwe Pharmaceuticals Ltd, Mr Fox, placed an advertisement in the national and local newspapers where he announced that the company would like to offer an out-of-court settlement and compensate the affected farmers for the losses suffered as a result of using the company's vaccination.

The company lawyers and the experts on animal medication (based on experience from representing other pharmaceutical companies facing similar charges) estimated as at the end of the year that an out-of-court settlement would probably cost the company approximately R30 million.

Indwe Pharmaceuticals Ltd plans to structure the settlement (should it be accepted by the farmers) by paying four annual instalments of R7 500 000 each, commencing on 31 December 20.6. Assume a pre-tax interest rate of 15% where applicable in your answer.

Required

Discuss whether a provision in respect of the out-of-court settlement should be recognised in the financial statements of Indwe Pharmaceuticals Ltd for the year ended 31 December 20.5. (Source: UJ)

Note: Ignore presentation and disclosure issues in your answer.

The solution must comply with the requirements of International Financial Reporting Standards (IFRS).

IAS 38 & SIC 32

Intangible assets

❑ QUESTIONS AND SOLUTIONS

IAS 38.1	Advice – research and development costs
IAS 38.2	Amortisation, impairment and tax
IAS 38.3	Amortisation, impairment and disclosure of development costs
IAS 38.4	Theory – capitalisation of costs
IAS 38.5	Capitalisation of costs and SIC 32

❑ QUESTIONS

IAS 38.6	Journal entries
IAS 38.7	Recognition, amortisation and disclosure of development costs
IAS 38.8	Amortisation and disclosure of development costs
IAS 38.9	Theory – capitalisation of costs and SIC 32
IAS 38.10	Indefinite useful life, subsequent expenditure and change in estimate
IAS 38.11	Recognition and measurement of website costs and SIC 32

Note: Any references to the definition of an asset within the context of an intangible asset refers to the definition of an asset as stipulated in IAS 38, and not as stipulated in the new (2018) Conceptual Framework, due to the fact that the IASB did not include changes to the new Conceptual Framework in IAS 38 (see footnote to the definition of an asset in IAS 38.8).

❑ QUESTION IAS 38.1

Snap Ltd, a pharmaceutical company, recently started a research division in one of its factories.

The total costs of R55 000 in respect of the new division, incurred by Snap Ltd for the current year, were paid as follows:

	Rand
Salaries	
Chemists	25 000
Additional technical personnel appointed	5 000
Administrative personnel	1 000
Consulting fees	
Initial payment for the sharing of knowledge with respect to remedy 'V'	5 000
General consulting work	3 000
Direct costs	
Tablets, chemicals and raw materials	3 000
Patents and licences	1 000
Sundry	2 000
General expenses	
General overheads	5 000
Costs of partitions in the new division	3 000
Depreciation of equipment	2 000
	55 000

Additional information

The total expenditure of R55 000 may be grouped into the following categories:
[R24 000 (refer point 1) + R16 000 (refer to point 2) + R15 000 (refer to point 3) = R55 000]

1. The division incurred the following work with regard to the development of five potential new remedies:

Remedy	Cost incurred Rand
'V' – It is expected that it will be marketed within the next six months	9 000
'I' – Project has been halted after initial work	5 000
'G' – It is expected that it will be marketed within the next year or two	6 000
'S' – In an early stage of development	3 000
'X' – In an early stage of development	1 000
	24 000

2. The division also undertook testing and quality control with regard to existing products, of which development had been completed in prior years. The total costs amounted to R16 000.

3. The remainder of the division's expenditure, namely R15 000, is in respect of general research undertaken in order to formulate potential new products which could be manufactured in the future.

The costs (R55 000) were accounted for in the financial statements of Snap Ltd by debiting a fifth thereof against profit for the year. The remainder was shown in the statement of financial position under 'Research and development costs – in process'.

A minute of a recent directors' meeting during which the above matter was discussed indicates that the board of directors plan to write off a fifth of the R55 000 to profit each year.

Required

Discuss how the costs should be recognised and measured in accordance with the requirements of International Financial Reporting Standards (IFRS). No reference to the Conceptual Framework is required. Also indicate why the current recognition and measurement are not acceptable.

❖ **Suggested solution IAS 38.1**

Reasons why not acceptable

The accounting treatment for research and development costs is prescribed by IAS 38.

Such is the nature of research that there is no certainty that future economic benefits will be realised from the specific expenditure on research. Research costs will therefore be recognised as an expense in the period in which they are incurred and will not be recognised as an asset (IAS 38.54).

The development costs of a project must be recognised as an expense in the period in which they are incurred unless all of the following criteria are met (IAS 38.57):

- The technical feasibility of completing the product or process so that it will be available for sale or use can be demonstrated.
- The entity intends to complete the product or process and sell or use it.
- The entity's ability to use or sell the product or process can be demonstrated.
- Details are available of how the intangible asset will generate probable future economic benefits: the existence of a market for the product of the intangible asset or the intangible asset itself or, if it is to be used internally rather than sold, its usefulness to the entity can be demonstrated.
- Adequate resources exist, or their availability can be demonstrated, to complete the intangible asset and market or use the intangible asset.
- The costs attributable to the intangible asset can be separately identified and reliably measured.

The amount of development costs recognised as an asset must then be amortised and recognised as an expense on a systematic basis so as to reflect the pattern in which the related economic benefits are recognised. The arbitrary allocation of five years by the board of directors is thus not acceptable.

Amortisation may only commence once the product or process is available for use. Snap Ltd's amortisation before the intangible assets were available for use is thus not acceptable.

Correct accounting treatment	**Capitalise as asset Rand**	**Recognise as expense Rand**
Development expenses:		
'V' (capitalise both the R5 000 sharing of knowledge cost and the (R9 000 – R5 000) R4 000 other cost) (1)	9 000	–
'I', 'S', and 'X' (2)	–	9 000
'G' (1)	6 000	–
Research costs	–	15 000
Quality control and testing	–	16 000
	15 000	40 000

(1) If assumed that all the requirements in IAS 38.57 have been met, the costs can be capitalised as an asset.
(2) 5 000 + 3 000 + 1 000 = 9 000

The R15 000 will not be amortised until the asset is ready for use, but should annually be tested for impairment in accordance with IAS 36.10(a).

❑ QUESTION IAS 38.2

On 1 January 20.2, C Net Ltd obtained a licence to operate a cell phone network for a period of 25 years. The total cost of the licence amounted to R5 million. The licence is amortised on the straight-line basis over a period of 25 years, as it is expected that economic benefits relating to the licence will flow to the entity over this period. The licence has no residual value as no active market exists for such licences.

On 31 December 20.2, it is estimated that the licence will generate cash inflow amounting to R1,5 million per annum. The annual cash outflow required to generate the inflow amounts to R650 000. An after-tax discount rate of 14,4% is regarded as appropriate. The expected future cash flow is less than the original estimate because a similar licence was awarded to a major competitor on 31 July 20.2. The licence can be sold on 31 December 20.2 for R4 million. Assume that all the cash flows occur on the last day of every year.

Assume that the South African Revenue Service does not allow a deduction of the cost of the licence. Assume a tax rate of 28%. The correct profit before tax for the 20.2 year after taking the above information into account amounted to R3 million.

Required

Disclose the above information in the notes that will accompany the financial statements of C Net Ltd for the year ended 31 December 20.2 in accordance with the requirements of International Financial Reporting Standards (IFRS). Ignore comparative amounts. Assume all amounts to be material. The tax rate reconciliation must be presented in percentages (%).

❖ **Suggested solution IAS 38.2**

Calculations

1. **Impairment loss**

	Rand
Carrying amount at 31 December 20.2 (1)	4 800 000
Recoverable amount (higher of R4 000 000 and R4 196 539 (2))	(4 196 539)
Impairment loss	603 461

(1) 5 000 000 – (5 000 000/25) = 4 800 000
(2) i = 14,4%/72% (pre-tax rate); n = 24; PMT = – (1 500 000 – 650 000); PV = 4 196 539

Disclosure

C NET LTD
NOTES FOR THE YEAR ENDED 31 DECEMBER 20.2

1. **Accounting policy**

The financial statements are prepared on the historical cost basis in accordance with the requirements of International Financial Reporting Standards (IFRS). The following are the principal accounting policies which are consistent in all material respects with those applied in previous years unless otherwise stated:

1.1 **Intangible assets**

Licences purchased separately are initially recognised at cost. Licences are disclosed at cost less accumulated amortisation and accumulated impairment losses. Licences have a finite useful life and are amortised on the straight-line basis over 25 years.

2. **Intangible assets**

	Rand
Licence (purchased):	
Carrying amount at 1 January 20.2	–
Additions: purchased separately	5 000 000
Amortisation (1)	(200 000)
Impairment loss recognised in profit or loss (see note 3) (calc 1)	(603 461)
Carrying amount at 31 December 20.2	4 196 539
Gross carrying amount	5 000 000
Accumulated amortisation and impairment losses	(803 461)
Remaining useful life (only if material)	24 years

(1) 5 000 000/25 = 200 000

3. **Profit before tax**

Profit before tax is stated after taking into account the following:

	Rand
Expenses	
Amortisation of intangible assets (included in other expenses) (1)	200 000
Impairment loss – licence (included in other expenses) (calc 1)	603 461

Impairment loss on licences

An impairment loss amounting to R603 461 was recognised on the licence granted to operate the cell phone network. This impairment loss is the result of a second licence being awarded to another cell phone network company. The recoverable amount represents value in use, based on a discount rate of 20% (2).

(1) 5 000 000/25 = 200 000
(2) 14.4%/72% = 20%

4. Income tax expense

	Rand
Major components of tax expense:	
Normal SA tax	
Current tax – current year (1)	1 064 969

Reconciliation of standard rate to effective rate	**%**
Applicable (statutory) tax rate	28,00
Tax effect of expenses not deductible for tax purposes:	
– Amortisation of licence (2)	1,87
– Impairment loss (3)	5,63
Effective rate (4)	35,50

(1) (3 000 000 + 200 000 + 603 461) × 28% = 1 064 969
(2) 200 000/3 000 000 × 28% = 1,87%
(3) 603 461/3 000 000 × 28% = 5,63%
(4) 1 064 969/3 000 000 × 100 = 35,50%

❑ QUESTION IAS 38.3

Fols Ltd is a company operating in diversified industries with a 31 December year end. The following information regarding the development costs is applicable:

Ice machine

During the 20.5 financial year, development costs of R400 000 were incurred. During the current financial year a further amount of R300 000 was incurred on development costs. Assume that the necessary requirements were met to capitalise the development costs.

Production commenced on 1 July 20.6. The marketing division estimated the following production and sales at this date:

Year	Units	Cost of sales Rand	Sales Rand
20.6	5 000	400 000	500 000
20.7	10 000	1 100 000	1 400 000
20.8	11 000	1 200 000	1 600 000
20.9	9 000	690 000	900 000

On 31 December 20.6 the marketing division presented the following adjusted estimates:

Year	Units	Cost of sales Rand	Sales Rand
20.7	9 000	1 200 000	1 400 000
20.8	10 000	1 300 000	1 400 000
20.9	8 000	700 000	800 000

The sales for 20.6 realised as was predicted. The development costs are amortised on the basis of the expected sales value. In order to ensure the realisation of the sales for 20.8, an additional R30 000 marketing costs must be incurred during 20.8. This amount has not been included in the 20.8 cost of sales figure. Technological obsolescence necessitated the preparation of new estimates by the marketing division. Assume that all cash flow takes place annually on 31 December, and that a discount rate of 10% before tax is appropriate. A figure for fair value less costs of disposal is not available.

Microwave oven

During 20.4, research costs to the amount of R400 000 and development costs to the amount of R900 000 were incurred in respect of this product. The development costs complied with all the criteria for recognition as an asset and thus were capitalised in terms of International Financial Reporting Standards (IFRS). Production commenced on 1 September 20.4. These development costs were amortised based on the number of units produced per annum. It may be assumed that sales and production occur evenly. During 20.4 it was expected that production of this product will continue for a period of five years from 1 September 20.4.

On 1 September 20.5, production was halted due to a fault discovered in the production process. Thereafter, additional development costs to the amount of R80 000 were incurred up until 30 November 20.5, before the production foreman indicated to management that the fault appeared to be inherent to the process and that additional development costs estimated at R750 000 would have to be incurred before the fault would be eliminated. The costs of R80 000 were written off in full in 20.5 due to the uncertain circumstances. Management approved the recommendation and further decided that the development would be contracted out to an international research institute. On 5 December 20.5, a contract was entered into with Das Haus Research plc in the UK with the completion date set for 30 June 20.6. The success of tracing and neutralising the fault could not be determined at the 20.5 year end and future economic benefits were uncertain.

On 30 June 20.6, the research report from Das Haus Research plc was presented and stated that the fault in the production process could be neutralised. On this date the recoverable amount of the previous year's development costs was calculated as R800 000, using a pre-tax discount rate of 12%. The fee of R750 000 was paid on 1 August 20.6. Additional development costs of R400 000 were incurred from 1 July 20.6 until 31 October 20.6, and production commenced again on 1 November 20.6. At this date it was estimated that production would occur evenly over a remaining period of 34 months. On 31 December 20.6 there are no indications of impairment.

Polycole model P54

During 20.4 the following estimates pertaining to this product were presented and approved:

	Rand
Research costs incurred – 20.4	200 000
Development costs incurred – 20.4	600 000
Amortised in 20.4 (based on number of units sold)	60 000
Amortised in 20.5	150 000
Amortised in 20.6 (evenly)	170 000
Amortised in 20.7	140 000
Amortised in 20.8	80 000

The marketing division revised the product at the 20.5 year end and was of the opinion that the estimated future sales would be realised. There was therefore no indication of impairment.

During 20.6, a competitor released a similar, more technologically advanced product to the market. The result of this was that no sales of Polycole model P54 have occurred since 1 August 20.6. At the 20.6 year end the marketing division recommended that this product be withdrawn from the market.

Required

Show all the information relating to the research and development costs in the financial statements of Fols Ltd for the year ended 31 December 20.6 in accordance with the requirements of International Financial Reporting Standards (IFRS). Accounting policy notes are not required.

❖ **Suggested solution IAS 38.3**

Calculations

20.5	**A** **Rand**	**B** **Rand**	**C** **Rand**	**Total** **Rand**
Balance – 1 January 20.5 (2) (6)	–	840 000	540 000	1 380 000
Amortised (2)	–	(120 000)	(150 000)	(270 000)
Written off (3)	–	(720 000)	–	(720 000)
Incurred and capitalised 20.5	400 000	–	–	400 000
Balance – 31 December 20.5	400 000	–	390 000	790 000

The R80 000 in respect of project B spent until 30 November 20.5 was written off in full in 20.5 due to the uncertainty.

20.6	A Rand	B Rand	C Rand	Total Rand
Balance – 1 January 20.6	400 000	–	390 000	790 000
Written back (5)	–	720 000	–	720 000
Incurred and capitalised 20.6 (9)	300 000	1 150 000	–	1 450 000
Amortised (1) (4) (7)	(79 545)	(110 000)	(99 167)	(288 712)
Written off (calc 1) (8)	(305 655)	–	(290 833)	(596 488)
Balance – 31 December 20.6	314 800	1 760 000	–	2 074 800

A = Ice machine
B = Microwave oven
C = Polycole model P54

(1) 500 000/(500 000 + 1 400 000 + 1 600 000 + 900 000) × 700 000 = 79 545
(2) 900 000 – (900 000 × 4/60) = 840 000; 900 000 × 8/60 = 120 000 (only for eight months because amortisation calculated on number of units produced method)
(3) 840 000 – 120 000 = 720 000
(4) Number of months for amortising = 34
(750 000 + 400 000 + 720 000) × 2/34 = 110 000
(5) When reversing an impairment loss, the increased carrying amount may not exceed what the carrying amount would have been if no impairment loss was recognised in previous years – IAS 36.117. If no impairment loss was recognised i.r.o. the microwave oven, the carrying amount would still have been R720 000 as no amortisation took place because no production occurred. The recoverable amount of R800 000 is therefore limited to R720 000.

If no impairment loss was recognised on the microwave oven, amortisation would still have been provided on it for the period 1 September 20.5 to 30 June 20.6 even if it was not in use. In this question, however, the amortisation for this period is RNil, because amortisation is based on number of units produced and no units have been produced during this period.
(6) 600 000 – 60 000 = 540 000
(7) 170 000 × 7/12 = 99 167
(8) 390 000 – 99 167 = 290 833
(9) 750 000 + 400 000 = 1 150 000

Calculation 1

Additional write-off of development costs – A

The technical obsolescence of the machine is an indication of possible impairment, therefore it is necessary to test for impairment.

Estimated future economic benefits	Rand
20.7 (1)	200 000
20.8 (2)	70 000
20.9 (3)	100 000
	370 000

Value in use	**Rand**
20.7 200 000/1,1	181 818
20.8 70 000/(1,1 × 1,1)	57 851
20.9 100 000/(1,1 × 1,1 × 1,1)	75 131
	314 800

Or with use of a financial calculator:

CFi 0	=	0
CFi 1	=	200 000
CFi 2	=	70 000
CFi 3	=	100 000
i	=	10
∴ NPV	=	314 800

	Rand
Additional write-off of development costs (4)	305 655

(1) 1 400 000 – 1 200 000 = 200 000
(2) 1 400 000 – 1 300 000 – 30 000 = 70 000
(3) 800 000 – 700 000 = 100 000
(4) (400 000 + 300 000) – 79 545 – 314 800 = 305 655

Disclosure

FOLS LTD
STATEMENT OF FINANCIAL POSITION AS AT 31 DECEMBER 20.6

	Note	**20.6 Rand**	**20.5 Rand**
ASSETS			
Non-current assets			
Intangible assets	2	2 074 800	790 000

FOLS LTD
NOTES FOR THE YEAR ENDED 31 DECEMBER 20.6

2. Intangible assets

	20.6 Rand	**20.5 Rand**
Development costs (generated internally) (calc 1)		
Carrying amount at 1 January 20.6	790 000	1 380 000
Gross carrying amount (2)	1 900 000	1 500 000
Accumulated amortisation and impairment losses (3)	(1 110 000)	(120 000)
Amortisation (1)	(288 712)	(270 000)
Impairment losses recognised in profit or loss	(596 488)	(720 000)
Impairment loss reversed in profit or loss	720 000	–
Expenditure incurred	1 450 000	400 000
Carrying amount at 31 December 20.6	2 074 800	790 000
Gross carrying amount (4) (2)	3 350 000	1 900 000
Accumulated amortisation and impairment losses (5)	(1 275 200)	(1 110 000)

(Also disclose description, carrying amount and remaining amortisation period if individual intangible asset is material)

(1) 120 000 + 150 000 = 270 000
(2) 900 000 + 600 000 + 400 000 = 1 900 000
    900 000 + 600 000 = 1 500 000
(3) 60 000 + 60 000 + 270 000 + 720 000 = 1 110 000
    60 000 + 60 000 = 120 000
(4) 1 900 000 + 1 450 000 = 3 350 000
(5) 1 110 000 + 288 712 + 596 488 – 720 000 = 1 275 200

3. Profit before tax

Profit before tax is stated after taking into account the following:

	20.6 Rand	**20.5 Rand**
Expenses		
Included in cost of sales:		
– Development costs – amortised (1)	288 712	270 000
– directly written off	–	80 000
– Impairment loss i.r.o. development costs	596 488	720 000
Income		
Reversal of impairment loss i.r.o. development costs – included in cost of sales	720 000	–

Impairment losses

During 20.5 development costs i.r.o. a microwave oven amounting to R720 000 were written off due to the discovery of a fault in the production process. The defect was identified and corrected after additional research and development costs had been expended. Production once again commenced during the year, which led to development costs of R720 000 being written back. The recoverable amount of the microwave oven's development costs is the value in use, which was calculated by using a discount rate of 12%.

During 20.6 a competitor launched a technologically advanced product into the market which resulted in one of the company's products (Polycole model P54) being withdrawn from the market as no further sales occurred. Development costs of R290 833 were written off in relation to this.

Development costs amounting to R305 655 were written off due to expected lower future economic benefits on account of technological obsolescence of one of the company's products – an ice machine. The recoverable amount of these development costs is the value in use, which was calculated by using a discount rate of 10%.

❑ QUESTION IAS 38.4

The financial director of Touch Ltd approached you for advice regarding the following issues:

1. Touch Ltd has been in business for a number of years and has established a portfolio of loyal customers. The financial director wants to include this portfolio of customers in the statement of financial position as an intangible asset as he is of the opinion that Touch Ltd is worth more than what is reflected by the company's current net asset value.

2. Market research has indicated that there is a need for a shocking device that can be used for self-defence. Two prototypes were developed during the year at a cost of R21 000. A final choice between the two prototypes will be made early in the next financial year. The financial director wants to capitalise the R21 000 as an asset.

3. R25 000 was spent during the current year to generate a trademark internally. It is expected that the benefits from the trademark will flow to the entity over a period of 10 years. The company therefore wants to capitalise the trademark and amortise it over 10 years.

4. Early in the current year a new production process was brought into use. Personnel were trained for three months to operate the new system. The total training expenditure amounted to R22 000. The new system will be in use for at least eight years, and therefore the company wants to capitalise the training expenditure and amortise it over eight years.

5. Advertising costs amounting to R43 000 were incurred during the year i.r.o. radio and television advertisements. The objective of these advertisements was to introduce to the public two new products of Touch Ltd. It is expected that the demand for these products will last for approximately three years. As the economic benefits will flow to the entity over a three-year period, the financial director wants to capitalise the advertising costs and then amortise them over three years.

Required

Indicate in each of the above cases whether or not the relevant costs may be capitalised. Motivate your answer in accordance with the requirements of International Financial Reporting Standards (IFRS). Assume all amounts are material. Reference to the Conceptual Framework of 2018 is not required.

❖ Suggested solution IAS 38.4

1. Internally generated goodwill may not be recognised as an asset as it is not an identifiable resource controlled by the entity. An entity may expect that customers will continue to trade with the entity in future, but has no control over the future economic benefits from customer relationships and loyalty. Goodwill can also not be measured reliably at cost. Differences between the market value of an entity and the carrying amount of its identifiable net assets may capture a range of factors that affect the value of the entity. However, such differences cannot be considered to represent the cost of the goodwill controlled by the entity (IAS 38.48, .50, .16). Touch Ltd may therefore not capitalise the goodwill.

2. The design, construction and testing of pre-production prototypes is regarded as development activities (IAS 38.59(a)). Development costs may only be capitalised if the following can be demonstrated (IAS 38.57):
   - The technical feasibility of completing the intangible asset so that it will be available for use or sale.
   - The intention to complete the intangible asset, and use or sell it.
   - The ability to use or sell the intangible asset.
   - How the intangible asset will generate probable future economic benefits. Among other things, the entity must demonstrate the existence of a market for the output of the intangible asset or for the intangible asset itself or, if it is to be used internally, the usefulness of the intangible asset.
   - The availability of adequate technical, financial and other resources to complete the development, and to use or sell the intangible asset.
   - The ability to reliably measure the expenditure attributable to the intangible asset during its development.

   If all these requirements are met, Touch Ltd may capitalise the development costs amounting to R21 000.

3. Internally generated trademarks may not be recognised as intangible assets as their development costs cannot be distinguished from the cost of developing the business as a whole (IAS 38.63, .64). The costs must therefore be recognised as an expense in profit or loss.

4. An asset must be controlled by an entity before it meets the definition of an intangible asset. Although an entity may be able to identify staff skills leading to future economic benefits from training and may also expect that such staff will continue to make their skills available to the entity in future, an entity usually has insufficient control over the expected future economic benefits arising from a team of skilled staff to consider that these items meet the definition of an intangible asset (IAS 38.15). Therefore the training expenditure may not be capitalised (IAS 38.69(b)).

5. In some cases expenditure is incurred to provide future economic benefits to an entity, but no intangible asset is created that can be recognised. IAS 38.69(c) specifically mentions expenditure on advertising and promotional activities as an example of such expenditure. It is not certain enough that economic benefits associated with the expenses will flow to the entity and therefore the amount will be expensed in the statement of profit or loss and other comprehensive income. (Also refer to IAS 38.29(a)).

❑ QUESTION IAS 38.5

Eggs Galore (Pty) Ltd is a company trading in decorated ostrich eggs and has a December year end. Owing to an extensive overseas market in African artefacts, Eggs Galore (Pty) Ltd decided to export its products.

In order for Eggs Galore (Pty) Ltd to enter the export market, the development of a website for its own use was necessitated. Potential export customers can visit the website to place orders and complete transactions in a secure web environment.

During May and June 20.1, the management of Eggs Galore (Pty) Ltd investigated and planned the development of their own website. Costs incurred during this period were as follows:

	Rand
Travelling expenses	8 000
Consultation fees	27 000

Viability studies concluded that the website would lead to a substantial improvement in profitability.

During July to November 20.1, a firm of web consultants was employed to complete the website, and the following costs were incurred:

	Rand
Content development costs and programming	130 000
Graphic design costs incurred for operation as intended by management	35 000

The website was successfully completed and implemented on 31 December 20.1. Assume that all the requirements of IAS 38.57 have been met for the capitalisation of website costs. Although the future economic benefits of the website could not be accurately measured, it was estimated they would only flow to the entity for a period of four years due to the rapid change in technology.

Required

a. Advise the management of Eggs Galore (Pty) Ltd on whether the costs incurred in connection with the website should be capitalised or whether it should be expensed. Your answer must be substantiated by referring to the requirements of International Financial Reporting Standards (IFRS).
b. Calculate the carrying amount of the website at 31 December 20.2.
c. How will your answer in part a. change if the website is developed solely to promote and advertise the entity's products?

❖ **Suggested solution IAS 38.5**

a. SIC 32 concludes that a website, developed by an entity for its own use, is an internally generated intangible asset subject to the requirements for recognition in IAS 38 being:

- an identifiable asset that will generate probable future economic benefits; and
- the costs of the asset can be reliably measured.

The planning stage of the website is similar to the research phase in IAS 38.54 – .56. Expenditure incurred in this stage will be recognised as an expense when it is incurred. Travelling costs of R8 000 and consultation fees paid of R27 000 will therefore be expensed in the profit or loss of Eggs Galore (Pty) Ltd for the current year.

The application, infrastructure development and graphic design, as well as the content development stages, are similar in nature to the development phase in IAS 38.57 – .64. Expenditure incurred in the development phase will be recognised as an expense in the period in which it is incurred unless all of the following criteria are met (IAS 38.57) (which implies capitalisation of development costs):

- The technical feasibility of completing the website so that it will be available for use.
- The intention to complete the website for use.
- The ability to use the website.
- How the website will generate probable future economic benefits.
- The availability of adequate technical, financial and other resources to complete the development of the website.
- The ability to reliably measure the expenditure attributable to the website during the development.

The expenditure incurred during July to November being content development costs and programming of R130 000, as well as graphic design costs of R35 000, will be capitalised as an internally generated intangible asset and be amortised on a systematic basis to reflect the pattern in which the related economic benefits are recognised. Owing to the rapid change in technology, the period of economic benefit from the current website is estimated at four years.

b.

	Rand
Content development costs and programming	130 000
Graphic design costs	35 000
Cost of website	165 000
Amortisation 20.1 (1)	(41 250)
Carrying amount	123 750

(1) 165 000/4 = 41 250

c. If the website is solely or primarily developed for promoting and advertising the entity's own products, the entity is not able to demonstrate how the website will generate probable future economic benefits. Consequently, all expenditure on developing such a website will be recognised as an expense when incurred.

❑ QUESTION IAS 38.6

Avon Ltd, a company listed on the JSE Ltd, has a 30 September year end. The company is involved in a number of different business activities.

1. On 1 December 20.3, Avon Ltd obtained a fishing quota, which entitles the company to fish sardines on the east coast of South Africa for a three-year period, starting on 1 January 20.4. The company incurred the following expenditure to obtain the fishing quota:

	Rand
Travel and entertainment expenses	20 000
Legal costs	55 000
Net salary (after deductions of R20 000) paid to an employee involved in the negotiation process	60 000
Licence fee paid to the Department of Fisheries to obtain the quota	235 000

The calculation of the recoverable amount of the fishing quota showed that the recoverable amount exceeded the carrying amount on 30 September 20.4.

2. Avon Ltd developed a new medicine for the treatment of a flu virus. Research costs of R2 500 000 were incurred for the year ended 30 September 20.3 for this purpose. From 1 October 20.3 to 15 November 20.3 a further amount of R35 000 was spent on research.

   On the basis of the research findings, testing of the medicine started from 16 November 20.3. Clinical trials were undertaken from 16 November 20.3 to 31 January 20.4 at a cost of R750 000, but it could not be determined with certainty during this period whether the medicine would actually be able to kill the flu virus. From 1 February 20.4 to 30 June 20.4, further clinical trials were done at a cost of R1 050 000. The clinical trials that were performed from 1 February 20.4 to 30 June 20.4, were completed successfully and confirmed that the new medicine will be able to kill the flu virus. The distribution of the medicine was approved by the Medicines Control Council on 30 June 20.4 and the manufacturing of the new medicine commenced on 1 July 20.4.

   The marketing department determined that the demand for the new medicine is so great that the recoverable amount was conservatively estimated at R80 million over a period of 15 years.

3. During the year ended 30 September 20.4, Avon Ltd spent R65 000 on the development of a customer list. It was expected that the benefits obtained from the customer list would accrue to the company over a period of 10 years.

4. Avon Ltd owns a patent with a cost of R450 000, which is used to manufacture an organic insect killer. The useful life of the patent was estimated at 15 years, and on 1 October 20.3 the carrying amount of the patent amounted to R390 000. The fair value of the patent in an active market amounted to R300 000 on 30 September 20.4, since another organic insect-killer patent was also approved and the competitor already obtained a large share of the market.

5. All intangible assets of Avon Ltd are amortised over their estimated useful life according to the straight-line method.

6. Assume the South African Revenue Service allows a deduction of 25% per annum (not apportioned for part of the year) on the following:

   - All costs incurred on the acquisition of the fish quota;
   - All research and development costs on the development of the new medicine for a flu virus;

- All costs for the development of a customer list; and
- All costs regarding patents.

7. Assume a tax rate of 28%. The deferred tax asset on 30 September 20.3 amounted to R339 150. There are no other temporary differences, non-taxable items or non-deductible items except for those arising from the above information.

8. The company is considered to be a going concern and it is certain, beyond reasonable doubt, that there will be sufficient future taxable income to recover deferred tax assets.

Required

Prepare the general journal entries (cash transactions included) of Avon Ltd for all the above transactions for the year ended 30 September 20.4 in accordance with the requirements of International Financial Reporting Standards (IFRS). Round all calculated amounts to the nearest rand.

❑ QUESTION IAS 38.7

A specialised engineering company, Gert Ltd, has a research and development department which is involved in various projects. The company's year-end is 30 June. Details of the projects are given below.

Project Dynamo

Three researchers were allocated to the project during the first three months of the financial year ended 30 June 20.4 with the aim of developing an alternative to the light switch. The researchers did not achieve any success and the research was therefore suspended. The costs allocated to this project amounted to R180 000.

Project Litho

During the financial year ended 30 June 20.4 the researchers in the team developed a new apparatus to do welding. The apparatus will ensure improved efficiency and increased safety. The researchers are of the opinion that the product will prove to be highly successful as safety in the workplace is a high priority for the trade unions. The research costs for the financial year amounted to R20 000. The development costs for the financial year ended 30 June 20.4 amounted to R670 000 (assume that the requirements of IAS 38.57 have been met) and are made up as follows: salaries R500 000, local consultants R50 000, raw materials R30 000, and the installation of plant for production R90 000. The plant is of a specialised nature, and will have no scrap value once the product is no longer manufactured. The project was completed on 30 June 20.4 and production commenced on 1 July 20.4.

The research department is of the opinion that demand for the product will only last three years due to ever-changing technology. There were no indications of impairment.

Project Flash

Various researchers worked on this project during the 20.3 financial year in order to develop an improved lawnmower. This project was then suspended due to the fact that this was not a high-priority research project. At that stage the project did not have a commercial marketing value and the amount of R350 000 was also treated as such. The research on this project resumed on 1 January 20.4. All the requirements for the capitalisation of development costs in accordance with IAS 38.57 had already been met by 1 February 20.4. The costs incurred for 20.4 were as follows:

	Rand
Research costs	600 000
Development costs	1 500 000

Additional development costs incurred from 1 July 20.4 to 31 August 20.4 amounted to R500 000. Production commenced on 1 September 20.4 in an existing plant. It is expected that the full costs incurred on this project during the financial years 20.3 to 20.5 will be recovered, and that the economic benefits of the project can be expected to be enjoyed for the next five years.

Project Romario

The development costs incurred on this project until 30 June 20.3 amounted to R700 000. During the year ended 30 June 20.4 a further R900 000 of development costs were incurred. During the year ended 30 June 20.5 development costs of R500 000 were incurred and the project was completed on 30 November 20.4. Production, however, only commenced on 1 January 20.5 in an existing plant. On 15 October 20.2 the research and development department presented a report on a feasibility study and concluded that the development of this new product would lead to a substantial improvement in profitability. The future economic benefits could not be accurately determined at that date although the estimates calculated indicated that the profit on sale of this product would cover the costs of development several times. The development costs incurred from 20.3 to 20.5 met all the requirements for capitalisation in terms of IAS 38.57. Economic benefits of the project can be expected for five years.

Project Limbo

The development of this project commenced on 1 July 20.3 and was completed on 1 February 20.4 at a cost of R570 000. Production commenced immediately in an existing plant. The development costs incurred met all the requirements for capitalisation in terms of IAS 38.57 on 1 July 20.3.

The marketing division estimated that 50 000 units of product Limbo can be manufactured and sold per financial year. The expected period of demand for product Limbo is five years.

The knowledge obtained during the development of product Limbo can be sold at the end of the five years for R20 000. An agreement with a third party to that effect has already been signed.

Required

Disclose intangible assets and profit before tax in the notes that will accompany the financial statements of Gert Ltd for the year ended 30 June 20.5, in accordance with the requirements of International Financial Reporting Standards (IFRS). Use a column for each project and assume that there were no impairment losses identified during annual impairment testing (where appropriate). The total column in the intangible asset note is not required.

❑ QUESTION IAS 38.8

Blerts Ltd is a company operating in the electronics and related industries, and has a year end of 31 December. The organisation has its own research and development department and makes use of local and international research institutes.

The following information is relevant to development costs which have been recognised as assets:

Electronic dart board

Development costs capitalised on 31 December 20.3 amounted to R400 000. A further amount of R400 000 was incurred during the current financial year on development costs. All conditions of IAS 38.57 have been met to ensure that the items can be capitalised. Production commenced on 1 July 20.4. It is expected that the economic benefits that will be enjoyed by the company will far exceed the development costs expended by the company.

The marketing division estimated that the product will have a limited useful marketing life and estimated the sales in units as follows:

20.4	–	40 000
20.5	–	100 000
20.6	–	60 000
20.7	–	30 000
20.8	–	20 000

The full production is sold during the relevant period of production and there is no inventory on hand. Amortisation of development costs is based on estimated sale of units.

Hi-fi amplifier

The development costs of this product were incurred, and development was also completed during 20.1. The amount capitalised up to 31 December 20.1 amounted to R900 000. The production commenced on 1 January 20.2. At that date the economic benefits were expected to be enjoyed by the company for five years. The estimate of economic benefits was revised on 31 December 20.4 and was still considered to be relevant. This intangible asset is amortised on a straight-line basis and there are no indications of impairment.

Mainframe system Mil

The development of this product was completed during 20.3 at a cost of R5 million. Management decided that, due to the material nature of the creation of this product, the development costs shall be capitalised as part of the cost of the inventory. The market demand for this product has been estimated to be only 10 units. The amortisation of the development costs is based on units produced. During 20.3 only one product was manufactured and this was on hand at year end. During 20.4, four Mil systems were manufactured of which two were in inventory at 31 December 20.4. The system that was in inventory at 31 December 20.3 was sold during the 20.4 financial year.

The following information is available:

- Cost of production for 20.3 (excluding the capitalised development costs) amounted to R900 000.
- Cost of production for 20.4 – four systems (excluding the capitalised development costs) amounted to R3 900 000.

There are no indications of any impairment in respect of mainframe system Mil.

Patents

Separately purchased patents with a cost of R1 million and accumulated amortisation of R333 333 at 31 December 20.3 are also held by the company. The patents are amortised on a straight-line basis over a period of 30 years, as the patents are registered for that period. It is expected that the product covered by the patents will have an expected selling life of 40 years. There are no indications that the patents might be impaired.

Required

a. Show how the intangible assets will be disclosed in the financial statements of Blerts Ltd for the year ended 31 December 20.4 in accordance with the requirements of International Financial Reporting Standards (IFRS). Accounting policy notes are required. Ignore the note on the preparation of the financial statements and compliance with International Financial Reporting Standards (IFRS). Ignore comparative amounts.
b. Calculate the carrying amount of inventories at 31 December 20.4.

❑ QUESTION IAS 38.9

The following is a list of costs incurred by Véju Ltd during their 28 February 20.2 financial year:

1. Véju Ltd operates an existing website for its own use. The costs to develop the website were capitalised in the previous year as an intangible asset as it complied with IAS 38.57 at that time. However, Véju Ltd acquired copyrights during the development of the website and these costs are now amortised over the existing economic life of the website. Amortisation costs of the copyrights amounts to R2 500 for the year. This reflects the pattern in which the economic benefits are consumed.

2. During the current year Véju Ltd paid R230 000 to Compusult (Pty) Ltd to secure the above-mentioned website. Previously the website was used mainly to advertise the products of Véju Ltd, but is now being integrated with the accounting function of Véju Ltd to incorporate the placement, as well as payment, of orders. These costs incurred prolonged the functioning of the website with an additional four years and will substantially improve profitability in future.

3. During the securing of the website, one of the design staff members of Compusult (Pty) Ltd worked for a month on a relatively high-risk approach to speed up the process of securing the website on request of Véju Ltd. His efforts proved fruitless and his salary for the period amounted to R30 000. This amount is not included in the R230 000 payment mentioned in note 2.

4. Véju Ltd's accounting software package complies with the recognition criteria of an intangible asset. After upgrading the website, it was necessary to modify the existing accounting software package to make it operate at its original assessed performance standard. These costs amounted to R150 000.

5. Training costs amounting to R13 000 were paid by Véju Ltd to train personnel on the accounting treatment and processing of orders placed on the new secure website.

6. Advertisements were placed in all leading newspapers amounting to R55 000, advertising the new secure webpage of Véju Ltd.

7. Véju Ltd has an extensive customer list indicating all loyal supporting customers of Véju Ltd. The directors are of the opinion that this list is worth at least R100 000 to their opposition, and want to capitalise the list at R150 000.

8. Véju Ltd had a cocktail and presentation evening to expand the goodwill of Véju Ltd within their existing customer base. Expenditure of R25 000 was incurred.

9. To entertain future VIP customers of Véju Ltd, the company applied for a fishing quota with the Natal Parks Board. The company incurred the following costs during the year in an attempt to obtain the quota:

	Rand
• Travelling and accommodation costs (excluding VAT)	10 900
• Legal costs (excluding VAT)	12 000

On 28 February 20.2 it was still not certain whether their application for the fishing quota had been successful.

Required

Indicate in each of the above cases whether or not the relevant costs can be capitalised or whether they should be expensed. Motivate your answer in accordance with the requirements of International Financial Reporting Standards (IFRS). Assume all amounts to be material.

❑ QUESTION IAS 38.10

On 1 January 20.0, Radio Ltd acquired a broadcasting licence for R600 000. This licence is renewable every five years if the entity complies with the relevant legislative requirements. The licence may be renewed indefinitely at little cost. Radio Ltd intends to renew the licence indefinitely, and evidence supports its ability to do so. Historically, there has been no compelling challenge to the licence renewal. The technology used in broadcasting is not expected to be replaced by other technology at any time in the foreseeable future.

On 1 January 20.5, Radio Ltd renewed the licence at a cost of R5 000.

On 1 January 20.6 the licensing authority decided that it will no longer renew broadcasting licences, but will rather auction them. It is expected that the costs to obtain a licence will be significantly higher in future. In spite of this, Radio Ltd still expects that the licence will continue to contribute to net cash inflows until it expires, and there is no other indication of impairment.

Assume that all amounts are material.

Required

a. Indicate, with reasons, what the useful life of the broadcasting licence was up to 20.5 and whether it should be amortised or not.
b. Discuss the correct recognition and measurement of the subsequent expenditure of R5 000 on 1 January 20.5.
c. Disclose the above information in the notes that will accompany the financial statements of Radio Ltd for the year ended 31 December 20.6 in accordance with the requirements of International Financial Reporting Standards (IFRS). Accounting policy notes are not required.

❑ QUESTION IAS 38.11

The Distance CA Ltd is a private university which was incorporated at the end of 20.15. Subsequent to its incorporation, Distance CA Ltd developed a new e-learning management system used by students and staff at Distance CA Ltd. Details in connection with this include the following:

E-learning management system

Distance CA Ltd developed a first of its kind e-learning management system that is used by students and staff at Distance CA Ltd. The reasoning behind the development of the e-learning management system was to facilitate communication, study content sharing and assessment, as well as to save on operating costs, such as photocopying of study material and printing of study guides which can be provided electronically on the e-learning management system in the future.

Since Distance CA Ltd has never used any e-learning management system, Distance CA Ltd decided on 1 January 20.16 to first undertake a feasibility study. The results of the feasibility study were favourable and indicated that the staff and students were in favour of such a system, and Distance CA Ltd could save a substantial amount on operating costs if such a system is implemented. Based on these findings, Distance CA Ltd continued and defined the hardware and software specifications needed to operate such a system. The total cost incurred in connection with the feasibility study and in defining the latter specifications amounted to R145 000.

The next step was to purchase all the hardware and to develop the software applications needed to operate the e-learning management system. The cost to purchase the hardware, and to develop the software application, which included several web servers and the outsourcing of various specialists in e-learning management system development, amounted to R1 100 000 and R800 000 respectively.

After completion of the above, a graphic designer was appointed to design the appearance of the e-learning management system. This service included the actual homepage, not requiring login details, as well as the appearance of the actual system after a student or staff member logged into the system. The graphic designer was also responsible for taking and editing the photographs of Distance CA Ltd that appear on the homepage of the e-learning management system. The costs in connection with designing the appearance of the system and for taking and editing the photographs amounted to R35 000 and R9 500 respectively. Displaying the photographs of Distance CA Ltd on the homepage of the e-learning management system was seen by management as an opportunity to indirectly advertise Distance CA Ltd to attract more students as the homepage is accessible and can be viewed without requiring any login details through the official Distance CA Ltd website and various search engines such as Google, Yahoo and Ask. Thereafter, the content of the e-learning management system was developed which included the various functionalities required. These included the announcement, resources, tests and quizzes and other functionalities. The total costs to develop the content amounted to R350 000.

After completion of all of the above, the newly developed e-learning management system was tested to identify any glitches in the system at a total cost of R10 000. After the identified glitches were rectified at no additional cost, the system was ready for use on 1 July 20.17 and was launched on 1 August 20.17 after all the Distance CA Ltd staff was trained on using the e-learning management system at a total cost of R125 000.

The e-learning management system has been used effectively ever since it was taken into use. Various updates have been made to the graphics at a total cost of R120 000. Another functionality referred to as the eGuide was developed and incorporated into the e-learning management system at a total cost of R100 000. The total useful life of the e-learning management system was initially estimated to be five years with no residual value and remained unchanged to date.

The e-learning management system meets the definition of an internally generated intangible asset in terms of IAS 38 *Intangible Assets*.

The financial manager provided you with the following calculation of the cost of the e-learning management system used to calculate the amortisation expense for 20.19:

Line items	**Rand**
Feasibility study and defining of hardware and software specifications	145 000
Purchase of all the hardware	1 100 000
Development of the software applications	800 000
Graphic designer: Designing the system	-
Graphic designer: Photographs	9 500
Content development	350 000
Testing	10 000
Training of staff	125 000
Subsequent updates of graphics	120 000
eGuide developed and implemented	-
Cost on 30 June 2019	**2 659 500**

Required

Briefly discuss the correctness of including or excluding each line item in the cost calculation prepared by the financial manager of Distance CA Ltd in connection with the e-learning management system provided above. Provide a brief reason to support your answer above for each of the line items in the calculation. Limit your reasons to the requirements of the International Financial Reporting Standards (IFRS).

(Recognition – NWU adjusted)

IAS 40

Investment property

❑ QUESTIONS AND SOLUTIONS

IAS 40.1	Classification and measurement of investment property: discussion
IAS 40.2	Classification of investment property (hotel): discussion
IAS 40.3	Simple investment property with operating leases: preparation of investment property, profit before taxation and operating lease disclosure notes
IAS 40.4#	Transfer from owner-occupied property to investment property with deferred tax implications: journal entries
IAS 40.5#	Transfer from investment property to owner-occupied property with deferred tax implications: journal entries

❑ QUESTIONS

IAS 40.6	Investment property using the fair value model and cost model with deferred tax and operating leases: preparation of notes on investment property, income tax, profit before taxation, deferred taxation and operating leases
IAS 40.7	Acquisition and construction of investment property with deferred tax implications: calculation of fair value adjustments and deferred tax and preparation of investment property disclosure note
IAS 40.8#	Transfer from owner-occupied property to investment property with deferred tax implications: preparation of disclosure notes and calculation of deferred tax
IAS 40.9	Subsidiary owns investment property and leases it to holding company: consolidation journal entries with and without deferred tax

 # These questions contain topics or principles that were at an awareness level of proficiency in the ITC syllabus of SAICA, at the time of publishing this book.

❑ QUESTION IAS 40.1

Wasser Ltd, a manufacturing concern, utilised surplus funds to purchase an office building in the central business district of Pretoria. The capacity of the building is 10 000 m^2 and is fully let. The estimated useful life at the date of completion was 30 years.

Required

Briefly discuss the accounting treatment of the above office building in the financial statements of Wasser Ltd to comply with the requirements of International Financial Reporting Standards (IFRS). Disclosure requirements are not to be discussed.

❖ Suggested solution IAS 40.1

Classification

The office building must be classified as investment property since the building is fully let. *Investment property* is defined as property (land or a building, or part of a building, or both) held (by an owner or by a lessee) to earn rentals and/or for capital appreciation, rather than for:

- use in the production or supply of goods or services or for administrative purposes; or
- sale in the ordinary course of the business.

Measurement at recognition

Investment property must be measured initially at its cost. The cost of a purchased investment property comprises its purchase price and any directly attributable expenditure such as professional fees for legal services, property transfer taxes and other transaction costs.

Measurement after initial recognition

Investment properties must be measured using either the fair value or the cost model.

Fair value is the price that would be received to sell an asset or paid to transfer a liability in an orderly transaction between market participants at the measurement date. The fair value of an investment property must therefore reflect market conditions at the reporting date. Any gain or loss arising from a change in the fair value of the investment property must be included in profit or loss for the period in which it arises.

If the investment property is measured by using the cost model according to IAS 16, it must be measured at cost less any accumulated depreciation and accumulated impairment losses to account for the land and the building classified as investment property. The office building would be depreciated over 30 years.

❑ QUESTION IAS 40.2

Peter Ltd owns a piece of land with hotel buildings thereon. This property is leased out to a well-known hotel group under an operating lease.

Required

Discuss comprehensively whether the directors of Peter Ltd must account for the land and hotel buildings as investment property to comply with the requirements of International Financial Reporting Standards (IFRS).

❖ Suggested solution IAS 40.2

Investment property is defined as property (land or a building, or part of a building, or both) held (by an owner or by a lessee) to earn rentals and/or for capital appreciation, rather than for:

- use in the production or supply of goods or services or for administrative purposes; or
- sale in the ordinary course of the business.

Owner-occupied property is property held (by an owner or by a lessee) for use in the production or supply of goods or services or for administrative purposes.

Judgment is needed to determine whether a hotel qualifies as an investment property as ancillary services are rendered to the guests of the hotel. These services might make up such a significant component of the arrangement as a whole that it might be argued that the hotel is actually used in the rendering of services and must therefore be accounted for as owner-occupied. This is often the case with an owner-managed hotel, where the owner is exposed to variations in the cash flows generated by the operations of the hotel.

The property referred to in the question is, however, not owner-managed but rented out to a well-known hotel group under an operating lease. The ancillary services are therefore provided not by the company, but by the hotel group. As no significant ancillary services are provided and rental income is generated by the property, it must be accounted for as an investment property.

❑ QUESTION IAS 40.3

Fern Ltd is a company that cultivates exotic plants.

The following investment properties are owned by the company:

Date acquired	**Description**	**Cost** **Rand**	**Fair value 31 Dec 20.6** **Rand**	**Fair value 31 Dec 20.5** **Rand**
1 January 20.5	Vacant land	1 200 000	1 260 000	1 220 000
1 March 20.6	Hothouse	300 000	330 000	–
1 July 20.6	Office building	550 000	575 000	–

Additional information

1. It is the company's policy to account for investment property using the fair value model.

2. The vacant land is situated in Cape Town and is held for long-term capital appreciation.

3. The hothouse and the office building are situated in Johannesburg and are leased out in terms of non-cancellable operating lease agreements for a period of five years from the dates they were acquired. The hothouse and office building were leased out at a monthly rental of R3 500 and R4 000 respectively during the 20.6 financial year.

4. Repairs and maintenance of R7 500 were incurred on the hothouse during the 20.6 financial year.

5. During January 20.6, an amount of R45 500 was spent to combat a sudden locust plague that broke out on the vacant land.

6. During November 20.6, expenditure of R45 000 was incurred for the hothouse. This expenditure will increase the future benefits expected from the hothouse.

7. The above properties were valued by Mrs B. Dlamini, an independent sworn appraiser who has recent experience in the location and category of the properties being valued. The valuer determined the fair value of the properties based on current prices in an active market for similar properties in the same location and condition, and subject to similar lease and other contracts.

8. Ignore all tax implications.

Required

Provide the investment property, profit before taxation and the operating leases disclosure notes in the financial statements of Fern Ltd for the year ended 31 December 20.6 in accordance with the requirements of International Financial Reporting Standards (IFRS). Comparative amounts are not required.

❖ **Suggested solution IAS 40.3**

FERN LTD
NOTES FOR THE YEAR ENDED 31 DECEMBER 20.6

1. Accounting policy

The financial statements have been prepared in accordance with the requirements of International Financial Reporting Standards (IFRS) and on the historical cost basis, except for investment property which is accounted for at fair value. The following are the principal accounting policies which are consistent in all material respects with those applied in previous years, unless otherwise stated:

1.1 Investment property

Investment property is accounted for by applying the fair value model. All property held to earn rentals or for capital appreciation, or both, is classified as investment property. The fair value of investment property is determined at reporting date by an independent sworn appraiser based on current prices in an active market for similar properties in the same location and condition.

1.2 Leased assets

Leases under which the risks and rewards incidental to ownership of a leased asset are effectively retained by the lessor are classified as operating leases. Lease income from operating leases is recognised in income on a straight-line basis over the lease term.

2. Investment property

	20.6
	Rand
Carrying amount on 1 January 20.6	1 220 000
Additions: acquisitions (1)	850 000
Additions: capitalised subsequent expenditure	45 000
Fair value adjustment (2)	50 000
Carrying amount on 31 December 20.6 (3)	2 165 000

(1) 300 000 + 550 000 = 850 000
(2) (1 260 000 – 1 220 000) + (330 000 – 300 000 – 45 000) + (575 000 – 550 000) = 50 000
(3) 1 260 000 + 330 000 + 575 000 = 2 165 000

Investment property is leased out in terms of non-cancellable operating lease agreements for a period of five years from their acquisition date (refer to note 4).

3. Profit before tax

	Rand
Profit before tax is stated after taking the following into account:	
Income	
Rental income from investment property (1)	59 000
Expenses	
Direct operating expenses arising from investment property that generated rental income	7 500
Direct operating expenses arising from investment property that did not generate rental income	45 500

(1) (3 500 × 10) + (4 000 × 6) = 59 000

4. Operating leases

Maturity analysis of undiscounted receivable operating lease payments on the reporting date:

	20.6
	Rand
For 20.7 (3 500 × 12) + (4 000 × 12)	90 000
For 20.8	90 000
For 20.9	90 000
For 20.10	90 000
For 20.11 (3 500 × 2) + (4 000 × 6)	31 000
	391 000

❑ QUESTION IAS 40.4#

On 1 September 20.3, Zero Ltd acquired a new manufacturing property and decided to lease the old property to another manufacturing company in terms of an operating lease agreement. The details of the property leased out are as follows:

	Rand
Cost	
Land	500 000
Buildings	1 200 000
Accumulated depreciation on buildings – 1 January 20.3	240 000
Tax base of buildings – 1 January 20.3	1 020 000
Fair value – 1 September 20.3	
Land	630 000
Buildings	1 210 000
Fair value – 31 December 20.3	
Land	650 000
Buildings	1 235 000

Owner-occupied property is accounted for by using the cost model while investment property is accounted for by using the fair value model. The company depreciates owner-occupied buildings on the straight-line basis over 15 years with an RNil estimated residual value. Upon review of the depreciation method, useful life and residual value of the building at 31 December 20.2, it was found they did not differ from previous estimates.

The South African Revenue Service allows an annual building allowance of 5%, not apportioned for part of the year.

Assume the following:

- A normal tax rate of 30% and that 66.6% of capital gains realised by the company on disposal of property will be taxable.
- It is probable that sufficient taxable income will be earned in the future against which any deferred tax assets can be utilised.
- The costs of the respective assets on acquisition reflect their 'base cost' for capital gains tax purposes.
- Depreciable investment properties are not held within a business model whose objective is to consume substantially all the economic benefits embodied in the investment property over time.

Ignore VAT.

Required

Prepare the journal entries in respect of the above-mentioned property for the year ended 31 December 20.3.

Your answer should comply with the requirements of International Financial Reporting Standards (IFRS).

❖ Suggested solution IAS 40.4#

	Rand Dr/(Cr)
1 September 20.3	
Depreciation (P or L) (1)	53 333
Accumulated depreciation: Buildings (SFPos)	(53 333)
Recognition of depreciation while property is owner-occupied	
Accumulated depreciation: Buildings (SFPos) (2)	293 333
Building at cost (SFPos)	(1 200 000)*
Building at revalued amount (SFPos)	1 210 000*
Gain on revaluation (OCI) (balancing)	(303 333)
Revaluation of building	

* These amounts could also have been journalised on a net basis.

	Rand Dr/(Cr)
Land at cost (SFPos)	(500 000)
Land at revalued amount (SFPos)	630 000
Gain on revaluation (OCI) (balancing)	(130 000)
Revaluation of land	
Income tax on items in OCI (OCI) (3)	116 974
Deferred tax (SFPos)	(116 974)
Deferred tax on revaluation of land and buildings	
Investment property (SFPos) (4)	1 840 000
Land at revalued amount (SFPos)	(630 000)
Building at revalued amount (SFPos)	(1 210 000)
Transfer of owner-occupied property to investment property	
Deferred tax (SFPos)	1 002
Income tax on items in OCI (OCI) (5)	(1 002)
Adjustment to deferred tax on revaluation of buildings due to change in intention from use to sale (IAS 12.51C)	
31 December 20.3	
Investment property (SFPos) (6)	45 000
Fair value adjustment (P or L)	(45 000)
Fair value adjustment at year-end	
Income tax expense – deferred (P or L) (calc 1)	10 991
Deferred tax (SFPos)	(10 991)
Deferred tax due to depreciation, building allowance and fair value adjustment	

(1) 1 200 000/15 × 8/12 = 53 333
(2) 240 000 + 53 333 = 293 333
(3) {[(630 000 – 500 000) × 66.6%] + [1 210 000 – (1 200 000 – 293 333)]} × 30% = 116 974
(4) 630 000 + 1 210 000 = 1 840 000
(5) (1 210 000 – 1 200 000) × 33.4% × 30% = 1 002
(6) (1 235 000 + 650 000) – (1 210 000 + 630 000) = 45 000

Calculation: deferred tax

31 December 20.2

	A Rand	B Rand	C Rand	D Rand	E Rand	F Rand	G Rand
Owner occupied property							
Land	500 000	500 000	–	–	–	500 000	Exempt
Building	1200 000	1200 000	–	–	1200 000	–	–
Depreciation/wear - and-tear (1) (2)	(240 000)	(240 000)	–	–	(180 000)	(60 000)	18 000
Deferred tax asset	960 000	960 000	–	–	1 020 000	440 000	18 000

31 December 20.3

	A Rand	B Rand	C Rand	D Rand	E Rand	F Rand	G Rand
Owner-occupied property transferred to investment property							
Land							
Balance on 1 Jan 20.3	500 000	500 000	–	–	–	500 000	Exempt
Revaluation 1 Sept 20.3 (3) (4)	130 000	–	130 000	–	–	130 000	(25 974)
Transferred to investment property	630 000	500 000	130 000	–	–	630 000	(25 974)
FV adjustment 31 Dec 20.3 (5) (6)	20 000	–	–	20 000	–	20 000	(3 996)
Deferred tax liability	650 000	500 000	130 000	20 000	–	650 000	(29 970)

	A Rand	B Rand	C Rand	D Rand	E Rand	F Rand	G Rand
Building							
Balance on 1 Jan 20.3	960 000	960 000	–	–	1020 000	(60 000)	18 000
Depreciation/wear-and-tear (7) (8) (9)	(53 333)	(53 333)	–	–	(60 000)	6 667	(2 000)
Revaluation 1 Sept 20.3 (10) (11)	303 333	–	303 333	–	–	303 333	(89 998)
Transfer to investment property	1 210 000	906 667	303 333	–	960 000	250 000	(73 998)
FV adjustment 31 Dec 20.3 (12) (13)	25 000	–	–	25 000	–	25 000	(4 995)
Deferred tax Liability	1 235 000	906 667	303 333	25 000	960 000	275 000	(78 993)

A	=	**Total**
B	=	**Historical**
C	=	**Revaluation**
D	=	**Fair value adjustment**
E	=	**Tax base**
F	=	**Temporary difference**
G	=	**Deferred tax**
FV	=	**Fair value**

	Rand
Total deferred tax liability 31 Dec 20.3 (14)	(108 963)
Total deferred tax asset 31 Dec 20.2	18 000
Movement for the year	126 963
Transfer from revaluation surplus (15)	(115 972)
Movement in profit or loss (Dr)	10 991

(1) (1 200 000 – 1 020 000) = 180 000
(2) 60 000 × 30% = 18 000
(3) (630 000 – 500 000) = 130 000
(4) 130 000 × 66.6% × 30% = 25 974
(5) (650 000 – 630 000) = 20 000
(6) 20 000 × 66.6% × 30% = 3 996
(7) (1 200 000/15 × 8/12) = 53 333
(8) (1 200 000 × 5%) = 60 000
(9) 6 667 × 30% = 2 000
(10) [1 210 000 – (960 000 – 53 333)] = 303 333
(11) [(1 210 000 – 1 200 000) × 66.6% × 30%] + (293 333 × 30%) = 89 998
(12) (1 235 000 – 1 210 000) = 25 000
(13) 25 000 × 66.6% × 30% = 4 995
(14) 78 993 + 29 970 = 108 963
(15) 25 974 + 89 998 = 115 972

❑ QUESTION IAS 40.5[#]

On 1 March 20.4, Zero Ltd occupied their manufacturing property that was previously leased to another manufacturer. The company applies the fair value model to account for investment property and the cost model to account for property, plant and equipment. Details of the property are as follows:

	Rand
Cost	
Land	3 200 000
Buildings	6 800 000
Fair value – 1 January 20.4	
Land	3 600 000
Buildings	6 950 000
Fair value – 1 March 20.4	
Land	3 680 000
Buildings	7 200 000
Tax base of buildings on 1 January 20.4	5 780 000

It is the company's policy to depreciate buildings on a straight-line basis and on 1 March 20.4 the remaining useful life of the buildings was estimated at 15 years. Upon review of the depreciation method, useful life and residual value of the buildings at 31 December 20.4, it was found they did not differ from previous estimates.

The South African Revenue Service grants an annual building allowance of 5%, not apportioned for part of a year.

Assume the following:

- A normal tax rate of 30% and that 66.6% of capital gains realised by the company on disposal of property will be taxable; and
- that the costs of the respective assets reflect their 'base cost' for capital gains tax purposes.
- Depreciable investment properties are not held within a business model whose objective is to consume substantially all the economic benefits embodied in the investment property over time.

Ignore VAT.

Required

Prepare the journal entries in respect of the above-mentioned property for the year ended 31 December 20.4.

Your answer must comply with the requirements of International Financial Reporting Standards (IFRS).

❖ **Suggested solution IAS 40.5**[#]

1 March 20.4

	Rand Dr/(Cr)
Investment property (SFPos) (1)	330 000
Fair value adjustment (P or L)	(330 000)
Fair value adjustment on 1 March 20.4	
Land (SFPos)	3 680 000
Buildings (SFPos)	7 200 000
Investment property (SFPos)	(10 880 000)
Transfer from investment property to owner-occupied property	
31 December 20.4	
Depreciation (P or L) (2)	400 000
Accumulated depreciation: Buildings (SFPos)	(400 000)
Depreciation for the 10 months ending 31 December 20.4	
Income tax expense – deferred (P or L) (calc 1)	88 014
Deferred tax (SFPos)	(88 014)
Deferred tax due to depreciation, building allowance and fair value adjustment	

(1) (3 680 000 + 7 200 000) – (3 600 000 + 6 950 000) = 330 000

(2) 7 200 000/15 × 10/12 = 400 000

Calculation

1. **Deferred tax**	**Carrying amount Rand**	**Tax base Rand**	**Temporary difference Rand**	**Deferred tax Rand**
31 December 20.3				
Investment property				
Land (1)	3 600 000	3 200 000	400 000	79 920
Building (2)	6 950 000	5 780 000	1 170 000	335 970
Deferred tax liability at year-end				415 890
31 December 20.4				
Property, plant and equipment				
Land (3)	3 680 000	3 200 000	480 000	95 904
Building (4) (5) (6)	6 800 000	5 440 000	1 360 000	408 000
Deferred tax liability at year-end				503 904
Deferred tax liability at beginning of year				(415 890)
Deferred tax recognised in profit or loss – 20.4 (Dr)				88 014

(1) 400 000 × 66.6% × 30% = 79 920
(2) [(6 950 000 – 6 800 000) × 66.6% × 30%] + [(6 800 000 – 5 780 000) × 30%] = 335 970
(3) 480 000 × 66.6% × 30% = 95 904
(4) 7 200 000 – (7 200 000/15 × 10/12) = 6 800 000
(5) 5 780 000 – (6 800 000 × 5%) = 5 440 000
(6) 1 360 000 × 30% = 408 000 (intention is now use)

❑ QUESTION IAS 40.6

Redge Ltd owns a factory property which was leased out to a manufacturer from 1 January 20.2 in terms of an operating lease agreement at R3 000 per month for 10 years. This property was acquired on 1 January 20.2 at a cost of R400 000, of which R50 000 was attributable to the land and R350 000 to the building. On 1 February 20.6, the building was repainted at a cost of R8 000. The South African Revenue Service grants a 5% annual building allowance, not apportioned for part of a year, in respect of the property. The fair values of this property at the beginning and end of the current financial year were as follows:

	Rand
31 December 20.5	
Land	80 000
Building	405 000
31 December 20.6	
Land	87 000
Building	410 000

On 1 December 20.6 the company bought a piece of vacant land for R120 000. It is still uncertain what this land will be used for, but a decision regarding the matter will be taken early in the next financial year. On 28 December 20.6, R2 000 was spent to combat a sudden rat plague that broke out on this property. The fair value of this vacant land increased to R122 000 on 31 December 20.6.

The fair values of the above properties were determined by Mr Y. Manyana, an independent valuer who holds a recognised and relevant professional qualification and has recent experience in the location and category of the properties being valued. The valuer determined the fair value of these properties based on current prices in an active market for similar property in the same location and condition, and subject to similar lease and other contracts.

Where investment property is accounted for using the cost model; depreciation is provided for on the straight-line basis over 25 years with an RNil estimated residual value.

The company's profit before tax, after taking into account all the above information, amounted to R720 000.

Ignore VAT.

Assume the following:

- A normal tax rate of 30% and that 66.6% of capital gains realised by the company on disposal of property will be taxable.
- The costs of the respective assets at acquisition reflect their 'base cost' for capital gains tax purposes.
- All operating expenditure in respect of investment property is deductible for tax purposes.
- The depreciation method and estimates in respect of the useful life and residual value of the factory building remained unchanged throughout the period of ownership.
- Depreciable investment properties are not held within a business model whose objective is to consume substantially all the economic benefits embodied in the investment property over time.

Required

Provide the investment property, income tax, profit before taxation, deferred taxation and operating leases notes in the financial statements of Redge Ltd for the year ended 31 December 20.6, based respectively on the following assumptions:

a. Investment property is accounted for by applying the fair value model.
b. Investment property is accounted for by applying the cost model.

Your answer should comply with the requirements of International Financial Reporting Standards (IFRS). Comparative amounts are not required.

❑ QUESTION IAS 40.7

Slowjo Ltd owns an office block in Pretoria that is leased to Jojo Ltd in terms of a non-cancellable operating lease agreement. This office block was acquired on 1 January 20.1 for R750 000, of which R120 000 was attributable to the land and R630 000 to the building. On 31 December 20.2 the fair value of the land amounted to R155 000, and that of the building to R645 000. On 1 December 20.3, Slowjo Ltd began to use two offices, which comprise approximately 2% of the building's floor space, for its own purposes. It is the company's policy to depreciate owner-occupied office buildings on the straight-line basis over 20 years.

On 1 March 20.3 a piece of land was bought for which the future use has not yet been determined. This property is situated in Johannesburg. Transfer duties amounting to R10 000 were paid immediately. Although the seller of the property does not usually sell on credit, he agreed that Slowjo Ltd would only pay an amount of R95 000 for the land on 28 February 20.4.

On 1 July 20.3 the company bought an office building at an auction for R202 000 of which R120 000 was attributable to the land and R82 000 to the building. The reduced price resulted from the neglected state of the building. The management of Slowjo Ltd, however, felt that this building had good potential as it is situated close to the Centurion lake, and therefore decided to renovate the building and lease it to tenants as furnished offices. During the following month the building was repainted at a cost of R5 000, the carpets were replaced at a cost of R12 000, and broken tiles were replaced at a cost of R7 500. On 1 August 20.3 the furniture for the offices was bought for R42 000, after which the tenants moved in.

A valuer supplied the following fair values on 31 December 20.3:

	Rand
Land in Pretoria (market price)	159 000
Building in Pretoria (market price)	652 000
Land in Johannesburg (market price)	98 000
Land in Centurion (market price)	120 000
Building in Centurion (discounted lease payments)	150 000

Costs of approximately 10% of the fair values will have to be incurred to dispose of the properties.

The company accounts for investment properties according to the fair value model. Furniture is depreciated over eight years on the straight-line basis.

The South African Revenue Service allows wear and tear on furniture at 10% per annum on the straight-line basis.

A fair discount rate before tax is 10% per annum, compounded annually.

Assume the following:

- A normal tax rate of 30% and that 66.6% of capital gains will be taxable.
- The actual cost price paid for the land reflects its 'base cost' for capital gains tax purposes.

- Depreciable investment properties are not held within a business model whose objective is to consume substantially all the economic benefits embodied in the investment property over time.

Required

a. Calculate the fair value adjustment on investment property for the year ended 31 December 20.3.
b. Calculate deferred tax in the statement of profit or loss and other comprehensive income (profit or loss) for the year ended 31 December 20.3.
c. Disclose the reconciliation between the carrying amount of investment property at the beginning and end of the year ended 31 December 20.3 in the investment property note. Comparative amounts are not required.

Your answer must comply with the requirements of International Financial Reporting Standards (IFRS).

❑ QUESTION IAS 40.8#

On 1 July 20.4, a new factory property was acquired by Invest Ltd at a total cost of R1 200 000, of which R250 000 was attributable to the land and the rest (R950 000) to the buildings. Subsequently it was decided to lease the previously used property to a manufacturing company from that date onwards in terms of an operating lease agreement, at a monthly rental of R5 000. This property was purchased on 1 January 20.0 at a cost of R80 000 for the land and R500 000 for the buildings. On 1 July 20.4 the fair value of this property amounted to R690 000, of which R110 000 was attributable to the land and R580 000 to the buildings. Owing to the good location of the property the fair value increased to R115 000 for the land and R590 000 for the buildings by 31 December 20.4.

During 20.2, the company acquired vacant land for R100 000 with an original intention to hold it for long-term capital appreciation. However, in the previous financial year the company commenced with the construction of a factory building on this vacant land with the purpose of leasing the factory building to a manufacturer once construction was completed. The construction expenses for the factory building were incurred as follows on the following dates:

30 September 20.3 – payment of R50 000 to contractor
31 December 20.3 – payment of R35 000 to contractor
31 July 20.4 – final payment of R40 000 to contractor

At 31 December 20.2 and 31 December 20.3, the fair value of this vacant land amounted to R125 000 and R135 000 respectively. At 31 December 20.3 the fair value of the factory building under construction amounted to R85 000.

From 1 August 20.4, the property was leased out in terms of an operating lease agreement at R2 000 per month. At 31 December 20.4 the fair value of these land and buildings amounted to R140 000 and R145 000 respectively.

It is the company's policy to account for property, plant and equipment using the cost model, while investment property is accounted for using the fair value model.

Depreciation on buildings is provided for on the straight-line basis over 25 years with residual values estimated at RNil.

The company regards a revaluation surplus as realised when the underlying asset is sold or withdrawn from use.

The profit before tax, after taking into account all the information above, amounts to R800 000.

The South African Revenue Service grants an annual building allowance of 5%, not apportioned for part of the year.

Assume the following:

- A normal tax rate of 30% and that 66.6% of capital gains realised by the company on disposal of property will be taxable.
- Depreciable investment properties are held within a business model whose objective is to consume substantially all the economic benefits embodied in the investment property over time.
- The costs of the respective assets at acquisition reflect their 'base cost' for capital gains tax purposes.
- The depreciation method and estimates of the useful life and residual values of the buildings have remained unchanged even on the date of change in use as well as throughout the period of ownership.

Required

a. Disclose the following notes of Invest Ltd for the year ended 31 December 20.4:
   - Property, plant and equipment
   - Investment property
   - Profit before tax
b. Calculate the deferred tax expense in the statement of profit or loss and other comprehensive income (profit or loss) for the year ended 31 December 20.4.
c. Disclose the income tax expense note to the statement of profit or loss and other comprehensive income (profit or loss) for the year ended 31 December 20.4.

Your answer must comply with the requirements of International Financial Reporting Standards (IFRS). Comparative amounts are not required.

❑ QUESTION IAS 40.9

On 1 January 20.1, H Ltd acquired an 80% interest in S Ltd. On the same day S Ltd bought land with factory buildings on it for R1 300 000, of which R500 000 was attributable to the land. These buildings have a useful life of 25 years. The property was immediately leased to H Ltd at a market-related rental. The fair value of the property on 31 December 20.1 was R1 400 000 (R540 000 i.r.o. land) and on 31 December 20.2 it was R1 550 000 (R600 000 i.r.o. land). The group accounts for property, plant and equipment according to the cost model in terms of IAS 16, while the fair value model is used for investment property.

The South African Revenue Service grants a 5% annual allowance on the factory buildings, not apportioned for part of a year.

Assume the following:

- A normal tax rate of 27% and that 50% of capital gains are taxable.
- Depreciable investment properties are held within a business model whose objective is to consume substantially all the economic benefits embodied in the investment property over time.
- The cost of the land and buildings on acquisition reflect their 'base cost' for capital gains tax purposes.

Required

a. Prepare the consolidation journal(s) required in respect of the above-mentioned property on 31 December 20.2. Ignore deferred tax.

b. Prepare the consolidation journal(s) required in respect of deferred tax on 31 December 20.2.

Your answer must comply with the requirements of International Financial Reporting Standards (IFRS).

IFRS 2

Share-based payment

❑ QUESTIONS AND SOLUTIONS

IFRS 2.1	Basic equity-settled and cash-settled share-based payment, cancellation: journal entries
IFRS 2.2	Share appreciation rights: journal entries
IFRS 2.3	Choice transaction accounted for as equity-settled share-based payment: journal entries

❑ QUESTIONS

IFRS 2.4	Choice transaction accounted for as cash-settled share-based payment: journal entries
IFRS 2.5[#]	Equity-settled and cash-settled share-based payment – market conditions, non-market conditions, repricing and group statements: classification and accounting treatment discussion and journal entries
IFRS 2.6	Equity-settled share-based payment: measurement discussion
IFRS 2.7[#]	Modified equity-settled share-based payment transaction that has been incorrectly recorded as a cash-settled share-based payment transaction: correcting journal entries
IFRS 2.8[@]	Equity-settled share-based payment arrangement of a subsidiary acquired in a business combination – acquirer did not replace the share-based payment arrangement: presentation of non-controlling interest in the statement of changes in equity

[@] *This question contains topics or principles that were not included in the ITC syllabus of SAICA at the time of publishing this book but might still be included in university syllabi.*

[#] *These questions contain topics or principles that were at an awareness level of proficiency in the ITC syllabus of SAICA at the time of publishing this book.*

❑ QUESTION IFRS 2.1

Colorado Ltd grants 10 000 rights to each of its three directors on the condition that the directors stay in the employment of Colorado Ltd for three years.

During year 2, one of the directors resigned.

The fair values of a right are as follows:

	Rand
Grant date	10,00
End of year 1	11,00
End of year 2	12,00
End of year 3	13,00

Required

Provide the journal entries in the records of Colorado Ltd over the three-year vesting period under each of the following assumptions:

a. The rights are options to ordinary shares in Colorado Ltd.
b. The rights are rights to a cash payment based on the share price of Colorado Ltd.
c. The rights are options to ordinary shares in Colorado Ltd, but the grant is cancelled at the end of year 2 in exchange for cash compensation of R13,50 per option paid to each director. The director who resigned did so before the cancellation.

Your answers must comply with International Financial Reporting Standards (IFRS). Ignore taxation.

❖ Suggested solution IFRS 2.1

a.

	Rand Dr/(Cr)
Year 1	
Directors' remuneration (P or L) (1)	100 000
Share-based payment reserve (Equity)	(100 000)
Recognition of equity-settled share-based payment in the first year of the vesting period	
Year 2	
Directors' remuneration (P or L) (2)	33 333
Share-based payment reserve (Equity)	(33 333)
Recognition of equity-settled share-based payment in the second year of the vesting period	
Year 3	
Directors' remuneration (P or L) (3)	66 667
Share-based payment reserve (Equity)	(66 667)
Recognition of equity-settled share-based payment in the third year of the vesting period	

(1) 10 000 × 3 × R10 × 1/3 = 100 000
(2) (10 000 × 2 × R10 × 2/3) – 100 000 = 33 333
(3) (10 000 × 2 × R10 × 3/3) – 100 000 – 33 333 = 66 667

b.

	Rand Dr/(Cr)
Year 1	
Directors' remuneration (P or L) (1)	110 000
Cash-settled share-based payment liability (SFPos)	(110 000)
Recognition of cash-settled share-based payment in the first year of the vesting period	
Year 2	
Directors' remuneration (P or L) (2)	50 000
Cash-settled share-based payment liability (SFPos)	(50 000)
Recognition of cash-settled share-based payment in the second year of the vesting period	
Year 3	
Directors' remuneration (P or L) (3)	100 000
Cash-settled share-based payment liability (SFPos)	(100 000)
Recognition of cash-settled share-based payment in the third year of the vesting period	

(1) 10 000 × 3 × R11 × 1/3 = 110 000
(2) (10 000 × 2 × R12 × 2/3) – 110 000 = 50 000
(3) (10 000 × 2 × R13 × 3/3) – 110 000 – 50 000 = 100 000

c.

	Rand Dr/(Cr)
Year 1	
Directors' remuneration (P or L) (1)	100 000
Share-based payment reserve (Equity)	(100 000)
Recognition of equity-settled share-based payment in the first year of the vesting period	
Year 2	
Directors' remuneration (P or L) (2)	100 000
Share-based payment reserve (Equity)	(100 000)
Accelerated vesting of the equity-settled share-based payment upon cancellation of the grant in the second year of the vesting period	
Share-based payment reserve (Equity) (3)	200 000
Directors' remuneration (P or L) (4)	30 000
Retained earnings (5)	40 000
Bank (6)	(270 000)
Buy-back of rights upon cancellation of the grant	

(1) 10 000 × 3 × R10 × 1/3 = 100 000
(2) (10 000 × 2 × R10 × 3/3) – 100 000 = 100 000
(3) 100 000 + 100 000 = 200 000 (balance of reserve end year 2 bought back)

(4) (13,50 – 12) × 10 000 × 2 = 30 000 (excess payment above fair value recognised as an expense)

(5) (12 – 10) × 10 000 × 2 = 40 000 (payment above balance of reserve up to fair value is also treated as a buy-back of equity; retained earnings are adjusted because the share-based payment reserve is already extinguished)

(6) 13,50 × 10 000 × 2 = 270 000

❑ QUESTION IFRS 2.2

On 1 January 20.7, Maine Ltd granted 20 share appreciation rights to each of its 400 employees. The rights entitle the employee to receive a cash payment equal to the intrinsic value of the rights on the exercise date. Only the employees in the company's employ on 1 January 20.7 are entitled to the grant, and the rights will vest after the rendering of two years of service.

In 20.7, five employees resigned, and three new employees were appointed. It was anticipated that a further two employees would resign in 20.8. In 20.8, four employees resigned, and one new employee was appointed. On 31 December 20.8, 60% of the employees exercised their rights.

The following information is relevant:

	Fair value per right Rand	Maine Ltd share price Rand	Strike price of rights* Rand
1 January 20.7	65	81	20
31 December 20.7	60	77	20
31 December 20.8	57	75	20

* The employee, therefore, 'pays' the strike price but also 'receives' a cash payment equal to the Maine Ltd share price.

Required

Provide the journal entries in the records of Maine Ltd for the year ended 31 December 20.8. Your answer must comply with International Financial Reporting Standards (IFRS). Ignore taxation.

❖ Suggested solution IFRS 2.2

	Rand Dr/(Cr)
31 December 20.8	
Employee benefits expense (P or L) (1)	200 556
Cash-settled share-based payment liability	(200 556)
Recognition of share-based payment in the second year of the vesting period	
Cash-settled share-based payment liability (1)	258 060
Bank	(258 060)
Cash payment to employees that exercised their rights	

(1)	20.8 expense:	
	Rights not yet exercised ((400 – 5 – 4) × 20 × 57* × 40%)	178 296
	Rights exercised ((400 – 5 – 4) × 20 × (75 – 20)* × 60%)	258 060
		436 356
	Less: 20.7 cumulative ((400 – 5 – 2) × 20 × 60 × 1/2)	(235 800)
	20.8 expense	200 556

Alternative calculation:

(1)	20.8 expense:	
	Opening balance: 20.7 cumulative ((400 – 5 – 2) × 20 × 60 × 1/2)	235 800
	Less: Rights exercised ((400 – 5 – 4) × 20 × (75 – 20)* × 60%)	(258 060)
	Adjusted carrying amount	(21 260)
	Closing balance: Rights not yet exercised ((400 – 5 – 4) × 20 × 57* × 40%)	178 296
	20.8 expense	200 556

* The fair value of the rights not yet exercised differs from the fair value of the rights exercised. The fair value of the rights exercised equals their intrinsic value (share price less strike price) because time value no longer plays a role when the rights are exercised.

❑ QUESTION IFRS 2.3

On 1 July 20.6, Delaware Ltd granted one of its managers the right to receive a cash payment equal to the value of 10 000 shares or 11 000 actual shares in the company. The settlement date is 30 June 20.9 on the condition that the company still employs the manager at that stage. The company has the right to choose the method of settlement. If the company chooses to settle in shares, the shares must be held for two years after the vesting date.

The fair value of Delaware Ltd is determined every year by a reputable firm of appraisers. The following fair values per share were determined:

1 July 20.6	R30
30 June 20.7	R31
30 June 20.8	R35
30 June 20.9	R40

The value of the shares to be issued in terms of the grant was R27 per share on the grant date (lower than the share price due to the vesting conditions). On 30 June 20.9, the company decided on a settlement in shares. Due to the post-vesting transfer condition, the fair value of the issued shares amounted to R38 per share on 30 June 20.9.

Delaware Ltd has no legal or constructive obligation to settle in cash.

Required

Provide the journal entries for the three years ended 30 June 20.7, 30 June 20.8 and 30 June 20.9 in the records of Delaware Ltd. Your answer must comply with International Financial Reporting Standards (IFRS). Ignore taxation.

❖ **Suggested solution IFRS 2.3**

	Rand Dr/(Cr)
30 June 20.7	
Employee benefits expense (P or L) (1)	99 000
Share-based payment reserve (Equity)	(99 000)
Recognition of share-based payment in the first year of the vesting period	
30 June 20.8	
Employee benefits expense (P or L) (2)	99 000
Share-based payment reserve (Equity)	(99 000)
Recognition of share-based payment in the second year of the vesting period	
30 June 20.9	
Employee benefits expense (P or L) (3)	99 000
Share-based payment reserve (Equity)	(99 000)
Recognition of share-based payment in the third year of the vesting period	
Employee benefits expense (P or L) (4)	18 000
Share-based payment reserve (Equity)	(18 000)
Recognition of additional expense because the alternative with the higher fair value is chosen	
Share-based payment reserve (Equity) (5)	315 000
Share capital	(315 000)
Issuing of shares to the manager in terms of the grant	

(1) 11 000 × R27 × 1/3 = 99 000
(2) (11 000 × R27 × 2/3) – 99 000 = 99 000
(3) (11 000 × R27 × 3/3) – 99 000 – 99 000 = 99 000
(4) (11 000 × R38) – (10 000 × R40) = 18 000
(5) (99 000 × 3) + 18 000 = 315 000

❑ **QUESTION IFRS 2.4**

On 1 July 20.0, Energex Ltd granted each of its 200 employees the right to receive either 1 200 Energex Ltd ordinary shares or a cash payment equal to the actual market price of 1 000 Energex Ltd ordinary shares, upon condition that they remain in the employ of Energex Ltd for three years from the grant date. Energex Ltd can choose how the arrangement will be settled but has a past established practice of settling in cash. However, should Energex Ltd chooses to settle in shares, the shares must be held for at least one year after the vesting date. During the year ended 30 June 20.1, 10 employees resigned, and it was expected that another seven would resign in the two years to follow. During the year ended 30 June 20.2, five employees resigned, and it is expected that another four will resign during the next year.

The following information applies to the shares of Energex Ltd:

	Fair value of shares in terms of this specific grant*	Actual market share price
1 July 20.0	R10	R12
30 June 20.1	R14	R15
30 June 20.2	R12	R13

* The fair value is lower than the actual share price due to post-vesting share transfer restrictions imposed through the conditions of this grant.

Required

Provide the journal entries of the share-based payment scheme in the records of Energex Ltd for the year ended 30 June 20.2 to comply with the requirements of International Financial Reporting Standards (IFRS). Ignore taxation.

❑ QUESTION IFRS 2.5#

Detroit Ltd is a company that manufactures and sells cars in South Africa. Many years ago, Detroit Ltd acquired a 75% interest in Phoenix Ltd, a company that also manufactures cars and sells its products across the country. Both companies are listed on the JSE Ltd and have a 31 December financial year-end.

On 1 January 20.0, Phoenix Ltd granted 20 000 options to ordinary shares in Detroit Ltd to each of its four divisional managers. Phoenix Ltd independently initiated the scheme. All the managers accepted the grant. The grant is, however, subject to the following conditions:

- Condition 1: Each manager should remain in the company's employment for at least three years from when the options were granted.
- Condition 2: The company's share price should exceed R30 per share at the end of the three years.
- Condition 3: During each of the three years, the divisional sales that each manager is responsible for should increase by at least 6% compared to the immediately preceding year. The moment this does not happen, the manager loses the full grant.

The expectation is that no manager will leave the company's employment before the options vest. It is, however, expected that only three of the four managers will comply with Condition 3. On 31 December 20.1, the divisional managers were also worried that the share price of Phoenix Ltd might not reach the R30 per share requirement on 31 December 20.2.

Due to a decrease in the share price, the company decided to reprice the options on 30 June 20.1. The immediate change in fair value of the option due to repricing was R5 on 30 June 20.1.

Other information relating to the fair value of the options follows:

	Exercise price (strike price)	Fair value taking into account the share price condition	Fair value not taking into account the share price condition
	Rand/option	Rand/option	Rand/option
1 January 20.0	30,00	18,00	19,00
31 December 20.0	30,00	14,00	14,50
30 June 20.1	30,00 repriced to 24,00	13,00 (without repricing)	13,50 (without repricing)
31 December 20.1	24,00	12,00	13,00

It is group policy to reclassify any equity originating from share-based payment transactions to retained earnings if market conditions are not satisfied on the vesting date.

Required

a. Discuss how the share-based payment transaction shall be classified in the financial statements of both Phoenix Ltd and the Detroit Ltd Group (consolidated financial statements).
b. Provide the journal entries to account for the share-based payment arrangement in the accounting records of Phoenix Ltd for the year ended 31 December 20.0 and 31 December 20.1.
c. Provide the pro forma consolidation journal entries to account for the share-based payment arrangement in the group's financial statements for the year ended 31 December 20.1. Ignore journals for non-controlling interest on the normal profit that pulls through from Phoenix Ltd's trial balance.
d. Briefly discuss how the accounting treatment would have differed if **Detroit Ltd** granted options to Detroit Ltd shares to the employees of Phoenix Ltd. Your answer must address the treatment for Detroit Ltd, Phoenix Ltd and the Detroit Ltd Group.

Your answers must comply with International Financial Reporting Standards (IFRS). Ignore taxation.

❑ QUESTION IFRS 2.6

The recently appointed head of finance of Masakhe Ltd, a construction company, proposed implementing a broad-based employee share ownership plan on 1 October 20.6. In terms of the proposal, Masakhe Ltd will issue 250 share options (one share option will entitle the holder thereof to one Masakhe Ltd share) to each of its employees, subject to the following conditions:

- A five-year service condition;
- A 15% increase in the earnings of Masakhe Ltd over the five years;
- The share price of Masakhe Ltd must double by 30 September 20.11; and
- The share option holder must pay a strike price of R70 per option to exercise an option.

The following reliably estimated fair values per option are available:

Date	Taking into account the possibility that the required 15% increase in the earnings of Masakhe Ltd is reached	Taking into account the possibility that the required 15% increase in the earnings of Masakhe Ltd is reached and that the share price of Masakhe Ltd doubles	Taking into account the possibility that the share price of Masakhe Ltd doubles
1 October 20.6	R144	R146	R145
31 December 20.6	R152	R154	R153

The Human Resources department provided the following estimated number of employees (to whom the share options were granted) to still be in the employ of Masakhe Ltd on 30 September 20.11:

Date	Number
1 October 20.6	510
31 December 20.6	490

Required

Draft an e-mail to be sent to the board of directors of Masakhe Ltd in which you explain the correct measurement of the employee benefit expense to be disclosed in the profit before taxation note of Masakhe Ltd for the year ended 31 December 20.6.

❑ QUESTION IFRS 2.7#

On 1 July 20.2, Bourke (Pty) Ltd implemented a Broad-Based Economic Empowerment share-based payment arrangement. In terms of the arrangement, share options were granted to all 102 of Bourke (Pty) Ltd's employees to compensate them (in addition to their current salaries) for services rendered, provided that the employee is still in the employ of Bourke (Pty) Ltd at 30 June 20.6 (on which date the options will vest). Employees will be given two years after the vesting date to exercise their options.

The terms and conditions of the share based payment arrangement further provided for the following:

- A performance condition also exists in terms of which the share options will only vest if Bourke (Pty) Ltd's profit after tax increases by more than 5% per year until 30 June 20.6;
- Each employee is entitled to 500 share options with an exercise price of R15 per share option; and
- When exercised, each share option will entitle the holder to one share in Bourke (Pty) Ltd.

The following projected profit after tax amounts were received from Bourke (Pty) Ltd's financial manager:

Year-end	June 20.2 Rand	June 20.3 Rand	June 20.4 Rand	June 20.5 Rand	June 20.6 Rand
Profit after tax	9 000 000	10 000 000	10 750 000	11 610 000	12 650 000

On 1 September 20.3, after months of ongoing strikes about wage disputes, Bourke (Pty) Ltd agreed to decrease the exercise price from R15 to R12,50 per share option. The vesting period remained unchanged.

The fair value per share option measured reliably on each date was as follows:

	Taking into account the possibility that the required profit after tax is reached		Without taking into account the possibility that the required profit after tax is reached	
Date	**Before being repriced**	**After being repriced**	**Before being repriced**	**After being repriced**
	Rand	**Rand**	**Rand**	**Rand**
1 July 20.2	4,50	Not applicable	5,00	Not applicable
30 June 20.3	13,50	Not applicable	15,00	Not applicable
1 September 20.3	27,50	38,50	30,00	41,00
30 June 20.4	46,50	55,50	50,00	59,00

The actual number of employees on each date, and the corresponding estimate of the number of employees (to whom the options were granted) to still be employed by Bourke (Pty) Ltd on 30 June 20.6, are as follows:

Date	**Actual**	**Estimate for 30 June 20.6**
1 July 20.2	102	93
30 June 20.3	97	88
1 September 20.3	85	80
30 June 20.4	80	70

You confirmed with the financial manager of Bourke (Pty) Ltd that the Broad-Based Economic Empowerment share-based payment arrangement had been accounted for as a cash-settled share-based payment transaction in the annual financial statements and draft pre-closing trial balance of Bourke (Pty) Ltd for the 20.3 and 20.4 financial years. The effect of the error effect is considered material, and no journal entries have yet been processed to correct the error.

Required

Based on the information provided, prepare the correcting journal entries necessary to accurately reflect the Broad-Based Economic Empowerment share-based payment arrangement in the books of Bourke (Pty) Ltd for the financial year ended 30 June 20.4. Ignore the effects of taxation arising from this transaction.

❑ QUESTION IFRS 2.8[@]

On 1 May 20.5, McNortan Ltd purchased an 80%-controlling interest in McWayne (Pty) Ltd representing a business combination as defined in IFRS 3. On the acquisition date, McWayne (Pty) Ltd had an active equity-settled share-based payment plan in terms of which share options were granted to its employees:

Grant date	Number of share options issued[1]	Service condition	Performance condition
1 January 20.5	100 per employee	Four years of completed service	25% increase in earnings over the four years

[1] One share option entitles the employee to one share of McWayne (Pty) Ltd.

McNortan Ltd did not replace McWayne (Pty) Ltd's share options with its own share options at the acquisition date. The fair value per share option measured reliably on each date was estimated as follows:

Date	Fair value per option per the McWayne (Pty) Ltd grant	
	Taking into account ...	Without taking into account ...
	... the possibility that the options will not vest if the required 25% increase in the earnings of McWayne (Pty) Ltd will not be reached	
1 January 20.5	R155,00	R157,00
1 May 20.5	R160,00	R162,00
31 December 20.5	R163,00	R165,00
31 December 20.6	R166,00	R167,50

The number of employees (that were granted the options) expected to still be in the employ of McWayne (Pty) Ltd when the options vest were estimated as follows:

Date	Employees[2]
1 January 20.5	150
1 May 20.5	153
31 December 20.5	149
31 December 20.6	152

[2] Subsequent changes in the estimated number of employees do not reflect circumstances that existed at the acquisition date.

It was expected that the required 25% increase in the earnings of McWayne (Pty) Ltd would be reached at all times.

Required

Prepare an extract of the non-controlling interest column in the consolidated statement of changes in equity of the McNortan Ltd Group for the year ended 31 December 20.6 as it relates to the share-based payment plan of McWayne (Pty) Ltd.

IFRS 3

Business combinations

Note: As this chapter and the chapter on IFRS 10 both deal with similar issues, the questions on these two chapters are integrated and such questions are presented as part of the chapter on IFRS 10.

IFRS 5

Non-current assets held for sale and discontinued operations

PART A: NON-CURRENT ASSETS HELD FOR SALE

❑ **QUESTIONS AND SOLUTIONS**

PART B: DISCONTINUED OPERATIONS

❑ **QUESTIONS AND SOLUTIONS**

❑ **QUESTIONS**

PART A: NON-CURRENT ASSETS HELD FOR SALE

❑ QUESTION IFRS 5.1

Sally Ltd owns a machine with a carrying amount of R150 000 on 31 December 20.3. On this date management decided to sell the machine for R160 000 (fair value) by 28 February 20.4 and a non-cancellable contract was entered into with a buyer. Costs in respect of the sales transaction will amount to R15 000. Assume that all the criteria of IFRS 5 for the classification of the asset as a non-current asset held for sale, have been met on 31 December 20.3.

Required

a. Determine the amount at which the machine should be presented in the statement of financial position as at 31 December 20.3.
b. Discuss the classification and measurement of the machine at 31 December 20.3.

Your answer must comply with the requirements of International Financial Reporting Standards (IFRS).

❖ Suggested solution IFRS 5.1

a. Amount presented in statement of financial position	**Rand**
Carrying amount of machine at 31 December 20.3	150 000
Fair value less costs to sell at 31 December 20.3 (1)	145 000
Amount presented in statement of financial position (lower of the two)	145 000

(1) 160 000 – 15 000 = 145 000

b. The machine met all the criteria of IFRS 5 for classification as a non-current asset held for sale on 31 December 20.3. The machine should therefore be transferred from non-current assets to current assets (non-current assets held for sale) and should then be measured at the lower of its carrying amount and fair value less costs to sell (IFRS 5.15). The 'held-for-sale' machine will thus be written down from R150 000 to R145 000 and an impairment loss of R5 000 will be recognised in profit or loss for 20.3.

❑ QUESTION IFRS 5.2

On 1 January 20.2 (beginning of the year), Charly Ltd owns a vehicle with an original cost price of R200 000 and accumulated depreciation of R40 000. Charly Ltd writes off depreciation on vehicles at 10% per annum in accordance with the straight-line method.

On 30 April 20.2, management decided to dispose of the vehicle within the next year and all the criteria of IFRS 5 for the classification of the asset as held for sale were met on this date. The fair value less costs to sell of the vehicle amounted to R125 000 on 30 April 20.2. At 31 December 20.2 (reporting date) the vehicle had not been sold yet and the fair value less costs to sell remained unchanged.

Required

a. List all the criteria set out in IFRS 5 which must be met before a non-current asset can be classified as held for sale.

b. Calculate the amount that must be presented under 'Non-current assets classified as held for sale' in the statement of financial position of Charly Ltd as at 31 December 20.2 as well as the amount of the impairment loss (if any) that must be recognised in profit or loss in respect of the asset for the year ended 31 December 20.2.

Your answer must comply with the requirements of International Financial Reporting Standards (IFRS).

❖ **Suggested solution IFRS 5.2**

a. The criteria that must be met before a non-current asset can be classified as held for sale

- An entity shall classify a non-current asset (or disposal group) as held for sale if its carrying amount will be recovered principally through a sale transaction rather than through continuing use (IFRS 5.6).
- For this to be the case, the asset (or disposal group) must be available for immediate sale in its present condition subject only to terms that are usual and customary for the sale of such assets (or disposal group) and its sale must be highly probable (IFRS 5.7).
- For the sale to be highly probable (IFRS 5.8):
  - The appropriate level of management must be committed to a plan to sell the asset (or disposal group) and an active programme to locate a buyer and complete the plan must have been initiated.
  - The asset (or disposal group) must be actively marketed for sale at a price that is reasonable in relation to its current fair value.
  - The sale should be expected to qualify for recognition as a completed sale within one year from date of classification, unless acceptable grounds for extending the period, as set out in IFRS 5.9, exist.
  - Actions required to complete the plan should indicate that it is unlikely that significant changes to the plan will be made or that the plan will be withdrawn.
  - The probability of shareholders' approval (if applicable) should be considered.

b. Carrying amount at 30 April 20.2	**Rand**
Carrying amount at 1 January 20.2 (1)	160 000
Depreciation up to 30 April 20.2 (2)	(6 667)
Carrying amount at 30 April 20.2	153 333
Fair value less costs to sell (given)	(125 000)
Impairment loss recognised in profit or loss	28 333

(1) 200 000 – 40 000 = 160 000
(2) 200 000 × 10% × 4/12 = 6 667

A non-current asset classified as held for sale must be measured at the lower of its carrying amount and fair value less costs to sell (IFRS 5.15). The vehicle will therefore be presented at R125 000 under 'Non-current assets classified as held for sale' in the statement of financial position as at 31 December 20.2.

❑ QUESTION IFRS 5.3

Howzit Ltd owns a number of assets, including the below-mentioned items. The two items do not form part of a disposal group.

- Investment property carried at fair value of R760 000 on 1 January 20.3 (beginning of the year). The fair value of the investment property is R780 000 on 30 June 20.3, while costs to sell the property amount to R25 000 on that date. These amounts remained unchanged at reporting date.
- Machinery with a cost price of R300 000 and a carrying amount of R180 000 on 1 January 20.3. The machinery is depreciated at 10% per annum in accordance with the straight-line method. The fair value less costs to sell of the machinery amounts to R155 000 on 30 June 20.3 and remained unchanged at reporting date.

On 30 June 20.3, management decided to dispose of the above-mentioned assets within the next year. All the criteria of IFRS 5 for the classification of the assets as non-current assets held for sale, were met on 30 June 20.3. At 31 December 20.3 (reporting date), the assets had not been sold yet.

Required

Calculate the amount that must be presented as 'Non-current assets classified as held for sale' in the statement of financial position of Howzit Ltd as at 31 December 20.3.

Your answer must comply with the requirements of International Financial Reporting Standards (IFRS).

❖ Suggested solution IFRS 5.3

Amount presented as non-current assets held for sale	**Rand**
Machinery (calc 1)	155 000
Investment property (calc 2)	780 000
	935 000

Calculations

1. Machinery	**Rand**
Carrying amount at 1 January 20.3	180 000
Depreciation up to 30 June 20.3 (1)	(15 000)
Carrying amount at 30 June 20.3	165 000
Fair value less costs to sell (given)	(155 000)
Impairment loss recognised in profit or loss	10 000

(1) 300 000 × 10% × 6/12 = 15 000

A non-current asset classified as held for sale must be measured at the lower of its carrying amount and fair value less costs to sell (IFRS 5.15). The machinery will therefore be presented at R155 000 under 'Non-current assets classified as held for sale' in the statement of financial position as at 31 December 20.3.

2. Investment property

Investment property accounted for in accordance with the fair value model of IAS 40, falls outside the measurement scope of IFRS 5 and should, after classification as held for sale, still be measured in accordance with its applicable IFRS (IFRS 5.2).

The investment property classified as held for sale shall consequently be measured at its fair value of R780 000 and the new carrying amount of R780 000 (fair value) will not be compared to the fair value less costs to sell of R755 000 (1).

(1) 780 000 – 25 000 = 755 000

❑ QUESTION IFRS 5.4

Darana Ltd has a 28 February reporting date and decided on 30 November 20.4, to dispose of a disposal group within the next 12 months. All the criteria of IFRS 5 for the disposal group to be classified as held for sale have been met on 30 November 20.4. The carrying amounts of the items included in the disposal group are as follows:

- Land (at 1 March 20.4)
  Carrying amount R100 000

- Factory building (at 1 March 20.4)
  Carrying amount R600 000 (depreciation: reducing balance at 5% per annum)

- Plant (at 1 March 20.4)
  Carrying amount R250 000 (depreciation: reducing balance at 15% per annum)

- Inventories (at 30 November 20.4)
  Cost price R60 000 (net realisable value: R50 000)

- Trade and other payables (at 30 November 20.4) R30 000

- Share investments (at 30 November 20.4)
  Fair value R100 000

Additional information

1. The fair value less costs to sell of the disposal group amounted to R980 000 on 30 November 20.4. Other costs associated with selling the disposal group were as follows:

	Rand
• Capital gains tax on sale of disposal group	50 000
• Finance costs	5 000

2. The share investments are accounted for at fair value through profit or loss.

Required

a. Determine the amount of the impairment loss, if any, that will be recognised in respect of the disposal group of Darana Ltd on 30 November 20.4.
b. Allocate the impairment loss to the individual items in the disposal group on 30 November 20.4.

Your answer must comply with the requirements of International Financial Reporting Standards (IFRS).

❖ **Suggested solution IFRS 5.4**

a. Impairment loss in respect of disposal group

	Rand
Land at cost	100 000
Factory building (1)	577 500
Plant (2)	221 875
Inventories (net realisable value since lower than cost)	50 000
Trade and other payables	(30 000)
Share investments (fair value)	100 000
Carrying amount of disposal group at 30 November 20.4	1 019 375
Fair value less costs to sell of disposal group at 30 November 20.4 (3)	980 000
Impairment loss	39 375

(1) 600 000 – (600 000 × 5% × 9/12) = 577 500
(2) 250 000 – (250 000 × 15% × 9/12) = 221 875
(3) Finance costs and tax are specifically excluded from costs to sell i.t.o. Appendix A to IFRS 5.

Note: The carrying amount of all assets and liabilities in the disposal group must, immediately before classification as held for sale, be measured in accordance with the applicable IFRSs (IFRS 5.18). Thereafter, the disposal group as a whole will be remeasured at the lower of carrying amount and fair value less costs to sell (IFRS 5.15).

b. Allocation of impairment loss

The impairment loss is only allocated to non-current assets that fall within the measurement scope of IFRS 5 and the allocation will be done in accordance with IAS 36 (IFRS 5.23).

Total carrying amount of non-current assets that fall within the measurement scope of IFRS 5:

	Rand
Land	100 000
Factory building	577 500
Plant	221 875
	899 375

Allocation	**Carrying amount on date of classification Rand**	**Impairment loss allocated Rand**	**Carrying amount after impairment loss Rand**
Land (1)	100 000	4 378	95 622
Factory building (2)	577 500	25 283	552 217
Plant (3)	221 875	9 714	212 161
Inventories	50 000	–	50 000
Trade and other payables	(30 000)	–	(30 000)
Share investments	100 000	–	100 000
	1 019 375	39 375	980 000

(1) 39 375 × 100 000/899 375 = 4 378
(2) 39 375 × 577 500/899 375 = 25 283
(3) 39 375 × 221 875/899 375 = 9 714

❑ QUESTION IFRS 5.5

Smart Talk Ltd has a disposal group that was classified as held for sale on 30 September 20.4. On date of classification, an impairment loss of R49 000 was recognised in accordance with IFRS 5 in respect of the disposal group. No impairment losses were previously recognised in accordance with IAS 36 in respect of any of the assets in the disposal group.

On 30 September 20.4 the carrying amounts of the items included in the disposal group (after recognition of the impairment loss) were as follows:

Carrying amounts at 30 September 20.4	**Rand**
Land	98 000
Factory building (depreciation: reducing balance at 5% per annum)	450 000
Plant (depreciation: reducing balance at 10% per annum)	190 000
Inventories	80 000
Trade and other payables	(30 000)
Share investments	100 000
	888 000

The following information was applicable at 31 December 20.4 (reporting date):

- The net realisable value of inventory amounted to R50 000.
- R15 000 in respect of trade and other payables as at 30 September 20.4, was repaid.
- The fair value of share investments increased with R20 000.
- The fair value of the disposal group amounted to R985 000 at 31 December 20.4, while costs associated with the sale amounted to R30 000.

Required

a. Calculate the amount of the impairment loss or reversal of impairment loss (if any) that should be recognised in respect of the disposal group of Smart Talk Ltd on 31 December 20.4.

b. Allocate the impairment loss/(reversal) to the individual assets in the disposal group on 31 December 20.4.

Your answer must comply with the requirements of International Financial Reporting Standards (IFRS).

❖ **Suggested solution IFRS 5.5**

a. Impairment loss/reversal

	Rand
Land	98 000
Factory building (1)	450 000
Plant (1)	190 000
Inventories (at net realisable value since lower than cost)	50 000
Trade and other payables (2)	(15 000)
Share investments (3)	120 000
Revised carrying amount of disposal group at 31 December 20.4	893 000
Fair value less costs to sell of disposal group at 31 December 20.4 (4)	955 000
Gain on remeasurement to fair value less costs to sell	62 000

Reversal of impairment loss is limited to impairment losses previously recognised in accordance with IAS 36 and IFRS 5 i.r.o. non-current assets in the disposal group (IFRS 5.22).

Therefore, impairment loss reversed	49 000

(1) Depreciation must be ceased after classification as held for sale (IFRS 5.25).
(2) 30 000 – 15 000 = 15 000
(3) 100 000 + 20 000 = 120 000
(4) 985 000 – 30 000 = 955 000

b. Allocation of reversal of impairment loss

	Rand
Land (1)	6 507
Factory building (2)	29 878
Plant (3)	12 615
	49 000

(1) 49 000 × 98 000/(98 000 + 450 000 + 190 000) = 6 507
(2) 49 000 × 450 000/(98 000 + 450 000 + 190 000) = 29 878
(3) 49 000 × 190 000/(98 000 + 450 000 + 190 000) = 12 615

❑ **QUESTION IFRS 5.6**

On 1 March 20.5 (beginning of the year), Reggie Ltd classified a plant as held for sale since it met all the criteria of IFRS 5 for classification as a non-current asset held for sale on that date. On 1 March 20.5 the carrying amount of the plant, after classification as a non-current asset held for sale, amounted to R560 000. The original cost price of the plant was R800 000 on 1 December 20.3 and depreciation on plant is written off at 20% per annum in accordance with the straight-line method. No impairment losses were previously recognised in accordance with IAS 36 in respect of the plant.

Owing to an increased demand in Reggie Ltd's products, the directors decided on 30 June 20.5 to no longer dispose of the plant. On 30 June 20.5, the recoverable amount of the plant amounted to R555 000 and the remaining useful life of the plant was estimated to be 3,5 years.

Required

a. Calculate the amount at which the plant must be measured at 30 June 20.5 due to the decision to no longer sell the plant, as well as the adjustment to the carrying amount on that date.
b. Calculate the amount of depreciation to be recognised in respect of the plant for the year ended 28 February 20.6.

Your answer must comply with the requirements of International Financial Reporting Standards (IFRS).

❖ **Suggested solution IFRS 5.6**

a. Carrying amount at 30 June 20.5 and amount of adjustment

Since the asset is no longer classified as held for sale, the plant should be measured at the lower of what its carrying amount would have been had it never been classified as held for sale and its recoverable amount (IFRS 5.27).

Carrying amount of plant on 30 June 20.5 if the plant had never been classified as held for sale:

	Rand
Cost price – 1 December 20.3	800 000
Depreciation (800 000 × 20% × 3/12)	(40 000)
Carrying amount – 28 February 20.4	760 000
Depreciation (800 000 × 20%)	(160 000)
Carrying amount – 28 February 20.5	600 000
Depreciation (800 000 × 20% × 4/12)	(53 333)
Carrying amount – 30 June 20.5	546 667
Recoverable amount – 30 June 20.5	555 000

Therefore, measure at R546 667

Adjustment to existing carrying amount on 30 June 20.5:

	Rand
Carrying amount on 30 June 20.5	560 000
Carrying amount on 30 June 20.5 – no longer held for sale	546 667
Adjustment to carrying amount	13 333

b. Depreciation for the year ended 28 February 20.6

546 667/3,5 × 8/12 = R104 127

❑ QUESTION IFRS 5.7

On 28 February 20.5, City News Ltd decided to dispose of part of its assets and directly associated liabilities in order to focus on its core products. The disposal groups identified would normally form part of the production segment. It is expected that the actual sale of the assets and liabilities will take place during May 20.5. The assets and associated liabilities meet all the criteria of IFRS 5 to be classified as a disposal group held for sale. There are two disposal groups and the amounts presented are the carrying amounts at 28 February 20.5, **after** classification as held for sale and **after** related impairment losses:

	Additional information	**Disposal group 1 Rand**	**Disposal group 2 Rand**
Property, plant and equipment	1	4 900 000	1 700 000
Share investment at fair value through other comprehensive income	2	1 400 000	–
Liabilities	3	(2 400 000)	(900 000)
Net carrying amount of disposal group		3 900 000	800 000

Additional information

1. Impairment losses of R800 000 (Group 1 = R500 000 and Group 2 = R300 000) were recognised against plant and R200 000 (Group 1 = R140 000 and Group 2 = R60 000) against vehicles, to arrive at the carrying amounts reflected above. The major classes of assets are plant and vehicles with their respective carrying amounts of R5 280 000 and R1 320 000, after taking the impairment losses into account.

2. Since acquisition of the share investment, an amount of R400 000 (credit) has been recognised in other comprehensive income on remeasurement of the financial asset to fair value.

3. The liabilities comprise deferred tax of R400 000 for each disposal group and the remainder is long-term borrowings.

Required

Present the given information in the statement of financial position of City News Ltd as at 28 February 20.5 and prepare the 'Disposal group classified as held for sale' note that will accompany the statement of financial position of City News Ltd as at 28 February 20.5. Your answer must comply with the requirements of International Financial Reporting Standards (IFRS). No comparative amounts are required.

(UNISA – adapted)

❖ **Suggested solution IFRS 5.7**

CITY NEWS LTD
STATEMENT OF FINANCIAL POSITION AS AT 28 FEBRUARY 20.5

	Notes	20.5 Rand
ASSETS		
Non-current assets		X XXX XXX
Current assets		8 000 000
Non-current assets and disposal groups classified as held for sale (1)	2	8 000 000
Total assets		X XXX XXX
EQUITY AND LIABILITIES		
Total equity		X XXX XXX
Equity in respect of non-current assets and disposal groups classified as held for sale		400 000
Total liabilities		X XXX XXX
Non-current liabilities		X XXX XXX
Deferred tax (2)		800 000
Current liabilities		X XXX XXX
Liabilities in respect of disposal groups classified as held for sale (3)	2	2 500 000
Total equity and liabilities		XX XXX XXX

(1) 4 900 000 + 1 700 000 + 1 400 000 = 8 000 000
(2) 400 000 + 400 000 = 800 000
(3) (2 400 000 – 400 000) + (900 000 – 400 000) = 2 500 000

CITY NEWS LTD
NOTES FOR THE YEAR ENDED 28 FEBRUARY 20.5

2. Non-current assets and disposal groups classified as held for sale

A decision to dispose of two groups of assets and related liabilities was taken during February 20.5 with the objective to focus on the core products of the company. It is expected that the assets of the disposal groups will be sold for cash and that the disposal will be completed by the end of May 20.5. The disposal groups comprise the following:

	Rand
Assets	
Plant	5 280 000
Vehicles	1 320 000
Share investment	1 400 000
	8 000 000
Liabilities	
Long-term borrowings (4)	2 500 000
	2 500 000

(4) (2 400 000 – 400 000) + (900 000 – 400 000) = 2 500 000

A total impairment loss of R1 000 000 (5) was recognised on initial classification of the disposal group as held for sale and this amount is included in the 'Other expenses' line item in profit or loss. The disposal groups were previously reported as part of the production segment.

(5) 800 000 + 200 000 = 1 000 000

PART B: DISCONTINUED OPERATIONS

❑ QUESTION IFRS 5.8

Delta Ltd is a furniture distributor and obtains some of its products from a furniture factory which is operated as a department of the company. The furniture factory represents a single major line of business which operates independently and also maintains independent financial records.

Upon further investigation, it was found that the factory was not economical and that Delta Ltd could obtain the same products at a lower price from other existing suppliers. On 30 June 20.5, the board of directors formally decided to discontinue the factory operations and to sell the factory. A public announcement to this effect was made on the same day, after the approval of a disposal plan. The assets and associated liabilities of the factory operations were also classified as a disposal group held for sale on this date, since the assets and associated liabilities were available for immediate sale in their current condition and the sale was intended to be completed within one year. All the other criteria of IFRS 5 to classify the disposal group as held for sale, were also met on this date.

The following is the trial balance of the factory operations:

	A **Rand** **Dr/(Cr)**	**B** **Rand** **Dr/(Cr)**	**C** **Rand** **Dr/(Cr)**
Revenue	–	(600 000)	(1 000 000)
Cost of sales	–	560 000	900 000
Rent (short-term)	–	12 000	20 000
Salaries	8 000	21 000	62 000
Bad debts (credit losses)	15 000	2 000	3 000
Termination of short-term lease contract	2 500	–	–
Sundry expenses	–	14 000	18 000
Inventories written off	3 750	–	–
Trade and other payables	–	(65 000)	(95 000)
Trade receivables			
Delta Ltd	3 000	3 000	5 000
Other	–	82 000	70 000
Head office account	(33 250)	(69 000)	(33 000)
Bank	1 000	(35 000)	30 000
Inventories	–	75 000	20 000

A = **6 months to 31 December 20.5**
B = **6 months to 30 June 20.5**
C = **12 months to 31 December 20.4**

Delta Ltd did not have any inventories on hand that were purchased from the factory at the respective trial balance dates.

The reporting date of Delta Ltd is 31 December.

All income and expenses are taxable or tax deductible and the tax rate for 20.4 and 20.5 is 27%.

Required

a. Explain to the accountant of Delta Ltd whether the furniture factory qualifies as a discontinued operation and if so, from which date the results of the operation should be presented separately.
b. If it is assumed that the furniture factory is a discontinued operation, calculate the results of the discontinued operation that should be presented separately for the years ended 31 December 20.4 and 20.5. A complete statement of profit or loss and other comprehensive income is not required.

Your answer must comply with the requirements of International Financial Reporting Standards (IFRS).

❖ **Suggested solution IFRS 5.8**

a. Discontinued operation and initial disclosure event

In terms of IFRS 5.32, a discontinued operation is a component of an entity that either has been disposed of or is classified as held for sale, and:

- represents a separate major line of business or geographical area of operations;
- is part of a single coordinated plan to dispose of a separate major line of business or geographical area of operations; or
- is a subsidiary acquired exclusively with a view to sell.

In terms of IFRS 5.31, a component of an entity comprises operations and cash flows that can be clearly distinguished, operationally and for financial reporting purposes, from the rest of the entity.

The furniture factory therefore qualifies as a discontinued operation since:

- it is a component of the entity (it is operated independently and maintains independent financial records, therefore it can be clearly distinguished operationally and for financial reporting purposes from the rest of the entity);
- it was classified as held for sale (the furniture factory was classified as held for sale on 30 June 20.5); and
- it represents a separate major line of business (given).

The results of the discontinued operation should be presented separately from the date on which it was classified as held for sale or, if earlier, from the date of disposal.

In this case, the results of the furniture factory should be presented separately as from 30 June 20.5, which is the date of classification as held for sale.

Note: If the initial disclosure event occurs in the current financial year, the comparative amounts in the statement of profit or loss and other comprehensive income should be restated so that the **results** of the discontinued operation are also presented separately for the previous period (IFRS 5.34).

b. Results of the discontinued operation

	20.5 Rand	20.4 Rand
Revenue	600 000	1 000 000
Expenses	(638 250)	(1 003 000)
Cost of sales	560 000	900 000
Rent	12 000	20 000
Salaries (1)	29 000	62 000
Credit losses (2)	17 000	3 000
Termination costs	2 500	–
Inventories written off	3 750	–
Sundry expenses	14 000	18 000
Profit before tax	(38 250)	(3 000)
Tax benefit (27%)	10 328	810

(1) 8 000 + 21 000 = 29 000
(2) 15 000 + 2 000 = 17 000

Note: In this question there is no information regarding the fair value less costs to sell of the disposal group, therefore the disposal group could not be remeasured to its fair value less costs to sell. The after-tax profit or loss on the measurement of a disposal group or non-current asset held for sale to fair value less costs to sell as well as the after-tax profit or loss on disposal of assets or disposal groups that form part of the discontinued operation, will normally be included in the results of the discontinued operation.

❑ QUESTION IFRS 5.9

All the information of question IFRS 5.8 is applicable. The following is the statement of profit or loss and other comprehensive income of Delta Ltd for the years ended 31 December 20.4 and 20.5. The results of the factory operations are not included in the results for 20.5 as shown below. All factory inventories had been sold by the reporting date.

	20.5 Rand	20.4 Rand
Revenue	2 700 000	3 000 000
Cost of sales	(2 160 000)	(2 500 000)
Gross profit	540 000	500 000
Other expenses	(350 000)	(325 000)
Profit before tax	190 000	175 000
Income tax expense	(57 000)	(52 500)
Profit for the year	133 000	122 500
Other comprehensive income	–	–
Total comprehensive income for the year	133 000	122 500

Required

Prepare the statement of profit or loss and other comprehensive income of Delta Ltd for the year ended 31 December 20.5 in accordance with the requirements of International Financial Reporting Standards (IFRS). The analysis as required by IFRS 5 must be presented on the face of the statement of profit or loss and other comprehensive income and no notes are required.

❖ **Suggested solution IFRS 5.9**

DELTA LTD
STATEMENT OF PROFIT OR LOSS AND OTHER COMPREHENSIVE INCOME FOR THE YEAR ENDED 31 DECEMBER 20.5

	20.5 Rand	20.4 Rand
Continuing operations		
Revenue (1)	2 700 000	2 000 000
Cost of sales (2)	(2 160 000)	(1 600 000)
Gross profit	540 000	400 000
Other expenses (3)	(350 000)	(222 000)
Profit before tax	190 000	178 000
Income tax expense (4)	(57 000)	(53 310)
Profit for the year from continuing operations	133 000	124 690
Discontinued operations		
Revenue	600 000	1 000 000
Expenses	(638 250)	(1 003 000)
Profit before tax	(38 250)	(3 000)
Income tax benefit	10 328	810
Loss for the year from discontinued operations	(27 922)	(2 190)
Profit for the year	105 078	122 500
Other comprehensive income	–	–
Total comprehensive income for the year	105 078	122 500

(1) 20.5: Given
20.4: 3 000 000 – 1 000 000 = 2 000 000
(2) 20.5: Given
20.4: 2 500 000 – 900 000 = 1 600 000
(3) 20.5 Given
20.4: 325 000 – (20 000 + 62 000 + 3 000 + 18 000) = 222 000
(4) 20.5: Given
20.4: 52 500 + 810 = 53 310

Note: According to IFRS 5.33(a), an entity should present a single amount on the face of the statement of profit or loss and other comprehensive income, comprising the total of:

- the post-tax profit or loss of discontinued operations; and
- the post-tax gain or loss recognised on either the measurement to fair value less costs to sell or on the disposal of assets or disposal groups of the discontinued operations.

IFRS 5.33(b) also requires the following analysis of the single amount:

- the revenue, expenses and pre-tax profit or loss of the discontinued operation, as well as the related tax expense; and
- the gain or loss recognised on either the measurement to fair value less costs to sell or on the disposal of assets or disposal groups of the discontinued operation, as well as the related tax expense.

The analysis may be presented in the notes or on the face of the statement of profit or loss and other comprehensive income.

❑ QUESTION IFRS 5.10

The following is the statement of profit or loss and other comprehensive income of Golf Ltd for the year ended 31 December 20.8 (before any adjustments in respect of discontinued operations):

	20.8 Rand	20.7 Rand
Revenue	18 000 000	14 000 000
Cost of sales	(14 400 000)	(11 200 000)
Gross profit	3 600 000	2 800 000
Other expenses	(3 000 000)	(2 150 000)
Profit before tax	600 000	650 000
Income tax expense	(181 350)	(195 000)
Profit for the year	418 650	455 000
Other comprehensive income	–	–
Total comprehensive income for the year	418 650	455 000

Golf Ltd mainly operates in Gauteng and the Free State. On 1 October 20.8, the directors of Golf Ltd formally decided to discontinue and dispose of its distribution branch in KwaZulu-Natal and made a public announcement in this regard. On 1 October 20.8, a binding sales agreement was entered into with Yesplease Ltd in terms of which all the assets and related liabilities (excluding the head office account, bank overdraft and any provisions) of the KwaZulu-Natal branch would be transferred to Yesplease Ltd on 28 February 20.9. The assets and related liabilities of the KwaZulu-Natal branch that will be transferred to Yesplease Ltd met all the criteria of IFRS 5 to be classified as a disposal group held for sale on 1 October 20.8. Assume that the fair value less costs to sell of the disposal group was equal to the carrying amount thereof at all times. The KwaZulu-Natal branch was previously reported as part of the KwaZulu-Natal geographical segment.

The following is the trial balance of the KwaZulu-Natal branch:

	A Rand Dr/(Cr)	B Rand Dr/(Cr)	C Rand Dr/(Cr)	D Rand Dr/(Cr)
Revenue	(85 500)	(641 250)	(1 781 250)	(2 500 000)
Cost of sales	70 350	525 740	1 396 500	2 000 000
Other expenses	101 150	148 510	402 750	475 000
Inventories	65 000	120 000	414 000	463 000
Trade receivables	150 000	215 000	375 000	530 000
Trade and other payables	(115 000)	(235 000)	(589 000)	(593 000)
Bank	(77 000)	(88 000)	(198 000)	(411 000)
Property, plant and equipment (carrying amount and tax base)	1 325 000	1 325 000	1 325 000	1 375 000
Head office account	(1 419 000)	(1 355 000)	(1 345 000)	(1 339 000)

A = 1 January 20.9 – 28 February 20.9 (projected amounts)
B = 1 October 20.8 – 31 December 20.8
C = 1 January 20.8 – 30 September 20.8
D = 1 January 20.7 – 31 December 20.7

The following items that relate to the discontinuance are included in 'Other expenses' for the three months ended 31 December 20.8:

	Rand
Employee termination costs paid (tax deductible)	8 000
Penalty paid on cancellation of short-term lease agreements (not tax deductible)	4 500

Assume a tax rate of 27% for both 20.7 and 20.8.

Required

a. Discuss (with reasons) whether or not the discontinuance of Golf Ltd's operations in KwaZulu-Natal can be treated as a discontinued operation.
b. If it is assumed that the KwaZulu-Natal branch is a discontinued operation, prepare the statement of profit or loss and other comprehensive income as well as the 'Disposal group classified as held for sale' note of Golf Ltd for the year ended 31 December 20.8. The analysis required by IFRS 5 must be presented on the face of the statement of profit or loss and other comprehensive income and no other notes are required.

Your answer must comply with the requirements of International Financial Reporting Standards (IFRS).

❖ **Suggested solution IFRS 5.10**

a. Identification of discontinued operation

The KwaZulu-Natal branch consists of operations and cash flows that can clearly be distinguished operationally and for financial reporting purposes from the rest of the entity. It is therefore a component of Golf Ltd's business that was classified as held for sale and:

- represents a separate geographical area of operations; and
- is part of a single coordinated plan to dispose of a separate geographical area of operations.

The branch therefore meets the requirements of IFRS 5.31 and IFRS 5.32 and hence can be treated as a discontinued operation.

b. Presentation in the statement of profit or loss and other comprehensive income

GOLF LTD
STATEMENT OF PROFIT OR LOSS AND OTHER COMPREHENSIVE INCOME FOR THE YEAR ENDED 31 DECEMBER 20.8

	20.8 Rand	20.7 Rand
Continuing operations		
Revenue (1)	15 577 500	11 500 000
Cost of sales (2)	(12 477 760)	(9 200 000)
Gross profit	3 099 740	2 300 000
Other expenses (3)	(2 448 740)	(1 675 000)
Profit before tax	651 000	625 000
Income tax expense (4)	(175 770)	(168 750)
Profit for the year from continuing operations	475 230	456 250
Discontinued operations		
Revenue (5)	2 422 500	2 500 000
Expenses (6)	(2 473 500)	(2 475 000)
Profit/(loss) before tax	(51 000)	25 000
Income tax benefit/(expense) (7)	12 555	(6 750)
Profit/(loss) after tax	(38 445)	18 250
Profit/(loss) on remeasurement to fair value less costs to sell	–	–
Impairment loss on remeasurement of disposal group	–	–
Income tax benefit	–	–
Profit/(loss) for the year from discontinued operations	(38 445)	18 250
Profit for the year	436 785	474 500
Other comprehensive income	–	–
Total comprehensive income for the year	436 785	474 500

(1) 18 000 000 – 641 250 – 1 781 250 = 15 577 500;
14 000 000 – 2 500 000 = 11 500 000
(2) 14 400 000 – 525 740 – 1 396 500 = 12 477 760;
11 200 000 – 2 000 000 = 9 200 000
(3) 3 000 000 – 148 510 – 402 750 = 2 448 740;
2 150 000 – 475 000 = 1 675 000
(4) 651 000 × 27% = 175 770;
625 000 × 27% = 168 750
(5) 641 250 + 1 781 250 = 2 422 500
(6) 525 740 + 1 396 500 + 148 510 + 402 750 = 2 473 500;
2 000 000 + 475 000 = 2 475 000
(7) [(51 000) + 4 500] × 27% = 12 555;
25 000 × 27% = 6 750

GOLF LTD
NOTES FOR THE YEAR ENDED 31 DECEMBER 20.8

2. Disposal group classified as held for sale

A decision to dispose of a group of assets and related liabilities of the KwaZulu-Natal branch was taken on 1 October 20.8. On that date a binding sales agreement regarding the assets and liabilities was entered into and it is expected that the disposal group will be sold for cash. The disposal will be completed by 28 February 20.9. The disposal group comprises the following:

	Rand
Assets	
Property, plant and equipment	1 325 000
Inventories	120 000
Trade receivables	215 000
	1 660 000
Liabilities	
Trade and other payables	235 000

No impairment loss was recognised in respect of the disposal group. The disposal group was previously reported as part of the KwaZulu-Natal geographical segment.

❑ QUESTION IFRS 5.11

SAPU Ltd's operating results have shown a setback due to losses incurred by its Upington factory. As a result, the directors approved a formal plan on 30 June 20.5 to immediately market and sell the Upington factory. A public announcement of the plan was also made on this date. The intention is to sell all the assets and related liabilities (including any provisions) of the factory in one single transaction. The assets and liabilities of the Upington factory met all the criteria of IFRS 5 to be classified as a disposal group held for sale on 30 June 20.5. SAPU Ltd has a 28 February reporting date.

On 30 June 20.5 the assets of the Upington factory were as follows:

Current assets	**A**	**B**
	Rand	**Rand**
Inventories	351 500	230 000
Trade receivables	594 850	490 000

A = Cost price or carrying amount
B = Expected value if operation is sold on 30 June 20.5

The difference between the carrying amount and expected value of trade receivables arose as a result of bad debts (credit losses). Assume that both the loss on inventories (write-down to net realisable value) as well as the bad debts (credit losses) are deductible for tax purposes.

Property, plant and equipment	**A**	**B**	**C**
	Rand	**Rand**	**Rand**
Plant and machinery	645 600	382 300	192 500
Other	141 350	84 750	49 300

A = Cost price
B = Accumulated depreciation at 1 March 20.5
C = Tax base at 28 February 20.5

Depreciation on plant and machinery is written off in accordance with the straight-line method at 20% per annum and at 15% per annum on other property, plant and equipment. Up to 30 June 20.5, the South African Revenue Service allowed wear and tear on the cost price of all assets at 15% per annum (apportioned for part of a year) according to the straight-line method. From 1 July 20.5, the assets were no longer used in the production of income.

The fair value of the disposal group was R939 900 on 30 June 20.5 and the expected costs to sell were R50 000.

The Upington operation earned a gross profit, excluding depreciation and fixed overheads, of R110 000 for the period 1 March 20.5 to 28 February 20.6, consisting of revenue of R1 240 000 and cost of sales of R1 130 000. The fixed overheads for the period 1 March 20.5 to 28 February 20.6 were as follows:

	Rand
Local salaries and wages	160 000
Other local expenses	30 000
Rent (short-term)	30 000
Head office administrative costs	10 000
	230 000

Payments to personnel as a result of the termination of services (**in addition** to those mentioned above), were estimated at R75 000 on 30 June 20.5 and will only be paid during March 20.6. Assume that this amount is not deductible for tax purposes.

Up to 28 February 20.6, R490 000 was received in respect of trade receivables. The net realisable value of inventories remained unchanged.

The fair value less costs to sell of the disposal group of the Upington factory amounted to R385 000 on 28 February 20.6.

On 28 February 20.6 there were two potential buyers, but no sales contracts were entered into.

Assume a tax rate of 27% and that the entity has sufficient taxable income from continuing operations on 28 February 20.6, against which any tax losses from discontinued operations can be utilised.

Required

a. Calculate the profit/loss on the discontinuance of the Upington operations to be presented in the statement of profit or loss and other comprehensive income of SAPU Ltd for the year ended 28 February 20.6.
b. Prepare the statement of profit or loss and other comprehensive income (only in respect of the discontinued operation) as well as the 'Disposal group classified as held for sale' note of SAPU Ltd for the year ended 28 February 20.6. The analysis as required by IFRS 5 must be shown on the face of the statement of profit or loss and other comprehensive income and no other notes are required. Comparative amounts are not required.
c. Discuss how the disposal group will be presented on the face of the statement of financial position of SAPU Ltd as at 28 February 20.6.

Your answer must comply with the requirements of International Financial Reporting Standards (IFRS).

❖ **Suggested solution IFRS 5.11**

a. Profit/loss from discontinued operations

	Rand
Gross profit	110 000
Fixed overheads	(230 000)
Depreciation	(50 108)
– Plant and machinery (1)	(43 040)
– Other assets (2)	(7 068)
Termination benefits (movement in provision)	(75 000)
Loss on inventories (3)	(121 500)
Credit losses (4)	(104 850)
Loss before tax	(471 458)
Income tax benefit (calc 1)	107 043
Loss after tax	(364 415)
Profit/(loss) on remeasurement to fair value less costs to sell	(29 048)
– Impairment loss on remeasurement of disposal group (calc 3)	(39 792)
– Income tax benefit (5)	10 744
Loss for the year	(393 463)

(1) 645 600 × 20% × 4/12 = 43 040
(2) 141 350 × 15% × 4/12 = 7 068
(3) 230 000 – 351 500 = (121 500)
(4) 490 000 – 594 850 = (104 850)
(5) 39 792 × 27% = 10 744

Calculations

1. Tax calculation (excluding impairment losses)

	Rand
Loss before tax (excluding impairment losses)	(471 458)
Non-taxable/deductible items	
• Termination benefits (movement in provision)	75 000
Temporary differences	10 760
• Depreciation	50 108
• Wear-and-tear allowance	
– Plant and machinery (1)	(32 280)
– Other assets (2)	(7 068)
Tax loss	(385 698)
Current tax benefit (385 698 × 27%)	104 138
Movement in deferred tax (excluding impairment loss) (calc 2)	2 905
	107 043

(1) 645 600 × 15% × 4/12 = 32 280
(2) 141 350 × 15% × 4/12 = 7 068

2. Deferred tax

	Carrying amount Rand	Tax base Rand	Temporary difference Rand	Deferred tax Rand (Dr)/Cr
28 February 20.5				
Plant and machinery (1)	263 300	192 500	70 800	19 116
Other assets (2)	56 600	49 300	7 300	1 971
	319 900	241 800	78 100	21 087
28 February 20.6				
Plant and machinery (3)	187 774	160 220	27 554	7 440
Other assets (4)	42 226	42 232	(6)	(2)
	230 000	202 452	27 548	7 438

(1) 645 600 – 382 300 = 263 300
(2) 141 350 – 84 750 = 56 600
(3) 263 300 – 43 040 – 32 486 (calc 3) = 187 774
192 500 – 32 280 = 160 220
(4) 56 600 – 7 068 – 7 306 (calc 3) = 42 226
49 300 – 7 068 = 42 232

Movement in deferred excluding impairment losses	**Rand**
Total movement in deferred tax attributable to discontinued operations (7 438 – 21 087)	13 649
Movement attributable to impairment loss [39 792 (calc 3) × 27%]	(10 744)
	2 905

3. Disposal group

30 June 20.5	**Rand**
Inventories (net realisable value)	230 000
Trade receivables (credit losses of R104 850 written off)	490 000
Plant and machinery (1)	220 260
Other assets (2)	49 532
Provision for termination benefits	(75 000)
Carrying amount of disposal group at 30 June 20.5	914 792
Fair value less costs to sell (3)	889 900
Impairment loss (4)	24 892

Impairment loss allocated as follows:

• Plant and machinery (5)	20 322
• Other assets (6)	4 570
	24 892

(1) 645 600 – 382 300 – (645 600 × 0,2 × 4/12) = 220 260
(2) 141 350 – 84 750 – (141 350 × 0,15 × 4/12) = 49 532
(3) 939 900 – 50 000 = 889 900
(4) 914 792 – 889 900 = 24 892
(5) 24 892 × 220 260/(220 260 + 49 532) = 20 322
(6) 24 892 × 49 532/(220 260 + 49 532) = 4 570

28 February 20.6	Rand
Inventories	230 000
Trade receivables (1)	–
Plant and machinery (2)	199 938
Other assets (3)	44 962
Provision for termination benefits	(75 000)
Carrying amount of disposal group at 28 February 20.6	399 900
Fair value less costs to sell	385 000
Impairment loss (4)	14 900
Impairment loss allocated as follows:	
• Plant and machinery (5)	12 164
• Other assets (6)	2 736
	14 900

Total impairment loss for the period (pre-tax)

Plant and machinery (7)	32 486
Other assets (8)	7 306
	39 792

(1) 490 000 – 490 000 = Nil
(2) 220 260 – 20 322 = 199 938
(3) 49 532 – 4 570 = 44 962
(4) 399 900 – 385 000 = 14 900
(5) 14 900 × 199 938/(199 938 + 44 962) = 12 164
(6) 14 900 × 44 962/(199 938 + 44 962) = 2 736
(7) 20 322 + 12 164 = 32 486
(8) 4 570 + 2 736 = 7 306

b. Presentation and disclosure

SAPU LTD
STATEMENT OF PROFIT OR LOSS AND OTHER COMPREHENSIVE INCOME FOR THE YEAR ENDED 28 FEBRUARY 20.6

	Rand
Discontinued operations	
Revenue	1 240 000
Expenses (1)	(1 711 458)
Loss before tax	(471 458)
Income tax benefit (part a.)	107 043
Loss after tax	(364 415)
Profit/(loss) on remeasurement to fair value less costs to sell (part a.)	(29 048)
Impairment loss on remeasurement of disposal group	(39 792)
Income tax benefit	10 744
Profit/(loss) for the year from discontinued operations	(393 463)

(1) 1 130 000 + 230 000 + 50 108 + 75 000 + 121 500 + 104 850 = 1 711 458 (part a.)

SAPU LTD
NOTES FOR THE YEAR ENDED 28 FEBRUARY 20.6

2. Disposal group classified as held for sale

A decision to dispose of the assets and related liabilities of the Upington factory was taken on 30 June 20.5 after a disposal plan for the operations of the Upington factory had been approved. It is expected that the disposal group will be sold for cash and that the disposal will be completed at the beginning of the new financial year. The Upington factory was previously reported as part of the xxx segment. The disposal group comprises:

	Rand
Assets	
Plant and machinery (part a.)	187 774
Other assets (part a.)	42 226
Inventories	230 000
	460 000
Liabilities	
Provision for termination benefits	75 000

c. The assets of the disposal group will be presented under current assets in the line item 'Disposal group classified as held for sale', in the statement of financial position as at 28 February 20.6. The liabilities of the disposal group will be presented under current liabilities in the line item 'Liabilities in respect of disposal group classified as held for sale'.

❑ QUESTION IFRS 5.12

Digit Ltd is a furniture distributor that purchases all its furniture from a furniture factory, which is operated as a department of the company. The furniture factory, of which the results were previously reported as part of the Gauteng geographical segment, was not profitable. Digit Ltd's distribution department can purchase similar furniture at lower prices from external suppliers.

On 15 September 20.5, the board of directors approved a detailed formal disposal plan for the discontinuance of the factory department and made a public announcement in this regard on the same date. An active marketing plan regarding the once-off sale of the assets and liabilities of the factory was initiated on 31 January 20.6 and a binding sales agreement in respect of the assets and liabilities, including any provisions made in respect of the discontinuance, was concluded on the same date. It is expected that the plan for the discontinuance and disposal of the furniture factory will be completed by 30 April 20.6.

Digit Ltd has a 28 February reporting date.

The following information is presented to you on 28 February 20.6 (before taking into account any adjustments relating to the discontinuance):

The results of the furniture factory	**1 Mar 20.5 to 31 Jan 20.6 Rand Dr/(Cr)**	**1 Feb 20.6 to 28 Feb 20.6 Rand Dr/(Cr)**
Revenue	(1 890 000)	(150 000)
Cost of sales	1 700 000	170 000
Other expenses	350 000	40 000
Finance costs	37 600	3 400

Discontinuance costs of the furniture factory	**1 Feb 20.6 to 28 Feb 20.6 (Actual) Rand**	**1 Mar 20.6 to 30 Apr 20.6 (Estimated) Rand**
Direct costs of discontinuance	51 000	32 000
Termination benefits for employees	40 000	120 000
Fine (cancellation of short-term rental agreement)	–	15 000
Operating loss	–	65 000

Results of the furniture distribution department	**1 Mar 20.5 to 28 Feb 20.6 Rand Dr/(Cr)**
Revenue	(3 400 000)
Cost of sales	1 800 000
Other expenses	650 000
Finance costs	35 000

Other balances at 28 February 20.6	**Furniture factory Rand**	**Furniture distribution department Rand**
Plant and equipment (Carrying amount at 1 March 20.5)	480 000	360 000
Current assets	330 000	250 000
Non-current liabilities	180 000	280 000
Current liabilities	200 000	70 000

Additional information

1. Assume that the direct costs of discontinuance are deductible for tax purposes when incurred, while all other discontinuance costs are not deductible for tax purposes.

2. The following information regarding the plant and equipment for both the furniture factory and furniture distribution department is available:

	Furniture factory	Furniture distribution department
Date acquired	1 March 20.3	1 March 20.3
Cost price	R800 000	R600 000
Depreciation	20% per annum, straight-line	20% per annum, straight-line
Wear-and-tear allowance	R200 000 per annum, not allocated pro rata for part of a year	R150 000 per annum not allocated pro rata for part of a year

Digit Ltd accounts for all property, plant and equipment in accordance with the cost model. No depreciation has been recognised for the current financial year.

3. The current assets consist mainly of trade receivables. One of the debtors of the furniture factory was declared insolvent and liquidated on 31 January 20.6. A total amount of R50 000 was outstanding and Digit Ltd will receive 40 cents in the rand of the outstanding amount after reporting date. This information has not yet been taken into account in the results and other balances of the furniture factory for the current financial year. The South African Revenue Service will allow the bad debt (credit loss) as a deduction in the current financial year.

4. The assets and liabilities of the furniture factory met all the criteria of IFRS 5 to be classified as a disposal group held for sale on 31 January 20.6. On 31 January 20.6, the fair value less costs to sell of the disposal group was determined to be R70 000, based on the sales agreement. The fair value less costs to sell of the disposal group remained unchanged on 28 February 20.6.

5. Assume a tax rate of 27%.

6. There are no other non-taxable income, non-deductible expenses or temporary differences other than those that are evident from the above information.

Required

a. Prepare the statement of profit or loss and other comprehensive income of Digit Ltd for the year ended 28 February 20.6. The analysis as required by IFRS 5 must be presented on the face of the statement of profit or loss and other comprehensive income (only those notes indicated in part b. are required).
b. Prepare the following notes to the financial statements of Digit Ltd for the year ended 28 February 20.6:
   - Income tax expense (ignore the tax rate reconciliation)
   - Disposal group classified as held for sale

Your answer must comply with the requirements of International Financial Reporting Standards (IFRS). **Ignore** comparative amounts. Round all calculations to the nearest rand.

(UNISA – adapted)

❖ **Suggested solution IFRS 5.12**

a. **Statement of profit or loss and other comprehensive income**

DIGIT LTD
STATEMENT OF PROFIT OR LOSS AND OTHER COMPREHENSIVE INCOME FOR THE YEAR ENDED 28 FEBRUARY 20.6

	Rand
Continuing operations	
Revenue	3 400 000
Cost of sales	(1 800 000)
Gross profit	1 600 000
Other expenses (1)	(770 000)
Finance costs	(35 000)
Profit before tax	795 000
Income tax expense (calc 1)	(214 650)
Profit for the year from continuing operations	580 350
Discontinued operations	
Revenue (3)	2 040 000
Expenses (4)	(2 735 667)
Profit/(loss) before tax	(695 667)
Income tax benefit (calc 3)	140 580
Profit/(loss) after tax	(555 087)
Profit/(loss) on remeasurement to fair value less costs to sell	(11 923)
Impairment loss on remeasurement of disposal group (calc 5)	(16 333)
Income tax benefit (7)	4 410
Loss for the year from discontinued operations	(567 010)
Profit for the year (8)	13 340
Other comprehensive income	–
Total comprehensive income for the year	13 340

(1) 650 000 + 120 000 (2) = 770 000
(2) 600 000 × 20% = 120 000 (depreciation)
(3) 1 890 000 + 150 000 = 2 040 000
(4) (1 700 000 + 170 000) + (350 000 + 40 000) + (37 600 + 3 400) + (32 000 + 120 000 + 15 000 + 51 000 + 40 000) + 146 667 (5) + 30 000 (6) = 2 735 667
(5) 800 000 × 20% × 11/12 = 146 667 (depreciation)
(6) 50 000 × 60% = 30 000 (credit losses)
(7) 16 333 × 27% = 4 410
(8) 580 350 – 567 010 = 13 340

b. Notes

DIGIT LTD
NOTES FOR THE YEAR ENDED 28 FEBRUARY 20.6

2. Income tax expense

	Rand
Major components of the tax expense:	
Current tax expense – current year (1)	60 210
Deferred tax expense – current year (2)	9 450
	69 660

(1) 206 550 (calc 1) – 146 340 (calc 3) = 60 210
(2) 8 100 (calc 2) + 1 350 (calc 4) = 9 450

3. Disposal group classified as held for sale

A decision to dispose of the assets and liabilities of the furniture factory was taken on 15 September 20.5 after a formal detailed plan for the discontinuance of the furniture factory was approved. The plan regarding the once-off sale of the assets and liabilities reached a stage of completion on 31 January 20.6 after a binding sales agreement had been entered into. It is expected that the plan for the discontinuance will be completed by 30 April 20.6. The disposal group was previously reported as part of the Gauteng geographical segment.

The disposal group consists of the following:

	Rand
Assets	
Plant and equipment (1)	317 000
Current assets (2)	300 000
	617 000
Liabilities	
Non-current liabilities	180 000
Current liabilities	200 000
Provision for discontinuance (calc 5)	167 000
	547 000

(1) 480 000 – 146 667 (depreciation) – 16 333 (calc 5) = 317 000
(2) 330 000 – 30 000 (credit losses) = 300 000

Calculations

1. Tax calculation - continuing operations

		Rand
Profit before tax		795 000
Non-taxable/non-deductible items		–
Temporary differences		(30 000)
Depreciation (1)	120 000	
Wear-and-tear allowance (given)	(150 000)	
Taxable income		765 000
Current tax (2)		206 550
Deferred tax (calc 2)		8 100
		214 650

(1) 600 000 × 20% = 120 000
(2) 765 000 × 27% = 206 550

2. Deferred tax – continuing operations

	Carrying amount Rand	Tax base Rand	Temporary difference Rand	Deferred tax Rand (Dr)/Cr
28 February 20.5				
Plant and equipment (1)	360 000	300 000	60 000	16 200
	360 000	300 000	60 000	16 200
28 February 20.6				
Plant and equipment (2)	240 000	150 000	90 000	24 300
	240 000	150 000	90 000	24 300

Movement in deferred tax through profit or loss: 24 300 – 16 200 = 8 100

(1) 600 000 – (600 000 × 20% × 2) = 360 000
600 000 – (150 000 × 2) = 300 000
(2) 360 000 – 120 000 (calc 1) = 240 000
300 000 – 150 000 = 150 000

3. Tax calculation – discontinued operation

		Rand
Loss before tax (excluding impairment loss) (1)		(695 667)
Non-taxable/non-deductible items		175 000
Fine	15 000	
Termination benefits (movement in provision) (2)	160 000	
Temporary differences		(21 333)
Provision for direct costs	32 000	
Depreciation (3)	146 667	
Wear-and-tear allowance (given)	(200 000)	
Taxable income		(542 000)
Current tax benefit (542 000 × 27%)		(146 340)
Movement in deferred tax (excluding impairment loss) (calc 4)		5 760
		(140 580)

(1) Per statement of profit or loss and other comprehensive income
(2) 120 000 + 40 000 = 160 000
(3) 800 000 × 20% × 11/12 = 146 667

4. Deferred tax – discontinued operation

	Carrying amount Rand	Tax base Rand	Temporary difference Rand	Deferred tax Rand (Dr)/Cr
28 February 20.5				
Plant and equipment (1)	480 000	400 000	80 000	21 600
	480 000	400 000	80 000	21 600

	Carrying amount Rand	Tax base Rand	Temporary difference Rand	Deferred tax Rand (Dr)/Cr
28 February 20.6				
Plant and equipment (2)	317 000	200 000	117 000	31 590
Provision for direct costs	(32 000)	–	(32 000)	(8 640)
Provision for termination benefits	(120 000)	(120 000)	–	–
Provision for fine	(15 000)	(15 000)	–	–
	150 000	65 000	85 000	22 950

(1) 800 000 – (800 000 × 20% × 2) = 480 000;
800 000 – (200 000 × 2) = 400 000

(2) 480 000 – 146 667 (calc 3) – 16 333 (calc 5) = 317 000;
400 000 – 200 000 = 200 000

Movement in deferred tax excluding impairment loss	**Rand**
Total movement in deferred tax attributable to discontinued operation (22 950 – 21 600)	1 350
Movement attributable to impairment loss [16 333 (calc 5) × 27%]	4 410
	5 760

5. **Disposal group**

	Rand
Plant and equipment (1)	333 333
Current assets (2)	300 000
Non-current liabilities	(180 000)
Current liabilities	(200 000)
Provision for discontinuance (3)	(167 000)
Carrying amount of disposal group on 31 January 20.6	86 333
Fair value less costs to sell	70 000
Impairment loss (allocated to property, plant and equipment)	16 333

(1) 480 000 – 146 667 (depreciation) = 333 333
(2) 330 000 – (50 000 × 60%) = 300 000
(3) 32 000 + 120 000 + 15 000 = 167 000

❑ QUESTION IFRS 5.13

Karp Ltd is a listed company with a 31 December reporting date.

On 1 January 20.4, the company announced a formal plan to discontinue a segment (clothing operation) and to sell the assets of the operation due to a decreasing demand for the company's products. The following information is available:

The formal discontinuation date (suspension of production) is 15 November 20.4 and the plant will be available for immediate sale in its current condition on that date. The plant and inventories were actively marketed to independent parties from that date and are expected to be realised in separate transactions. The disposal date is expected to be early in the new financial year. The plant met all the criteria of IFRS 5 to be classified as a non-current asset held for sale on 15 November 20.4.

The results of the discontinued operation for the year ended 31 December 20.4 are as follows:

	1 Jan 20.4 – 15 Nov 20.4 Rand	16 Nov 20.4 – 31 Dec 20.4 Rand
Revenue	700 000	100 000
Cost of sales	(400 000)	(50 000)
Gross profit	300 000	50 000
Other expenses	(150 000)	(80 000)
Profit/(loss) before tax	150 000	(30 000)

Inventories consist of raw materials with a carrying amount of R60 000 on 15 November 20.4 and a net realisable value of R70 000 on that date. The net realisable value of the raw materials remained unchanged at reporting date.

The carrying amount and tax base of the plant amounted to R600 000 on 1 January 20.4 and the fair value less costs to sell amounted to R100 000 on 15 November 20.4. The fair value less costs to sell remained unchanged at reporting date.

Plant is depreciated at 20% per annum in accordance with the reducing balance method for both accounting and tax purposes. Assume that the tax allowances were only granted up to the date of suspension of production.

Additional information

1. The profit before tax for the year ended 31 December 20.4 includes depreciation.
2. The estimated profit before tax for the period 1 January 20.5 up to the date of disposal, amounts to R80 000.
3. Assume a tax rate of 27%.

Required

Prepare the statement of profit or loss and other comprehensive income (only in respect of discontinued operations) as well as the 'Non-current assets classified as held for sale' note of Karp Ltd for the year ended 31 December 20.4, in accordance with the requirements of International Financial Reporting Standards (IFRS). The analysis as required by IFRS 5 must be presented on the face of the statement of profit or loss and other comprehensive income and no other notes are required. Comparative amounts can be ignored.

❑ QUESTION IFRS 5.14

Boxom Ltd is a company with diversified operations. During the financial year ended 28 February 20.5, a serious levelling off in the clothing industry arose which led to the board of directors formally deciding to suspend all operations of the clothing division from 15 January 20.5. All the assets and liabilities of the clothing division will be sold in a single transaction early in the next financial year. A public announcement to this effect was made on 15 January 20.5.

Information for the year ended 28 February 20.5 is as follows:

	Continuing operations Rand	Clothing division Rand
The profit/(loss) before tax (before taking into account impairment losses) for the year ended 28 February 20.5 is as follows:		
1 March 20.4 to 15 January 20.5	1 680 000	(50 000)
16 January 20.5 to 28 February 20.5	220 000	5 000
Revenue for 20.5 is made up as follows:		
1 March 20.4 to 15 January 20.5	3 800 000	500 000
16 January 20.5 to 28 February 20.5	435 000	200 000
Cost of sales for 20.5 is made up as follows:		
1 March 20.4 to 15 January 20.5	1 570 000	360 000
16 January 20.5 to 28 February 20.5	140 000	135 000
Other expenses for 20.5 (including depreciation) are made up as follows:		
1 March 20.4 to 15 January 20.5	550 000	190 000
16 January 20.5 to 28 February 20.5	75 000	60 000

The assets of the discontinued operation met all the criteria of IFRS 5 to be classified as a disposal group held for sale on 15 January 20.5 and consist of the following:

	Carrying amount Rand
Raw materials	120 000
Finished products	180 000
Plant (carrying amount on 1 March 20.4)	600 000

The fair value less costs to sell of the disposal group amounted to R480 000 on 15 January 20.5. This amount remained unchanged at reporting date.

Plant is depreciated at 20% per annum in accordance with the reducing balance method for both accounting and tax purposes. The tax base of the plant of the clothing division amounted to R540 000 on 1 March 20.4. Assume that the tax allowances were only granted up to the date of suspension of production.

Assume a tax rate of 27%. There are no other temporary differences, non-taxable items or non-deductible items, other than those arising from the above information.

Required

Prepare the statement of profit or loss and other comprehensive income as well as the 'Disposal group classified as held for sale' note of Boxom Ltd for the year ended 28 February 20.5, in accordance with the requirements of International Financial Reporting Standards (IFRS). The analysis as required by IFRS 5 must be disclosed in the notes to the financial statements and no other notes are required. Comparative amounts can be ignored.

IFRS 7

Financial instruments: disclosure

Note:	As this chapter and the chapter on IFRS 9 both deal with financial instruments, the questions on these two chapters are integrated and such questions are presented as part of the chapter on IFRS 9.

IFRS 8

Operating segments

❑ QUESTIONS AND SOLUTIONS

❑ QUESTIONS

@ *These questions contain topics or principles that were not included in the ITC syllabus of SAICA at the time of publishing this book, but might still be included in university syllabi.*
Please note: the whole IFRS 8 is not included in the ITC syllabus of SAICA.

❑ QUESTION IFRS 8.1@

1. Are the following statements true or false?

   a. The requirements of this standard are compulsory for listed companies only.

   b. When both the parent's separate financial statements and the consolidated financial statements are presented, segment information need only be provided in respect of the consolidated financial statements.

   c. An operating segment may take the form of a department.

   d. A corporate headquarters that does not earn revenues is an operating segment.

   e. The term 'chief operating decision maker' refers to a manager with a specific title.

   f. An operating segment usually has a segment manager.

   g. An entity does not present comparative amounts for a reportable segment if that segment did not satisfy the criteria for reportability in the prior period.

   h. An entity must disclose the identities of its major customers.

2. The following segment information is available:

Operating segments	**I** **Rand**	**II** **Rand**	**III** **Rand**	**IV** **Rand**
Consolidated revenue				
Sales to customers	10 000	40 000	20 000	4 000
Inter-segment sales	5 000	–	12 000	6 000

The entity includes all sales for internal accounting purposes.

Required

Which of the above segments are reportable segments in accordance with the requirements of IFRS 8?

3. The following consolidated segment information is available:

Operating segments	**A** **Rand**	**B** **Rand**	**C** **Rand**	**D** **Rand**
Total identifiable assets				
Tangible assets	100 000	280 000	40 000	20 000
Intangible assets	40 000	20 000	20 000	10 000
Total	140 000	300 000	60 000	30 000

Tangible assets of R70 000 cannot be allocated to operating segments.

Required

Which of the above segments are reportable segments in accordance with IFRS 8?

4. The following consolidated segment information is available:

Operating segments	**A Rand**	**B Rand**	**C Rand**
Revenue	800 000	600 000	400 000
Expenses	600 000	300 000	100 000

The following items must still be accounted for:

	Rand
Interest received (relating to segment A)	40 000
Interest paid (in the ratio of segment A:B:C = 3:2:1)	60 000
Income tax expense (not reviewed by the chief operating decision maker)	400 000
Share of profit of associate (relating to segment C)	300 000

Required

Which of the above segments are reportable segments in accordance with IFRS 8?

❖ **Suggested solution IFRS 8.1**[@]

1.

a.	True	(IFRS 8.2)
b.	True	(IFRS 8.4)
c.	True	(IFRS 8.5)
d.	False	(IFRS 8.6)
e.	False	(IFRS 8.7)
f.	True	(IFRS 8.9)
g.	False	(IFRS 8.18)
h.	False	(IFRS 8.34)

2.

Operating segments	**Sales to customers Rand**	**Inter-segment sales Rand**	**Combined revenue Rand**
Segment I	10 000	5 000	15 000
Segment II	40 000	–	40 000
Segment III	20 000	12 000	32 000
Segment IV	4 000	6 000	10 000
Total	74 000	23 000	97 000

Segments I, II, III and IV will be disclosed as each segment's revenue is more than 10% of the total combined revenue (IFRS 8.13). Even though the majority of the revenue of segment IV is not earned from sales to external customers, it is still a reportable segment (IFRS 8.13 and IFRS 8.IN12).

3. Operating segments

	Identifiable assets Rand
Segment A	140 000
Segment B	300 000
Segment C	60 000
Segment D	30 000
Total segment assets	530 000
Unallocated assets	70 000
Consolidated	600 000

Segments A (140/530) = 26%, B (300/530) = 57% and C (60/530) = 11% will be disclosed because their assets are more than 10% of the total combined assets (IFRS 8.13).

4. Operating segments

	A Rand	B Rand	C Rand	Total Rand
Revenue	800 000	600 000	400 000	1 800 000
Expenses	(600 000)	(300 000)	(100 000)	(1 000 000)
Interest received	40 000	–	–	40 000
Interest paid (1)	(30 000)	(20 000)	(10 000)	(60 000)
Share of profit of associate	–	–	300 000	300 000
	210 000	280 000	590 000	1 080 000
210 000/1 080 000	19%			
280 000/1 080 000		26%		
590 000/1 080 000			55%	

(1) 60 000 × 3/6 = 30 000; 60 000 × 2/6 = 20 000; 60 000 × 1/6 = 10 000

Segments A, B and C will be disclosed (IFRS 8.13). Interest received and paid are included in the profit or loss of an operating segment if reviewed by the chief operating decision maker (assumed because no information to the contrary was given) (IFRS 8.23 and IFRS 8.IN17). The same applies to the share of profit of associate (IFRS 8.23). The income tax expense is not included in this case because it is not reviewed by the chief operating decision maker (IFRS 8.23).

❑ QUESTION IFRS 8.2@

The following information was extracted from the records of Monorcos Ltd, a company listed on the JSE Ltd:

Operating segments (determined by management)

- Diamonds
- Industrial
- Energy

Geographical areas

- Europe
- Africa (outside South Africa)
- South Africa

Other information (for 20.1)	**Diamonds Rand**	**Industrial Rand**	**Energy Rand**
Sales to external customers	700 000	500 000	300 000
Inter-segment sales	–	20 000	–
Total assets	600 000	300 000	200 000
Liabilities	400 000	100 000	100 000
Expenses	400 000	300 000	200 000
Sundry	350 000	260 000	180 000
Depreciation	20 000	25 000	12 000
Research	30 000	15 000	8 000
Capital expenditure incurred on non-current assets	100 000	80 000	30 000
Number of employees	6 000	2 000	1 500

	Europe Rand	**Africa Rand**	**South Africa Rand**
Sales to external customers	600 000	500 000	400 000
Transfers between areas	–	40 000	–
Non-current assets	320 000	240 000	350 000

ABRIDGED STATEMENT OF PROFIT OR LOSS AND OTHER COMPREHENSIVE INCOME FOR THE YEAR ENDED 31 DECEMBER 20.1

	Rand
Revenue	1 500 000
Cost of sales	(500 000)
Gross profit	1 000 000
Other expenses	(412 000)
Finance costs	(40 000)
Share of profit of associate	200 000
Profit before tax	748 000
Income tax expense	(200 000)
Profit for the year	548 000
Other comprehensive income	
Items that will not be reclassified to profit or loss	
Gain on property revaluation	–
Total comprehensive income for the year	548 000
Profit/total comprehensive income attributable to:	
Owners of the parent	448 000
Non-controlling interest	100 000
	548 000

The following information was also obtained:

1. Assets not allocated to a segment amounted to R60 000 and include an investment in an associate of R35 000. This is the only associate of Monorcos Ltd.

2. General expenses incurred and not allocated to a segment amounted to R20 000.

3. Monorcos Ltd is engaged in:
   a. Kaolin mining
   b. Road construction
   c. Diamond mining
   d. Oil production
   e. Coal mining

4. The inter-segment pricing is at market value.

5. The profit adjustment in respect of inter-segment transactions amounts to R12 000.

6. Income tax expense is not reviewed by the chief operating decision maker.

7. Only the liabilities of the Diamonds segment are interest bearing.

8. Except for certain amounts not allocated to segments as indicated above, Monorcos Ltd applies the same accounting policies to its segment reporting as for the entity as a whole.

9. Revenue from one customer of the Diamonds segment represents R200 000 of the total revenue of Monorcos Ltd.

Required

Disclose the segment information for Monorcos Ltd in accordance with IFRS 8 *Operating Segments*.

❖ **Suggested solution IFRS 8.2**[@]

MONORCOS LTD

Types of products and services from which segments derive their revenues

The company operates in the following segments:

Diamonds
    Mining of diamonds
Industrial
    Kaolin mining
    Road construction
Energy
    Oil production
    Coal mining.

Measurement of segment information

Inter-segment transfers are priced at market value. Income tax expense and all amounts regarding investments in associate entities are not allocated to operating segments. In all other material respects, Monorcos Ltd generally applies the same accounting policies to its segment reporting as for the entity as a whole.

Information regarding operating segments for the year ended 31 December 20.1:

	Diamonds Rand	Industrial Rand	Energy Rand	Total Rand
Revenue from external customers	700 000	500 000	300 000	1 500 000
Inter-segment revenue	–	20 000	–	20 000
Interest expense	40 000	–	–	40 000
Depreciation	20 000	25 000	12 000	57 000
Segment profit (1)	260 000	220 000	100 000	580 000
Segment assets	600 000	300 000	200 000	1 100 000
Segment liabilities	400 000	100 000	100 000	600 000
Capital expenditure incurred on non-current assets	100 000	80 000	30 000	210 000

(1) 700 000 – 400 000 – 40 000 = 260 000; 520 000 – 300 000 = 220 000; 300 000 – 200 000 = 100 000

Reconciliations of reportable segment revenues, profit or loss, assets and liabilities

	Rand
Revenue	
Total revenue for reportable segments	1 520 000
Elimination of inter-segment revenue	(20 000)
Entity's revenue	1 500 000
Profit	
Total profit for reportable segments	580 000
Elimination of inter-segment profits	(12 000)
Unallocated expenses	(20 000)
Share of profit of associate	200 000
Profit before income tax expense	748 000
Assets	
Total assets for reportable segments	1 100 000
Investment in associate not allocated	35 000
Other unallocated assets	25 000
Entity's assets	1 160 000

Geographical information	Europe Rand	Africa Rand	South Africa Rand	Total Rand
Revenue	600 000	500 000	400 000	1 500 000
Non-current assets	320 000	240 000	350 000	910 000

Information about major customers

Revenue from one customer of the Diamonds segment represents R200 000 of the total revenue of the entity.

❑ QUESTION IFRS 8.3@

The following segment information from the consolidated financial statements of Jerry Ltd for the years ended 31 December 20.6 and 20.7 is available:

Operating segments	**A** **Rand**	**B** **Rand**	**C** **Rand**	**D** **Rand**
Sales to customers				
20.6	750 000	313 000	160 000	591 000
20.7	865 000	412 000	271 000	603 000
Total assets				
20.6	1 250 000	865 000	512 000	908 000
20.7	1 310 000	913 000	596 000	1 002 000
Results of operations				
20.6 profit/(loss)	365 000	245 000	6 000	(286 000)
20.7 profit/(loss)	483 000	297 000	224 000	(15 000)

Segment B is a wholly owned subsidiary acquired in 20.6. Its method of accounting for inventory differs from that used by the rest of the group. In 20.7 the accounting policy was changed to bring it in line with the group, which resulted in the profits of 20.6 being restated by a surplus of R5 000. This change is not reflected in the segment information given above.

The company has not changed the basis for segment reporting and it is expected that the current trend in results will continue.

The company operates in one geographical area only.

Required

By using the given information only, show how the segment information should be disclosed in the consolidated financial statements of the group for the year ended 31 December 20.7. Your solution must comply with the requirements of IFRS 8 *Operating Segments.*

❖ Suggested solution IFRS 8.3@

JERRY LTD GROUP
SEGMENT REPORT FOR THE YEAR ENDED 31 DECEMBER 20.7

Operating segments

Jerry Ltd and its subsidiaries operate in the following segments:

- Segment A
- Segment B
- Segment C
- Segment D

The group operates in one geographical area only.

Information concerning the operating segments for the year ended 31 December 20.7 is as follows:

	A Rand	B Rand	C Rand	D Rand	Total Rand
20.6					
Revenue	750 000	313 000	160 000	591 000	1 814 000
Profit/(loss) (1)	365 000	250 000	6 000	(286 000)	335 000
Assets (2)	1 250 000	870 000	512 000	908 000	3 540 000
20.7					
Revenue	865 000	412 000	271 000	603 000	2 151 000
Profit/(loss)	483 000	297 000	224 000	(15 000)	989 000
Assets	1 310 000	913 000	596 000	1 002 000	3 821 000

The accounting policy of Segment B has been changed in respect of inventory in order to comply with group policy. The comparative amounts have been restated by the resultant surplus of R5 000.

Note: Further disclosures in other notes to the financial statements may be required in terms of IAS 8.

(1) 245 000 + 5 000 = 250 000
(2) 865 000 + 5 000 = 870 000

❑ QUESTION IFRS 8.4@

Bishop Ltd is a listed company which has to date published segment results only for retail and wholesale sales in its financial statements. The company also manufactures a wide range of consumables, and has retail and wholesale distribution points in Australia, the UK and South Africa. The company possesses a number of sawmills and supplies wood to the wholesale market in South Africa.

Required

Taking the circumstances of Bishop Ltd into account, discuss in broad terms the following aspects of segment reporting:

a. The segments which should be included in the segment report.
b. The information relating to each segment which should be disclosed in the segment report.

❖ Suggested solution IFRS 8.4@

a. Segments to be included in the segment report

Broad guidelines

The following should be covered by the discussion:

- Discussion of the core principle of operating segments (IFRS 8.1).
- Definition of 'operating segment' (IFRS 8.5 and Appendix A).

- An operating segment has discrete financial information which is reviewed by the chief operating decision maker.
- Not every part of an entity is necessarily an operating segment, for example a corporate headquarters or functional departments that do not earn revenues, or the revenues are only incidental to the activities of the entity (IFRS 8.6).
- The determination of operating segments is dependent on a certain amount of judgment (IFRS 8.8).
- Generally, an operating segment has a segment manager (IFRS 8.9).
- In this case, Bishop Ltd may identify operating segments based on the type of products or based on the geographical location. The entity will determine which of these sets of components constitute the operating segments by reference to the core principle (IFRS 8.10).
- Identification of reportable operating segments is based on applying the aggregation criteria (IFRS 8.12) and the quantitative thresholds (IFRS 8.13). According to the latter, segments are reported if their revenue, profit or loss or assets are 10% or more of the combined revenue, profit or loss or assets. Reportable segments must represent at least 75% of the entity's total revenues (IFRS 8.15).

Possible segments

Based on type of product

- Manufacturing
- Wholesale
- Retail
- Sawmill and wood section

Based on geographical area

- South Africa
- UK
- Australia

b. Information which must be disclosed in the financial statements

- Factors that management used to identify the entity's reportable segments (IFRS 8.22(a)) and their judgments in applying the aggregation criteria (IFRS 8.22(aa)).
- Description of the types of products and services from which each reportable segment derives its revenues (IFRS 8.22(b)).
- Information about reportable segment profit or loss, assets and liabilities, if reviewed by the chief operating decision maker (IFRS 8.23, .24):
  - Revenue from external customers;
  - Inter-segment revenues;
  - Interest revenue;
  - Interest expense;
  - Depreciation and amortisation;
  - Material items that are separately disclosed in terms of IAS 1;
  - Share of profit of associates or joint ventures accounted for by the equity method;
  - Income tax expense or income;
  - Segment profit or loss;
  - Other material non-cash items;

- Total assets;
- Additions to reportable segment non-current assets;
- Investments in associates and joint ventures accounted for by the equity method; and
- Liabilities.

- Measurement of operating segment profit or loss, assets and liabilities, including the basis of accounting for inter-segment transactions and changes in measurement methods from prior periods (IFRS 8.27).
- Reconciliations of the total of reportable segments' revenue, profit or loss, assets, liabilities and other material items to the corresponding amounts for the entity as a whole (IFRS 8.28).
- Entity-wide disclosures:
  - Information about products and services (IFRS 8.32)
  - Information about geographical areas (IFRS 8.33)
  - Information about major customers (IFRS 8.34).

❑ QUESTION IFRS 8.5[@]

The following are details of the operations of three companies in the same group:

Cicero Ltd and Viceroy Ltd are manufacturers, while Icarus Ltd is partially responsible for the marketing of their products. The total sales of Icarus Ltd resulted from goods purchased from Cicero Ltd and Viceroy Ltd in the ratio 60:40. Icarus Ltd purchases goods at cost price plus 25% and at the reporting date had R325 000 inventory on hand of which 60% was purchased from Cicero Ltd. Approximately 30% of Cicero Ltd's sales are to Icarus Ltd. Viceroy Ltd is situated in Taiwan, while Cicero Ltd and Icarus Ltd operate in Gauteng.

The following information is taken from the records and financial statements of the companies for the year ended 31 December 20.3:

STATEMENTS OF FINANCIAL POSITION

	Cicero Ltd Rand	Viceroy Ltd Rand	Icarus Ltd Rand
Property, plant and equipment	3 500 000	1 000 000	500 000
Goodwill	–	–	37 000
Net current assets/(liabilities)	(600 000)	75 000	83 000
Long-term borrowings	(1 780 000)	–	–
Intragroup loans dr/(cr)	800 000	–	(800 000)

STATEMENTS OF PROFIT OR LOSS AND OTHER COMPREHENSIVE INCOME

	Cicero Ltd Rand	Viceroy Ltd Rand	Icarus Ltd Rand
Revenue	85 000 000	32 000 000	51 000 000
Profit	975 000	342 000	205 000

Interest on intragroup loans amounted to R120 000 for both Cicero Ltd and Icarus Ltd. Cicero Ltd paid interest on long-term borrowings amounting to R267 000. Interest has already been taken into account in the calculation of profit. The profit of Cicero Ltd includes an amount of R52 000 received as share of profit of associates and a dividend of R100 000 received from Icarus Ltd.

The Cicero Ltd group identifies operating segments based on the type of product or service.

Interest, dividends and the related investments and liabilities are not reviewed by the chief operating decision maker because the Cicero Ltd group regards these items as of a non-operating nature.

The group has no customers from which it earns revenues that represent 10% or more of the total revenue of the group.

Required

Disclose all segment information for the Cicero Ltd group for the year ended 31 December 20.3 in accordance with the requirements of IFRS 8 *Operating Segments.*

❑ QUESTION IFRS 8.6@

The following is the segment information in respect of Joker Ltd for the year ended 30 June 20.8:

	Assets Rand	**Profit Rand**	**Revenue Rand**
20.7			
Manufacturing	15 000 000	500 000	8 000 000
Mining	150 000 000	7 000 000	90 000 000
Agriculture	35 000 000	680 000	15 000 000
South Africa	165 000 000	7 000 000	88 000 000
Rest of Africa	25 000 000	1 000 000	20 000 000
Europe	10 000 000	180 000	5 000 000
20.8			
Manufacturing	14 000 000	900 000	21 000 000
Mining	153 000 000	6 500 000	95 000 000
Agriculture	31 000 000	920 000	32 000 000
South Africa	161 000 000	6 890 000	92 000 000
Rest of Africa	11 000 000	500 000	12 000 000
Europe	26 000 000	930 000	44 000 000

Additional information

1. During the year the company changed its accounting policy in respect of inventory in the South Africa segment. This change resulted in a decrease of R1 100 000 in respect of profit for 20.7. This amount has not been corrected in the 20.7 figures. The new policy was used in the preparation of the 20.8 figures.
2. The company identifies operating segments on the basis of geographical location.
3. Management does not regard comparative amounts as of continuing significance once a segment no longer meets the criteria for reportability in a specific year.

Required

a. Discuss which of the operating segments are reportable in both 20.7 and 20.8. Show all supporting calculations.
b. Disclose the segment information of Joker Ltd for the year ended 30 June 20.8 so as to comply with the requirements of IFRS 8 *Operating Segments*. Use only the information given.

❑ QUESTION IFRS 8.7[@]

Martina Ltd, Steffi Ltd and Monica Ltd are all listed on the JSE Ltd. Steffi Ltd and Monica Ltd are wholly owned subsidiaries of Martina Ltd. The following information is relevant:

Extracts from the financial statements at 28 February 20.2:

	Martina Ltd Rand	**Steffi Ltd Rand**	**Monica Ltd Rand**
Revenue	500 000 000	250 000 000	70 000 000
Property, plant and equipment	20 463 000	45 221 000	7 000 000
Profit before tax	1 500 000	510 000	225 000
15% long-term borrowings – interest bearing	500 000	–	–
Trading inventory	224 000	148 000	300 000
Other current assets	150 000	245 000	126 000

Martina Ltd and Monica Ltd operate primarily in Pretoria and Cape Town (the South Africa segment), while Steffi Ltd operates primarily in Maputo (the Mozambique segment). Martina Ltd and Steffi Ltd are manufacturers of hardware, while Monica Ltd operates as a general dealer.

The long-term borrowings were incurred on 1 March 20.1, and no redemption of capital has taken place since then.

Monica Ltd purchases all its inventory from Martina Ltd and Steffi Ltd in the ratio of approximately 70:30. The closing inventory of Monica Ltd will also be in the same ratio. Sales to Monica Ltd take place at cost plus 20%. Approximately 40% of the sales of both companies, being Martina Ltd and Steffi Ltd, are supplied to Monica Ltd.

The chief operating decision maker assesses the performance of segments based on their geographical location.

The Martina Ltd group accounts for segment information by using the group accounting policies. Interest expense is regularly reviewed by management to assess the performance of operating segments. Income tax expense is, however, not reviewed.

Revenue from one South African customer represents 12% of the total revenue of the Martina Ltd group.

Required

a. Calculate the consolidated revenue, profit before tax and total assets as they will appear in the group statements for the year ended 28 February 20.2.
b. Prepare the segment report of the Martina Ltd group for the year ended 28 February 20.2 in accordance with the requirements of IFRS 8 *Operating Segments.*

❑ QUESTION IFRS 8.8[@]

Nkosi Ltd is a company in the electronics industry and is listed on the JSE Ltd. The company has various subsidiaries in the same industry. The group has five operating segments, namely Computers, Cell phones, Television, Radio and Appliances. The following segment information for the year ended 31 December 20.8 was extracted from the consolidated records of the Nkosi Ltd Group:

	Computers	**Cell phones**	**Television**	**Radio**	**Appliances**
	Rand	**Rand**	**Rand**	**Rand**	**Rand**
Sales	5 880 000	4 800 000	1 404 000	1 248 000	1 200 000
Profit/(loss) before tax	720 000	540 000	126 000	144 000	(120 000)
Plant at carrying amount	960 000	720 000	204 000	176 000	180 000
Total equity	1 200 000	960 000	240 000	264 000	258 000
Total liabilities	4 200 000	3 360 000	960 000	900 000	984 000

The following information for the Nkosi Ltd group is also available:

ABRIDGED CONSOLIDATED STATEMENT OF PROFIT OR LOSS AND OTHER COMPREHENSIVE INCOME FOR THE YEAR ENDED 31 DECEMBER 20.8

	Rand
Revenue	14 132 000
Cost of sales	(11 305 600)
Gross profit	2 826 400
Other expenses	(1 505 400)
Finance costs	(121 000)
Share of profit of associate	280 000
Profit before tax	1 480 000
Income tax expense	(414 400)
Profit for the year	1 065 600

	Rand
Other comprehensive income	
Items that will not be reclassified to profit or loss	
Gain on property revaluation	144 000
Total comprehensive income for the year	1 209 600
Profit attributable to:	
Owners of the parent	906 600
Non-controlling interest	159 000
	1 065 600
Total comprehensive income attributable to:	
Owners of the parent	1 050 600
Non-controlling interest	159 000
	1 209 600

Additional information

1. All segments operate in South Africa, except for the Computers segment, which also produces some computer products for the Canadian market. Approximately 20% of the revenue of the Computers segment represents sales to Canada. All of this revenue is derived from a single Canadian customer.

2. The difference between the total combined revenue of all segments and the consolidated revenue of the Nkosi Ltd group is due to inter-segment sales included in the revenue of the Television segment.

3. All inter-segment sales take place at a profit of 20% on the selling price. The closing inventory of the Cell phones segment includes R250 000 of parts inventory that was purchased from the Computers segment. The remaining difference between the total combined profit of all segments and the consolidated profit of the Nkosi Ltd Group is due to head office expenses not allocated to operating segments.

4. Other expenses include an amount of R300 000 for depreciation on buildings. The Nkosi Ltd group allocates depreciation to operating segments on the basis of the size of the floor area used by each segment. The floor area used by each segment is as follows:

	m^2
Computers	20 000
Cell phones	15 000
Television	6 000
Radio	5 000
Appliances	4 000
Total	50 000

5. The segment assets include non-current assets of R9 966 000 and current assets of R2 100 000 in respect of South African operations, and current assets of R640 000 in respect of Canadian operations.

6. The profit of the Television segment includes an impairment loss on plant amounting to R75 000.

7. The only capital expenditure incurred during the year was the purchase of a new delivery vehicle for the Computers segment amounting to R200 000.

8. The Nkosi Ltd group applies its group accounting policies to segment reporting, except that the share of profit of associates and income tax expense are not allocated to operating segments.

9. All finance costs relate to interest paid on the bank overdraft of the Cell phones segment. This amount has already been taken into account in determining the segment profit.

Required

a. Discuss which of the operating segments of the Nkosi Ltd Group is reportable in terms of IFRS 8 *Operating Segments*. Show all relevant calculations. Round all percentages to one decimal point.
b. Assuming that the Computers, Cell phones and Television segments are reportable, disclose all information required by IFRS 8 *Operating Segments*.

IAS 32, IFRS 9, IFRS 7, IFRS 13, IFRIC 10 & IFRIC 19

Financial instruments

Note: This chapter does not address current tax or deferred tax on financial instruments.

❑ QUESTIONS AND SOLUTIONS

IFRS 9.1	Equity instruments (IAS 32): discussion of accounting treatment
IFRS 9.2	Equity (IAS 32): discussion of transaction costs and calculation of SFPos carrying amount
IFRS 9.3	Equity instruments (IAS 32 and IFRS 7): discussion of classification and disclosure
IFRS 9.4	Financial assets and liabilities (IAS 32): discussion of classification and presentation (including offsetting)
IFRS 9.5	Classification and measurement of various items: discussion
IFRS 9.6	Theoretical aspects of accounting for speculative derivatives: discussion
IFRS 9.7	Investment in debt instrument at amortised cost or fair value through other comprehensive income: journal entries and calculation of SFPos carrying amounts
IFRS 9.8	Fair value adjustments for different categories of financial assets: journal entries
IFRS 9.9	Options used for speculative and hedging purposes: journal entries
IFRS 9.10	Impairment of financial asset: journal entries
IFRS 9.11[@]	Integrated question (IFRS 9 & IAS 32): discussion and journal entries

❑ QUESTIONS

IFRS 9.12[#]	Equity instruments (IAS 32): discussion of classification
IFRS 9.13	Equity instruments: presentation and journal entries
IFRS 9.14	Financial assets and liabilities (IFRS 9 & IAS 32): discussion of accounting treatment and presentation (including offsetting)
IFRS 9.15	Futures – speculative and commercial hedging: journal entries
IFRS 9.16	Options: discussion of classification, journal entries
IFRS 9.17	Recognition of transactions dealing with non-financial assets (inventory) as opposed to financial assets (derivative – FEC): journal entries
IFRS 9.18	Initial and subsequent accounting for several classes of financial instruments: journal entries and calculation of SFPos carrying amount

IFRS 9.19	Measurement of financial instruments: discussion
IFRS 9.20#	Integrated question (IFRS 9 & IAS 32): discussion and journal entries
IFRS 9.21#	Initial and subsequent accounting for several classes of financial instruments: journal entries and calculation of SFPos carrying amount
IFRS 9.22	Fair value measurement and impairment of several classes of financial assets: journal entries and calculation of SFPos carrying amount
IFRS 9.23	Extinguishing financial liability with equity instruments (IFRIC 19): journal entries

@ *These questions contain topics or principles that were not included in the ITC syllabus of SAICA at the time of publishing this book, but might still be included in university syllabi.*

These questions contain topics or principles that were at an awareness level of proficiency in the ITC syllabus of SAICA, at the time of publishing this book.

❑ QUESTION IFRS 9.1

Bon-Bon Ltd issued the following preference shares:

Type 1

The preference shares are convertible into ordinary shares on a one-to-one basis at the discretion of the issuer. The preference share dividends are cumulative but not compulsory. The issuer, Bon-Bon Ltd, has no contractual obligation to deliver cash or another financial asset to another party.

Type 2

The preference shares are convertible into debentures at the issuer's discretion; therefore, there is no current contractual obligation on the board of directors of Bon-Bon Ltd to do this conversion, i.e. transfer cash or another financial asset to another party. The preference share dividends are cumulative but not compulsory. Consequently, it appears as if these shares must be classified as equity.

However, since the interest on debentures is deductible for tax purposes, while preference dividends are not deductible, and in the light of the (assumed) 20% dividend rate on the preference shares, it is probable that this choice for conversion into preference shares will be exercised. In pursuing economic compulsion, the directors believe these preference shares should be classified as a financial liability.

Required

Briefly discuss how each type of preference share should be classified, presented and disclosed in the financial statements of Bon-Bon Ltd in accordance with the requirements of International Financial Reporting Standards (IFRS).

❖ Suggested solution IFRS 9.1

The accounting treatment and disclosure are as follows:

Type 1

The shares are classified as an equity instrument since they bear no contractual obligation to deliver cash or another financial asset, and the number of shares to be issued is fixed. All the presentation and disclosure requirements for ordinary and preference shares in terms of IAS 1, IAS 32 and IFRS 7 must be met. The shares are consequently included in share capital on initial recognition, and the dividends paid will be treated as dividends paid in the statement of changes in equity. The conditions relating to conversion should also be disclosed in the notes to the financial statements (IAS 1.79(a), IAS 1.106(d), IAS 32.35, IFRS 7.7).

Type 2

Economic compulsion has no bearing on classifying financial instruments as liabilities or equity. As there is no contractual obligation to deliver cash, the instrument should be classified as equity. They are presented and disclosed the same as for Type 1.

❑ QUESTION IFRS 9.2

On 1 July 20.0, Venus Ltd listed its existing 25 000 000 issued ordinary shares on the JSE Ltd.

In addition, it was decided to issue 500 000 compulsory convertible debentures of R1 each on the same date. These debentures bear interest at 9% per annum, compounded annually, until conversion on 30 June 20.3. On that date (30 June 20.3), the debentures will be converted into ordinary shares on a one-for-one basis. Similar debentures without conversion rights bear interest at 13% per annum, compounded annually.

The following costs were incurred in respect of the listing of the shares and the issue of the convertible debentures:

		Rand
Listing of shares		3 000 000
JSE listing costs	1 500 000	
Sponsors and advisors' costs	1 000 000	
Internal administrative costs	500 000	
Debenture issue		25 000
Sponsors and advisors' costs	17 000	
Securities transfer tax	5 000	
Internal administrative costs	3 000	
		3 025 000

Required

a. Discuss the accounting treatment of the transaction costs related to the share listing and the debenture issue in complying with International Financial Reporting Standards (IFRS). Mention amounts in your answer.

b. Calculate the finance costs to be recognised in the statement of profit or loss and other comprehensive income for the year ended 30 June 20.1, as well as the amortised cost balance of the debenture liability on the same date.

❖ Suggested solution IFRS 9.2

a.

IAS 32.35, 37 – .39 deals with the costs of equity transactions.

The costs of an equity transaction consist only of those external incremental costs directly attributable to the equity transaction that would otherwise have been avoided (see IAS 32.37). Internal administrative costs, therefore, do not form part of the cost of an equity transaction.

The transaction costs of an equity transaction (excluding internal administrative costs) must be accounted for as a reduction in equity (IAS 32.37).

Listing of shares
IAS 32 does not specifically exclude listing costs. The transaction costs of the listing of shares will be accounted for as follows:

- The internal administrative costs (R500 000) are recognised as an expense in profit or loss since only external costs can be costs of an equity transaction.

- The listing costs and sponsors and advisors' costs (R2 500 000) will be deducted from equity, net of any related income tax benefit. (IAS 32.35; IAS 32.39)

Debentures issued
IAS 32.38 states that transaction costs incurred on the issue of a compound instrument should be allocated to the different components of the instrument based on the proceeds of the components of the instrument.

The convertible debentures are a compound instrument as described in IAS 32.28.

The transaction costs of the debentures will be accounted for as follows:
- The internal administrative costs (R3 000) are recognised as an expense in profit or loss since only external costs can be costs of an equity transaction.
- The securities transfer tax and costs for sponsors and advisors (R22 000) must be allocated to the components based on the proceeds of the convertible debenture issue.

Split instrument into components at initial recognition:			**Rand**
Liability			*106 252
PMT	=	500 000 × 9% = 45 000	
i	=	13%	
n	=	3	
FV	=	0 (conversion to equity)	
Comp PV	=	?*	
Equity (balancing figure)			393 748
Total instrument			500 000

Allocate external costs (25 000 – 3 000) according to relative proceeds:

	Weight	**Costs**
Liability component	106 252	4 675
Equity component	393 748	17 325
	500 000	22 000

The R17 325 related to equity is shown as a reduction in the statement of changes in equity.

Extract from the statement of changes in equity	**Equity component of convertible debentures Rand**
Balance on 1 July 20.0	–
Changes in equity for 20.1	
Issue of convertible debentures	393 748
Transaction costs	(17 325)
Balance on 30 June 20.1	376 423

The external costs allocated to the liability component will be amortised as part of the liability and should not be initially recognised in profit or loss (IFRS 9.5.1.1).

b.

Recalculate the effective interest rate of the liability:

PV	=	106 252 – 4 675 = 101 577
PMT	=	45 000
n	=	3
Comp i	=	15,69%

Finance charges for 20.1

101 577 × 15,69% = 15 937

Balance of liability on 30 June 20.1	**Rand**
Initial amount of liability (106 252 – 4 675)	101 577
Interest paid (cash)	(45 000)
Interest recognised in profit or loss	15 937
Liability on 30 June 20.1	72 514

❑ QUESTION IFRS 9.3

The financial manager of Renox Limited approaches you for advice on IAS 32 *Financial instruments: Presentation.* He provides the following information:

- In order to obtain funding, the company sourced a convertible loan of R4,2 million from a financial institution. The loan bears interest at 15% per annum, compounded annually, and is repayable in equal instalments over eight years. The loan is convertible, at the option of the financial institution (holder), upon the repayment of each instalment into a fixed number of ordinary shares of Renox Limited. The conversion will take place at one ordinary share for every R10,00 of the repaid debt.

  Of the R4,2 million, R4 million relates to a loan without a conversion option and R200 000 to the conversion option.

- Renox Limited also issued debentures of R6 million. The debentures bear interest at 15,5% per annum, compounded annually, and are settled after 10 years if they are not converted into shares. Settlement or conversion are based on the share price of Renox: If the share price of Renox Limited remains below R12,00 per share, the debentures are convertible into ordinary shares at one ordinary share for every R12,00 of the repayable debt. If the share price of Renox Limited equals or increases to above R12,00 per share, the debentures will be settled in cash.

The current market value of Renox Ltd's ordinary shares is R8 per share.

Required

a. Discuss how each transaction should initially be classified (equity or liability) in the financial statements of Renox Limited in terms of IAS 32.
b. Discuss which information should be disclosed in respect of every transaction in terms of IFRS 7.

Your answer must comply with International Financial Reporting Standards (IFRS) requirements.

❖ Suggested solution IFRS 9.3

a. Principles

The **substance** of a financial instrument, rather than its legal form, regulates its classification in the statement of financial position of the issuer (IAS 32.15).

The classification is done when the instrument is **initially** recognised (IAS 32.15) and is not changed until the financial instrument is derecognised (removed) from the statement of financial position.

In order to determine the classification, the following definitions are essential:

IAS 32.16 states that an instrument is an **equity instrument** if, and only if, both conditions (a) and (b) below are met:

(a) The instrument includes no contractual obligation (i) to deliver cash or another financial asset to another entity; or (ii) to exchange financial assets or financial liabilities with another entity under conditions that are potentially unfavourable to the issuer, and

(b) If the instrument will or may be settled in the issuer's own equity instruments, it is: (i) a non-derivative that includes no contractual obligation for the issuer to deliver a variable number of its own equity instruments; or (ii) n/a.

A **financial liability** is any liability that is a contractual obligation:

- to deliver cash or another financial asset to another entity; or
- to exchange financial instruments with another entity on conditions that are potentially unfavourable.

Other components of the definitions are not given here as they are not applicable.

The critical characteristic in the distinction between a financial liability and an equity instrument is a **contractual obligation,** as discussed above.

Application

Loan

The loan consists of two components:

- Loan of R4 million
- Conversion option to purchase shares for R200 000*

IAS 32 stipulates that where a financial instrument contains both a liability and an equity element, the elements must be **classified separately** (IAS 32.28).

The loan of R4 million represents a **liability**, i.e. a contractual obligation to deliver cash or another financial asset.

* The conversion option of R200 000 represents an **equity instrument** – a purchase option that grants the holder the right to convert the instrument into a fixed number of ordinary shares for a fixed amount of cash in Renox Ltd's own equity instruments within a specified period of time.

Debentures

IAS 32.25 stipulates that where a financial instrument requires the entity to deliver cash or another financial asset, or otherwise to settle it in such a way that it would be a financial liability in the event of the **occurrence or non-occurrence of uncertain future events** (or on the outcome of uncertain circumstances) that are beyond the control of both the issuer and the holder of the instrument, the issuer of such an instrument does not have the unconditional right to avoid delivering cash or another financial asset (or otherwise to settle it in such a way that it would be a financial liability) (contingent settlement provisions). Therefore, it will be classified as a financial liability of the issuer, unless the part of the contingent settlement provision that could require settlement in cash or another financial asset (or otherwise in such a way that it would be a financial liability), is not genuine.

The interest on the debenture over its lifetime is considered a financial liability as this is a contractual obligation to deliver cash. The contingent settlement provision at the end of the instrument's life is genuine as the share price may increase above R12,00. Therefore, the contingent settlement in cash is classified as a financial liability of the issuer. However, there is the potential that Renox will have to convert the debentures into a fixed number of shares. The latter points to an equity instrument. The debenture will therefore be classified as a **compound instrument**, with the liability portion consisting of the present value of the interest and settlement discounted at a market-related rate without a conversion option. The balancing amount would constitute the equity portion.

b. The following must be disclosed in terms of IFRS 7:

- IFRS 7.8: The carrying amount of financial liabilities measured at amortised cost (R4 000 000).
- IFRS 7.20(b): The total interest expense (calculated using the effective interest method) for financial liabilities that are not at fair value through profit or loss.
- IFRS 7.21: The accounting policies used in preparing the financial statements and that are relevant to an understanding of the financial statements, including the treatment of:
  - long-term loans and the liability portion of the convertible debentures carried at amortised cost; and
  - the purchase option.
- IFRS 7.31: The nature and extent of risks, arising from the financial instruments, to which the entity is exposed during the period and at the reporting date, and how the entity manages those risks.
- IFRS 7.33-34 applied: The exposure to interest rate risk, including:
  - contractual repricing dates, where applicable;
  - effective interest rates, when applicable for both the loan and the debentures (as interest rates are fixed in both instances).
- IFRS 7.39: Exposure to liquidity risk, including:
  - contractual repricing dates.

(**Note:** The disclosure requirements of IFRS 13.91-99 were not addressed as this was not required, and none of the above instruments is normally carried at fair value after initial recognition).

❑ QUESTION IFRS 9.4

The managing director of Conglomerate Ltd has suggested a transaction which he believes would reduce the effective after-tax interest rate on a five-year loan of R200 million granted to Lucky Ltd, a wholly owned subsidiary of Conglomerate Ltd.

The transaction requires, among other things, that Lucky Ltd issues debentures of R200 million to Insuro Ltd, a large insurance company. Lucky Ltd invests the proceeds of the debentures in preference shares to the value of R200 million, which are issued by a company in the Insuro group.

The managing director believes that the debentures and preference shares do not have to be presented and disclosed in the group annual financial statements of Conglomerate Ltd since the substance of the transactions is to improve the after-tax return. He mentions that should the preference shares and debentures be disclosed in the consolidated financial statements as assets and liabilities, various financing ratios would be adversely affected, and he would not enter into the transaction. (QE 1992 – adapted)

Required

Discuss whether you agree with the presentation and disclosure as suggested by the managing director. The correct classification and presentation (if applicable) should also be discussed. Your answer must comply with International Financial Reporting Standards (IFRS) requirements.

❖ **Suggested solution IFRS 9.4**

The above series of transactions represents two separate transactions:

- The debentures are issued to Insuro Ltd (thus a financial liability); and
- The proceeds are then invested in preference shares of another company in the Insuro group (thus a financial asset).

In terms of IAS 32.42, a financial asset and a financial liability may only be offset, and the net amount presented in the statement of financial position when:

- A legally enforceable right exists to set off the recognised amounts; and
- The intention is either to settle on a net basis or to realise the asset and settle the liability simultaneously.

No indication is given in the fact pattern as to whether such a legally enforceable right exists; therefore, the debentures and preference shares must be presented separately in the annual financial statements of Lucky Ltd and in the consolidated financial statements.

The preference shares taken up by Lucky Ltd must be classified as either a financial asset at fair value through profit or loss or elected as a financial asset at fair value through other comprehensive income. Fair value adjustments will be accounted for according to the initial classification, either through profit or loss or through other comprehensive income. The preference shares must be presented under 'Non-current assets' in the statement of financial position.

The debentures must be classified as a financial liability measured at amortised cost and presented under 'Non-current liabilities' in the statement of financial position. The disclosure requirements of IFRS 7 must be adhered to.

❑ **QUESTION IFRS 9.5**

Discuss how each of the following items should be classified and measured initially and subsequently to that for accounting purposes in terms of IFRS 9:

- Trade receivables, held to collect contractual cash flows due*
- Allowance account ('provision') for credit losses ('doubtful debts')

- Investment in shares, but not held for speculative purposes or otherwise elected
- Quoted/listed investment in municipal bonds, held to collect contractual cash flows due*
- Derivative assets
- Long-term borrowings not held for trading or otherwise designated
- Trade payables not otherwise designated

** Assume that interest is solely compensation for the time value of money and credit risk associated with the principal amount outstanding.*

❖ **Suggested solution IFRS 9.5**

- **Trade receivables**

Trade receivables are classified as measured at amortised cost because it is a debt instrument held within a business model to collect contractual cash flows that are solely payments of principal and interest on the principal outstanding on the specified dates (IFRS 9.4.1.2).

Trade receivables with a significant financing component per IFRS 15 are measured at fair value at initial recognition, including transaction costs directly attributable to this financial asset (IFRS 9.5.1.1). Subsequently, they are measured (according to the initial classification) at amortised cost (IFRS 9.5.2.1).

Trade receivables that do not have a significant financing component in accordance with IFRS 15 are initially and subsequently measured at the transaction price as defined in IFRS 15, or when the entity applies the practical expedient in accordance with IFRS 15.63 (IFRS 9.5.1.3).

The entity must also apply the impairment requirements to trade receivables, as it is a financial asset measured at amortised cost (IFRS 9.4.1.1 and IFRS 9.5.2.1).

- **Allowance account for credit losses**

Allowance account for credit losses is an impairment loss adjustment (IFRS 9.5.5). A credit loss is the difference between all contractual cash flows that are due to an entity in accordance with the contract and all the cash flows that the entity expects to receive (i.e. all cash shortfalls), discounted at the original effective interest rate (or credit-adjusted effective interest rate for purchased or originated credit-impaired financial assets[@]). Expected credit losses are the weighted average of credit losses with the respective risks of a default (non-payment) occurring as the weights. An entity recognises a loss allowance for expected credit losses in every reporting period and not only when there is an indicator of impairment. The allowance account (balance) is measured at each reporting date, as follows:

- If the credit risk* on a financial asset has increased significantly since initial recognition: at an amount equal to the lifetime expected credit losses; or
- If the credit risk on a financial asset has not increased significantly since initial recognition: at an amount equal to 12-month expected credit losses. The latter is the portion of lifetime expected credit losses that represent the expected credit losses that result from default events (i.e. events causing non-payment) on a financial instrument that is possible within the 12 months after the reporting date (i.e. the effect of the entire credit loss on an asset weighted by the probability that this loss will occur in the next 12 months) (IFRS 9.B5.5.43).

Short-term receivables are normally not discounted, as the effect of the time value of money is usually immaterial, therefore, the allowance account for credit losses on such receivables is also not discounted.

* *The risk that one party to a financial instrument will cause a financial loss for the other party by failing to discharge an obligation (IFRS 7 Appendix A)*

@ *Not in the SAICA syllabus.*

- **Investment in shares (non-speculative)**

  The investment in shares is classified as a financial asset at fair value through profit or loss since it is an equity instrument that is not held for trading or elected at initial recognition as measured at fair value through other comprehensive income (IFRS 9.5.7.5).

  The investment is initially measured at fair value on the date of acquisition, excluding directly attributable transaction costs (IFRS 9.5.1.1).

  Subsequently, the investment is measured according to the initial classification at fair value through profit or loss (IFRS 9.5.2.1).

- **Quoted/listed investment in municipal bonds**

  The investment in municipal bonds is classified as measured at amortised cost because it is a debt instrument held within a business model with the objective to collect contractual cash flows that are solely payments of principal and interest on the principal outstanding on specified dates (IFRS 9.4.1.2).

  The municipal bonds investment is initially measured at fair value, including directly attributable transaction costs (IFRS 9.5.1.1).

  Subsequently, according to the initial classification, the municipal bonds investment is measured at amortised cost (IFRS 9.5.2.1) by using the effective interest method (IFRS 9.5.4).

  The entity must also apply the impairment requirements to the investment in municipal bonds, as it is a financial asset measured at amortised cost (IFRS 9.4.1.1 and IFRS 9.5.2.1).

- **Derivative assets**

  Derivatives that are assets are classified as measured at fair value through profit or loss since they are geared, and therefore do not have cash flows that are solely payments of principal and interest on principal outstanding on specified dates. Moreover, the derivatives are not equity instruments (IFRS 9.4.1.4). Derivatives are initially measured (according to the initial classification) at fair value (IFRS 9.5.1.1), excluding directly attributable transaction costs. After that, they are measured at fair value through profit or loss (IFRS 9.5.2.1).

- **Long-term borrowings**

  Long-term borrowings are financial liabilities classified as measured at amortised cost since they are not held for trading or otherwise designated (IFRS 9.4.2.1). Initially, financial liabilities are measured at fair value less directly attributable transaction costs (since the cost is a debit, the costs are deducted) (IFRS 9.5.1.1). After that, they are measured at amortised cost (IFRS 9.5.3.1).

- **Trade payables**

  These trade payables are financial liabilities classified as measured at amortised cost using the effective interest method (the default classification) because they do not constitute one of the exceptions per IFRS 9.4.2.1.

  Trade payables should (as with long-term borrowings) initially be measured at fair value less attributable transaction costs (IFRS 9.5.1.1), using the effective interest method, and after that at amortised cost (IFRS 9.5.3.1).

❑ QUESTION IFRS 9.6

You are the auditor of Pricey Parts Ltd, a motor car spare parts supplier. During your audit for the year ended 31 December 20.2, you were responsible for the review of the following item in the statement of financial position:

Deferred loss on bankers' acceptance future	R150 000

This *speculative* instrument was entered into in an attempt to improve reported profits. The amount represents a loss incurred by the year-end on a bankers' acceptance future. The initial entry done by Pricey Parts Ltd was Dr Deferred loss on banker's acceptance future and Cr Future (liability).

Given the current International Financial Reporting Standards (IFRS), you do not agree with the accounting entry processed by your client.

Required

Draft a letter to the management of the company explaining why you disagree with the accounting entry of the item detailed above. Your letter should also recommend the proposed accounting treatment and detail its effect on the statement of profit or loss and other comprehensive income for the year ended 31 December 20.2. (QE 1991 – adapted)

❖ Suggested solution IFRS 9.6

Letter: Heading and introduction

Futures are derivatives because they require only a small initial investment (or no investment at all), their value changes in response to the change in an interest rate, foreign exchange rate, share price, commodity price, etc., and they are settled at a future date (definition in IFRS 9 Appendix A).

IFRS 9.4.2.1(a) stipulates that derivatives that are liabilities shall be subsequently measured at fair value with changes in the fair value recognised in profit or loss.

Since the bankers' acceptance future was entered into for speculative purposes, the loss (representing the fair value change) should be recognised as an expense in profit or loss in the statement of profit or loss and other comprehensive income. A loss on the bankers' acceptance future may, therefore, not be deferred to the statement of financial position.

[Not required:]
The loss included in profit or loss should be disclosed separately in the note to profit before tax (IFRS 7.20(a)(i)).

Letter: Conclusion

❑ QUESTION IFRS 9.7

A company purchased 3 000 listed debentures at R190,00 per debenture at the beginning of 20.1. The debentures are 10% R200 debentures and are redeemable at par at the end of 20.3.

Transaction costs amounted to R2 000. Interest is payable annually at the end of the year, and you may assume that the purchase price is at fair value.

The debentures are held within a business model with the objective to collect contractual cash flows that are solely payments of principal and interest on the principal outstanding on the specified dates. Assume that interest is solely compensation for the time value of money and credit risk associated with the principal amount outstanding.

Required

a. Journalise the effect of the transaction for 20.1 to 20.3.
b. Calculate the amortised cost of the debenture investment for 20.1 to 20.3.
c. If it is assumed that the debentures are held within a business model with the objective to collect contractual cash flows **and** sell the financial assets, and the contractual terms of the financial asset give rise to cash flows that are solely payments of principal and interest on the principal amount outstanding, journalise the effect of the transaction for 20.1 to 20.3. Assume that the year-end fair values for the debentures for 20.1 to 20.3 are R582 000, R590 000 and R600 000, respectively.
d. Assume that the debentures in c. above are sold at the end of 20.2 for their fair value of R590 000. Journalise the effect of the transaction on the date of sale.

Your answer should comply with International Financial Reporting Standards (IFRS) requirements.

❖ Suggested solution IFRS 9.7

The debenture investment is classified as a financial asset measured at amortised cost.

Calculations

			Rand
1.	**Cost**		
	Initial payment (3 000 × R190) (fair value)		570 000
	Transaction costs		2 000
			572 000

			Rand (outflow)
2.	**Cash flow**		
	1 Jan 20.1		(572 000)
	31 Dec 20.1	(600 000 × 10%)	60 000
	31 Dec 20.2	(600 000 × 10%)	60 000
	31 Dec 20.3	[(600 000 × 10%) + 600 000]	660 000

OR

n	=	3
PMT	=	600 000 × 10% = 60 000
FV	=	600 000
PV	=	–572 000
Comp i	=	11,94099%

3. Effective interest rate	11,94099%

a. Journals

	Rand Dr/(Cr)
1 January 20.1	
Debentures at amortised cost (SFPos)	570 000
Bank	(570 000)
Purchase of debentures	
1 January 20.1	
Debentures at amortised cost (SFPos)	2 000
Bank	(2 000)
Transaction costs capitalised	
31 December 20.1	
Debentures at amortised cost (SFPos)	68 302
Interest received (P or L)	(68 302)
Recognise effective interest accrued @ 11,94099% (1)	
31 December 20.1	
Bank (2)	60 000
Debentures at amortised cost (SFPos)	(60 000)
Coupon interest actually received	
31 December 20.2	
Debentures at amortised cost (SFPos)	69 294
Interest received (P or L) (3)	(69 294)
Recognise effective interest accrued	
31 December 20.2	
Bank	60 000
Debentures at amortised cost (SFPos)	(60 000)
Coupon interest actually received	
31 December 20.3	
Debentures at amortised cost (SFPos)	70 404
Interest received (P or L) (4)	(70 404)
Recognise effective interest accrued	
31 December 20.3	
Bank	660 000
Debentures at amortised cost (SFPos)	(660 000)
Receive coupon interest and repayment at redemption	

b. Amortised cost at the end of 20.1 to 20.3

	20.1 Rand	20.2 Rand	20.3 Rand
Initial recognition (570 000 + 2 000)	572 000	–	–
Amortised cost end of the previous year	–	580 302	589 596
Interest accrued (effective) (1) (3) (4)	68 302	69 294	70 404
Interest received (coupon) (2)	(60 000)	(60 000)	(60 000)
Capital redemption	–	–	(600 000)
Amortised cost end of year	580 302	589 596	Nil

(1) 572 000 × 11,94099% = 68 302
(2) 600 000 × 10% = 60 000
(3) (572 000 + 68 302 – 60 000) × 11,94099% = 69 294
(4) (580 302 + 69 294 – 60 000) × 11,94099% = 70 404

c. Journals

IFRS 9.5.7.11 states that, if a financial asset is measured at fair value through other comprehensive income, the amounts that are recognised in profit or loss are the same as those that would have been recognised in profit or loss if the financial asset had been measured at amortised cost. Consequently, the same journal entries as in **b.** above would be recorded, with an additional journal to account for the fair value adjustment through other comprehensive income.

	Rand Dr/(Cr)
1 January 20.1	
Debentures at fair value through other comprehensive income (SFPos)	570 000
Bank	(570 000)
Purchase of debentures	
1 January 20.1	
Debentures at fair value through other comprehensive income (SFPos)	2 000
Bank	(2 000)
Transaction costs capitalised	
31 December 20.1	
Debentures at fair value through other comprehensive income (SFPos)	68 302
Interest received (P or L)	(68 302)
Recognise effective interest accrued @ 11,94099% (1)	
31 December 20.1	
Bank (2)	60 000
Debentures at fair value through other comprehensive income (SFPos)	(60 000)
Coupon interest actually received	
31 December 20.1	
Debentures at fair value through other comprehensive income (SFPos)	1 698
Fair value adjustment (OCI)	(1 698)
Recognise the fair value adjustment (3)	

	Rand Dr/(Cr)
31 December 20.2	
Debentures at fair value through other comprehensive income (SFPos)	69 294
Interest received (P or L) (4)	(69 294)
Recognise effective interest accrued	
31 December 20.2	
Bank	60 000
Debentures at fair value through other comprehensive income (SFPos)	(60 000)
Coupon interest actually received	
31 December 20.2	
Fair value adjustment (OCI)	1 294
Debentures at fair value through other comprehensive income (SFPos)	(1 294)
Recognise the fair value adjustment (5)	
31 December 20.3	
Debentures at fair value through other comprehensive income (SFPos)	70 404
Interest received (P or L) (6)	(70 404)
Recognise effective interest accrued	
31 December 20.3	
Fair value adjustment (OCI)	404
Debentures at fair value through other comprehensive income (SFPos)	(404)
Recognise the fair value adjustment (7)	
31 December 20.3	
Bank	660 000
Debentures at fair value through other comprehensive income (SFPos)	(660 000)
Receive coupon interest and repayment at redemption	

Calculation	**20.1 Rand**	**20.2 Rand**	**20.3 Rand**
Initial recognition (570 000 + 2 000)	572 000	–	–
Carrying amount end of the previous year	–	582 000	590 000
Interest accrued (effective) (1) (4) (6)	68 302	69 294	70 404
Interest received (coupon) (2)	(60 000)	(60 000)	(60 000)
Carrying amount before fair value adjustment	580 302	591 294	600 404
Fair value adjustment (OCI) (3) (5) (7)	1 698	(1 294)	(404)
Fair value at end of the year	582 000	590 000	600 000
Capital redemption	–	–	(600 000)
Carrying amount end of the year	582 000	590 000	Nil

(1) 572 000 × 11,94099% = 68 302
(2) 600 000 × 10% = 60 000
(3) 582 000 – 580 302 = 1 698
(4) (572 000 + 68 302 – 60 000) × 11,94099% = 69 294
(5) 590 000 – 591 294 = (1 294)

(6) (580 302 + 69 294 – 60 000) × 11,94099% = 70 404
(7) 600 000 – 600 404 = (404)

d. Sale of debenture measured at fair value through other comprehensive income

When the asset is sold, the contractual rights to the cash flows expire, and the entity must derecognise the financial asset (IFRS 9.3.2.3). IFRS 9.5.7.10 states that when the financial asset is derecognised, the cumulative gain or loss previously recognised in other comprehensive income is reclassified from equity to profit or loss as a reclassification adjustment (see IAS 1).

	Rand Dr/(Cr)
31 December 20.2	
Bank	590 000
Debentures at fair value through other comprehensive income (SFPos)	(590 000)
Derecognise the financial asset	
31 December 20.2	
Fair value adjustment (OCI) (1)	404
Fair value adjustment (P or L)	(404)
Reclassification adjustment	

(1) Cumulative amount in OCI upon reclassification to P or L: 1 698 – 1 294 = 404

❑ QUESTION IFRS 9.8

Fair Ltd acquired 10 000 ordinary shares on the JSE Ltd for R100 000 (fair value) with related transaction costs of R1 000. The fair value of the investment is R120 000 at year-end.

Required

Journalise the initial recognition and fair value adjustment at year-end if the share investment is classified as:
a. At fair value through profit or loss;
b. At fair value through other comprehensive income.

Your answer must comply with International Financial Reporting Standards (IFRS) requirements.

❖ Suggested solution IFRS 9.8

a.

	Rand Dr/(Cr)
Purchase date	
Investment – at fair value through profit or loss (SFPos)	100 000
Bank	(100 000)
Purchase cost *excluding* transaction costs	
Transaction costs (P or L)	1 000
Bank	(1 000)
Recognising transaction costs separately	
Year-end	
Investment – at fair value through profit or loss (SFPos)	20 000
Fair value adjustment on share investment (P or L) (1)	(20 000)
Fair value adjustment at year-end	

b.

Purchase date	
Investment – at fair value through other comprehensive income (SFPos)	101 000
Bank (2)	(101 000)
Purchase costs, including transaction costs	
Year-end	
Investment – at fair value through other comprehensive income (SFPos)	19 000
Mark-to-market reserve (OCI) (3)	(19 000)
Fair value adjustment at year-end	

(1) 120 000 – 100 000 = 20 000
(2) 100 000 + 1 000 = 101 000
(3) 120 000 – 101 000 = 19 000

❑ QUESTION IFRS 9.9

A company purchases 200 options on 1 January 20.5 to acquire shares in a specific company. The purchase price is R9 per option. Transaction costs associated with the purchase were R20 in total. The maturity date of the options was 31 March 20.5, and the exercise (strike) price (to purchase shares) was R350 per share. The fair value of an option on 31 March 20.5 was R25 and that of a share R375.

The company's initial intention was to settle the options gross (i.e. acquire the options to purchase the shares). The company does not apply hedge accounting. The year-end of the company is 28 February 20.5. On that date, the fair value of an option was R16 and that of a share R357.

Required

The journal entries if:

a. The options are not exercised;
b. The options are exercised.

Your answer must comply with International Financial Reporting Standards (IFRS) requirements.

❖ **Suggested solution IFRS 9.9**

		Rand Dr/(Cr)
a.	**1 January 20.5**	
	Options (SFPos) (1)	1 800
	Bank	(1 800)
	Purchase of options	
	Transaction costs (P or L)	20
	Bank	(20)
	Expense transaction costs	
	28 February 20.5	
	Options (SFPos) (2)	1 400
	Fair value adjustment on options (P or L)	(1 400)
	Remeasure options to fair value	
	31 March 20.5	
	Options (SFPos) (3)	1 800
	Fair value adjustment on options (P or L)	(1 800)
	Remeasure options to fair value at maturity	
	Options expensed (P or L)	5 000
	Options (SFPos)	(5 000)
	Expense option asset at the expiry date	
	Note: The net effect in profit or loss is:	
	Fair value adjustments	3 200
	Options written off	(5 000)
	Net loss	(1 800)

(1) 200 × R9 = 1 800
(2) (200 × R16) – 1 800 = 1 400
(3) (200 × R25) – (1 800 + 1 400) = 1 800

The net loss is equal to the original purchase price of the options.

b. If the shares were purchased, the journal entries on 1 January 20.5 and 28 February 20.5 would be the same. The journals on 31 March 20.5 will be:

	Rand Dr/(Cr)
31 March 20.5	
Options (SFPos)	1 800
Fair value adjustment on options (P or L)	(1 800)
Remeasure to fair value at purchase of shares (Same as the previous journal)	
Investment in shares (SFPos) (1)	75 000
Bank	(70 000)
Options (SFPos)	(5 000)
Purchase shares at the option price	

(1) 200 × R375 = 75 000 (initially recognised at fair value)

❑ QUESTION IFRS 9.10

Nita Ltd purchased 1 000 listed debentures at R760 per debenture at the beginning of 20.1. The debentures are 10% R800 debentures and are redeemable at par at the end of 20.4.

Transaction costs amounted to R5 000. Interest is payable annually at the end of the year, and you may assume that the purchase price is at fair value.

The debentures are held within a business model with the objective to collect contractual cash flows that are solely payments of principal and interest on the principal outstanding on the specified dates. Assume that interest is solely compensation for the time value of money and credit risk associated with the principal amount outstanding.

All contractual cash flows were received unless otherwise indicated. Considering the probability of default, time value of money and other supporting information, management made the following assessments concerning the debentures' credit risk:

Date of assessment	**Credit risk as assessed by management**	**12-month expected credit losses**	**Lifetime expected credit losses**
		Rand	**Rand**
31 December 20.1	**Performing:** No significant increase in credit risk since initial recognition.	23 150	100 000
31 December 20.2	**Under-performing:** There has been a significant increase in credit risk since initial recognition.	23 400	101 500
1 January 20.3	**Non-performing:** Management obtained objective evidence that the issuer of the debentures is in financial trouble and considers the investment to be credit-impaired.	23 400	101 500
31 December 20.3	**Non-performing:** There is still objective evidence of credit impairment at the reporting date.	23 700	150 750

Required

a. Journalise the effect of the transaction for 20.1 to 20.3.
b. Calculate the amortised cost of the debenture investment for 20.1 to 20.3.
c. Journalise the effect of the transaction for 20.4 if you assume that default occurs on 31 December 20.4 and that Nita Ltd received a coupon interest payment of R50 000 and a capital redemption amount of R665 000 on that date. Also, assume that management has judged that there is no prospect of recovering any outstanding contractual cash flows.

Your answer should comply with International Financial Reporting Standards (IFRS) requirements.

❖ Suggested solution IFRS 9.10

The debenture investment is classified as a financial asset at amortised cost. The amortised cost of the financial asset is measured as the difference between the gross carrying amount and the allowance for expected credit losses.

Calculations

		Rand
1.	**Cost**	
	Initial payment (1 000 × R760) (fair value)	760 000
	Transaction costs	5 000
		765 000

		Rand (outflow)/ inflow
2.	**Cash flows**	
	1 January 20.1	(765 000)
	31 December 20.1 (800 000 × 10%)	80 000
	31 December 20.2 (800 000 × 10%)	80 000
	31 December 20.3 (800 000 × 10%)	80 000
	31 December 20.4 [(800 000 × 10%) + 800 000]	880 000

OR

n	=	4
PMT	=	800 000 × 10% = 80 000
FV	=	800 000
PV	=	–765 000
Comp i	=	11,4229%

3.	**Effective interest rate**	11,4229%

a. Journals

	Rand Dr/(Cr)
1 January 20.1	
Debentures at gross carrying amount (SFPos)	760 000
Bank	(760 000)
Purchase of debentures	
Debentures at gross carrying amount (SFPos)	5 000
Bank	(5 000)
Transaction costs recognised	
31 December 20.1	
Debentures at gross carrying amount (SFPos)	87 385
Interest received (P or L) (1)	(87 385)
Recognise effective interest accrued	
Bank (2)	80 000
Debentures at gross carrying amount (SFPos)	(80 000)
Coupon interest actually received	
Expected credit losses (P or L) (5)	23 150
Allowance for expected credit losses (SFPos)	(23 150)
Recognise expected credit losses	

	Rand Dr/(Cr)
31 December 20.2	
Debentures at gross carrying amount (SFPos)	88 229
Interest received (P or L) (3)	(88 229)
Recognise effective interest accrued	
Bank	80 000
Debentures at gross carrying amount (SFPos)	(80 000)
Coupon interest actually received	
Expected credit losses (P or L) (6)	78 350
Allowance for expected credit losses (SFPos)	(78 350)
Recognise movement in expected credit losses	
1 January 20.3	
No entries needed (7)	
31 December 20.3	
Debentures at gross carrying amount (SFPos)	89 169
Interest received* (P or L) (4)	(89 169)
Recognise effective interest accrued	
Bank	80 000
Debentures at gross carrying amount (SFPos)	(80 000)
Coupon interest actually received	
Interest received* (P or L) (8)	11 594
Allowance for expected credit losses (SFPos)	(11 594)
Recognise interest accrued	
Expected credit losses (P or L) (9)	37 656
Allowance for expected credit losses (SFPos)	(37 656)
Recognise movement in expected credit losses	

* Net interest = 89 169 – 11 594 = 77 575

b. Amortised cost at the end of 20.1 to 20.3

	20.1 Rand	20.2 Rand	20.3 Rand
Initial recognition (760 000 + 5 000)	765 000	–	–
Gross carrying amount end of previous year	–	772 385	780 614
Interest accrued (effective) (1) (3) (4)	87 385	88 229	89 169
Interest received in cash (2)	(80 000)	(80 000)	(80 000)
Capital redemption	–	–	–
Gross carrying amount end of year	772 385	780 614	789 783
Allowance for expected credit losses	(23 150)	(101 500)	(150 750)
Balance at end of previous year	–	(23 150)	(101 500)
Interest on expected credit losses (8)	–	–	(11 594)
Movement in expected credit losses recognised during the year (5) (6) (9)	(23 150)	(78 350)	(37 656)
Amortised cost at the end of the year	749 235	679 114	639 033

(1) 765 000 × 11,4229% = 87 385
(2) 800 000 × 10% = 80 000
(3) (765 000 + 87 385 – 80 000) × 11,4229% = 88 229
(4) (772 385 + 88 229 – 80 000) × 11,4229% = 89 169
(5) No significant increase in credit risk since initial recognition – use 12-month expected credit losses (IFRS 9 par. 5.5.5).
(6) Significant increase in credit risk – use lifetime expected credit losses (IFRS 9 par. 5.5.3). 101 500 – 23 150 = 78 350. No interest is recognised on the allowance for expected credit losses for 20.2 (interest calculated on the gross carrying amount only).
(7) On 1 January 20.3, the allowance for expected credit losses is already reflected at lifetime expected credit losses.
(8) The financial asset is credit-impaired from 1 January 20.3, and interest on the opening balance of the allowance for expected credit losses should be recognised. 101 500 × 11,4229% = 11 594. This interest reduces the interest recognised on the gross carrying amount so that the total interest is calculated on a net basis as required in IFRS 9.
(9) The financial asset is credit-impaired – use lifetime expected credit losses. 150 750 – (101 500 + 11 594) = 37 656.

c. Journals

	Rand Dr/(Cr)
31 December 20.4	
Debentures at gross carrying amount (SFPos)	90 216
Interest received* (P or L) (1)	(90 216)
Recognise effective interest accrued	
Bank	50 000
Debentures at gross carrying amount (SFPos)	(50 000)
Coupon interest actually received	
Interest received* (P or L) (2)	17 220
Allowance for expected credit losses (SFPos)	(17 220)
Recognise interest accrued	
Bank	665 000
Credit loss (P or L) (4)	164 999
Debentures at gross carrying amount (SFPos) (3)	(829 999)
Recognise capital redemption and derecognise financial asset	
Allowance for expected credit losses (SFPos) (5)	167 970
Expected credit losses (P or L)	(167 970)
Reversal of allowance for expected credit losses	

* Net interest = 90 216 – 17 220 = 72 996

(1) 789 783 × 11,4229% = 90 216
(2) 150 750 × 11,4229% = 17 220
(3) 789 783 + 90 216 – 50 000 = 829 999
(4) 829 999 – 665 000 = 164 999
(5) 150 750 + 17 220 = 167 970

❑ QUESTION IFRS 9.11[@]

The following information relates to Ko Samet Ltd for the year ended 28 February 20.2:

Share capital

500 000	Ordinary shares.
100 000	Redeemable preference shares of R2,00 each. These shares pay dividends at a market-related rate of 10% per annum that are not within the entity's discretion. Of the shares, 50% will be redeemed at par for cash on 28 February 20.3, while the remainder will be redeemed on 31 August 20.4.
50 000	Debentures of R10,00 each, issued at R11,00 per debenture on 28 February 20.2. Interest at a fixed rate is payable annually on the face value. The debentures must be converted on 28 February 20.5 into five ordinary shares for each debenture held on 28 February 20.5.

Inventory

Ko Samet Ltd placed an order to purchase inventory (highly probable forecast transaction) from the US for $46 000 on 10 January 20.2. To manage the currency risks of the company, management immediately took out a forward exchange contract (FEC) for this inventory purchase, which expires three months later on the settlement date. The goods were shipped free on board (FOB) on 20 February 20.2, and the creditor was paid on 10 April 20.2. On 20 February 20.2, the forward rate for an FEC maturing on 10 April 20.2 amounted to R12,38, while at year-end, an FEC maturing on 10 April 20.2 traded at R12,49. The hedge of the foreign currency creditor is accounted for as a fair value hedge.

Foreign loan

Ko Samet Ltd finances some of its activities with funds from the US. Owing to current market conditions and projections, it appears as if the rand will not appreciate in the near future. The board of directors decided to hedge the company against future exchange losses that may arise from the repayment of this foreign loan (i.e. the future cash flows are hedged).

The company entered into a six-month FEC on 1 January 20.2 for $300 000. This FEC covers the semi-annual instalment that is payable on 1 July 20.2. The total amount due comprises $300 000, of which $72 000 relates to interest. An equivalent FEC traded at R12,80 on 28 February 20.2.

The applicable exchange rates are as follows:

Date	Spot rate $1 = R	Six months FEC $1 = R	Three months FEC $1 = R
1 January 20.2	11,20	12,50	12,20
10 January 20.2	11,29	12,55	12,32
20 February 20.2	11,35		
28 February 20.2	11,45		

Ignore the time value of money. Assume that all qualifying hedging criteria are adhered to.

Required

a. Discuss the correct accounting classification and presentation of the preference shares and debentures in the financial statements of Ko Samet Ltd for the year ended 28 February 20.2 in accordance with IAS 32.
b. Supply the journal entries regarding the purchase of inventory for the year ended 28 February 20.2. Ignore taxation.
c. Journalise the hedging of the instalment on the foreign loan, as well as the recording of the finance costs for the year ended 28 February 20.2. Ignore taxation.

(UNISA – adapted)

❖ **Suggested solution IFRS 9.11@**

a. Classification of preference shares and debentures

IAS 32.15 requires that the issuer of a financial instrument classifies it in its components as a liability or as equity in accordance with the substance of the contractual arrangement on initial recognition. The substance, rather than the legal form, governs its classification.

An equity instrument and financial liability are described as follows:

Equity instrument – see definition in IAS 32.16.

Financial liability – see definition in IAS 32.11.

Preference shares

The preference shares are redeemable in cash on a predetermined date and create an obligation for the issuer to deliver cash to the holders, thus meeting the definition of a financial liability. Since the dividend payment is compulsory and therefore a financial liability, the instrument complies with the description of a financial liability in both instances. The instrument shall therefore be classified as a liability (substance over form) in its entirety.

The preference shares redeemable on 28 February 20.3 (12 months after year-end) (50% × 100 000 × R2 = R100 000) shall be presented as a current liability.

The preference shares redeemable on 31 August 20.4 (50% × 100 000 × R2 = R100 000) shall be presented as part of non-current liabilities.

Dividends paid on the preference shares shall be classified as part of finance costs since the classification of a financial instrument in the statement of financial position drives the classification of its related statement of profit or loss and other comprehensive income items.

Debentures

There is a contractual obligation to deliver cash, namely, to pay interest on the debentures up to 28 February 20.5, and this obligation represents a **financial liability.** The compulsory conversion to ordinary shares gives rise to an **equity instrument** since the issue of a company's own shares includes no contractual obligation to deliver cash or another financial asset, and the company has no contractual obligation to deliver a variable number of its own shares. The debentures are, therefore, a **compound instrument**.

The present value of the future obligatory interest payments should be presented as a liability on 28 February 20.2 in the SFPos. Consequently, the total issue price of the debentures (50 000 × R11,00 = R550 000) less the present value of the future interest payment on 28 February 20.2 should be presented as equity in the SoFP.

b. Inventory

	Rand Dr/(Cr)
10 January 20.2	
No entry since the FEC has no fair value at the time of issuance.	
20 February 20.2	
Determine the limit of the amount that may be taken to equity in terms of IFRS 9.6.5.11(a):	
Loss on change of future cash flows up to 20 February 20.2 (1)	(2 760)
Gain on FEC (2)	2 760
Effectiveness: 2 760/2 760 (for illustration purposes only)	100%
Journal entries:	
FEC asset (derivative instrument) (SFPos)	2 760
Deferred hedging reserve (OCI) (2)	(2 760)
Fair value adjustment (cash flow hedge – inventory not yet recorded)	
Inventory (SFPos) (3)	522 100
Payables (SFPos)	(522 100)
Creditor recorded at spot rate on transaction date	
Deferred hedging reserve (OCI)	2 760
Inventory (SFPos)	(2 760)
Hedging gain transferred to inventory on transaction date	
28 February 20.2	
Foreign exchange difference (P or L)	4 600
Payables (SFPos) (4)	(4 600)
Restate creditor at closing rate at year-end	
FEC asset (SFPos)	5 060
Foreign exchange difference (P or L) (5)	(5 060)
Fair value adjustment of FEC (now a fair value hedge) (6)	

(1) $46 000 × (R11,35 – R11,29) = 2 760
(2) $46 000 × (R12,38 – R12,32) = 2 760
(3) $46 000 × R11,35 = 522 100
(4) $46 000 × (R11,45 – R11,35) = 4 600
(5) $46 000 × (R12,49 – R12,38) = 5 060
(6) Effectiveness now 91% – 110% (4 600/5 060) – for illustration purposes only

c. Foreign loan

Instalment payable	1 July 20.2
Capital (300 000 – 72 000)	$228 000
Interest (given)	$72 000
Forward rate	R12,50
Equivalent FEC rate	R12,80

	Rand Dr/(Cr)
28 February 20.2	
Finance costs (P or L) (1)	271 800
Interest accrued (SFPos)	(271 800)
Interest accrual at year-end	
Foreign exchange difference (P or L) (2)	3 000
Interest accrued	(3 000)
Exchange adjustment on accrued interest	
FEC asset (3)	90 000
Deferred hedging gain (OCI)	(90 000)
Fair value adjustment of the FEC at year-end	
Deferred hedging gain (OCI) (4)	75 600
Foreign exchange difference (P or L)	(75 600)
Reclassify gain to profit or loss as the underlying loan affects profit or loss	

(1) $72 000 × 2/6 × [(R11,45 + R11,20)/2] = 271 800
(2) $72 000 × 2/6 × [(R11,45 – R11,20)/2] = 3 000
(3) $300 000 × (R12,50 – R12,80) = 90 000
(4) 90 000 × [(72 000 × 2/6) + 300 000 – 72 000]/300 000 = 75 600

❑ QUESTION IFRS 9.12#

The following is a list of independent instruments:

1. Non-cumulative preferences shares that are not redeemable with discretionary dividend payments.
2. Cumulative preference shares that are compulsory redeemable with compulsory dividend payments.
3. Compulsory convertible debentures convertible into a fixed number of ordinary shares on a specific date.
4. Debentures which are convertible into a fixed number of ordinary shares at the option of the holder thereof.
5. An option issued by a company granting the right to acquire a fixed number of shares in that company at a fixed price.

Required

Briefly classify each instrument as either equity or a liability in the issuer's books. Your answer must comply with International Financial Reporting Standards (IFRS) requirements.

❑ QUESTION IFRS 9.13

A Ltd, a company with a 31 December year-end, purchased the following shares:

Company	B Ltd
Number of shares purchased	10 000
Purchase date	30 June 20.3

Fair value per share

–	30 June 20.3	R15,00
–	31 December 20.4	R17,00
–	31 December 20.5	R12,00
–	31 December 20.6	R13,50
–	30 June 20.7	R9,50
–	31 December 20.7	R13,80

The investment has, on initial recognition, been correctly classified as a financial asset at fair value through other comprehensive income.

Required

a. Prepare extracts of the statement of profit or loss and other comprehensive income of A Ltd for the year ended 31 December **20.6** to reflect the movements on the investment in B Ltd.
b. The company prepares interim financial statements on 30 June. On 30 June 20.7, the directors believed that the investment was impaired. Prepare the journal entries relating to this investment for the year ended 31 December **20.7**.

❑ QUESTION IFRS 9.14

Plex-Fame Ltd has invested R143 million in government bonds. The government bonds are held within a business model with the objective to collect contractual cash flows that are solely payments of principal and interest on the principal outstanding on the specified dates. Interest on the government bonds is solely compensation for the time value of money and credit risk associated with the principal amount outstanding.

During the past year, a portion of these bonds was set aside to cover interest and principal obligations on the company's loan of US $25 million. The loan is not held for trading or otherwise designated.

When the loan agreement was signed, Plex-Fame Ltd entered into a forward contract to buy US dollars for the same amounts as the capital obligations under the loan and for the same dates on which the obligations will mature. Plex-Fame Ltd does not apply hedge accounting.

The financial director believes that, in substance, the debt has been settled, and consequently, both the bonds and the loan have been derecognised (removed) from the company's statement of financial position.

Required

Discuss the appropriate accounting treatment and presentation of the above in terms of the requirements of International Financial Reporting Standards (IFRS) (QE 1991 – adapted).

❑ QUESTION IFRS 9.15

ABC Ltd incurred the following two transactions:

- On 1 May 20.1, 20 industrial share index futures were purchased for speculative purposes and were classified at fair value through profit or loss. The industrial share index on 1 May 20.1 was 2 400. Transaction costs were R200, and the margin deposit was R40 000. The 20 futures were sold on 15 July 20.1. The mark-to-market indexes are as follows:

30 June 20.1	2 650
15 July 20.1	2 740

- The company held industrial shares for speculative purposes and classified these as at fair value through profit or loss. A decline in the share prices is anticipated, and consequently, the company decided to hedge itself against the possible decline. On 1 May 20.1, 15 industrial share index futures were sold. The contracts matured on 1 August 20.1, and 15 contracts were entered into. Transaction costs were R150. The margin deposit was R50 000. The company does not apply hedge accounting. The mark-to-market indexes are as follows:

1 May 20.1	3 150
30 June 20.1	3 100
1 August 20.1	3 020

The year-end of the company is 30 June 20.1. Each index point represents R10 in value. Gains and losses are settled daily.

Required

Journalise the transactions. Your answer must comply with International Financial Reporting Standards (IFRS) requirements.

❑ QUESTION IFRS 9.16

B Ltd purchased 5 000 options for R32 500. The options give the right to buy 5 000 shares in PHB Pilliton Ltd at R130 (market price at the purchase date of options) per share, with associated transaction costs of R500. These purchased options expire on 30 June 20.7. PHB Pilliton's shares traded at R150 per share at year-end (31 December 20.6), and the fair value per option increased to R26,50 **per option**.

Required

a. Discuss in detail in which category of financial instruments the options should be classified.
b. Journalise the above transactions on initial recognition, as well as at year-end, with journal narrations. Your answer must comply with International Financial Reporting Standards (IFRS) requirements.

❑ QUESTION IFRS 9.17

Bambi Ltd entered into the following transactions during the year ended 31 December 20.6:

Transaction 1

On 15 April 20.6, 10 000 units of inventory, which are generally available in the market, were ordered from a supplier by way of a non-cancellable contract at R10 per unit. The R100 000 will be paid within 30 days after receiving the inventory. The inventory was delivered on 30 April 20.6 and paid for on 30 May 20.6. The market price of the generally available inventory increased by R2 per unit on 20 May 20.6.

Transaction 2

An FEC was entered into on 30 November 20.6 in which $150 000 will be purchased on 30 January 20.7 at R6,20 per $. At year-end, the exchange rates are as follows:

	$		Rand
Spot rate	1	=	6,22
Forward rate (similar contract)	1	=	6,30

Bambi Ltd does not apply hedge accounting.

Required

Journalise the above transactions (also cash transactions) in detail for the year ended 31 December 20.6 and explain in respect of each transaction why it was accounted for on the specific date. Your answer must comply with International Financial Reporting Standards (IFRS) requirements. Journal narrations are not required.

❑ QUESTION IFRS 9.18

Bimba Ltd entered into several transactions during the year ended 31 December 20.6:

Transaction 1

On 2 February 20.6, 5 000 listed shares in Specky Ltd were purchased for R100 000, with brokerage amounting to R500. These shares form part of a portfolio of financial instruments managed together and showed a pattern of short-term profit taking in the recent past. The company does not intend to sell these shares in the near future. On 31 December 20.6, the shares were trading at R19 per share on the JSE Ltd.

Transaction 2

On 16 April 20.6, 6 000 unlisted shares in Specter Ltd were purchased for R60 000, with brokerage amounting to R500 and regulatory fees of R200. The company intends to sell these unlisted shares when they get a higher price. Because these are unlisted shares, a quoted price on an active market is not available, and it is also clear from other evidence that it is not possible to measure the fair value of these shares because of insufficient recent information. On 31 December 20.6, it was still impossible to determine these shares' fair value. It was however established that the cost price of the shares represents the best estimate of their fair value.

Transaction 3

On 1 July 20.6 (and redeemable on 30 June 20.10), 500 000 12% R1 listed government bonds were purchased for R555 604, while the market rate for instruments with similar terms and conditions is currently 10% per annum. The government bonds are redeemable at a premium of 7%, interest is paid annually in arrears on 30 June, and the associated transaction costs are the following: brokerage = R1 000, regulatory fees = R400 and management time spent = R2 000. The government bonds are held within a business model whose objective is achieved by **both** collecting contractual cash flows (that are solely payments of principal and interest on the principal outstanding on the specified dates) and selling the bonds. Interest on government bonds is solely a compensation for the time value of money, the credit risk associated with the principal amount outstanding and a reasonable profit margin. On 31 December 20.6, the fair value of these bonds amounted to R605 132.

Transaction 4

On 2 October 20.6, 7 500 listed shares in Notty Ltd were purchased for R150 000 with brokerage amounting to R750. Notty Ltd is a major supplier of Bimba Ltd and, due to their strategic importance, Bimba Ltd does not intend to sell these shares in the near future and has elected at initial recognition to account for the changes in the fair value in other comprehensive income. On 31 December 20.6, these shares were trading at R21 per share on the JSE Ltd.

Required

Provide journal entries for each of these transactions for the year ended 31 December 20.6, as well as the statement of financial position amounts as at 31 December 20.6. In each case, indicate in what financial asset category you would classify the item. Your answer must comply with International Financial Reporting Standards (IFRS) requirements. Journal narrations are not required.

❑ QUESTION IFRS 9.19

You are a senior technical advisor at a large professional services firm. One of your clients needs your advice on the measurement of financial instruments.

Required

Answer the following questions that your client has raised:

a. At what value would transactions in financial assets and liabilities normally be accounted for at initial recognition?
b. When should the bid price be used, and when should the offer price be used?
c. If the current bid and offer prices are unavailable in an active market, how would the fair value be determined under these circumstances?

❑ QUESTION IFRS 9.20#

On 1 January 20.0, when the ruling market interest rate was 12%, Casheeze Ltd purchased the following securities:

	Fair value at acquisition Rand
10% R1 000 debentures (redeemable at par) from Moneyshort Ltd with a maturity date of 31 December 20.9. These debentures are listed, and Casheeze Ltd holds the debentures within a business model with the objective to collect contractual cash flows that are solely payments of principal and interest on the principal outstanding on the specified dates. Interest on the debentures is solely a compensation for the time value of money and credit risk associated with the principal amount outstanding.	887
14% R5 000 debentures with a maturity date of 31 December 20.4 and maturing at par, from Breakeven Ltd. Casheeze Ltd, expects that interest rates will fall in the short term and that they will then be able to realise a gain on the sale of the debentures.	5 360
100 ordinary shares in Quickbuck Ltd. Casheeze Ltd anticipates that the share price will rise by 10%, at which point the shares will be sold.	2 200

	Fair value at acquisition Rand
150 ordinary shares in Riskfree Ltd. Casheeze Ltd has no immediate plans to sell the shares, irrespective of movements in fair value.	5 600

Assume transaction costs are R60 in each case.

Additional information

1. Interest rates have fallen to 10% on 31 December 20.0, boosting the fair value of Breakeven Ltd's debentures to R5 634. Casheeze Ltd's policy is to account for interest income separately from fair value adjustments.
2. At the end of 20.0, the fair values of the investments in Quickbuck Ltd and Riskfree Ltd are R2 700 and R5 190, respectively.
3. Assume that Casheeze Ltd did not designate the instruments as either at fair value through profit or loss or elected as at fair value through other comprehensive income if they would generally have been classified differently.
4. Ignore taxes.

Required

a. State which category each of the above-mentioned financial instruments would be classified into and how they should be measured on initial recognition and subsequent to that.
b. Prepare the journal entries (also for cash transactions) for the year ended 31 December 20.0 for all the transactions mentioned above in the books of Casheeze Ltd. Show the purchase price and transaction costs separately.
c. On 1 July 20.1, 75 of the ordinary shares in Riskfree Ltd were sold for R30 per share. Prepare the journal entries to record the transaction mentioned above in the books of Casheeze Ltd.
d. On 1 September 20.1, Quickbuck Ltd had a capitalisation issue of one share for every 10 ordinary shares held.
   i. Prepare the journal entries to record the transaction mentioned above in the books of Casheeze Ltd.
   ii. Calculate the value of each share after the capitalisation issue if the fair value of the investment is still R2 700.
e. On 31 December 20.1, when the interest rate was 8%, the directors changed their intention regarding the investment in Breakeven Ltd. The investment will now be held until maturity in order to collect contractual cash flows. Prepare the journal entry/ies to record the above-mentioned change in intention in the accounting records of Casheeze Ltd.
f. On 31 December 20.1, Casheeze Ltd established that Moneyshort Ltd is experiencing financial difficulties due to mismanagement and that there is a 100% chance that only 50% of the future cash flows of the debentures will be paid out. Prepare the journal entry/ies to account for the above-mentioned information on 31 December 20.1.

(UNISA – adapted)

❑ QUESTION IFRS 9.21#

Mambo Ltd entered into the following transactions during the year ended 31 December 20.6:

Transaction 1

Credit sales to the amount of R2 million were made to debtors after ensuring, through credit control procedures, that these receivables are of exceptionally high quality. The effect of the time value of money is insignificant.

Transaction 2

At the beginning of the year, a debit loan of R1 million with a term of five years was granted to a supplier of essential raw materials in respect of the production process of Mambo Ltd. Mambo Ltd is convinced that the granting of the loan will lead to a long and prosperous relationship (at least for five years) between the two companies. The loan was granted at an interest rate of 8%, while the current market rate for loans with similar terms, conditions and credit rating is 12%. Transaction costs associated with the loan amount to R1 000. Interest is payable annually in arrears, and the capital is repayable in full after five years.

Transaction 3

A debit loan of R1,5 million for a term of four years was made at the beginning of the year to a supplier of a less essential raw material in the production process of Mambo Ltd. The loan was granted at an interest rate of 12%, while the current market rate for loans with similar terms, conditions and credit rating is also 12%. Transaction costs associated with the loan amount to R1 500. Interest is payable annually in arrears, and the capital is repayable in full after four years.

Required

Provide in each case all the journal entries related to the above transactions for the year ended 31 December 20.6 as well as the balances at year-end as they would appear in the statement of financial position of Mambo Ltd. Your answer must comply with International Financial Reporting Standards (IFRS) requirements. Journal narrations are not required.

❑ QUESTION IFRS 9.22

Dumbo Ltd is a financially healthy company with massive cash reserves. Consequently, the board of directors decided to acquire several financial assets, and on 31 December 20.6 (year-end), the company held several such investments. The following information relates to these investments, and you may, in all cases, assume that these investments were acquired at fair value:

Investment 1: 20 000 shares in Busy Bee Ltd

These shares were acquired on 1 June 20.6 at R12,50 per share with associated transaction costs amounting to R2 500. Dumbo Ltd intends to sell them as soon as the return on the original capital outlay is sufficient – they, therefore, speculate with these shares. In the meantime, the share market has dropped drastically, and at year-end (31 December 20.6), these shares were trading at R11,00 per share. The shares were not designated to any specific financial asset category on initial recognition but were classified based on the entity's business model.

Investment 2: 30 000 shares in Ecdon Ltd

These shares were acquired on 1 January 20.5 at R10,50 per share with associated transaction costs of R3 000. Dumbo Ltd originally intended to hold them for 10 years to secure maximum capital growth and dividends from this investment and elected to designate this investment as at fair value through other comprehensive income. Owing to favourable economic predictions in respect of the South African economy and the nature of the product of Ecdon Ltd, it was expected that the business and value of shares would show extreme growth for at least 10 years, and consequently, good dividends would be paid. However, due to flooding the market with similar imported Chinese products at prices much lower than those at which Ecdon Ltd could manufacture their products, the share price of Ecdon Ltd had dropped to R9,50 by 31 December 20.5 and to R7,00 by 31 December 20.6.

Early in 20.5, Ecdon Ltd petitioned the government for import protection on its products, and by the end of December 20.5, it appeared as if the government would implement the import protection. However, on 1 April 20.6, a new director-general was appointed by the Department of Trade and Industry and by 30 December 20.6, this department announced in a press release that they would not implement import protection measures for the products of Ecdon Ltd. According to the press release, the free market should be left to sort out the matter.

Investment 3: 150 000 shares in Small Fry Ltd

According to the financial director, this is an extremely risky investment in a new company that should show brilliant growth in the short term and therefore must be treated as a speculative investment. The shares do not trade in an active market. The shares were purchased on 1 March 20.6 at R2 per share, and brokerage amounted to R2 800, while the financial director spent time to the value of R2 000 on the evaluation of the target company and the purchase transaction. On 31 December 20.6, the board of directors gathered the following information:

- Annual estimated cash flows from this asset (directors' best estimate) for an indeterminable period is R25 000 per year.
- Directors' best estimate of the rate of return on investments with a similar risk profile is 10% per annum.

Investment 4: 1 000 8% listed R1 000 municipal bonds in the Kimberley Metro (Sol Plaatje Municipality)

The investment in R1 000 bonds was made on 1 January 20.4 for strategic reasons. The bonds are held within a business model with the objective to collect contractual cash flows that are solely payments of principal and interest on the principal outstanding on the specified dates until their maturity date on 31 December 20.13. Interest on the bonds is solely a compensation for the time value of money, the credit risk associated with the principal amount outstanding and other basic lending risks and costs. The investment has not been designated as any other financial asset category. The fair value (transaction price) of the bonds (to be redeemed at par) on 1 January 20.4 was R877 109, and the market interest rate for similar bonds at that stage was 10% per annum. The associated transaction costs in respect of the investment were R2 000. The bonds were not credit-impaired on the purchase date, and credit risk was assessed as insignificant. The 12-month' expected credit losses were estimated as RNil.

On 28 December 20.6, the financial director of Dumbo Ltd received a letter from Kimberley Metro which indicated that the Metro would be forced to reduce the original benefits promised at the time of the bond issue. This action is unavoidable due to the long drought in the Northern Cape, as well as the refusal of municipal taxpayers to pay their municipal levies that are in arrears. According to this letter, the Metro will have to reduce the interest paid on these debentures to 6%, while the eventual redemption will no longer take place at par but at 86% of the original par value of the bonds.

Required

a. Identify the level in the fair value hierarchy (see IFRS 13) of Investment 3.
b. Provide all the related journal entries (cash transactions included) regarding the above investments from initial recognition to 31 December 20.6.
c. Provide, for each of the above investments, the carrying amount in the statement of financial position of Dumbo Ltd for the year ended 31 December 20.6.
d. Provide the carrying amount of Investment 4 as at 31 December 20.7 and also at 31 December 20.13 (immediately before redemption).

Your answer must comply with International Financial Reporting Standards (IFRS) requirements. Round off all amounts to the nearest rand.

❑ QUESTION IFRS 9.23

InDebt Ltd has a financial liability of R400 000 in favour of Capital Ltd. During 20.9, InDebt Ltd experienced financial difficulties, and its board of directors decided to approach Capital Ltd with a debt-for-equity swap offer. If accepted, the liability will be settled in full by issuing ordinary shares in InDebt Ltd.

The debt-for-equity swap offer was accepted on 30 June 20.9, on which date the R400 000 liability was settled in full by issuing 32 000 ordinary InDebt Ltd shares at its fair value of R12,50 per share.

You may assume that the interest on the liability was paid up at all times and that the interest rate on the liability was market related. InDebt Ltd and Capital Ltd are not related.

Required

a. Provide the journal entries for the above debt-for-equity swap transaction on 30 June 20.9.
b. Provide the journal entries for the above debt-for-equity swap transaction if InDebt Ltd decides to issue 33 000 shares at R12,50 in full and final settlement of the liability.

IFRS 10, IFRS 12, IFRS 3 & IAS 27

Consolidated financial statements and separate financial statements

---

❑ QUESTIONS AND SOLUTIONS

IFRS 10.1	Theory – separate versus individual financial statements
IFRS 10.2[@]	Theory – when to consolidate and when not
IFRS 10.3[@]	Accounting for investments in subsidiaries, joint ventures and associates in separate financial statements and the effect on consolidated financial statements
IFRS 10.4	Theory – potential ordinary shares and the issue of control
IFRS 10.5	Theory – structured entities and entities with different year ends

❑ QUESTIONS

IFRS 10.6	Disposal of a portion of a subsidiary
IFRS 10.7[#]	IFRS 3 Business combinations (acquisition of an equity interest)
IFRS 10.8[@]	Investment entities
IFRS 10.9[@]	IFRS 3 Business combinations – integration (acquisition of an equity interest)
IFRS 10.10	IFRS 3 Business combinations – integration (acquisition of assets and liabilities)

[@] *These questions contain topics or principles that were not included in the ITC syllabus of SAICA at the time of publishing this book, but might still be included in university syllabi.*

[#] *This question contains topics or principles that were at an awareness level of proficiency in the ITC syllabus of SAICA, at the time of publishing this book.*

❑ QUESTION IFRS 10.1

Acc Ltd is a company holding shares in several other companies. However, the level of control in respect of none of these investments leads to these investments being classified as either a subsidiary (IAS 27/IFRS 10), joint venture or associate (IAS 28).

Bac Ltd is a company with investments in the shares of several other companies and each of these investments can be classified as a subsidiary, joint venture or associate in terms of the relevant International Financial Reporting Standards (IFRS).

Required

Indicate, with reasons, whether the financial statements (not consolidated financial statements) of Acc and Bac Ltd containing these investment accounts can be classified as separate financial statements or not.

❖ Suggested solution IFRS 10.1

The financial statements of **Acc** Ltd cannot be classified as separate financial statements as none of the investments held can be classified as subsidiaries, joint ventures or associates (IAS 27.4 and .7). The financial statements of Acc Ltd can rather possibly be called 'individual' financial statements, to distinguish them from separate financial statements.

The financial statements of **Bac** Ltd can be classified as separate financial statements, as all the investments held by this parent, venturer or investor can be classified as either subsidiaries, joint ventures or associates (IAS 27.7).

❑ QUESTION IFRS 10.2@

Required

When should investments in subsidiaries be consolidated by a parent and when not?

❖ Suggested solution IFRS 10.2@

In terms of IFRS 10.2(a) and IFRS 10.4, the consolidated financial statements of a group should consolidate **all subsidiaries** of the parent (i.e. all entities **controlled** by the parent).

However, a parent need **not present consolidated financial statements** if and only if:

- the parent is itself a wholly owned subsidiary, or a partly owned subsidiary of another entity and its other owners, including those not otherwise entitled to vote, have been informed about, and do not object to, the parent not presenting consolidated financial statements; and
- the parent's debt or equity instruments are not traded in a public market; and
- the parent did not file, nor is it in the process of filing, its financial statements with a securities commission or other regulatory organisation for the purpose of issuing any class of instruments in a public market; and
- the ultimate or any intermediate parent of the parent produces consolidated financial statements available for public use that comply with International Financial Reporting Standards.

IFRS 10.4B states that a parent that is an investment entity shall not present consolidated financial statements if it measures all of its subsidiaries at fair value in accordance with IFRS 10.31.

❑ QUESTION IFRS 10.3@

Parent Ltd owns two subsidiaries namely One Ltd and Two Ltd. The investments in these subsidiaries appear in the statement of financial position in the company's separate financial statements and these subsidiaries must be consolidated in the consolidated financial statements of the Parent Ltd Group.

The following financial information is available in respect of these investments in subsidiaries as at 31 December 20.5:

	Cost Rand	**Fair value Rand**
One Ltd	100 000	200 000
Two Ltd	130 000	180 000

According to IAS 27.10, investments in subsidiaries, joint ventures and associates can be accounted for, amongst others, at cost or at fair value in accordance with IFRS 9.

Investments accounted for at cost shall be accounted for in accordance with IFRS 5 when they are classified as held for sale in accordance with IFRS 5. The measurement of investments accounted for in accordance with IFRS 9 is not changed in such circumstances.

Assume an income tax rate of 27% and that 80% of capital gains are taxed. Also assume that the deferred tax balance, apart from any balances arising from these items, amounts to RNil.

Required

a. State at what amounts the investments in One Ltd and Two Ltd should be presented in the statement of financial position in the separate financial statements of Parent Ltd as at 31 December 20.5, if Parent Ltd elected as its accounting policy to show investments in subsidiaries in its own (separate) financial statements **at cost.** Also state what other line items in the statement of financial position will be affected by the decision to carry these investments at cost and provide the related amounts.
b. State at what amounts the investments in One Ltd and Two Ltd should be presented in the statement of financial position in the separate financial statements of Parent Ltd as at 31 December 20.5, if Parent Ltd made an irrevocable election to show investments in these subsidiaries in its own (separate) financial statements at **fair value through other comprehensive income** (IFRS 9.5.7.5). Also state what other line items on the statement of financial position will be affected by the decision to carry these investments at fair value through other comprehensive income, and provide the relevant amounts.
c. If Parent Ltd rather elected to show investments in these subsidiaries in its own (separate) financial statements at **fair value through profit or loss**, draft the journal entries required in the separate financial statements of Parent Ltd to account for the movement in fair value.
d. Provide the consolidation journal entries that will arise from carrying the investments in the subsidiaries at cost, at fair value through other comprehensive income and at fair value through profit or loss respectively. Assume that the fair value adjustments were processed in the current financial year.
e. Discuss whether Parent Ltd may elect to carry the investment in One Ltd at cost and that of Two Ltd at fair value in its separate financial statements.
f. Identify any other allowable method(s) of measuring the investments in subsidiaries in the separate financial statements of Parent Ltd.

❖ **Suggested solution IFRS 10.3@**

a. The accounting policy selected, is to carry the investments at **cost** in the separate financial statements of Parent Ltd:

- Investment in One Ltd R100 000
- Investment in Two Ltd R130 000

No other line items in the statement of financial position will be affected at year end.

b. The accounting policy selected is to carry the investments at **fair value through other comprehensive income** in the separate financial statements of Parent Ltd:

- Investment in One Ltd R200 000
- Investment in Two Ltd R180 000

Since these investments are not held for trading Parent Ltd can make an election in terms of IFRS 9.5.7.5 to present all changes in fair value in other comprehensive income. Consequently other line items to be affected would be the mark-to-market reserve and deferred tax.

The mark-to-market reserve would be R117 600 (1).

(1) [(200 000 – 100 000) × 78,4%] + [(180 000 – 130 000) × 78,4%] = R117 600

The deferred tax line item in the statement of financial position would be R32 400 (2).

(2) [(200 000 – 100 000) × 21.6%] + [(180 000 – 130 000) × 21.6%] = R32 400

c. The accounting policy selected is to carry the investments at **fair value through profit or loss** in the separate financial statements of Parent Ltd:

- Investment in One Ltd R200 000
- Investment in Two Ltd R180 000

Since Parent Ltd has not made an election in terms of IFRS 9.5.7.5 to present all changes in fair value in other comprehensive income, all fair value changes are recognised in profit or loss. Consequently the journal entry Parent Ltd would process to account for the movement in fair value in its **separate financial statements** would be as follows:

	Rand Dr/(Cr)
Investment in One Ltd (1)	100 000
Investment in Two Ltd (2)	50 000
Fair value adjustment (P or L)	(150 000)
Accounting for the movement in fair value of the investments in profit or loss	
Deferred tax (P or L) (3)	32 400
Deferred tax (SFPos) (3)	(32 400)
Accounting for the deferred tax at capital gains tax rate	

(1) 200 000 – 100 000 = R100 000
(2) 180 000 – 130 000 = R50 000
(3) 150 000 × 21.6% = R32 400

d. Consolidation journal entries

If the accounting policy of Parent Ltd is to carry these investments at **cost:**

The investment will be eliminated at cost in the consolidated financial statements. No additional consolidation journal entries will be required.

If the accounting policy of Parent Ltd is to carry these investments **at fair value through other comprehensive income**, then the following additional pro forma journal entry will be required in addition to eliminating the investment at cost:

	Rand Dr/(Cr)
Fair value adjustment (OCI)	150 000
Income tax on items in OCI (OCI)	(32 400)
Deferred tax (SFPos)	32 400
Investment in One Ltd	(100 000)
Investment in Two Ltd	(50 000)
Restoring the investments in subsidiaries to cost before eliminating these investments against the equity at acquisition of subsidiaries	

If the accounting policy of Parent Ltd is to carry these investments **at fair value through profit or loss,** then the following pro forma journal entry will be required in addition to eliminating the investment at cost:

	Rand Dr/(Cr)
Fair value adjustment (P or L)	150 000
Investment in One Ltd	(100 000)
Investment in Two Ltd	(50 000)
Deferred tax (SFPos)	32 400
Deferred tax (P or L)	(32 400)
Restoring the investments in subsidiaries to cost before eliminating these investments against the equity at acquisition of subsidiaries	

e. In terms of IAS 27.10, the same accounting policy should be applied for each category of investments. Consequently, all investments in subsidiaries must either be accounted for at cost or at fair value, while all investments in, for example, associates should be accounted for at either cost or fair value. The investment in One Ltd may therefore not be carried at cost if at the same time the investment in Two Ltd is carried at fair value, therefore both must either be carried at cost or both must be carried at fair value.

f. IAS 27.10(c) also allows the equity method to account for the investments in the separate financial statements.

❑ QUESTION IFRS 10.4

Blue Bull Ltd recently acquired a 40% interest in Sharks Ltd. On the same date, Blue Bull Ltd also acquired options to purchase a further 20% interest in Sharks Ltd. These options are exercisable, at the option of Blue Bull Ltd, at any time during the next three years.

During the audit of Blue Bull Ltd it was mentioned that there may be a possibility that Sharks Ltd would need to be consolidated as a subsidiary in the financial statements of Blue Bull Ltd. Sharks Ltd has shown good financial performance during the year resulting in these options being in the money (fair value of the shares are greater than the current exercise price of the options). Blue Bull Ltd has the financial ability to exercise these options.

Required

Briefly discuss whether Sharks Ltd needs to be consolidated as a subsidiary in the financial statements of Blue Bull Ltd.

❖ **Suggested solution IFRS 10.4**

IFRS 10 describes a subsidiary as an entity that is controlled by another entity. It should therefore be determined whether Blue Bull Ltd has control over Sharks Ltd to determine whether it should be consolidated.

Control arises when the investor is exposed, or has rights, to variable returns from its involvement with the investee and has the ability to affect those returns through its power over the investee (IFRS 10.6).

An investor has power over an investee when the investor has existing rights that give it the current ability to direct relevant activities of the investee (IFRS 10.10). An investor with the current ability to direct the relevant activities has the power even if its rights to direct have not been exercised (IFRS 10.12).

Current (40%) as well as potential (20%) voting rights should be considered when determining if an investor has power over an investee (IFRS 10.B50).

In assessing whether it has power, an investor considers only substantive rights whereby the holder must have the practical ability to exercise the right (IFRS 10.B22). Barriers that prevent the holder from exercising such rights include but are not limited to: an exercise price that creates a financial barrier that would prevent or deter the holder from exercising such rights (IFRS 10.B23(a)(ii)). The holder of potential voting rights shall consider the exercise price of the instrument in assessing whether it has power over the investee (IFRS 10.B23(c)).

Blue Bull Ltd has the current ability to exercise these options (currently exercisable and has the financial ability to exercise) and the options are in the money which would not deter Blue Bull Ltd from exercising its options. Blue Bull Ltd therefore controls Sharks Ltd and should consolidate Sharks Ltd in its consolidated annual financial statements.

It should be kept in mind that only 40% of the subsidiary (actual share ownership) will be consolidated (non-controlling interest will thus be 60%).

❑ **QUESTION IFRS 10.5**

The directors of Stella Ltd recently approached you with the following questions:

a. 'We recently incorporated an entity (Finance Ltd) who is principally engaged in providing a source of long-term capital to us (Stella Ltd). We hold only 10% of the voting rights in the entity. Should we consolidate the entity?'
b. 'The above entity's year end differs by two months from our year end. What effect will this have on the consolidation?'

Required

Answer the directors of Stella Ltd in a memorandum.

❖ **Suggested solution IFRS 10.5**

To : Directors of Stella Ltd
Subject : Consolidation questions
From : Your auditor

a. If Stella Ltd controls Finance Ltd it should consolidate Finance Ltd.

Control arises when the investor is exposed, or has rights, to variable returns from its involvement with the investee and has the ability to affect those returns through its power over the investee (IFRS 10.6). Power arises from rights. Sometimes assessing power is straightforward, such as when power over an investee is obtained directly and solely from voting rights arising from equity instruments such as shares. In other cases, the assessment will be more complex and require more than one factor to be considered (IFRS 10.11).

Other factors to consider include:

- The purpose and design of the investee;
- The relevant activities and how decisions about them are made;
- Whether the rights of the investor give it the current ability to direct relevant activities;
- Whether the investor is exposed, or has rights, to variable returns from its involvement in the investee; and
- Whether the investor has the ability to use its power over the investee to affect the amount of the investor's returns (IFRS 10.B3).

In assessing the purpose and design of the investee, an investor shall consider the involvement and decisions made at the investee's **inception** as part of its design and evaluate whether the transaction terms and features of the involvement provide the investor with rights that are sufficient to give it power (IFRS 10.B51).

Finance Ltd appears to be what is often described in practice as a 'special purpose entity' or 'special purpose vehicle'. Finance Ltd was incorporated by Stella Ltd with the view of providing finance primarily to Stella Ltd which, by lack of further information, may indicate that Stella Ltd controls Finance Ltd for the following reasons:

- Stella Ltd was involved in the purpose and design of Finance Ltd at inception by incorporating Finance Ltd;
- The relevant activities of Finance Ltd are to provide finance to Stella Ltd and these activities are decided upon by Stella Ltd;
- Stella Ltd is exposed to variable returns from the financing activities of Finance Ltd; and
- Stella Ltd can use its power over Finance Ltd to affect its returns.

A structured entity is an entity that has been designed so that voting or similar rights are not the dominant factor in deciding who controls the entity (IFRS 12 Appendix A).

Finance Ltd is a structured entity controlled by Stella Ltd that needs to be consolidated in the group annual financial statements.

b. According to IFRS 10.B92, the financial statements of the parent and its subsidiaries used in the preparation of the consolidated financial statements shall be prepared as of the same date.

When the end of the reporting period of the parent is different from that of the subsidiary, the subsidiary prepares, for consolidation purposes, additional financial statements as of the same date as the financial statements of the parent unless it is impractical to do so.

If it is impractical, the subsidiary shall adjust its financial statements for the effects of significant transactions or events that occur between the subsidiary's reporting date and the parent's reporting date. The difference between the reporting dates shall be no more than three months. The length of the reporting periods and any difference between the ends of the reporting periods shall be the same from period to period.

Stella Ltd would therefore instruct Finance Ltd to either prepare additional financial statements or adjust their financial statements for all significant transactions and events during the two-month period. The latter option is acceptable because the requirement of three months is not exceeded, provided that it is impractical to prepare additional financial statements.

Please contact me should you have any further queries.

❑ QUESTION IFRS 10.6

Holder Ltd acquired an 80% controlling interest in Sub Ltd on 1 January 20.5. This was the incorporation date of Sub Ltd.

Holder Ltd sold 25% of its share (i.e. has 60% left) in Sub Ltd on 1 January 20.8 for R50 000.

The trial balances of Holder Ltd and Sub Ltd as at 31 December 20.8, the companies' financial year end, showed the following amounts:

	Holder Ltd Rand	**Sub Ltd Rand**
Share capital	200 000	100 000
Retained earnings	375 000	125 000
Long-term loan	–	30 000
Trade and other payables	75 000	15 000
Current portion of long-term loan	–	5 000
Profit for the year	45 000	20 000
Gain on sale of investment in Sub Ltd	30 000	–
	725 000	295 000
Property, plant and equipment	225 000	200 000
Investment in Sub Ltd at cost price	60 000	–
Other investments	90 000	–
Inventory	50 000	25 000
Trade and other receivables	100 000	40 000
Cash and cash equivalents	200 000	30 000
	725 000	295 000

The Holder Ltd Group measures non-controlling interest at their proportional share of the net assets of the subsidiary.

Required

a. Calculate the equity adjustment the group will recognise on the partial sale of their interest in Sub Ltd.
b. Prepare the consolidated statement of financial position as at 31 December 20.8, as well as the statement of changes in equity for the year ended 31 December 20.8, of the Holder Ltd Group.
   - Notes are not required.
   - Comparative amounts are not required.
c. Briefly discuss what the effect will be in the consolidated as well as the separate financial statements if Holder Ltd sold 50% of its interest in Sub Ltd, and not only 25%. Assume a selling price of R100 000 and that the fair value of the remaining 40% interest in Sub Ltd is R95 000.

❑ QUESTION IFRS 10.7#

Hercules Ltd is a JSE-listed investment company. Hercules Ltd has investments in most industry sectors, but had never in the past invested in the mining industry because a suitable opportunity has never arisen. However, during the current financial year (ended 30 June 20.1) the board became aware of a struggling mining company, Minerals (Pty) Ltd, which was incorporated two years ago. According to Hercules Ltd the biggest 'asset' of Minerals (Pty) Ltd is a prospecting right in respect of platinum that was granted by the government shortly after incorporation. However, due to a lack of funding and management expertise, Minerals (Pty) Ltd could not as of yet make noticeable progress with prospecting.

The board of Hercules Ltd therefore approached the existing shareholders of Minerals (Pty) Ltd on 14 August 20.0 and made an offer on a 51% interest in Minerals (Pty) Ltd. The shareholders of Minerals (Pty) Ltd were willing to trade their controlling interest for a non-controlling interest to gain access to funding via Hercules Ltd. Negotiations were finalised by the end of December and both parties agreed on 1 January 20.1 that Hercules Ltd acquires a 51% interest in Minerals (Pty) Ltd from the previous shareholders.

In spite of a valuation of R26 million that was conducted recently, Minerals (Pty) Ltd recognised the cost price of the prospecting right as an expense because the probable inflow of economic benefits could not be demonstrated due to the above problems. The prospecting right had a nine-year remaining term as of 1 January 20.1.

Minerals (Pty) Ltd had already (before take-over by Hercules Ltd) appointed contractors to carry out prospecting activities and purchased various mining equipment and vehicles for this purpose. Minerals (Pty) Ltd has 22 full-time employees in its service.

The purchase price of the 51% interest will be settled by Hercules Ltd in favour of the previous shareholders as follows:

- A cash payment of R1 500 000 on 1 January 20.1.
- Mining equipment with a value of R7 600 000. The equipment was purchased by Hercules Ltd in December 20.0 for R5 500 000 and it was not yet ready for use as at 1 January 20.1, the date on which it was transferred to the previous shareholders.
- A cash payment of R4 000 000 on 1 January 20.3.
- An additional payment in the form of platinum futures that will be transferred on 1 January 20.3 if platinum reserves of more than the sector norm are found at that

stage. This possible payment is correctly classified as 'at fair value through profit or loss' in terms of IFRS 9 and had a fair value of R2 000 000 on 1 January 20.1, which decreased to R1 700 000 on 30 June 20.1.

- 5 000 ordinary shares in Hercules Ltd, issued at 1 January 20.1. Issue costs amounted to R2 500.

Hercules Ltd's share price fluctuated as follows:

1 January 20.1	R220.50
30 June 20.1	R228.60

The trial balances of Minerals (Pty) Ltd on the respective dates were as follows:

	01/01/20.1 Rand	**30/06/20.1 Rand**
Mining equipment	1 860 000	1 840 000
Vehicles	544 000	532 000
Share capital	(1 000 000)	(1 000 000)
Long-term loans (at various banks)	(1 400 000)	(1 400 000)
Bank overdraft	(253 456)	(380 877)
Accumulated loss at the beginning of each six-months period	224 654	249 456
Net loss for the six months ended on the respective dates	24 802	159 421

Minerals (Pty) Ltd signed a guarantee of R1 400 000 for the debt of Sapphire (Pty) Ltd, a third party. Because the possibility of outflow of economic benefits was estimated to be less probable, Minerals (Pty) Ltd only disclosed this guarantee as a contingent liability. The fair value of the obligation for Minerals (Pty) Ltd was estimated to be R900 000 on 1 January 20.1 (not deductible for tax purposes). The estimate systematically increased to R1 100 000 by 30 June 20.1 due to circumstances that arose after the acquisition date.

A suitable pre-tax discount rate amounts to 10% per annum where applicable.

Assume that all profits/losses accrued evenly except where the contrary is stated.

Assume a tax rate of 28%. Ignore any form of taxation other than income tax.

Non-controlling interest is measured according to the proportional method.

Hercules Ltd carries investments in subsidiaries at cost in its separate financial statements in accordance with IAS 27.

Required

a. Briefly discuss whether IFRS 3 is applicable to the acquisition of Minerals (Pty) Ltd and also the resulting recognition and measurement of the prospecting right.
b. Provide the journal entries in the separate records of Hercules Ltd only on 1 January 20.1 and only in respect of the acquisition of Minerals (Pty) Ltd. Ignore tax implications for this part.
c. Assuming that IFRS 3 is indeed applicable, provide all pro forma journal entries for the year ended 30 June 20.1 that are needed to account for Minerals (Pty) Ltd in the consolidated financial statements of the Hercules Ltd group.

Your answers must comply with International Financial Reporting Standards (IFRS).
(NWU – adapted)

❑ QUESTION IFRS 10.8@

Investcor Ltd, a listed entity, was incorporated on 1 January 20.4 by issuing equity shares to various unrelated shareholders. Investcor Ltd would utilise these funds to purchase various investments that would yield investment income and potential for capital appreciation, as documented in the issuing prospectus.

At year end, 31 December 20.4, Investcor Ltd had the following investments:
- 10% equity interest in F1 (Pty) Ltd
- 40% equity interest in A1 (Pty) Ltd
- 60% equity interest in S1 (Pty) Ltd
- 80% equity interest in S2 (Pty) Ltd
- 100% ownership of an investment property

Investcor Ltd also owns a property used by the Investcor Ltd staff as offices.

Investcor Ltd exercises significant influence over A1 (Pty) Ltd in accordance with IAS 28 and has a controlling interest in S1 (Pty) Ltd and S2 (Pty) Ltd in accordance with IFRS 10.

Investcor Ltd has an investment exit strategy whereby it disposes of all investments within three years.

Investcor Ltd carries investments in equity shares and investment property at fair value in accordance with IFRS 9 and IAS 40 respectively. Owner-occupied property is accounted for using the cost model in terms of IAS 16. Investcor Ltd reports to shareholders on a monthly basis using the above-mentioned values.

Required

a. Discuss whether Investcor Ltd needs to prepare consolidated annual financial statements.
b. Briefly discuss the classification and measurement in the separate financial statements of Investcor Ltd for the investments listed above.

❑ QUESTION IFRS 10.9@

Attitude (Pty) Ltd holds a controlling interest in the ordinary shares of Positive (Pty) Ltd and Indifferent (Pty) Ltd. All entities in the group have a 31 December 20.5 year end.

Positive (Pty) Ltd

Attitude (Pty) Ltd acquired 240 000 ordinary shares in Positive (Pty) Ltd on 1 January 20.1 from a former shareholder when the retained earnings balance and revaluation surplus balance were R110 000 (credit balance) and R28 800, respectively.

The purchase price transferred to the previous owners of the shares in Positive (Pty) Ltd was settled as follows:
- A cash payment of R247 303 on 1 January 20.1; and
- The issue of 30 000 7% compulsory redeemable debentures on 1 January 20.1 with a face value of R10 each. The debentures are redeemable in five years from their issue date at a premium of 10% on their face value. Interest is paid annually in arrears. All companies in the group have an incremental borrowing rate of 8,1% after tax. Attitude (Pty) Ltd correctly accounts for this financial instrument at amortised cost.

Attitude (Pty) Ltd accounts for the non-controlling interest in Positive (Pty) Ltd at fair value. The fair value of the non-controlling interest at acquisition was R129 520.

On 1 January 20.1, Positive (Pty) Ltd had an in-progress development asset capitalised in its records at R120 000 relating to a self-help kit for mothers called 'Making motherhood magical'. The IAS 38 criteria for capitalisation were satisfied in full. The fair value of this development asset ('Making motherhood magical') is R260 000 and various market participants have offered to buy it for that value.

Positive (Pty) Ltd has not recorded any amortisation on the development asset as it has not yet started producing the 'Making motherhood magical' self-help kit nor did Positive (Pty) Ltd recognise any impairment loss on the development asset in its separate financial statements due to its fair value less costs to sell being higher than its carrying amount.

The Attitude Group is not planning to use this self-help kit, as it directly competes with an existing package that Attitude (Pty) Ltd is marketing called 'Magnificent moms'.

Positive (Pty) Ltd makes use of billboards to advertise its products. Mr Happy Face (the chief marketing director) is of the opinion that the Positive (Pty) Ltd brand name has great value and they want to capitalise it in the separate financial statements of Positive (Pty) Ltd. They even registered the brand name to prevent other entities from trading under this brand name. They appointed a brand name valuation expert, who reported back that the fair value of the Positive (Pty) Ltd brand name amounted to R200 000 on 1 January 20.1. Management expects this brand name to have a remaining useful life of 16 years from 1 January 20.1.

Most of Positive (Pty) Ltd's sales are cash sales and Positive (Pty) Ltd has never had significant issues with accounts receivable not being recoverable.

Assume that all intangible assets have tax consequences at the statutory company tax rate.

Not all packages are perceived to be as effective as the Positive (Pty) Ltd advertisements make consumers believe. This has led to a couple of pending lawsuits. Below follows an extract from the 31 December 20.0 financial statements – contingent liability note:

Claim for monetary damages due to a class action by customers advocating that the self-help packages were not as effective as advertised. The claim represents a present obligation that is unlikely to lead to an outflow of economic benefits. The estimated fair value of the claim is R50 000 on the acquisition date.

By 31 December 20.5, the latter claim was still pending and the fair value remained unchanged.

You may assume that the claim is deductible for income tax purposes.

All other identifiable assets and liabilities of Positive (Pty) Ltd were fairly valued in terms of IFRS 3 at the acquisition date.

The investment in Positive (Pty) Ltd has never been impaired in the separate financial statements of Attitude (Pty) Ltd.

Indifferent (Pty) Ltd

On 30 June 20.2, Attitude (Pty) Ltd acquired a 65% controlling equity interest in the ordinary shares of Indifferent (Pty) Ltd for R300 000 which was paid in cash. On this date, Indifferent (Pty) Ltd had a retained earnings balance of R40 000 (credit balance). The fair value of the non-controlling interest at acquisition was R158 000. Attitude accounts for the non-controlling interest in Indifferent (Pty) Ltd at fair value. All identifiable assets and liabilities were fairly valued in terms of IFRS 3 at the acquisition date.

On 1 July 20.5, Indifferent (Pty) Ltd bought back 50 000 of its own shares at R6 per share (39 500 shares were bought back from Attitude (Pty) Ltd). The share buyback has been accounted for correctly in the separate financial statements of Indifferent (Pty) Ltd and Attitude (Pty) Ltd.

Indifferent (Pty) Ltd incurs income and expenses evenly throughout the year.

Revaluations are performed at the end of the year.

Attitude accounts for its investments in subsidiaries at cost in its separate annual financial statements.

Assume a normal tax rate of 28% with a capital gains inclusion rate of 80%.

All companies in the group realise revaluation surpluses upon the derecognition of the revalued assets.

The trial balances of the companies as at 31 December 20.5 showed the following amounts:

Trial balance at 31 December 20.5

	Attitude Dr/(Cr) Rand	**Positive Dr/(Cr) Rand**	**Indifferent Dr/(Cr) Rand**
Share capital	(280 000)	(300 000)	(350 000)
Retained earnings: beginning of year	(320 000)	(310 000)	(280 000)
Retained earnings: buyback of shares	–	–	250 000
Revaluation surplus	–	(28 800)	–
Investment in Indifferent at cost	254 423	–	–
Investment in Positive at cost	518 080	–	–
Deferred tax	(17 000)	(35 000)	25 600
Property, plant and equipment	606 721	1 224 137	575 320
Intangible assets	330 000	270 000	125 000
Inventories	12 000	46 875	105 000
Accounts receivable	54 400	75 000	15 000
Financial liabilities	(800 000)	(750 000)	(250 000)
Accounts payable	(210 000)	(93 750)	(40 000)
Bank	285 000	11 778	(58 000)
Revenue	(1 100 000)	(850 000)	(970 000)
Cost of sales	770 000	662 000	679 000
Other income	(285 000)	(25 000)	–
Expenses	45 523	24 000	112 000
Finance charges	80 000	75 000	25 000

	Attitude Dr/(Cr) Rand	Positive Dr/(Cr) Rand	Indifferent Dr/(Cr) Rand
Income tax expense	55 854	34 000	42 000
Other comprehensive income – revaluation of plant	–	(42 000)	(36 000)
Income tax on revaluation of plant	–	11 760	10 080
Dividends paid	–	–	20 000
Profit for the year	**(433 623)**	**(80 000)**	**(112 000)**

The issued number of shares at 31 December 20.5 was 600 000 for Attitude (Pty) Ltd, 300 000 for Positive (Pty) Ltd and 350 000 for Indifferent (Pty) Ltd.

Dividends were declared and paid on 30 June 20.5.

Required

a. Compute the goodwill that arose at the acquisition of Positive (Pty) Ltd in accordance with IFRS 3.
b. Provide the pro forma journal entries needed to consolidate Indifferent (Pty) Ltd as part of the Attitude Group for the year ended 31 December 20.5.

(NWU – adapted)

❑ QUESTION IFRS 10.10

MM (Pty) Ltd decided to acquire all the assets and liabilities of SS (Pty) Ltd, a company in the entertainment industry, on 22 March 20.17. All the individual assets and liabilities of SS (Pty) Ltd were transferred to MM (Pty) Ltd on 31 March 20.17. MM (Pty) Ltd, therefore, obtained control, as defined in IFRS 10, over these assets and liabilities on 31 March 20.17. The acquisition of the assets and liabilities by MM (Pty) Ltd met the definition of acquiring a business, as defined in IFRS 3, on 31 March 20.17.

The purchase price settled by MM (Pty) Ltd, to the previous owners of SS (Pty) Ltd, consisted of the following:

- An immediate cash payment of R4 130 000 paid on 31 March 20.17.
- The transfer of three fleet vehicles originally obtained by MM (Pty) Ltd on 1 July 20.14. The correctly calculated carrying amount and fair value of the vehicles in the separate financial statements of MM (Pty) Ltd amounted to R1 355 200 and R850 000 (in total) respectively on the acquisition date. Each vehicle had a total useful life of 10 years for MM (Pty) Ltd. The residual value was regarded as being immaterial. These estimates remained unchanged to date.
- MM (Pty) Ltd issued 250 000 ordinary shares to the former owners. These shares were correctly classified as equity instruments in terms of IAS 32 in the separate financial statements of MM (Pty) Ltd. The fair value on the acquisition date was R1,00 per share. These shares were only issued a week later when the fair value was R1,20 per share. Cost to issue these shares amounted to R0,10 per share and was paid by MM (Pty) Ltd.

- A further cash payment of R1 100 000 payable on 31 March 20.18 if the total concert revenue over the next financial year increases by 15%. The current growth rate is 16% per year and it is expected that this trend will continue into the future. The fair value of this payment was reliably determined as being R1 250 000 on 31 March 2017.
- MM (Pty) Ltd incurred lawyer fees amounting to R30 000 in drafting the purchase agreement.

The carrying amounts and fair values of all the assets and liabilities of SS (Pty) Ltd consisted of the following on the acquisition date:

Description	**Carrying amount Dr/(Cr) Rand**	**Fair value Dr/(Cr) Rand**
Property, plant and equipment – Land and Buildings	4 500 000	4 500 000
Property, plant and equipment – Concert equipment	1 380 000	1 380 000
Intangible assets – Liquor license	250 000	380 000
Intangible assets – Goodwill*	350 000	350 000
Trade payables	(190 000)	(190 000)

* The goodwill arose during a business combination, as defined in IFRS 3, between SS (Pty) Ltd and an unrelated third party a number of years ago.

SS (Pty) Ltd also has a very experienced and dedicated workforce. The purchase agreement specifically stated that the roles, responsibilities, remuneration and benefits of the employees will remain the same as with SS (Pty) Ltd. The estimated fair value of this workforce amounted to R1 450 000 on the acquisition date.

While attending the meeting where the purchase agreement was signed, the chief executive officer (CEO) of MM (Pty) Ltd also had a look at the latest audited financial statements of SS (Pty) Ltd for the financial year ended 28 February 20.17. The CEO noted that SS (Pty) Ltd disclosed a contingent liability in connection with a claim from a client. The client sued SS (Pty) Ltd due to alleged irregularities on the poker tables by the dealer, which resulted in the client losing R150 000. After a discussion with the prior financial manager of SS (Pty) Ltd, the CEO confirmed that SS (Pty) Ltd did not have any present obligation in terms of IAS 37, but that a possible obligation did exist on 28 February 20.17. To date, the case has yet to go to court nor has the internal investigation into these allegations been completed. The fair value of this possible payment was reliably determined to be R160 000 on 31 March 20.17.

The only journal entry processed by MM (Pty) Ltd to account for the acquisition of SS (Pty) Ltd in the separate financial statements of MM (Pty) Ltd on 31 March 20.17 is the following:

	Dr/(Cr) Rand
Property, plant and equipment – Concert equipment (SFPos)	1 380 000
Intangible assets – Liquor licence (SFPos)	250 000
Intangible assets – Goodwill (SFPos)	350 000
Intangible assets – Workforce (SFPos)	1 450 000
Intangible assets – Acquisition-related costs (SFPos)	[N2]30 000
Transaction costs (P or L) (250 000 × 0.10)	[N3]25 000
Goodwill (SFPos) (balancing figure)	(9 600)
Bank (SFPos) (30 000* + 25 000**)	(55 000)
Gain on transfer of vehicles (P or L) (1 355 200 – 850 000)	(505 200)
Property, plant and equipment – Vehicles (SFPos)	(1 355 200)
Share capital (equity) (250 000 × 1.20)	(300 000)
Financial liability – Contingent payment (SFPos)	(1 100 000)
Provision (SFPos)	(160 000)
Recognition of acquisition of SS (Pty) Ltd on 31 March 20.17	

* Transaction costs on the issue of the ordinary shares as part of the consideration paid.
** Lawyer's fees on drafting the purchase agreement.

The CEO of MM (Pty) Ltd is currently very uncertain about the correctness of the journal entry processed and requires your insights on this matter. You may assume that all casting and calculations are correct.

Required

a. Identify and discuss any errors and omissions you noted within the journal entry processed to account for the acquisition of SS (Pty) Ltd in the separate financial statements of MM (Pty) Ltd on 31 March 20.17. Each error or omission identified should be supported by a brief reason from IAS 32 or IFRS 3. You are not required to re-perform the goodwill calculation or to provide correcting journal entries, i.e. only comment (identify and discuss) on the given journal entry as it is presented above. Ignore taxation.

(NWU – adapted)

IFRS 11 & IFRS 12

Joint arrangements

❑ **QUESTIONS AND SOLUTIONS**

IFRS 11.1[@]	Joint operation and joint venture, investment accounted for at cost in separate financial statements, intragroup loan, no tax consequences: preparation of consolidated financial statements with no comparative amounts or notes; only retained earnings column in statement of changes in equity
IFRS 11.2[@]	Joint operation, investment accounted for at fair value in separate financial statements, intragroup loan and sale of inventory; no tax consequences: preparation of consolidated financial statements with no comparative amounts or notes; only retained earnings column in statement of changes in equity
IFRS 11.3[@]	Joint venture, investment accounted for at fair value in separate financial statements, deferred tax and capital gains tax consequences: journal entries for interest in joint venture using equity method; preparation of consolidated financial statements with no comparative amounts or notes; only retained earnings column in statement of changes in equity; disclosure of joint venture in terms of IFRS 12

❑ **QUESTIONS**

IFRS 11.4[@]	Joint operation, investment accounted for at cost in separate financial statements, goodwill at acquisition, intragroup loan, sale of inventory, sale of depreciable property, plant and equipment and other transactions; tax consequences: preparation of consolidated financial statements with no comparative amounts or notes; only retained earnings column in statement of changes in equity
IFRS 11.5	Joint arrangements: discussion of classification.

Note: There are more questions on the application of the equity method in the chapter on IAS 28.

[@] *These questions contain topics or principles that were not included in the ITC syllabus of SAICA at the time of publishing this book, but might still be included in university syllabi.*

❑ QUESTION IFRS 11.1@

Hawson Ltd decided with three other parties to form a company, Stanford Ltd. A contractual arrangement between the parties stipulates that they exercise joint control over Stanford Ltd since the unanimous consent of all four parties are required when taking decisions about the company's activities. Each of the parties owns an equal shareholding in Stanford Ltd.

On 1 January 20.2 Hawson Ltd made a loan of R100 000 to Stanford Ltd which is repayable after 10 years. Interest is payable annually in arrears at a rate of 15% per annum.

The summarised financial statements of both companies at 31 December 20.2 are as follows:

STATEMENTS OF FINANCIAL POSITION AS AT 31 DECEMBER 20.2

	Hawson Ltd Rand	Stanford Ltd Rand
ASSETS		
Non-current assets	1 050 000	150 000
Property, plant and equipment	900 000	150 000
Share investment in Stanford Ltd	50 000	–
Loan to Stanford Ltd	100 000	–
Current assets	450 000	200 000
Total assets	1 500 000	350 000
EQUITY AND LIABILITIES		
Total equity	1 500 000	250 000
Share capital	1 000 000	200 000
Retained earnings	500 000	50 000
Non-current liabilities		
Long-term borrowings	–	100 000
Total equity and liabilities	1 500 000	350 000

STATEMENTS OF PROFIT OR LOSS AND OTHER COMPREHENSIVE INCOME FOR THE YEAR ENDED 31 DECEMBER 20.2

	Hawson Ltd Rand	Stanford Ltd Rand
Profit before finance income/cost	485 000	60 000
Finance income	15 000	–
Finance costs	–	(15 000)
Profit for the year	500 000	45 000
Other comprehensive income	–	–
Total comprehensive income for the year	500 000	45 000

EXTRACTS FROM STATEMENTS OF CHANGES IN EQUITY FOR THE YEAR ENDED 31 DECEMBER 20.2

Retained earnings	Hawson Ltd Rand	Stanford Ltd Rand
Balance at 1 January 20.2	100 000	20 000
Changes in equity for 20.2		
Profit/Total comprehensive income for the year	500 000	45 000
Dividends	(100 000)	(15 000)
Balance at 31 December 20.2	500 000	50 000

Additional information

1. Ignore all forms of tax for both companies.
2. The share investment in Stanford Ltd was accounted for at cost in the above-mentioned financial statements of Hawson Ltd.

Required

Prepare the consolidated financial statements of the Hawson Ltd group for the year ended 31 December 20.2 to comply with the requirements of International Financial Reporting Standards (IFRS) if it is assumed that:

a. The joint arrangement is classified as a joint operation. The contractual arrangement stipulates that assets, liabilities, income and expenses are divided in accordance with the shareholding of the joint operators.
b. The joint arrangement is classified as a joint venture.

Comparative amounts and notes are not required. Only the retained earnings column of the consolidated statement of changes in equity is required.

❖ **Suggested solution IFRS 11.1@**

a. Joint operation

In accordance with IFRS 11.20, a joint operator shall recognise the following in its financial statements in relation to its interest in a joint operation:

- its assets, including its share of any assets held jointly;
- its liabilities, including its share of any liabilities incurred jointly;
- its revenue from the sale of its share of the output arising from the joint operation;
- its share of the revenue from the sale of the output by the joint operation;
- its expenses, including its share of any expenses incurred jointly.

This treatment will be the same for both the separate and consolidated financial statements of the operator.

HAWSON LTD GROUP
CONSOLIDATED STATEMENT OF FINANCIAL POSITION AS AT 31 DECEMBER 20.2

	Rand
ASSETS	
Non-current assets	1 012 500
Property, plant and equipment (1)	937 500
Loan to joint operation (Stanford Ltd) (2)	75 000
Current assets (3)	500 000
Total assets	1 512 500
EQUITY AND LIABILITIES	
Equity attributable to owners of the parent	1 512 500
Share capital	1 000 000
Retained earnings	512 500
Total equity and liabilities	1 512 500

(1) 900 000 + (25% × 150 000) = 937 500
(2) 100 000 – (25% × 100 000) = 75 000 or 100 000 × 75% = 75 000
(3) 450 000 + (25% × 200 000) = 500 000

HAWSON LTD GROUP
CONSOLIDATED STATEMENT OF PROFIT OR LOSS AND OTHER COMPREHENSIVE INCOME FOR THE YEAR ENDED 31 DECEMBER 20.2

	Rand
Other income	
Profit before other income (4)	496 250
Other income (5)	11 250
Profit for the year	507 500
Other comprehensive income	–
Total comprehensive income for the year	507 500

(4) 485 000 + (25% × 60 000) – (25% × 15 000 dividend received) = 496 250
(5) 15 000 – (25% × 15 000) = 11 250

HAWSON LTD GROUP
CONSOLIDATED STATEMENT OF CHANGES IN EQUITY FOR THE YEAR ENDED 31 DECEMBER 20.2

	Retained earnings Rand
Balance at 1 January 20.2 (6)	105 000
Changes in equity for 20.2	
Profit/Total comprehensive income for the year	507 500
Dividends	(100 000)
Balance at 31 December 20.2	512 500

(6) 100 000 + (25% × 20 000) = 105 000

b. Joint venture

According to IFRS 11.24, a joint venturer shall account for its interest in a joint venture as an investment using the equity method in IAS 28.

HAWSON LTD GROUP
CONSOLIDATED STATEMENT OF FINANCIAL POSITION AS AT 31 DECEMBER 20.2

	Rand
ASSETS	
Non-current assets	1 062 500
Property, plant and equipment	900 000
Investment in joint venture (Stanford Ltd) (1)	62 500
Loan to joint venture (Stanford Ltd)	100 000
Current assets	450 000
Total assets	1 512 500
EQUITY AND LIABILITIES	
Equity attributable to owners of the parent	1 512 500
Share capital	1 000 000
Retained earnings	512 500
Total equity and liabilities	1 512 500

(1) 50 000 (cost) + (25% × 50 000 post-acquisition portion of net assets) = 62 500

HAWSON LTD GROUP
CONSOLIDATED STATEMENT OF PROFIT OR LOSS AND OTHER COMPREHENSIVE INCOME FOR THE YEAR ENDED 31 DECEMBER 20.2

	Rand
Profit before finance cost (2)	481 250
Finance income	15 000
Share of profit of joint venture (3)	11 250
Profit for the year	507 500
Other comprehensive income	–
Total comprehensive income for the year	507 500

(2) 485 000 – (25% × 15 000 dividend from joint venture) = 481 250
(3) 45 000 × 25% = 11 250

HAWSON LTD GROUP
CONSOLIDATED STATEMENT OF CHANGES IN EQUITY FOR THE YEAR ENDED 31 DECEMBER 20.2

	Retained earnings Rand
Balance at 1 January 20.2 (4)	105 000
Changes in equity for 20.2	
Profit/Total comprehensive income for the year	507 500
Dividends	(100 000)
Balance at 31 December 20.2 (5)	512 500

(4) 100 000 + (25% × 20 000) = 105 000
(5) 500 000 + (25% × 50 000) = 512 500

❑ QUESTION IFRS 11.2@

The following are abridged trial balances of PA Ltd and MA Ltd at 30 June 20.3:

	PA Ltd Rand Dr/(Cr)	MA Ltd Rand Dr/(Cr)
Share capital (100 000; 80 000 shares)	(100 000)	(80 000)
Mark-to-market reserve	(15 000)	–
Retained earnings	(21 000)	(14 500)
Profit before tax	(17 000)	(10 500)
Trade and other payables	(84 000)	(26 000)
Loan from PA Ltd	–	(10 000)
Property, plant and equipment	80 000	42 000
Investment in MA Ltd – Shares at fair value	60 000	–
– Loan	10 000	–
Inventory	10 000	30 000
Trade receivables	65 000	60 000
Income tax expense	7 000	5 000
Dividends paid	5 000	4 000

Additional information

1. On 1 July 20.0 PA Ltd acquired 40 000 shares in MA Ltd, on which date MA Ltd's retained earnings amounted to R7 000. PA Ltd accounts for the share investment in MA Ltd at fair value with changes in fair value recognised in other comprehensive income. The other 40 000 shares in MA Ltd are held by Skoonma Ltd. PA Ltd and Skoonma Ltd exercise joint control over MA Ltd in terms of a contractual agreement. Assume that this joint arrangement has been correctly classified as a joint operation. The contractual arrangement stipulates that all assets, liabilities, income and expenses are divided according to the shareholding of the joint operators.

2. Revenue for the two companies was as follows:

	Rand
PA Ltd	170 000
MA Ltd (70% from PA Ltd)	110 000

3. PA Ltd purchases all its inventory from MA Ltd at a profit margin of 25% on cost price. The opening inventory of PA Ltd amounted to R7 500.

4. Ignore the effect of deferred tax.

5. Goodwill is not impaired.

Required

a. Prepare the consolidation journal entry in respect of the correction of the value of the investment in MA Ltd for the purposes of the preparation of the consolidated financial statements of the PA Ltd group for the year ended 30 June 20.3.

b. Prepare the consolidated statement of financial position, the consolidated statement of profit or loss and other comprehensive income and the consolidated statement of changes in equity (only the column for retained earnings) of the PA Ltd group for the year ended 30 June 20.3. Your solution must comply with the requirements of International Financial Reporting Standards (IFRS). Notes and comparative amounts are not required.

❖ **Suggested solution IFRS 11.2@**

a. Consolidation journal entry	**Rand Dr/(Cr)**
Mark-to-market reserve	15 000
Investment in shares of MA Ltd	(15 000)

b. Consolidated financial statements

PA LTD GROUP
CONSOLIDATED STATEMENT OF FINANCIAL POSITION AS AT 30 JUNE 20.3

	Rand
ASSETS	
Non-current assets	107 500
Property, plant and equipment (1)	101 000
Goodwill (2)	1 500
Loan to joint operation (MA Ltd) (3)	5 000
Current assets	119 000
Inventory (4)	24 000
Trade receivables (5)	95 000
Total assets	226 500
EQUITY AND LIABILITIES	
Equity attributable to owners of the parent	129 500
Share capital (6)	100 000
Retained earnings	29 500
Current liabilities	
Trade and other payables (7)	97 000
Total equity and liabilities	226 500

(1) 80 000 + (0,5 × 42 000) = 101 000
(2) 45 000 – [0,5 × (80 000 + 7 000)] = 1 500 goodwill at acquisition

(3) 10 000 – 5 000 = 5 000
(4) 10 000 – (0,5 × 2 000) + (0,5 × 30 000) = 24 000
(5) 65 000 + (0,5 × 60 000) = 95 000
(6) 100 000 + (0,5 × 80 000) – 40 000 (at acquisition of interest) = 100 000
(7) 84 000 + (0,5 × 26 000) = 97 000

PA LTD GROUP
CONSOLIDATED STATEMENT OF PROFIT OR LOSS AND OTHER COMPREHENSIVE INCOME FOR THE YEAR ENDED 30 JUNE 20.3

	Rand
Revenue (8)	186 500
Cost of sales	xxx
Gross profit	xxx
Other expenses	xxx
Profit before tax (9)	20 000
Income tax expense (10)	(9 500)
Profit for the year	10 500
Other comprehensive income	–
Total comprehensive income for the year	10 500

(8) 170 000 + [0,5 × (110 000 × 0,3)] = 186 500
(9) 17 000 – 2 000 (dividends received) + [(10 500 + 1 500 – 2 000) × 0,5] = 20 000
(10) 7 000 + (0,5 × 5 000) = 9 500

PA LTD GROUP
CONSOLIDATED STATEMENT OF CHANGES IN EQUITY FOR THE YEAR ENDED 30 JUNE 20.3

	Retained earnings Rand
Balance at 1 July 20.2 (11)	24 000
Changes in equity for 20.3	
Profit/Total comprehensive income for the year	10 500
Dividends (12)	(5 000)
Balance at 30 June 20.3	29 500

(11) 21 000 + [0,5 × (14 500 – 1 500 – 7 000)] = 24 000
(12) 5 000 + (0,5 × 4 000) – 2 000 (dividends received) = 5 000

Calculation

1. **Unrealised profit in inventory**	Rand
Opening inventory (1)	1 500
Closing inventory (2)	2 000

(1) 25/125 × 7 500 = 1 500
(2) 25/125 × 10 000 = 2 000

❑ QUESTION IFRS 11.3@

On 1 January 20.7 Avril Ltd acquired 45% of the share capital of Blink (Pty) Ltd for R49 500. On this date, the equity of Blink (Pty) Ltd consisted of the following:

	Rand
Share capital (100 000 shares)	100 000
Retained earnings	10 000

In terms of a contractual arrangement Avril Ltd exercises joint control over Blink (Pty) Ltd. The contractual arrangement determines that the parties have rights to the net assets of Blink (Pty) Ltd and, as a result, the arrangement has been classified as a joint venture.

You are provided with the following financial statements:

STATEMENTS OF FINANCIAL POSITION AS AT 31 DECEMBER 20.9

	Avril Ltd	Blink (Pty) Ltd
	Rand	Rand
ASSETS		
Non-current assets	1 064 500	120 000
Property, plant and equipment	1 000 000	120 000
Share investment in Blink (Pty) Ltd	64 500	–
Current assets	230 000	120 000
Inventory	200 000	110 000
Cash and cash equivalents	30 000	10 000
Total assets	1 294 500	240 000
EQUITY AND LIABILITIES		
Total equity	1 291 728	240 000
Share capital	500 000	100 000
Retained earnings	779 500	140 000
Mark-to-market reserve	12 228	–
Non-current liabilities		
Deferred tax	2 772	–
Total equity and liabilities	1 294 500	240 000

STATEMENTS OF PROFIT OR LOSS AND OTHER COMPREHENSIVE INCOME FOR THE YEAR ENDED 31 DECEMBER 20.9

	Avril Ltd Rand	Blink (Pty) Ltd Rand
Profit before tax	450 000	160 000
Income tax expense	(130 000)	(40 000)
Profit for the year	320 000	120 000
Other comprehensive income	–	–
Total comprehensive income for the year	320 000	120 000

EXTRACTS FROM STATEMENTS OF CHANGES IN EQUITY FOR THE YEAR ENDED 31 DECEMBER 20.9

Retained earnings	Avril Ltd Rand	Blink (Pty) Ltd Rand
Balance at 1 January 20.9	559 500	60 000
Changes in equity for 20.9		
Profit/Total comprehensive income for the year	320 000	120 000
Dividends	(100 000)	(40 000)
Balance at 31 December 20.9	779 500	140 000

Additional information

1. Avril Ltd accounts for the share investment in Blink (Pty) Ltd at fair value and recognises changes in its fair value in other comprehensive income in accordance with IFRS 9.5.7.5.
2. Assume a tax rate of 28% and that 66% of capital gains are taxable.

Required

a. Provide the journal entries in the consolidated financial statements of the Avril Ltd group for the year ended 31 December 20.9, to account for the interest in the joint venture using the equity method. Narrations are not required.
b. Prepare the consolidated financial statements of the Avril Ltd group for the year ended 31 December 20.9. Your answer must comply with the requirements of International Financial Reporting Standards (IFRS). Comparative amounts and notes are not required and only the retained earnings column in the statement of changes in equity is required.
c. Prepare the notes for the year ended 31 December 20.9 of the Avril Ltd group, relating to the joint venture, to comply with the disclosure requirements of IFRS 12.

❖ **Suggested solution IFRS 11.3@**

a. Journal entries

	Rand Dr/(Cr)
Mark-to-market reserve (1)	12 228
Deferred tax (SFPos) (2)	2 772
Share investment in Blink (Pty) Ltd (3)	(15 000)
Share investment in Blink (Pty) Ltd	58 500
Dividends received (4)	18 000
Retained earnings – opening balance (5)	(22 500)
Share of profit of joint venture (6)	(54 000)

(1) 64 500 – 49 500 – (15 000 × 66% × 28%) = 12 228
(2) 15 000 × 66% × 28% = 2 772
(3) 64 500 – 49 500 = 15 000
(4) 40 000 × 45% = 18 000
(5) (60 000 – 10 000) × 45% = 22 500
(6) 120 000 × 45% = 54 000

b. **AVRIL LTD GROUP**
CONSOLIDATED STATEMENT OF FINANCIAL POSITION AS AT 31 DECEMBER 20.9

	Rand
ASSETS	
Non-current assets	1 108 000
Property, plant and equipment	1 000 000
Investment in joint venture (1)	108 000
Current assets	230 000
Inventory	200 000
Cash and cash equivalents	30 000
Total assets	1 338 000
EQUITY AND LIABILITIES	
Equity attributable to owners of the parent	1 338 000
Share capital	500 000
Retained earnings	838 000
Non-current liabilities	–
Total equity and liabilities	1 338 000

(1) 64 500 – 15 000 + 58 500 = 108 000

AVRIL LTD GROUP
CONSOLIDATED STATEMENT OF PROFIT OR LOSS AND OTHER COMPREHENSIVE INCOME FOR THE YEAR ENDED 31 DECEMBER 20.9

	Rand
Profit before tax (2)	432 000
Share of profit of joint venture (3)	54 000
Income tax expense	(130 000)
Profit for the year	356 000
Other comprehensive income	–
Total comprehensive income for the year	356 000

(2) 450 000 – 18 000 (dividend received) = 432 000
(3) 120 000 × 45% = 54 000

AVRIL LTD GROUP
CONSOLIDATED STATEMENT OF CHANGES IN EQUITY FOR THE YEAR ENDED 31 DECEMBER 20.9

Retained earnings	**Rand**
Balance at 1 January 20.9 (4)	582 000
Changes in equity for 20.9	
Profit/Total comprehensive income for the year	356 000
Dividends	(100 000)
Balance at 31 December 20.9	838 000

(4) 559 500 + 22 500 = 582 000

c. **AVRIL LTD GROUP**
NOTES FOR THE YEAR ENDED 31 DECEMBER 20.9

1. Accounting policy

1.1 Joint ventures

Joint arrangements are classified as joint ventures when the parties that exercise joint control, have rights to the net assets of the arrangement.

Interests in joint ventures are accounted for as investments using the equity method.

2. Joint ventures

The entity has a 45% interest in a joint venture, Blink (Pty) Ltd. A contractual arrangement between the entity and the other shareholders determines that the parties have joint control over Blink (Pty) Ltd as the unanimous consent of all parties is required when making decisions about the company's activities.

The activities of the joint venture are strategic to the entity.

The joint venture's principal place of business and country of incorporation is the Republic of South Africa.

The investment in the joint venture is accounted for using the equity method.

Remarks

- The above-mentioned disclosure requirements are outlined in IFRS 12.21.
- IFRS 12.21b(ii) further requires the disclosure of summarised financial information relating to the joint venture (see IFRS 12.B12(b) for the specific line items).
- IFRS 12.7 also requires the disclosure of information about the significant judgments and assumptions made to determine:
  - whether the entity has joint control over another entity;
  - the type of joint arrangement (joint operation or joint venture) when it is structured through a separate entity.

❑ QUESTION IFRS 11.4[@]

Alfa Ltd, a listed company, and four other construction companies each have a 20% holding in a jointly controlled entity, Group 5 Ltd. Alfa Ltd acquired the holding on 1 January 20.3 for R28 000, on which date Group 5 Ltd's retained earnings amounted to R15 000. A contractual arrangement between the shareholders stipulates that all the parties exercise joint control over Group 5 Ltd. Assume that the arrangement has been correctly classified as a joint operation.

The following abridged financial statements are available:

STATEMENTS OF PROFIT OR LOSS AND OTHER COMPREHENSIVE INCOME FOR THE YEAR ENDED 31 DECEMBER 20.8

	Alfa Ltd Rand	Group 5 Ltd Rand
Profit before interest and investment income	948 200	146 700
Investment income	25 600	–
Finance charges	(63 800)	(9 300)
Profit before tax	910 000	137 400
Income tax expense	(365 000)	(53 600)
Profit for the year	545 000	83 800
Other comprehensive income	–	–
Total comprehensive income for the year	545 000	83 800

EXTRACTS FROM STATEMENTS OF CHANGES IN EQUITY FOR THE YEAR ENDED 31 DECEMBER 20.8

Retained earnings	Alfa Ltd Rand	Group 5 Ltd Rand
Balance at 1 January 20.8	791 000	55 000
Changes in equity for 20.8		
Profit/Total comprehensive for the year	545 000	83 800
Dividends paid on 30 June 20.8	(500 000)	(12 000)
Balance at 31 December 20.8	836 000	126 800

STATEMENTS OF FINANCIAL POSITION AS AT 31 DECEMBER 20.8

	Alfa Ltd Rand	Group 5 Ltd Rand
ASSETS		
Non-current assets		
Property, plant and equipment	2 393 800	169 600
Cost price	8 423 600	284 000
Accumulated depreciation	(6 029 800)	(114 400)
Investment in Group 5 Ltd	67 000	–
Shares	28 000	–
Long-term liabilities	39 000	–
Current assets	5 432 100	247 600
Total assets	7 892 900	417 200
EQUITY AND LIABILITIES		
Total equity	5 799 000	226 800
Share capital – ordinary	4 960 000	100 000
Share premium	3 000	–
Retained earnings	836 000	126 800

	Alfa Ltd Rand	Group 5 Ltd Rand
Non-current liabilities	505 000	92 000
Deferred tax	105 000	24 000
Long-term borrowings	400 000	68 000
Current liabilities	1 588 900	98 400
Total equity and liabilities	7 892 900	417 200

Additional information

1. The above financial statements were prepared without taking into account the relationship between the two companies.

2. Alfa Ltd is responsible for the day-to-day management of Group 5 Ltd for an agreed management fee.

3. The long-term loan of R39 000 to Group 5 Ltd was granted on 1 January 20.6 and is repayable after eight years in one payment. The loan carries interest at 10% per annum. Included in the current liabilities of Group 5 Ltd, is the total interest due to Alfa Ltd for the past year. On 14 January 20.9 the interest was paid in cash to Alfa Ltd. Alfa Ltd has already accrued for the interest.

4. On 31 December 20.8 Alfa Ltd sold depreciable property, plant and equipment with a carrying amount of R45 000 to Group 5 Ltd at a profit of R15 000. The original cost price of the assets was R70 000.

5. Included in the profit before interest and investment income of Group 5 Ltd, are the following expenses:

	Rand
Management fee paid to Alfa Ltd	80 000
Short-term rental paid for office buildings of Alfa Ltd	10 000

6. During September 20.8, Group 5 Ltd sold inventory with a cost price of R71 000 to Alfa Ltd for R87 000. All such inventory has subsequently been sold by Alfa Ltd.

7. The tax rate for the companies has remained unchanged at 27% for the past number of years.

8. Goodwill is not impaired.

Required

Prepare the abridged consolidated statement of financial position, statement of profit or loss and other comprehensive income and statement of changes in equity (retained earnings column only) of the Alfa Ltd group for the year ended 31 December 20.8 to comply with the requirements of International Financial Reporting Standards (IFRS). Comparative amounts, earnings per share and notes are not required.

❑ QUESTION IFRS 11.5

Four companies, Romeo Ltd, Uniform Ltd, Sierra Ltd and Tango Ltd entered into an agreement in terms of which they created a purchase consortium. They want to use the consortium to negotiate better inventory prices.

The agreement stipulates that each of the parties will have a 25% interest in the consortium and that it will be under their joint control. The unanimous consent of all four parties is required when decisions are made about the activities of the consortium.

Required

Briefly discuss the type of joint arrangement the purchase consortium should be classified as if assumed that:

a. The consortium will **not** be structured through a separate 'vehicle' (entity).
b. The consortium will be structured through a separate 'vehicle' (entity), RUST Ltd. Assume that the memorandum of incorporation and the contractual arrangement stipulate that the assets and liabilities of the newly formed entity will be the assets and liabilities of that entity and that the shareholders do not have the rights to and obligations for the assets and liabilities of RUST Ltd.

   Your answer should be based only on the information provided and you do not need to consider other facts and circumstances.

IFRS 12

Disclosure of interests in other entities

Note:	As this chapter and the chapters on IAS 28, IFRS 10 and IFRS 11 all deal with interests in other entities, the questions on these chapters are integrated and such questions are presented as part of the chapters on IAS 28, IFRS 10 and IFRS 11.

IFRS 13

Fair value measurement

Note:	IFRS 13 provides extensive guidance on the measurement of fair value. The standard affects most other standards that require fair value measurement and/or disclosure, therefore the questions on this standard are integrated with various other standards and such questions are presented as part of other chapters. Especially refer to the chapter on IFRS 9 where some of the principles in IFRS 13 are specifically addressed.

IFRS 15

Revenue from contracts with customers

❑ QUESTIONS AND SOLUTIONS

❑ QUESTIONS

❑ QUESTION IFRS 15.1

Consider the following transactions:

1. An early settlement discount is granted on a sale of goods to a creditworthy customer which has a proven record of paying within settlement terms.

2. Goods are sold to a customer at a transaction price inclusive of VAT. The entity (seller) and the customer are registered as VAT vendors.

3. Goods are sold to a customer, subject to a 60-day money-back guarantee if the customer is not completely satisfied with the goods. The entity (seller) expects that 5% of the goods sold will be returned and refunded within 60 days after a sale is made.

4. Ten vehicles are sold to a customer. Registration and licensing of the vehicles in the customer's name have been completed. The customer already paid for the vehicles, however, the customer requested that the vehicles be kept at the dealer's premises until the customer is ready to collect them.

Required

Briefly discuss the appropriate treatment of each of the transactions above to comply with the requirements of IFRS 15 *Revenue from Contracts with Customers*.

❖ Suggested solution IFRS 15.1

1. Early settlement discounts granted

Revenue is recognised at the amount of the transaction price (which excludes estimates of variable consideration that are constrained) (IFRS 15.46), which an entity expects to be entitled to in exchange for transferring promised goods or services to a customer (IFRS 15 Appendix A). Constraining estimates of variable consideration entails that variable consideration will only be included in the transaction price to the extent that it is highly probable that a significant reversal in the amount of cumulative revenue recognised will not occur when the uncertainty associated with the variable consideration is subsequently resolved (IFRS 15.56).

An early settlement discount is a form of variable consideration (IFRS 15.51) that is considered in determining the transaction price (IFRS 15.48). The customer usually pays within settlement terms (which is supported by a proven early settlement record), and the entity expects that the discount will be granted to this customer. The transaction price, net of the early settlement discount, will be recognised as revenue on the date control over the goods transfers to the customer.

2. Transaction price inclusive of VAT

The transaction price is the amount of consideration to which an entity expects to be entitled in exchange for transferring promised goods or services to a customer, excluding amounts collected on behalf of third parties (for example, some sales taxes) (IFRS 15.47).

VAT is collected on behalf of the tax authority, the South African Revenue Service, and output VAT is recognised as a separate liability at the VAT payable amount. The transaction price excluding VAT will be recognised as revenue on the date control over the goods transfers to the customer.

3. 60-day money-back guarantee

Revenue is recognised at the amount of the transaction price (IFRS 15.46), which an entity expects to be entitled to in exchange for transferring promised goods or services to a customer (IFRS 15 Appendix A).

The entity (seller) expects that 5% of the goods sold will be returned and refunded within 60 days after a sale is made, therefore the entity expects to be entitled to 95% of the initial proceeds received. Consequently, the entity will recognise 95% of the initial proceeds received as revenue on the date control over the goods transfers to the customer. The entity shall recognise a separate refund liability for the remaining 5% of the initial proceeds received (IFRS 15.B21).

95% of the cost of the goods is recognised as cost of sales and a separate refund asset is recognised for the remaining 5% of the cost of the goods on the date control over the goods transfers to the customer (IFRS 15.B21).

4. Bill-and-hold arrangement

A bill-and-hold arrangement is a contract under which an entity bills a customer for a product, but the entity retains physical possession of the product until it is transferred to the customer at a point in time in the future. The customer requested the dealer to keep the vehicles at its premises until the customer is ready to collect them (IFRS 15.B79).

This represents a bill-and-hold arrangement and the customer may obtain control of the vehicles even though the vehicles remain in the dealer's physical possession. As vehicle licensing and registration have been completed, the customer probably controls the vehicles from this date even though physical possession has not been taken. In this case, the customer has the ability to direct the use of, and obtain substantially all of the remaining benefits from, the vehicles even though it has decided not to exercise its right to take physical possession of the vehicles on registration date. Consequently, the entity does not control the vehicles anymore. Instead, the entity provides custodial services to the customer which might be a separate performance obligation if it can be argued that these services are distinct. The entity (seller) may therefore recognise the revenue from the sale of the vehicles on the day the vehicles are licensed and registered in the customer's name even though delivery has not been taken by the customer.

❑ QUESTION IFRS 15.2

The following unrelated cases are presented to you:

a. Bezt Clothing Ltd has a lay-bye sales option (i.e. some goods are set aside for a customer upon payment of a deposit and delivery is taken upon receipt of the final payment). Experience has shown that customers have the intention of completing the lay-bye sales and most such sales are completed. Bezt Clothing Ltd does not keep the lay-bye sales separate and can sell the lay-bye clothing to other customers and replace it with the same items from its shelves when the customer collects its lay-bye items. The following information is available:

- On 5 January 20.3 a lay-bye sale of clothing amounting to R500, which was identified and ready for delivery, was made to Mr Steyn. He paid a deposit of R100 on the same date.

- The balance of the outstanding amount was paid as follows:
  - 6 February 20.3 – R150
  - 18 March 20.3 – R250

The clothing was delivered on 18 March 20.3.

b. JV Tyres Ltd sells tyres to the public.
- On 4 January 20.3 Thabo ordered four tyres from JV Tyres Ltd. JV Tyres Ltd did not have the specific tyres Thabo wanted on hand and had to order the tyres.
- On 6 January 20.3 JV Tyres Ltd received the tyres. JV Tyres Ltd invoiced Thabo on this date after the tyres were set aside in the storeroom and labelled 'Sold to Thabo – do not sell'.
- Thabo asked JV Tyres Ltd if they could keep the tyres until 10 January 20.3 when he would come and collect them.
- Thabo collected and paid for the tyres on 13 January 20.3.

Required

On which date should revenue be recognised in each of the above independent cases to comply with the requirements of IFRS 15? Provide brief reasons for your answers.

❖ **Suggested solution IFRS 15.2**

a. The revenue should be recognised on 18 March 20.3 which is the date the customer obtains control of the clothing (IFRS 15.31). Control is not transferred to the customer before this date as Bezt Clothing Ltd can still sell the lay-bye clothing to other customers and replace it with the same items, i.e. before 18 March 20.3 the customer does not have the ability to direct the use of the clothing (IFRS 15.33).

b. A bill-and-hold arrangement is a contract under which an entity bills a customer for a product, but the entity retains physical possession of the product until it is transferred to the customer at a point in time in the future (IFRS 15.B79). Thabo entered into a 'bill-and-hold' arrangement with JV Tyres Ltd and the revenue from the sale of the tyres should be recognised on 6 January 20.3, which is the date Thabo obtained control of the tyres. On 6 January 20.3 the arrangement is substantive (Thabo requested the arrangement), the tyres were identified as belonging to Thabo, the tyres were ready for physical transfer to Thabo and from this date JV Tyres Ltd cannot sell the tyres to another customer (IFRS 15.B81).

❑ QUESTION IFRS 15.3

Repairs Ltd is an electrical contractor that also sells, repairs and installs electronic devices. Repairs Ltd also offers short training courses and apprentice contracts to any person who wants to become an electrician.

The following transactions occurred in the records of Repairs Ltd for the year ended 30 June 20.9:

	Rand
1. Repair services	76 000
2. Sales of equipment	103 000
3. Installation fees received	37 000
Included in this is an amount of R1 500 for an installation which has not been started on 30 June 20.9.	

	Rand
4. Sale of equipment by Repairs Ltd on behalf of another firm Repairs Ltd receives a commission of 15% on all these consignment inventory sales.	67 000
5. Course fees received for training of electrician apprentices The course takes place from 1 June 20.9 to 31 August 20.9. Course fees of R2 400 are still outstanding at 30 June 20.9. Repairs Ltd expects to collect the full amount still outstanding.	9 600

Required

Calculate the amount of revenue that should be recognised for the year ended 30 June 20.9 in respect of the above transactions to comply with the requirements of IFRS.

❖ **Suggested solution IFRS 15.3**

The following amounts should be included in revenue:

	Rand
Repair services	76 000
Sales of equipment	103 000
Installations (1)	35 500
Commission (2)	10 050
Course fees (3)	4 000
Total revenue	228 550

(1) 37 000 – 1 500 = 35 500
(2) 67 000 × 0,15 = 10 050
(3) (9 600 + 2 400) × 1/3 = 4 000

❑ **QUESTION IFRS 15.4**

Lion's Head Ltd sells food, electronic devices, houseware and clothing. Lion's Head Ltd is a registered VAT vendor and only sells to creditworthy customers. Its sales amount comprises the following for the year ended 31 December 20.2:

	Note	Rand
Invoice value of sale of goods (including VAT at 15%)		805 000
Instalments received on lay-bye sales (including VAT at 15%)	1	115 000
Consignment sales value of all inventories on consignment	2	40 000
Trade discounts received		30 000
Sales on approval at invoice value (including VAT at 15%)	3	45 600
		1 035 600

Notes:

1. Total lay-bye sales for the year were R115 000 (including VAT). Only 50% of the goods sold under a lay-bye agreement during the year ended 31 December 20.2 have been taken by customers. Lion's Head Ltd removes the goods sold under a lay-bye agreement from it shelves and it is not allowed to sell these goods to any other customers during the lay-bye period.

2. The R40 000 sales value of all consignment inventory excludes VAT. The 'inventory on consignment at cost' account shows a balance of R5 000 on hand as at 31 December 20.2. All consignment sales are made by agents and the sales take place at a gross profit of 20% on selling price. The agents are entitled to a commission of 10% of the sales value once the consignment inventory is sold.

3. Sales subject to approval are accounted for separately. Invoices with a VAT-inclusive value of R20 727 relate to goods accepted by the customer. A further amount of R13 773 (VAT inclusive) is presumed to be accepted, as the time period for rejection has elapsed. Based on past experience and the nature of the goods sold, Lion's Head Ltd cannot objectively say that the remainder of the goods will necessarily be accepted by the customers.

Required

a. Calculate the amount of revenue that should be recognised in the records of Lion's Head Ltd for the year ended 31 December 20.2.

❖ **Suggested solution IFRS 15.4**

The following amounts should be included in revenue:

	Rand
Sale of goods (1)	700 000
Lay-bye sales (2)	100 000
Consignment inventory sales (3) (4)	30 375
Trade discount received (5)	–
Sales subject to customer acceptance (6)	30 000
Total revenue	860 375

(1) 805 000 × 100/115 = 700 000
The VAT is collected on behalf of the South African Revenue Service and the transaction price exclusive of VAT should be recognised as revenue (IFRS 15.47).

(2) 115 000 × 100/115 = 100 000
The customers have the ability to prevent Lion's Head Ltd from selling the lay-bye goods to other customers. Sales revenue from lay-bye goods exclusive of VAT can therefore be recognised in full.

(3) 5 000 × 100/80 = 6 250
Inventory on consignment with a selling price of R6 250 should be excluded from sales as the inventory is unsold at year end (IFRS 15.B77).

(4) 40 000 – 6 250 = 33 750 × 90% = 30 375
Lion's Head Ltd is only entitled to the transaction price excluding the commission amount due to the agents.

(5) Trade discount received should not be recognised as revenue, but as a reduction of the initial recognition of inventory purchased (IAS 2).

(6) (20 727 + 13 773) × 100/115 = 30 000
Only the sales (exclusive of VAT) of accepted goods and the goods where the rejection period has elapsed can be recognised as revenue (IFRS 15.38(e) & .B84).

❑ QUESTION IFRS 15.5

Chick Chefs Ltd manufactures and sells expensive professional kitchen utensils. On 1 November 20.0, Chick Chefs Ltd sold a set of kitchen knives to Mr Du Toit for R65 000 on credit. In order to motivate Mr Du Toit to settle the outstanding amount promptly, Chick Chefs Ltd offered him a settlement discount of 10% should he settle the outstanding amount by 31 December 20.0. Mr Du Toit has a record of paying within terms.

On 1 November 20.0, Chick Chefs Ltd also offered Mr Du Toit a service to sharpen his knives every two months for a period of two years after transaction date. The total stand-alone selling price of this service amounts to R12 000, and it was agreed that Mr Du Toit would settle the amount as and when the sharpenings are performed (all sharpenings have equal values). Mr Du Toit handed in his knives on 31 December 20.0 for the first sharpening, and Chick Chefs Ltd returned the sharpened knives to him on the same date, after he paid for this service.

Mr Du Toit also purchased a set of pans on 1 November 20.0 with a cash selling price of R30 000 on that date. No settlement discount was offered on this transaction, since it was agreed that Mr Du Toit would settle the outstanding amount by making two-monthly instalments of R3 000 each payable in arrears for a period of two years, i.e. R3 000 × 12 (2 years; 6 instalments per year).

The first instalment is payable on 31 December 20.0. On 1 November 20.0, Chick Chefs Ltd determined that Mr Du Toit's borrowing rate was 17,538% per year.

Mr Du Toit made an electronic payment transfer of R62 500 to Chick Chefs Ltd on 31 December 20.0. This amount is made up as follows:

	Rand
Set of kitchen knives (1)	58 500
Knife sharpening service (2)	1 000
Instalment on set of pans	3 000
Total	62 500

(1) 65 000 × 90% = 58 500
(2) 12 000/12 two-monthly periods = 1 000

You may ignore VAT and income tax implications.

Required

a. Journalise the above revenue transactions in the records of Chick Chefs Ltd on 1 November 20.0.
b. Journalise the above revenue transactions in the records of Chick Chefs Ltd on 31 December 20.0.

Journal narrations are not required and the solution must comply with the requirements of IFRS.

❖ **Suggested solution IFRS 15.5**

	Rand Dr/(Cr)
a. 1 November 20.0	
Receivables (SFPos) (1)	88 500
Revenue (P or L)	(88 500)
(1) 58 500 + 30 000 = 88 500	
b. 31 December 20.0	
Receivables (SFPos)	877
Finance income (P or L) (1)	(877)
Bank (SFPos)	62 500
Receivables (SFPos) (2)	(61 500)
Revenue (P or L)	(1 000)

(1) Interest for the period 1 November 20.0 to 31 December 20.0 on sale of pans:
I = 17,538% per year/6 (two-monthly instalments) = 2,923%
N = 12
PMT = 3 000
Comp PV = 30 000 (or given)
Thus interest for the two months ending 31 December 20.0 = R877 (R30 000 × 2,923%)

(2) 58 500 + 3 000 instalment paid = 61 500

❑ **QUESTION IFRS 15.6**

Digital Television Broadcasting Corporation (DTBC) Ltd, a South African company and provider of pay channel TV, entered into the following transaction with one of its customers, an Internet company, Incredible Web Services (IWS) Ltd:

DTBC Ltd would broadcast the normal IWS Ltd advertisement during December 20.9 on its pay channel and in exchange IWS Ltd would add a DTBC Ltd advertisement by means of a 'banner' during December 20.9 on IWS Ltd's website.

The marketing directors of both companies felt that it was not necessary for the exchange of invoices since both companies provide advertising services and the value of the advertisements was considered to be equal.

Required

Discuss, with reasons, whether the treatment of the above transaction (i.e. not issuing an invoice and not recognising advertising revenue in the records of DTBC Ltd) is correct and in accordance with the requirements of IFRS 15. In addition, briefly discuss the appropriate measurement of this transaction in the records of DTBC Ltd if you do not agree with the treatment above.

❖ **Suggested solution IFRS 15.6**

DTBC Ltd entered into what is referred to as a 'barter transaction' to provide advertising services in exchange for receiving advertising services from its customer (in this case IWS Ltd).

IFRS 15.5(d) states that non-monetary exchanges between entities in the same line of business to facilitate sales to customers or potential customers are scoped out of the standard. However, this scope exemption is not applicable to DTBC Ltd, as it is not in the same line of business as IWS Ltd. DTBC Ltd is a pay channel TV provider and IWS Ltd is an Internet company.

Furthermore, IFRS 15.9(d) requires an entity to account for a contract with a customer that is within the scope of IFRS 15 when, amongst other things, the contract has commercial substance (e.g. the future cash flows are expected to change because goods or services are exchanged for goods or services that are of a different nature or value). It is clear from the above that although DTBC Ltd and IWS Ltd both provide advertising services, the services are dissimilar and the transaction has commercial substance. Therefore, DTBC Ltd should account for the contract with IWS Ltd that is within the scope of IFRS 15.

The treatment of this transaction (i.e. not issuing an invoice and not recognising advertising revenue in the records of DTBC Ltd) is thus incorrect and not in accordance with the requirements of IFRS 15.

The consideration received by DTBC Ltd for the broadcasting of a TV advertisement is an advertising service from IWS Ltd and therefore of a non-cash nature. IFRS 15.66 requires revenue in this case to be measured at the fair value of the non-cash consideration received, i.e. the advertising service received from IWS Ltd. When the fair value of the services received cannot be estimated reliably, the revenue is measured at the fair value of the services provided (see IFRS 15.67). The issue is therefore whether DTBC Ltd can reliably measure revenue at the fair value of the advertising services received or provided in this barter transaction.

Revenue from a barter transaction involving advertising can most likely not be measured reliably at the fair value of advertising services received as information to estimate such a fair value may be limited. However, since DTBC Ltd is a pay channel provider, it is likely that it will be able to reliably determine the fair value of the advertising services it provides in the barter transaction.

Revenue from this transaction will probably be measured at the fair value of the advertising services DTBC Ltd provides.

❑ QUESTION IFRS 15.7

Group2Save (Pty) Ltd, with a 31 December financial year end, operates in more than 50 cities in 35 different countries. Group2Save (Pty) Ltd contracts with suppliers to sell their goods on its website on behalf of the suppliers. Group2Save (Pty) Ltd advertises and sells the goods on its website through featured discounted daily deals.

Through collective buying power, the suppliers can increase their sales volumes substantially. A risk with this business model is that a successful deal could temporarily swamp a small supplier with too many customers, risking a possibility that customers will be dissatisfied, or that there will not be enough goods to meet the demand of customers.

Group2Save (Pty) Ltd employs a sizeable number of creative staff who draft descriptions for the deals. These employees and the suppliers of the deals jointly determine the prices at which the deals will be sold to customers.

Customers that are signed up for daily deals, receive an e-mail providing details of unbeatable deals at discounted prices in the country and city they selected upon registration. Unlike classified advertising, the customer does not pay an upfront fee to participate in the deals.

Should the customer be interested in a particular deal, they select the link (as provided in the e-mail), which then takes them directly to the Group2Save (Pty) Ltd website from which they can purchase Group2Save (Pty) Ltd vouchers to be redeemed at a wide range of suppliers who will deliver the goods or services directly to them.

Each deal is available for only 24 hours; after which it is automatically removed from the website. Group2Save (Pty) Ltd requires payment from customers before orders are processed and voucher confirmations are issued. As soon as a voucher has been issued, no changes can be made to it and no refunds will be given. The voucher states that it is valid for six months from the date of purchase whereafter it will expire without being refunded. Group2Save (Pty) Ltd does not purchase vouchers in advance from suppliers; instead, it purchases vouchers only after they were purchased by the customers on the website.

Group2Save (Pty) Ltd keeps 10% of the cash purchase price of the vouchers. As part of their buyer satisfaction programme, Group2Save (Pty) Ltd will assist the customers to get in touch with the suppliers who are responsible for fulfilling obligations associated with the vouchers, including remedies for dissatisfaction with the goods or services. Group2Save (Pty) Ltd does not guarantee inventory availability.

Required

Discuss the recognition of revenue in the financial statements of Group2Save (Pty) Ltd, if it is assumed that a contract with a customer that is within the scope of IFRS 15 already exists between the respective parties (i.e. you need not discuss the criteria for identifying a contract with a customer).

❑ QUESTION IFRS 15.8

Trade Store CC, a general dealer, only sells to creditworthy customers. Trade Store CC's accountant included the following transactions in its revenue line item of R781 340 for the year ended 31 December 20.8, however, she is not certain if her treatment of these transactions is correct:

1. Lay-bye sales

Cash payments received on the following lay-bye sales were included in full in revenue:

Invoice number	Selling price Rand	Balance outstanding Rand
3161	355	65
4031	171	104

Trade Store CC can sell the lay-bye goods to other customers and replace them with the same items during the lay-bye period.

2. Bill-and-hold arrangement

Invoice number 4136 amounting to R363 was emailed to a customer on 15 December 20.8 when Trade Store CC informed him that his goods were booked out and ready for collection. (Trade Store CC may not sell these goods to other customers.) The customer informed Trade Store CC that he was on leave and would only be able to collect the goods at the end of January 20.9. The full invoice amount was included in revenue.

3. Branch sales

On 15 December 20.8, inventory with a sales value of R27 300 was delivered to one of Trade Store CC's branches. Trade Store CC included the full sales value in its revenue for the year ended 31 December 20.8. As at 31 December 20.8, the branch still had 90% of the inventory on hand.

4. Consignment inventory

Consignment inventory with a sales value of R9 000 was sent to a butchery. As at 31 December 20.8, the butchery sold inventory with a sales value of R5 000. Trade Store CC included the full R9 000 in its revenue for the year ended 31 December 20.8.

5. Undelivered goods

Goods with a selling price of R3 600, invoiced on 31 December 20.8 and included in revenue above, have not yet been delivered nor is there a signed receipt for them.

Required

Calculate the amount of revenue that Trade Store CC may recognise for the year ended 31 December 20.8. The solution must comply with the requirements of IFRS. Ignore VAT.

❑ QUESTION IFRS 15.9

Pamco Ltd is a manufacturer of various machines. It also sells spares for the machines and has been in the business for many years. On 1 August 20.8, Pamco Ltd entered into a written agreement with Precision Ltd for the supply of machinery to be used in Precision Ltd's production process.

The cash selling price of the machinery was R1 250 000, however, it was agreed that a deposit of R275 000 would be paid immediately, and the remaining debt would be settled in three equal instalments on the following dates: 31 January 20.9, 31 July 20.9 and 31 January 20.10. Interest would be charged at 6% below prime on the outstanding balance. The machinery would be delivered to Precision Ltd, who would also be responsible for its installation, on 31 August 20.8.

The contract also included a clause for the sale of spares for the machinery. The spares are to be despatched in two equal batches. The first delivery will be on 30 November 20.8 and the second delivery will take place on 28 February 20.9. The selling price of each batch of spares is R75 800, and if Precision Ltd settles the debt on receipt of the goods, it will be entitled to a 5% settlement discount like Pamco Ltd's other customers of machine spares receive.

Required

a. Discuss the recognition of revenue from the sale of the machinery and the spares in accordance with IFRS 15 in the records of Pamco Ltd for the year ended 31 January 20.9. Assume the machinery and the spares are separate performance obligations that are not satisfied over time (i.e. you need not discuss the criteria for identifying separate performance obligations and whether the performance obligations are satisfied over time).
b. Discuss the measurement of revenue from the sale of the machinery and the spares in accordance with IFRS 15 in the records of Pamco Ltd for the year ended 31 January 20.9. Calculations are not required.

❑ QUESTION IFRS 15.10

Nqutu Ltd is a South African listed company that manufactures and distributes ethnic jewellery countrywide as well as in the United Kingdom. Nqutu Ltd's head office is situated in KwaZulu-Natal and its jewellery range includes beaded necklaces, bangles and earrings.

If Nqutu Ltd's customers open a Nqutu Ltd club account at a fixed monthly fee of R100, they will receive free marketing material showcasing Nqutu Ltd's latest jewellery designs, a service to polish their Nqutu Ltd jewellery in the first two years after purchase (note 1) and earn points that can be redeemed on future purchases from Nqutu Ltd (note 2).

Note 1
From past experience, approximately 30% of all jewellery sold to account holders is handed in for polishing in the first year after selling date, and approximately 50% of jewellery sold is handed in for polishing in the second year after selling date.

Note 2
Points will be earned as the account holders purchase Nqutu Ltd goods. Customers may decide when and how they want to redeem their points. The points structure works as follows:

Number of points	Nqutu Ltd goods qualified for
5 000	Eight beaded serviette rings
10 000	Matching necklace and bracelet
15 000	Deluxe Nqutu hamper

Required

Briefly discuss the recognition of the fixed monthly fee in the records of Nqutu Ltd in accordance with the requirements of IFRS. You may assume that a contract with a customer, that is within the scope of IFRS 15, already exists between the respective parties and that there are two separate performance obligations (the polishing service and the sale of points) in a contract with an account holder (i.e. you need not discuss the criteria for identifying a contract with a customer and if the marketing material is a separate performance obligation).

(UJ – adapted)

❑ QUESTION IFRS 15.11

Consider the following independent cases of various companies in the construction industry:

Case A

Zondi Ltd incurred R200 000 of costs in connection with winning a successful bid on a contract to build a new bridge over the Khamanzi River near Greytown in KZN. The costs were incurred during the proposal and contract negotiations, and include the initial bridge design.

Required

Briefly discuss how Zondi Ltd should account for the costs incurred.

Case B

Gumede Ltd entered into a contract with a customer to build an office building. Amongst others, the following costs were incurred:

	Rand
Transport heavy equipment to the building site	65 000
Direct costs related to supplies, equipment, material and labour (building phase)	500 000
Costs related to abnormal wastage of materials	40 000

Gumede Ltd expects to recover all incurred costs under the contract.

Required

Briefly discuss how Gumede Ltd should account for the costs incurred.

Case C

Mbobo Ltd entered into a contract to build a dam for the South African government. The total contract price is R100 million, with a performance bonus of R40 million that will be paid based on the timing of completion. The amount of the performance bonus decreases by 10% per week for every week beyond the agreed-upon completion date.

Mbobo Ltd concluded that the expected value method is most predictive in estimating the amount of variable consideration that the company is expected to be entitled to. Management estimates that there is a 60% probability that the contract will be completed by the agreed-upon completion date, a 30% probability that it will be completed one week late, and a 10% probability that it will be completed two weeks late.

Required

Calculate the transaction price of the dam for purposes of measuring revenue in the records of Mbobo Ltd.

❑ QUESTION IFRS 15.12

BMW Klerksdorp (Pty) Ltd sells BMW vehicles. The contract with the customer includes the sale of a vehicle and a motor plan that are both distinct performance obligations in the contract. On 30 March 20.5, BMW Klerksdorp (Pty) Ltd purchased a BMW 318i M Sport Automatic at a cost of R219 380 (excluding transport cost) from BMW SA Ltd in anticipation of a promotional offer to be advertised during April 20.5. Transport cost of R2 500 (per vehicle, settled in cash) was incurred by BMW Klerksdorp (Pty) Ltd to transport the vehicle from BMW SA Ltd to BMW Klerksdorp (Pty) Ltd.

The promotional offer advertised during April 20.5 read as follows:

Driving a BMW is all about choice and the power to choose. Now, with our latest offers, you have more power to choose the finance option that suits you and your lifestyle.

At the end of your contract term you will be left with a number of options:

- **Option A:** After paying an initial deposit of 5,5% and 36 monthly instalments of only R5 999, refinance the outstanding balance; or
- **Option B:** Buy the brand new BMW 318i M Sport Automatic at its cash selling price of only R439 000 and choose to sell the vehicle back to a BMW dealer, after 36 months, at a guaranteed cash future value (GFV) of R205 000. This option gives the vehicle's end-of-term value in advance, protecting you from unexpected depreciation.

Included in Options A and B are an innovative motor plan, which is offered on all new BMWs. The three-year/60 000-km service and maintenance motor plan covers repair work to all major components, beyond the standard new vehicle warranty.

Terms and conditions

- *Maintenance and service work are required every 20 000 km.*
- *All options are subject to the payment of an additional cash administration fee of R1 750, paid in advance, to get the vehicle ready for delivery.*
- *Cash selling prices exclude licence and registration fees.*
- *Customers choosing Option A are contractually indebted to either settle the outstanding balance of R215 000 in cash, equal to the estimated market value, in one final balloon payment, or refinance the estimated outstanding balance at the end of the 36-months contract.*
- *The GFV buy-back option will only be available to customers driving less than 20 000 km in a 12-month period, i.e. customers driving more than 20 000 km in a 12-month period are in breach of the contract terms and are consequently, from that date, not entitled to request the buy-back after 36 months.*

Additional information:

- The expected maintenance and service costs to be incurred by BMW Klerksdorp (Pty) Ltd for the service of a BMW 318i M Sport Automatic are as follows:

	Expected cost per service Rand
First maintenance and service	8 000
Second maintenance and service	6 000
Third maintenance and service	13 000
Total expected service costs	**27 000**

- The stand-alone selling price for the motor plan is not directly observable; however, it can be estimated by taking expected cost per service plus a profit margin of 45%.
- The average customer drives +/- 20 000 km in a 12-month period.

Required

Prepare the journal entries required to record the purchase and sale of one BMW 318i M Sport Automatic vehicle, financed under Option B, for the years ended 30 June 20.5 and 30 June 20.6 in the records of BMW Klerksdorp (Pty) Ltd, under the following assumptions:

a. At contract inception, BMW Klerksdorp (Pty) Ltd expected that the customer will drive less than the average of 20 000 km in a 12-month period, return the vehicle after 36 months and request the dealer to repurchase it at its GFV; and
b. On 15 November 20.5, the customer brought the vehicle in for its first 20 000 km service. From this date, BMW Klerksdorp (Pty) Ltd updated its initial estimate to now reflect the observable evidence that the customer breached the contract terms.

Assume that the payment received in advance for the motor plan arises for reasons other than the provision of finance. Ignore taxation.

IFRS 16

Leases

❑ QUESTIONS AND SOLUTIONS

IFRS 16.1	Low-value lease – discussion; equalisation of lease payments; journal entries with tax implications (lessee)
IFRS 16.2	Low-value lease – equalisation of lease payments; journal entries without tax implications; disclosure in the notes (lessee)
IFRS 16.3	Normal lease – calculation of interest rate implicit in the lease; preparation of amortisation table; journal entries; calculation of current and deferred tax; presentation in the financial statements (lessee)
IFRS 16.4	Normal lease – calculation of lease instalments (lessee)
IFRS 16.5#	Sale and leaseback – journal entries without tax implications; disclosure in the property, plant and equipment note (lessee)
IFRS 16.6	Normal lease – Calculation of amount used for the initial measurement of the right-of-use asset and lease liability, taking into consideration the interest rate implicit in the lease or the lessee's incremental borrowing rate; preparation of amortisation tables (lessee)
IFRS 16.7	Finance lease – Calculation of various line items; journal entries with tax implications (lessor)
IFRS 16.8#	Finance lease – manufacturer/dealer: presentation in financial statements and disclosure in notes, with tax implications (lessor)
IFRS 16.9	Operating lease – presentation in financial statements and disclosure in notes, with tax implications (lessor)
IFRS 16.10	Operating lease – incentives: journal entries; disclosure in the 'profit before tax' note; without tax implications (lessor)
IFRS 16.11	Identification of a lease where the legal form is not a lease: brief theory

❑ QUESTIONS

IFRS 16.12	Classification between operating and finance lease (lessor); discussion of accounting treatment (lessee and lessor)
IFRS 16.13	Low-value lease – journal entries; presentation and disclosure; deferred taxation (lessee)
IFRS 16.14	Normal lease – calculation of deferred tax; journal entries; presentation and disclosure (lessee)
IFRS 16.15#	Sale and leaseback – journal entries without tax implications; presentation and disclosure (lessee)
IFRS 16.16#	Normal lease – lease modification: interest rate and instalment change; presentation and disclosure, with deferred tax implications (lessee)
IFRS 16.17	Instalment sales agreement – journal entries with tax implications, including VAT; presentation and disclosure (purchaser)
IFRS 16.18#	Finance lease – manufacturer/dealer with lease modification: interest rate and instalment change; journal entries without tax implications (lessor)
IFRS 16.19	Discussion on classification as finance or operating lease; presentation and disclosure of finance lease, with tax implications (lessor)

IFRS 16.20	Instalment sales agreement – journal entries with deferred tax implications as well as VAT; presentation in financial statements and disclosure in 'net investment in the instalment sales agreement' note (seller)
IFRS 16.21[#]	Finance lease – manufacturer/dealer: not at market rate; journal entries; presentation and disclosure, including tax implications (lessor)
IFRS 16.22	Identification of a lease where the legal form is not a lease: comprehensive discussion of recognition and measurement (lessee)

[#] *These questions contain topics or principles that were at an awareness level of proficiency in the ITC syllabus of SAICA, at the time of publishing this book.*

❑ QUESTION IFRS 16.1

A toy manufacturer leased a low-value machine on 1 January 20.0 for a period of five years. The expected useful life of the machine is 11 years. The lease instalments are R400 per month for the first two years and R300 per month thereafter. The lessee has the option at the end of the lease term of extending the lease period for a further three years at R10 per month.

The tax rate is 27% for the full term of the lease. You may assume that the option to extend the lease will be exercised. You may also assume that the company has elected to account for the lease of the low-value item in accordance with IFRS 16.6. The financial year end is 31 December.

Ignore VAT.

Required

a. Explain, with reasons, how the lease payments in respect of the lease must be recognised as an expense.
b. Journalise the lease transactions (cash transactions included) over the full lease period. Journal narrations are not required. Your answer must comply with the requirements of International Financial Reporting Standards (IFRS).
(UP – adapted)

❖ Suggested solution IFRS 16.1

a. According to paragraph 5(b) of IFRS 16, a lessee may elect not to apply the normal accounting requirements to leases of which the underlying asset is of a low value. Paragraph 6 explains that, in such a case, the lessee shall recognise the lease payments as an expense on a straight-line basis over the lease term (or another systematic basis, if that basis is more representative of the pattern of the lessee's benefit).

The cash flow basis is not considered to be another systematic basis representative of the time pattern of the benefits from use of the asset.

Therefore, the lease payments must be recognised on a straight-line basis over the lease term and not on the basis of cash flows.

b. Journal entries

Year:	1 and 2 Rand Dr/(Cr)	3, 4 and 5 Rand Dr/(Cr)	6, 7 and 8 Rand Dr/(Cr)
Lease expenses (P or L) (1) (2) (3)	4 800	3 600	120
Bank (SFPos)	(4 800)	(3 600)	(120)
Prepaid lease expenses (SFPos) (4) (5) (6)	2 205	1 005	(2 475)
Lease expenses (P or L)	(2 205)	(1 005)	2 475
Alternative – combined journal entry:			
Lease expenses (P or L) (7)	2 595	2 595	2 595
Prepaid lease expenses (SFPos) (4) (5) (6)	2 205	1 005	(2 475)
Bank (SFPos)	(4 800)	(3 600)	(120)

Year:	1 and 2 Rand Dr/(Cr)	3, 4 and 5 Rand Dr/(Cr)	6, 7 and 8 Rand Dr/(Cr)
Income tax expense (P or L) (8)	595	271	(668)
Deferred tax (SFPos)	(595)	(271)	668

(1) 400 × 12 months = 4 800
(2) 300 × 12 months = 3 600
(3) 10 × 12 months = 120
(4) 4 800 – 2 595* = 2 205
(5) 3 600 – 2 595* = 1 005
(6) 2 595* – 120 (amortisation of deferred expenditure) = 2 475
(7) See calculation 1
(8) See calculation 2

* See calculation 1

Proof of accuracy

Prepaid lease expenses	**Rand**
Provided years 1 and 2 (1)	4 410
Provided years 3 to 5 (2)	3 015
	7 425
Reversed years 6 to 8 (3)	(7 425)
	Nil

(1) 2 years × 2 205 = 4 410
(2) 3 years × 1 005 = 3 015
(3) 3 years × 2 475 = 7 425

Calculations

1. Equalising of lease instalments (straight-lining)	**Rand**
Lease instalments years 1 and 2 (1)	9 600
Lease instalments years 3 to 5 (2)	10 800
Lease instalments (for extended period) years 6 to 8 (3)	360
Total lease instalments	20 760
Thus: lease expense per year (4)	2 595

(1) (400 × 12 months) × 2 years = 9 600
(2) (300 × 12 months) × 3 years = 10 800
(3) (10 × 12 months) × 3 years = 360
(4) 20 760 / 8 years = 2 595

2. Deferred tax		Carrying amount Rand	Tax base Rand	Temporary difference Rand	Deferred tax Rand Dr/(Cr)	Movement in P or L Rand Dr/(Cr)
Prepaid lease expense						
Year 1	– movement	2 205				595
	– balance	2 205	–	2 205	(595)	
Year 2	– movement	2 205				595
	– balance	4 410	–	4 410	(1 191)	
Year 3	– movement	1 005				271
	– balance	5 415	–	5 415	(1 462)	
Year 4	– movement	1 005				271
	– balance	6 420	–	6 420	(1 733)	
Year 5	– movement	1 005				271
	– balance	7 425	–	7 425	(2 005)	
Year 6	– movement	(2 475)				(668)
	– balance	4 950	–	4 950	(1 337)	
Year 7	– movement	(2 475)				(668)
	– balance	2 475	–	2 475	(668)	
Year 8	– movement	(2 475)				(668)
	– balance	–	–	–	–	

❑ QUESTION IFRS 16.2

Jasa Ltd, a handbag manufacturer, has various low-value items of property, plant and equipment held under non-cancellable lease agreements. The financial year end is 28 February.

Extracts from the non-cancellable lease agreements

1. **Nef Bank**

   - Asset leased – vehicle
   - Period of lease – 1 July 20.1 to 30 June 20.6
   - First lease premium – R3 000 (payable in advance) on 1 July 20.1
   - Monthly lease instalments (payable in arrears) thereafter – R400

2. **Stan Bank**

   - Asset leased – office equipment
   - Period of lease – 1 January 20.0 to 31 December 20.3
   - Monthly lease instalments (payable in arrears) – R285

   On termination of the lease agreement the company made a cash offer of R1 000 (fair value) for the office equipment. The offer was accepted.

Additional information

Depreciation is recognised on property, plant and equipment according to the straight-line method using the following rates:

- Vehicles – 20%
- Office equipment – 20%

Jasa Ltd has elected to account for the leases of the low-value items in accordance with IFRS 16.6.

Ignore current and deferred tax as well as VAT. Assume all amounts are material.

Required

a. Journalise all relevant transactions (cash transactions included) for the year ended 28 February 20.4 in compliance with the requirements of International Financial Reporting Standards (IFRS).

b. Prepare the disclosure required, in terms of the requirements of International Financial Reporting Standards (IFRS), for the year ended 28 February 20.4. Comparative amounts are not required.

❖ **Suggested solution IFRS 16.2**

a. Journal entries

	Rand Dr/(Cr)
Nef Bank	
Lease expenses (P or L) (1)	4 800
Bank (SFPos)	(4 800)
Being lease payments for 12 months at R400 per month	
Lease expenses (P or L) (2)	600
Lease expenses accrued (SFPos)	(600)
Being portion of initial payment apportioned over period of contract	
Alternative – combined journal entry:	
Lease expenses (P or L) (see calculation 1)	5 400
Bank (SFPos) (1)	(4 800)
Lease expenses accrued (SFPos) (2)	(600)
Stan Bank	
Lease expenses (P or L) (3)	2 850
Bank (SFPos)	(2 850)
Being lease payments for 10 months at R285 per month	
Office equipment (SFPos)	1 000
Bank (SFPos)	(1 000)
Being purchase of equipment on termination of the lease agreement	
Depreciation (P or L) (4)	33
Accumulated depreciation (SFPos)	(33)
Being depreciation for two months	

(1) $12 \times 400 = 4\,800$

(2) $5\,400 - 4\,800 = 600$

(3) $10 \times 285 = 2\,850$

(4) $1\,000 \times 20\% \times 2 / 12 = 33$

Calculations

Equalising (straight-lining) of lease payments

1. **Nef Bank**	**Rand**
First lease payment in advance	3 000
Total monthly lease payments (1)	24 000
Total lease expense over lease term	27 000
Thus: lease expense per month (2)	450
Thus: lease expense per year (3)	5 400

(1) (400 × 12 months) × 5 years = 24 000
(2) 27 000 / 60 months = 450
(3) 450 × 12 months = 5 400

b. Disclosure

JASA LTD
NOTES FOR THE YEAR ENDED 28 FEBRUARY 20.4

1. Accounting policy

1.1 Property, plant and equipment

Property, plant and equipment are accounted for at cost less accumulated depreciation. Depreciation is recognised over the expected useful lives of the assets on the straight-line method.

The following rates are applicable:
Vehicles – 20%
Office equipment – 20%

2. Property, plant and equipment	**Rand**
Equipment	
Carrying amount beginning of year	-
Cost	-
Accumulated depreciation	-
Additions	1 000
Depreciation	(33)
Carrying amount end of year	967
Cost	1 000
Accumulated depreciation	(33)

3. Profit before tax	**Rand**
Profit before tax is stated after taking the following into account:	
Lease expenses (see note 4)	8 250
Depreciation	33

4. Leases

The company elected not to capitalise leases of low-value assets, but to recognise the lease payments on a straight-line basis over the lease term. Included in profit before tax (see note 3) is an amount of R8 250 in respect of lease expenses. The total cash outflow for the leases for the year was R7 650 (1).

Significant lease arrangements (shown here only in respect of the lease of the vehicle for illustrative purposes):
- Lease is for a vehicle.
- Lease term is five years and commenced on 1 July 20.1.
- Lease payments are R400 per month payable monthly in arrears.
- First payment is payable on 31 July 20.1.
- Lease premium of R3 000 payable in advance on 1 July 20.1.

(1) 4 800 + 2 850 = 7 650

❑ QUESTION IFRS 16.3

The following details relate to the use of a machine acquired by Bewer Ltd in terms of a lease agreement:

- Date of commencement of agreement – 1 July 20.1.
- Cash price – R150 000, which is the same as the fair value on the commencement date.
- Lease period – three years.
- Payments of R36 250 are payable half-yearly, in arrears.
- There are no guaranteed or unguaranteed residual values.
- No initial direct costs have been incurred by the lessee or the lessor.
- Ownership of the machine passes to Bewer Ltd at the end of the lease agreement.

The machine was available for use and brought into use on 1 July 20.1. Machinery is depreciated at 20% per annum on a straight-line basis.

The company's financial year ends on 30 June. Profit before tax, before taking the effect of the lease into account, is R150 000 for each year of the agreement.

Assume a tax rate of 27% and ignore VAT.

Required

a. Calculate the interest rate implicit in the lease.
b. Prepare an amortisation table for the lease.
c. Journalise all relevant transactions (cash transactions included), other than for tax, over the lease term. Journal narrations are not required. Your answer must be in compliance with the requirements of International Financial Reporting Standards (IFRS).
d. Calculate the current and deferred tax that must be provided for in respect of the lease agreement over the term of the lease in accordance with the requirements of International Financial Reporting Standards (IFRS).
e. Present all the relevant amounts in the financial statements of Bewer Ltd over the term of the lease agreement so as to comply with the requirements of International Financial Reporting Standards (IFRS). Notes are not required.

❖ Suggested solution IFRS 16.3

a. The interest rate implicit in the lease is calculated using a financial calculator

Input:	150 000	PV
	0	FV
	6	N
	(36 250)	PMT
	COMP	I
	=	11,7734% per half year
	=	23,5468% per year

b. Amortisation table

	Instalment Rand	Interest Rand	Capital Rand	Balance Rand
Cash price	–	–	–	150 000
Instalment 1 (1) (2) (3)	36 250	17 660	18 590	131 410
Instalment 2	36 250	15 471	20 779	110 631
Instalment 3	36 250	13 025	23 225	87 406
Instalment 4	36 250	10 291	25 959	61 447
Instalment 5	36 250	7 234	29 016	32 431
Instalment 6	36 250	3 819	32 431	–
	217 500	67 500	150 000	Nil

(1) 150 000 × 23,5468% × 6 / 12 = 17 660
(2) 36 250 – 17 660 = 18 590
(3) 150 000 – 18 590 = 131 410

Alternative

Make use of the AMRT function (or similar function) on the financial calculator to calculate the capital (principal) and interest components of each relevant instalment, or for a number of instalments combined, based on the inputs in part a.

Different procedures are used for different financial calculators and therefore the procedure is not illustrated here. Your lecturer will be able to help you with this.

c. Journal entries

Year	20.4 Rand Dr/(Cr)	20.3 Rand Dr/(Cr)	20.2 Rand Dr/(Cr)
Right-of-use asset (SFPos)	–	–	150 000
Lease liability (SFPos)	–	–	(150 000)
Finance cost (P or L) (1)	11 053	23 316	33 131
Lease liability (SFPos) (2)	61 447	49 184	39 369
Bank (SFPos)	(72 500)	(72 500)	(72 500)

Year	20.4 Rand Dr/(Cr)	20.3 Rand Dr/(Cr)	20.2 Rand Dr/(Cr)
Depreciation (P or L) (3)	30 000	30 000	30 000
Accumulated depreciation (SFPos)	(30 000)	(30 000)	(30 000)

(1) 17 660 + 15 471 = 33 131
(2) 18 590 + 20 779 = 39 369
(3) 150 000 × 20% = 30 000 (see IFRS 16.32)

d. Current and deferred tax

Current tax

Year end – 30 June	20.4 Rand	20.3 Rand	20.2 Rand
Profit (given)	150 000	150 000	150 000
Depreciation	(30 000)	(30 000)	(30 000)
Finance charges	(11 053)	(23 316)	(33 131)
Profit before tax	108 947	96 684	86 869
Temporary differences	(31 447)	(19 184)	(9 369)
Depreciation	30 000	30 000	30 000
Finance costs	11 053	23 316	33 131
Lease payments	(72 500)	(72 500)	(72 500)
Taxable income	77 500	77 500	77 500
Current tax (1)	20 925	20 925	20 925

(1) 77 500 × 27% = 20 925

Deferred tax	Carrying amount Rand	Tax base Rand	Temporary difference Rand	Deferred tax Rand Dr/(Cr)	Movement in P or L Rand Dr/(Cr)
30 June 20.2					
Right-of-use asset	120 000	–	120 000	(32 400)	
Lease liability	110 631	–	110 631	29 870	
				(2 530)	2 530
30 June 20.3					
Right-of-use asset	90 000	–	90 000	(24 300)	
Lease liability	61 447	–	61 447	16 591	
				(7 709)	5 179
30 June 20.4					
Right-of-use asset	60 000	–	60 000	(16 200)	
Lease liability	–	–	–	–	
				(16 200)	8 491

Total income tax expense	**20.4 Rand**	**20.3 Rand**	**20.2 Rand**
Current tax expense	20 925	20 925	20 925
Deferred tax expense	8 491	5 179	2 530
	29 416	26 104	23 455

e. **Presentation**

BEWER LTD
STATEMENT OF FINANCIAL POSITION AS AT 30 JUNE

	20.4 Rand	**20.3 Rand**	**20.2 Rand**
ASSETS			
Non-current assets			
Right-of-use asset	60 000	90 000	120 000
EQUITY AND LIABILITIES			
Non-current liabilities	16 200	7 709	63 977
Lease liability	–	–	61 447
Deferred tax	16 200	7 709	2 530
Current liabilities	20 925	82 372	70 109
Current portion of lease liability	–	61 447	49 184
Current tax payable	20 925	20 925	20 925

BEWER LTD
STATEMENT OF PROFIT OR LOSS AND OTHER COMPREHENSIVE INCOME FOR THE YEAR ENDED 30 JUNE

	20.4 Rand	**20.3 Rand**	**20.2 Rand**
Profit before tax	108 947	96 684	86 869
Income tax expense	(29 416)	(26 104)	(23 455)
Profit for the year	79 531	70 580	63 414
Other comprehensive income	–	–	–
Total comprehensive income for the year	79 531	70 580	63 414

❑ QUESTION IFRS 16.4

Puntkop Ltd concluded a lease agreement for the purchase of certain production machinery on 1 July 20.1. The following information is available:

- Contract date – 1 July 20.1.
- Cash price – R120 000, which is the same as its fair value on the contract date.
- The interest rate implicit in the lease is 22,7759%.
- Lease period – two years.
- Instalments are payable half-yearly in arrears as from 31 December 20.1.
- There are no guaranteed or unguaranteed residual values.
- No initial direct costs have been incurred by the lessee or the lessor.

The company's financial year end is 30 June. Ignore VAT.

Required

Calculate the half-yearly instalment.

❖ Suggested solution IFRS 16.4

Half-yearly instalment

The half-yearly instalment is calculated using a financial calculator.

Input:	(120 000)	PV	
	0	FV	
	4	N	
	11,38795	I	(1)
	COMP	PMT	
	=	39 000	

(1) 22,7759% per year/two payments a year = 11,38795% per payment

❑ QUESTION IFRS 16.5#

The summarised draft trial balance of Topper Ltd at 31 March 20.3 is as follows:

	Rand Dr/(Cr)
Plant and machinery at cost	183 000
Accumulated depreciation – 31 March 20.2	(31 000)
Deferred tax – 31 March 20.2	(13 440)
Trade receivables	197 744
Trade and other payables	(100 000)
Sale and leaseback agreement	(18 400)
Profit before tax and depreciation	(81 000)
Income tax expense (81 000 × 30%)	24 300
Retained earnings – 31 March 20.2	(60 204)
Share capital	(101 000)

Additional information

1. On 1 April 20.2 the company obtained cash funds by entering into a sale and leaseback agreement.

   The machine relating to this transaction was originally purchased and brought into use on 2 December 20.1 and had an economic life of five years with no residual value.

   The machine was included in the trial balance at 1 April 20.2 at the following amounts:

	Rand
Cost	34 000
Accumulated depreciation	2 267

   This machine had a fair value of R33 000 at 1 April 20.2 and was sold for this amount and leased back on the following terms:

Payments are to be made as follows:	**Rand**
1 April 20.2	5 000
31 March 20.3	9 600
31 March 20.4	10 450
31 March 20.5	14 086

   On expiry of the lease the machine will once again become the property of the company.

   The interest rate implicit in the lease is 9,9% p.a. There are no guaranteed or unguaranteed residual values, and no initial direct costs have been incurred by the lessee or the lessor.

2. The company depreciates machinery at 20% per annum according to the straight-line method. No purchases took place during the year.

3. The company has **not** elected to apply the recognition exemption (see IFRS 16.5) on leases of low-value assets.

4. The company presents right-of-use assets together with property, plant and equipment on the face of the statement of financial position (see IFRS 16.47(a)).

Ignore VAT and taxation.

Required

a. Prepare the journal entries (cash transactions included) to account for the sale and leaseback agreement for the year ended 31 March 20.3. Journal narrations are not required, and your answer must comply with the requirements of International Financial Reporting Standards (IFRS).
b. Prepare the property, plant and equipment note for the year ended 31 March 20.3 in accordance with the requirements of International Financial Reporting Standards (IFRS). Comparative amounts are not required.
c. Prepare the journal entry in respect of the sale transaction if three annual lease payments of R8 000 were payable in arrears and no prepayment was made on 1 April 20.2, while the interest rate implicit in the lease remains unchanged at 9,9% per annum.

❖ Suggested solution IFRS 16.5#

a. Journal entries

	Rand Dr/(Cr)
Accumulated depreciation (SFPos) (1)	2 267
Machinery (SFPos) (1)	(34 000)
Right-of-use asset (SFPos) (2)	31 733
Bank (SFPos) (3)	33 000
Lease obligation (SFPos) (4)	(33 000)
Gain on transfer of rights (P or L) (5)	–
Finance costs (P or L) (6)	2 772
Lease obligation (SFPos) (7)	11 828
Bank (SFPos) (8)	(14 600)
Depreciation (P or L) (9)	6 800
Accumulated depreciation on right-of-use asset (SFPos) (9)	(6 800)

(1) Amounts given for 'old' asset
(2) (34 000 – 2 267)/33 000 × 33 000 = 31 733 (right of use of 'old' asset retained)
(3) Cash proceeds received
(4) This is the present value of the lease payments (as given in the question) discounted at 9.9% per annum by using the cash flow function of a financial calculator (CF_0 = 5 000; CF_1 = 9 600; CF_2 = 10 450; CF_3 = 14 086)
(5) (1 267 (calc. 10 below)/33 000) × (33 000 – 33 000) = 0
(6) Amortisation table per calculation 1
(7) 5 000 + 6 828 = 11 828 per calculation 1
(8) 5 000 + 9 600 = 14 600 per calculation 1
(9) 4 months expired useful life (2 December 20.1 to 1 April 20.1)
5 years – 4 months = 56 months remaining useful life
31 733/56 months × 12 = 6 800
(10) 33 000 (fair value of machine) – 31 733 (carrying amount of machine on sale date) = 1 267

Calculations

1. Amortisation table	Instalment Rand	Capital Rand	Interest Rand	Balance Rand
1 Apr 20.2	–	–	–	33 000
1 Apr 20.2	5 000	5 000	–	28 000
31 Mar 20.3 (1) (2)	9 600	6 828	2 772	21 172
31 Mar 20.4	10 450	8 354	2 096	12 818
31 Mar 20.5	14 086	12 818	1 268	–
	39 136	33 000	6 136	

(1) 28 000 × 9,9% = 2 772
(2) 9 600 – 2 772 = 6 828

b. **TOPPER LTD**
NOTES FOR THE YEAR ENDED 31 MARCH 20.3

2. Property, plant and equipment

	Right-of-use assets: machinery Rand	Other machinery Rand	Total Rand
Carrying amount – opening balance	–	152 000	152 000
Cost price	–	183 000	183 000
Accumulated depreciation	–	(31 000)	(31 000)
Additions (1)	31 733	–	31 733
Disposals (2)	–	(31 733)	(31 733)
Depreciation (3) (4)	(6 800)	(29 800)	(36 600)
Carrying amount – closing balance	24 933	90 467	115 400
Cost price (5)	31 733	149 000	180 733
Accumulated depreciation (6)	(6 800)	(58 533)	(65 333)

(1) Refer calculations under journals per part a.
(2) 34 000 – 2 267 = 31 733
(3) Refer calculations under journals per part a.
(4) (183 000 – 34 000) × 20% = 29 800
(5) 183 000 – 34 000 = 149 000
(6) 31 000 + 29 800 – 2 267 = 58 533

c. **Amended journal entry: sale transaction**

	Rand Dr/(Cr)
Accumulated depreciation (1)	2 267
Machinery (1)	(34 000)
Right-of-use asset (2)	19 165
Bank (3)	33 000
Lease obligation (4)	(19 930)
Gain on transfer of rights (P or L) (5)	(502)

(1) Amounts given for 'old' asset
(2) (34 000 – 2 267) / 33 000 × 19 930 (calc. 4 below) = 19 165 (right of use of 'old' asset retained)
(3) Cash proceeds received
(4) PMT 8 000
I 9.9%
N 3
Comp PV = 19 930
(5) 1 267 (6) / 33 000 × (33 000 – 19 930) = 502
(6) 33 000 (fair value of machine) – 31 733 (carrying amount of machine on sale date) = 1 267

❑ QUESTION IFRS 16.6

You are presented with the following information in respect of a lease agreement:

Annual instalment payable in arrears	R30 000
Residual value guarantee	R50 000
Unguaranteed residual value	R5 000
Lease term	4 years
Fair value of asset leased at the commencement date	R125 000

No initial direct costs have been incurred by the lessee or the lessor.

Ignore VAT.

Required

a. Calculate the amount at which the right-of-use asset and related liability will initially be recognised in the books of the lessee.
b. Prepare the amortisation table for the lessee in accordance with part a above.
c. Assume that the lessee did not have enough information about the unguaranteed residual value and could not calculate the interest rate implicit in the lease. Its own incremental borrowing rate is 13,5% per year. Calculate the amount at which the right-of-use asset and related liability will initially be recognised in the books of the lessee.
d. Prepare the amortisation table for the lessee in accordance with part c above.

❖ Suggested solution IFRS 16.6

a. Asset and liability recognised in books of lessee using interest rate implicit in the lease

Asset and liability measured at the present value of lease payments discounted at interest rate implicit in the lease: R121 861 (calculations 1 and 2)

1. Firstly, the interest rate implicit in lease needs to be calculated:

PV	=	125 000
PMT	=	(30 000)
FV (1)	=	(55 000)
N	=	4
Therefore I	=	12,3413% per year

(1) 50 000 (residual value guarantee) + 5 000 (unguaranteed residual value) = 55 000

Note: Even though the lessee does not capitalise the unguaranteed residual value as part of the asset and related liability, it must still be taken into account in calculating the interest rate implicit in the lease (refer IFRS 16 Appendix A – definition of 'interest rate implicit in the lease').

2. Now the lessee's lease payments (excluding the unguaranteed residual value) must be discounted at 12,3413% to determine the present value.

PMT	=	(30 000)
FV	=	(50 000) (guaranteed residual value only)
N	=	4
I	=	12,3413% (calculation 1)
Therefore PV	=	121 861

b. Amortisation table for lessee

	Instalment Rand	Capital Rand	Interest Rand	Balance Rand
				121 861
Year 1	30 000	14 961	15 039	106 900
Year 2	30 000	16 807	13 193	90 093
Year 3	30 000	18 881	11 119	71 212
Year 4	30 000	21 212	8 788	50 000
	120 000	71 861	48 139	

c. Asset and liability recognised in books of lessee using incremental borrowing rate

PMT	=	(30 000)
FV	=	(50 000) (guaranteed residual value only)
N	=	4
I	=	13,5%
Therefore PV	=	118 444

Therefore, the asset and liability will be measured initially at R118 444.

d. Amortisation table for lessee

	Instalment Rand	Capital Rand	Interest Rand	Balance Rand
				118 444
Year 1	30 000	14 010	15 990	104 434
Year 2	30 000	15 901	14 099	88 533
Year 3	30 000	18 048	11 952	70 485
Year 4	30 000	20 485	9 515	50 000
	120 000	68 444	51 556	

❑ QUESTION IFRS 16.7

The following information was extracted from the records of Ben Ltd for the year ended 31 December 20.1:

Lease agreement with Raka Ltd

Machine leased by Raka Ltd from Ben Ltd on 2 January 20.1 in terms of a finance lease:

Guaranteed residual value	–	R6 000
Unguaranteed residual value	–	RNil
Lease term	–	3 years
Instalments (payable annually in arrears)	–	R78 800
Commencement date of lease term	–	2 January 20.1

No initial direct costs were incurred by the lessee or the lessor.

The interest rate implicit in the lease is 16,2744% per year.

The lessee obtains ownership of the machine at the end of the lease term.

The machine was acquired by Ben Ltd on 1 January 20.1 at a cost of R180 000. The fair value of the machine on 2 January 20.1 was R180 000.

Tax information:

- Wear-and-tear allowance (straight-line) on machinery – 33,33%
- Tax rate (20.1 – 20.3) – 30%

Ignore VAT.

Required

a. Calculate the following amounts for disclosure in the financial statements of Ben Ltd for the years ended 31 December 20.1 to 20.3 for the lease agreement with Raka Ltd in accordance with the requirements of International Financial Reporting Standards (IFRS):
   1. Finance income
   2. Unearned finance income
   3. Gross investment in the lease
   4. Income tax expense/income
   5. Deferred tax asset/liability

   Note: All amounts must be rounded off to the nearest rand. Financial statements and notes are not required.

b. Prepare the journal entries for all transactions (including cash transactions) to account for the above agreement in accordance with the requirements of International Financial Reporting Standards (IFRS) in the financial statements of Ben Ltd over the lease term. Journal narrations are not required.

❖ Suggested solution IFRS 16.7

Agreement with Raka Ltd

a.	**Amounts to be disclosed**	**20.1 Rand**	**20.2 Rand**	**20.3 Rand**
1.	Finance income (calc 2)	29 294	21 237	11 869
2.	Unearned finance income (calc 3)	33 106	11 869	Nil
3.	Gross investment (calc 3)	163 600	84 800	Nil
4.	Current tax expense (calc 4)	5 640	5 640	7 440
	Deferred tax expense/(income) (calc 5)	3 148	731	(3 879)
	Income tax expense	8 788	6 371	3 561
5.	Deferred tax liability balance (calc 5)	3 148	3 879	Nil

Calculations

1. Determination of value used for initial recognition

FV = (6 000)
N = 3
PMT = (78 800)
I = 16,2744%
Therefore PV = 180 000

Thus, net investment in lease on 2 January 20.1 is R180 000.

2. Amortisation table: Allocation of finance income

Date	**Instalment Rand**	**Capital Rand**	**Interest Rand**	**Balance Rand**
2 Jan 20.1	–	–	–	180 000
31 Dec 20.1 (1) (2)	78 800	49 506	29 294	130 494
31 Dec 20.2	78 800	57 563	21 237	72 931
31 Dec 20.3	78 800	66 931	11 869	6 000
31 Dec 20.3	6 000	6 000	–	–
	242 400	180 000	62 400	

(1) 180 000 × 16,2744% = 29 294
(2) 78 800 – 29 294 = 49 506

3. **Carrying amount of investment in lease**	**20.1 Rand**	**20.2 Rand**	**20.3 Rand**
Gross investment before instalment paid (1)	242 400	163 600	84 800
Less: Instalment	(78 800)	(78 800)	(84 800)
Gross investment after instalment paid	163 600	84 800	Nil
Less: Unearned finance income	(33 106)	(11 869)	Nil
Unearned finance income: beginning (2)	(62 400)	(33 106)	(11 869)
Finance income earned (2)	29 294	21 237	11 869
Net investment in lease	130 494	72 931	Nil

(1) (78 800 × 3) + 6 000 = 242 400
242 400 – 78 800 = 163 600
163 600 – 78 800 = 84 800
(2) Refer amortisation table calculation 2

4. **Taxable income**	**20.1 Rand**	**20.2 Rand**	**20.3 Rand**
Finance income (1)	29 294	21 237	11 869
Profit before tax	29 294	21 237	11 869
Add: Instalment received (2)	78 800	78 800	84 800
Less: Wear-and-tear allowance (3)	(60 000)	(60 000)	(60 000)
Less: Finance income (1)	(29 294)	(21 237)	(11 869)
Taxable income	18 800	18 800	24 800
Current tax at 30%	5 640	5 640	7 440

(1) Refer amortisation table calculation 2
(2) 20.1 and 20.2: 78 800 (given)
20.3: 78 800 + 6 000 (guaranteed residual value) = 84 800
(3) 180 000 × 33,33% = 60 000

5. Deferred tax

Deferred tax	**Carrying amount Rand**	**Tax base Rand**	**Temporary difference Rand**	**Deferred tax Rand Dr/(Cr)**	**Movement in P or L Rand Dr/(Cr)**
31 Dec 20.1					
Investment in lease (1)(2)	130 494	120 000	10 494	(3 148)	
				(3 148)	3 148
31 Dec 20.2					
Investment in lease (1)(3)	72 931	60 000	12 931	(3 879)	
				(3 879)	731
31 Dec 20.3					
Investment in lease	–	–	–	–	
				–	(3 879)

(1) Refer amortisation table calculation 2
(2) 180 000 – (180 000 × 33,33%) = 120 000
(3) 180 000 – (180 000 × 33,33% × 2 years) = 60 000

b. Journal entries

	20.1 Rand Dr/(Cr)	20.2 Rand Dr/(Cr)	20.3 Rand Dr/(Cr)
Gross investment in lease (SFPos)	242 400	–	–
Unearned finance income (SFPos)	(62 400)	–	–
Machinery (SFPos)	(180 000)	–	–
Bank (SFPos)	78 800	78 800	84 800
Gross investment in lease (SFPos)	(78 800)	(78 800)	(84 800)
Unearned finance income (SFPos)	29 294	21 237	11 869
Finance income (P or L)	(29 294)	(21 237)	(11 869)
Income tax expense (P or L)	3 148	731	(3 879)
Deferred tax (liability)/asset (SFPos)	(3 148)	(731)	3 879
Income tax expense (P or L)	5 640	5 640	7 440
Current tax owing (SFPos)	(5 640)	(5 640)	(7 440)

❑ QUESTION IFRS 16.8#

Charlie Ltd is a manufacturer and trader of industrial machinery with a 31 December year end. During 20.5 the company leased a machine (cost R310 000) to Delta Ltd for a period of five years. Charlie Ltd invoices similar machines at a profit of 20% on the selling price.

Assume that the fair value of the machinery is the same as the selling price.

The lease agreement with Delta Ltd includes the following provisions:

- The date of commencement of the lease term is 1 July 20.5.
- Instalments amount to R105 000 per annum.
- Instalments are payable in advance on 1 July of each year.
- The machine will be used in a manufacturing process.
- The interest rate implicit in the lease is 17,9921% per annum.
- There are no guaranteed or unguaranteed residual values.
- No initial direct costs have been incurred by the lessee or the lessor.

Additional information

1. The lease agreement with Delta Ltd is the first and only agreement concluded by Charlie Ltd for the financial year ended 31 December 20.5. The company has decided to make greater use of this kind of financing for sales in the future.

2. Wear-and tear-allowances are 20% per annum and are calculated according to the straight-line method.

3. The tax rate for 20.5 and 20.6 was 30%.

4. Ignore VAT.

5. The following items appeared in the trial balance of Charlie Ltd before taking the lease agreement with Delta Ltd into account:

	20.6 Rand Dr/(Cr)	20.5 Rand Dr/(Cr)
Revenue	(900 000)	(1 000 000)
Cost of sales	400 000	400 000
Other expenses	100 000	100 000
Income tax expense		
Current	150 000	200 000
Deferred	(30 000)	(50 000)
Retained earnings – 31 December 20.4		(275 571)
Deferred tax balance	(145 000)	(175 000)

Required

Using only the information provided above, prepare the applicable extracts from the statement of profit or loss and other comprehensive income and statement of financial position of Charlie Ltd for the year ended 31 December 20.6. Prepare only those notes which refer to the lease agreement and related taxation. All the disclosure must comply with the requirements of International Financial Reporting Standards (IFRS).

❖ **Suggested solution IFRS 16.8#**

Calculations

1. **Value used by lessor for initial recognition of revenue**

Lower of:
- Fair value = R387 500 (R310 000 × 100/80)
- Present value of future lease instalments

Set calculator on BGN		
PMT	=	(105 000)
FV	=	0
N	=	5
I	=	17,9921%
Therefore PV	=	387 500

Thus the fair value is the same as the PV of R387 500, and sales revenue will be recognised at R387 500.

2. **Total finance income**

	Rand
Cost	310 000
Profit (1)	77 500
Selling price (2) (same as fair value)	387 500
Finance income	137 500
Gross investment in the lease (3)	525 000

(1) 310 000/80 × 20 = 77 500
(2) 310 000/80 × 100 = 387 500
(3) 105 000 × 5 = 525 000

3. Amortisation table: Allocation of finance income

Date	Instalment Rand	Capital Rand	Interest Rand	Balance Rand
1 Jul 20.5	–	–	–	387 500
1 Jul 20.5	105 000	105 000	–	282 500
1 Jul 20.6 (1) (2)	105 000	54 172	50 828	228 328
1 Jul 20.7	105 000	63 919	41 081	164 409
1 Jul 20.8	105 000	75 419	29 581	88 990
1 Jul 20.9	105 000	88 990	16 010	–
	525 000	387 500	137 500	

(1) (282 500 × 17,9921%) = 50 828
(2) 105 000 – 50 828 = 54 172

4. Calculation of taxable income (related to finance lease agreement)

	20.6 Rand	20.5 Rand
Revenue (1)	–	387 500
Cost of sales (2)	–	(310 000)
Finance income (3)	45 955	25 414
Profit before tax resulting from finance lease	45 955	102 914
Add: Lease instalments (given)	105 000	105 000
Less: Wear-and-tear allowance (4)	(77 500)	(38 750)
Less: Finance income (3)	(45 955)	(25 414)
Taxable income for finance lease	27 500	143 750

(1) Sales price – refer calculation 1
(2) Cost of machinery leased (given)
(3) 20.5: 50 828 (refer amortisation table calc 3) × 6 / 12 months = 25 414
20.6: 50 828 × 6 / 12 months + 41 081 × 6 / 12 months = 45 955
(4) 20.5: 387 500 × 20% × 6 / 12 months = 38 750
20.6: 387 500 × 20% × 12 / 12 months = 77 500

Note: For manufacturers/traders, SARS will tax the lessor in year 1 of the lease agreement (20.5) on the difference between the recoupment amount (the market value = cash selling price) (R387 500) and the cost of sales amount (cash cost to lessor) (R310 000) of the asset that was inventory, but which now becomes a capital asset that is leased out (on which a wear-and-tear allowance is calculated). As the selling price and cost of sales are already included in the accounting profit before tax, no further adjustment is required when calculating taxable income.

5. Calculation of current tax

	20.6 Rand	20.5 Rand
Taxable income on other profit or loss items before finance lease agreement accounted for (1)	500 000	666 667
Taxable income for finance lease (calc 4)	27 500	143 750
Taxable profit	527 500	810 417
Current tax at 30%	158 250	243 125

(1) Current income tax expense divided by the tax rate
20.6: 150 000 / 30% = 500 000
20.5: 200 000 / 30% = 666 667

6. Deferred tax calculation

	Carrying amount Rand		Tax base Rand		Temporary difference Rand	Deferred tax Rand Dr/(Cr)		Movement in P or L Rand (Dr)/Cr	
20.5									
Other						(175 000)	(1)		
Lease debtors	307 914	(2)	348 750	(3)	40 836	12 251			
						(162 749)		62 251	(4)
20.6									
Other						(145 000)	(1)		
Lease debtors	248 869	(5)	271 250	(6)	22 381	6 714			
						(138 286)		24 463	(7)

(1) Given
(2) 282 500 + 50 828 × 6 / 12 months = 307 914 (refer calc 3 and note 2)
(3) 387 500 × 20% × 4,5 years remaining for wear-and-tear allowance = 348 750 **or**
387 500 – 38 750 wear-and-tear allowance = 348 750
(4) 50 000 deferred tax expense + 12 251 = 62 251
(5) 228 328 + 41 081 × 6 / 12 months = 248 869 (refer calc 3 and note 2)
(6) 387 500 × 20% × 3,5 years remaining for wear-and-tear allowance = 271 250 **or**
387 500 – (38 750 + 77 500) wear-and-tear allowance = 271 250 **or**
348 750 (tax base 20.5) – 77 500 (wear-and-tear allowance 20.6) = 271 250
(7) 162 750 – 138 286 = 24 464 **or**
30 000 (given) – 5 537 (decrease in lease debtors deferred tax) = 24 463

Disclosure

CHARLIE LTD
STATEMENT OF FINANCIAL POSITION AS AT 31 DECEMBER 20.6

	Note	20.6 Rand	20.5 Rand
ASSETS			
Non-current assets			
Net investment in finance lease	2	164 409	228 328
Current assets			
Net investment in finance lease	2	63 919	54 172
Trade and other receivables	2	20 541	25 414
EQUITY AND LIABILITIES			
Non-current liabilities			
Deferred tax	3	138 286	162 749
Current liabilities			
Current tax payable		158 250	243 125

CHARLIE LTD
STATEMENT OF PROFIT OR LOSS AND OTHER COMPREHENSIVE INCOME FOR THE YEAR ENDED 31 DECEMBER 20.6

	Note	20.6 Rand	20.5 Rand
Revenue (1)		900 000	1 387 500
Cost of sales (2)		(400 000)	(710 000)
Gross profit		500 000	677 500
Other expenses		(100 000)	(100 000)
Other income (3)		45 955	25 414
Profit before tax		445 955	602 914
Income tax expense	4	(133 787)	(180 874)
Profit for the year		312 168	422 040
Other comprehensive income		–	–
Total comprehensive income for the year		312 168	422 040

(1) 1 000 000 + 387 500 (refer calc 1) = 1 387 500
(2) 400 000 + 310 000 = 710 000
(3) 20.5: 50 828 (refer amortisation table calc 3) × 6 / 12 months = 25 414
20.6: 50 828 × 6 / 12 months + 41 081 × 6 / 12 months = 45 955

CHARLIE LTD
STATEMENT OF CHANGES IN EQUITY FOR THE YEAR ENDED 31 DECEMBER 20.6

	Share capital Rand	Retained earnings Rand	Total Rand
Balance at 1 January 20.5	xx xxx	275 571	275 571
Changes in equity for 20.5			
Total comprehensive income for the year	–	422 040	422 040
Profit for the year	–	422 040	422 040
Other comprehensive income	–	–	–
Balance at 31 December 20.5	xx xxx	697 611	697 611
Changes in equity for 20.6			
Total comprehensive income for the year	–	312 168	312 168
Profit for the year	–	312 168	312 168
Other comprehensive income	–	–	–
Balance at 31 December 20.6	xx xxx	1 009 779	1 009 779

CHARLIE LTD
NOTES FOR THE YEAR ENDED 31 DECEMBER 20.6

1. Accounting policy

1.1 Finance lease agreements

Finance leases are recognised as receivables and measured initially at the present value of future lease payments. Finance income on lease agreements is recognised using the effective interest method.

2. Net investment in finance lease

Reconciliation of net investment in finance lease from the beginning to the end of the year:

	20.6 Rand	20.5 Rand
Balance at the beginning of the year	307 914	–
New leases entered into (1)	–	387 500
Reversal of finance income previously accrued (2)	(25 414)	–
Capital repayments (3)	(54 172)	(105 000)
Finance income accrued (2) (4)	20 541	25 414
Balance at the end of the year	248 869	307 914
Balance represented by:		
Finance income accrued (included in trade receivables)	20 541	25 414
Present value of lease payments (included in the net investment in the lease) (3)	228 328	282 500

Maturity analysis of undiscounted finance lease payments receivable as at the reporting date and reconciliation thereof to the net investment:

20.6	Gross investment	Unearned finance income	Net investment
	Rand	Rand	Rand
For 20.7 (3)	105 000	(41 081)	63 919
For 20.8 (3)	105 000	(29 581)	75 419
For 20.9 (3)	105 000	(16 010)	88 990
Total net investment	315 000	(86 672)	228 328
Finance income accrued (4)			20 541
Total finance lease debtors			248 869

20.5	Gross investment	Unearned finance income	Net investment
	Rand	Rand	Rand
For 20.6 (3)	105 000	(50 828)	54 172
For 20.7 (3)	105 000	(41 081)	63 919
For 20.8 (3)	105 000	(29 581)	75 419
For 20.9 (3)	105 000	(16 010)	88 990
Total net investment	420 000	(137 500)	282 500
Finance income accrued (2)			25 414
Total finance lease debtors			307 914

Significant lease arrangements:
- Lease is in respect of machinery.
- Lease term is five years and commenced on 1 July 20.5.
- Lease payments are R105 000 per year.
- Lease payments are payable annually in advance.
- First lease payment payable on 1 July 20.5.
- Interest rate implicit in the lease is 17,9921%.

(1) Refer to calculation 1 above
(2) 50 828 (refer amortisation table calc 3) × 6 / 12 months = 25 414
(3) Per amortisation table: refer to calculation 3 above
(4) 41 081 (refer amortisation table calc 3) × 6 / 12 months = 20 541

3. Income tax expense

	20.6	20.5
	Rand	Rand
Major components of tax expense		
Current tax expense – current	158 250	243 125
Deferred tax expense – current	(24 463)	(62 251)
	133 787	180 874

4. Deferred tax

	20.6	20.5
	Rand	Rand
Analysis of temporary differences		
Finance leases	(6 714)	(12 251)
Others (no details provided)	145 000	175 000
	138 286	162 749

❑ QUESTION IFRS 16.9

Kamstra Leasing Ltd leases a machine which cost R500 000 to Pypers Manufacturers Ltd. The non-cancellable operating lease agreement was concluded on 1 January 20.1. Kamstra Leasing Ltd had purchased this machine on 31 December 20.0.

The following information has been extracted from the lease contract:

- Lease period is five years;
- Lease instalment is R180 000 per annum, payable in arrears; and
- Selling price is R600 000.

The wear-and-tear allowance is 25% straight-line. The tax rate is 30%.

Machinery is depreciated at 20% per annum according to the straight-line method.

Required

Disclose the operating lease in the financial statements of Kamstra Leasing Ltd for the years ended 31 December 20.1 to 20.5 so as to comply with the requirements of International Financial Reporting Standards (IFRS).

❖ Suggested solution IFRS 16.9

Calculations

Depreciation	**20.1 Rand**	**20.2 Rand**	**20.3 Rand**	**20.4 Rand**	**20.5 Rand**
20% × 500 000	100 000	100 000	100 000	100 000	100 000

Accounting profit	**20.1 Rand**	**20.2 Rand**	**20.3 Rand**	**20.4 Rand**	**20.5 Rand**
Lease income	180 000	180 000	180 000	180 000	180 000
Depreciation	(100 000)	(100 000)	(100 000)	(100 000)	(100 000)
Profit before tax	80 000	80 000	80 000	80 000	80 000

Current tax	**20.1 Rand**	**20.2 Rand**	**20.3 Rand**	**20.4 Rand**	**20.5 Rand**
Profit before tax	80 000	80 000	80 000	80 000	80 000
Add: Depreciation	100 000	100 000	100 000	100 000	100 000
Less: Wear-and-tear allowance machine (1)	(125 000)	(125 000)	(125 000)	(125 000)	-
Taxable profit	55 000	55 000	55 000	55 000	180 000
Tax rate	30%	30%	30%	30%	30%
Current tax expense	(16 500)	(16 500)	(16 500)	(16 500)	(54 000)

Carrying amount – machine	**20.1 Rand**	**20.2 Rand**	**20.3 Rand**	**20.4 Rand**	**20.5 Rand**
Cost/carrying amount	500 000	400 000	300 000	200 000	100 000
Depreciation	(100 000)	(100 000)	(100 000)	(100 000)	(100 000)
Carrying amount	400 000	300 000	200 000	100 000	–

Tax base – machine	**20.1 Rand**	**20.2 Rand**	**20.3 Rand**	**20.4 Rand**	**20.5 Rand**
Cost/tax base	500 000	375 000	250 000	125 000	–
Wear-and-tear allowance	(125 000)	(125 000)	(125 000)	(125 000)	–
Tax base	375 000	250 000	125 000	–	–
Taxable temporary difference	25 000	50 000	75 000	100 000	–

Deferred tax	**20.1 Rand Dr/(Cr)**	**20.2 Rand Dr/(Cr)**	**20.3 Rand Dr/(Cr)**	**20.4 Rand Dr/(Cr)**	**20.5 Rand Dr/(Cr)**
Closing deferred tax liability (2)	(7 500)	(15 000)	(22 500)	(30 000)	–
Opening deferred tax liability	–	(7 500)	(15 000)	(22 500)	(30 000)
Deferred tax expense/(income)	7 500	7 500	7 500	7 500	(30 000)

Income tax expense	**20.1 Rand**	**20.2 Rand**	**20.3 Rand**	**20.4 Rand**	**20.5 Rand**
Current taxation	16 500	16 500	16 500	16 500	54 000
Deferred tax	7 500	7 500	7 500	7 500	(30 000)
Income tax expense	24 000	24 000	24 000	24 000	24 000

(1) 500 000 × 25% = 125 000
(2) Temporary difference × 30%

Disclosure

KAMSTRA LEASING LTD
STATEMENT OF FINANCIAL POSITION AS AT 31 DECEMBER

	20.1 Rand	**20.2 Rand**	**20.3 Rand**	**20.4 Rand**	**20.5 Rand**
ASSETS					
Non-current assets					
Property, plant and equipment (note 2)	400 000	300 000	200 000	100 000	–
EQUITY AND LIABILITIES					
Non-current liabilities					
Deferred tax	7 500	15 000	22 500	30 000	–

KAMSTRA LEASING LTD
STATEMENT OF PROFIT OR LOSS AND OTHER COMPREHENSIVE INCOME FOR THE YEAR ENDED 31 DECEMBER

	Note	20.1 Rand	20.2 Rand	20.3 Rand	20.4 Rand	20.5 Rand
Profit before tax		80 000	80 000	80 000	80 000	80 000
Income tax expense	3	(24 000)	(24 000)	(24 000)	(24 000)	(24 000)
Profit for the year		56 000	56 000	56 000	56 000	56 000
Other comprehensive income		–	–	–	–	–
Total comprehensive income for the year		56 000	56 000	56 000	56 000	56 000

KAMSTRA LEASING LTD
NOTES FOR THE YEAR ENDED 31 DECEMBER

1. Accounting policies

1.1 Property, plant and equipment

Property, plant and equipment are carried at cost less accumulated depreciation. Machinery is depreciated at 20% per annum according to the straight-line method.

2. Property, plant and equipment	20.1 Rand	20.2 Rand	20.3 Rand	20.4 Rand	20.5 Rand
Carrying amount beginning of year	500 000	400 000	300 000	200 000	100 000
Cost	500 000	500 000	500 000	500 000	500 000
Accumulated depreciation	–	(100 000)	(200 000)	(300 000)	(400 000)
Depreciation	(100 000)	(100 000)	(100 000)	(100 000)	(100 000)
Carrying amount end of year	400 000	300 000	200 000	100 000	–
Cost	500 000	500 000	500 000	500 000	500 000
Accumulated depreciation	(100 000)	(200 000)	(300 000)	(400 000)	(500 000)

3. Income tax expense	20.1 Rand	20.2 Rand	20.3 Rand	20.4 Rand	20.5 Rand
Major components of tax expense:					
Current tax expense	16 500	16 500	16 500	16 500	54 000
Deferred tax expense	7 500	7 500	7 500	7 500	(30 000)
	24 000	24 000	24 000	24 000	24 000

4. Operating lease

Maturity analysis of undiscounted operating lease payments receivable as at the reporting date:

	20.1 Rand	20.2 Rand	20.3 Rand	20.4 Rand	20.5 Rand
For 20.2	180 000	–	–	–	–
For 20.3	180 000	180 000	–	–	–
For 20.4	180 000	180 000	180 000	–	–
For 20.5	180 000	180 000	180 000	180 000	–
	720 000	540 000	360 000	180 000	–

Significant lease arrangements:
– Lease is in respect of a machine.
– Lease term is five years and commences on 1 January 20.1.
– Lease instalments are R180 000 payable annually in arrears.
– First payment was payable on 31 December 20.1.

☐ QUESTION IFRS 16.10

On 1 July 20.5, Vision Ltd (lessor) entered into an operating lease agreement with Euro Ltd (lessee) in respect of a factory building for a four-year period. The annual lease instalment is R150 000 for the first two years and R120 000 for the last two years. Vision Ltd agreed to pay the relocation costs of Euro Ltd as an incentive to Euro Ltd for entering into the lease. The relocation costs amounted to R50 000.

Ignore all tax implications.

Required

a. Prepare the journal entries (cash transactions included) to account for the operating lease agreement in the books of Vision Ltd for the financial year ended 30 June 20.6. Your answer must comply with the requirements of International Financial Reporting Standards (IFRS). Journal narrations are not required.

b. Disclose the operating lease in the 'Profit before tax' note for Vision Ltd for the year ended 30 June 20.6 in accordance with the requirements of International Financial Reporting Standards (IFRS). Assume that all amounts are material. Comparative amounts are not required.

❖ **Suggested solution IFRS 16.10**

Calculations

Calculation of annual operating lease income

	Rand
Total rental over lease term (1)	540 000
Lease incentive – relocation costs paid by lessor	(50 000)
	490 000
Equalised lease income per year – including lease incentive (2)	122 500
Equalised lease income per year – excluding lease incentive (3)	135 000

(1) (150 000 × 2) + (120 000 × 2) = 540 000
(2) 490 000 / 4 years = 122 500
(3) 540 000 / 4 years = 135 000

a. Journal entries

	Rand Dr/(Cr)
Prepaid expenses (SFPos)	50 000
Bank (SFPos)	(50 000)
Bank (SFPos)	150 000
Operating lease income (P or L)	(135 000)
Income received in advance (SFPos)	(15 000)
Operating lease income (P or L) (1)	12 500
Prepaid expenses (SFPos) (1)	(12 500)

(1) 50 000 / 4 years = 12 500

b. Disclosure

VISION LTD
NOTES FOR THE YEAR ENDED 30 JUNE 20.6

1. Profit before tax

	Rand
Profit before tax is stated after the following items have been taken into account:	
Income	
Operating lease income	122 500
– Operating lease instalment	135 000
– Operating lease incentive cost amortised	(12 500)

❑ QUESTION IFRS 16.11

IFRS 16 also covers arrangements that do not take the legal form of a lease, but which in substance may convey a right to use an asset in return for a payment or a series of payments for an agreed period of time.

Required

List the two criteria that, if present in an arrangement, would cause the arrangement to contain a lease transaction in substance, regardless of whether or not the legal form is a lease. Also name two examples of arrangements that might contain a lease even if the legal form is not a lease.

❖ Suggested solution IFRS 16.11

The two criteria that are relevant for the identification of a lease are:

- The customer (lessee) has, throughout the period of use, the right to obtain substantially all of the economic benefits from use of the identified asset (IFRS 16 Appendix B.B9(a)); and
- The customer (lessee) has, throughout the period of use, the right to direct the use of the identified asset (IFRS 16 Appendix B.B9(b)).

If both criteria are met, the arrangement contains a lease that must be accounted for in terms of IFRS 16.

Examples:

- The outsourcing of production (e.g. where a specific manufacturing plant is used for the exclusive benefit of the customer, and the customer has the right to direct the use thereof).
- A transport contract (e.g. where the vast majority of kilometres travelled by a truck is used to transport goods for a single customer, and the customer has the right to direct the use).

❑ QUESTION IFRS 16.12

For each of the cases below, explain (from the perspective of the lessor) whether the lease is a finance or an operating lease. Then explain how the lease transaction will be recognised and measured in the financial statements of both the lessor and the lessee so as to comply with the requirements of International Financial Reporting Standards (IFRS):

1. Grootbou (Pty) Ltd erects office buildings on a contract basis. For this purpose, Grootbou (Pty) Ltd concluded a contract for five years to lease a crane from Crane Ltd. At the end of the lease contract, Grootbou (Pty) Ltd will purchase the crane at a nominal amount. The useful life and the economic life of the crane are both six years.

2. Grootbou (Pty) Ltd has fallen behind on its contract schedule. To catch up the lost time, Grootbou (Pty) Ltd concluded a second contract with Crisis Ltd for the lease of another crane. The contract period is one year. Crisis Ltd is liable for all maintenance work on the crane, and on expiry of the contract retains ownership of the crane.

3. Sitso Ltd manufactures steel products. It requires a special welding machine (2XII) for the completion of a contract. Sitso Ltd concluded a lease contract for the lease of a 2XII from Weld Ltd for nine months.

   Sitso Ltd also tendered for another contract which will require the exclusive use of a 2XII. If this contract is awarded to Sitso Ltd, the 2XII will be needed for a further period of five years. Taking into account these circumstances, an option clause was written into the original contract for the lease of the 2XII for a further five years, whereafter the 2XII will be acquired for a nominal amount.

   If Sitso Ltd does not need the 2XII after the expiry of the first contract (nine-month period), the machine may be returned to Weld Ltd if it is in a good condition.

   If the renewal option is exercised, the lessee (Sitso Ltd) will be responsible for repairs and maintenance of the 2XII, but until then these are the responsibility of the lessor (Weld Ltd).

   It is still uncertain if the second production contract will be awarded to Sitso Ltd.

❑ QUESTION IFRS 16.13

Van Damme Construction Ltd specialises in the building of dams and has a 31 December year end. Van Damme Construction Ltd's latest contract, which commenced on 2 January 20.5, includes the building of an entrance road to a dam.

On 1 July 20.5, the company entered into a non-cancellable lease for 24 months in respect of a small (low-value) machine, which will also be needed in building the road. The cost price of the machine amounts to R50 000.

Since Van Damme Construction Ltd will only receive progress payments at a later stage, the lease payments were structured as follows:

	Rand
At the commencement of the lease – lump sum amount	600
First 6 months – per month	200
Next 12 months – per month	300
Last 6 months – per month	1 000

The tax rate is 27%. Assume that the credit balance on the deferred tax account (excluding the above transaction) is due to temporary differences on capital assets and the balance is RNil at 1 January 20.5, R8 000 at 31 December 20.5, and R7 000 at 31 December 20.6.

Ignore current tax and VAT.

Van Damme Construction Ltd elected to comply with the requirements of International Financial Reporting Standards (IFRS) and also elected to account for the lease of low-value items in accordance with IFRS 16.6.

Option 1: Assume that the lump sum payment of R600 is deductible for tax purposes when the payment is made.

Option 2: Assume that the lump sum payment of R600 is deductible for tax purposes in equal, unapportioned annual amounts over the lease term.

Required

a. Prepare the journal entries (including cash transactions) resulting from the above transactions for the years ended 31 December 20.5 and 20.6 for both options 1 and 2 as indicated below. Your answer must be in compliance with the requirements of International Financial Reporting Standards (IFRS).

b. Prepare the required disclosure in accordance with IFRS 16 for the year ended 31 December 20.6. Also provide the presentation of deferred tax on the face of the statement of financial position. This is required for both options 1 and 2.

❑ QUESTION IFRS 16.14

Road Runner (Pty) Ltd sells and fits tyres and exhaust systems for vehicles.

- Road Runner (Pty) Ltd entered into a lease agreement for the acquisition of a new hydraulic jack for installation in the workshop.
- The effective date of the agreement is 31 March 20.2.
- The hydraulic jack was brought into use on 31 March 20.2.
- The fair value of the jack was R250 000 on 31 March 20.2.
- The lease period is four years.
- The instalments amount to R21 455 per quarter, payable in arrears.
- The interest rate implicit in the lease agreement is 16% per annum.
- There are no guaranteed or unguaranteed residual values.
- No initial direct costs have been incurred by the lessee or the lessor.
- Road Runner (Pty) Ltd depreciates workshop equipment at 20% per annum using the straight-line method.
- Road Runner (Pty) Ltd will acquire ownership of the hydraulic jack at the end of the lease term.
- The South African Revenue Service allows wear and tear at 20% per annum using the straight-line method for similar types of equipment.
- The tax rate is 30%.
- Ignore current tax and VAT.
- Assume that the entity will have sufficient future taxable profits to justify the recognition of a deferred tax asset.
- The company's financial year end is 31 December.

Required

a. Calculate the deferred tax that must be provided for 20.2 and 20.3 in respect of the lease agreement in accordance with the requirements of International Financial Reporting Standards (IFRS).

b. Journalise all relevant transactions (including cash transactions) for the financial years ended 31 December 20.2 and 31 December 20.3 in order to comply with the requirements of International Financial Reporting Standards (IFRS).

c. Disclose all relevant items in the financial statements of Road Runner (Pty) Ltd for the years ended 31 December 20.2 and 31 December 20.3 so as to comply with the requirements of International Financial Reporting Standards (IFRS). Notes are required.

❑ QUESTION IFRS 16.15#

Cashstrap Ltd is a manufacturer facing cash flow difficulties. It has one major asset, a manufacturing plant, which the directors have decided to sell and then lease back in terms of a lease agreement, to enable them to continue using the plant.

Details relating to the plant are as follows:

	Rand
Cost price (paid to a supplier)	800 000
Carrying amount at date of sale	500 000
Fair value at date of sale for which asset was sold	600 000
Historical depreciation rate per annum	20%, straight-line method

The finance company paid Cashstrap Ltd R600 000 for its plant on 1 March 20.7 (the commencement date of the lease).

Details relating to the lease agreement are:

Lease payments – paid monthly in arrears	R19 000
Lease period	48 months

There are no guaranteed or unguaranteed residual values and no initial direct costs have been incurred by the lessee or the lessor. On the date of the sale the remaining useful life of the plant was re-estimated to be four years.

The company presents right-of-use assets together with property, plant and equipment on the face of the statement of financial position (see IFRS 16.47(a)).

Cashstrap Ltd has a financial year that ends on 28 February.

Ignore all tax implications.

Required

a. Prepare all the journal entries (including cash transactions) relating to the sale and subsequent leaseback of the plant for the financial year ended 28 February 20.8 ensuring compliance with the requirements of International Financial Reporting Standards (IFRS).
b. Provide the disclosure relating to the sale and leaseback in the financial statements of Cashstrap Ltd for the financial year ended 28 February 20.8 so as to comply with the requirements of International Financial Reporting Standards (IFRS). The only accounting policy note required is that relating to leases.
c. Indicate, in respect of the sale transaction only, how the journal entry would have differed if the plant had a fair value of R570 000 on the date of sale.

❑ QUESTION IFRS 16.16

Robberg Ltd operates an earth-moving business. The use of earth-moving equipment was obtained on 1 January 20.5 through a lease agreement.

Extracts from the lease agreement are as follows:

Lease term	5 years
Cash price of equipment, which is the same as fair value on the commencement date	R500 000
Scrap value	RNil
Interest rate implicit in the lease – per annum	Prime plus 2%
Lease payments	Annually in arrears

There are no guaranteed or unguaranteed residual values, and no initial direct costs have been incurred by the lessee or the lessor.

In terms of the contract, the interest rate (and therefore the instalments) are linked to the prime interest rate. The prime interest rate was 18% on the date that the lease was entered into but decreased to 16% on 31 December 20.6. Finance charges are recognised using the effective interest method. The equipment is depreciated at 20% per annum using the straight-line method.

Assume a tax rate of 30% and that there are no temporary differences other than those resulting from the above information, and that it would be appropriate to create a debit balance on the deferred tax account if necessary.

Ignore VAT.

Required

Disclose the effects of this lease agreement in the financial statements of Robberg Ltd for the financial year ended 31 December 20.7 so as to comply with the requirements of International Financial Reporting Standards (IFRS). Accounting policy notes are not required.

❑ QUESTION IFRS 16.17

Luxor Ltd entered into an instalment sales agreement on 1 January 20.6 to acquire a manufacturing machine. The contract stipulates the following:

Cash purchase price of machine (including VAT at 15%)	R230 000
Period	48 months
Number of instalments (six-monthly, payable in arrears on 30 June and 31 December)	8
Interest rate implicit in the contract	21% per annum
Instalments	R30 539
Deposit – 20% of cash price (excluding VAT)	R40 000

None of the parties to this agreement has incurred any initial direct costs.

Luxor Ltd immediately pays over the VAT to the seller. The applicable VAT rate is 15%.

The fair value of the machine on 1 January 20.6 is the same as its cash purchase price excluding VAT.

The company provides for depreciation at 25% per annum using the reducing balance method and is registered for VAT purposes. VAT is claimed immediately and finance costs on instalment sales agreements are recognised using the effective interest method.

Tax is calculated at 30% per annum. Wear-and-tear allowances are calculated at 20% per annum using the straight-line method. There are no other temporary differences. Assume that the company will have sufficient taxable profits for the recognition of any deferred tax assets.

Required

a. Prepare all the journal entries applicable to the above transactions (including cash transactions) for Luxor Ltd for the two years ended 31 December 20.6 and 20.7 in order to comply with the requirements of International Financial Reporting Standards (IFRS).
b. Disclose all relevant information applicable to the above transactions in the financial statements for the year ended 31 December 20.7 so as to comply with the requirements of International Financial Reporting Standards (IFRS). No accounting policy or tax notes are required.

❑ QUESTION IFRS 16.18#

DKW Ltd manufactures and distributes manufacturing machinery for use in the motor industry and uses the perpetual inventory system. During 20.3, equipment was leased to Ossewa Ltd. The details are as follows:

Cost of the equipment	R130 000
Cash selling price (same as fair value)	R162 500
Lease conditions – five equal annual instalments, payable in arrears	
Interest rate per annum	Prime plus 5%
Commencement date of contract	1 July 20.3

In terms of the contract, the interest rate and therefore the instalments are linked to the prime interest rate. At commencement of the contract, prime was 20% per year. On 1 July 20.6 the prime rate decreased to 17% per year.

At the end of the lease term, ownership of the machine will transfer to the lessee.

DKW Ltd's financial year end is 31 December.

Ignore all tax implications.

Required

Prepare the journal entries (cash transactions included) in the books of DKW Ltd for this lease agreement for the years ended 31 December 20.3 to 31 December 20.8 in compliance with the requirements of International Financial Reporting Standards (IFRS).

❑ QUESTION IFRS 16.19

Jonkershoek Investments Ltd decided to expand its operations and become involved in the leasing of equipment. For this purpose a front-end loader was purchased on 1 March 20.3. A contract was then concluded with an earth-moving contractor, Bamco (Pty) Ltd, in terms of which the front-end loader is leased out for a period of four years from 1 March 20.3 on the following conditions:

Lease instalments – payable monthly in advance by Bamco (Pty) Ltd	R4 250
Lease period	48 months
Residual value guarantee (payable at end of lease contract)	R40 000
No unguaranteed residual value.	

Bamco (Pty) Ltd is responsible for the maintenance and insurance of the front-end loader. Bamco (Pty) Ltd incurred initial direct costs of R5 000 in respect of this agreement. No initial direct costs were incurred by Jonkershoek Investments Ltd.

The interest rate implicit in the lease is 16,8% per annum.

The useful life of the front-end loader is estimated to be five years and depreciation is provided for by using the straight-line method with no residual value (assume that this treatment is correct). Assume that the South African Revenue Service allows wear and tear on the cost price of this type of leased machinery at 20% per annum on the straight-line method (without taking into account any residual values).

The tax rate has remained constant at 30%. Assume that Jonkershoek Investments Ltd has had no transactions other than those related to this lease agreement with Bamco (Pty) Ltd.

Ignore VAT.

Required

a. Indicate, with reasons, whether the lease transaction concluded by Jonkershoek Investments Ltd with Bamco (Pty) Ltd is a finance lease or an operating lease in terms of IFRS 16.
b. Disclose the lease transaction and related items in the statement of profit or loss and other comprehensive income and statement of financial position of Jonkershoek Investments Ltd for the year ended 28 February 20.5 in accordance with the requirements of International Financial Reporting Standards (IFRS). Accounting policy notes are not required.

❑ QUESTION IFRS 16.20

Abu Ltd, a manufacturer of machinery, sold a machine under an instalment sales agreement to Edfu Ltd on 1 January 20.6. The provisions of the agreement are as follows:

Selling price – cash (excluding VAT)	R200 000
Cost price	R160 000
VAT (at 15%)	R30 000
Term	48 months
Number of instalments (receivable in arrears)	8
Interest rate implicit in the contract	21% p.a.
Instalments	R30 539
Instalment payment dates	30 June/31 December
Deposit (on cash selling price)	20%

VAT is paid over immediately by the buyer to the seller (Abu Ltd). The applicable VAT rate is 15%.

Depreciation on machinery is provided for at 20% per annum on the straight-line method. Inventories are accounted for using a perpetual inventory system.

Assume that the South African Revenue Service includes the profit on instalment sales agreements in taxable income in proportion to the capital repayments received during a particular year. The portion of the profit that relates to future capital repayments will be taxed in future tax years.

The applicable tax rate is 30%.

Abu Ltd is registered for VAT purposes.

Required

a. Prepare the journal entries, other than for current tax, for Abu Ltd for the two years ended 31 December 20.6 and 20.7 (include all cash transactions). Journal narrations are not required. Your answer must comply with the requirements of International Financial Reporting Standards (IFRS).
b. Disclose the information regarding this transaction in the financial statements of Abu Ltd for the year ended 31 December 20.7 so as to comply with the requirements of International Financial Reporting Standards (IFRS). Provide only the following note:
   - Net investment in instalment sales agreement (debtors).

❑ QUESTION IFRS 16.21#

Giza Ltd sells or leases manufacturing machinery under finance lease agreements, depending on the customer's needs. On 1 January 20.4 the following lease agreement was concluded with Esua Ltd:

Four annual instalments, payable in arrears	R35 030 each
Interest rate	15% p.a.
Selling price at normal profit margin (same as fair value)	R100 010

Additional information

1. Giza Ltd's cost price for the applicable machine was R60 000.
2. A market-related interest rate for the specific transaction would be 20% per annum.
3. The loss of finance income is recovered by an increase in gross profit on the sale.
4. Wear and tear is allowed at 20% per annum on the straight-line method (assume for purposes of this question that the wear and tear is based on the selling price for accounting purposes).
5. The current tax rate is 30%.
6. A perpetual inventory system is used.
7. Assume that there are sufficient future taxable profits to enable the recognition of any deferred tax assets.

8. Ignore VAT.

Required

a. Prepare the journal entries (including cash transactions) for the two years ended 31 December 20.4 and 20.5 for Giza Ltd. Journal narrations are not required. Your answer must comply with the requirements of International Financial Reporting Standards (IFRS).
b. Disclose all relevant information regarding this transaction for Giza Ltd for the year ended 31 December 20.5 so as to comply with the requirements of International Financial Reporting Standards (IFRS).

❑ QUESTION IFRS 16.22

Incredible (Pty) Ltd is a motorcar manufacturer located in Johannesburg. The directors of the company declared in the financial statements that Incredible (Pty) Ltd adheres to International Financial Reporting Standards (IFRS).

The most recent financial reporting period of Incredible (Pty) Ltd ended on 30 June 20.8.

During the 20.7 financial year, Incredible (Pty) Ltd has decided to develop a new product line of environmentally friendly motor vehicles. The directors have identified a gap in the market due to the sudden consciousness by the public of the environmental problems arising from global warming. These motor vehicles will boast a built-in solar panel on the roof and make use of hybrid petrol/solar power engines. The engines will also have a special component that limits the emission of harmful gases.

Incredible (Pty) Ltd has already acquired the patents to manufacture these motor vehicles. However, Incredible (Pty) Ltd does not have the necessary capacity and intellectual capital to manufacture these motor vehicles by itself. Another company, Fabulous Ltd, has however been involved in the industry of environmentally friendly motor vehicles for many years. The directors of Incredible (Pty) Ltd approached Fabulous Ltd regarding their plans to manufacture the new product line and, after months of negotiations, Incredible (Pty) Ltd entered into an agreement with Fabulous Ltd with the following terms:

- The agreement commences on 1 May 20.8 and runs for a period of eight years.
- Fabulous Ltd will specifically erect a new production plant on Incredible (Pty) Ltd's premises. The production plant is owned by Fabulous Ltd.
- The production plant will be used to manufacture environmentally friendly motor vehicles on behalf of Incredible (Pty) Ltd. Any spare capacity in the production plant that are not required for Incredible (Pty) Ltd's purposes may be used for Fabulous Ltd's own needs, limited to a maximum of 10% of the total capacity of the plant.
- Incredible (Pty) Ltd will provide all production workers necessary to operate the plant. Fabulous Ltd is however responsible for managing the plant in accordance with criteria set by Incredible (Pty) Ltd which could at any time be amended by Incredible (Pty) Ltd.

The fixed monthly charge that Incredible (Pty) Ltd has to pay to Fabulous Ltd in respect of this arrangement amounts to R650 000 (excluding other input costs like materials and labour that are incurred by Incredible (Pty) Ltd).

Incredible (Pty) Ltd has to pay the R650 000 every month, regardless of the quantity of output produced from the plant. The fair value of the plant is estimated at R28 million. The plant is expected to be usable for a period of 22 years and Fabulous Ltd intends to make it available to other companies or for its own use after the eight-year period of the agreement has lapsed.

A market-related lending interest rate is currently 17% per annum.

Ignore taxation and VAT.

Required

Discuss the correct recognition and measurement of the agreement with Fabulous Ltd in the records of Incredible (Pty) Ltd for the year ended 30 June 20.8.

www.ingramcontent.com/pod-product-compliance
Ingram Content Group UK Ltd.
Pitfield, Milton Keynes, MK11 3LW, UK
UKHW062009041026
15591UKWH00017B/1247

9 781485 132